MySQL®

Administrator's Guide and Language Reference

MySQL®

Administrator's Guide
and Language Reference

MySQL AB

800 East 96th Street, Indianapolis, Indiana 46240 USA

MySQL® Administrator's Guide and Language Reference

International Standard Book Number: 0-672-32870-4

Library of Congress Catalog Card Number: 2005934932

Printed in the United States of America

First Printing: April 2006

09   08   07   06   4   3   2   1

Trademarks

All terms mentioned in this book that are known to be trademarks or service marks have been appropriately capitalized. Pearson Education cannot attest to the accuracy of this information. Use of a term in this book should not be regarded as affecting the validity of any trademark or service mark.

Warning and Disclaimer

Every effort has been made to make this book as complete and as accurate as possible, but no warranty or fitness is implied. The information provided is on an "as is" basis. The author and the publisher shall have neither liability nor responsibility to any person or entity with respect to any loss or damages arising from the information contained in this book or from the use of the CD or programs accompanying it.

Bulk Sales

Pearson Education offers excellent discounts on this book when ordered in quantity for bulk purchases or special sales. For more information, please contact

U.S. Corporate and Government Sales

1-800-382-3419

corpsales@pearsontechgroup.com

For sales outside of the U.S., please contact

International Sales

international@pearsoned.com

ASSOCIATE PUBLISHER Mark Taber	MANAGING EDITOR Charlotte Clapp	PROOFREADER Mike Henry	MULTIMEDIA DEVELOPER Dan Scherf
ACQUISITIONS EDITOR Shelley Johnston	PROJECT EDITOR Andy Beaster	PUBLISHING COORDINATOR Vanessa Evans	DESIGNER Gary Adair
DEVELOPMENT EDITOR Damon Jordan	INDEXER Heather McNeill		PAGE LAYOUT Bronkella Publishing

MySQL® Press is the exclusive publisher of technology books and materials that have been authorized by MySQL AB. MySQL Press books are written and reviewed by the world's leading authorities on MySQL technologies, and are edited, produced, and distributed by the Que/Sams Publishing group of Pearson Education, the worldwide leader in integrated education and computer technology publishing. For more information on MySQL Press and MySQL Press books, please go to **www.mysqlpress.com**.

MYSQL HQ
MySQL AB
Banagårdsgatan 8
S-753 20 Uppsala
Sweden

GERMANY, AUSTRIA, AND SWITZERLAND
MySQL GmbH
Radlkoferstrasse 2
81373 München
Germany

FRANCE
MySQL AB (France)
123, rue du Faubourg St. Antoine
75011, Paris
France

UNITED STATES
MySQL Inc.
2510 Fairview Avenue East
Seattle, WA 98102
USA

FINLAND
MySQL Finland Ab
Laaksotie/Dalvägen 10
02700 Kaunianen/Grankulla
Finland

MySQL® AB develops and supports a family of high-performance, affordable database products—including MySQL Network, a comprehensive set of certified software and premium support services. MySQL AB is the sole owner of the MySQL server source code, the MySQL trademark, and the mysql.com domain. For more MySQL information and downloads, please visit **www.mysql.com**.

- Training information: **www.mysql.com/training**
- Support services: **www.mysql.com/support**
- Consulting services: **www.mysql.com/consulting**

About this Book

The *MySQL Administrator's Guide and Language Reference* is made up of those sections in the MySQL Reference Manual (available online in several formats and languages at `http://dev.mysql.com`) that focus on administering MySQL and on the SQL language used to perform database operations in MySQL.

The original MySQL Reference Manual was written by Michael "Monty" Widenius and David Axmark, and it is currently maintained by the documentation team in the MySQL development department.

These members of the documentation team helped produce this book: Stefan Hinz (lead), Paul DuBois, Mike Hillyer, and Jon Stephens.

We Want to Hear from You!

As the reader of this book, *you* are our most important critic and commentator. We value your opinion and want to know what we're doing right, what we could do better, what areas you'd like to see us publish in, and any other words of wisdom you're willing to pass our way.

You can email or write me directly to let me know what you did or didn't like about this book—as well as what we can do to make our books stronger.

Please note that I cannot help you with technical problems related to the topic of this book, and that due to the high volume of mail I receive, I might not be able to reply to every message.

When you write, please be sure to include this book's title and author as well as your name and phone number or email address. I will carefully review your comments and share them with the author and editors who worked on the book.

E-mail: mysqlpress@pearsoned.com

Mail: Mark Taber
          Associate Publisher
          Pearson Education/MySQL Press
          800 East 96th Street
          Indianapolis, IN 46240 USA

Contents At a Glance

MySQL Administrator's Guide

MySQL Language Reference (on the CD-ROM)

Table of Contents—MySQL Administrator's Guide

Table of Contents—MySQL Language Reference (On CD-ROM)

General Information

The MySQL® software delivers a very fast, multi-threaded, multi-user, and robust SQL (Structured Query Language) database server. MySQL Server is intended for mission-critical, heavy-load production systems as well as for embedding into mass-deployed software. MySQL is a registered trademark of MySQL AB.

The MySQL software is dual licensed. Users can choose to use the MySQL software as an Open Source product under the terms of the GNU General Public License (`http://www.fsf.org/licenses/`) or can purchase a standard commercial license from MySQL AB. See `http://www.mysql.com/company/legal/licensing/` for more information on our licensing policies.

The following list describes some sections of particular interest in this manual:

- For a discussion about the capabilities of the MySQL Database Server, see Section 1.4.2, "The Main Features of MySQL."
- For installation instructions, see Chapter 2, "Installing and Upgrading MySQL." For information about upgrading MySQL, see Section 2.10, "Upgrading MySQL."
- For information about configuring and administering MySQL Server, see Chapter 4, "Database Administration."
- For information about setting up replication servers, see Chapter 5, "Replication."
- For benchmarking information, see the `sql-bench` benchmarking directory in your MySQL distribution.
- For a history of new features and bugfixes, see the change history in the online "MySQL Reference Manual" at `http://dev.mysql.com/doc/`.
- For future plans, see Section 1.6, "MySQL Development Roadmap."

Important:

To report errors (often called "bugs"), please use the instructions at Section 1.8, "How to Report Bugs or Problems."

If you have found a sensitive security bug in MySQL Server, please let us know immediately by sending an email message to `security@mysql.com`.

1.1 About This Manual

This is the Reference Manual for the MySQL Database System, version 5.0. It is not intended for use with older versions of the MySQL software due to the many functional and other differences between MySQL 5.0 and previous versions. If you are using a version 4.1 release of the MySQL software, please refer to the "MySQL 3.23, 4.0, 4.1 Reference Manual," which covers the 3.23, 4.0, and 4.1 series of MySQL software releases. Differences between minor versions of MySQL 5.0 are noted in the present text with reference to release numbers (5.0.*x*).

Because this manual serves as a reference, it does not provide general instruction on SQL or relational database concepts. It also does not teach you how to use your operating system or command-line interpreter.

The MySQL Database Software is under constant development, and the Reference Manual is updated frequently as well. The most recent version of the manual is available online in searchable form at `http://dev.mysql.com/doc/`. Other formats also are available there, including HTML, PDF, and Windows CHM versions.

The Reference Manual source files are written in DocBook XML format. The HTML version and other formats are produced automatically, primarily using the DocBook XSL stylesheets. For information about DocBook, see `http://docbook.org/`.

If you have any suggestions concerning additions or corrections to this manual, please send them to the documentation team at `docs@mysql.com`.

This manual was originally written by David Axmark and Michael "Monty" Widenius. It is maintained by the MySQL Documentation Team, consisting of Paul DuBois, Stefan Hinz, Mike Hillyer, and Jon Stephens.

The copyright to this manual is owned by the Swedish company MySQL AB. MySQL® and the MySQL logo are registered trademarks of MySQL AB. Other trademarks and registered trademarks referred to in this manual are the property of their respective owners, and are used for identification purposes only.

1.2 Conventions Used in This Manual

This manual uses certain typographical conventions:

- `Text in this style` is used for SQL statements; database, table, and column names; program listings and source code; and environment variables. Example: "To reload the grant tables, use the `FLUSH PRIVILEGES` statement."
- **`Text in this style`** indicates input that you type in examples.
- `Text in this style` indicates the names of executable programs and scripts, examples being `mysql` (the MySQL command line client program) and `mysqld` (the MySQL server executable).

- *Text in this style* is used for variable input for which you should substitute a value of your own choosing.
- Filenames and directory names are written like this: "The global `my.cnf` file is located in the `/etc` directory."
- Character sequences are written like this: "To specify a wildcard, use the '`%`' character."
- *Text in this style* is used for emphasis.
- **Text in this style** is used in table headings and to convey especially strong emphasis.

When commands are shown that are meant to be executed from within a particular program, the prompt shown preceding the command indicates which command to use. For example, `shell>` indicates a command that you execute from your login shell, and `mysql>` indicates a statement that you execute from the `mysql` client program:

```
shell> type a shell command here
mysql> type a mysql statement here
```

The "shell" is your command interpreter. On Unix, this is typically a program such as `sh`, `csh`, or `bash`. On Windows, the equivalent program is `command.com` or `cmd.exe`, typically run in a console window.

When you enter a command or statement shown in an example, do not type the prompt shown in the example.

Database, table, and column names must often be substituted into statements. To indicate that such substitution is necessary, this manual uses *db_name*, *tbl_name*, and *col_name*. For example, you might see a statement like this:

```
mysql> SELECT col_name FROM db_name.tbl_name;
```

This means that if you were to enter a similar statement, you would supply your own database, table, and column names, perhaps like this:

```
mysql> SELECT author_name FROM biblio_db.author_list;
```

SQL keywords are not case sensitive and may be written in any lettercase. This manual uses uppercase.

In syntax descriptions, square brackets ('[' and ']') indicate optional words or clauses. For example, in the following statement, `IF EXISTS` is optional:

```
DROP TABLE [IF EXISTS] tbl_name
```

When a syntax element consists of a number of alternatives, the alternatives are separated by vertical bars ('|'). When one member from a set of choices *may* be chosen, the alternatives are listed within square brackets ('[' and ']'):

```
TRIM([[BOTH | LEADING | TRAILING] [remstr] FROM] str)
```

When one member from a set of choices *must* be chosen, the alternatives are listed within braces ('{' and '}'):

```
{DESCRIBE | DESC} tbl_name [col_name | wild]
```

An ellipsis (...) indicates the omission of a section of a statement, typically to provide a shorter version of more complex syntax. For example, INSERT ... SELECT is shorthand for the form of INSERT statement that is followed by a SELECT statement.

An ellipsis can also indicate that the preceding syntax element of a statement may be repeated. In the following example, multiple reset_option values may be given, with each of those after the first preceded by commas:

```
RESET reset_option [,reset_option] ...
```

Commands for setting shell variables are shown using Bourne shell syntax. For example, the sequence to set the CC environment variable and run the configure command looks like this in Bourne shell syntax:

```
shell> CC=gcc ./configure
```

If you are using csh or tcsh, you must issue commands somewhat differently:

```
shell> setenv CC gcc
shell> ./configure
```

1.3 Overview of MySQL AB

MySQL AB is the company of the MySQL founders and main developers. MySQL AB was originally established in Sweden by David Axmark, Allan Larsson, and Michael "Monty" Widenius.

We are dedicated to developing the MySQL database software and promoting it to new users. MySQL AB owns the copyright to the MySQL source code, the MySQL logo and (registered) trademark, and this manual. See Section 1.4, "Overview of the MySQL Database Management System."

The MySQL core values show our dedication to MySQL and Open Source.

These core values direct how MySQL AB works with the MySQL server software:

- To be the best and the most widely used database in the world
- To be available and affordable by all
- To be easy to use
- To be continuously improved while remaining fast and safe
- To be fun to use and improve
- To be free from bugs

These are the core values of the company MySQL AB and its employees:

- We subscribe to the Open Source philosophy and support the Open Source community
- We aim to be good citizens
- We prefer partners that share our values and mindset
- We answer email and provide support
- We are a virtual company, networking with others
- We work against software patents

The MySQL Web site (`http://www.mysql.com/`) provides the latest information about MySQL and MySQL AB.

By the way, the "AB" part of the company name is the acronym for the Swedish "aktiebolag," or "stock company." It translates to "MySQL, Inc." In fact, MySQL, Inc. and MySQL GmbH are examples of MySQL AB subsidiaries. They are located in the United States and Germany, respectively.

1.4 Overview of the MySQL Database Management System

MySQL, the most popular Open Source SQL database management system, is developed, distributed, and supported by MySQL AB. MySQL AB is a commercial company, founded by the MySQL developers. It is a second generation Open Source company that unites Open Source values and methodology with a successful business model.

The MySQL Web site (`http://www.mysql.com/`) provides the latest information about MySQL software and MySQL AB.

- MySQL is a database management system.

  A database is a structured collection of data. It may be anything from a simple shopping list to a picture gallery or the vast amounts of information in a corporate network. To add, access, and process data stored in a computer database, you need a database management system such as MySQL Server. Since computers are very good at handling large amounts of data, database management systems play a central role in computing, as standalone utilities, or as parts of other applications.

- MySQL is a relational database management system.

  A relational database stores data in separate tables rather than putting all the data in one big storeroom. This adds speed and flexibility. The SQL part of "MySQL" stands for "Structured Query Language." SQL is the most common standardized language used to access databases and is defined by the ANSI/ISO SQL Standard. The SQL standard has been evolving since 1986 and several versions exist. In this manual, "SQL-92" refers to the standard released in 1992, "SQL:1999" refers to the standard released in 1999, and "SQL:2003" refers to the current version of the standard. We use the phrase "the SQL standard" to mean the current version of the SQL Standard at any time.

- MySQL software is Open Source.

  Open Source means that it is possible for anyone to use and modify the software. Anybody can download the MySQL software from the Internet and use it without paying anything. If you wish, you may study the source code and change it to suit your needs. The MySQL software uses the GPL (GNU General Public License), http://www.fsf.org/licenses/, to define what you may and may not do with the software in different situations. If you feel uncomfortable with the GPL or need to embed MySQL code into a commercial application, you can buy a commercially licensed version from us. See the MySQL Licensing Overview for more information (http://www.mysql.com/company/legal/licensing/).

- The MySQL Database Server is very fast, reliable, and easy to use.

  If that is what you are looking for, you should give it a try. MySQL Server also has a practical set of features developed in close cooperation with our users. You can find a performance comparison of MySQL Server with other database managers on our benchmark page. See Section 6.1.4, "The MySQL Benchmark Suite."

  MySQL Server was originally developed to handle large databases much faster than existing solutions and has been successfully used in highly demanding production environments for several years. Although under constant development, MySQL Server today offers a rich and useful set of functions. Its connectivity, speed, and security make MySQL Server highly suited for accessing databases on the Internet.

- MySQL Server works in client/server or embedded systems.

  The MySQL Database Software is a client/server system that consists of a multi-threaded SQL server that supports different backends, several different client programs and libraries, administrative tools, and a wide range of application programming interfaces (APIs).

  We also provide MySQL Server as an embedded multi-threaded library that you can link into your application to get a smaller, faster, easier-to-manage standalone product.

- A large amount of contributed MySQL software is available.

  It is very likely that your favorite application or language supports the MySQL Database Server.

The official way to pronounce "MySQL" is "My Ess Que Ell" (not "my sequel"), but we don't mind if you pronounce it as "my sequel" or in some other localized way.

1.4.1 History of MySQL

We started out with the intention of using the mSQL database system to connect to our tables using our own fast low-level (ISAM) routines. However, after some testing, we came to the conclusion that mSQL was not fast enough or flexible enough for our needs. This resulted in a new SQL interface to our database but with almost the same API interface as mSQL. This API was designed to allow third-party code that was written for use with mSQL to be ported easily for use with MySQL.

The derivation of the name MySQL is not clear. Our base directory and a large number of our libraries and tools have had the prefix "my" for well over 10 years. However, co-founder Monty Widenius's daughter is also named My. Which of the two gave its name to MySQL is still a mystery, even for us.

The name of the MySQL Dolphin (our logo) is "Sakila," which was chosen by the founders of MySQL AB from a huge list of names suggested by users in our "Name the Dolphin" contest. The winning name was submitted by Ambrose Twebaze, an Open Source software developer from Swaziland, Africa. According to Ambrose, the feminine name Sakila has its roots in SiSwati, the local language of Swaziland. Sakila is also the name of a town in Arusha, Tanzania, near Ambrose's country of origin, Uganda.

1.4.2 The Main Features of MySQL

The following list describes some of the important characteristics of the MySQL Database Software. See also Section 1.6, "MySQL Development Roadmap," for more information about current and upcoming features.

Internals and Portability:

- Written in C and C++.
- Tested with a broad range of different compilers.
- Works on many different platforms. See Section 2.1.1, "Operating Systems Supported by MySQL."
- Uses GNU Automake, Autoconf, and Libtool for portability.
- APIs for C, C++, Eiffel, Java, Perl, PHP, Python, Ruby, and Tcl are available.
- Fully multi-threaded using kernel threads. It can easily use multiple CPUs if they are available.
- Provides transactional and non-transactional storage engines.
- Uses very fast B-tree disk tables (MyISAM) with index compression.
- Relatively easy to add other storage engines. This is useful if you want to add an SQL interface to an in-house database.
- A very fast thread-based memory allocation system.
- Very fast joins using an optimized one-sweep multi-join.
- In-memory hash tables, which are used as temporary tables.
- SQL functions are implemented using a highly optimized class library and should be as fast as possible. Usually there is no memory allocation at all after query initialization.

- The MySQL code is tested with Purify (a commercial memory leakage detector) as well as with Valgrind, a GPL tool (`http://developer.kde.org/~sewardj/`).
- The server is available as a separate program for use in a client/server networked environment. It is also available as a library that can be embedded (linked) into standalone applications. Such applications can be used in isolation or in environments where no network is available.

Data Types:

- Many data types: signed/unsigned integers 1, 2, 3, 4, and 8 bytes long, `FLOAT`, `DOUBLE`, `CHAR`, `VARCHAR`, `TEXT`, `BLOB`, `DATE`, `TIME`, `DATETIME`, `TIMESTAMP`, `YEAR`, `SET`, `ENUM`, and OpenGIS spatial types.
- Fixed-length and variable-length records.

Statements and Functions:

- Full operator and function support in the `SELECT` and `WHERE` clauses of queries. For example:

```
mysql> SELECT CONCAT(first_name, ' ', last_name)
    -> FROM citizen
    -> WHERE income/dependents > 10000 AND age > 30;
```

- Full support for SQL `GROUP BY` and `ORDER BY` clauses. Support for group functions (`COUNT()`, `COUNT(DISTINCT ...)`, `AVG()`, `STD()`, `SUM()`, `MAX()`, `MIN()`, and `GROUP_CONCAT()`).
- Support for `LEFT OUTER JOIN` and `RIGHT OUTER JOIN` with both standard SQL and ODBC syntax.
- Support for aliases on tables and columns as required by standard SQL.
- `DELETE`, `INSERT`, `REPLACE`, and `UPDATE` return the number of rows that were changed (affected). It is possible to return the number of rows matched instead by setting a flag when connecting to the server.
- The MySQL-specific `SHOW` command can be used to retrieve information about databases, database engines, tables, and indexes.
- The `EXPLAIN` command can be used to determine how the optimizer resolves a query.
- Function names do not clash with table or column names. For example, `ABS` is a valid column name. The only restriction is that for a function call, no spaces are allowed between the function name and the '(' that follows it.
- You can mix tables from different databases in the same query (as of MySQL 3.22).

Security:

- A privilege and password system that is very flexible and secure, and that allows host-based verification. Passwords are secure because all password traffic is encrypted when you connect to a server.

Scalability and Limits:

- Handles large databases. We use MySQL Server with databases that contain 50 million records. We also know of users who use MySQL Server with 60,000 tables and about 5,000,000,000 rows.

- Up to 64 indexes per table are allowed (32 before MySQL 4.1.2). Each index may consist of 1 to 16 columns or parts of columns. The maximum index width is 1000 bytes (500 before MySQL 4.1.2). An index may use a prefix of a column for `CHAR`, `VARCHAR`, `BLOB`, or `TEXT` column types.

Connectivity:

- Clients can connect to the MySQL server using TCP/IP sockets on any platform. On Windows systems in the NT family (NT, 2000, XP, or 2003), clients can connect using named pipes. On Unix systems, clients can connect using Unix domain socket files.

- In MySQL versions 4.1 and higher, Windows servers also support shared-memory connections if started with the `--shared-memory` option. Clients can connect through shared memory by using the `--protocol=memory` option.

- The Connector/ODBC (MyODBC) interface provides MySQL support for client programs that use ODBC (Open Database Connectivity) connections. For example, you can use MS Access to connect to your MySQL server. Clients can be run on Windows or Unix. MyODBC source is available. All ODBC 2.5 functions are supported, as are many others.

- The Connector/J interface provides MySQL support for Java client programs that use JDBC connections. Clients can be run on Windows or Unix. Connector/J source is available.

- MySQL Connector/NET enables developers to easily create .NET applications that require secure, high-performance data connectivity with MySQL. It implements the required ADO.NET interfaces and integrates into ADO.NET aware tools. Developers can build applications using their choice of .NET languages. MySQL Connector/NET is a fully managed ADO.NET driver written in 100% pure C#.

Localization:

- The server can provide error messages to clients in many languages. See Section 4.11.2, "Setting the Error Message Language."

- Full support for several different character sets, including `latin1` (cp1252), `german`, `big5`, `ujis`, and more. For example, the Scandinavian characters 'å', 'ä' and 'ö' are allowed in table and column names. Unicode support is available as of MySQL 4.1.

- All data is saved in the chosen character set. All comparisons for normal string columns are case-insensitive.

- Sorting is done according to the chosen character set (using Swedish collation by default). It is possible to change this when the MySQL server is started. To see an example of very advanced sorting, look at the Czech sorting code. MySQL Server supports many different character sets that can be specified at compile time and runtime.

Clients and Tools:

- MySQL Server has built-in support for SQL statements to check, optimize, and repair tables. These statements are available from the command line through the `mysqlcheck` client. MySQL also includes `myisamchk`, a very fast command-line utility for performing these operations on `MyISAM` tables. See Chapter 4, "Database Administration."

- All MySQL programs can be invoked with the `--help` or `-?` options to obtain online assistance.

1.4.3 MySQL Stability

This section addresses the questions *"How stable is MySQL Server?"* and *"Can I depend on MySQL Server in this project?"* We will try to clarify these issues and answer some important questions that concern many potential users. The information in this section is based on data gathered from the mailing lists, which are very active in identifying problems as well as reporting types of use.

The original code stems back to the early 1980s. It provides a stable code base, and the `ISAM` table format used by the original storage engine remains backward-compatible. At TcX, the predecessor of MySQL AB, MySQL code has worked in projects since mid-1996, without any problems. When the MySQL Database Software initially was released to a wider public, our new users quickly found some pieces of untested code. Each new release since then has had fewer portability problems, even though each new release has also had many new features.

Each release of the MySQL Server has been usable. Problems have occurred only when users try code from the "gray zones." Naturally, new users don't know what the gray zones are; this section therefore attempts to document those areas that are currently known. The descriptions mostly deal with Versions 3.23 and later of MySQL Server.

The MySQL Server design is multi-layered with independent modules. Some of the newer modules are listed here with an indication of how well-tested each of them is:

- Replication (Stable)

  Large groups of servers using replication are in production use, with good results. Work on enhanced replication features is continuing.

- InnoDB tables (Stable)

  The `InnoDB` transactional storage engine has been stable since version 3.23.49. `InnoDB` is being used in large, heavy-load production systems.

- BDB tables (Stable)

  The `Berkeley DB` code is very stable, but we are still improving the `BDB` transactional storage engine interface in MySQL Server.

- Full-text searches (Stable)

    Full-text searching is widely used. Important feature enhancements were added in MySQL 4.0 and 4.1.

- MyODBC 3.51 (Stable)

    MyODBC 3.51 uses ODBC SDK 3.51 and is in wide production use. Some issues brought up appear to be application-related and independent of the ODBC driver or underlying database server.

1.4.4 How Large MySQL Tables Can Be

MySQL 3.22 had a 4GB (4 gigabyte) limit on table size. With the MyISAM storage engine in MySQL 3.23, the maximum table size was increased to 65536 terabytes ($256^7 - 1$ bytes). With this larger allowed table size, the maximum effective table size for MySQL databases is usually determined by operating system constraints on file sizes, not by MySQL internal limits.

The InnoDB storage engine maintains InnoDB tables within a tablespace that can be created from several files. This allows a table to exceed the maximum individual file size. The tablespace can include raw disk partitions, which allows extremely large tables. The maximum tablespace size is 64TB.

The following table lists some examples of operating system file-size limits. This is only a rough guide and is not intended to be definitive. For the most up-to-date information, be sure to check the documentation specific to your operating system.

Operating System	File-Size Limit
Linux 2.2-Intel 32-bit	2GB (LFS: 4GB)
Linux 2.4+	(using ext3 filesystem) 4TB
Solaris 9/10	16TB
NetWare w/NSS filesystem	8TB
Win32 w/ FAT/FAT32	2GB/4GB
Win32 w/ NTFS	2TB (possibly larger)
MacOS X w/ HFS+	2TB

On Linux 2.2, you can get MyISAM tables larger than 2GB in size by using the Large File Support (LFS) patch for the ext2 filesystem. On Linux 2.4, patches also exist for ReiserFS to get support for big files (up to 2TB). Most current Linux distributions are based on kernel 2.4 or higher and include all the required LFS patches. With JFS and XFS, petabyte and larger files are possible on Linux. However, the maximum available file size still depends on several factors, one of them being the filesystem used to store MySQL tables.

For a detailed overview about LFS in Linux, have a look at Andreas Jaeger's "Large File Support in Linux" page at http://www.suse.de/~aj/linux_lfs.html.

Windows users please note: FAT and VFAT (FAT32) are *not* considered suitable for production use with MySQL. Use NTFS instead.

By default, MySQL creates MyISAM tables with an internal structure that allows a maximum size of about 4GB. You can check the maximum table size for a MyISAM table with the SHOW TABLE STATUS statement or with myisamchk -dv *tbl_name*.

If you need a MyISAM table that is larger than 4GB and your operating system supports large files, the CREATE TABLE statement supports AVG_ROW_LENGTH and MAX_ROWS options. You can also change these options with ALTER TABLE to increase a table's maximum allowable size after the table has been created.

Other ways to work around file-size limits for MyISAM tables are as follows:

- If your large table is read-only, you can use myisampack to compress it. myisampack usually compresses a table by at least 50%, so you can have, in effect, much bigger tables. myisampack also can merge multiple tables into a single table. See Section 7.4, "myisampack—Generate Compressed, Read-Only MyISAM Tables."

- MySQL includes a MERGE library that allows you to handle a collection of MyISAM tables that have identical structure as a single MERGE table. See Section 8.3, "The MERGE Storage Engine."

1.4.5 Year 2000 Compliance

The MySQL Server itself has no problems with Year 2000 (Y2K) compliance:

- MySQL Server uses Unix time functions that handle dates into the year 2037 for TIMESTAMP values. For DATE and DATETIME values, dates through the year 9999 are accepted.

- All MySQL date functions are implemented in one source file, sql/time.cc, and are coded very carefully to be year 2000-safe.

- In MySQL, the YEAR data type can store the years 0 and 1901 to 2155 in one byte and display them using two or four digits. All two-digit years are considered to be in the range 1970 to 2069, which means that if you store 01 in a YEAR column, MySQL Server treats it as 2001.

The following simple demonstration illustrates that MySQL Server has no problems with DATE or DATETIME values through the year 9999, and no problems with TIMESTAMP values until after the year 2030:

```
mysql> DROP TABLE IF EXISTS y2k;
Query OK, 0 rows affected (0.00 sec)

mysql> CREATE TABLE y2k (date DATE,
    ->                    date_time DATETIME,
    ->                    time_stamp TIMESTAMP);
Query OK, 0 rows affected (0.01 sec)
```

```
mysql> INSERT INTO y2k VALUES
    -> ('1998-12-31','1998-12-31 23:59:59','1998-12-31 23:59:59'),
    -> ('1999-01-01','1999-01-01 00:00:00','1999-01-01 00:00:00'),
    -> ('1999-09-09','1999-09-09 23:59:59','1999-09-09 23:59:59'),
    -> ('2000-01-01','2000-01-01 00:00:00','2000-01-01 00:00:00'),
    -> ('2000-02-28','2000-02-28 00:00:00','2000-02-28 00:00:00'),
    -> ('2000-02-29','2000-02-29 00:00:00','2000-02-29 00:00:00'),
    -> ('2000-03-01','2000-03-01 00:00:00','2000-03-01 00:00:00'),
    -> ('2000-12-31','2000-12-31 23:59:59','2000-12-31 23:59:59'),
    -> ('2001-01-01','2001-01-01 00:00:00','2001-01-01 00:00:00'),
    -> ('2004-12-31','2004-12-31 23:59:59','2004-12-31 23:59:59'),
    -> ('2005-01-01','2005-01-01 00:00:00','2005-01-01 00:00:00'),
    -> ('2030-01-01','2030-01-01 00:00:00','2030-01-01 00:00:00'),
    -> ('2040-01-01','2040-01-01 00:00:00','2040-01-01 00:00:00'),
    -> ('9999-12-31','9999-12-31 23:59:59','9999-12-31 23:59:59');
Query OK, 14 rows affected, 2 warnings (0.00 sec)
Records: 14  Duplicates: 0  Warnings: 2

mysql> SELECT * FROM y2k;
+------------+---------------------+---------------------+
| date       | date_time           | time_stamp          |
+------------+---------------------+---------------------+
| 1998-12-31 | 1998-12-31 23:59:59 | 1998-12-31 23:59:59 |
| 1999-01-01 | 1999-01-01 00:00:00 | 1999-01-01 00:00:00 |
| 1999-09-09 | 1999-09-09 23:59:59 | 1999-09-09 23:59:59 |
| 2000-01-01 | 2000-01-01 00:00:00 | 2000-01-01 00:00:00 |
| 2000-02-28 | 2000-02-28 00:00:00 | 2000-02-28 00:00:00 |
| 2000-02-29 | 2000-02-29 00:00:00 | 2000-02-29 00:00:00 |
| 2000-03-01 | 2000-03-01 00:00:00 | 2000-03-01 00:00:00 |
| 2000-12-31 | 2000-12-31 23:59:59 | 2000-12-31 23:59:59 |
| 2001-01-01 | 2001-01-01 00:00:00 | 2001-01-01 00:00:00 |
| 2004-12-31 | 2004-12-31 23:59:59 | 2004-12-31 23:59:59 |
| 2005-01-01 | 2005-01-01 00:00:00 | 2005-01-01 00:00:00 |
| 2030-01-01 | 2030-01-01 00:00:00 | 2030-01-01 00:00:00 |
| 2040-01-01 | 2040-01-01 00:00:00 | 0000-00-00 00:00:00 |
| 9999-12-31 | 9999-12-31 23:59:59 | 0000-00-00 00:00:00 |
+------------+---------------------+---------------------+
14 rows in set (0.00 sec)
```

The final two TIMESTAMP column values are zero because the year values (2040, 9999) exceed the TIMESTAMP maximum. The TIMESTAMP data type, which is used to store the current time, supports values that range from '1970-01-01 00:00:00' to '2030-01-01 00:00:00' on 32-bit machines (signed value). On 64-bit machines, TIMESTAMP handles values up to 2106 (unsigned value).

Although MySQL Server itself is Y2K-safe, you may run into problems if you use it with applications that are not Y2K-safe. For example, many old applications store or manipulate years using two-digit values (which are ambiguous) rather than four-digit values. This problem may be compounded by applications that use values such as 00 or 99 as "missing" value indicators. Unfortunately, these problems may be difficult to fix because different applications may be written by different programmers, each of whom may use a different set of conventions and date-handling functions.

Thus, even though MySQL Server has no Y2K problems, *it is the application's responsibility to provide unambiguous input.* See the "MySQL Language Reference" for MySQL Server's rules for dealing with ambiguous date input data that contains two-digit year values.

1.5 Overview of the MaxDB Database Management System

MaxDB is a heavy-duty enterprise database. The database management system is SAP-certified.

MaxDB is the new name of a database management system formerly called SAP DB. In 2003 SAP AG and MySQL AB joined a partnership and re-branded the database system to MaxDB. The development of MaxDB has continued since then as it was done before—through the SAP developer team.

MySQL AB cooperates closely with the MaxDB team at SAP around delivering improvements to the MaxDB product. Joint efforts include development of new native drivers to enable more efficient usage of MaxDB in the Open Source community, and improvement of documentation to expand the MaxDB user base. Interoperability features between MySQL and MaxDB database also are seen as important. For example, the new MaxDB Synchronization Manager supports data synchronization from MaxDB to MySQL.

The MaxDB database management system does not share a common code-base with the MySQL database management system. The MaxDB and MySQL database management systems are independent products provided by MySQL AB.

MySQL AB offers a complete portfolio of Professional Services for MaxDB.

1.5.1 What Is MaxDB?

MaxDB is an ANSI SQL-92 (entry level) compliant relational database management system (RDBMS) from SAP AG, that is delivered by MySQL AB as well. MaxDB fulfills the needs for enterprise usage: safety, scalability, high concurrency, and performance. It runs on all major operating systems. Over the years it has proven able to run SAP R/3 and terabytes of data in 24×7 operation.

The database development started in 1977 as a research project at the Technical University of Berlin. In the early 1980s it became a database product that subsequently was owned by Nixdorf, Siemens Nixdorf, Software AG, and today by SAP AG. Along the way, it has been named VDN, Reflex, Supra 2, DDB/4, Entire SQL-DB-Server, and ADABAS D. In 1997, SAP took over the software from Software AG and renamed it to SAP DB. Since October 2000, SAP DB sources additionally were released as Open Source under the GNU General Public License.

In 2003, SAP AG and MySQL AB formed a partnership and re-branded the database system to MaxDB.

1.5.2 History of MaxDB

The history of MaxDB goes back to SAP DB, SAP AG's DBMS. That is, MaxDB is a re-branded and enhanced version of SAP DB. For many years, MaxDB has been used for small, medium, and large installations of the mySAP Business Suite and other demanding SQL applications requiring an enterprise-class DBMS with regard to the number of users, the transactional workload, and the size of the database.

SAP DB was meant to provide an alternative to third-party database systems such as Oracle, Microsoft SQL Server, and DB2 by IBM. In October 2000, SAP AG released SAP DB under the GNU GPL license, thus making it Open Source software.

Today, MaxDB is used in about 3,500 SAP customer installations worldwide. Moreover, the majority of all DBMS installations on Unix and Linux within SAP's IT department rely on MaxDB. MaxDB is tuned toward heavy-duty online transaction processing (OLTP) with several thousand users and database sizes ranging from several hundred GB to multiple TB.

In 2003, SAP and MySQL concluded a partnership and development cooperation agreement. As a result, SAP's database system SAP DB has been delivered under the name of MaxDB by MySQL since the release of version 7.5 (November 2003).

Version 7.5 of MaxDB is a direct advancement of the SAP DB 7.4 code base. Therefore, the MaxDB software version 7.5 can be used as a direct upgrade of previous SAP DB versions starting 7.2.04 and higher.

The former SAP DB development team at SAP AG is responsible, now as before, for developing and supporting MaxDB. MySQL AB cooperates closely with the MaxDB team at SAP around delivering improvements to the MaxDB product, see Section 1.5, "Overview of the MaxDB Database Management System." Both SAP AG and MySQL AB handle the sale and distribution of MaxDB. The advancement of MaxDB and the MySQL Server leverages synergies that benefit both product lines.

MaxDB is subjected to SAP AG's complete quality assurance process before it is shipped with SAP solutions or provided as a download from the MySQL site.

1.5.3 Features of MaxDB

MaxDB is a heavy-duty, SAP-certified Open Source database for OLTP and OLAP usage which offers high reliability, availability, scalability, and a very comprehensive feature set. It is targeted for large mySAP Business Suite environments and other applications that require maximum enterprise-level database functionality and complements the MySQL database server.

MaxDB operates as a client/server product. It was developed to meet the needs of installations in OLTP and Data Warehouse/OLAP/Decision Support scenarios and offers these benefits:

- **Easy configuration and administration:** GUI-based Installation Manager and Database Manager as single administration tools for DBMS operations
- **Around-the-clock operation, no planned downtimes, no permanent attendance required:** Automatic space management, no need for reorganizations
- **Sophisticated backup and restore capabilities:** Online and incremental backups, recovery wizard to guide you through the recovery scenario
- **Supports large number of users, database sizes in the terabytes, and demanding workloads:** Proven reliability, performance, and scalability
- **High availability:** Cluster support, standby configuration, hot standby configuration

1.5.4 Licensing and Support

MaxDB can be used under the same licenses available for the other products distributed by MySQL AB. Thus, MaxDB is available under the GNU General Public License, and a commercial license. For more information on licensing, see `http://www.mysql.com/company/legal/licensing/`.

MySQL AB offers MaxDB technical support to non-SAP customers. MaxDB support is available on various levels (Basic, Silver, and Gold), which expand from unlimited email/web-support to 24×7 phone support for business critical systems.

MySQL AB also offers Licenses and Support for MaxDB when used with SAP Applications, like SAP NetWeaver and mySAP Business Suite. For more information on licenses and support for your needs, please contact MySQL AB. (See `http://www.mysql.com/company/contact/`.)

Consulting and training services are available. MySQL gives classes on MaxDB at regular intervals. See `http://www.mysql.com/training/` for a list of classes.

1.5.5 Feature Differences Between MaxDB and MySQL

MaxDB is MySQL AB's SAP-certified database. The MaxDB database server complements the MySQL AB product portfolio. Some MaxDB features are not available on the MySQL database management server and vice versa.

The following list summarizes the main differences between MaxDB and MySQL; it is not complete.

- MaxDB runs as a client/server system. MySQL can run as a client/server system or as an embedded system.

- MaxDB might not run on all platforms supported by MySQL.

- MaxDB uses a proprietary network protocol for client/server communication. MySQL uses either TCP/IP (with or without SSL encryption), sockets (under Unix-like systems), or named pipes or shared memory (under Windows NT-family systems).

- MaxDB supports stored procedures and functions. MySQL 5.0 and up also supports stored procedures and function and functions. MaxDB supports programming of triggers through an SQL extension. MySQL 5.0 supports triggers. MaxDB contains a debugger for stored procedure languages, can cascade nested triggers, and supports multiple triggers per action and row.

- MaxDB is distributed with user interfaces that are text-based, graphical, or Web-based. MySQL is distributed with text-based user interfaces only; graphical user interfaces (MySQL Query Browser, MySQL Administrator) are shipped separately from the main distributions. Web-based user interfaces for MySQL are offered by third parties.

- MaxDB supports a number of programming interfaces that also are supported by MySQL. For developing with MaxDB, the MaxDB ODBC Driver, SQL Database Connectivity (SQLDBC), JDBC Driver, Perl and Python modules and a MaxDB PHP extension, which provides access to MySQL MaxDB databases using PHP, are available.

  Third-party programming interfaces: Support for OLE DB, ADO, DAO, RDO and .NET through ODBC. MaxDB supports embedded SQL with C/C++.

- MaxDB includes administrative features that MySQL does not have: job scheduling by time, event, and alert, and sending messages to a database administrator on alert thresholds. (MySQL has scheduling support starting with version 5.1.6.)

1.5.6 Interoperability Features Between MaxDB and MySQL

MaxDB and MySQL are independent database management servers. The interoperation of the systems is possible in a way that the systems can exchange their data. To exchange data between MaxDB and MySQL, you can use the import and export tools of the systems or the MaxDB Synchronization Manager. The import and export tools can be used to transfer data in an infrequent, manual fashion. The MaxDB Synchronization Manager offers faster, automatic data transfer capabilities.

The MaxDB Loader can be used to export data and object definitions. The Loader can export data using MaxDB internal, binary formats and text formats (CSV). Data exported from MaxDB in text formats can be imported into MySQL using the `mysqlimport` client program. To export MySQL data, you can use either `mysqldump` to create `INSERT` statements or `SELECT ... INTO OUTFILE` to create a text file (CSV). Use the MaxDB Loader to import the data files generated by MySQL.

Object definitions can be exchanged between the systems using MaxDB Loader and the MySQL tool `mysqldump`. As the SQL dialects of both systems differ slightly and MaxDB has features currently not supported by MySQL like SQL constraints, we recommend hand-tuning the definition files. The `mysqldump` tool offers an option `--compatible=maxdb` to produce output that is compatible with MaxDB to make porting easier.

The MaxDB Synchronization Manager is available as part of MaxDB 7.6. The Synchronization Manager supports creation of asynchronous replication scenarios between several MaxDB instances. However, interoperability features also are planned, so that the Synchronization Manager supports replication to and from a MySQL server.

In the first release, the Synchronization Manager supports inserting data into MySQL. This means that initially only replication from MaxDB to MySQL is supported. In the course of 2005, exporting of data from a MySQL server to the Synchronization Manager will be added, thus adding support for MySQL to MaxDB replication scenarios.

1.5.7 MaxDB-Related Links

The main page for MaxDB information is `http://www.mysql.com/products/maxdb`, which provides details about the features of the MaxDB database management systems and has pointers to available documentation.

The "MySQL Reference Manual" does not contain any MaxDB documentation other than the introduction given in this section. MaxDB has its own documentation, which is called the MaxDB library and is available at `http://dev.mysql.com/doc/maxdb/index.html`.

MySQL AB runs a community mailing list on MaxDB; see `http://lists.mysql.com/maxdb`. The list shows a vivid community discussion. Many of the core developers contribute to it. Product announcements are sent to the list.

A Web forum on MaxDB is available at `http://forums.mysql.com/`. The forum focuses on MaxDB questions not related to SAP applications.

1.6 MySQL Development Roadmap

This section provides a snapshot of the MySQL development roadmap, including major features implemented in or planned for various MySQL releases. The following sections provide information for each release series.

The current production release series is MySQL 5.0, which was declared stable for production use as of MySQL 5.0.15, released in October 2005. The previous production release series was MySQL 4.1, which was declared stable for production use as of MySQL 4.1.7, released in October 2004. "Production status" means that future 5.0 and 4.1 development is limited only to bugfixes. For the older MySQL 4.0 and 3.23 series, only critical bugfixes are made.

Active MySQL development is currently taking place in the MySQL 5.0 and 5.1 release series, and new features are being added only to the latter.

Before upgrading from one release series to the next, please see the notes in Section 2.10, "Upgrading MySQL."

The most requested features and the versions in which they were implemented or are scheduled for implementation are summarized in the following table:

Feature	MySQL Series
Foreign keys	3.23 (for the `InnoDB` storage engine)
Unions	4.0
Subqueries	4.1
R-trees	4.1 (for the `MyISAM` storage engine)
Stored procedures	5.0
Views	5.0
Cursors	5.0
XA transactions	5.0
Foreign keys	5.2 (implemented in 3.23 for `InnoDB`)
Triggers	5.0 and 5.1
Partitioning	5.1
Pluggable storage engine API	5.1
Row-based replication	5.1

1.6.1 What's New in MySQL 5.0

The following features are implemented in MySQL 5.0:

- **`BIT` Data Type**: Can be used to store numbers in binary notation.
- **Cursors**: Elementary support for server-side cursors.
- **Information Schema**: The introduction of the `INFORMATION_SCHEMA` database in MySQL 5.0 provided a standards-compliant means for accessing the MySQL Server's metadata; that is, data about the databases (schemas) on the server and the objects which they contain.
- **Instance Manager**: Can be used to start and stop the MySQL Server, even from a remote host. See Section 4.5, "`mysqlmanager`—The MySQL Instance Manager."
- **Precision Math**: MySQL 5.0 introduced stricter criteria for acceptance or rejection of data, and implemented a new library for fixed-point arithmetic. These contributed to a much higher degree of accuracy for mathematical operations and greater control over invalid values.

- **Storage Engines**: Storage engines added in MySQL 5.0 include ARCHIVE and FEDERATED. See Section 8.8, "The ARCHIVE Storage Engine," and Section 8.7, "The FEDERATED Storage Engine."

- **Stored Routines**: Support for named stored procedures and stored functions was implemented in MySQL 5.0.

- **Strict Mode and Standard Error Handling**: MySQL 5.0 added a strict mode whereby it follows standard SQL in a number of ways in which it did not previously. Support for standard SQLSTATE error messages was also implemented. See Section 4.2.5, "The Server SQL Mode."

- **Triggers**: MySQL 5.0 added limited support for triggers.

- **VARCHAR Data Type**: The maximum effective length of a VARCHAR column was increased to 65,532 bytes, and stripping of trailing whitespace was eliminated.

- **Views**: MySQL 5.0 added support for named, updatable views. See Section 1.9.5.6, "Views."

- **XA Transactions**.

- **Performance Enhancements**: A number of improvements were made in MySQL 5.0 to improve the speed of certain types of queries and in the handling of certain types. These include:

  - MySQL 5.0 introduces a new "greedy" optimizer that can greatly reduce the time required to arrive at a query execution plan. This is particularly noticeable where several tables are to be joined and no good join keys can otherwise be found. Without the greedy optimizer, the complexity of the search for an execution plan is calculated as $N!$, where N is the number of tables to be joined. The greedy optimizer reduces this to $N!/(D-1)!$, where D is the depth of the search. Although the greedy optimizer does not guarantee the best possible of all execution plans (this is currently being worked on), it can reduce the time spent arriving at an execution plan for a join involving a great many tables—30, 40, or more—by a factor of as much as 1,000. This should eliminate most if not all situations where users thought that the optimizer had hung when trying to perform joins across many tables.

  - Use of the *Index Merge* method to obtain better optimization of AND and OR relations over different keys. (Previously, these were optimized only where both relations in the WHERE clause involved the same key.) This also applies to other one-to-one comparison operators (>, <, and so on), including = and the IN operator. This means that MySQL can use multiple indexes in retrieving results for conditions such as WHERE key1 > 4 OR key2 < 7 and even combinations of conditions such as WHERE (key1 > 4 OR key2 < 7) AND (key3 >= 10 OR key4 = 1). See Section 6.2.6, "Index Merge Optimization."

- A new equality detector finds and optimizes "hidden" equalities in joins. For example, a `WHERE` clause such as

  ```
  t1.c1=t2.c2 AND t2.c2=t3.c3 AND t1.c1 < 5
  ```

  can be reduced to

  ```
  t1.c1=t3.c3 AND t2.c2 < 5 AND t3.c3 < 5
  ```

  These optimizations can be applied with any combination of `AND` and `OR` operators. See Section 6.2.10, "Nested Join Optimization," and Section 6.2.11, "Outer Join Simplification."

- Optimization of `NOT IN` and `NOT BETWEEN` relations, reducing or eliminating table scans for queries making use of them by mean of range analysis. The performance of MySQL with regard to these relations now matches its performance with regard to `IN` and `BETWEEN`.

- The `VARCHAR` data type as implemented in MySQL 5.0 is more efficient than in previous versions, due to the elimination of the old (and nonstandard) removal of trailing spaces during retrieval.

- The addition of a true `BIT` column type; this type is much more efficient for storage and retrieval of Boolean values than the workarounds required in MySQL in versions previous to 5.0.

- **Performance Improvements in the `InnoDB` Storage Engine**:
  - New compact storage format which can save up to 20% of the disk space required in previous MySQL/`InnoDB` versions.
  - Faster recovery from a failed or aborted `ALTER TABLE`.
  - Faster implementation of `TRUNCATE`.

  (See Section 8.2, "The `InnoDB` Storage Engine.")

- **Performance Improvements in the `NDBCluster` Storage Engine**:
  - Faster handling of queries that use `IN` and `BETWEEN`.
  - **Condition pushdown**: In cases involving the comparison of an unindexed column with a constant, this condition is "pushed down" to the cluster where it is evaluated in all partitions simultaneously, eliminating the need to send non-matching records over the network. This can make such queries 10 to 100 times faster than in MySQL 4.1 Cluster.

    See Section 6.2.1, "Optimizing Queries with `EXPLAIN`," for more information.

  (See Chapter 9, "MySQL Cluster.")

For those wishing to take a look at the bleeding edge of MySQL development, we make our BitKeeper repository for MySQL publicly available. See Section 2.8.3, "Installing from the Development Source Tree."

1.7 MySQL Information Sources

This section lists sources of additional information that you may find helpful, such as the MySQL mailing lists and user forums, and Internet Relay Chat.

1.7.1 MySQL Mailing Lists

This section introduces the MySQL mailing lists and provides guidelines as to how the lists should be used. When you subscribe to a mailing list, you receive all postings to the list as email messages. You can also send your own questions and answers to the list.

To subscribe to or unsubscribe from any of the mailing lists described in this section, visit `http://lists.mysql.com/`. For most of them, you can select the regular version of the list where you get individual messages, or a digest version where you get one large message per day.

Please *do not* send messages about subscribing or unsubscribing to any of the mailing lists, because such messages are distributed automatically to thousands of other users.

Your local site may have many subscribers to a MySQL mailing list. If so, the site may have a local mailing list, so that messages sent from `lists.mysql.com` to your site are propagated to the local list. In such cases, please contact your system administrator to be added to or dropped from the local MySQL list.

If you wish to have traffic for a mailing list go to a separate mailbox in your mail program, set up a filter based on the message headers. You can use either the `List-ID:` or `Delivered-To:` headers to identify list messages.

The MySQL mailing lists are as follows:

- `announce`

    This list is for announcements of new versions of MySQL and related programs. This is a low-volume list to which all MySQL users should subscribe.

- `mysql`

    This is the main list for general MySQL discussion. Please note that some topics are better discussed on the more-specialized lists. If you post to the wrong list, you may not get an answer.

- `bugs`

    This list is for people who want to stay informed about issues reported since the last release of MySQL or who want to be actively involved in the process of bug hunting and fixing. See Section 1.8, "How to Report Bugs or Problems."

- `internals`

    This list is for people who work on the MySQL code. This is also the forum for discussions on MySQL development and for posting patches.

- `mysqldoc`

  This list is for people who work on the MySQL documentation: people from MySQL AB, translators, and other community members.

- `benchmarks`

  This list is for anyone interested in performance issues. Discussions concentrate on database performance (not limited to MySQL), but also include broader categories such as performance of the kernel, filesystem, disk system, and so on.

- `packagers`

  This list is for discussions on packaging and distributing MySQL. This is the forum used by distribution maintainers to exchange ideas on packaging MySQL and on ensuring that MySQL looks and feels as similar as possible on all supported platforms and operating systems.

- `java`

  This list is for discussions about the MySQL server and Java. It is mostly used to discuss JDBC drivers such as MySQL Connector/J.

- `win32`

  This list is for all topics concerning the MySQL software on Microsoft operating systems, such as Windows 9x, Me, NT, 2000, XP, and 2003.

- `myodbc`

  This list is for all topics concerning connecting to the MySQL server with ODBC.

- `gui-tools`

  This list is for all topics concerning MySQL graphical user interface tools such as MySQL Administrator and MySQL Query Browser.

- `cluster`

  This list is for discussion of MySQL Cluster.

- `dotnet`

  This list is for discussion of the MySQL server and the .NET platform. It is mostly related to MySQL Connector/Net.

- `plusplus`

  This list is for all topics concerning programming with the C++ API for MySQL.

- `perl`

  This list is for all topics concerning Perl support for MySQL with `DBD::mysql`.

If you're unable to get an answer to your questions from a MySQL mailing list or forum, one option is to purchase support from MySQL AB. This puts you in direct contact with MySQL developers.

The following table shows some MySQL mailing lists in languages other than English. These lists are not operated by MySQL AB.

- `mysql-france-subscribe@yahoogroups.com`

    A French mailing list.

- `list@tinc.net`

    A Korean mailing list. To subscribe, email `subscribe mysql your@email.address` to this list.

- `mysql-de-request@lists.4t2.com`

    A German mailing list. To subscribe, email `subscribe mysql-de your@email.address` to this list. You can find information about this mailing list at `http://www.4t2.com/mysql/`.

- `mysql-br-request@listas.linkway.com.br`

    A Portuguese mailing list. To subscribe, email `subscribe mysql-br your@email.address` to this list.

- `mysql-alta@elistas.net`

    A Spanish mailing list. To subscribe, email `subscribe mysql your@email.address` to this list.

1.7.1.1 Guidelines for Using the Mailing Lists

Please don't post mail messages from your browser with HTML mode turned on. Many users don't read mail with a browser.

When you answer a question sent to a mailing list, if you consider your answer to have broad interest, you may want to post it to the list instead of replying directly to the individual who asked. Try to make your answer general enough that people other than the original poster may benefit from it. When you post to the list, please make sure that your answer is not a duplication of a previous answer.

Try to summarize the essential part of the question in your reply. Don't feel obliged to quote the entire original message.

When answers are sent to you individually and not to the mailing list, it is considered good etiquette to summarize the answers and send the summary to the mailing list so that others may have the benefit of responses you received that helped you solve your problem.

1.7.2 MySQL Community Support at the MySQL Forums

The forums at `http://forums.mysql.com/` are an important community resource. Many forums are available, grouped into these general categories:

- Migration
- MySQL Usage
- MySQL Connectors
- Programming Languages

- Tools
- 3rd-Party Applications
- Storage Engines
- MySQL Technology
- SQL Standards
- Business

1.7.3 MySQL Community Support on Internet Relay Chat (IRC)

In addition to the various MySQL mailing lists and forums, you can find experienced community people on Internet Relay Chat (IRC). These are the best networks/channels currently known to us:

- **freenode** (see `http://www.freenode.net/` for servers)
- `#mysql` is primarily for MySQL questions, but other database and general SQL questions are welcome. Questions about PHP, Perl, or C in combination with MySQL are also common.

If you are looking for IRC client software to connect to an IRC network, take a look at xChat (`http://www.xchat.org/`). X-Chat (GPL licensed) is available for Unix as well as for Windows platforms (a free Windows build of X-Chat is available at `http://www.silverex.org/download/`).

1.8 How to Report Bugs or Problems

Before posting a bug report about a problem, please try to verify that it is a bug and that it has not been reported already:

- Start by searching the MySQL online manual at `http://dev.mysql.com/doc/`. We try to keep the manual up to date by updating it frequently with solutions to newly found problems. The change history (`http://dev.mysql.com/doc/mysql/en/news.html`) can be particularly useful since it is quite possible that a newer version contains a solution to your problem.
- If you get a parse error for a SQL statement, please check your syntax closely. If you can't find something wrong with it, it's extremely likely that your current version of MySQL Server doesn't support the syntax you are using. If you are using the current version and the manual doesn't cover the syntax that you are using, MySQL Server doesn't support your statement. In this case, your options are to implement the syntax yourself or email `licensing@mysql.com` and ask for an offer to implement it.

  If the manual covers the syntax you are using, but you have an older version of MySQL Server, you should check the MySQL change history to see when the syntax was implemented. In this case, you have the option of upgrading to a newer version of MySQL Server.

- Search the bugs database at `http://bugs.mysql.com/` to see whether the bug has been reported and fixed.
- Search the MySQL mailing list archives at `http://lists.mysql.com/`. See Section 1.7.1, "MySQL Mailing Lists."
- You can also use `http://www.mysql.com/search/` to search all the Web pages (including the manual) that are located at the MySQL AB Web site.

If you can't find an answer in the manual, the bugs database, or the mailing list archives, check with your local MySQL expert. If you still can't find an answer to your question, please use the following guidelines for reporting the bug.

The normal way to report bugs is to visit `http://bugs.mysql.com/`, which is the address for our bugs database. This database is public and can be browsed and searched by anyone. If you log in to the system, you can enter new reports. If you have no Web access, you can generate a bug report by using the `mysqlbug` script described at the end of this section.

Bugs posted in the bugs database at `http://bugs.mysql.com/` that are corrected for a given release are noted in the change history.

If you have found a sensitive security bug in MySQL, you can send email to `security@ mysql.com`.

To discuss problems with other users, you can use one of the MySQL mailing lists. Section 1.7.1, "MySQL Mailing Lists."

Writing a good bug report takes patience, but doing it right the first time saves time both for us and for yourself. A good bug report, containing a full test case for the bug, makes it very likely that we will fix the bug in the next release. This section helps you write your report correctly so that you don't waste your time doing things that may not help us much or at all. Please read this section carefully and make sure that all the information described here is included in your report.

Preferably, you should test the problem using the latest production or development version of MySQL Server before posting. Anyone should be able to repeat the bug by just using `mysql test < script_file` on your test case or by running the shell or Perl script that you include in the bug report. Any bug that we are able to repeat has a high chance of being fixed in the next MySQL release.

It is most helpful when a good description of the problem is included in the bug report. That is, give a good example of everything you did that led to the problem and describe, in exact detail, the problem itself. The best reports are those that include a full example showing how to reproduce the bug or problem.

Remember that it is possible for us to respond to a report containing too much information, but not to one containing too little. People often omit facts because they think they know the cause of a problem and assume that some details don't matter. A good principle to follow is that if you are in doubt about stating something, state it. It is faster and less troublesome to write a couple more lines in your report than to wait longer for the answer if we must ask you to provide information that was missing from the initial report.

The most common errors made in bug reports are (a) not including the version number of the MySQL distribution that you use, and (b) not fully describing the platform on which the MySQL server is installed (including the platform type and version number). These are highly relevant pieces of information, and in 99 cases out of 100, the bug report is useless without them. Very often we get questions like, "Why doesn't this work for me?" Then we find that the feature requested wasn't implemented in that MySQL version, or that a bug described in a report has been fixed in newer MySQL versions. Errors often are platform-dependent. In such cases, it is next to impossible for us to fix anything without knowing the operating system and the version number of the platform.

If you compiled MySQL from source, remember also to provide information about your compiler if it is related to the problem. Often people find bugs in compilers and think the problem is MySQL-related. Most compilers are under development all the time and become better version by version. To determine whether your problem depends on your compiler, we need to know what compiler you used. Note that every compiling problem should be regarded as a bug and reported accordingly.

If a program produces an error message, it is very important to include the message in your report. If we try to search for something from the archives, it is better that the error message reported exactly matches the one that the program produces. (Even the lettercase should be observed.) It is best to copy and paste the entire error message into your report. You should never try to reproduce the message from memory.

If you have a problem with Connector/ODBC (MyODBC), please try to generate a trace file and send it with your report.

If your report includes long query output lines from test cases that you run with the `mysql` command-line tool, you can make the output more readable by using the `--vertical` option or the `\G` statement terminator. The EXPLAIN SELECT example later in this section demonstrates the use of `\G`.

Please include the following information in your report:

- The version number of the MySQL distribution you are using (for example, MySQL 5.0.19). You can find out which version you are running by executing `mysqladmin version`. The `mysqladmin` program can be found in the `bin` directory under your MySQL installation directory.
- The manufacturer and model of the machine on which you experience the problem.
- The operating system name and version. If you work with Windows, you can usually get the name and version number by double-clicking your My Computer icon and pulling down the "Help/About Windows" menu. For most Unix-like operating systems, you can get this information by executing the command `uname -a`.

- Sometimes the amount of memory (real and virtual) is relevant. If in doubt, include these values.

- If you are using a source distribution of the MySQL software, include the name and version number of the compiler that you used. If you have a binary distribution, include the distribution name.

- If the problem occurs during compilation, include the exact error messages and also a few lines of context around the offending code in the file where the error occurs.

- If `mysqld` died, you should also report the statement that crashed `mysqld`. You can usually get this information by running `mysqld` with query logging enabled, and then looking in the log after `mysqld` crashes.

- If a database table is related to the problem, include the output from the `SHOW CREATE TABLE` *db_name.tbl_name* statement in the bug report. This is a very easy way to get the definition of any table in a database. The information helps us create a situation matching the one that you have experienced.

- For performance-related bugs or problems with `SELECT` statements, you should always include the output of `EXPLAIN SELECT ...`, and at least the number of rows that the `SELECT` statement produces. You should also include the output from `SHOW CREATE TABLE` *tbl_name* for each table that is involved. The more information you provide about your situation, the more likely it is that someone can help you.

The following is an example of a very good bug report. The statements are run using the `mysql` command-line tool. Note the use of the `\G` statement terminator for statements that would otherwise provide very long output lines that are difficult to read.

```
mysql> SHOW VARIABLES;
mysql> SHOW COLUMNS FROM ...\G
        <output from SHOW COLUMNS>
mysql> EXPLAIN SELECT ...\G
        <output from EXPLAIN>
mysql> FLUSH STATUS;
mysql> SELECT ...;
        <A short version of the output from SELECT,
        including the time taken to run the query>
mysql> SHOW STATUS;
        <output from SHOW STATUS>
```

- If a bug or problem occurs while running `mysqld`, try to provide an input script that reproduces the anomaly. This script should include any necessary source files. The more closely the script can reproduce your situation, the better. If you can make a reproducible test case, you should upload it to be attached to the bug report.

If you can't provide a script, you should at least include the output from `mysqladmin variables extended-status processlist` in your report to provide some information on how your system is performing.

- If you can't produce a test case with only a few rows, or if the test table is too big to be included in the bug report (more than 10 rows), you should dump your tables using `mysqldump` and create a `README` file that describes your problem. Create a compressed archive of your files using `tar` and `gzip` or `zip`, and use FTP to transfer the archive to `ftp://ftp.mysql.com/pub/mysql/upload/`. Then enter the problem into our bugs database at `http://bugs.mysql.com/`.

- If you believe that the MySQL server produces a strange result from a statement, include not only the result, but also your opinion of what the result should be, and an explanation describing the basis for your opinion.

- When you provide an example of the problem, it's better to use the table names, variable names, and so forth that exist in your actual situation than to come up with new names. The problem could be related to the name of a table or variable. These cases are rare, perhaps, but it is better to be safe than sorry. After all, it should be easier for you to provide an example that uses your actual situation, and it is by all means better for us. If you have data that you don't want to be visible to others in the bug report, you can use FTP to transfer it to `ftp://ftp.mysql.com/pub/mysql/upload/`. If the information is really top secret and you don't want to show it even to us, go ahead and provide an example using other names, but please regard this as the last choice.

- Include all the options given to the relevant programs, if possible. For example, indicate the options that you use when you start the `mysqld` server, as well as the options that you use to run any MySQL client programs. The options to programs such as `mysqld` and `mysql`, and to the `configure` script, are often key to resolving problems and are very relevant. It is never a bad idea to include them. If your problem involves a program written in a language such as Perl or PHP, please include the language processor's version number, as well as the version for any modules that the program uses. For example, if you have a Perl script that uses the `DBI` and `DBD::mysql` modules, include the version numbers for Perl, `DBI`, and `DBD::mysql`.

- If your question is related to the privilege system, please include the output of `mysqlaccess`, the output of `mysqladmin reload`, and all the error messages you get when trying to connect. When you test your privileges, you should first run `mysqlaccess`. After this, execute `mysqladmin reload version` and try to connect with the program that gives you trouble. `mysqlaccess` can be found in the `bin` directory under your MySQL installation directory.

- If you have a patch for a bug, do include it. But don't assume that the patch is all we need, or that we can use it, if you don't provide some necessary information such as test cases showing the bug that your patch fixes. We might find problems with your patch or we might not understand it at all. If so, we can't use it.

  If we can't verify the exact purpose of the patch, we won't use it. Test cases help us here. Show that the patch handles all the situations that may occur. If we find a borderline case (even a rare one) where the patch won't work, it may be useless.

- Guesses about what the bug is, why it occurs, or what it depends on are usually wrong. Even the MySQL team can't guess such things without first using a debugger to determine the real cause of a bug.

- Indicate in your bug report that you have checked the reference manual and mail archive so that others know you have tried to solve the problem yourself.

- If the problem is that your data appears corrupt or you get errors when you access a particular table, you should first check your tables and then try to repair them with CHECK TABLE and REPAIR TABLE or with myisamchk. See Chapter 4, "Database Administration."

  If you are running Windows, please verify the value of lower_case_table_names using the SHOW VARIABLES LIKE 'lower_case_table_names' command. This variable affects how the server handles lettercase of database and table names.

- If you often get corrupted tables, you should try to find out when and why this happens. In this case, the error log in the MySQL data directory may contain some information about what happened. (This is the file with the .err suffix in the name.) See Section 4.12.1, "The Error Log." Please include any relevant information from this file in your bug report. Normally mysqld should *never* crash a table if nothing killed it in the middle of an update. If you can find the cause of mysqld dying, it's much easier for us to provide you with a fix for the problem.

- If possible, download and install the most recent version of MySQL Server and check whether it solves your problem. All versions of the MySQL software are thoroughly tested and should work without problems. We believe in making everything as backward-compatible as possible, and you should be able to switch MySQL versions without difficulty. See Section 2.1.2, "Choosing Which MySQL Distribution to Install."

If you have no Web access and cannot report a bug by visiting http://bugs.mysql.com/, you can use the mysqlbug script to generate a bug report (or a report about any problem). mysqlbug helps you generate a report by determining much of the following information automatically, but if something important is missing, please include it with your message. mysqlbug can be found in the scripts directory (source distribution) and in the bin directory under your MySQL installation directory (binary distribution).

1.9 MySQL Standards Compliance

This section describes how MySQL relates to the ANSI/ISO SQL standards. MySQL Server has many extensions to the SQL standard, and here you can find out what they are and how to use them. You can also find information about functionality missing from MySQL Server, and how to work around some of the differences.

The SQL standard has been evolving since 1986 and several versions exist. In this manual, "SQL-92" refers to the standard released in 1992, "SQL:1999" refers to the standard released in 1999, and "SQL:2003" refers to the current version of the standard. We use the phrase "the SQL standard" or "standard SQL" to mean the current version of the SQL standard at any time.

One of our main goals with the product is to continue to work toward compliance with the SQL standard, but without sacrificing speed or reliability. We are not afraid to add extensions to SQL or support for non-SQL features if this greatly increases the usability of MySQL Server for a large segment of our user base. The HANDLER interface is an example of this strategy.

We continue to support transactional and non-transactional databases to satisfy both mission-critical 24/7 usage and heavy Web or logging usage.

MySQL Server was originally designed to work with medium-sized databases (10–100 million rows, or about 100MB per table) on small computer systems. Today MySQL Server handles terabyte-sized databases, but the code can also be compiled in a reduced version suitable for hand-held and embedded devices. The compact design of the MySQL server makes development in both directions possible without any conflicts in the source tree.

Currently, we are not targeting real-time support, although MySQL replication capabilities offer significant functionality.

MySQL supports high-availability database clustering using the NDBCluster storage engine. See Chapter 9, "MySQL Cluster."

XML support is to be implemented in a future version of the database server.

1.9.1 What Standards MySQL Follows

Our aim is to support the full ANSI/ISO SQL standard, but without making concessions to speed and quality of the code.

ODBC levels 0-3.51.

1.9.2 Selecting SQL Modes

The MySQL server can operate in different SQL modes, and can apply these modes differentially for different clients. This capability enables each application to tailor the server's operating mode to its own requirements.

SQL modes control aspects of server operation such as what SQL syntax MySQL should support and what kind of data validation checks it should perform. This makes it easier to use MySQL in different environments and to use MySQL together with other database servers.

You can set the default SQL mode by starting mysqld with the --sql-mode="*mode_value*" option. Beginning with MySQL 4.1, you can also change the mode at runtime by setting the sql_mode system variable with a SET [SESSION|GLOBAL] sql_mode='*mode_value*' statement.

For more information on setting the SQL mode, see Section 4.2.5, "The Server SQL Mode."

1.9.3 Running MySQL in ANSI Mode

You can tell mysqld to run in ANSI mode with the --ansi startup option. Running the server in ANSI mode is the same as starting it with the following options:

```
--transaction-isolation=SERIALIZABLE --sql-mode=ANSI
```

As of MySQL 4.1.1, you can achieve the same effect at runtime by executing these two statements:

```
SET GLOBAL TRANSACTION ISOLATION LEVEL SERIALIZABLE;
SET GLOBAL sql_mode = 'ANSI';
```

You can see that setting the sql_mode system variable to 'ANSI' enables all SQL mode options that are relevant for ANSI mode as follows:

```
mysql> SET GLOBAL sql_mode='ANSI';
mysql> SELECT @@global.sql_mode;
        -> 'REAL_AS_FLOAT,PIPES_AS_CONCAT,ANSI_QUOTES,IGNORE_SPACE,ANSI'
```

Note that running the server in ANSI mode with --ansi is not quite the same as setting the SQL mode to 'ANSI'. The --ansi option affects the SQL mode and also sets the transaction isolation level. Setting the SQL mode to 'ANSI' has no effect on the isolation level.

See Section 1.9.2, "Selecting SQL Modes," and Section 4.2.1, "mysqld Command Options."

1.9.4 MySQL Extensions to Standard SQL

MySQL Server supports some extensions that you probably won't find in other SQL DBMSs. Be warned that if you use them, your code won't be portable to other SQL servers. In some cases, you can write code that includes MySQL extensions, but is still portable, by using comments of the following form:

```
/*! MySQL-specific code */
```

In this case, MySQL Server parses and executes the code within the comment as it would any other SQL statement, but other SQL servers will ignore the extensions. For example, MySQL Server recognizes the STRAIGHT_JOIN keyword in the following statement, but other servers will not:

```
SELECT /*! STRAIGHT_JOIN */ col1 FROM table1,table2 WHERE ...
```

If you add a version number after the '!' character, the syntax within the comment is executed only if the MySQL version is greater than or equal to the specified version number. The TEMPORARY keyword in the following comment is executed only by servers from MySQL 3.23.02 or higher:

```
CREATE /*!32302 TEMPORARY */ TABLE t (a INT);
```

The following descriptions list MySQL extensions, organized by category.

- Organization of data on disk

  MySQL Server maps each database to a directory under the MySQL data directory, and maps tables within a database to filenames in the database directory. This has a few implications:

  - Database and table names are case sensitive in MySQL Server on operating systems that have case-sensitive filenames (such as most Unix systems).

  - You can use standard system commands to back up, rename, move, delete, and copy tables that are managed by the `MyISAM` storage engine. For example, it is possible to rename a `MyISAM` table by renaming the `.MYD`, `.MYI`, and `.frm` files to which the table corresponds. (Nevertheless, it is preferable to use `RENAME TABLE` or `ALTER TABLE ... RENAME` and let the server rename the files.)

  Database and table names cannot contain pathname separator characters ('/', '\').

- General language syntax

  - By default, strings can be enclosed by either '"' or '‘', not just by '‘'. (If the `ANSI_QUOTES` SQL mode is enabled, strings can be enclosed only by '‘' and the server interprets strings enclosed by '"' as identifiers.)

  - Use of '\' as an escape character in strings.

  - In SQL statements, you can access tables from different databases with the `db_name.tbl_name` syntax. Some SQL servers provide the same functionality but call this `User space`. MySQL Server doesn't support tablespaces such as used in statements like this: `CREATE TABLE ralph.my_table...IN my_tablespace`.

- SQL statement syntax

  - The `ANALYZE TABLE`, `CHECK TABLE`, `OPTIMIZE TABLE`, and `REPAIR TABLE` statements.

  - The `CREATE DATABASE`, `DROP DATABASE`, and `ALTER DATABASE` statements.

  - The `DO` statement.

  - `EXPLAIN SELECT` to obtain a description of how tables are processed by the query optimizer.

  - The `FLUSH` and `RESET` statements.

  - The `SET` statement.

  - The `SHOW` statement. As of MySQL 5.0, the information produced by many of the MySQL-specific `SHOW` statements can be obtained in more standard fashion by using `SELECT` to query `INFORMATION_SCHEMA`.

  - Use of `LOAD DATA INFILE`. In many cases, this syntax is compatible with Oracle's `LOAD DATA INFILE`.

  - Use of `RENAME TABLE`.

  - Use of `REPLACE` instead of `DELETE` plus `INSERT`.

- Use of CHANGE *col_name*, DROP *col_name*, or DROP INDEX, IGNORE or RENAME in ALTER TABLE statements. Use of multiple ADD, ALTER, DROP, or CHANGE clauses in an ALTER TABLE statement.

- Use of index names, indexes on a prefix of a column, and use of INDEX or KEY in CREATE TABLE statements.

- Use of TEMPORARY or IF NOT EXISTS with CREATE TABLE.

- Use of IF EXISTS with DROP TABLE and DROP DATABASE.

- The capability of dropping multiple tables with a single DROP TABLE statement.

- The ORDER BY and LIMIT clauses of the UPDATE and DELETE statements.

- INSERT INTO ... SET *col_name* = ... syntax.

- The DELAYED clause of the INSERT and REPLACE statements.

- The LOW_PRIORITY clause of the INSERT, REPLACE, DELETE, and UPDATE statements.

- Use of INTO OUTFILE or INTO DUMPFILE in SELECT statements.

- Options such as STRAIGHT_JOIN or SQL_SMALL_RESULT in SELECT statements.

- You don't need to name all selected columns in the GROUP BY clause. This gives better performance for some very specific, but quite normal queries.

- You can specify ASC and DESC with GROUP BY, not just with ORDER BY.

- The ability to set variables in a statement with the := assignment operator:

```
mysql> SELECT @a:=SUM(total),@b=COUNT(*),@a/@b AS avg
    -> FROM test_table;
mysql> SELECT @t1:=(@t2:=1)+@t3:=4,@t1,@t2,@t3;
```

- Data types
  - The MEDIUMINT, SET, and ENUM data types, and the various BLOB and TEXT data types.
  - The AUTO_INCREMENT, BINARY, NULL, UNSIGNED, and ZEROFILL data type attributes.

- Functions and operators
  - To make it easier for users who migrate from other SQL environments, MySQL Server supports aliases for many functions. For example, all string functions support both standard SQL syntax and ODBC syntax.
  - MySQL Server understands the || and && operators to mean logical OR and AND, as in the C programming language. In MySQL Server, || and OR are synonyms, as are && and AND. Because of this nice syntax, MySQL Server doesn't support the standard SQL || operator for string concatenation; use CONCAT() instead. Because CONCAT() takes any number of arguments, it's easy to convert use of the || operator to MySQL Server.
  - Use of COUNT(DISTINCT *value_list*) where *value_list* has more than one element.
  - String comparisons are case-insensitive by default, with sort ordering determined by the collation of the current character set, which is latin1 (cp1252 West European) by default. If you don't like this, you should declare your columns with

the BINARY attribute or use the BINARY cast, which causes comparisons to be done using the underlying character code values rather then a lexical ordering.

- The % operator is a synonym for MOD(). That is, N % M is equivalent to MOD(N,M). % is supported for C programmers and for compatibility with PostgreSQL.

- The =, <>, <=,<, >=,>, <<, >>, <=>, AND, OR, or LIKE operators may be used in expressions in the output column list (to the left of the FROM) in SELECT statements. For example:

```
mysql> SELECT col1=1 AND col2=2 FROM my_table;
```

- The LAST_INSERT_ID() function returns the most recent AUTO_INCREMENT value.

- LIKE is allowed on numeric values.

- The REGEXP and NOT REGEXP extended regular expression operators.

- CONCAT() or CHAR() with one argument or more than two arguments. (In MySQL Server, these functions can take a variable number of arguments.)

- The BIT_COUNT(), CASE, ELT(), FROM_DAYS(), FORMAT(), IF(), PASSWORD(), ENCRYPT(), MD5(), ENCODE(), DECODE(), PERIOD_ADD(), PERIOD_DIFF(), TO_DAYS(), and WEEKDAY() functions.

- Use of TRIM() to trim substrings. Standard SQL supports removal of single characters only.

- The GROUP BY functions STD(), BIT_OR(), BIT_AND(), BIT_XOR(), and GROUP_CONCAT().

For a prioritized list indicating when new extensions are added to MySQL Server, you should consult the online MySQL development roadmap at http://dev.mysql.com/doc/mysql/en/roadmap.html.

1.9.5 MySQL Differences from Standard SQL

We try to make MySQL Server follow the ANSI SQL standard and the ODBC SQL standard, but MySQL Server performs operations differently in some cases:

- For VARCHAR columns, trailing spaces are removed when the value is stored. (This is fixed in MySQL 5.0.3.)

- In some cases, CHAR columns are silently converted to VARCHAR columns when you define a table or alter its structure. (This is fixed in MySQL 5.0.3.)

- There are several differences between the MySQL and standard SQL privilege systems. For example, in MySQL, privileges for a table are not automatically revoked when you delete a table. You must explicitly issue a REVOKE statement to revoke privileges for a table.

- The CAST() function does not support cast to REAL or BIGINT.

- Standard SQL requires that a HAVING clause in a SELECT statement be able to refer to columns in the GROUP BY clause. This cannot be done before MySQL 5.0.2.

1.9.5.1 Subquery Support

MySQL 4.1 and up supports subqueries and derived tables. A "subquery" is a SELECT statement nested within another statement. A "derived table" (an unnamed view) is a subquery in the FROM clause of another statement.

For MySQL versions older than 4.1, most subqueries can be rewritten using joins or other methods.

1.9.5.2 SELECT INTO TABLE

MySQL Server doesn't support the SELECT ... INTO TABLE Sybase SQL extension. Instead, MySQL Server supports the INSERT INTO ... SELECT standard SQL syntax, which is basically the same thing. For example:

```
INSERT INTO tbl_temp2 (fld_id)
    SELECT tbl_temp1.fld_order_id
    FROM tbl_temp1 WHERE tbl_temp1.fld_order_id > 100;
```

Alternatively, you can use SELECT ... INTO OUTFILE or CREATE TABLE ... SELECT.

As of MySQL 5.0, you can use SELECT ... INTO with user-defined variables. The same syntax can also be used inside stored routines using cursors and local variables.

1.9.5.3 Transactions and Atomic Operations

MySQL Server (version 3.23-max and all versions 4.0 and above) supports transactions with the InnoDB and BDB transactional storage engines. InnoDB provides *full* ACID compliance. See Chapter 8, "Storage Engines and Table Types." For information about InnoDB differences from standard SQL with regard to treatment of transaction errors, see Section 8.2.15, "InnoDB Error Handling."

The other non-transactional storage engines in MySQL Server (such as MyISAM) follow a different paradigm for data integrity called "atomic operations." In transactional terms, MyISAM tables effectively always operate in AUTOCOMMIT=1 mode. Atomic operations often offer comparable integrity with higher performance.

Because MySQL Server supports both paradigms, you can decide whether your applications are best served by the speed of atomic operations or the use of transactional features. This choice can be made on a per-table basis.

As noted, the trade-off for transactional versus non-transactional storage engines lies mostly in performance. Transactional tables have significantly higher memory and disk space requirements, and more CPU overhead. On the other hand, transactional storage engines such as InnoDB also offer many significant features. MySQL Server's modular design allows the concurrent use of different storage engines to suit different requirements and deliver optimum performance in all situations.

But how do you use the features of MySQL Server to maintain rigorous integrity even with the non-transactional MyISAM tables, and how do these features compare with the transactional storage engines?

- If your applications are written in a way that is dependent on being able to call ROLLBACK rather than COMMIT in critical situations, transactions are more convenient. Transactions also ensure that unfinished updates or corrupting activities are not committed to the database; the server is given the opportunity to do an automatic rollback and your database is saved.

  If you use non-transactional tables, MySQL Server in almost all cases allows you to resolve potential problems by including simple checks before updates and by running simple scripts that check the databases for inconsistencies and automatically repair or warn if such an inconsistency occurs. Note that just by using the MySQL log or even adding one extra log, you can normally fix tables perfectly with no data integrity loss.

- More often than not, critical transactional updates can be rewritten to be atomic. Generally speaking, all integrity problems that transactions solve can be done with LOCK TABLES or atomic updates, ensuring that there are no automatic aborts from the server, which is a common problem with transactional database systems.

- To be safe with MySQL Server, regardless of whether you use transactional tables, you only need to have backups and have binary logging turned on. When that is true, you can recover from any situation that you could with any other transactional database system. It is always good to have backups, regardless of which database system you use.

The transactional paradigm has its benefits and its drawbacks. Many users and application developers depend on the ease with which they can code around problems where an abort appears to be necessary, or is necessary. However, even if you are new to the atomic operations paradigm, or more familiar with transactions, do consider the speed benefit that non-transactional tables can offer on the order of three to five times the speed of the fastest and most optimally tuned transactional tables.

In situations where integrity is of highest importance, MySQL Server offers transaction-level reliability and integrity even for non-transactional tables. If you lock tables with LOCK TABLES, all updates stall until integrity checks are made. If you obtain a READ LOCAL lock (as opposed to a write lock) for a table that allows concurrent inserts at the end of the table, reads are allowed, as are inserts by other clients. The newly inserted records are not be seen by the client that has the read lock until it releases the lock. With INSERT DELAYED, you can write inserts that go into a local queue until the locks are released, without having the client wait for the insert to complete. See Section 6.3.3, "Concurrent Inserts."

"Atomic," in the sense that we mean it, is nothing magical. It only means that you can be sure that while each specific update is running, no other user can interfere with it, and there can never be an automatic rollback (which can happen with transactional tables if you are not very careful). MySQL Server also guarantees that there are no dirty reads.

Following are some techniques for working with non-transactional tables:

- Loops that need transactions normally can be coded with the help of LOCK TABLES, and you don't need cursors to update records on the fly.
- To avoid using ROLLBACK, you can employ the following strategy:
    1. Use LOCK TABLES to lock all the tables you want to access.
    2. Test the conditions that must be true before performing the update.
    3. Update if the conditions are satisfied.
    4. Use UNLOCK TABLES to release your locks.

    This is usually a much faster method than using transactions with possible rollbacks, although not always. The only situation this solution doesn't handle is when someone kills the threads in the middle of an update. In that case, all locks are released but some of the updates may not have been executed.

- You can also use functions to update records in a single operation. You can get a very efficient application by using the following techniques:
    - Modify columns relative to their current value.
    - Update only those columns that actually have changed.

For example, when we are updating customer information, we update only the customer data that has changed and test only that none of the changed data, or data that depends on the changed data, has changed compared to the original row. The test for changed data is done with the WHERE clause in the UPDATE statement. If the record wasn't updated, we give the client a message: "Some of the data you have changed has been changed by another user." Then we show the old row versus the new row in a window so that the user can decide which version of the customer record to use.

This gives us something that is similar to column locking but is actually even better because we only update some of the columns, using values that are relative to their current values. This means that typical UPDATE statements look something like these:

```
UPDATE tablename SET pay_back=pay_back+125;
```

```
UPDATE customer
  SET
    customer_date='current_date',
    address='new address',
    phone='new phone',
    money_owed_to_us=money_owed_to_us-125
  WHERE
    customer_id=id AND address='old address' AND phone='old phone';
```

This is very efficient and works even if another client has changed the values in the pay_back or money_owed_to_us columns.

- In many cases, users have wanted LOCK TABLES or ROLLBACK for the purpose of managing unique identifiers. This can be handled much more efficiently without locking or rolling back by using an AUTO_INCREMENT column and either the LAST_INSERT_ID() SQL function or the mysql_insert_id() C API function.

You can generally code around the need for row-level locking. Some situations really do need it, and InnoDB tables support row-level locking. Otherwise, with MyISAM tables, you can use a flag column in the table and do something like the following:

```
UPDATE tbl_name SET row_flag=1 WHERE id=ID;
```

MySQL returns 1 for the number of affected rows if the row was found and row_flag wasn't 1 in the original row. You can think of this as though MySQL Server changed the preceding statement to:

```
UPDATE tbl_name SET row_flag=1 WHERE id=ID AND row_flag <> 1;
```

1.9.5.4 Stored Routines and Triggers

Stored procedures and functions are implemented beginning with MySQL 5.0.

Basic trigger functionality is implemented beginning with MySQL 5.0.2, with further development planned for MySQL 5.1.

1.9.5.5 Foreign Keys

In MySQL Server 3.23.44 and up, the InnoDB storage engine supports checking of foreign key constraints, including CASCADE, ON DELETE, and ON UPDATE. See Section 8.2.6.4, "FOREIGN KEY Constraints."

For storage engines other than InnoDB, MySQL Server parses the FOREIGN KEY syntax in CREATE TABLE statements, but does not use or store it. In the future, the implementation will be extended to store this information in the table specification file so that it may be retrieved by mysqldump and ODBC. At a later stage, foreign key constraints will be implemented for MyISAM tables as well.

Foreign key enforcement offers several benefits to database developers:

- Assuming proper design of the relationships, foreign key constraints make it more difficult for a programmer to introduce an inconsistency into the database.
- Centralized checking of constraints by the database server makes it unnecessary to perform these checks on the application side. This eliminates the possibility that different applications may not all check the constraints in the same way.
- Using cascading updates and deletes can simplify the application code.
- Properly designed foreign key rules aid in documenting relationships between tables.

Do keep in mind that these benefits come at the cost of additional overhead for the database server to perform the necessary checks. Additional checking by the server affects performance, which for some applications may be sufficiently undesirable as to be avoided if possible. (Some major commercial applications have coded the foreign key logic at the application level for this reason.)

MySQL gives database developers the choice of which approach to use. If you don't need foreign keys and want to avoid the overhead associated with enforcing referential integrity, you can choose another storage engine instead, such as MyISAM. (For example, the MyISAM storage engine offers very fast performance for applications that perform only INSERT and SELECT operations. In this case, the table has no holes in the middle and the inserts can be performed concurrently with retrievals. See Section 6.3.3, "Concurrent Inserts.")

If you choose not to take advantage of referential integrity checks, keep the following considerations in mind:

- In the absence of server-side foreign key relationship checking, the application itself must handle relationship issues. For example, it must take care to insert rows into tables in the proper order, and to avoid creating orphaned child records. It must also be able to recover from errors that occur in the middle of multiple-record insert operations.

- If ON DELETE is the only referential integrity capability an application needs, you can achieve a similar effect as of MySQL Server 4.0 by using multiple-table DELETE statements to delete rows from many tables with a single statement.

- A workaround for the lack of ON DELETE is to add the appropriate DELETE statements to your application when you delete records from a table that has a foreign key. In practice, this is often as quick as using foreign keys and is more portable.

Be aware that the use of foreign keys can sometimes lead to problems:

- Foreign key support addresses many referential integrity issues, but it is still necessary to design key relationships carefully to avoid circular rules or incorrect combinations of cascading deletes.

- It is not uncommon for a DBA to create a topology of relationships that makes it difficult to restore individual tables from a backup. (MySQL alleviates this difficulty by allowing you to temporarily disable foreign key checks when reloading a table that depends on other tables. See Section 8.2.6.4, "FOREIGN KEY Constraints." As of MySQL 4.1.1, mysqldump generates dump files that take advantage of this capability automatically when they are reloaded.)

Note that foreign keys in SQL are used to check and enforce referential integrity, not to join tables. If you want to get results from multiple tables from a SELECT statement, you do this by performing a join between them:

```
SELECT * FROM t1 INNER JOIN t2 ON t1.id = t2.id;
```

The FOREIGN KEY syntax without ON DELETE ... is often used by ODBC applications to produce automatic WHERE clauses.

1.9.5.6 Views

Views (including updatable views) are implemented beginning with MySQL Server 5.0.1.

Views are useful for allowing users to access a set of relations (tables) as if it were a single table, and limiting their access to just that. Views can also be used to restrict access to rows (a subset of a particular table). For access control to columns, you can also use the sophisticated privilege system in MySQL Server. See Section 4.8, "The MySQL Access Privilege System."

In designing an implementation of views, our ambitious goal, as much as is possible within the confines of SQL, has been full compliance with "Codd's Rule #6" for relational database systems: "All views that are theoretically updatable, should in practice also be updatable."

1.9.5.7 '--' as the Start of a Comment

Standard SQL uses the C syntax /* this is a comment */ for comments, and MySQL Server supports this syntax as well. MySQL also support extensions to this syntax that allow MySQL-specific SQL to be embedded in the comment, as described in the "MySQL Language Reference."

Standard SQL uses '--' as a start-comment sequence. MySQL Server uses '#' as the start comment character. MySQL Server 3.23.3 and up also supports a variant of the '--' comment style. That is, the '--' start-comment sequence must be followed by a space (or by a control character such as a newline). The space is required to prevent problems with automatically generated SQL queries that use constructs such as the following, where we automatically insert the value of the payment for !payment!:

```
UPDATE account SET credit=credit-!payment!
```

Consider about what happens if payment has a negative value such as -1:

```
UPDATE account SET credit=credit--1
```

credit--1 is a legal expression in SQL, but '--' is interpreted as the start of a comment, part of the expression is discarded. The result is a statement that has a completely different meaning than intended:

```
UPDATE account SET credit=credit
```

The statement produces no change in value at all! This illustrates that allowing comments to start with '--' can have serious consequences.

Using our implementation of requiring a following space for '--' to be recognized as a start-comment sequence in MySQL Server 3.23.3 and up, credit--1 is actually safe.

Another safe feature is that the `mysql` command-line client ignores lines that start with '--'.

The following information is relevant only if you are running a MySQL version earlier than 3.23.3:

If you have an SQL script in a text file that contains '--' comments, you should use the `replace` utility as follows to convert the comments to use '#' characters before executing the script:

```
shell> replace " --" " #" < text-file-with-funny-comments.sql \
         | mysql db_name
```

That is safer than executing the script in the usual way:

```
shell> mysql db_name < text-file-with-funny-comments.sql
```

You can also edit the script file "in place" to change the '--' comments to '#' comments:

```
shell> replace " --" " #" -- text-file-with-funny-comments.sql
```

Change them back with this command:

```
shell> replace " #" " --" -- text-file-with-funny-comments.sql
```

See Section 7.16, "`replace`—A String-Replacement Utility."

1.9.6 How MySQL Deals with Constraints

MySQL allows you to work both with transactional tables that allow rollback and with non-transactional tables that do not. Because of this, constraint handling is a bit different in MySQL than in other DBMSs. We must handle the case when you have inserted or updated a lot of rows in a non-transactional table for which changes cannot be rolled back when an error occurs.

The basic philosophy is that MySQL Server tries to produce an error for anything that it can detect while parsing a statement to be executed, and tries to recover from any errors that occur while executing the statement. We do this in most cases, but not yet for all.

The options MySQL has when an error occurs are to stop the statement in the middle or to recover as well as possible from the problem and continue. By default, the server follows the latter course. This means, for example, that the server may coerce illegal values to the closest legal values.

Beginning with MySQL 5.0.2, several SQL mode options are available to provide greater control over handling of bad data values and whether to continue statement execution or abort when errors occur. Using these options, you can configure MySQL Server to act in a more traditional fashion that is like other DBMSs that reject improper input. The SQL mode can be set globally at server startup to affect all clients. Individual clients can set the SQL mode at runtime, which enables each client to select the behavior most appropriate for its requirements. See Section 4.2.5, "The Server SQL Mode."

The following sections describe how MySQL Server handles different types of constraints.

1.9.6.1 PRIMARY KEY and UNIQUE Index Constraints

Normally, an error occurs when you try to INSERT or UPDATE a row that causes a primary key, unique key, or foreign key violation. If you are using a transactional storage engine such as InnoDB, MySQL automatically rolls back the statement. If you are using a non-transactional storage engine, MySQL stops processing the statement at the row for which the error occurred and leaves any remaining rows unprocessed.

If you want to ignore such key violations, MySQL supports an IGNORE keyword for INSERT and UPDATE. In this case, MySQL ignores any key violations and continues processing with the next row.

You can get information about the number of rows actually inserted or updated with the mysql_info() C API function. In MySQL 4.1 and up, you also can use the SHOW WARNINGS statement.

Currently, only InnoDB tables support foreign keys. See Section 8.2.6.4, "FOREIGN KEY Constraints." Foreign key support in MyISAM tables is scheduled for implementation in MySQL 5.2. See Section 1.6, "MySQL Development Roadmap."

1.9.6.2 Constraints on Invalid Data

Before MySQL 5.0.2, MySQL is forgiving of illegal or improper data values and coerces them to legal values for data entry. In MySQL 5.0.2 and up, that remains the default behavior, but you can change the server SQL mode to select more traditional treatment of bad values such that the server rejects them and aborts the statement in which they occur. Section 4.2.5, "The Server SQL Mode."

This section describes the default (forgiving) behavior of MySQL, as well as the newer strict SQL mode and how it differs.

If you are not using strict mode, whenever you insert an "incorrect" value into a column, such as a NULL into a NOT NULL column or a too-large numeric value into a numeric column, MySQL sets the column to the "best possible value" instead of producing an error. The following rules describe in more detail how this works:

- If you try to store an out of range value into a numeric column, MySQL Server instead stores zero, the smallest possible value, or the largest possible value, whichever is closest to the invalid value.

- For strings, MySQL stores either the empty string or as much of the string as can be stored in the column.

- If you try to store a string that doesn't start with a number into a numeric column, MySQL Server stores 0.

- Invalid values for ENUM and SET columns are handled as described in Section 1.9.6.3, "ENUM and SET Constraints."

- MySQL allows you to store certain incorrect date values into DATE and DATETIME columns (such as '2000-02-31' or '2000-02-00'). The idea is that it's not the job of the SQL server to validate dates. If MySQL can store a date value and retrieve exactly the same value, MySQL stores it as given. If the date is totally wrong (outside the server's ability to store it), the special "zero" date value '0000-00-00' is stored in the column instead.

- If you try to store NULL into a column that doesn't take NULL values, an error occurs for single-row INSERT statements. For multiple-row INSERT statements or for INSERT INTO ... SELECT statements, MySQL Server stores the implicit default value for the column data type. In general, this is 0 for numeric types, the empty string (' ') for string types, and the "zero" value for date and time types.

- If an INSERT statement specifies no value for a column, MySQL inserts its default value if the column definition includes an explicit DEFAULT clause. If the definition has no such DEFAULT clause, MySQL inserts the implicit default value for the column data type.

The reason for using the preceding rules in non-strict mode is that we can't check these conditions until the statement has begun executing. We can't just roll back if we encounter a problem after updating a few rows, because the storage engine may not support rollback. The option of terminating the statement is not that good; in this case, the update would be "half done," which is probably the worst possible scenario. In this case, it's better to "do the best you can" and then continue as if nothing happened.

In MySQL 5.0.2 and up, you can select stricter treatment of input values by using the STRICT_TRANS_TABLES or STRICT_ALL_TABLES SQL modes:

```
SET sql_mode = 'STRICT_TRANS_TABLES';
SET sql_mode = 'STRICT_ALL_TABLES';
```

STRICT_TRANS_TABLES enables strict mode for transactional storage engines, and also to some extent for non-transactional engines. It works like this:

- For transactional storage engines, bad data values occurring anywhere in a statement cause the statement to abort and roll back.

- For non-transactional storage engines, a statement aborts if the error occurs in the first row to be inserted or updated. (When the error occurs in the first row, the statement can be aborted to leave the table unchanged, just as for a transactional table.) Errors in rows after the first do not abort the statement, because the table has already been changed by the first row. Instead, bad data values are adjusted and result in warnings rather than errors. In other words, with STRICT_TRANS_TABLES, a wrong value causes MySQL to roll back all updates done so far, if that can be done without changing the table. But once the table has been changed, further errors result in adjustments and warnings.

For even stricter checking, enable STRICT_ALL_TABLES. This is the same as STRICT_TRANS_TABLES except that for non-transactional storage engines, errors abort the statement even for bad data in rows following the first row. This means that if an error occurs partway through a multiple-row insert or update for a non-transactional table, a partial update results. Earlier rows are inserted or updated, but those from the point of the error on are not. To avoid this for non-transactional tables, either use single-row statements or else use STRICT_TRANS_TABLES if conversion warnings rather than errors are acceptable. To avoid problems in the first place, do not use MySQL to check column content. It is safest (and often faster) to let the application ensure that it passes only legal values to the database.

With either of the strict mode options, you can cause errors to be treated as warnings by using INSERT IGNORE or UPDATE IGNORE rather than INSERT or UPDATE without IGNORE.

1.9.6.3 ENUM and SET Constraints

ENUM and SET columns provide an efficient way to define columns that can contain only a given set of values. However, before MySQL 5.0.2, ENUM and SET columns do not provide true constraints on entry of invalid data:

- ENUM columns always have a default value. If you specify no default value, it is NULL for columns that can have NULL; otherwise it is the first enumeration value in the column definition.

- If you insert an incorrect value into an ENUM column or if you force a value into an ENUM column with IGNORE, it is set to the reserved enumeration value of 0, which is displayed as an empty string in string context.

- If you insert an incorrect value into a SET column, the incorrect value is ignored. For example, if the column can contain the values 'a', 'b', and 'c', an attempt to assign 'a,x,b,y' results in a value of 'a,b'.

As of MySQL 5.0.2, you can configure the server to use strict SQL mode. See Section 4.2.5, "The Server SQL Mode." With strict mode enabled, the definition of a ENUM or SET column does act as a constraint on values entered into the column. An error occurs for values that do not satisfy these conditions:

- An ENUM value must be one of those listed in the column definition, or the internal numeric equivalent thereof. The value cannot be the error value (that is, 0 or the empty string). For a column defined as ENUM('a','b','c'), values such as '', 'd', or 'ax' are illegal and are rejected.

- A SET value must be the empty string or a value consisting only of the values listed in the column definition separated by commas. For a column defined as SET('a','b','c'), values such as 'd' or 'a,b,c,d' are illegal and are rejected.

Errors for invalid values can be suppressed in strict mode if you use INSERT IGNORE or UPDATE IGNORE. In this case, a warning is generated rather than an error. For ENUM, the value is inserted as the error member (0). For SET, the value is inserted as given except that any invalid substrings are deleted. For example, 'a,x,b,y' results in a value of 'a,b'.

2

Installing and Upgrading MySQL

This chapter describes how to obtain and install MySQL. A summary of the procedure follows and later sections provide the details. If you plan to upgrade an existing version of MySQL to a newer version rather than install MySQL for the first time, see Section 2.10, "Upgrading MySQL," for information about upgrade procedures and about issues that you should consider before upgrading.

1. **Determine whether your platform is supported.** Please note that not all supported systems are equally suitable for running MySQL. On some platforms it is much more robust and efficient than others. See Section 2.1.1, "Operating Systems Supported by MySQL," for details.

2. **Choose which distribution to install.** Several versions of MySQL are available, and most are available in several distribution formats. You can choose from pre-packaged distributions containing binary (precompiled) programs or source code. When in doubt, use a binary distribution. We also provide public access to our current source tree for those who want to see our most recent developments and help us test new code. To determine which version and type of distribution you should use, see Section 2.1.2, "Choosing Which MySQL Distribution to Install."

3. **Download the distribution that you want to install.** For instructions, see Section 2.1.3, "How to Get MySQL." To verify the integrity of the distribution, use the instructions in Section 2.1.4, "Verifying Package Integrity Using MD5 Checksums or GnuPG."

4. **Install the distribution.** To install MySQL from a binary distribution, use the instructions in Section 2.2, "Standard MySQL Installation Using a Binary Distribution." To install MySQL from a source distribution or from the current development source tree, use the instructions in Section 2.8, "MySQL Installation Using a Source Distribution."

   If you encounter installation difficulties, see Section 2.12, "Operating System–Specific Notes," for information on solving problems for particular platforms.

5. **Perform any necessary post-installation setup.** After installing MySQL, read Section 2.9, "Post-Installation Setup and Testing." This section contains important information

about making sure the MySQL server is working properly. It also describes how to secure the initial MySQL user accounts, *which have no passwords* until you assign passwords. The section applies whether you install MySQL using a binary or source distribution.

6. If you want to run the MySQL benchmark scripts, Perl support for MySQL must be available. See Section 2.13, "Perl Installation Notes."

2.1 General Installation Issues

Before installing MySQL, you should do the following:

1. Determine whether MySQL runs on your platform.

2. Choose a distribution to install.

3. Download the distribution and verify its integrity.

This section contains the information necessary to carry out these steps. After doing so, you can use the instructions in later sections of the chapter to install the distribution that you choose.

2.1.1 Operating Systems Supported by MySQL

This section lists the operating systems on which you can expect to be able to run MySQL.

We use GNU Autoconf, so it is possible to port MySQL to all modern systems that have a C++ compiler and a working implementation of POSIX threads. (Thread support is needed for the server. To compile only the client code, the only requirement is a C++ compiler.) We use and develop the software ourselves primarily on Linux (SuSE and Red Hat), FreeBSD, and Sun Solaris (versions 8 and 9).

MySQL has been reported to compile successfully on the following combinations of operating system and thread package. Note that for many operating systems, native thread support works only in the latest versions.

- AIX 4.x, 5.x with native threads.
- Amiga.
- BSDI 2.x with the MIT-pthreads package.
- BSDI 3.0, 3.1 and 4.x with native threads.
- Digital Unix 4.x with native threads.
- FreeBSD 2.x with the MIT-pthreads package.
- FreeBSD 3.x and 4.x with native threads.
- FreeBSD 4.x with LinuxThreads.
- HP-UX 10.20 with the DCE threads or the MIT-pthreads package.
- HP-UX 11.x with the native threads.

- Linux 2.0+ with LinuxThreads 0.7.1+ or `glibc` 2.0.7+ for various CPU architectures.
- Mac OS X.
- NetBSD 1.3/1.4 Intel and NetBSD 1.3 Alpha (requires GNU make).
- Novell NetWare 6.0 and 6.5.
- OpenBSD 2.5 and with native threads. OpenBSD earlier than 2.5 with the MIT-pthreads package.
- OS/2 Warp 3, FixPack 29 and OS/2 Warp 4, FixPack 4.
- SCO OpenServer 5.0.X with a recent port of the FSU Pthreads package.
- SCO Openserver 6.0.x.
- SCO UnixWare 7.1.x.
- SGI Irix 6.x with native threads.
- Solaris 2.5 and above with native threads on SPARC and x86.
- SunOS 4.x with the MIT-pthreads package.
- Tru64 Unix.
- Windows 9x, Me, NT, 2000, XP, and Windows Server 2003.

Not all platforms are equally well-suited for running MySQL. How well a certain platform is suited for a high-load mission-critical MySQL server is determined by the following factors:

- General stability of the thread library. A platform may have an excellent reputation otherwise, but MySQL is only as stable as the thread library it calls, even if everything else is perfect.
- The capability of the kernel and the thread library to take advantage of symmetric multi-processor (SMP) systems. In other words, when a process creates a thread, it should be possible for that thread to run on a CPU different from the original process.
- The capability of the kernel and the thread library to run many threads that acquire and release a mutex over a short critical region frequently without excessive context switches. If the implementation of `pthread_mutex_lock()` is too anxious to yield CPU time, this hurts MySQL tremendously. If this issue is not taken care of, adding extra CPUs actually makes MySQL slower.
- General filesystem stability and performance.
- If your tables are large, performance is affected by the capability of the filesystem to deal with large files at all and to deal with them efficiently.
- Our level of expertise here at MySQL AB with the platform. If we know a platform well, we enable platform-specific optimizations and fixes at compile time. We can also provide advice on configuring your system optimally for MySQL.
- The amount of testing we have done internally for similar configurations.

- The number of users that have run MySQL successfully on the platform in similar configurations. If this number is high, the likelihood of encountering platform-specific surprises is much smaller.

Based on the preceding criteria, the best platforms for running MySQL at this point are x86 with SuSE Linux using a 2.4 or 2.6 kernel, and ReiserFS (or any similar Linux distribution) and SPARC with Solaris (2.7-9). FreeBSD comes third, but we really hope it joins the top club once the thread library is improved. We also hope that at some point we are able to include into the top category all other platforms on which MySQL currently compiles and runs, but not quite with the same level of stability and performance. This requires some effort on our part in cooperation with the developers of the operating systems and library components that MySQL depends on. If you are interested in improving one of those components, are in a position to influence its development, and need more detailed instructions on what MySQL needs to run better, send an email message to the MySQL internals mailing list. See Section 1.7.1, "MySQL Mailing Lists."

Please note that the purpose of the preceding comparison is not to say that one operating system is better or worse than another in general. We are talking only about choosing an OS for the specific purpose of running MySQL. With this in mind, the result of this comparison might be different if other factors were considered. In some cases, the reason one OS is better for MySQL than another might simply be that we have been able to put more effort into testing and optimizing for a particular platform. We are just stating our observations to help you decide which platform to use for running MySQL.

2.1.2 Choosing Which MySQL Distribution to Install

When preparing to install MySQL, you should decide which version to use. MySQL development occurs in several release series, and you can pick the one that best fits your needs. After deciding which version to install, you can choose a distribution format. Releases are available in binary or source format.

2.1.2.1 Choosing Which Version of MySQL to Install

The first decision to make is whether you want to use a production (stable) release or a development release. In the MySQL development process, multiple release series co-exist, each at a different stage of maturity:

- MySQL 5.1 is the next development release series and is the series in which new features are to be implemented. Beta releases are available now to allow widespread testing by interested users.
- MySQL 5.0 is the current stable (production-quality) release series. New releases are issued for bugfixes only; no new features are being added that could effect stability.
- MySQL 4.1 is the previous stable (production-quality) release series. New releases are issued for critical bugfixes and security fixes. No significant new features are to be added to this series.

- MySQL 4.0 and 3.23 are the old stable (production-quality) release series. These versions are now retired, so new releases are issued only to fix extremely critical bugs (primarily security issues).

We do not believe in a complete code freeze because this prevents us from making bugfixes and other fixes that must be done. By "somewhat frozen" we mean that we may add small things that should not affect anything that currently works in a production release. Naturally, relevant bugfixes from an earlier series propagate to later series.

Normally, if you are beginning to use MySQL for the first time or trying to port it to some system for which there is no binary distribution, we recommend going with the production release series. Currently, this is MySQL 5.0. All MySQL releases, even those from development series, are checked with the MySQL benchmarks and an extensive test suite before being issued.

If you are running an older system and want to upgrade, but do not want to take the chance of having a non-seamless upgrade, you should upgrade to the latest version in the same release series you are using (where only the last part of the version number is newer than yours). We have tried to fix only fatal bugs and make only small, relatively "safe" changes to that version.

If you want to use new features not present in the production release series, you can use a version from a development series. Note that development releases are not as stable as production releases.

If you want to use the very latest sources containing all current patches and bugfixes, you can use one of our BitKeeper repositories. These are not "releases" as such, but are available as previews of the code on which future releases are to be based.

The MySQL naming scheme uses release names that consist of three numbers and a suffix; for example, **mysql-5.0.12-beta**. The numbers within the release name are interpreted as follows:

- The first number (**5**) is the major version and describes the file format. All MySQL 5 releases have the same file format.
- The second number (**0**) is the release level. Taken together, the major version and release level constitute the release series number.
- The third number (**12**) is the version number within the release series. This is incremented for each new release. Usually you want the latest version for the series you have chosen.

For each minor update, the last number in the version string is incremented. When there are major new features or minor incompatibilities with previous versions, the second number in the version string is incremented. When the file format changes, the first number is increased.

Release names also include a suffix to indicates the stability level of the release. Releases within a series progress through a set of suffixes to indicate how the stability level improves. The possible suffixes are:

- **alpha** indicates that the release contains new features that have not been thoroughly tested. Known bugs should be documented in the News section of the online "MySQL Reference Manual" at `http://dev.mysql.com/doc/mysql/en/news.html`. Most alpha releases implement new commands and extensions. Active development that may involve major code changes can occur in an alpha release. However, we do conduct testing before issuing a release.

- **beta** means that the release is intended to be feature-complete and that all new code has been tested. No major new features that are added. There should be no known critical bugs. A version changes from alpha to beta when there have been no reported fatal bugs within an alpha version for at least a month and we have no plans to add any new features that could make previously implemented features unreliable.

  All APIs, externally visible structures, and columns for SQL statements will not change during future beta, release candidate, or production releases.

- **rc** is a release candidate; that is, a beta that has been around for a while and seems to work well. Only minor fixes are added. (A release candidate is what formerly was known as a "gamma release.")

- If there is no suffix, it means that the version has been run for a while at many different sites with no reports of critical repeatable bugs other than platform-specific bugs. Only critical bugfixes are applied to the release. This is what we call a production (stable) or "General Availability" (GA) release.

MySQL uses a naming scheme that is slightly different from most other products. In general, it is usually safe to use any version that has been out for a couple of weeks without being replaced by a new version within the same release series.

All releases of MySQL are run through our standard tests and benchmarks to ensure that they are relatively safe to use. Because the standard tests are extended over time to check for all previously found bugs, the test suite keeps getting better.

All releases have been tested at least with these tools:

- An internal test suite

  The `mysql-test` directory contains an extensive set of test cases. We run these tests for virtually every server binary.

- The MySQL benchmark suite

  This suite runs a range of common queries. It is also a test to determine whether the latest batch of optimizations actually made the code faster. See Section 6.1.4, "The MySQL Benchmark Suite."

- The `crash-me` test

  This test tries to determine what features the database supports and what its capabilities and limitations are. See Section 6.1.4, "The MySQL Benchmark Suite."

We also test the newest MySQL version in our internal production environment, on at least one machine. We have more than 100GB of data to work with.

2.1.2.2 Choosing a Distribution Format

After choosing which version of MySQL to install, you should decide whether to use a binary distribution or a source distribution. In most cases, you should probably use a binary distribution, if one exists for your platform. Binary distributions are available in native format for many platforms, such as RPM files for Linux or PKG package installers for Mac OS X. Distributions also are available as Zip archives or compressed `tar` files.

Reasons to choose a binary distribution include the following:

- Binary distributions generally are easier to install than source distributions.
- To satisfy different user requirements, we provide two different binary versions. One is compiled with the core feature set. The other (MySQL-Max) is compiled with an extended feature set. Both versions are compiled from the same source distribution. All native MySQL clients can connect to servers from either MySQL version.

  The extended MySQL binary distribution is identified by the `-max` suffix and is configured with the same options as `mysqld-max`. See Section 4.3, "The `mysqld-max` Extended MySQL Server."

  For RPM distributions, if you want to use the `MySQL-Max` RPM, you must first install the standard `MySQL-server` RPM.

Under some circumstances, you may be better off installing MySQL from a source distribution:

- You want to install MySQL at some explicit location. The standard binary distributions are ready to run at any installation location, but you might require even more flexibility to place MySQL components where you want.
- You want to configure `mysqld` to ensure that features are available that might not be included in the standard binary distributions. Here is a list of the most common extra options that you may want to use to ensure feature availability:
  - `--with-innodb`
  - `--with-berkeley-db` (not available on all platforms)
  - `--with-libwrap`
  - `--with-named-z-libs` (this is done for some of the binaries)
  - `--with-debug[=full]`
- You want to configure `mysqld` without some features that are included in the standard binary distributions. For example, distributions normally are compiled with support for all character sets. If you want a smaller MySQL server, you can recompile it with support for only the character sets you need.
- You have a special compiler (such as `pgcc`) or want to use compiler options that are better optimized for your processor. Binary distributions are compiled with options that should work on a variety of processors from the same processor family.

- You want to use the latest sources from one of the BitKeeper repositories to have access to all current bugfixes. For example, if you have found a bug and reported it to the MySQL development team, the bugfix is committed to the source repository and you can access it there. The bugfix does not appear in a release until a release actually is issued.

- You want to read (or modify) the C and C++ code that makes up MySQL. For this purpose, you should get a source distribution, because the source code is always the ultimate manual.

- Source distributions contain more tests and examples than binary distributions.

2.1.2.3 How and When Updates Are Released

MySQL is evolving quite rapidly and we want to share new developments with other MySQL users. We try to produce a new release whenever we have new and useful features that others also seem to have a need for.

We also try to help users who request features that are easy to implement. We take note of what our licensed users want, and we especially take note of what our support customers want and try to help them in this regard.

No one is *required* to download a new release. The News section helps you determine whether the new release has something you really want. See the News section of the online "MySQL Reference Manual" at http://dev.mysql.com/doc/mysql/en/news.html.

We use the following policy when updating MySQL:

- Releases are issued within each series. For each release, the last number in the version is one more than the previous release within the same series.

- Production (stable) releases are meant to appear about 1–2 times a year. However, if small bugs are found, a release with only bugfixes is issued.

- Working releases/bugfixes to old releases are meant to appear about every 4–8 weeks.

- Binary distributions for some platforms are made by us for major releases. Other people may make binary distributions for other systems, but probably less frequently.

- We make fixes available as soon as we have identified and corrected small or noncritical but annoying bugs. The fixes are available immediately from our public BitKeeper repositories, and are included in the next release.

- If by any chance a fatal bug is found in a release, our policy is to fix it in a new release as soon as possible. (We would like other companies to do this, too!)

2.1.2.4 Release Philosophy—No Known Bugs in Releases

We put a lot of time and effort into making our releases bug-free. We haven't released a single MySQL version with any *known* fatal repeatable bugs. (A "fatal" bug is something that crashes MySQL under normal usage, produces incorrect answers for normal queries, or has a security problem.)

We have documented all open problems, bugs, and issues that are dependent on design decisions.

Our aim is to fix everything that is fixable without making a stable MySQL version less stable. In certain cases, this means we can fix an issue in the development versions, but not in the stable (production) version. Naturally, we document such issues so that users are aware of them.

Here is a description of our build process:

- We monitor bugs from our customer support list, the bugs database at `http://bugs.mysql.com/`, and the MySQL external mailing lists.
- All reported bugs for live versions are entered into the bugs database.
- When we fix a bug, we always try to make a test case for it and include it into our test system to ensure that the bug can never recur without being detected. (About 90% of all fixed bugs have test cases.)
- We create test cases for each new feature that we add to MySQL.
- Before we start to build a new MySQL release, we ensure that all reported repeatable bugs for that MySQL version (3.23.x, 4.0.x, 4.1.x, 5.0.x, 5.1.x, and so on) are fixed. If something is impossible to fix due to some internal design decision in MySQL, we document this in the manual.
- We do a build on all platforms for which we support binaries and run our test suite and benchmark suite on all of them.
- We do not publish a binary for a platform for which the test or benchmark suite fails. If the problem is due to a general error in the source, we fix it and do the build plus tests on all systems again from scratch.
- The build and test process takes a week. If we receive a report regarding a fatal bug during this process (for example, one that causes a core dump), we fix the problem and restart the build process.
- After publishing the binaries on `http://dev.mysql.com/`, we send out an announcement message to the `mysql` and `announce` mailing lists. See Section 1.7.1, "MySQL Mailing Lists." The announcement message contains a list of all changes to the release and any known problems with the release. The **Known Problems** section in the release notes has been needed for only a handful of releases.
- To quickly give our users access to the latest MySQL features, we try to produce a new MySQL release every 4–8 weeks. Source code snapshots are built daily and are available at `http://downloads.mysql.com/snapshots.php`.
- If, despite our best efforts, we receive any bug reports after a release is issued that a critical problem exists for the build on a specific platform, we fix it at once and build a new `'a'` release for that platform. Thanks to our large user base, problems are found and resolved very quickly.

- Our track record for making stable releases is quite good. In the last 150 releases, we had to do a new build for fewer than 10 of them. In three of these cases, the bug was a faulty glibc library on one of our build machines that took us a long time to track down.

2.1.2.5 MySQL Binaries Compiled by MySQL AB

As a service of MySQL AB, we provide a set of binary distributions of MySQL that are compiled on systems at our site or on systems where supporters of MySQL kindly have given us access to their machines.

In addition to the binaries provided in platform-specific package formats, we offer binary distributions for a number of platforms in the form of compressed tar files (.tar.gz files). See Section 2.2, "Standard MySQL Installation Using a Binary Distribution."

The RPM distributions for MySQL 5.0 releases that we make available through our Web site are generated by MySQL AB.

For Windows distributions, see Section 2.3, "Installing MySQL on Windows."

These distributions are generated using the script Build-tools/Do-compile, which compiles the source code and creates the binary tar.gz archive using scripts/make_binary_distribution.

For information about the compilers and options used to build these binaries, see the section in the online "MySQL Reference Manual" at http://dev.mysql.com/doc/mysql/en/mysql-binaries.html. This information can also be obtained by looking at the variables COMP_ENV_INFO and CONFIGURE_LINE inside the script bin/mysqlbug of every binary tar file distribution.

Anyone who has more optimal options for any of the following configure commands can mail them to the MySQL internals mailing list. See Section 1.7.1, "MySQL Mailing Lists."

If you want to compile a debug version of MySQL, you should add --with-debug or --with-debug=full to the following configure commands and remove any -fomit-frame-pointer options.

2.1.3 How to Get MySQL

Check our downloads page at http://dev.mysql.com/downloads/ for information about the current version of MySQL and for downloading instructions. For a complete up-to-date list of MySQL download mirror sites, see http://dev.mysql.com/downloads/mirrors.html. You can also find information there about becoming a MySQL mirror site and how to report a bad or out-of-date mirror.

Our main mirror is located at http://mirrors.sunsite.dk/mysql/.

2.1.4 Verifying Package Integrity Using MD5 Checksums or GnuPG

After you have downloaded the MySQL package that suits your needs and before you attempt to install it, you should make sure that it is intact and has not been tampered with. MySQL AB offers three means of integrity checking:

- MD5 checksums
- Cryptographic signatures using GnuPG, the GNU Privacy Guard
- For RPM packages, the built-in RPM integrity verification mechanism

The following sections describe how to use these methods.

If you notice that the MD5 checksum or GPG signatures do not match, first try to download the respective package one more time, perhaps from another mirror site. If you repeatedly cannot successfully verify the integrity of the package, please notify us about such incidents, including the full package name and the download site you have been using, at webmaster@ mysql.com or build@mysql.com. Do not report downloading problems using the bug-reporting system.

2.1.4.1 Verifying the MD5 Checksum

After you have downloaded a MySQL package, you should make sure that its MD5 check-sum matches the one provided on the MySQL download pages. Each package has an individual checksum that you can verify with the following command, where *package_name* is the name of the package you downloaded:

```
shell> md5sum package_name
```

Example:

```
shell> md5sum mysql-standard-5.0.19-linux-i686.tar.gz
aaab65abbec64d5e907dcd41b8699945  mysql-standard-5.0.19-linux-i686.tar.gz
```

You should verify that the resulting checksum (the string of hexadecimal digits) matches the one displayed on the download page immediately below the respective package.

Note: Make sure to verify the checksum of the *archive file* (for example, the .zip or .tar.gz file) and not of the files that are contained inside of the archive.

Note that not all operating systems support the md5sum command. On some, it is simply called md5, and others do not ship it at all. On Linux, it is part of the **GNU Text Utilities** package, which is available for a wide range of platforms. You can download the source code from http://www.gnu.org/software/textutils/ as well. If you have OpenSSL installed, you can use the command openssl md5 *package_name* instead. A Windows implementation of the md5 command-line utility is available from http://www.fourmilab.ch/md5/. winMd5Sum is a graphical MD5 checking tool that can be obtained from http://www.nullriver.com/index/ products/winmd5sum.

2.1.4.2 Signature Checking Using GnuPG

Another method of verifying the integrity and authenticity of a package is to use cryptographic signatures. This is more reliable than using MD5 checksums, but requires more work.

At MySQL AB, we sign MySQL downloadable packages with GnuPG (GNU Privacy Guard). GnuPG is an Open Source alternative to the well-known Pretty Good Privacy (PGP) by Phil Zimmermann. See http://www.gnupg.org/ for more information about GnuPG and how to obtain and install it on your system. Most Linux distributions ship with GnuPG installed by default. For more information about GnuPG, see http://www.openpgp.org/.

To verify the signature for a specific package, you first need to obtain a copy of MySQL AB's public GPG build key, which you can download from http://www.keyserver.net/. The key that you want to obtain is named build@mysql.com. Alternatively, you can cut and paste the key directly from the following text:

```
Key ID:
pub  1024D/5072E1F5 2003-02-03
     MySQL Package signing key (www.mysql.com) <build@mysql.com>
Fingerprint: A4A9 4068 76FC BD3C 4567  70C8 8C71 8D3B 5072 E1F5


Public Key (ASCII-armored):

-----BEGIN PGP PUBLIC KEY BLOCK-----
Version: GnuPG v1.0.6 (GNU/Linux)
Comment: For info see http://www.gnupg.org
```

```
mQGiBD4+owwRBAC14GIfUfCyEDSIePvEW3SAFUdJBtoQHH/nJKZyQT7h9bPlUWC3
RODjQReyCITRrdwyrKUGku2FmeVGwn2u2WmDMNABLnpprWPkBdCk96+OmSLN9brZ
fw2vOUgCmYv2hWOhyDHuvYlQA/BThQoADgj8AW6/OLo7V1W9/8VuHPOgQwCgvzV3
BqOxRznNCRCRxAuAuVztHRcEAJooQK1+iSiunZMYD1WufeXfshc57S/+yeJkegNW
hxwR9pRWVArNYJdDRT+rf2RUe3vpquKNQU/hnEIUHJRQqYHo8gTxvxXNQc7fJYLV
K2HtkrPbP72vwsEKMYYhhr0eKCbtLGfls9krjJ6sBgACyP/Vb7hiPwxh6rDZ7ITnE
kYpXBACmWpP8NJTkamEnPCia2ZoOHODANwpUkP43I7jsDmgtobZX9qnrAXw+uNDI
QJEXM6FSbiOLLtZciNlYsafwAPEOMDKpMqAK6IyisNtPvaLd8lHObPAnWqcyefep
rvOsxxqUEMcM3o7wwgfN83POkDasDbs3pjwPhxvhz6//62zQJ7Q7TXlTUUwgUGFj
a2FnZSBzaWduaW5nIGtleSAod3d3Lm15c3FsLmNvbSkgPGJ1aWxkQG15c3FsLmNv
bT6IXQQTEQIAHQUCPj6jDAUJCWYBgAULBwoDBAMVAwIDFgIBAheAAAoJEIxxjTtQ
cuH1cY4AnilUwTXn8MatQOiGOa/bPxrvK/gCAJ4oinSNZRYTnblChwFaazt7PF3q
zIhMBBMRAgAMBQI+PqPRBYMJZgC7AAoJEElQ4SqycpHyJOEAn1mxHijft00bKXvu
cSo/pECUmppiAJ41M9MRVj5VcdH/KN/KjRtW6tHFPYhMBBMRAgAMBQI+QoIDBYMJ
YiKJAAoJELb1zU3GuiQ/lpEAoIhpp6BozKI8p6eaabzF5MlJH58pAKCu/ROofK8J
Eg2aLos+5zEYrB/LsrkCDQQ+PqMdEAgA7+GJfxbMdY4wslPnjH9rF4N2qfWsEN/l
xaZoJYc3a6MO2WCnHl6ahT2/tBK2w1QI4YFteR47gCvtgb6OlJHffOo2HfLmRDRi
Rjd1DTCHqeyX7CHhcghj/dNRlW2ZOl5QFEcmV9UOVhp3aFfWC4Ujfs3LU+hkAWzE
7zaD5cH9J7yv/6xuZVw411x0h4UqsTcWMuOiM1BzELqX1DY7LwoPEb/O9Rkbf4fm
Le11EzIaCa4PqARXQZc4dhSinMt6K3X4BrRsKTfozBu74F47D8Ilbf5vSYHbuE5p
```

```
/1oIDznkg/p8kW+3FxuWrycciqFTcNz215yyX39LXFnlLzKUb/F5GwADBQf+Lwqq
a8CGrRfsOAJxim63CHfty5mUc5rUSnTslGYEIOCR1BeQauyPZbPDsDD9MZ1ZaSaf
anFvwFG6Llx9xkU7tzq+vKLoWkm4u5xf3vn55VjnSd1aQ9eQnUcXiL4cnBGoTbOW
I39EcyzgslzBdC++MPjcQTcA7p6JUVsP6oAB3FQWg54tuUoOEc8bsM8b3Ev42Lmu
QT5NdKHGwHsXTPtl0klk4bQk4OajHsiy1BMahpT27jWjJlMiJc+IWJOmghkKHt92
6s/ymfdf5HkdQ1cyvsz5tryVI3Fx78XeSYfQvuuwqp2H139pXGEkgOn6KdUOetdZ
Whe70YGNPw1yjWJT1IhMBBgRAgAMBQI+PqMdBQkJZgGAAAoJEIxxjTtQcuH17p4A
n3r1QpVC9yhnW2cSAjq+kr72GXOeAJ4295kl6NxYEuFApmr1+OuUq/SlsQ==
=YJkx
-----END PGP PUBLIC KEY BLOCK-----
```

To import the build key into your personal public GPG keyring, use `gpg --import`. For example, if you have saved the key in a file named `mysql_pubkey.asc`, the import command looks like this:

```
shell> gpg --import mysql_pubkey.asc
```

After you have downloaded and imported the public build key, download your desired MySQL package and the corresponding signature, which also is available from the download page. The signature file has the same name as the distribution file with an `.asc` extension. For example:

Distribution file	`mysql-standard-5.0.19-linux-i686.tar.gz`
Signature file	`mysql-standard-5.0.19-linux-i686.tar.gz.asc`

Make sure that both files are stored in the same directory and then run the following command to verify the signature for the distribution file:

```
shell> gpg --verify package_name.asc
```

Example:

```
shell> gpg --verify mysql-standard-5.0.19-linux-i686.tar.gz.asc
gpg: Signature made Tue 12 Jul 2005 23:35:41 EST using DSA key ID 5072E1F5
gpg: Good signature from "MySQL Package signing key (www.mysql.com)
<build@mysql.com>"
```

The `Good signature` message indicates that everything is all right. You can ignore any `insecure memory` warning you might obtain.

See the GPG documentation for more information on how to work with public keys.

2.1.4.3 Signature Checking Using RPM

For RPM packages, there is no separate signature. RPM packages have a built-in GPG signature and MD5 checksum. You can verify a package by running the following command:

```
shell> rpm --checksig package_name.rpm
```

Example:

```
shell> rpm --checksig MySQL-server-5.0.19-0.i386.rpm
MySQL-server-5.0.19-0.i386.rpm: md5 gpg OK
```

Note: If you are using RPM 4.1 and it complains about (GPG) NOT OK (MISSING KEYS: GPG#5072e1f5), even though you have imported the MySQL public build key into your own GPG keyring, you need to import the key into the RPM keyring first. RPM 4.1 no longer uses your personal GPG keyring (or GPG itself). Rather, it maintains its own keyring because it is a system-wide application and a user's GPG public keyring is a user-specific file. To import the MySQL public key into the RPM keyring, first obtain the key as described in Section 2.1.4.2, "Signature Checking Using GnuPG." Then use rpm --import to import the key. For example, if you have saved the public key in a file named mysql_pubkey.asc, import it using this command:

```
shell> rpm --import mysql_pubkey.asc
```

If you need to obtain the MySQL public key, see Section 2.1.4.2, "Signature Checking Using GnuPG."

2.1.5 Installation Layouts

This section describes the default layout of the directories created by installing binary or source distributions provided by MySQL AB. A distribution provided by another vendor might use a layout different from those shown here.

For MySQL 5.0 on Windows, the default installation directory is C:\Program Files\MySQL\MySQL Server 5.0. (Some Windows users prefer to install in C:\mysql, the directory that formerly was used as the default. However, the layout of the subdirectories remains the same.) The installation directory has the following subdirectories:

Directory	Contents of Directory
bin	Client programs and the mysqld server
data	Log files, databases
Docs	Documentation
examples	Example programs and scripts
include	Include (header) files
lib	Libraries
scripts	Utility scripts
share	Error message files

Installations created from MySQL AB's Linux RPM distributions result in files under the following system directories:

Directory	Contents of Directory
/usr/bin	Client programs and scripts
/usr/sbin	The mysqld server
/var/lib/mysql	Log files, databases
/usr/share/doc/packages	Documentation
/usr/include/mysql	Include (header) files
/usr/lib/mysql	Libraries
/usr/share/mysql	Error message and character set files
/usr/share/sql-bench	Benchmarks

On Unix, a tar file binary distribution is installed by unpacking it at the installation location you choose (typically /usr/local/mysql) and creates the following directories in that location:

Directory	Contents of Directory
bin	Client programs and the mysqld server
data	Log files, databases
docs	Documentation, ChangeLog
include	Include (header) files
lib	Libraries
scripts	mysql_install_db
share/mysql	Error message files
sql-bench	Benchmarks

A source distribution is installed after you configure and compile it. By default, the installation step installs files under /usr/local, in the following subdirectories:

Directory	Contents of Directory
bin	Client programs and scripts
include/mysql	Include (header) files
info	Documentation in Info format
lib/mysql	Libraries
Libexec	The mysqld server
share/mysql	Error message files
sql-bench	Benchmarks and crash-me test
Var	Databases and log files

Within its installation directory, the layout of a source installation differs from that of a binary installation in the following ways:

- The mysqld server is installed in the libexec directory rather than in the bin directory.
- The data directory is var rather than data.
- mysql_install_db is installed in the bin directory rather than in the scripts directory.

- The header file and library directories are include/mysql and lib/mysql rather than include and lib.

You can create your own binary installation from a compiled source distribution by executing the scripts/make_binary_distribution script from the top directory of the source distribution.

2.2 Standard MySQL Installation Using a Binary Distribution

The next several sections cover the installation of MySQL on platforms where we offer packages using the native packaging format of the respective platform. (This is also known as performing a "binary install.") However, binary distributions of MySQL are available for many other platforms as well. See Section 2.7, "Installing MySQL on Other Unix-Like Systems," for generic installation instructions for these packages that apply to all platforms.

See Section 2.1, "General Installation Issues," for more information on what other binary distributions are available and how to obtain them.

2.3 Installing MySQL on Windows

A native Windows distribution of MySQL has been available from MySQL AB since version 3.21 and represents a sizable percentage of the daily downloads of MySQL. This section describes the process for installing MySQL on Windows.

Note: If you are upgrading MySQL from an existing installation older than MySQL 4.1.5, you must first perform the procedure described in Section 2.3.14, "Upgrading MySQL on Windows."

To run MySQL on Windows, you need the following:

- A 32-bit Windows operating system such as 9x, Me, NT, 2000, XP, or Windows Server 2003.

   A Windows NT–based operating system (NT, 2000, XP, 2003) permits you to run the MySQL server as a service. The use of a Windows NT–based operating system is strongly recommended. See Section 2.3.11, "Starting MySQL as a Windows Service."

   Generally, you should install MySQL on Windows using an account that has administrator rights. Otherwise, you may encounter problems with certain operations such as editing the PATH environment variable or accessing the Service Control Manager.

- TCP/IP protocol support.
- Enough space on the hard drive to unpack, install, and create the databases in accordance with your requirements (generally a minimum of 200 megabytes is recommended).

There may also be other requirements, depending on how you plan to use MySQL:

- If you plan to connect to the MySQL server via ODBC, you need a Connector/ODBC driver.
- If you need tables with a size larger than 4GB, install MySQL on an NTFS or newer filesystem. Don't forget to use MAX_ROWS and AVG_ROW_LENGTH when you create tables.

MySQL for Windows is available in several distribution formats:

- Binary distributions are available that contain a setup program that installs everything you need so that you can start the server immediately. Another binary distribution format contains an archive that you simply unpack in the installation location and then configure yourself. For details, see Section 2.3.1, "Choosing An Installation Package."
- The source distribution contains all the code and support files for building the executables using the Visual Studio 7.1 compiler system.

Generally speaking, you should use a binary distribution that includes an installer. It is simpler to use than the others, and you need no additional tools to get MySQL up and running. The installer for the Windows version of MySQL, combined with a GUI Configuration Wizard, automatically installs MySQL, creates an option file, starts the server, and secures the default user accounts.

The following section describes how to install MySQL on Windows using a binary distribution. To use an installation package that does not include an installer, follow the procedure described in Section 2.3.5, "Installing MySQL from a Noinstall Zip Archive." To install using a source distribution, see Section 2.8.6, "Installing MySQL from Source on Windows."

MySQL distributions for Windows can be downloaded from http://dev.mysql.com/downloads/. See Section 2.1.3, "How to Get MySQL."

2.3.1 Choosing an Installation Package

For MySQL 5.0, there are three installation packages to choose from when installing MySQL on Windows:

- **The Essentials Package**: This package has a filename similar to mysql-essential-5.0.19-win32.msi and contains the minimum set of files needed to install MySQL on Windows, including the Configuration Wizard. This package does not include optional components such as the embedded server and benchmark suite.
- **The Complete Package**: This package has a filename similar to mysql-5.0.19-win32.zip and contains all files needed for a complete Windows installation, including the Configuration Wizard. This package includes optional components such as the embedded server and benchmark suite.
- **The Noinstall Archive**: This package has a filename similar to mysql-noinstall-5.0.19-win32.zip and contains all the files found in the Complete install package, with the exception of the Configuration Wizard. This package does not include an automated installer, and must be manually installed and configured.

The Essentials package is recommended for most users. It is provided as an .msi file for use with the Windows Installer. The Complete and Noinstall distributions are packaged as Zip archives. To use them, you must have a tool that can unpack .zip files.

Your choice of install package affects the installation process you must follow. If you choose to install either the Essentials or Complete install packages, see Section 2.3.2, "Installing MySQL with the Automated Installer." If you choose to install MySQL from the Noinstall archive, see Section 2.3.5, "Installing MySQL from a Noinstall Zip Archive."

2.3.2 Installing MySQL with the Automated Installer

New MySQL users can use the MySQL Installation Wizard and MySQL Configuration Wizard to install MySQL on Windows. These are designed to install and configure MySQL in such a way that new users can immediately get started using MySQL.

The MySQL Installation Wizard and MySQL Configuration Wizard are available in the Essentials and Complete install packages. They are recommended for most standard MySQL installations. Exceptions include users who need to install multiple instances of MySQL on a single server host and advanced users who want complete control of server configuration.

2.3.3 Using the MySQL Installation Wizard

2.3.3.1 Introduction to the Installation Wizard

MySQL Installation Wizard is an installer for the MySQL server that uses the latest installer technologies for Microsoft Windows. The MySQL Installation Wizard, in combination with the MySQL Configuration Wizard, allows a user to install and configure a MySQL server that is ready for use immediately after installation.

The MySQL Installation Wizard is the standard installer for all MySQL server distributions, version 4.1.5 and higher. Users of previous versions of MySQL need to shut down and remove their existing MySQL installations manually before installing MySQL with the MySQL Installation Wizard. See Section 2.3.3.7, "Upgrading MySQL with the Installation Wizard," for more information on upgrading from a previous version.

Microsoft has included an improved version of its Microsoft Windows Installer (MSI) in the recent versions of Windows. MSI has become the de-facto standard for application installations on Windows 2000, Windows XP, and Windows Server 2003. The MySQL Installation Wizard makes use of this technology to provide a smoother and more flexible installation process.

The Microsoft Windows Installer Engine was updated with the release of Windows XP; those using a previous version of Windows can reference this Microsoft Knowledge Base article (http://support.microsoft.com/default.aspx?scid=kb;EN-US;292539) for information on upgrading to the latest version of the Windows Installer Engine.

In addition, Microsoft has introduced the WiX (Windows Installer XML) toolkit recently. This is the first highly acknowledged Open Source project from Microsoft. We have switched to WiX because it is an Open Source project and it allows us to handle the complete Windows installation process in a flexible manner using scripts.

Improving the MySQL Installation Wizard depends on the support and feedback of users like you. If you find that the MySQL Installation Wizard is lacking some feature important to you, or if you discover a bug, please report it in our bugs database using the instructions given in Section 1.8, "How to Report Bugs or Problems."

2.3.3.2 Downloading and Starting the MySQL Installation Wizard

The MySQL installation packages can be downloaded from `http://dev.mysql.com/downloads/`. If the package you download is contained within a Zip archive, you need to extract the archive first.

The process for starting the wizard depends on the contents of the installation package you download. If there is a `setup.exe` file present, double-click it to start the installation process. If there is an `.msi` file present, double-click it to start the installation process.

2.3.3.3 Choosing an Install Type

There are three installation types available: **Typical**, **Complete**, and **Custom**.

The **Typical** installation type installs the MySQL server, the `mysql` command-line client, and the command-line utilities. The command-line clients and utilities include `mysqldump`, `myisamchk`, and several other tools to help you manage the MySQL server.

The **Complete** installation type installs all components included in the installation package. The full installation package includes components such as the embedded server library, the benchmark suite, support scripts, and documentation.

The **Custom** installation type gives you complete control over which packages you wish to install and the installation path that is used. See Section 2.3.3.4, "The Custom Install Dialog," for more information on performing a custom install.

If you choose the **Typical** or **Complete** installation types and click the `Next` button, you advance to the confirmation screen to verify your choices and begin the installation. If you choose the **Custom** installation type and click the `Next` button, you advance to the custom installation dialog, described in Section 2.3.3.4, "The Custom Install Dialog."

2.3.3.4 The Custom Install Dialog

If you wish to change the installation path or the specific components that are installed by the MySQL Installation Wizard, choose the **Custom** installation type.

A tree view on the left side of the custom install dialog lists all available components. Components that are not installed have a red X icon; components that are installed have a gray icon. To change whether a component is installed, click on that component's icon and choose a new option from the drop-down list that appears.

You can change the default installation path by clicking the `Change...` button to the right of the displayed installation path.

After choosing your installation components and installation path, click the Next button to advance to the confirmation dialog.

2.3.3.5 The Confirmation Dialog

Once you choose an installation type and optionally choose your installation components, you advance to the confirmation dialog. Your installation type and installation path are displayed for you to review.

To install MySQL if you are satisfied with your settings, click the Install button. To change your settings, click the Back button. To exit the MySQL Installation Wizard without installing MySQL, click the Cancel button.

After installation is complete, you have the option of registering with the MySQL Web site. Registration gives you access to post in the MySQL forums at forums.mysql.com (http:// forums.mysql.com), along with the ability to report bugs at bugs.mysql.com (http://bugs. mysql.com) and to subscribe to our newsletter. The final screen of the installer provides a summary of the installation and gives you the option to launch the MySQL Configuration Wizard, which you can use to create a configuration file, install the MySQL service, and configure security settings.

2.3.3.6 Changes Made by MySQL Installation Wizard

Once you click the Install button, the MySQL Installation Wizard begins the installation process and makes certain changes to your system which are described in the sections that follow.

Changes to the Registry

The MySQL Installation Wizard creates one Windows registry key in a typical install situation, located in HKEY_LOCAL_MACHINE\SOFTWARE\MySQL AB.

The MySQL Installation Wizard creates a key named after the major version of the server that is being installed, such as MySQL Server 5.0. It contains two string values, Location and Version. The Location string contains the path to the installation directory. In a default installation it contains C:\Program Files\MySQL\MySQL Server 5.0\. The Version string contains the release number. For example, for an installation of MySQL Server 5.0.19, the key contains a value of 5.0.19.

These registry keys are used to help external tools identify the installed location of the MySQL server, preventing a complete scan of the hard-disk to determine the installation path of the MySQL server. The registry keys are not required to run the server, and if you install MySQL using the noinstall Zip archive, the registry keys are not created.

Changes to the Start Menu

The MySQL Installation Wizard creates a new entry in the Windows Start menu under a common MySQL menu heading named after the major version of MySQL that you have installed. For example, if you install MySQL 5.0, the MySQL Installation Wizard creates a MySQL Server 5.0 section in the Start menu.

The following entries are created within the new `Start` menu section:

- `MySQL Command Line Client`: This is a shortcut to the `mysql` command-line client and is configured to connect as the `root` user. The shortcut prompts for a `root` user password when you connect.

- `MySQL Server Instance Config Wizard`: This is a shortcut to the MySQL Configuration Wizard. Use this shortcut to configure a newly installed server, or to reconfigure an existing server.

- `MySQL Documentation`: This is a link to the MySQL server documentation that is stored locally in the MySQL server installation directory. This option is not available when the MySQL server is installed using the Essentials installation package.

Changes to the File System

The MySQL Installation Wizard by default installs the MySQL 5.0 server to `C:\Program Files\MySQL\MySQL Server 5.0`, where `Program Files` is the default location for applications in your system, and `5.0` is the major version of your MySQL server. This is the recommended location for the MySQL server, replacing the former default location `C:\mysql`.

By default, all MySQL applications are stored in a common directory at `C:\Program Files\MySQL`, where `Program Files` is the default location for applications in your Windows installation. A typical MySQL installation on a developer machine might look like this:

```
C:\Program Files\MySQL\MySQL Server 5.0
C:\Program Files\MySQL\MySQL Administrator 1.0
C:\Program Files\MySQL\MySQL Query Browser 1.0
```

This approach makes it easier to manage and maintain all MySQL applications installed on a particular system.

2.3.3.7 Upgrading MySQL with the Installation Wizard

The MySQL Installation Wizard can perform server upgrades automatically using the upgrade capabilities of MSI. That means you do not need to remove a previous installation manually before installing a new release. The installer automatically shuts down and removes the previous MySQL service before installing the new version.

Automatic upgrades are available only when upgrading between installations that have the same major and minor version numbers. For example, you can upgrade automatically from MySQL 4.1.5 to MySQL 4.1.6, but not from MySQL 4.1 to MySQL 5.0.

See Section 2.3.14, "Upgrading MySQL on Windows."

2.3.4 Using the Configuration Wizard

2.3.4.1 Introduction to the Configuration Wizard

The MySQL Configuration Wizard helps automate the process of configuring your server under Windows. The MySQL Configuration Wizard creates a custom `my.ini` file by asking you a series of questions and then applying your responses to a template to generate a my.ini file that is tuned to your installation.

The MySQL Configuration Wizard is included with the MySQL 5.0 server, and is currently available for Windows users only.

The MySQL Configuration Wizard is to a large extent the result of feedback MySQL AB has received from many users over a period of several years. However, if you find that it lacks some feature important to you, please report it in our bugs database using the instructions given in Section 1.8, "How to Report Bugs or Problems."

2.3.4.2 Starting the MySQL Configuration Wizard

The MySQL Configuration Wizard is typically launched from the MySQL Installation Wizard, as the MySQL Installation Wizard exits. You can also launch the MySQL Configuration Wizard by clicking the MySQL Server Instance Config Wizard entry in the MySQL section of the Windows Start menu.

Alternatively, you can navigate to the bin directory of your MySQL installation and launch the MySQLInstanceConfig.exe file directly.

2.3.4.3 Choosing a Maintenance Option

If the MySQL Configuration Wizard detects an existing my.ini file, you have the option of either reconfiguring your existing server, or removing the server instance by deleting the my.ini file and stopping and removing the MySQL service.

To reconfigure an existing server, choose the Re-configure Instance option and click the Next button. Your existing my.ini file is renamed to my*timestamp*.ini.bak, where *timestamp* is the date and time at which the existing my.ini file was created. To remove the existing server instance, choose the Remove Instance option and click the Next button.

If you choose the Remove Instance option, you advance to a confirmation window. Click the Execute button. The MySQL Configuration Wizard stops and removes the MySQL service, and then deletes the my.ini file. The server installation and its data folder are not removed.

If you choose the Re-configure Instance option, you advance to the Configuration Type dialog where you can choose the type of installation that you wish to configure.

2.3.4.4 Choosing a Configuration Type

When you start the MySQL Configuration Wizard for a new MySQL installation, or choose the Re-configure Instance option for an existing installation, you advance to the Configuration Type dialog.

There are two configuration types available: Detailed Configuration and Standard Configuration. The Standard Configuration option is intended for new users who want to get started with MySQL quickly without having to make many decisions about server configuration. The Detailed Configuration option is intended for advanced users who want more fine-grained control over server configuration.

If you are new to MySQL and need a server configured as a single-user developer machine, the `Standard Configuration` should suit your needs. Choosing the `Standard Configuration` option causes the MySQL Configuration Wizard to set all configuration options automatically with the exception of `Service Options` and `Security Options`.

The `Standard Configuration` sets options that may be incompatible with systems where there are existing MySQL installations. If you have an existing MySQL installation on your system in addition to the installation you wish to configure, the `Detailed Configuration` option is recommended.

To complete the `Standard Configuration`, please refer to the sections on `Service Options` and `Security Options` in Section 2.3.4.11, "The Service Options Dialog," and Section 2.3.4.12, "The Security Options Dialog," respectively.

2.3.4.5 The `Server Type` Dialog

There are three different server types available to choose from. The server type that you choose affects the decisions that the MySQL Configuration Wizard makes with regard to memory, disk, and processor usage.

- `Developer Machine:` Choose this option for a typical desktop workstation where MySQL is intended only for personal use. It is assumed that many other desktop applications are running. The MySQL server is configured to use minimal system resources.

- `Server Machine:` Choose this option for a server machine where the MySQL server is running alongside other server applications such as FTP, email, and Web servers. The MySQL server is configured to use a moderate portion of the system resources.

- `Dedicated MySQL Server Machine:` Choose this option for a server machine that is intended to run only the MySQL server. It is assumed that no other applications are running. The MySQL server is configured to use all available system resources.

2.3.4.6 The `Database Usage` Dialog

The `Database Usage` dialog allows you to indicate the storage engines that you expect to use when creating MySQL tables. The option you choose determines whether the `InnoDB` storage engine is available and what percentage of the server resources are available to `InnoDB`.

- `Multifunctional Database:` This option enables both the `InnoDB` and `MyISAM` storage engines and divides resources evenly between the two. This option is recommended for users who use both storage engines on a regular basis.

- `Transactional Database Only:` This option enables both the `InnoDB` and `MyISAM` storage engines, but dedicates most server resources to the `InnoDB` storage engine. This option is recommended for users who use `InnoDB` almost exclusively and make only minimal use of `MyISAM`.

- `Non-Transactional Database Only:` This option disables the `InnoDB` storage engine completely and dedicates all server resources to the `MyISAM` storage engine. This option is recommended for users who do not use `InnoDB`.

2.3.4.7 The `InnoDB Tablespace` Dialog

Some users may want to locate the `InnoDB` tablespace files in a different location than the MySQL server data directory. Placing the tablespace files in a separate location can be desirable if your system has a higher capacity or higher performance storage device available, such as a RAID storage system.

To change the default location for the `InnoDB` tablespace files, choose a new drive from the drop-down list of drive letters and choose a new path from the drop-down list of paths. To create a custom path, click the ... button.

If you are modifying the configuration of an existing server, you must click the `Modify` button before you change the path. In this situation you must move the existing tablespace files to the new location manually before starting the server.

2.3.4.8 The `Concurrent Connections` Dialog

To prevent the server from running out of resources, it is important to limit the number of concurrent connections to the MySQL server that can be established. The `Concurrent Connections` dialog allows you to choose the expected usage of your server, and sets the limit for concurrent connections accordingly. It is also possible to set the concurrent connection limit manually.

- `Decision Support (DSS)/OLAP`: Choose this option if your server does not require a large number of concurrent connections. The maximum number of connections is set at 100, with an average of 20 concurrent connections assumed.
- `Online Transaction Processing (OLTP)`: Choose this option if your server requires a large number of concurrent connections. The maximum number of connections is set at 500.
- `Manual Setting`: Choose this option to set the maximum number of concurrent connections to the server manually. Choose the number of concurrent connections from the drop-down box provided, or enter the maximum number of connections into the drop-down box if the number you desire is not listed.

2.3.4.9 The `Networking and Strict Mode Options` Dialog

Use the `Networking Options` dialog to enable or disable TCP/IP networking and to configure the port number that is used to connect to the MySQL server.

TCP/IP networking is enabled by default. To disable TCP/IP networking, uncheck the box next to the `Enable TCP/IP Networking` option.

Port 3306 is used by default. To change the port used to access MySQL, choose a new port number from the drop-down box or type a new port number directly into the drop-down box. If the port number you choose is in use, you are prompted to confirm your choice of port number.

Set the `Server SQL Mode` to either enable or disable strict mode. Enabling strict mode (default) makes MySQL behave more like other database management systems. *If you run applications that rely on MySQL's old "forgiving" behavior, make sure to either adapt those applications or to disable strict mode.* For more information about strict mode, see Section 4.2.5, "The Server SQL Mode."

2.3.4.10 The `Character Set` Dialog

The MySQL server supports multiple character sets and it is possible to set a default server character set that is applied to all tables, columns, and databases unless overridden. Use the `Character Set` dialog to change the default character set of the MySQL server.

- `Standard Character Set`: Choose this option if you want to use `latin1` as the default server character set. `latin1` is used for English and many Western European languages.

- `Best Support For Multilingualism`: Choose this option if you want to use `utf8` as the default server character set. This is a Unicode character set that can store characters from many different languages.

- `Manual Selected Default Character Set / Collation`: Choose this option if you want to pick the server's default character set manually. Choose the desired character set from the provided drop-down list.

2.3.4.11 The `Service Options` Dialog

On Windows NT–based platforms, the MySQL server can be installed as a Windows service. When installed this way, the MySQL server can be started automatically during system startup, and even restarted automatically by Windows in the event of a service failure.

The MySQL Configuration Wizard installs the MySQL server as a service by default, using the service name `MySQL`. If you do not wish to install the service, uncheck the box next to the `Install As Windows Service` option. You can change the service name by picking a new service name from the drop-down box provided or by entering a new service name into the drop-down box.

To install the MySQL server as a service but not have it started automatically at startup, uncheck the box next to the `Launch the MySQL Server Automatically` option.

2.3.4.12 The `Security Options` Dialog

It is strongly recommended that you set a root password for your MySQL server, and the MySQL Configuration Wizard requires by default that you do so. If you do not wish to set a `root` password, uncheck the box next to the `Modify Security Settings` option.

To set the `root` password, enter the desired password into both the `New root password` and `Confirm` boxes. If you are reconfiguring an existing server, you need to enter the existing `root` password into the `Current root password` box.

To prevent `root` logins from across the network, check the box next to the `Root May Only Connect from Localhost` option. This increases the security of your `root` account.

To create an anonymous user account, check the box next to the `Create an Anonymous Account` option. Creating an anonymous account can decrease server security and cause login and permission difficulties. For this reason, it is not recommended.

2.3.4.13 The `Confirmation` Dialog

The final dialog in the MySQL Configuration Wizard is the `Confirmation` dialog. To start the configuration process, click the `Execute` button. To return to a previous dialog, click the `Back` button. To exit the MySQL Configuration Wizard without configuring the server, click the `Cancel` button.

After you click the `Execute` button, the MySQL Configuration Wizard performs a series of tasks whose progress is displayed onscreen as the tasks are performed.

The MySQL Configuration Wizard first determines configuration file options based on your choices using a template prepared by MySQL AB developers and engineers. This template is named `my-template.ini` and is located in your server installation directory.

The MySQL Configuration Wizard then writes these options to a `my.ini` file. The final location of the `my.ini` file is displayed next to the `Write configuration file` task.

If you chose to create a service for the MySQL server, the MySQL Configuration Wizard creates and starts the service. If you are reconfiguring an existing service, the MySQL Configuration Wizard restarts the service to apply your configuration changes.

If you chose to set a `root` password, the MySQL Configuration Wizard connects to the server, sets your new `root` password and applies any other security settings you may have selected.

After the MySQL Configuration Wizard has completed its tasks, a summary is displayed. Click the `Finish` button to exit the MySQL Configuration Wizard.

2.3.4.14 The Location of the `my.ini` File

The MySQL Configuration Wizard places the `my.ini` file in the installation directory for the MySQL server. This helps associate configuration files with particular server instances.

To ensure that the MySQL server knows where to look for the `my.ini` file, an argument similar to this is passed to the MySQL server as part of the service installation: `--defaults-file="C:\Program Files\MySQL\MySQL Server 5.0\my.ini"`. Here, `C:\Program Files\MySQL\MySQL Server 5.0` is replaced with the installation path to the MySQL Server.

The `--defaults-file` option instructs the MySQL server to read the specified file for configuration options when it starts.

2.3.4.15 Editing the `my.ini` File

To modify the `my.ini` file, open it with a text editor and make any necessary changes. You can also modify the server configuration with the MySQL Administrator (`http://www.mysql.com/products/administrator/`) utility.

MySQL clients and utilities such as the `mysql` and `mysqldump` command-line clients are not able to locate the `my.ini` file located in the server installation directory. To configure the client and utility applications, create a new `my.ini` file in the `C:\WINDOWS` or `C:\WINNT` directory (whichever is applicable to your Windows version).

2.3.5 Installing MySQL from a Noinstall Zip Archive

Users who are installing from the Noinstall package can use the instructions in this section to manually install MySQL. The process for installing MySQL from a Zip archive is as follows:

1. Extract the archive to the desired install directory
2. Create an option file
3. Choose a MySQL server type
4. Start the MySQL server
5. Secure the default user accounts

This process is described in the sections that follow.

2.3.6 Extracting the Install Archive

To install MySQL manually, do the following:

1. If you are upgrading from a previous version please refer to Section 2.3.14, "Upgrading MySQL on Windows," before beginning the upgrade process.

2. If you are using a Windows NT–based operating system such as Windows NT, Windows 2000, Windows XP, or Windows Server 2003, make sure that you are logged in as a user with administrator privileges.

3. Choose an installation location. Traditionally, the MySQL server is installed in `C:\mysql`. The MySQL Installation Wizard installs MySQL under `C:\Program Files\MySQL`. If you do not install MySQL at `C:\mysql`, you must specify the path to the install directory during startup or in an option file. See Section 2.3.7, "Creating an Option File."

4. Extract the install archive to the chosen installation location using your preferred Zip archive tool. Some tools may extract the archive to a folder within your chosen installation location. If this occurs, you can move the contents of the subfolder into the chosen installation location.

2.3.7 Creating an Option File

If you need to specify startup options when you run the server, you can indicate them on the command line or place them in an option file. For options that are used every time the server starts, you may find it most convenient to use an option file to specify your MySQL configuration. This is particularly true under the following circumstances:

- The installation or data directory locations are different from the default locations (C:\Program Files\MySQL\MySQL Server 5.0 and C:\Program Files\MySQL\MySQL Server 5.0\data).

- You need to tune the server settings.

When the MySQL server starts on Windows, it looks for options in two files: the my.ini file in the Windows directory, and the C:\my.cnf file. The Windows directory typically is named something like C:\WINDOWS or C:\WINNT. You can determine its exact location from the value of the WINDIR environment variable using the following command:

```
C:\> echo %WINDIR%
```

MySQL looks for options first in the my.ini file, and then in the my.cnf file. However, to avoid confusion, it's best if you use only one file. If your PC uses a boot loader where C: is not the boot drive, your only option is to use the my.ini file. Whichever option file you use, it must be a plain text file.

You can also make use of the example option files included with your MySQL distribution. Look in your install directory for files such as my-small.cnf, my-medium.cnf, my-large.cnf, and my-huge.cnf, which you can rename and copy to the appropriate location for use as a base configuration file.

An option file can be created and modified with any text editor, such as Notepad. For example, if MySQL is installed in E:\mysql and the data directory is in E:\mydata\data, you can create an option file containing a [mysqld] section to specify values for the basedir and datadir parameters:

```
[mysqld]
# set basedir to your installation path
basedir=E:/mysql
# set datadir to the location of your data directory
datadir=E:/mydata/data
```

Note that Windows pathnames are specified in option files using (forward) slashes rather than backslashes. If you do use backslashes, you must double them:

```
[mysqld]
# set basedir to your installation path
basedir=E:\\mysql
# set datadir to the location of your data directory
datadir=E:\\mydata\\data
```

On Windows, the MySQL installer places the data directory directly under the directory where you install MySQL. If you would like to use a data directory in a different location, you should copy the entire contents of the data directory to the new location. For example, if MySQL is installed in `C:\Program Files\MySQL\MySQL Server 5.0`, the data directory is by default in `C:\Program Files\MySQL\MySQL Server 5.0\data`. If you want to use `E:\mydata` as the data directory instead, you must do two things:

1. Move the entire data directory and all of its contents from `C:\Program Files\MySQL\MySQL Server 5.0\data` to `E:\mydata`.

2. Use a `--datadir` option to specify the new data directory location each time you start the server.

2.3.8 Selecting a MySQL Server Type

The following table shows the available servers for Windows in MySQL 5.0:

Binary	Description
mysqld-debug	Compiled with full debugging and automatic memory allocation checking, as well as InnoDB and BDB support.
mysqld	Optimized binary with InnoDB support.
mysqld-nt	Optimized binary for Windows NT, 2000, and XP with support for named pipes.
mysqld-max	Optimized binary with support for InnoDB and BDB support.
mysqld-max-nt	Like mysqld-max, but compiled with support for named pipes.

All of the preceding binaries are optimized for modern Intel processors, but should work on any Intel i386–class or higher processor.

All Windows MySQL 5.0 servers have support for symbolic linking of database directories.

MySQL supports TCP/IP on all Windows platforms. The mysqld-nt and mysql-max-nt servers support named pipes on Windows NT, 2000, XP, and 2003. However, the default is to use TCP/IP regardless of platform. (Named pipes are slower than TCP/IP in many Windows configurations.)

Use of named pipes is subject to these conditions:

*   Named pipes are enabled only if you start the server with the `--enable-named-pipe` option. It is necessary to use this option explicitly because some users have experienced problems with shutting down the MySQL server when named pipes were used.

*   Named-pipe connections are allowed only by the mysqld-nt or mysqld-max-nt servers, and only if the server is run on a version of Windows that supports named pipes (NT, 2000, XP, 2003).

*   These servers can be run on Windows 98 or Me, but only if TCP/IP is installed; named-pipe connections cannot be used.

*   These servers cannot be run on Windows 95.

Note: Most of the examples in this manual use `mysqld` as the server name. If you choose to use a different server, such as `mysqld-nt`, make the appropriate substitutions in the commands that are shown in the examples.

2.3.9 Starting the Server for the First Time

This section gives a general overview of starting the MySQL server. The following sections provide more specific information for starting the MySQL server from the command line or as a Windows service.

The information here applies primarily if you installed MySQL using the `Noinstall` version, or if you wish to configure and test MySQL manually rather than with the GUI tools.

The examples in these sections assume that MySQL is installed under the default location of `C:\Program Files\MySQL\MySQL Server 5.0`. Adjust the pathnames shown in the examples if you have MySQL installed in a different location.

On NT-based systems such as Windows NT, 2000, XP, or 2003, clients have two options. They can use TCP/IP, or they can use a named pipe if the server supports named-pipe connections. For MySQL to work with TCP/IP on Windows NT 4, you must install service pack 3 (or newer).

On Windows 95, 98, or Me, MySQL clients always connect to the server using TCP/IP. (This allows any machine on your network to connect to your MySQL server.) Because of this, you must make sure that TCP/IP support is installed on your machine before starting MySQL. You can find TCP/IP on your Windows CD-ROM.

Note that if you are using an old Windows 95 release (for example, OSR2), it is likely that you have an old Winsock package; MySQL requires Winsock 2. You can get the newest Winsock from `http://www.microsoft.com/`. Windows 98 has the new Winsock 2 library, so it is unnecessary to update the library.

MySQL for Windows also supports shared-memory connections if the server is started with the `--shared-memory` option. Clients can connect through shared memory by using the `--protocol=memory` option.

For information about which server binary to run, see Section 2.3.8, "Selecting a MySQL Server type."

Testing is best done from a command prompt in a console window (or "DOS window"). In this way you can have the server display status messages in the window where they are easy to see. If something is wrong with your configuration, these messages make it easier for you to identify and fix any problems.

To start the server, enter this command:

```
C:\> "C:\Program Files\MySQL\MySQL Server 5.0\bin\mysqld" --console
```

For servers that include `InnoDB` support, you should see the following messages as the server starts:

```
InnoDB: The first specified datafile c:\ibdata\ibdata1 did not exist:
InnoDB: a new database to be created!
InnoDB: Setting file c:\ibdata\ibdata1 size to 209715200
InnoDB: Database physically writes the file full: wait...
InnoDB: Log file c:\iblogs\ib_logfile0 did not exist: new to be created
InnoDB: Setting log file c:\iblogs\ib_logfile0 size to 31457280
InnoDB: Log file c:\iblogs\ib_logfile1 did not exist: new to be created
InnoDB: Setting log file c:\iblogs\ib_logfile1 size to 31457280
InnoDB: Log file c:\iblogs\ib_logfile2 did not exist: new to be created
InnoDB: Setting log file c:\iblogs\ib_logfile2 size to 31457280
InnoDB: Doublewrite buffer not found: creating new
InnoDB: Doublewrite buffer created
InnoDB: creating foreign key constraint system tables
InnoDB: foreign key constraint system tables created
011024 10:58:25  InnoDB: Started
```

When the server finishes its startup sequence, you should see something like this, which indicates that the server is ready to service client connections:

```
mysqld: ready for connections
Version: '5.0.19'  socket: ''  port: 3306
```

The server continues to write to the console any further diagnostic output it produces. You can open a new console window in which to run client programs.

If you omit the --console option, the server writes diagnostic output to the error log in the data directory (C:\Program Files\MySQL\MySQL Server 5.0\data by default). The error log is the file with the .err extension.

Note: The accounts that are listed in the MySQL grant tables initially have no passwords. After starting the server, you should set up passwords for them using the instructions in Section 2.9, "Post-Installation Setup and Testing."

2.3.10 Starting MySQL from the Windows Command Line

The MySQL server can be started manually from the command line. This can be done on any version of Windows.

To start the mysqld server from the command line, you should start a console window (or "DOS window") and enter this command:

```
C:\> "C:\Program Files\MySQL\MySQL Server 5.0\bin\mysqld"
```

The path used in the preceding example may vary depending on the install location of MySQL on your system.

On non-NT versions of Windows, this starts mysqld in the background. That is, after the server starts, you should see another command prompt. If you start the server this way on Windows NT, 2000, XP, or 2003, the server runs in the foreground and no command prompt appears until the server exits. Because of this, you should open another console window to run client programs while the server is running.

You can stop the MySQL server by executing this command:

```
C:\> "C:\Program Files\MySQL\MySQL Server 5.0\bin\mysqladmin" -u root shutdown
```

Note: If the MySQL root user account has a password, you need to invoke mysqladmin with the -p option and supply the password when prompted.

This command invokes the MySQL administrative utility mysqladmin to connect to the server and tell it to shut down. The command connects as the MySQL root user, which is the default administrative account in the MySQL grant system. Note that users in the MySQL grant system are wholly independent from any login users under Windows.

If mysqld doesn't start, check the error log to see whether the server wrote any messages there to indicate the cause of the problem. The error log is located in the C:\Program Files\MySQL\MySQL Server 5.0\data directory. It is the file with a suffix of .err. You can also try to start the server as mysqld --console; in this case, you may get some useful information on the screen that may help solve the problem.

The last option is to start mysqld with the --standalone and --debug options. In this case, mysqld writes a log file C:\mysqld.trace that should contain the reason why mysqld doesn't start.

Use mysqld --verbose --help to display all the options that mysqld understands.

2.3.11 Starting MySQL as a Windows Service

On the NT family (Windows NT, 2000, XP, 2003), the recommended way to run MySQL is to install it as a Windows service, whereby MySQL starts and stops automatically when Windows starts and stops. A MySQL server installed as a service can also be controlled from the command line using NET commands, or with the graphical Services utility.

The Services utility (the Windows Service Control Manager) can be found in the Windows Control Panel (under Administrative Tools on Windows 2000, XP, and Server 2003). To avoid conflicts, it is advisable to close the Services utility while performing server installation or removal operations from the command line.

Before installing MySQL as a Windows service, you should first stop the current server if it is running by using the following command:

```
C:\> "C:\Program Files\MySQL\MySQL Server 5.0\bin\mysqladmin" -u root shutdown
```

Note: If the MySQL root user account has a password, you need to invoke mysqladmin with the -p option and supply the password when prompted.

This command invokes the MySQL administrative utility mysqladmin to connect to the server and tell it to shut down. The command connects as the MySQL root user, which is the default administrative account in the MySQL grant system. Note that users in the MySQL grant system are wholly independent from any login users under Windows.

Install the server as a service using this command:

```
C:\> "C:\Program Files\MySQL\MySQL Server 5.0\bin\mysqld" --install
```

The service-installation command does not start the server. Instructions for that are given later in this section.

To make it easier to invoke MySQL programs, you can add the pathname of the MySQL bin directory to your Windows system PATH environment variable:

- On the Windows desktop, right-click on the My Computer icon, and select Properties.

- Next select the Advanced tab from the System Properties menu that appears, and click the Environment Variables button.

- Under System Variables, select Path, and then click the Edit button. The Edit System Variable dialogue should appear.

- Place your cursor at the end of the text appearing in the space marked Variable Value. (Use the End key to ensure that your cursor is positioned at the very end of the text in this space.) Then enter the complete pathname of your MySQL bin directory (for example, C:\Program Files\MySQL\MySQL Server 5.0\bin). Note that there should be a semicolon separating this path from any values present in this field. Dismiss this dialog, and each dialog in turn, by clicking OK until all of the dialogs that were opened have been dismissed. You should now be able to invoke any MySQL executable program by typing its name at the DOS prompt from any directory on the system, without having to supply the path. This includes the servers, the mysql client, and all MySQL command-line utilities such as mysqladmin and mysqldump.

  You should not add the MySQL bin directory to your Windows PATH if you are running multiple MySQL servers on the same machine.

Warning: You must exercise great care when editing your system PATH by hand; accidental deletion or modification of any portion of the existing PATH value can leave you with a malfunctioning or even unusable system.

The following additional arguments can be used in MySQL 5.0 when installing the service:

- You can specify a service name immediately following the --install option. The default service name is MySQL.

- If a service name is given, it can be followed by a single option. By convention, this should be --defaults-file=file_name to specify the name of an option file from which the server should read options when it starts.

  It is possible to use a single option other than --defaults-file, but this is discouraged. --defaults-file is more flexible because it enables you to specify multiple startup options for the server by placing them in the named option file. Also, in MySQL 5.0, use of an option different from --defaults-file is not supported until 5.0.3.

- As of MySQL 5.0.1, you can also specify a --local-service option following the service name. This causes the server to run using the LocalService Windows account that has limited system privileges. This account is available only for Windows XP or newer. If both --defaults-file and --local-service are given following the service name, they can be in any order.

For a MySQL server that is installed as a Windows service, the following rules determine the service name and option files that the server uses:

- If the service-installation command specifies no service name or the default service name (MySQL) following the --install option, the server uses the a service name of MySQL and reads options from the [mysqld] group in the standard option files.

- If the service-installation command specifies a service name other than MySQL following the --install option, the server uses that service name. It reads options from the group that has the same name as the service, and reads options from the standard option files.

  The server also reads options from the [mysqld] group from the standard option files. This allows you to use the [mysqld] group for options that should be used by all MySQL services, and an option group with the same name as a service for use by the server installed with that service name.

- If the service-installation command specifies a --defaults-file option after the service name, the server reads options only from the [mysqld] group of the named file and ignores the standard option files.

As a more complex example, consider the following command:

```
C:\> "C:\Program Files\MySQL\MySQL Server 5.0\bin\mysqld"
         --install MySQL --defaults-file=C:\my-opts.cnf
```

Here, the default service name (MySQL) is given after the --install option. If no --defaults-file option had been given, this command would have the effect of causing the server to read the [mysqld] group from the standard option files. However, because the --defaults-file option is present, the server reads options from the [mysqld] option group, and only from the named file.

You can also specify options as Start parameters in the Windows Services utility before you start the MySQL service.

Once a MySQL server has been installed as a service, Windows starts the service automatically whenever Windows starts. The service also can be started immediately from the Services utility, or by using a NET START MySQL command. The NET command is not case sensitive.

When run as a service, mysqld has no access to a console window, so no messages can be seen there. If mysqld does not start, check the error log to see whether the server wrote any messages there to indicate the cause of the problem. The error log is located in the MySQL data directory (for example, C:\Program Files\MySQL\MySQL Server 5.0\data). It is the file with a suffix of .err.

When a MySQL server has been installed as a service, and the service is running, Windows stops the service automatically when Windows shuts down. The server also can be stopped manually by using the `Services` utility, the `NET STOP MySQL` command, or the `mysqladmin shutdown` command.

You also have the choice of installing the server as a manual service if you do not wish for the service to be started automatically during the boot process. To do this, use the `--install-manual` option rather than the `--install` option:

```
C:\> "C:\Program Files\MySQL\MySQL Server 5.0\bin\mysqld" --install-manual
```

To remove a server that is installed as a service, first stop it if it is running by executing `NET STOP MYSQL`. Then use the `--remove` option to remove it:

```
C:\> "C:\Program Files\MySQL\MySQL Server 5.0\bin\mysqld" --remove
```

If `mysqld` is not running as a service, you can start it from the command line. For instructions, see Section 2.3.10, "Starting MySQL from the Windows Command Line."

Please see Section 2.3.13, "Troubleshooting a MySQL Installation Under Windows," if you encounter difficulties during installation.

2.3.12 Testing the MySQL Installation

You can test whether the MySQL server is working by executing any of the following commands:

```
C:\> "C:\Program Files\MySQL\MySQL Server 5.0\bin\mysqlshow"
C:\> "C:\Program Files\MySQL\MySQL Server 5.0\bin\mysqlshow" -u root mysql
C:\> "C:\Program Files\MySQL\MySQL Server 5.0\bin\mysqladmin" version status proc
C:\> "C:\Program Files\MySQL\MySQL Server 5.0\bin\mysql" test
```

If `mysqld` is slow to respond to TCP/IP connections from client programs, there is probably a problem with your DNS. In this case, start `mysqld` with the `--skip-name-resolve` option and use only `localhost` and IP numbers in the `Host` column of the MySQL grant tables.

You can force a MySQL client to use a named-pipe connection rather than TCP/IP by specifying the `--pipe` or `--protocol=PIPE` option, or by specifying . (period) as the host name. Use the `--socket` option to specify the name of the pipe if you do not want to use the default pipe name.

Note that if you have set a password for the `root` account, deleted the anonymous account, or created a new user account, you must use the appropriate `-u` and `-p` options with the commands shown above in order to connect with the MySQL Server. See Section 4.8.4, "Connecting to the MySQL Server."

For more information about `mysqlshow`, see Section 7.13, "`mysqlshow`—Display Database, Table, and Column Information."

2.3.13 Troubleshooting a MySQL Installation Under Windows

When installing and running MySQL for the first time, you may encounter certain errors that prevent the MySQL server from starting. The purpose of this section is to help you diagnose and correct some of these errors.

Your first resource when troubleshooting server issues is the error log. The MySQL server uses the error log to record information relevant to the error that prevents the server from starting. The error log is located in the data directory specified in your my.ini file. The default data directory location is C:\Program Files\MySQL\MySQL Server 5.0\data. See Section 4.12.1, "The Error Log."

Another source of information regarding possible errors is the console messages displayed when the MySQL service is starting. Use the NET START mysql command from the command line after installing mysqld as a service to see any error messages regarding the starting of the MySQL server as a service. See Section 2.3.11, "Starting MySQL as a Windows Service."

The following examples show other common error messages you may encounter when installing MySQL and starting the server for the first time:

- If the MySQL server cannot find the mysql privileges database or other critical files, you may see these messages:

```
System error 1067 has occurred.
Fatal error: Can't open privilege tables: Table 'mysql.host' doesn't exist
```

These messages often occur when the MySQL base or data directories are installed in different locations than the default locations (C:\Program Files\MySQL\MySQL Server 5.0 and C:\Program Files\MySQL\MySQL Server 5.0\data, respectively).

This situation may occur when MySQL is upgraded and installed to a new location, but the configuration file is not updated to reflect the new location. In addition, there may be old and new configuration files that conflict. Be sure to delete or rename any old configuration files when upgrading MySQL.

If you have installed MySQL to a directory other than C:\Program Files\MySQL\MySQL Server 5.0, you need to ensure that the MySQL server is aware of this through the use of a configuration (my.ini) file. The my.ini file needs to be located in your Windows directory, typically C:\WINDOWS or C:\WINNT. You can determine its exact location from the value of the WINDIR environment variable by issuing the following command from the command prompt:

```
C:\> echo %WINDIR%
```

An option file can be created and modified with any text editor, such as Notepad. For example, if MySQL is installed in E:\mysql and the data directory is D:\MySQLdata, you can create the option file and set up a [mysqld] section to specify values for the basedir and datadir parameters:

```
[mysqld]
# set basedir to your installation path
basedir=E:/mysql
# set datadir to the location of your data directory
datadir=D:/MySQLdata
```

Note that Windows pathnames are specified in option files using (forward) slashes rather than backslashes. If you do use backslashes, you must double them:

```
[mysqld]
# set basedir to your installation path
basedir=C:\\Program Files\\MySQL\\MySQL Server 5.0
# set datadir to the location of your data directory
datadir=D:\\MySQLdata
```

If you change the datadir value in your MySQL configuration file, you must move the contents of the existing MySQL data directory before restarting the MySQL server.

See Section 2.3.7, "Creating an Option File."

■ If you reinstall or upgrade MySQL without first stopping and removing the existing MySQL service and install MySQL using the MySQL Configuration Wizard, you may see this error:

```
Error: Cannot create Windows service for MySql. Error: 0
```

This occurs when the Configuration Wizard tries to install the service and finds an existing service with the same name.

One solution to this problem is to choose a service name other than mysql when using the Configuration Wizard. This allows the new service to be installed correctly, but leaves the outdated service in place. Although this is harmless, it is best to remove old services that are no longer in use.

To permanently remove the old mysql service, execute the following command as a user with administrative privileges, on the command line:

```
C:\> sc delete mysql
[SC] DeleteService SUCCESS
```

If the sc utility is not available for your version of Windows, download the delsrv utility from http://www.microsoft.com/windows2000/techinfo/reskit/tools/existing/delsrv-o.asp and use the delsrv mysql syntax.

2.3.14 Upgrading MySQL on Windows

This section lists some of the steps you should take when upgrading MySQL on Windows.

1. Review Section 2.10, "Upgrading MySQL," for additional information on upgrading MySQL that is not specific to Windows.

2. You should always back up your current MySQL installation before performing an upgrade. See Section 4.10.1, "Database Backups."

3. Download the latest Windows distribution of MySQL from `http://dev.mysql.com/downloads/`.

4. Before upgrading MySQL, you must stop the server. If the server is installed as a service, stop the service with the following command from the command prompt:

   ```
   C:\> NET STOP MYSQL
   ```

   If you are not running the MySQL server as a service, use the following command to stop it:

   ```
   C:\> "C:\Program Files\MySQL\MySQL Server 5.0\bin\mysqladmin" -u root shutdown
   ```

   Note: If the MySQL `root` user account has a password, you need to invoke `mysqladmin` with the `-p` option and supply the password when prompted.

5. When upgrading to MySQL 5.0 from a version previous to 4.1.5, or when upgrading from a version of MySQL installed from a Zip archive to a version of MySQL installed with the MySQL Installation Wizard, you must manually remove the previous installation and MySQL service (if the server is installed as a service).

   To remove the MySQL service, use the following command:

   ```
   C:\> C:\mysql\bin\mysqld --remove
   ```

   If you do not remove the existing service, the MySQL Installation Wizard may fail to properly install the new MySQL service.

6. If you are using the MySQL Installation Wizard, start the wizard as described in Section 2.3.3, "Using the MySQL Installation Wizard."

7. If you are installing MySQL from a Zip archive, extract the archive. You may either overwrite your existing MySQL installation (usually located at `C:\mysql`), or install it into a different directory, such as `C:\mysql5`. Overwriting the existing installation is recommended.

8. If you were running MySQL as a Windows service and you had to remove the service earlier in this procedure, reinstall the service. (See Section 2.3.11, "Starting MySQL as a Windows Service.")

9. Restart the server. For example, use `NET START MySQL` if you run MySQL as a service, or invoke `mysqld` directly otherwise.

10. If you encounter errors, see Section 2.3.13, "Troubleshooting a MySQL Installation Under Windows."

2.3.15 MySQL on Windows Compared to MySQL on Unix

MySQL for Windows has proven itself to be very stable. The Windows version of MySQL has the same features as the corresponding Unix version, with the following exceptions:

- **Windows 95 and threads**

  Windows 95 leaks about 200 bytes of main memory for each thread creation. Each connection in MySQL creates a new thread, so you shouldn't run `mysqld` for an extended time on Windows 95 if your server handles many connections! Newer versions of Windows don't suffer from this bug.

- **Limited number of ports**

  Windows systems have about 4,000 ports available for client connections, and after a connection on a port closes, it takes two to four minutes before the port can be reused. In situations where clients connect to and disconnect from the server at a high rate, it is possible for all available ports to be used up before closed ports become available again. If this happens, the MySQL server appears to be unresponsive even though it is running. Note that ports may be used by other applications running on the machine as well, in which case the number of ports available to MySQL is lower.

  For more information about this problem, see `http://support.microsoft.com/default.aspx?scid=kb;en-us;196271`.

- **Concurrent reads**

  MySQL depends on the `pread()` and `pwrite()` system calls to be able to mix `INSERT` and `SELECT`. Currently, we use mutexes to emulate `pread()` and `pwrite()`. We intend to replace the file-level interface with a virtual interface in the future so that we can use the `readfile()`/`writefile()` interface on NT, 2000, and XP to get more speed. The current implementation limits the number of open files that MySQL 5.0 can use to 2,048, which means that you cannot run as many concurrent threads on Windows NT, 2000, XP, and 2003 as on Unix.

- **Blocking read**

  MySQL uses a blocking read for each connection. That has the following implications if named-pipe connections are enabled:

  - A connection is not disconnected automatically after eight hours, as happens with the Unix version of MySQL.

  - If a connection hangs, it is not possible to break it without killing MySQL.

  - `mysqladmin kill` does not work on a sleeping connection.

  - `mysqladmin shutdown` cannot abort as long as there are sleeping connections.

  We plan to fix this problem in the future.

- **ALTER TABLE**

  While you are executing an `ALTER TABLE` statement, the table is locked from being used by other threads. This has to do with the fact that on Windows, you can't delete a file that is in use by another thread. In the future, we may find some way to work around this problem.

- **DROP TABLE**

  `DROP TABLE` on a table that is in use by a `MERGE` table does not work on Windows because the `MERGE` handler does the table mapping hidden from the upper layer of MySQL. Because Windows does not allow dropping files that are open, you first must flush all `MERGE` tables (with `FLUSH TABLES`) or drop the `MERGE` table before dropping the table.

- **DATA DIRECTORY** and **INDEX DIRECTORY**

  The DATA DIRECTORY and INDEX DIRECTORY options for CREATE TABLE are ignored on Windows, because Windows doesn't support symbolic links. These options also are ignored on systems that have a non-functional realpath() call.

- **DROP DATABASE**

  You cannot drop a database that is in use by some thread.

- **Killing MySQL from the Task Manager**

  On Windows 95, you cannot kill MySQL from the Task Manager or with the shutdown utility. You must stop it with mysqladmin shutdown.

- **Case-insensitive names**

  Filenames are not case sensitive on Windows, so MySQL database and table names are also not case sensitive on Windows. The only restriction is that database and table names must be specified using the same case throughout a given statement.

- **The '\' pathname separator character**

  Pathname components in Windows are separated by the '\' character, which is also the escape character in MySQL. If you are using LOAD DATA INFILE or SELECT ... INTO OUTFILE, use Unix-style filenames with '/' characters:

  ```
  mysql> LOAD DATA INFILE 'C:/tmp/skr.txt' INTO TABLE skr;
  mysql> SELECT * INTO OUTFILE 'C:/tmp/skr.txt' FROM skr;
  ```

  Alternatively, you must double the '\' character:

  ```
  mysql> LOAD DATA INFILE 'C:\\tmp\\skr.txt' INTO TABLE skr;
  mysql> SELECT * INTO OUTFILE 'C:\\tmp\\skr.txt' FROM skr;
  ```

- **Problems with pipes**

  Pipes do not work reliably from the Windows command-line prompt. If the pipe includes the character ^Z / CHAR(24), Windows thinks that it has encountered end-of-file and aborts the program.

  This is mainly a problem when you try to apply a binary log as follows:

  ```
  C:\> mysqlbinlog binary_log_file | mysql --user=root
  ```

  If you have a problem applying the log and suspect that it is because of a ^Z / CHAR(24) character, you can use the following workaround:

  ```
  C:\> mysqlbinlog binary_log_file --result-file=/tmp/bin.sql
  C:\> mysql --user=root --execute "source /tmp/bin.sql"
  ```

  The latter command also can be used to reliably read in any SQL file that may contain binary data.

- **Access denied for user error**

  If MySQL cannot resolve your hostname properly, you may get the following error when you attempt to run a MySQL client program to connect to a server running on the same machine:

  ```
  Access denied for user 'some_user'@'unknown'
  to database 'mysql'
  ```

  To fix this problem, you should create a file named \windows\hosts containing the following information:

  ```
  127.0.0.1        localhost
  ```

Here are some open issues for anyone who might want to help us improve MySQL on Windows:

- Add macros to use the faster thread-safe increment/decrement methods provided by Windows.

2.4 Installing MySQL on Linux

The recommended way to install MySQL on Linux is by using the RPM packages. The MySQL RPMs are currently built on a SuSE Linux 7.3 system, but should work on most versions of Linux that support rpm and use glibc. To obtain RPM packages, see Section 2.1.3, "How to Get MySQL."

MySQL AB does provide some platform-specific RPMs; the difference between a platform-specific RPM and a generic RPM is that a platform-specific RPM is built on the targeted platform and is linked dynamically whereas a generic RPM is linked statically with LinuxThreads.

Note: RPM distributions of MySQL often are provided by other vendors. Be aware that they may differ in features and capabilities from those built by MySQL AB, and that the instructions in this manual do not necessarily apply to installing them. The vendor's instructions should be consulted instead.

If you have problems with an RPM file (for example, if you receive the error Sorry, the host 'xxxx' could not be looked up), see Section 2.12, "Operating System–Specific Notes."

In most cases, you need to install only the MySQL-server and MySQL-client packages to get a functional MySQL installation. The other packages are not required for a standard installation. If you want to run a MySQL-Max server that has additional capabilities, you should also install the MySQL-Max RPM. However, you should do so only *after* installing the MySQL-server RPM. See Section 4.3, "The mysqld-max Extended MySQL Server."

If you get a dependency failure when trying to install MySQL packages (for example, error: removing these packages would break dependencies: libmysqlclient.so.10 is needed by ...), you should also install the MySQL-shared-compat package, which includes both the shared libraries for backward compatibility (libmysqlclient.so.12 for MySQL 4.0 and libmysqlclient.so.10 for MySQL 3.23).

Some Linux distributions still ship with MySQL 3.23 and they usually link applications dynamically to save disk space. If these shared libraries are in a separate package (for example, MySQL-shared), it is sufficient to simply leave this package installed and just upgrade the MySQL server and client packages (which are statically linked and do not depend on the shared libraries). For distributions that include the shared libraries in the same package as the MySQL server (for example, Red Hat Linux), you could either install our 3.23 MySQL-shared RPM, or use the MySQL-shared-compat package instead.

The following RPM packages are available:

- MySQL-server-VERSION.i386.rpm

  The MySQL server. You need this unless you only want to connect to a MySQL server running on another machine. Note: Server RPM files were called MySQL-VERSION. i386.rpm before MySQL 4.0.10. That is, they did not have -server in the name.

- MySQL-Max-VERSION.i386.rpm

  The MySQL-Max server. This server has additional capabilities that the one provided in the MySQL-server RPM does not. You must install the MySQL-server RPM first, because the MySQL-Max RPM depends on it.

- MySQL-client-VERSION.i386.rpm

  The standard MySQL client programs. You probably always want to install this package.

- MySQL-bench-VERSION.i386.rpm

  Tests and benchmarks. Requires Perl and the DBD::mysql module.

- MySQL-devel-VERSION.i386.rpm

  The libraries and include files that are needed if you want to compile other MySQL clients, such as the Perl modules.

- MySQL-shared-VERSION.i386.rpm

  This package contains the shared libraries (libmysqlclient.so*) that certain languages and applications need to dynamically load and use MySQL.

- MySQL-shared-compat-VERSION.i386.rpm

  This package includes the shared libraries for both MySQL 3.23 and MySQL 4.0. Install this package instead of MySQL-shared if you have applications installed that are dynamically linked against MySQL 3.23 but you want to upgrade to MySQL 4.0 without breaking the library dependencies. This package has been available since MySQL 4.0.13.

- MySQL-embedded-VERSION.i386.rpm

  The embedded MySQL server library (available as of MySQL 4.0).

- `MySQL-VERSION.src.rpm`

   This contains the source code for all of the previous packages. It can also be used to rebuild the RPMs on other architectures (for example, Alpha or SPARC).

To see all files in an RPM package (for example, a `MySQL-server` RPM), run a command like this:

```
shell> rpm -qpl MySQL-server-VERSION.i386.rpm
```

To perform a standard minimal installation, install the server and client RPMs:

```
shell> rpm -i MySQL-server-VERSION.i386.rpm
shell> rpm -i MySQL-client-VERSION.i386.rpm
```

To install only the client programs, install just the client RPM:

```
shell> rpm -i MySQL-client-VERSION.i386.rpm
```

RPM provides a feature to verify the integrity and authenticity of packages before installing them. If you would like to learn more about this feature, see Section 2.1.4, "Verifying Package Integrity Using MD5 Checksums or GnuPG."

The server RPM places data under the `/var/lib/mysql` directory. The RPM also creates a login account for a user named `mysql` (if one does not exist) to use for running the MySQL server, and creates the appropriate entries in `/etc/init.d/` to start the server automatically at boot time. (This means that if you have performed a previous installation and have made changes to its startup script, you may want to make a copy of the script so that you don't lose it when you install a newer RPM.) See Section 2.9.2.2, "Starting and Stopping MySQL Automatically," for more information on how MySQL can be started automatically on system startup.

If you want to install the MySQL RPM on older Linux distributions that do not support initialization scripts in `/etc/init.d` (directly or via a symlink), you should create a symbolic link that points to the location where your initialization scripts actually are installed. For example, if that location is `/etc/rc.d/init.d`, use these commands before installing the RPM to create `/etc/init.d` as a symbolic link that points there:

```
shell> cd /etc
shell> ln -s rc.d/init.d .
```

However, all current major Linux distributions should support the new directory layout that uses `/etc/init.d`, because it is required for LSB (Linux Standard Base) compliance.

If the RPM files that you install include `MySQL-server`, the `mysqld` server should be up and running after installation. You should be able to start using MySQL.

If something goes wrong, you can find more information in the binary installation section. See Section 2.7, "Installing MySQL on Other Unix-Like Systems."

Note: The accounts that are listed in the MySQL grant tables initially have no passwords. After starting the server, you should set up passwords for them using the instructions in Section 2.9, "Post-Installation Setup and Testing."

2.5 Installing MySQL on Mac OS X

You can install MySQL on Mac OS X 10.2.x ("Jaguar") or newer using a Mac OS X binary package in PKG format instead of the binary tarball distribution. Please note that older versions of Mac OS X (for example, 10.1.x) are **not** supported by this package.

The package is located inside a disk image (.dmg) file that you first need to mount by double-clicking its icon in the Finder. It should then mount the image and display its contents.

To obtain MySQL, see Section 2.1.3, "How to Get MySQL."

Note: Before proceeding with the installation, be sure to shut down all running MySQL server instances by either using the MySQL Manager Application (on Mac OS X Server) or via mysqladmin shutdown on the command line.

To actually install the MySQL PKG file, double-click on the package icon. This launches the Mac OS X Package Installer, which guides you through the installation of MySQL.

Due to a bug in the Mac OS X package installer, you may see this error message in the destination disk selection dialog:

```
You cannot install this software on this disk. (null)
```

If this error occurs, simply click the Go Back button once to return to the previous screen. Then click Continue to advance to the destination disk selection again, and you should be able to choose the destination disk correctly. We have reported this bug to Apple and it is investigating this problem.

The Mac OS X PKG of MySQL installs itself into /usr/local/mysql-*VERSION* and also installs a symbolic link, /usr/local/mysql, that points to the new location. If a directory named /usr/local/mysql exists, it is renamed to /usr/local/mysql.bak first. Additionally, the installer creates the grant tables in the mysql database by executing mysql_install_db.

The installation layout is similar to that of a tar file binary distribution; all MySQL binaries are located in the directory /usr/local/mysql/bin. The MySQL socket file is created as /tmp/mysql.sock by default. See Section 2.1.5, "Installation Layouts."

MySQL installation requires a Mac OS X user account named mysql. A user account with this name should exist by default on Mac OS X 10.2 and up.

If you are running Mac OS X Server, a version of MySQL should already be installed. The following table shows the versions of MySQL that ship with Mac OS X Server versions.

Mac OS X Server Version	MySQL Version
10.2-10.2.2	3.23.51
10.2.3-10.2.6	3.23.53
10.3	4.0.14
10.3.2	4.0.16
10.4.0	4.1.10a

This manual section covers the installation of the official MySQL Mac OS X PKG only. Make sure to read Apple's help information about installing MySQL: Run the "Help View" application, select "Mac OS X Server" help, do a search for "MySQL," and read the item entitled "Installing MySQL."

For pre-installed versions of MySQL on Mac OS X Server, note especially that you should start mysqld with safe_mysqld instead of mysqld_safe if MySQL is older than version 4.0.

If you previously used Marc Liyanage's MySQL packages for Mac OS X from http://www.entropy.ch, you can simply follow the update instructions for packages using the binary installation layout as given on his pages.

If you are upgrading from Marc's 3.23.xx versions or from the Mac OS X Server version of MySQL to the official MySQL PKG, you also need to convert the existing MySQL privilege tables to the current format, because some new security privileges have been added. See Section 4.6.2, "mysql_upgrade—Check Tables for MySQL Upgrade."

If you want MySQL to start automatically during system startup, you also need to install the MySQL Startup Item. It is part of the Mac OS X installation disk images as a separate installation package. Simply double-click the MySQLStartupItem.pkg icon and follow the instructions to install it.

Note that the Startup Item need be installed only once! There is no need to install it each time you upgrade the MySQL package later.

The Startup Item for MySQL is installed into /Library/StartupItems/MySQLCOM. (Before MySQL 4.1.2, the location was /Library/StartupItems/MySQL, but that collided with the MySQL Startup Item installed by Mac OS X Server.) Startup Item installation adds a variable MYSQLCOM=-YES- to the system configuration file /etc/hostconfig. If you want to disable the automatic startup of MySQL, simply change this variable to MYSQLCOM=-NO-.

On Mac OS X Server, the default MySQL installation uses the variable MYSQL in the /etc/hostconfig file. The MySQL AB Startup Item installer disables this variable by setting it to MYSQL=-NO-. This avoids boot time conflicts with the MYSQLCOM variable used by the MySQL AB Startup Item. However, it does not shut down a running MySQL server. You should do that yourself.

After the installation, you can start up MySQL by running the following commands in a terminal window. You must have administrator privileges to perform this task.

If you have installed the Startup Item, use this command:

```
shell> sudo /Library/StartupItems/MySQLCOM/MySQLCOM start
(Enter your password, if necessary)
(Press Control-D or enter "exit" to exit the shell)
```

If you don't use the Startup Item, enter the following command sequence:

```
shell> cd /usr/local/mysql
shell> sudo ./bin/mysqld_safe
(Enter your password, if necessary)
(Press Control-Z)
shell> bg
(Press Control-D or enter "exit" to exit the shell)
```

You should be able to connect to the MySQL server, for example, by running /usr/local/mysql/bin/mysql.

Note: The accounts that are listed in the MySQL grant tables initially have no passwords. After starting the server, you should set up passwords for them using the instructions in Section 2.9, "Post-Installation Setup and Testing."

You might want to add aliases to your shell's resource file to make it easier to access commonly used programs such as mysql and mysqladmin from the command line. The syntax for bash is:

```
alias mysql=/usr/local/mysql/bin/mysql
alias mysqladmin=/usr/local/mysql/bin/mysqladmin
```

For tcsh, use:

```
alias mysql /usr/local/mysql/bin/mysql
alias mysqladmin /usr/local/mysql/bin/mysqladmin
```

Even better, add /usr/local/mysql/bin to your PATH environment variable. For example, add the following line to your $HOME/.bashrc file if your shell is bash:

```
PATH=${PATH}:/usr/local/mysql/bin
```

Add the following line to your $HOME/.tcshrc file if your shell is tcsh:

```
setenv PATH ${PATH}:/usr/local/mysql/bin
```

If no .bashrc or .tcshrc file exists in your home directory, create it with a text editor.

If you are upgrading an existing installation, note that installing a new MySQL PKG does not remove the directory of an older installation. Unfortunately, the Mac OS X Installer does not yet offer the functionality required to properly upgrade previously installed packages.

To use your existing databases with the new installation, you'll need to copy the contents of the old data directory to the new data directory. Make sure that neither the old server nor the new one is running when you do this. After you have copied over the MySQL database files from the previous installation and have successfully started the new server, you should consider removing the old installation files to save disk space. Additionally, you should also remove older versions of the Package Receipt directories located in `/Library/Receipts/mysql-VERSION.pkg`.

2.6 Installing MySQL on NetWare

Porting MySQL to NetWare was an effort spearheaded by Novell. Novell customers should be pleased to note that NetWare 6.5 ships with bundled MySQL binaries, complete with an automatic commercial use license for all servers running that version of NetWare.

MySQL for NetWare is compiled using a combination of Metrowerks CodeWarrior for NetWare and special cross-compilation versions of the GNU autotools.

The latest binary packages for NetWare can be obtained at `http://dev.mysql.com/downloads/`. See Section 2.1.3, "How to Get MySQL."

To host MySQL, the NetWare server must meet these requirements:

- The latest Support Pack of NetWare 6.5 (`http://support.novell.com/filefinder/18197/index.html`) must be installed.
- The system must meet Novell's minimum requirements to run the respective version of NetWare.
- MySQL data and the program binaries must be installed on an NSS volume; traditional volumes are not supported.

To install MySQL for NetWare, use the following procedure:

1. If you are upgrading from a prior installation, stop the MySQL server. This is done from the server console, using the following command:

   `SERVER: mysqladmin -u root shutdown`

   Note: If the MySQL root user account has a password, you need to invoke `mysqladmin` with the `-p` option and supply the password when prompted.

2. Log on to the target server from a client machine with access to the location where you are installing MySQL.

3. Extract the binary package Zip file onto the server. Be sure to allow the paths in the Zip file to be used. It is safe to simply extract the file to `SYS:\`.

   If you are upgrading from a prior installation, you may need to copy the data directory (for example, `SYS:MYSQL\DATA`), as well as `my.cnf`, if you have customized it. You can then delete the old copy of MySQL.

4. You might want to rename the directory to something more consistent and easy to use. The examples in this manual use `SYS:MYSQL` to refer to the installation directory.

Note that MySQL installation on NetWare does not detect if a version of MySQL is already installed outside the NetWare release. Therefore, if you have installed the latest MySQL version from the Web (for example, MySQL 4.1 or later) in SYS:\MYSQL, you must rename the folder before upgrading the NetWare server; otherwise, files in SYS:\MySQL are overwritten by the MySQL version present in NetWare Support Pack.

5. At the server console, add a search path for the directory containing the MySQL NLMs. For example:

```
SERVER:  SEARCH ADD SYS:MYSQL\BIN
```

6. Initialize the data directory and the grant tables, if necessary, by executing mysql_install_db at the server console.

7. Start the MySQL server using mysqld_safe at the server console.

8. To finish the installation, you should also add the following commands to autoexec.ncf. For example, if your MySQL installation is in SYS:MYSQL and you want MySQL to start automatically, you could add these lines:

```
#Starts the MySQL 5.0.x database server
SEARCH ADD SYS:MYSQL\BIN
MYSQLD_SAFE
```

If you are running MySQL on NetWare 6.0, we strongly suggest that you use the --skip-external-locking option on the command line:

```
#Starts the MySQL 5.0.x database server
SEARCH ADD SYS:MYSQL\BIN
MYSQLD_SAFE --skip-external-locking
```

It is also necessary to use CHECK TABLE and REPAIR TABLE instead of myisamchk, because myisamchk makes use of external locking. External locking is known to have problems on NetWare 6.0; the problem has been eliminated in NetWare 6.5.

mysqld_safe on NetWare provides a screen presence. When you unload (shut down) the mysqld_safe NLM, the screen does not go away by default. Instead, it prompts for user input:

```
*<NLM has terminated; Press any key to close the screen>*
```

If you want NetWare to close the screen automatically instead, use the --autoclose option to mysqld_safe. For example:

```
#Starts the MySQL 5.0.x database server
SEARCH ADD SYS:MYSQL\BIN
MYSQLD_SAFE --autoclose
```

The behavior of mysqld_safe on NetWare is described further in Section 4.4.1, "mysqld_safe—MySQL Server Startup Script."

9. When installing MySQL, either for the first time or upgrading from a previous version, download and install the latest and appropriate Perl module and PHP extensions for NetWare:

   - Perl: `http://forge.novell.com/modules/xfcontent/downloads.php/perl/Modules/`
   - PHP: `http://forge.novell.com/modules/xfcontent/downloads.php/php/Modules/`

If there was an existing installation of MySQL on the NetWare server, be sure to check for existing MySQL startup commands in `autoexec.ncf`, and edit or delete them as necessary.

Note: The accounts that are listed in the MySQL grant tables initially have no passwords. After starting the server, you should set up passwords for them using the instructions in Section 2.9, "Post-Installation Setup and Testing."

2.7 Installing MySQL on Other Unix-Like Systems

This section covers the installation of MySQL binary distributions that are provided for various platforms in the form of compressed `tar` files (files with a `.tar.gz` extension). See Section 2.1.2.5, "MySQL Binaries Compiled by MySQL AB," for more information.

To obtain MySQL, see Section 2.1.3, "How to Get MySQL."

MySQL tar file binary distributions have names of the form `mysql-VERSION-OS.tar.gz`, where `VERSION` is a number (for example, `5.0.19`), and `OS` indicates the type of operating system for which the distribution is intended (for example, `pc-linux-i686`).

In addition to these generic packages, we also offer binaries in platform-specific package formats for selected platforms. See Section 2.2, "Standard MySQL Installation Using a Binary Distribution," for more information on how to install these.

You need the following tools to install a MySQL `tar` file binary distribution:

- GNU `gunzip` to uncompress the distribution.
- A reasonable `tar` to unpack the distribution. GNU `tar` is known to work. Some operating systems come with a pre-installed version of `tar` that is known to have problems. For example, Mac OS X tar and Sun tar are known to have problems with long filenames. On Mac OS X, you can use the pre-installed `gnutar` program. On other systems with a deficient `tar`, you should install GNU `tar` first.

If you run into problems and need to file a bug report, please use the instructions in Section 1.8, "How to Report Bugs or Problems."

The basic commands that you must execute to install and use a MySQL binary distribution are:

```
shell> groupadd mysql
shell> useradd -g mysql mysql
```

```
shell> cd /usr/local
shell> gunzip < /path/to/mysql-VERSION-OS.tar.gz | tar xvf -
shell> ln -s full-path-to-mysql-VERSION-OS mysql
shell> cd mysql
shell> scripts/mysql_install_db --user=mysql
shell> chown -R root  .
shell> chown -R mysql data
shell> chgrp -R mysql .
shell> bin/mysqld_safe --user=mysql &
```

Note: This procedure does not set up any passwords for MySQL accounts. After following the procedure, proceed to Section 2.9, "Post-Installation Setup and Testing."

A more detailed version of the preceding description for installing a binary distribution follows:

1. Add a login user and group for mysqld to run as:

   ```
   shell> groupadd mysql
   shell> useradd -g mysql mysql
   ```

   These commands add the mysql group and the mysql user. The syntax for useradd and groupadd may differ slightly on different versions of Unix, or they may have different names such as adduser and addgroup.

   You might want to call the user and group something else instead of mysql. If so, substitute the appropriate name in the following steps.

2. Pick the directory under which you want to unpack the distribution and change location into it. In the following example, we unpack the distribution under /usr/local. (The instructions, therefore, assume that you have permission to create files and directories in /usr/local. If that directory is protected, you must perform the installation as root.)

   ```
   shell> cd /usr/local
   ```

3. Obtain a distribution file using the instructions in Section 2.1.3, "How to Get MySQL." For a given release, binary distributions for all platforms are built from the same MySQL source distribution.

4. Unpack the distribution, which creates the installation directory. Then create a symbolic link to that directory:

   ```
   shell> gunzip < /path/to/mysql-VERSION-OS.tar.gz | tar xvf -
   shell> ln -s full-path-to-mysql-VERSION-OS mysql
   ```

   The tar command creates a directory named mysql-VERSION-OS. The ln command makes a symbolic link to that directory. This lets you refer more easily to the installation directory as /usr/local/mysql.

   With GNU tar, no separate invocation of gunzip is necessary. You can replace the first line with the following alternative command to uncompress and extract the distribution:

   ```
   shell> tar zxvf /path/to/mysql-VERSION-OS.tar.gz
   ```

5. Change location into the installation directory:

```
shell> cd mysql
```

You will find several files and subdirectories in the `mysql` directory. The most important for installation purposes are the `bin` and `scripts` subdirectories:

- The `bin` directory contains client programs and the server. You should add the full pathname of this directory to your `PATH` environment variable so that your shell finds the MySQL programs properly.
- The `scripts` directory contains the `mysql_install_db` script used to initialize the `mysql` database containing the grant tables that store the server access permissions.

6. If you have not installed MySQL before, you must create the MySQL grant tables:

```
shell> scripts/mysql_install_db --user=mysql
```

If you run the command as `root`, you must use the `--user` option as shown. The value of the option should be the name of the login account that you created in the first step to use for running the server. If you run the command while logged in as that user, you can omit the `--user` option.

After creating or updating the grant tables, you need to restart the server manually.

7. Change the ownership of program binaries to `root` and ownership of the data directory to the user that you run `mysqld` as. Assuming that you are located in the installation directory (`/usr/local/mysql`), the commands look like this:

```
shell> chown -R root  .
shell> chown -R mysql data
shell> chgrp -R mysql .
```

The first command changes the owner attribute of the files to the `root` user. The second changes the owner attribute of the data directory to the `mysql` user. The third changes the group attribute to the `mysql` group.

8. If you want MySQL to start automatically when you boot your machine, you can copy `support-files/mysql.server` to the location where your system has its startup files. More information can be found in the `support-files/mysql.server` script itself and in Section 2.9.2.2, "Starting and Stopping MySQL Automatically."

9. You can set up new accounts using the `bin/mysql_setpermission` script if you install the `DBI` and `DBD::mysql` Perl modules. For instructions, see Section 2.13, "Perl Installation Notes."

10. If you would like to use `mysqlaccess` and have the MySQL distribution in some non-standard location, you must change the location where `mysqlaccess` expects to find the `mysql` client. Edit the `bin/mysqlaccess` script at approximately line 18. Search for a line that looks like this:

```
$MYSQL     = '/usr/local/bin/mysql';     # path to mysql executable
```

Change the path to reflect the location where `mysql` actually is stored on your system. If you do not do this, a `Broken pipe` error will occur when you run `mysqlaccess`.

After everything has been unpacked and installed, you should test your distribution. To start the MySQL server, use the following command:

```
shell> bin/mysqld_safe --user=mysql &
```

If that command fails immediately and prints mysqld ended, you can find some information in the *host_name*.err file in the data directory.

More information about mysqld_safe is given in Section 4.4.1, "mysqld_safe—MySQL Server Startup Script."

Note: The accounts that are listed in the MySQL grant tables initially have no passwords. After starting the server, you should set up passwords for them using the instructions in Section 2.9, "Post-Installation Setup and Testing."

2.8 MySQL Installation Using a Source Distribution

Before you proceed with an installation from source, first check whether our binary is available for your platform and whether it works for you. We put a great deal of effort into ensuring that our binaries are built with the best possible options.

To obtain a source distribution for MySQL, Section 2.1.3, "How to Get MySQL."

MySQL source distributions are provided as compressed tar archives and have names of the form mysql-*VERSION*.tar.gz, where *VERSION* is a number like 5.0.19.

You need the following tools to build and install MySQL from source:

- GNU gunzip to uncompress the distribution.
- A reasonable tar to unpack the distribution. GNU tar is known to work. Some operating systems come with a pre-installed version of tar that is known to have problems. For example, Mac OS X tar and Sun tar are known to have problems with long filenames. On Mac OS X, you can use the pre-installed gnutar program. On other systems with a deficient tar, you should install GNU tar first.
- A working ANSI C++ compiler. gcc 2.95.2 or later, egcs 1.0.2 or later or egcs 2.91.66, SGI C++, and SunPro C++ are some of the compilers that are known to work. libg++ is not needed when using gcc. gcc 2.7.x has a bug that makes it impossible to compile some perfectly legal C++ files, such as sql/sql_base.cc. If you have only gcc 2.7.x, you must upgrade your gcc to be able to compile MySQL. gcc 2.8.1 is also known to have problems on some platforms, so it should be avoided if a new compiler exists for the platform.

  gcc 2.95.2 or later is recommended when compiling MySQL 3.23.x.
- A good make program. GNU make is always recommended and is sometimes required. If you have problems, we recommend GNU make 3.75 or newer.

If you are using a version of gcc recent enough to understand the -fno-exceptions option, it is *very important* that you use this option. Otherwise, you may compile a binary that crashes randomly. We also recommend that you use -felide-constructors and -fno-rtti along with -fno-exceptions. When in doubt, do the following:

```
CFLAGS="-O3" CXX=gcc CXXFLAGS="-O3 -felide-constructors \
       -fno-exceptions -fno-rtti" ./configure \
       --prefix=/usr/local/mysql --enable-assembler \
       --with-mysqld-ldflags=-all-static
```

On most systems, this gives you a fast and stable binary.

If you run into problems and need to file a bug report, please use the instructions in Section 1.8, "How to Report Bugs or Problems."

2.8.1 Source Installation Overview

The basic commands that you must execute to install a MySQL source distribution are:

```
shell> groupadd mysql
shell> useradd -g mysql mysql
shell> gunzip < mysql-VERSION.tar.gz | tar -xvf -
shell> cd mysql-VERSION
shell> ./configure --prefix=/usr/local/mysql
shell> make
shell> make install
shell> cp support-files/my-medium.cnf /etc/my.cnf
shell> cd /usr/local/mysql
shell> bin/mysql_install_db --user=mysql
shell> chown -R root  .
shell> chown -R mysql var
shell> chgrp -R mysql .
shell> bin/mysqld_safe --user=mysql &
```

If you start from a source RPM, do the following:

```
shell> rpmbuild --rebuild --clean MySQL-VERSION.src.rpm
```

This makes a binary RPM that you can install. For older versions of RPM, you may have to replace the command rpmbuild with rpm instead.

Note: This procedure does not set up any passwords for MySQL accounts. After following the procedure, proceed to Section 2.9, "Post-Installation Setup and Testing," for post-installation setup and testing.

A more detailed version of the preceding description for installing MySQL from a source distribution follows:

1. Add a login user and group for mysqld to run as:

   ```
   shell> groupadd mysql
   shell> useradd -g mysql mysql
   ```

These commands add the `mysql` group and the `mysql` user. The syntax for `useradd` and `groupadd` may differ slightly on different versions of Unix, or they may have different names such as `adduser` and `addgroup`.

You might want to call the user and group something else instead of `mysql`. If so, substitute the appropriate name in the following steps.

2. Pick the directory under which you want to unpack the distribution and change location into it.

3. Obtain a distribution file using the instructions in Section 2.1.3, "How to Get MySQL."

4. Unpack the distribution into the current directory:

```
shell> gunzip < /path/to/mysql-VERSION.tar.gz | tar xvf -
```

This command creates a directory named `mysql-VERSION`.

With GNU `tar`, no separate invocation of `gunzip` is necessary. You can use the following alternative command to uncompress and extract the distribution:

```
shell> tar zxvf /path/to/mysql-VERSION-OS.tar.gz
```

5. Change location into the top-level directory of the unpacked distribution:

```
shell> cd mysql-VERSION
```

Note that currently you must configure and build MySQL from this top-level directory. You cannot build it in a different directory.

6. Configure the release and compile everything:

```
shell> ./configure --prefix=/usr/local/mysql
shell> make
```

When you run `configure`, you might want to specify other options. Run `./configure --help` for a list of options. Section 2.8.2, "Typical `configure` Options," discusses some of the more useful options.

If `configure` fails and you are going to send mail to a MySQL mailing list to ask for assistance, please include any lines from `config.log` that you think can help solve the problem. Also include the last couple of lines of output from `configure`. To file a bug report, please use the instructions in Section 1.8, "How to Report Bugs or Problems."

If the compile fails, see Section 2.8.4, "Dealing with Problems Compiling MySQL," for help.

7. Install the distribution:

```
shell> make install
```

If you want to set up an option file, use one of those present in the `support-files` directory as a template. For example:

```
shell> cp support-files/my-medium.cnf /etc/my.cnf
```

You might need to run these commands as `root`.

If you want to configure support for `InnoDB` tables, you should edit the `/etc/my.cnf` file, remove the `#` character before the option lines that start with `innodb_...`, and modify the option values to be what you want. See Section 3.3.2, "Using Option Files," and Section 8.2.3, "`InnoDB` Configuration."

8. Change location into the installation directory:

```
shell> cd /usr/local/mysql
```

9. If you haven't installed MySQL before, you must create the MySQL grant tables:

```
shell> bin/mysql_install_db --user=mysql
```

If you run the command as `root`, you should use the `--user` option as shown. The value of the option should be the name of the login account that you created in the first step to use for running the server. If you run the command while logged in as that user, you can omit the `--user` option.

After using `mysql_install_db` to create the grant tables for MySQL, you must restart the server manually. The `mysqld_safe` command to do this is shown in a later step.

10. Change the ownership of program binaries to `root` and ownership of the data directory to the user that you run `mysqld` as. Assuming that you are located in the installation directory (`/usr/local/mysql`), the commands look like this:

```
shell> chown -R root    .
shell> chown -R mysql var
shell> chgrp -R mysql .
```

The first command changes the owner attribute of the files to the `root` user. The second changes the owner attribute of the data directory to the `mysql` user. The third changes the group attribute to the `mysql` group.

11. If you want MySQL to start automatically when you boot your machine, you can copy `support-files/mysql.server` to the location where your system has its startup files. More information can be found in the `support-files/mysql.server` script itself; see also Section 2.9.2.2, "Starting and Stopping MySQL Automatically."

12. You can set up new accounts using the `bin/mysql_setpermission` script if you install the `DBI` and `DBD::mysql` Perl modules. For instructions, see Section 2.13, "Perl Installation Notes."

After everything has been installed, you should test your distribution. To start the MySQL server, use the following command:

```
shell> /usr/local/mysql/bin/mysqld_safe --user=mysql &
```

If that command fails immediately and prints `mysqld ended`, you can find some information in the *host_name*`.err` file in the data directory.

More information about `mysqld_safe` is given in Section 4.4.1, "`mysqld_safe`—MySQL Server Startup Script."

Note: The accounts that are listed in the MySQL grant tables initially have no passwords. After starting the server, you should set up passwords for them using the instructions in Section 2.9, "Post-Installation Setup and Testing."

2.8.2 Typical `configure` Options

The `configure` script gives you a great deal of control over how you configure a MySQL source distribution. Typically you do this using options on the `configure` command line. You can also affect `configure` using certain environment variables. For a list of options supported by `configure`, run this command:

```
shell> ./configure --help
```

Some of the more commonly used `configure` options are described here:

- To compile just the MySQL client libraries and client programs and not the server, use the --without-server option:

```
shell> ./configure --without-server
```

  If you have no C++ compiler, mysql cannot be compiled (it is the one client program that requires C++). In this case, you can remove the code in `configure` that tests for the C++ compiler and then run ./configure with the --without-server option. The compile step should still try to build mysql, but you can ignore any warnings about mysql.cc. (If make stops, try make -k to tell it to continue with the rest of the build even if errors occur.)

- If you want to build the embedded MySQL library (libmysqld.a), use the --with-embedded-server option.

- If you don't want your log files and database directories located under /usr/local/var, use a `configure` command something like one of these:

```
shell> ./configure --prefix=/usr/local/mysql
shell> ./configure --prefix=/usr/local \
          --localstatedir=/usr/local/mysql/data
```

  The first command changes the installation prefix so that everything is installed under /usr/local/mysql rather than the default of /usr/local. The second command preserves the default installation prefix, but overrides the default location for database directories (normally /usr/local/var) and changes it to /usr/local/mysql/data.

  You can also specify the locations at server startup time by using a MySQL option file. See Section 3.3.2, "Using Option Files."

- If you are using Unix and you want the MySQL socket file location to be somewhere other than the default location (normally in the directory /tmp or /var/run), use a `configure` command like this:

```
shell> ./configure \
          --with-unix-socket-path=/usr/local/mysql/tmp/mysql.sock
```

The socket filename must be an absolute pathname. You can also change the location of mysql.sock at server startup by using a MySQL option file.

- If you want to compile statically linked programs (for example, to make a binary distribution, to get better performance, or to work around problems with some Red Hat Linux distributions), run configure like this:

```
shell> ./configure --with-client-ldflags=-all-static \
         --with-mysqld-ldflags=-all-static
```

- If you are using gcc and don't have libg++ or libstdc++ installed, you can tell configure to use gcc as your C++ compiler:

```
shell> CC=gcc CXX=gcc ./configure
```

When you use gcc as your C++ compiler, it does not attempt to link in libg++ or libstdc++. This may be a good thing to do even if you have those libraries installed. Some versions of them have caused strange problems for MySQL users in the past.

The following list indicates some compilers and environment variable settings that are commonly used with each one.

- gcc 2.7.2:

```
CC=gcc CXX=gcc CXXFLAGS="-O3 -felide-constructors"
```

- egcs 1.0.3a:

```
CC=gcc CXX=gcc CXXFLAGS="-O3 -felide-constructors \
-fno-exceptions -fno-rtti"
```

- gcc 2.95.2:

```
CFLAGS="-O3 -mpentiumpro" CXX=gcc CXXFLAGS="-O3 -mpentiumpro \
-felide-constructors -fno-exceptions -fno-rtti"
```

- pgcc 2.90.29 or newer:

```
CFLAGS="-O3 -mpentiumpro -mstack-align-double" CXX=gcc \
CXXFLAGS="-O3 -mpentiumpro -mstack-align-double \
-felide-constructors -fno-exceptions -fno-rtti"
```

In most cases, you can get a reasonably optimized MySQL binary by using the options from the preceding list and adding the following options to the configure line:

```
--prefix=/usr/local/mysql --enable-assembler \
--with-mysqld-ldflags=-all-static
```

The full configure line would, in other words, be something like the following for all recent gcc versions:

```
CFLAGS="-O3 -mpentiumpro" CXX=gcc CXXFLAGS="-O3 -mpentiumpro \
-felide-constructors -fno-exceptions -fno-rtti" ./configure \
--prefix=/usr/local/mysql --enable-assembler \
--with-mysqld-ldflags=-all-static
```

The binaries we provide on the MySQL Web site at `http://dev.mysql.com/downloads/` are all compiled with full optimization and should be perfect for most users. See Section 2.1.2.5, "MySQL Binaries Compiled by MySQL AB." There are some configuration settings you can tweak to build an even faster binary, but these are only for advanced users. See Section 6.5.4, "How Compiling and Linking Affects the Speed of MySQL."

If the build fails and produces errors about your compiler or linker not being able to create the shared library `libmysqlclient.so.N` (where *N* is a version number), you can work around this problem by giving the `--disable-shared` option to `configure`. In this case, `configure` does not build a shared `libmysqlclient.so.N` library.

- By default, MySQL uses the `latin1` (cp1252 West European) character set. To change the default set, use the `--with-charset` option:

```
shell> ./configure --with-charset=CHARSET
```

CHARSET may be one of `big5`, `cp1251`, `cp1257`, `czech`, `danish`, `dec8`, `dos`, `euc_kr`, `gb2312`, `gbk`, `german1`, `hebrew`, `hp8`, `hungarian`, `koi8_ru`, `koi8_ukr`, `latin1`, `latin2`, `sjis`, `swe7`, `tis620`, `ujis`, `usa7`, or `win1251ukr`. See Section 4.11.1, "The Character Set Used for Data and Sorting."

The default collation may also be specified. MySQL uses the `latin1_swedish_ci` collation by default. To change this, use the `--with-collation` option:

```
shell> ./configure --with-collation=COLLATION
```

To change both the character set and the collation, use both the `--with-charset` and `--with-collation` options. The collation must be a legal collation for the character set. (Use the `SHOW COLLATION` statement to determine which collations are available for each character set.)

If you want to convert characters between the server and the client, you should use the `SET NAMES` statement.

Warning: If you change character sets after having created any tables, you must run `myisamchk -r -q --set-collation=collation_name on every MyISAM table`. Your indexes may be sorted incorrectly otherwise. This can happen if you install MySQL, create some tables, and then reconfigure MySQL to use a different character set and reinstall it.

With the `configure` option `--with-extra-charsets=LIST`, you can define which additional character sets should be compiled into the server. *LIST* is one of the following:

  - A list of character set names separated by spaces
  - `complex` to include all character sets that can't be dynamically loaded
  - `all` to include all character sets into the binaries

- To configure MySQL with debugging code, use the `--with-debug` option:

```
shell> ./configure --with-debug
```

This causes a safe memory allocator to be included that can find some errors and that provides output about what is happening.

- If your client programs are using threads, you must compile a thread-safe version of the MySQL client library with the `--enable-thread-safe-client` configure option. This creates a `libmysqlclient_r` library with which you should link your threaded applications.

- It is possible to build MySQL 5.0 with large table support using the `--with-big-tables` option, beginning with MySQL 5.0.4.

  This option causes the variables used to keep table row counts to be stored using `unsigned long long` rather than `unsigned long`. What this does is to allow tables to hold up to approximately 1.844E+19 ($(2^{32})^2$) rows rather than 2^{32} (~4.295E+09) rows. Previously it was necessary to pass `-DBIG_TABLES` to the compiler manually in order to enable this feature.

- Options that pertain to particular operating systems can be found in the system-specific section of this manual. See Section 2.12, "Operating System–Specific Notes."

2.8.3 Installing from the Development Source Tree

Caution: You should read this section only if you are interested in helping us test our new code. If you just want to get MySQL up and running on your system, you should use a standard release distribution (either a binary or source distribution).

To obtain our most recent development source tree, first download and install the BitKeeper free client if you do not have it. The client can be obtained from `http://www.bitmover.com/bk-client.shar`.

To install the BitKeeper client on Unix, use these commands:

```
shell> sh bk-client.shar
shell> cd bk_client-1.1
shell> make all
shell> PATH=$PWD:$PATH
```

To install the BitKeeper client on Windows, use these instructions:

1. Download and install Cygwin from `http://cygwin.com/`.

2. Make sure gcc and make have been installed under Cygwin. You can test this by issuing `which gcc` and `which make` commands. If either one is not installed, run Cygwin's package manager, select gcc, make, or both, and install them.

3. Under Cygwin, execute these commands:

   ```
   shell> sh bk-client.shar
   shell> cd bk_client-1.1
   ```

   Then edit the Makefile and change the line that reads `$(CC) $(CFLAGS) -o sfio -lz sfio.c` to this:

   ```
   $(CC) $(CFLAGS) -o sfio sfio.c -lz
   ```

Now run the make command and set the path:

```
shell> make all
shell> PATH=$PWD:$PATH
```

The BitKeeper free client is shipped with its source code. The only documentation available for the free client is the source code itself.

After you have installed the BitKeeper client, you can access the MySQL development source tree:

1. Change location to the directory you want to work from, and then use the following command to make a local copy of the MySQL 5.0 branch:

```
shell> sfioball -r+ bk://mysql.bkbits.net/mysql-5.0 mysql-5.0
```

   In the preceding example, the source tree is set up in the mysql-5.0/ subdirectory of your current directory.

   The initial download of the source tree may take a while, depending on the speed of your connection. Please be patient.

2. You need GNU make, autoconf 2.58 (or newer), automake 1.8, libtool 1.5, and m4 to run the next set of commands. Even though many operating systems come with their own implementation of make, chances are high that the compilation fails with strange error messages. Therefore, it is highly recommended that you use GNU make (sometimes named gmake) instead.

   Fortunately, a large number of operating systems ship with the GNU toolchain preinstalled or supply installable packages of these. In any case, they can also be downloaded from the following locations:

   - http://www.gnu.org/software/autoconf/
   - http://www.gnu.org/software/automake/
   - http://www.gnu.org/software/libtool/
   - http://www.gnu.org/software/m4/
   - http://www.gnu.org/software/make/

   To configure MySQL 5.0, you also need GNU bison 1.75 or later. Older versions of bison may report this error:

```
sql_yacc.yy:#####: fatal error: maximum table size (32767) exceeded
```

   Note: The maximum table size is not actually exceeded; the error is caused by bugs in older versions of bison.

   The following example shows the typical commands required to configure a source tree. The first cd command changes location into the top-level directory of the tree; replace mysql-5.0 with the appropriate directory name.

```
shell> cd mysql-5.0
shell> aclocal; autoheader
```

```
shell> libtoolize --automake --force
shell> automake --force --add-missing; autoconf
shell> (cd innobase; aclocal; autoheader; autoconf; automake)
shell> (cd bdb/dist; sh s_all)
shell> ./configure  # Add your favorite options here
shell> make
```

Or you can use BUILD/autorun.sh as a shortcut for the following sequence of commands:

```
shell> aclocal; autoheader
shell> libtoolize --automake --force
shell> automake --force --add-missing; autoconf
shell> (cd innobase; aclocal; autoheader; autoconf; automake)
shell> (cd bdb/dist; sh s_all)
```

The command lines that change directory into the innobase and bdb/dist directories are used to configure the InnoDB and Berkeley DB (BDB) storage engines. You can omit these command lines if you to not require InnoDB or BDB support.

If you get some strange errors during this stage, verify that you really have libtool installed.

A collection of our standard configuration scripts is located in the BUILD/ subdirectory. You may find it more convenient to use the BUILD/compile-pentium-debug script than the preceding set of shell commands. To compile on a different architecture, modify the script by removing flags that are Pentium-specific.

3. When the build is done, run make install. Be careful with this on a production machine; the command may overwrite your live release installation. If you have another installation of MySQL, we recommend that you run ./configure with different values for the --prefix, --with-tcp-port, and --unix-socket-path options than those used for your production server.

4. Play hard with your new installation and try to make the new features crash. Start by running make test.

5. If you have gotten to the make stage, but the distribution does not compile, please enter the problem into our bugs database using the instructions given in Section 1.8, "How to Report Bugs or Problems." If you have installed the latest versions of the required GNU tools, and they crash trying to process our configuration files, please report that also. However, if you execute aclocal and get a command not found error or a similar problem, do not report it. Instead, make sure that all the necessary tools are installed and that your PATH variable is set correctly so that your shell can find them.

6. After initially copying the repository with sfioball to obtain the source tree, you should use update periodically to update your local copy. To do this any time after you have set up the repository, use this command:

```
shell> update bk://mysql.bkbits.net/mysql-5.0
```

7. You can examine the change history for the tree with all the diffs by viewing the BK/ChangeLog file in the source tree and looking at the ChangeSet descriptions listed there. To examine a particular changeset, you would have to use the sfioball command to extract two particular revisions of the source tree, and then use an external diff command to compare them. If you see some funny diffs or code that you have a question about, do not hesitate to send email to the MySQL internals mailing list. See Section 1.7.1, "MySQL Mailing Lists." Also, if you think you have a better idea on how to do something, send an email message to the list with a patch.

You can also browse changesets, comments, and source code online. To browse this information for MySQL 5.0, go to http://mysql.bkbits.net:8080/mysql-5.0.

2.8.4 Dealing with Problems Compiling MySQL

All MySQL programs compile cleanly for us with no warnings on Solaris or Linux using gcc. On other systems, warnings may occur due to differences in system include files. See Section 2.8.5, "MIT-pthreads Notes," for warnings that may occur when using MIT-pthreads. For other problems, check the following list.

The solution to many problems involves reconfiguring. If you do need to reconfigure, take note of the following:

- If configure is run after it has previously been run, it may use information that was gathered during its previous invocation. This information is stored in config.cache. When configure starts up, it looks for that file and reads its contents if it exists, on the assumption that the information is still correct. That assumption is invalid when you reconfigure.

- Each time you run configure, you must run make again to recompile. However, you may want to remove old object files from previous builds first because they were compiled using different configuration options.

To prevent old configuration information or object files from being used, run these commands before re-running configure:

```
shell> rm config.cache
shell> make clean
```

Alternatively, you can run make distclean.

The following list describes some of the problems when compiling MySQL that have been found to occur most often:

- If you get errors such as the ones shown here when compiling sql_yacc.cc, you probably have run out of memory or swap space:

```
Internal compiler error: program cc1plus got fatal signal 11
Out of virtual memory
Virtual memory exhausted
```

The problem is that gcc requires a huge amount of memory to compile sql_yacc.cc with inline functions. Try running configure with the --with-low-memory option:

```
shell> ./configure --with-low-memory
```

This option causes -fno-inline to be added to the compile line if you are using gcc and -O0 if you are using something else. You should try the --with-low-memory option even if you have so much memory and swap space that you think you can't possibly have run out. This problem has been observed to occur even on systems with generous hardware configurations, and the --with-low-memory option usually fixes it.

- By default, configure picks c++ as the compiler name and GNU c++ links with -lg++. If you are using gcc, that behavior can cause problems during configuration such as this:

```
configure: error: installation or configuration problem:
C++ compiler cannot create executables.
```

You might also observe problems during compilation related to g++, libg++, or libstdc++.

One cause of these problems is that you may not have g++, or you may have g++ but not libg++, or libstdc++. Take a look at the config.log file. It should contain the exact reason why your C++ compiler didn't work. To work around these problems, you can use gcc as your C++ compiler. Try setting the environment variable CXX to "gcc -O3". For example:

```
shell> CXX="gcc -O3" ./configure
```

This works because gcc compiles C++ source files as well as g++ does, but does not link in libg++ or libstdc++ by default.

Another way to fix these problems is to install g++, libg++, and libstdc++. However, we recommend that you not use libg++ or libstdc++ with MySQL because this only increases the binary size of mysqld without providing any benefits. Some versions of these libraries have also caused strange problems for MySQL users in the past.

- If your compile fails with errors such as any of the following, you must upgrade your version of make to GNU make:

```
making all in mit-pthreads
make: Fatal error in reader: Makefile, line 18:
Badly formed macro assignment
```

Or:

```
make: file `Makefile' line 18: Must be a separator (:
```

Or:

```
pthread.h: No such file or directory
```

Solaris and FreeBSD are known to have troublesome make programs.

GNU make 3.75 is known to work.

- If you want to define flags to be used by your C or C++ compilers, do so by adding the flags to the CFLAGS and CXXFLAGS environment variables. You can also specify the compiler names this way using CC and CXX. For example:

```
shell> CC=gcc
shell> CFLAGS=-O3
shell> CXX=gcc
shell> CXXFLAGS=-O3
shell> export CC CFLAGS CXX CXXFLAGS
```

See Section 2.1.2.5, "MySQL Binaries Compiled by MySQL AB," for more information.

- If you get errors such as those shown here when compiling mysqld, configure did not correctly detect the type of the last argument to accept(), getsockname(), or getpeername():

```
cxx: Error: mysqld.cc, line 645: In this statement, the referenced
     type of the pointer value ''length'' is ''unsigned long'',
     which is not compatible with ''int''.
new_sock = accept(sock, (struct sockaddr *)&cAddr, &length);
```

To fix this, edit the config.h file (which is generated by configure). Look for these lines:

```
/* Define as the base type of the last arg to accept */
#define SOCKET_SIZE_TYPE XXX
```

Change XXX to size_t or int, depending on your operating system. (You must do this each time you run configure because configure regenerates config.h.)

- The sql_yacc.cc file is generated from sql_yacc.yy. Normally, the build process does not need to create sql_yacc.cc because MySQL comes with a pre-generated copy. However, if you do need to re-create it, you might encounter this error:

```
"sql_yacc.yy", line xxx fatal: default action causes potential...
```

This is a sign that your version of yacc is deficient. You probably need to install bison (the GNU version of yacc) and use that instead.

- On Debian Linux 3.0, you need to install gawk instead of the default mawk if you want to compile MySQL with Berkeley DB support.

- If you need to debug mysqld or a MySQL client, run configure with the --with-debug option, and then recompile and link your clients with the new client library.

- If you get a compilation error on Linux (for example, SuSE Linux 8.1 or Red Hat Linux 7.3) similar to the following one, you probably do not have gtt installed:

```
libmysql.c:1329: warning: passing arg 5 of `gethostbyname_r' from
incompatible pointer type
libmysql.c:1329: too few arguments to function `gethostbyname_r'
libmysql.c:1329: warning: assignment makes pointer from integer
without a cast
make[2]: *** [libmysql.lo] Error 1
```

By default, the `configure` script attempts to determine the correct number of arguments by using g++ (the GNU C++ compiler). This test yields wrong results if g++ is not installed. There are two ways to work around this problem:

- Make sure that the GNU C++ g++ is installed. On some Linux distributions, the required package is called gpp; on others, it is named gcc-c++.

- Use gcc as your C++ compiler by setting the CXX environment variable to gcc:

  `export CXX="gcc"`

You must run `configure` again after making either of those changes.

2.8.5 MIT-pthreads Notes

This section describes some of the issues involved in using MIT-pthreads.

On Linux, you should *not* use MIT-pthreads. Use the installed LinuxThreads implementation instead.

If your system does not provide native thread support, you should build MySQL using the MIT-pthreads package. This includes older FreeBSD systems, SunOS 4.x, Solaris 2.4 and earlier, and some others. See Section 2.1.1, "Operating Systems Supported by MySQL."

MIT-pthreads is not part of the MySQL 5.0 source distribution. If you require this package, you need to download it separately from http://www.mysql.com/Downloads/Contrib/pthreads-1_60_beta6-mysql.tar.gz.

After downloading, extract this source archive into the top level of the MySQL source directory. It creates a new subdirectory named `mit-pthreads`.

- On most systems, you can force MIT-pthreads to be used by running `configure` with the `--with-mit-threads` option:

  `shell> ./configure --with-mit-threads`

  Building in a non-source directory is not supported when using MIT-pthreads because we want to minimize our changes to this code.

- The checks that determine whether to use MIT-pthreads occur only during the part of the configuration process that deals with the server code. If you have configured the distribution using `--without-server` to build only the client code, clients do not know whether MIT-pthreads is being used and use Unix socket file connections by default. Because Unix socket files do not work under MIT-pthreads on some platforms, this means you need to use `-h` or `--host` with a value other than `localhost` when you run client programs.

- When MySQL is compiled using MIT-pthreads, system locking is disabled by default for performance reasons. You can tell the server to use system locking with the `--external-locking` option. This is needed only if you want to be able to run two MySQL servers against the same data files, but that is not recommended, anyway.

- Sometimes the pthread `bind()` command fails to bind to a socket without any error message (at least on Solaris). The result is that all connections to the server fail. For example:

```
shell> mysqladmin version
mysqladmin: connect to server at '' failed;
error: 'Can't connect to mysql server on localhost (146)'
```

  The solution to this problem is to kill the `mysqld` server and restart it. This has happened to us only when we have forcibly stopped the server and restarted it immediately.

- With MIT-pthreads, the `sleep()` system call isn't interruptible with `SIGINT` (break). This is noticeable only when you run `mysqladmin --sleep`. You must wait for the `sleep()` call to terminate before the interrupt is served and the process stops.

- When linking, you might receive warning messages like these (at least on Solaris); they can be ignored:

```
ld: warning: symbol `_iob' has differing sizes:
    (file /my/local/pthreads/lib/libpthread.a(findfp.o) value=0x4;
file /usr/lib/libc.so value=0x140);
    /my/local/pthreads/lib/libpthread.a(findfp.o) definition taken
ld: warning: symbol `__iob' has differing sizes:
    (file /my/local/pthreads/lib/libpthread.a(findfp.o) value=0x4;
file /usr/lib/libc.so value=0x140);
    /my/local/pthreads/lib/libpthread.a(findfp.o) definition taken
```

- Some other warnings also can be ignored:

```
implicit declaration of function `int strtoll(...)'
implicit declaration of function `int strtoul(...)'
```

- We have not been able to make `readline` work with MIT-pthreads. (This is not necessary, but may be of interest to some.)

2.8.6 Installing MySQL from Source on Windows

These instructions describe how to build binaries from source for MySQL 5.0 on Windows. Instructions are provided for building binaries from a standard source distribution or from the BitKeeper tree that contains the latest development source.

Note: The instructions here are strictly for users who want to test MySQL on Windows from the latest source distribution or from the BitKeeper tree. For production use, MySQL AB does not advise using a MySQL server built by yourself from source. Normally, it is best to use precompiled binary distributions of MySQL that are built specifically for optimal performance on Windows by MySQL AB. Instructions for installing a binary distributions are available in Section 2.3, "Installing MySQL on Windows."

To build MySQL on Windows from source, you need the following compiler and resources available on your Windows system:

- Visual Studio 7.1 compiler system (VC++ 7.0)
- Between 3GB and 5GB disk space
- Windows 2000 or higher

The exact system requirements can be found here:
`http://msdn.microsoft.com/vstudio/productinfo/sysreqs/default.aspx`.

You also need a MySQL source distribution for Windows. There are two ways to obtain a source distribution:

1. Obtain a source distribution packaged by MySQL AB. These are available from `http://dev.mysql.com/downloads/`.

2. You can package a source distribution yourself from the latest BitKeeper developer source tree. If you plan to do this, you must create the package on a Unix system and then transfer it to your Windows system. (Some of the configuration and build steps require tools that work only on Unix.) The BitKeeper approach thus requires:

   - A system running Unix, or a Unix-like system such as Linux.
   - BitKeeper 3.0 installed on that system. See Section 2.8.3, "Installing from the Development Source Tree," for instructions how to download and install BitKeeper.

If you are using a Windows source distribution, you can go directly to Section 2.8.6.1, "Building MySQL Using VC++." To build from the BitKeeper tree, proceed to Section 2.8.6.2, "Creating a Windows Source Package from the Latest Development Source."

If you find something not working as expected, or you have suggestions about ways to improve the current build process on Windows, please send a message to the `win32` mailing list. See Section 1.7.1, "MySQL Mailing Lists."

2.8.6.1 Building MySQL Using VC++

Note: VC++ workspace files for MySQL 4.1 and above are compatible with Microsoft Visual Studio 2003 editions and tested by MySQL AB staff before each release.

Follow this procedure to build MySQL:

1. Create a work directory (for example, `C:\workdir`).
2. Unpack the source distribution in the aforementioned directory using `WinZip` or another Windows tool that can read `.zip` files.
3. Start Visual Studio.
4. From the `File` menu, select `Open Workspace`.
5. Open the `mysql.dsw` workspace you find in the work directory.
6. From the `Build` menu, select the `Set Active Configuration` menu.
7. Click over the screen selecting `mysqld - Win32 Debug` and click `OK`.
8. Press `F7` to begin the build of the debug server, libraries, and some client applications.

9. Compile the release version in the same way.

10. Debug versions of the programs and libraries are placed in the `client_debug` and `lib_debug` directories. Release versions of the programs and libraries are placed in the `client_release` and `lib_release` directories. Note that if you want to build both debug and release versions, you can select the `Build All` option from the `Build` menu.

11. Test the server. The server built using the preceding instructions expects that the MySQL base directory and data directory are `C:\mysql` and `C:\mysql\data` by default. If you want to test your server using the source tree root directory and its data directory as the base directory and data directory, you need to tell the server their pathnames. You can either do this on the command line with the `--basedir` and `--datadir` options, or by placing appropriate options in an option file. (See Section 3.3.2, "Using Option Files.") If you have an existing data directory elsewhere that you want to use, you can specify its pathname instead.

12. Start your server from the `client_release` or `client_debug` directory, depending on which server you want to use. The general server startup instructions are in Section 2.3, "Installing MySQL on Windows." You must adapt the instructions appropriately if you want to use a different base directory or data directory.

13. When the server is running in standalone fashion or as a service based on your configuration, try to connect to it from the `mysql` interactive command-line utility that exists in your `client_release` or `client_debug` directory.

When you are satisfied that the programs you have built are working correctly, stop the server. Then install MySQL as follows:

1. Create the directories where you want to install MySQL. For example, to install into `C:\mysql`, use these commands:

```
C:\> mkdir C:\mysql
C:\> mkdir C:\mysql\bin
C:\> mkdir C:\mysql\data
C:\> mkdir C:\mysql\share
C:\> mkdir C:\mysql\scripts
```

If you want to compile other clients and link them to MySQL, you should also create several additional directories:

```
C:\> mkdir C:\mysql\include
C:\> mkdir C:\mysql\lib
C:\> mkdir C:\mysql\lib\debug
C:\> mkdir C:\mysql\lib\opt
```

If you want to benchmark MySQL, create this directory:

```
C:\> mkdir C:\mysql\sql-bench
```

Benchmarking requires Perl support. See Section 2.13, "Perl Installation Notes."

2. From the `workdir` directory, copy into the `C:\mysql` directory the following directories:

```
C:\> cd \workdir
C:\workdir> copy client_release\*.exe C:\mysql\bin
C:\workdir> copy client_debug\mysqld.exe C:\mysql\bin\mysqld-debug.exe
C:\workdir> xcopy scripts\*.* C:\mysql\scripts /E
C:\workdir> xcopy share\*.* C:\mysql\share /E
```

If you want to compile other clients and link them to MySQL, you should also copy several libraries and header files:

```
C:\workdir> copy lib_debug\mysqlclient.lib C:\mysql\lib\debug
C:\workdir> copy lib_debug\libmysql.* C:\mysql\lib\debug
C:\workdir> copy lib_debug\zlib.* C:\mysql\lib\debug
C:\workdir> copy lib_release\mysqlclient.lib C:\mysql\lib\opt
C:\workdir> copy lib_release\libmysql.* C:\mysql\lib\opt
C:\workdir> copy lib_release\zlib.* C:\mysql\lib\opt
C:\workdir> copy include\*.h C:\mysql\include
C:\workdir> copy libmysql\libmysql.def C:\mysql\include
```

If you want to benchmark MySQL, you should also do this:

```
C:\workdir> xcopy sql-bench\*.* C:\mysql\bench /E
```

Set up and start the server in the same way as for the binary Windows distribution. See Section 2.3, "Installing MySQL on Windows."

2.8.6.2 Creating a Windows Source Package from the Latest Development Source

To create a Windows source package from the current BitKeeper source tree, use the instructions here. This procedure must be performed on a system running a Unix or Unix-like operating system because some of the configuration and build steps require tools that work only on Unix. For example, the following procedure is known to work well on Linux.

1. Copy the BitKeeper source tree for MySQL 5.0. For instructions on how to do this, see Section 2.8.3, "Installing from the Development Source Tree."

2. Configure and build the distribution so that you have a server binary to work with. One way to do this is to run the following command in the top-level directory of your source tree:

```
shell> ./BUILD/compile-pentium-max
```

3. After making sure that the build process completed successfully, run the following utility script from top-level directory of your source tree:

```
shell> ./scripts/make_win_src_distribution
```

This script creates a Windows source package to be used on your Windows system. You can supply different options to the script based on your needs. It accepts the following options:

- `--help`

  Display a help message.

- `--debug`

  Print information about script operations, do not create package.

- `--tmp`

  Specify the temporary location.

- `--suffix`

  The suffix name for the package.

- `--dirname`

  Directory name to copy files (intermediate).

- `--silent`

  Do not print verbose list of files processed.

- `--tar`

  Create `tar.gz` package instead of `.zip` package.

By default, `make_win_src_distribution` creates a Zip-format archive with the name `mysql-VERSION-win-src.zip`, where `VERSION` represents the version of your MySQL source tree.

4. Copy or upload the Windows source package that you have just created to your Windows machine. To compile it, use the instructions in Section 2.8.6.1, "Building MySQL Using VC++."

2.8.7 Compiling MySQL Clients on Windows

In your source files, you should include `my_global.h` before `mysql.h`:

```
#include <my_global.h>
#include <mysql.h>
```

`my_global.h` includes any other files needed for Windows compatibility (such as `windows.h`) if you compile your program on Windows.

You can either link your code with the dynamic `libmysql.lib` library, which is just a wrapper to load in `libmysql.dll` on demand, or link with the static `mysqlclient.lib` library.

The MySQL client libraries are compiled as threaded libraries, so you should also compile your code to be multi-threaded.

2.9 Post-Installation Setup and Testing

After installing MySQL, there are some issues that you should address. For example, on Unix, you should initialize the data directory and create the MySQL grant tables. On all platforms, an important security concern is that the initial accounts in the grant tables have no passwords. You should assign passwords to prevent unauthorized access to the MySQL server. Optionally, you can create time zone tables to enable recognition of named time zones.

The following sections include post-installation procedures that are specific to Windows systems and to Unix systems. Another section, Section 2.9.2.3, "Starting and Troubleshooting the MySQL Server," applies to all platforms; it describes what to do if you have trouble getting the server to start. Section 2.9.3, "Securing the Initial MySQL Accounts," also applies to all platforms. You should follow its instructions to make sure that you have properly protected your MySQL accounts by assigning passwords to them.

When you are ready to create additional user accounts, you can find information on the MySQL access control system and account management in Section 4.8, "The MySQL Access Privilege System," and Section 4.9, "MySQL User Account Management."

2.9.1 Windows Post-Installation Procedures

On Windows, the data directory and the grant tables do not have to be created. MySQL Windows distributions include the grant tables with a set of preinitialized accounts in the `mysql` database under the data directory. It is unnecessary to run the `mysql_install_db` script that is used on Unix. Regarding passwords, if you installed MySQL using the Windows Installation Wizard, you may have already assigned passwords to the accounts. (See Section 2.3.3, "Using the MySQL Installation Wizard.") Otherwise, use the password-assignment procedure given in Section 2.9.3, "Securing the Initial MySQL Accounts."

Before setting up passwords, you might want to try running some client programs to make sure that you can connect to the server and that it is operating properly. Make sure that the server is running (see Section 2.3.9, "Starting the Server for the First Time"), and then issue the following commands to verify that you can retrieve information from the server. The output should be similar to what is shown here:

```
C:\> C:\mysql\bin\mysqlshow
+-----------+
| Databases |
+-----------+
| mysql     |
| test      |
+-----------+
```

```
C:\> C:\mysql\bin\mysqlshow mysql
Database: mysql
+--------------------------+
|          Tables          |
+--------------------------+
| columns_priv             |
| db                       |
| func                     |
| help_category            |
| help_keyword             |
| help_relation            |
| help_topic               |
| host                     |
| proc                     |
| procs_priv               |
| tables_priv              |
| time_zone                |
| time_zone_leap_second    |
| time_zone_name           |
| time_zone_transition     |
| time_zone_transition_type |
| user                     |
+--------------------------+
```

```
C:\> C:\mysql\bin\mysql -e "SELECT Host,Db,User FROM db" mysql
+------+-------+------+
| host | db    | user |
+------+-------+------+
| %    | test% |      |
+------+-------+------+
```

If you are running a version of Windows that supports services and you want the MySQL server to run automatically when Windows starts, see Section 2.3.11, "Starting MySQL as a Windows Service."

2.9.2 Unix Post-Installation Procedures

After installing MySQL on Unix, you need to initialize the grant tables, start the server, and make sure that the server works satisfactorily. You may also wish to arrange for the server to be started and stopped automatically when your system starts and stops. You should also assign passwords to the accounts in the grant tables.

On Unix, the grant tables are set up by the mysql_install_db program. For some installation methods, this program is run for you automatically:

- If you install MySQL on Linux using RPM distributions, the server RPM runs mysql_install_db.

- If you install MySQL on Mac OS X using a PKG distribution, the installer runs `mysql_install_db`.

Otherwise, you'll need to run `mysql_install_db` yourself.

The following procedure describes how to initialize the grant tables (if that has not previously been done) and then start the server. It also suggests some commands that you can use to test whether the server is accessible and working properly. For information about starting and stopping the server automatically, see Section 2.9.2.2, "Starting and Stopping MySQL Automatically."

After you complete the procedure and have the server running, you should assign passwords to the accounts created by `mysql_install_db`. Instructions for doing so are given in Section 2.9.3, "Securing the Initial MySQL Accounts."

In the examples shown here, the server runs under the user ID of the `mysql` login account. This assumes that such an account exists. Either create the account if it does not exist, or substitute the name of a different existing login account that you plan to use for running the server.

1. Change location into the top-level directory of your MySQL installation, represented here by *BASEDIR*:

   ```
   shell> cd BASEDIR
   ```

   BASEDIR is likely to be something like `/usr/local/mysql` or `/usr/local`. The following steps assume that you are located in this directory.

2. If necessary, run the `mysql_install_db` program to set up the initial MySQL grant tables containing the privileges that determine how users are allowed to connect to the server. You'll need to do this if you used a distribution type for which the installation procedure doesn't run the program for you.

   Typically, `mysql_install_db` needs to be run only the first time you install MySQL, so you can skip this step if you are upgrading an existing installation, However, `mysql_install_db` does not overwrite any existing privilege tables, so it should be safe to run in any circumstances.

   To initialize the grant tables, use one of the following commands, depending on whether `mysql_install_db` is located in the `bin` or `scripts` directory:

   ```
   shell> bin/mysql_install_db --user=mysql
   shell> scripts/mysql_install_db --user=mysql
   ```

   The `mysql_install_db` script creates the server's data directory. Under the data directory, it creates directories for the `mysql` database that holds all database privileges and the `test` database that you can use to test MySQL. The script also creates privilege table entries for `root` accounts and anonymous-user accounts. The accounts have no passwords initially. A description of their initial privileges is given in Section 2.9.3, "Securing the Initial MySQL Accounts." Briefly, these privileges allow the MySQL root user to do anything, and allow anybody to create or use databases with a name of `test` or starting with `test_`.

It is important to make sure that the database directories and files are owned by the `mysql` login account so that the server has read and write access to them when you run it later. To ensure this, the `--user` option should be used as shown if you run `mysql_install_db` as root. Otherwise, you should execute the script while logged in as `mysql`, in which case you can omit the `--user` option from the command.

`mysql_install_db` creates several tables in the `mysql` database, including `user`, `db`, `host`, `tables_priv`, `columns_priv`, and `func`, as well as others. See Section 4.8, "The MySQL Access Privilege System," for a complete listing and description of these tables.

If you don't want to have the `test` database, you can remove it with `mysqladmin -u root drop test` after starting the server.

If you have trouble with `mysql_install_db` at this point, see Section 2.9.2.1, "Problems Running `mysql_install_db`."

3. Start the MySQL server:

```
shell> bin/mysqld_safe --user=mysql &
```

It is important that the MySQL server be run using an unprivileged (non-root) login account. To ensure this, the `--user` option should be used as shown if you run `mysql_safe` as system root. Otherwise, you should execute the script while logged in to the system as `mysql`, in which case you can omit the `--user` option from the command.

Further instructions for running MySQL as an unprivileged user are given in Section 4.7.5, "How to Run MySQL As a Normal User."

If you neglected to create the grant tables before proceeding to this step, the following message appears in the error log file when you start the server:

```
mysqld: Can't find file: 'host.frm'
```

If you have other problems starting the server, see Section 2.9.2.3, "Starting and Troubleshooting the MySQL Server."

4. Use `mysqladmin` to verify that the server is running. The following commands provide simple tests to check whether the server is up and responding to connections:

```
shell> bin/mysqladmin version
shell> bin/mysqladmin variables
```

The output from `mysqladmin version` varies slightly depending on your platform and version of MySQL, but should be similar to that shown here:

```
shell> bin/mysqladmin version
mysqladmin  Ver 14.12 Distrib 5.0.19, for pc-linux-gnu on i686
Copyright (C) 2000 MySQL AB & MySQL Finland AB & TCX DataKonsult AB
This software comes with ABSOLUTELY NO WARRANTY. This is free software,
and you are welcome to modify and redistribute it under the GPL license
```

```
Server version          5.0.19-Max
Protocol version        10
Connection              Localhost via UNIX socket
UNIX socket             /var/lib/mysql/mysql.sock
Uptime:                 14 days 5 hours 5 min 21 sec

Threads: 1  Questions: 366  Slow queries: 0
Opens: 0  Flush tables: 1  Open tables: 19
Queries per second avg: 0.000
```

To see what else you can do with mysqladmin, invoke it with the --help option.

5. Verify that you can shut down the server:

   ```
   shell> bin/mysqladmin -u root shutdown
   ```

6. Verify that you can start the server again. Do this by using mysqld_safe or by invoking mysqld directly. For example:

   ```
   shell> bin/mysqld_safe --user=mysql --log &
   ```

   If mysqld_safe fails, see Section 2.9.2.3, "Starting and Troubleshooting the MySQL Server."

7. Run some simple tests to verify that you can retrieve information from the server. The output should be similar to what is shown here:

   ```
   shell> bin/mysqlshow
   +-----------+
   | Databases |
   +-----------+
   | mysql     |
   | test      |
   +-----------+

   shell> bin/mysqlshow mysql
   Database: mysql
   +------------------------+
   |         Tables         |
   +------------------------+
   | columns_priv           |
   | db                     |
   | func                   |
   | help_category          |
   | help_keyword           |
   | help_relation          |
   | help_topic             |
   | host                   |
   | proc                   |
   | procs_priv             |
   | tables_priv            |
   | time_zone              |
   ```

```
| time_zone_leap_second     |
| time_zone_name            |
| time_zone_transition      |
| time_zone_transition_type |
| user                      |
+---------------------------+

shell> bin/mysql -e "SELECT Host,Db,User FROM db" mysql
+------+--------+------+
| host | db     | user |
+------+--------+------+
| %    | test   |      |
| %    | test_% |      |
+------+--------+------+
```

8. There is a benchmark suite in the `sql-bench` directory (under the MySQL installation directory) that you can use to compare how MySQL performs on different platforms. The benchmark suite is written in Perl. It requires the Perl DBI module that provides a database-independent interface to the various databases, and some other additional Perl modules:

```
DBI
DBD::mysql
Data::Dumper
Data::ShowTable
```

These modules can be obtained from CPAN (`http://www.cpan.org/`). See also Section 2.13.1, "Installing Perl on Unix."

The `sql-bench/Results` directory contains the results from many runs against different databases and platforms. To run all tests, execute these commands:

```
shell> cd sql-bench
shell> perl run-all-tests
```

If you don't have the `sql-bench` directory, you probably installed MySQL using RPM files other than the source RPM. (The source RPM includes the `sql-bench` benchmark directory.) In this case, you must first install the benchmark suite before you can use it. There are separate benchmark RPM files named `mysql-bench-VERSION-i386.rpm` that contain benchmark code and data.

If you have a source distribution, there are also tests in its `tests` subdirectory that you can run. For example, to run `auto_increment.tst`, execute this command from the top-level directory of your source distribution:

```
shell> mysql -vvf test < ./tests/auto_increment.tst
```

The expected result of the test can be found in the `./tests/auto_increment.res` file.

9. At this point, you should have the server running. However, none of the initial MySQL accounts have a password, so you should assign passwords using the instructions found in Section 2.9.3, "Securing the Initial MySQL Accounts."

The MySQL 5.0 installation procedure creates time zone tables in the mysql database. However, you must populate the tables manually using the instructions in Section 4.11.8, "MySQL Server Time Zone Support."

2.9.2.1 Problems Running mysql_install_db

The purpose of the mysql_install_db script is to generate new MySQL privilege tables. It does not overwrite existing MySQL privilege tables, and it does not affect any other data.

If you want to re-create your privilege tables, first stop the mysqld server if it's running. Then rename the mysql directory under the data directory to save it, and then run mysql_install_db. Suppose that your current directory is the MySQL installation directory and that mysql_install_db is located in the bin directory and the data directory is named data. To rename the mysql database and re-run mysql_install_db, use these commands.

```
shell> mv data/mysql data/mysql.old
shell> bin/mysql_install_db --user=mysql
```

When you run mysql_install_db, you might encounter the following problems:

- **mysql_install_db fails to install the grant tables**

    You may find that mysql_install_db fails to install the grant tables and terminates after displaying the following messages:

    ```
    Starting mysqld daemon with databases from XXXXXX
    mysqld ended
    ```

    In this case, you should examine the error log file very carefully. The log should be located in the directory XXXXXX named by the error message and should indicate why mysqld didn't start. If you do not understand what happened, include the log when you post a bug report. See Section 1.8, "How to Report Bugs or Problems."

- **There is a mysqld process running**

    This indicates that the server is running, in which case the grant tables have probably been created already. If so, there is no need to run mysql_install_db at all because it needs to be run only once (when you install MySQL the first time).

- **Installing a second mysqld server does not work when one server is running**

    This can happen when you have an existing MySQL installation, but want to put a new installation in a different location. For example, you might have a production installation, but you want to create a second installation for testing purposes. Generally the problem that occurs when you try to run a second server is that it tries to use a network interface that is in use by the first server. In this case, you should see one of the following error messages:

    ```
    Can't start server: Bind on TCP/IP port:
    Address already in use
    Can't start server: Bind on unix socket...
    ```

For instructions on setting up multiple servers, see Section 4.13, "Running Multiple MySQL Servers on the Same Machine."

- **You do not have write access to the `/tmp` directory**

  If you do not have write access to create temporary files or a Unix socket file in the default location (the `/tmp` directory), an error occurs when you run `mysql_install_db` or the `mysqld` server.

  You can specify different locations for the temporary directory and Unix socket file by executing these commands prior to starting `mysql_install_db` or `mysqld`, where *some_tmp_dir* is the full pathname to some directory for which you have write permission:

  ```
  shell> TMPDIR=/some_tmp_dir/
  shell> MYSQL_UNIX_PORT=/some_tmp_dir/mysql.sock
  shell> export TMPDIR MYSQL_UNIX_PORT
  ```

  Then you should be able to run `mysql_install_db` and start the server with these commands:

  ```
  shell> bin/mysql_install_db --user=mysql
  shell> bin/mysqld_safe --user=mysql &
  ```

  If `mysql_install_db` is located in the `scripts` directory, modify the first command to `scripts/mysql_install_db`.

There are some alternatives to running the `mysql_install_db` script provided in the MySQL distribution:

- If you want the initial privileges to be different from the standard defaults, you can modify `mysql_install_db` before you run it. However, it is preferable to use GRANT and REVOKE to change the privileges *after* the grant tables have been set up. In other words, you can run `mysql_install_db`, and then use `mysql -u root mysql` to connect to the server as the MySQL root user so that you can issue the necessary GRANT and REVOKE statements.

  If you want to install MySQL on several machines with the same privileges, you can put the GRANT and REVOKE statements in a file and execute the file as a script using `mysql` after running `mysql_install_db`. For example:

  ```
  shell> bin/mysql_install_db --user=mysql
  shell> bin/mysql -u root < your_script_file
  ```

  By doing this, you can avoid having to issue the statements manually on each machine.

- It is possible to re-create the grant tables completely after they have previously been created. You might want to do this if you're just learning how to use GRANT and REVOKE and have made so many modifications after running `mysql_install_db` that you want to wipe out the tables and start over.

  To re-create the grant tables, remove all the `.frm`, `.MYI`, and `.MYD` files in the mysql database directory. Then run the `mysql_install_db` script again.

- You can start `mysqld` manually using the `--skip-grant-tables` option and add the privilege information yourself using `mysql`:

```
shell> bin/mysqld_safe --user=mysql --skip-grant-tables &
shell> bin/mysql mysql
```

From `mysql`, manually execute the SQL commands contained in `mysql_install_db`. Make sure that you run `mysqladmin flush-privileges` or `mysqladmin reload` afterward to tell the server to reload the grant tables.

Note that by not using `mysql_install_db`, you not only have to populate the grant tables manually, you also have to create them first.

2.9.2.2 Starting and Stopping MySQL Automatically

Generally, you start the `mysqld` server in one of these ways:

- By invoking `mysqld` directly. This works on any platform.
- By running the MySQL server as a Windows service. This can be done on versions of Windows that support services (such as NT, 2000, XP, and 2003). The service can be set to start the server automatically when Windows starts, or as a manual service that you start on request. For instructions, see Section 2.3.11, "Starting MySQL as a Windows Service."
- By invoking `mysqld_safe`, which tries to determine the proper options for `mysqld` and then runs it with those options. This script is used on Unix and Unix-like systems. See Section 4.4.1, "`mysqld_safe`—MySQL Server Startup Script."
- By invoking `mysql.server`. This script is used primarily at system startup and shutdown on systems that use System V–style run directories, where it usually is installed under the name `mysql`. The `mysql.server` script starts the server by invoking `mysqld_safe`. See Section 4.4.2, "`mysql.server`—MySQL Server Startup Script."
- On Mac OS X, you can install a separate MySQL Startup Item package to enable the automatic startup of MySQL on system startup. The Startup Item starts the server by invoking `mysql.server`. See Section 2.5, "Installing MySQL on Mac OS X," for details.

The `mysqld_safe` and `mysql.server` scripts and the Mac OS X Startup Item can be used to start the server manually, or automatically at system startup time. `mysql.server` and the Startup Item also can be used to stop the server.

To start or stop the server manually using the `mysql.server` script, invoke it with `start` or `stop` arguments:

```
shell> mysql.server start
shell> mysql.server stop
```

Before `mysql.server` starts the server, it changes location to the MySQL installation directory, and then invokes `mysqld_safe`. If you want the server to run as some specific user, add an appropriate `user` option to the `[mysqld]` group of the `/etc/my.cnf` option file, as shown later in this section. (It is possible that you will need to edit `mysql.server` if you've installed a binary distribution of MySQL in a non-standard location. Modify it to cd into the proper directory before it runs mysqld_safe. If you do this, your modified version of mysql.server may be overwritten if you upgrade MySQL in the future, so you should make a copy of your edited version that you can re-install.)

mysql.server stop stops the server by sending a signal to it. You can also stop the server manually by executing mysqladmin shutdown.

To start and stop MySQL automatically on your server, you need to add start and stop commands to the appropriate places in your /etc/rc* files.

If you use the Linux server RPM package (MySQL-server-VERSION.rpm), the mysql.server script is installed in the /etc/init.d directory with the name mysql. You need not install it manually. See Section 2.4, "Installing MySQL on Linux," for more information on the Linux RPM packages.

Some vendors provide RPM packages that install a startup script under a different name such as mysqld.

If you install MySQL from a source distribution or using a binary distribution format that does not install mysql.server automatically, you can install it manually. The script can be found in the support-files directory under the MySQL installation directory or in a MySQL source tree.

To install mysql.server manually, copy it to the /etc/init.d directory with the name mysql, and then make it executable. Do this by changing location into the appropriate directory where mysql.server is located and executing these commands:

```
shell> cp mysql.server /etc/init.d/mysql
shell> chmod +x /etc/init.d/mysql
```

Older Red Hat systems use the /etc/rc.d/init.d directory rather than /etc/init.d. Adjust the preceding commands accordingly. Alternatively, first create /etc/init.d as a symbolic link that points to /etc/rc.d/init.d:

```
shell> cd /etc
shell> ln -s rc.d/init.d .
```

After installing the script, the commands needed to activate it to run at system startup depend on your operating system. On Linux, you can use chkconfig:

```
shell> chkconfig --add mysql
```

On some Linux systems, the following command also seems to be necessary to fully enable the mysql script:

```
shell> chkconfig --level 345 mysql on
```

On FreeBSD, startup scripts generally should go in /usr/local/etc/rc.d/. The rc(8) manual page states that scripts in this directory are executed only if their basename matches the *.sh shell filename pattern. Any other files or directories present within the directory are silently ignored. In other words, on FreeBSD, you should install the mysql.server script as /usr/local/etc/rc.d/mysql.server.sh to enable automatic startup.

As an alternative to the preceding setup, some operating systems also use /etc/rc.local or /etc/init.d/boot.local to start additional services on startup. To start up MySQL using this method, you could append a command like the one following to the appropriate startup file:

```
/bin/sh -c 'cd /usr/local/mysql; ./bin/mysqld_safe --user=mysql &'
```

For other systems, consult your operating system documentation to see how to install startup scripts.

You can add options for mysql.server in a global /etc/my.cnf file. A typical /etc/my.cnf file might look like this:

```
[mysqld]
datadir=/usr/local/mysql/var
socket=/var/tmp/mysql.sock
port=3306
user=mysql


[mysql.server]
basedir=/usr/local/mysql
```

The mysql.server script understands the following options: basedir, datadir, and pid-file. If specified, they *must* be placed in an option file, not on the command line. mysql.server understands only start and stop as command-line arguments.

The following table shows which option groups the server and each startup script read from option files:

Script	Option Groups
mysqld	[mysqld], [server], [mysqld-*major_version*]
mysqld_safe	[mysqld], [server], [mysqld_safe]
mysql.server	[mysqld], [mysql.server], [server]

[mysqld-*major_version*] means that groups with names like [mysqld-4.1] and [mysqld-5.0] are read by servers having versions 4.1.x, 5.0.x, and so forth. This feature can be used to specify options that can be read only by servers within a given release series.

For backward compatibility, mysql.server also reads the [mysql_server] group and mysqld_safe also reads the [safe_mysqld] group. However, you should update your option files to use the [mysql.server] and [mysqld_safe] groups instead when using MySQL 5.0.

See Section 3.3.2, "Using Option Files."

2.9.2.3 Starting and Troubleshooting the MySQL Server

This section provides troubleshooting suggestions for problems starting the server on Unix. If you are using Windows, see Section 2.3.13, "Troubleshooting a MySQL Installation Under Windows."

If you have problems starting the server, here are some things to try:

- Check the error log to see why the server does not start.
- Specify any special options needed by the storage engines you are using.
- Make sure that the server knows where to find the data directory.
- Make sure that the server can access the data directory. The ownership and permissions of the data directory and its contents must be set such that the server can read and modify them.
- Verify that the network interfaces the server wants to use are available.

Some storage engines have options that control their behavior. You can create a my.cnf file and specify startup options for the engines that you plan to use. If you are going to use storage engines that support transactional tables (InnoDB, BDB, NDB), be sure that you have them configured the way you want before starting the server:

- If you are using InnoDB tables, see Section 8.2.3, "InnoDB Configuration."
- If you are using BDB (Berkeley DB) tables, see Section 8.5.3, "BDB Startup Options."
- If you are using MySQL Cluster, see Section 9.4, "MySQL Cluster Configuration."

Storage engines will use default option values if you specify none, but it is recommended that you review the available options and specify explicit values for those for which the defaults are not appropriate for your installation.

When the mysqld server starts, it changes location to the data directory. This is where it expects to find databases and where it expects to write log files. The server also writes the pid (process ID) file in the data directory.

The data directory location is hardwired in when the server is compiled. This is where the server looks for the data directory by default. If the data directory is located somewhere else on your system, the server will not work properly. You can determine what the default path settings are by invoking mysqld with the --verbose and --help options.

If the default locations don't match the MySQL installation layout on your system, you can override them by specifying options to mysqld or mysqld_safe on the command line or in an option file.

To specify the location of the data directory explicitly, use the --datadir option. However, normally you can tell mysqld the location of the base directory under which MySQL is installed and it looks for the data directory there. You can do this with the --basedir option.

To check the effect of specifying path options, invoke mysqld with those options followed by the --verbose and --help options. For example, if you change location into the directory where mysqld is installed and then run the following command, it shows the effect of starting the server with a base directory of /usr/local:

```
shell> ./mysqld --basedir=/usr/local --verbose --help
```

You can specify other options such as --datadir as well, but note that --verbose and --help must be the last options.

Once you determine the path settings you want, start the server without --verbose and --help.

If mysqld is currently running, you can find out what path settings it is using by executing this command:

```
shell> mysqladmin variables
```

Or:

```
shell> mysqladmin -h host_name variables
```

host_name is the name of the MySQL server host.

If you get Errcode 13 (which means Permission denied) when starting mysqld, this means that the privileges of the data directory or its contents do not allow the server access. In this case, you change the permissions for the involved files and directories so that the server has the right to use them. You can also start the server as root, but this raises security issues and should be avoided.

On Unix, change location into the data directory and check the ownership of the data directory and its contents to make sure the server has access. For example, if the data directory is /usr/local/mysql/var, use this command:

```
shell> ls -la /usr/local/mysql/var
```

If the data directory or its files or subdirectories are not owned by the login account that you use for running the server, change their ownership to that account. If the account is named mysql, use these commands:

```
shell> chown -R mysql /usr/local/mysql/var
shell> chgrp -R mysql /usr/local/mysql/var
```

If the server fails to start up correctly, check the error log. Log files are located in the data directory (typically C:\Program Files\MySQL\MySQL Server 5.0\data on Windows, /usr/local/mysql/data for a Unix binary distribution, and /usr/local/var for a Unix source distribution). Look in the data directory for files with names of the form host_name.err and host_name.log, where host_name is the name of your server host. Then examine the last few lines of these files. On Unix, you can use tail to display them:

```
shell> tail host_name.err
shell> tail host_name.log
```

The error log should contain information that indicates why the server couldn't start. For example, you might see something like this in the log:

```
000729 14:50:10  bdb:  Recovery function for LSN 1 27595 failed
000729 14:50:10  bdb:  warning: ./test/t1.db: No such file or directory
000729 14:50:10  Can't init databases
```

This means that you did not start mysqld with the --bdb-no-recover option and Berkeley DB found something wrong with its own log files when it tried to recover your databases. To be able to continue, you should move the old Berkeley DB log files from the database directory to some other place, where you can later examine them. The BDB log files are named in sequence beginning with log.0000000001, where the number increases over time.

If you are running mysqld with BDB table support and mysqld dumps core at startup, this could be due to problems with the BDB recovery log. In this case, you can try starting mysqld with --bdb-no-recover. If that helps, you should remove all BDB log files from the data directory and try starting mysqld again without the --bdb-no-recover option.

If either of the following errors occurs, it means that some other program (perhaps another mysqld server) is using the TCP/IP port or Unix socket file that mysqld is trying to use:

```
Can't start server: Bind on TCP/IP port: Address already in use
Can't start server: Bind on unix socket...
```

Use ps to determine whether you have another mysqld server running. If so, shut down the server before starting mysqld again. (If another server is running, and you really want to run multiple servers, you can find information about how to do so in Section 4.13, "Running Multiple MySQL Servers on the Same Machine.")

If no other server is running, try to execute the command telnet *your_host_name* *tcp_ip_port_number*. (The default MySQL port number is 3306.) Then press Enter a couple of times. If you don't get an error message like telnet: Unable to connect to remote host: Connection refused, some other program is using the TCP/IP port that mysqld is trying to use. You'll need to track down what program this is and disable it, or else tell mysqld to listen to a different port with the --port option. In this case, you'll also need to specify the port number for client programs when connecting to the server via TCP/IP.

Another reason the port might be inaccessible is that you have a firewall running that blocks connections to it. If so, modify the firewall settings to allow access to the port.

If the server starts but you can't connect to it, you should make sure that you have an entry in /etc/hosts that looks like this:

```
127.0.0.1    localhost
```

This problem occurs only on systems that do not have a working thread library and for which MySQL must be configured to use MIT-pthreads.

If you cannot get mysqld to start, you can try to make a trace file to find the problem by using the --debug option.

2.9.3 Securing the Initial MySQL Accounts

Part of the MySQL installation process is to set up the `mysql` database that contains the grant tables:

- Windows distributions contain preinitialized grant tables that are installed automatically.
- On Unix, the grant tables are populated by the `mysql_install_db` program. Some installation methods run this program for you. Others require that you execute it manually. For details, see Section 2.9.2, "Unix Post-Installation Procedures."

The grant tables define the initial MySQL user accounts and their access privileges. These accounts are set up as follows:

- Accounts with the username `root` are created. These are superuser accounts that can do anything. The initial `root` account passwords are empty, so anyone can connect to the MySQL server as root—*without a password*—and be granted all privileges.
    - On Windows, one `root` account is created; this account allows connecting from the local host only. The Windows installer will optionally create an account allowing for connections from any host only if the user selects the `Enable root access from remote machines` option during installation.
    - On Unix, both `root` accounts are for connections from the local host. Connections must be made from the local host by specifying a hostname of `localhost` for one of the accounts, or the actual hostname or IP number for the other.
- Two anonymous-user accounts are created, each with an empty username. The anonymous accounts have no password, so anyone can use them to connect to the MySQL server.
    - On Windows, one anonymous account is for connections from the local host. It has all privileges, just like the `root` accounts. The other is for connections from any host and has all privileges for the `test` database and for other databases with names that start with `test`.
    - On Unix, both anonymous accounts are for connections from the local host. Connections must be made from the local host by specifying a hostname of `localhost` for one of the accounts, or the actual hostname or IP number for the other. These accounts have all privileges for the `test` database and for other databases with names that start with `test_`.

As noted, none of the initial accounts have passwords. This means that your MySQL installation is unprotected until you do something about it:

- If you want to prevent clients from connecting as anonymous users without a password, you should either assign a password to each anonymous account or else remove the accounts.
- You should assign a password to each MySQL `root` account.

The following instructions describe how to set up passwords for the initial MySQL accounts, first for the anonymous accounts and then for the root accounts. Replace "*newpwd*" in the examples with the actual password that you want to use. The instructions also cover how to remove the anonymous accounts, should you prefer not to allow anonymous access at all.

You might want to defer setting the passwords until later, so that you don't need to specify them while you perform additional setup or testing. However, be sure to set them before using your installation for production purposes.

To assign passwords to the anonymous accounts, connect to the server as root and then use either SET PASSWORD or UPDATE. In either case, be sure to encrypt the password using the PASSWORD() function.

To use SET PASSWORD on Windows, do this:

```
shell> mysql -u root
mysql> SET PASSWORD FOR ''@'localhost' = PASSWORD('newpwd');
mysql> SET PASSWORD FOR ''@'%' = PASSWORD('newpwd');
```

To use SET PASSWORD on Unix, do this:

```
shell> mysql -u root
mysql> SET PASSWORD FOR ''@'localhost' = PASSWORD('newpwd');
mysql> SET PASSWORD FOR ''@'host_name' = PASSWORD('newpwd');
```

In the second SET PASSWORD statement, replace *host_name* with the name of the server host. This is the name that is specified in the Host column of the non-localhost record for root in the user table. If you don't know what hostname this is, issue the following statement before using SET PASSWORD:

```
mysql> SELECT Host, User FROM mysql.user;
```

Look for the record that has root in the User column and something other than localhost in the Host column. Then use that Host value in the second SET PASSWORD statement.

The other way to assign passwords to the anonymous accounts is by using UPDATE to modify the user table directly. Connect to the server as root and issue an UPDATE statement that assigns a value to the Password column of the appropriate user table records. The procedure is the same for Windows and Unix. The following UPDATE statement assigns a password to both anonymous accounts at once:

```
shell> mysql -u root
mysql> UPDATE mysql.user SET Password = PASSWORD('newpwd')
    ->     WHERE User = '';
mysql> FLUSH PRIVILEGES;
```

After you update the passwords in the user table directly using UPDATE, you must tell the server to re-read the grant tables with FLUSH PRIVILEGES. Otherwise, the change goes unnoticed until you restart the server.

If you prefer to remove the anonymous accounts instead, do so as follows:

```
shell> mysql -u root
mysql> DELETE FROM mysql.user WHERE User = '';
mysql> FLUSH PRIVILEGES;
```

The DELETE statement applies both to Windows and to Unix. On Windows, if you want to remove only the anonymous account that has the same privileges as root, do this instead:

```
shell> mysql -u root
mysql> DELETE FROM mysql.user WHERE Host='localhost' AND User='';
mysql> FLUSH PRIVILEGES;
```

That account allows anonymous access but has full privileges, so removing it improves security.

You can assign passwords to the root accounts in several ways. The following discussion demonstrates three methods:

- Use the SET PASSWORD statement
- Use the mysqladmin command-line client program
- Use the UPDATE statement

To assign passwords using SET PASSWORD, connect to the server as root and issue two SET PASSWORD statements. Be sure to encrypt the password using the PASSWORD() function.

For Windows, do this:

```
shell> mysql -u root
mysql> SET PASSWORD FOR 'root'@'localhost' = PASSWORD('newpwd');
mysql> SET PASSWORD FOR 'root'@'%' = PASSWORD('newpwd');
```

For Unix, do this:

```
shell> mysql -u root
mysql> SET PASSWORD FOR 'root'@'localhost' = PASSWORD('newpwd');
mysql> SET PASSWORD FOR 'root'@'host_name' = PASSWORD('newpwd');
```

In the second SET PASSWORD statement, replace *host_name* with the name of the server host. This is the same hostname that you used when you assigned the anonymous account passwords.

To assign passwords to the root accounts using mysqladmin, execute the following commands:

```
shell> mysqladmin -u root password "newpwd"
shell> mysqladmin -u root -h host_name password "newpwd"
```

These commands apply both to Windows and to Unix. In the second command, replace *host_name* with the name of the server host. The double quotes around the password are not always necessary, but you should use them if the password contains spaces or other characters that are special to your command interpreter.

You can also use UPDATE to modify the user table directly. The following UPDATE statement assigns a password to both root accounts at once:

```
shell> mysql -u root
mysql> UPDATE mysql.user SET Password = PASSWORD('newpwd')
    ->       WHERE User = 'root';
mysql> FLUSH PRIVILEGES;
```

The UPDATE statement applies both to Windows and to Unix.

After the passwords have been set, you must supply the appropriate password whenever you connect to the server. For example, if you want to use mysqladmin to shut down the server, you can do so using this command:

```
shell> mysqladmin -u root -p shutdown
Enter password: (enter root password here)
```

To set up additional accounts, you can use the GRANT statement. For instructions, see Section 4.9.2, "Adding New User Accounts to MySQL."

2.10 Upgrading MySQL

As a general rule, we recommend that when upgrading from one release series to another, you should go to the next series rather than skipping a series. For example, if you currently are running MySQL 3.23 and wish to upgrade to a newer series, upgrade to MySQL 4.0 rather than to 4.1 or 5.0.

The following items form a checklist of things that you should do whenever you perform an upgrade:

- Before upgrading from MySQL 4.1 to 5.0, read Section 2.10.2, "Upgrading from MySQL 4.1 to 5.0") as well as the News section of the online "MySQL Reference Manual" at http://dev.mysql.com/doc/mysql/en/news.html. These provide information about features that are new in MySQL 5.0 or differ from those found in MySQL 4.1. If you wish to upgrade from a release series previous to MySQL 4.1, you should upgrade to each successive release series in turn until you have reached MySQL 4.1, and then proceed with the upgrade to MySQL 5.0. For information on upgrading from MySQL 4.1 or earlier releases, see the "MySQL 3.23, 4.0, 4.1 Reference Manual."

- Before you perform an upgrade, back up your databases, including the mysql database that contains the grant tables.

- Some releases of MySQL introduce incompatible changes to tables. (Our aim is to avoid these changes, but occasionally they are necessary to correct problems that would be worse than an incompatibility between releases.) Some releases of MySQL introduce changes to the structure of the grant tables to add new privileges or features.

  To avoid problems due to such changes, after you upgrade to a new version of MySQL, you should check your tables (and repair them if necessary), and update your grant tables to make sure that they have the current structure so that you can take advantage of any new capabilities. See Section 4.6.2, "`mysql_upgrade`—Check Tables for MySQL Upgrade."

- If you are running MySQL Server on Windows, see Section 2.3.14, "Upgrading MySQL on Windows."

- If you are using replication, see Section 5.7, "Upgrading a Replication Setup," for information on upgrading your replication setup.

- If you previously installed a MySQL-Max distribution that includes a server named `mysqld-max`, and then upgrade later to a non-Max version of MySQL, `mysqld_safe` still attempts to run the old `mysqld-max` server. If you perform such an upgrade, you should remove the old `mysqld-max` server manually to ensure that `mysqld_safe` runs the new `mysqld` server.

You can always move the MySQL format files and data files between different versions on the same architecture as long as you stay within versions for the same release series of MySQL. If you change the character set when running MySQL, you must run `myisamchk -r -q --set-collation=`*`collation_name`* on all `MyISAM` tables. Otherwise, your indexes may not be ordered correctly, because changing the character set may also change the sort order.

If you are cautious about using new versions, you can always rename your old `mysqld` before installing a newer one. For example, if you are using MySQL 4.1.13 and want to upgrade to 5.0.10, rename your current server from `mysqld` to `mysqld-4.1.13`. If your new `mysqld` then does something unexpected, you can simply shut it down and restart with your old `mysqld`.

If, after an upgrade, you experience problems with recompiled client programs, such as `Commands out of sync` or unexpected core dumps, you probably have used old header or library files when compiling your programs. In this case, you should check the date for your `mysql.h` file and `libmysqlclient.a` library to verify that they are from the new MySQL distribution. If not, recompile your programs with the new headers and libraries.

If problems occur, such as that the new `mysqld` server does not start or that you cannot connect without a password, verify that you do not have an old `my.cnf` file from your previous installation. You can check this with the `--print-defaults` option (for example, `mysqld --print-defaults`). If this command displays anything other than the program name, you have an active `my.cnf` file that affects server or client operation.

It is a good idea to rebuild and reinstall the Perl `DBD::mysql` module whenever you install a new release of MySQL. The same applies to other MySQL interfaces as well, such as the PHP `mysql` extension and the Python `MySQLdb` module.

2.10.1 Upgrading from MySQL 5.0 to 5.1

When upgrading a 5.0 installation to 5.0.10 or above, note that it is *necessary* to upgrade your grant tables. Otherwise, creating stored procedures and functions might not work. The procedure for doing this is described in Section 4.6.2, "`mysql_upgrade`—Check Tables for MySQL Upgrade."

Note: It is good practice to back up your data before installing any new version of software. Although MySQL works very hard to ensure a high level of quality, you should protect your data by making a backup. MySQL generally recommends that you dump and reload your tables from any previous version to upgrade to MySQL 5.1.

In general, you should do the following when upgrading from MySQL 5.0 to 5.1:

- Check the items in the change lists found later in this section to see whether any of them might affect your applications. Note particularly any that are marked **Incompatible change**. These result in incompatibilities with earlier versions of MySQL, and may require your attention *before you upgrade*.

- Some releases of MySQL introduce incompatible changes to tables. (Our aim is to avoid these changes, but occasionally they are necessary to correct problems that would be worse than an incompatibility between releases.) Some releases of MySQL introduce changes to the structure of the grant tables to add new privileges or features.

  To avoid problems due to such changes, after you upgrade to a new version of MySQL, you should check your tables (and repair them if necessary), and update your grant tables to make sure that they have the current structure so that you can take advantage of any new capabilities. See Section 4.6.2, "`mysql_upgrade`—Check Tables for MySQL Upgrade."

- Read the MySQL 5.1 change history to see what significant new features you can use in 5.1. See the News section of the online "MySQL Reference Manual" at `http://dev.mysql.com/doc/mysql/en/news.html`.

- If you are running MySQL Server on Windows, see Section 2.3.14, "Upgrading MySQL on Windows."

- If you are using replication, see Section 5.7, "Upgrading a Replication Setup," for information on upgrading your replication setup.

The following lists describe changes that may affect applications and that you should watch out for when upgrading to MySQL 5.1:

Server Changes:

- **Incompatible change**: The structure of FULLTEXT indexes has been changed in MySQL 5.1.6. After upgrading to MySQL 5.1.6 or greater, call the REPAIR TABLE statement for each table that contains any FULLTEXT indexes.

SQL Changes:

- **Incompatible change**: MySQL 5.1.6 introduces the TRIGGER privilege. Previously, the SUPER privilege was needed to create or drop triggers. Now those operations require the TRIGGER privilege. This is a security improvement because you no longer need to grant users the SUPER privilege to enable them to create triggers. However, the requirement that the account named in a trigger's DEFINER clause must have the SUPER privilege has changed to a requirement for the TRIGGER privilege. When upgrading from a previous version of MySQL 5.0 or 5.1 to MySQL 5.1.6 or newer, be sure to update your grant tables as described in Section 4.6.2, "`mysql_upgrade`—Check Tables for MySQL Upgrade." This process assigns the `TRIGGER` privilege to all accounts that had the `SUPER` privilege. If you fail to update the grant tables, triggers may fail when activated. (After updating the grant tables, you can revoke the `SUPER` privilege from those accounts that no longer otherwise require it.)

2.10.2 Upgrading from MySQL 4.1 to 5.0

Note: It is good practice to back up your data before installing any new version of software. Although MySQL works very hard to ensure a high level of quality, you should protect your data by making a backup. MySQL generally recommends that you dump and reload your tables from any previous version to upgrade to 5.0.

In general, you should do the following when upgrading from MySQL 4.1 to 5.0:

- Check the items in the change lists found later in this section to see whether any of them might affect your applications. Note particularly any that are marked **Incompatible change**. These result in incompatibilities with earlier versions of MySQL, and may require your attention *before you upgrade*.

- Some releases of MySQL introduce incompatible changes to tables. (Our aim is to avoid these changes, but occasionally they are necessary to correct problems that would be worse than an incompatibility between releases.) Some releases of MySQL introduce changes to the structure of the grant tables to add new privileges or features.

  To avoid problems due to such changes, after you upgrade to a new version of MySQL, you should check your tables (and repair them if necessary), and update your grant tables to make sure that they have the current structure so that you can take advantage of any new capabilities. See Section 4.6.2, "`mysql_upgrade`—Check Tables for MySQL Upgrade."

- Read the MySQL 5.0 change history to see what significant new features you can use in 5.0. See the News section of the online "MySQL Reference Manual" at `http://dev.mysql.com/doc/mysql/en/news.html`.

- If you are running MySQL Server on Windows, see Section 2.3.14, "Upgrading MySQL on Windows."

- MySQL 5.0 adds support for stored procedures. This support requires the `mysql.proc` table. To create this table, you should run the `mysql_upgrade` script as described in Section 4.6.2, "`mysql_upgrade`—Check Tables for MySQL Upgrade."

- MySQL 5.0 adds support for views. This support requires extra privilege columns in the `mysql.user` and `mysql.db` tables. To create these columns, you should run the `mysql_upgrade` script as described in Section 4.6.2, "`mysql_upgrade`—Check Tables for MySQL Upgrade."

- If you are using replication, see Section 5.7, "Upgrading a Replication Setup," for information on upgrading your replication setup.

Several visible behaviors have changed between MySQL 4.1 and MySQL 5.0 to make MySQL more compatible with standard SQL. These changes may affect your applications.

The following lists describe changes that may affect applications and that you should watch out for when upgrading to MySQL 5.0.

Server Changes:

- **Incompatible change**: The indexing order for end-space in TEXT columns for InnoDB and MyISAM tables has changed. Starting from 5.0.3, TEXT indexes are compared as space-padded at the end (just as MySQL sorts CHAR, VARCHAR and TEXT fields). If you have a index on a TEXT column, you should run CHECK TABLE on it. If the check reports errors, rebuild the indexes: Dump and reload the table if it is an InnoDB table, or run OPTIMIZE TABLE or REPAIR TABLE if it is a MyISAM table.

- **Incompatible change**: For BINARY columns, the pad value and how it is handled has changed as of MySQL 5.0.15. The pad value for inserts now is 0x00 rather than space, and there is no stripping of the pad value for selects.

- **Incompatible change**: The implementation of DECIMAL has changed in MySQL 5.0.3. You should make your applications aware of that change, which is described in the "MySQL Language Reference."

  A consequence of the change in handling of the DECIMAL and NUMERIC fixed-point data types is that the server is more strict to follow standard SQL. For example, a data type of DECIMAL(3,1) stores a maximum value of 99.9. Before MySQL 5.0.3, the server allowed larger numbers to be stored. That is, it stored a value such as 100.0 as 100.0. As of MySQL 5.0.3, the server clips 100.0 to the maximum allowable value of 99.9. If you have tables that were created before MySQL 5.0.3 and that contain floating-point data not strictly legal for the data type, you should alter the data types of those columns. For example:

  ```
  ALTER TABLE tbl_name MODIFY col_name DECIMAL(4,1);
  ```

- **Incompatible change**: MyISAM and InnoDB tables created with DECIMAL columns in MySQL 5.0.3 to 5.0.5 will appear corrupt after an upgrade to MySQL 5.0.6. (The same incompatibility will occur for these tables created in MySQL 5.0.6 after a downgrade to MySQL 5.0.3 to 5.0.5.) If you have such tables, check and repair them with mysql_upgrade after upgrading. See Section 4.6.2, "mysql_upgrade—Check Tables for MySQL Upgrade."

- **Incompatible change**: As of MySQL 5.0.3, the server by default no longer loads user-defined functions (UDFs) unless they have at least one auxiliary symbol (for example, an xxx_init or xxx_deinit symbol) defined in addition to the main function symbol. This behavior can be overridden with the --allow-suspicious-udfs option.

- **Incompatible change**: The update log has been removed in MySQL 5.0. If you had enabled it previously, you should enable the binary log instead.

- **Incompatible change**: Support for the ISAM storage engine has been removed in MySQL 5.0. If you have any ISAM tables, you should convert them *before* upgrading. For example, to convert an ISAM table to use the MyISAM storage engine, use this statement:

```
ALTER TABLE tbl_name ENGINE = MyISAM;
```

   Use a similar statement for every ISAM table in each of your databases.

- **Incompatible change**: Support for RAID options in MyISAM tables has been removed in MySQL 5.0. If you have tables that use these options, you should convert them before upgrading. One way to do this is to dump them with mysqldump, edit the dump file to remove the RAID options in the CREATE TABLE statements, and reload the dump file. Another possibility is to use CREATE TABLE new_tbl ... SELECT raid_tbl to create a new table from the RAID table. However, the CREATE TABLE part of the statement must contain sufficient information to re-create column attributes as well as indexes, or column attributes may be lost and indexes will not appear in the new table.

   The .MYD files for RAID tables in a given database are stored under the database directory in subdirectories that have names consisting of two hex digits in the range from 00 to ff. After converting all tables that use RAID options, these RAID-related subdirectories still will exist but can be removed. Verify that they are empty, and then remove them manually. (If they are not empty, there is some RAID table that has not been converted.)

- In MySQL 5.0.6, binary logging of stored routines and triggers was changed. This change has implications for security, replication, and data recovery, as discussed in the "MySQL Language Reference."

SQL Changes:

- **Incompatible change**: Previously, a lock wait timeout caused InnoDB to roll back the entire current transaction. As of MySQL 5.0.13, it rolls back only the most recent SQL statement.

- **Incompatible change**: The namespace for triggers has changed in MySQL 5.0.10. Previously, trigger names had to be unique per table. Now they must be unique within the schema (database). An implication of this change is that DROP TRIGGER syntax now uses a schema name instead of a table name (schema name is optional and, if omitted, the current schema will be used).

   When upgrading from a previous version of MySQL 5 to MySQL 5.0.10 or newer, you must drop all triggers and re-create them or DROP TRIGGER will not work after the upgrade. Here is a suggested procedure for doing this:

   1. Upgrade to MySQL 5.0.10 or later to be able to access trigger information in the INFORMATION_SCHEMA.TRIGGERS table. (It should work even for pre-5.0.10 triggers.)

   2. Dump all trigger definitions using the following SELECT statement:

```
SELECT CONCAT('CREATE TRIGGER ', t.TRIGGER_SCHEMA, '.', t.TRIGGER_NAME,
              ' ', t.ACTION_TIMING, ' ', t.EVENT_MANIPULATION, ' ON ',
          t.EVENT_OBJECT_SCHEMA, '.', t.EVENT_OBJECT_TABLE,
          ' FOR EACH ROW ', t.ACTION_STATEMENT, '//' )
INTO OUTFILE '/tmp/triggers.sql'
FROM INFORMATION_SCHEMA.TRIGGERS AS t;
```

The statement uses INTO OUTFILE, so you must have the FILE privilege. The file will be created on the server host. Use a different filename if you like. To be 100% safe, inspect the trigger definitions in the triggers.sql file, and perhaps make a backup of the file.

3. Stop the server and drop all triggers by removing all .TRG files in your database directories. Change location to your data directory and issue this command:

```
shell> rm */*.TRG
```

4. Start the server and re-create all triggers using the triggers.sql file. For the file created earlier, use these commands in the mysql program:

```
mysql> delimiter // ;
mysql> source /tmp/triggers.sql //
```

5. Use the SHOW TRIGGERS statement to check that all triggers were created successfully.

- **Incompatible change**: As of MySQL 5.0.15, the CHAR() function returns a binary string rather than a string in the connection character set. An optional USING *charset_name* clause may be used to produce a result in a specific character set instead. Also, arguments larger than 256 produce multiple characters. They are no longer interpreted modulo 256 to produce a single character each. These changes may cause some incompatibilities:

  - CHAR(ORD('A')) = 'a' is no longer true:

    ```
    mysql> SELECT CHAR(ORD('A')) = 'a';
    +----------------------+
    | CHAR(ORD('A')) = 'a' |
    +----------------------+
    |                    0 |
    +----------------------+
    ```

    To perform a case-insensitive comparison, you can produce a result string in a non-binary character set by adding a USING clause or converting the result:

    ```
    mysql> SELECT CHAR(ORD('A') USING latin1) = 'a';
    +-----------------------------------+
    | CHAR(ORD('A') USING latin1) = 'a' |
    +-----------------------------------+
    |                                 1 |
    +-----------------------------------+
    mysql> SELECT CONVERT(CHAR(ORD('A')) USING latin1) = 'a';
    +--------------------------------------------+
    | CONVERT(CHAR(ORD('A')) USING latin1) = 'a' |
    +--------------------------------------------+
    |                                          1 |
    +--------------------------------------------+
    ```

- CREATE TABLE ... SELECT CHAR(...) produces a VARBINARY column, not a VARCHAR column. To produce a VARCHAR column, use USING or CONVERT() as just described to convert the CHAR() result into a non-binary character set.

- Previously, the following statements inserted the value 0x00410041 ('AA' as a ucs2 string) into the table:

  ```
  CREATE TABLE t (ucs2_column CHAR(2) CHARACTER SET ucs2);
  INSERT INTO t VALUES (CHAR(0x41,0x41));
  ```

  As of MySQL 5.0.15, the statements insert a single ucs2 character with value 0x4141.

- **Incompatible change**: Beginning with MySQL 5.0.12, natural joins and joins with USING, including outer join variants, are processed according to the SQL:2003 standard. The changes include elimination of redundant output columns for NATURAL joins and joins specified with a USING clause and proper ordering of output columns. The precedence of the comma operator also now is lower compared to JOIN, LEFT JOIN, and so forth.

These changes make MySQL more compliant with standard SQL. However, they can result in different output columns for some joins. Also, some queries that appeared to work correctly prior to 5.0.12 must be rewritten to comply with the standard. For details about the scope of the changes and examples that show what query rewrites are necessary, see the "MySQL Language Reference."

- **Incompatible change**: Before MySQL 5.0.13, GREATEST(x,NULL) and LEAST(x,NULL) return x when x is a non-NULL value. As of 5.0.3, both functions return NULL if any argument is NULL, the same as Oracle. This change can cause problems for applications that rely on the old behavior.

- **Incompatible change**: Before MySQL 4.1.13/5.0.8, conversion of DATETIME values to numeric form by adding zero produced a result in YYYYMMDDHHMMSS format. The result of DATETIME+0 is now in YYYYMMDDHHMMSS.000000 format.

- Some keywords are reserved in MySQL 5.0 that were not reserved in MySQL 4.1.

- As of MySQL 5.0.3, DECIMAL columns are stored in a more efficient format. To convert a table to use the new DECIMAL type, you should do an ALTER TABLE on it. The ALTER TABLE also will change the table's VARCHAR columns to use the new VARCHAR data type. For information about possible incompatibilities with old applications, see the "MySQL Language Reference."

- MySQL 5.0.3 and up uses precision math when calculating with DECIMAL values (64 decimal digits) and for rounding exact-value numbers.

- Comparisons made between FLOAT or DOUBLE values that happened to work in MySQL 4.1 may not do so in 5.0. Values of these types are imprecise in all MySQL versions, and you are *strongly advised* to avoid such comparisons as WHERE col_name=some_double, *regardless of the MySQL version you are using.*

- As of MySQL 5.0.3, trailing spaces no longer are removed from values stored in VAR-CHAR and VARBINARY columns. The maximum lengths for VARCHAR and VARBINARY columns in MySQL 5.0.3 and later are 65,535 characters and 65,535 bytes, respectively.

  Note: If you create a table with new VARCHAR or VARBINARY columns in MySQL 5.0.3 or later, the table will not be usable if you downgrade to a version older than 5.0.3. Dump the table before downgrading and reload it after downgrading.

- As of MySQL 5.0.3, BIT is a separate data type, not a synonym for TINYINT(1).

- MySQL 5.0.2 adds several SQL modes that allow stricter control over rejecting records that have invalid or missing values. See Section 1.9.6.2, "Constraints on Invalid Data," and Section 4.2.5, "The Server SQL Mode." If you want to enable this control but continue to use MySQL's capability for storing incorrect dates such as '2004-02-31', you should start the server with --sql_mode=TRADITIONAL,ALLOW_INVALID_DATES.

- As of MySQL 5.0.2, the SCHEMA and SCHEMAS keywords are accepted as synonyms for DATABASE and DATABASES, respectively. (While "schemata" is grammatically correct and even appears in some MySQL 5.0 system database and table names, it cannot be used as a keyword.)

- User variables are not case sensitive in MySQL 5.0. In MySQL 4.1, SET @x = 0; SET @X = 1; SELECT @x; created two variables and returned 0. In MySQL 5.0, it creates one variable and returns 1.

- A new startup option named innodb_table_locks was added that causes LOCK TABLE to also acquire InnoDB table locks. This option is enabled by default. This can cause deadlocks in applications that use AUTOCOMMIT=1 and LOCK TABLES. If your application encounters deadlocks after upgrading, you may need to add innodb_table_locks=0 to your my.cnf file.

C API Changes:

- **Incompatible change**: Because the MySQL 5.0 server has a new implementation of the DECIMAL data type, a problem may occur if the server is used by older clients that still are linked against MySQL 4.1 client libraries. If a client uses the binary client/server protocol to execute prepared statements that generate result sets containing numeric values, an error will be raised: 'Using unsupported buffer type: 246'

  This error occurs because the 4.1 client libraries do not support the new MYSQL_TYPE_NEWDECIMAL type value added in 5.0. There is no way to disable the new DECIMAL data type on the server side. You can avoid the problem by relinking the application with the client libraries from MySQL 5.0.

- **Incompatible change**: The ER_WARN_DATA_TRUNCATED warning symbol was renamed to WARN_DATA_TRUNCATED in MySQL 5.0.3.

- The reconnect flag in the MYSQL structure is set to 0 by mysql_real_connect(). Only those client programs which did not explicitly set this flag to 0 or 1 after mysql_real_connect() experience a change. Having automatic reconnection enabled by default was considered too dangerous (due to the fact that table locks, temporary tables, user variables, and session variables are lost after reconnection).

2.10.3 Copying MySQL Databases to Another Machine

You can copy the `.frm`, `.MYI`, and `.MYD` files for `MyISAM` tables between different architectures that support the same floating-point format. (MySQL takes care of any byte-swapping issues.) See Section 8.1, "The `MyISAM` Storage Engine."

In cases where you need to transfer databases between different architectures, you can use `mysqldump` to create a file containing SQL statements. You can then transfer the file to the other machine and feed it as input to the `mysql` client.

Use `mysqldump --help` to see what options are available. If you are moving the data to a newer version of MySQL, you should use `mysqldump --opt` to take advantage of any optimizations that result in a dump file that is smaller and can be processed more quickly.

The easiest (although not the fastest) way to move a database between two machines is to run the following commands on the machine on which the database is located:

```
shell> mysqladmin -h 'other_hostname' create db_name
shell> mysqldump --opt db_name | mysql -h 'other_hostname' db_name
```

If you want to copy a database from a remote machine over a slow network, you can use these commands:

```
shell> mysqladmin create db_name
shell> mysqldump -h 'other_hostname' --opt --compress db_name | mysql db_name
```

You can also store the dump in a file, transfer the file to the target machine, and then load the file into the database there. For example, you can dump a database to a compressed file on the source machine like this:

```
shell> mysqldump --quick db_name | gzip > db_name.gz
```

Transfer the file containing the database contents to the target machine and run these commands there:

```
shell> mysqladmin create db_name
shell> gunzip < db_name.gz | mysql db_name
```

You can also use `mysqldump` and `mysqlimport` to transfer the database. For large tables, this is much faster than simply using `mysqldump`. In the following commands, `DUMPDIR` represents the full pathname of the directory you use to store the output from `mysqldump`.

First, create the directory for the output files and dump the database:

```
shell> mkdir DUMPDIR
shell> mysqldump --tab=DUMPDIR db_name
```

Then transfer the files in the `DUMPDIR` directory to some corresponding directory on the target machine and load the files into MySQL there:

```
shell> mysqladmin create db_name          # create database
shell> cat DUMPDIR/*.sql | mysql db_name  # create tables in database
shell> mysqlimport db_name DUMPDIR/*.txt  # load data into tables
```

Do not forget to copy the `mysql` database because that is where the grant tables are stored. You might have to run commands as the MySQL `root` user on the new machine until you have the `mysql` database in place.

After you import the `mysql` database on the new machine, execute `mysqladmin flush-privileges` so that the server reloads the grant table information.

2.11 Downgrading MySQL

This section describes what you should do to downgrade to an older MySQL version in the unlikely case that the previous version worked better than the new one.

If you are downgrading within the same release series (for example, from 4.1.13 to 4.1.12) the general rule is that you just have to install the new binaries on top of the old ones. There is no need to do anything with the databases. As always, however, it is always a good idea to make a backup.

The following items form a checklist of things you should do whenever you perform a downgrade:

- Read the upgrading section for the release series from which you are downgrading to be sure that it does not have any features you really need. Section 2.10, "Upgrading MySQL."
- If there is a downgrading section for that version, you should read that as well.

In most cases, you can move the MySQL format files and data files between different versions on the same architecture as long as you stay within versions for the same release series of MySQL.

If you downgrade from one release series to another, there may be incompatibilities in table storage formats. In this case, you can use `mysqldump` to dump your tables before downgrading. After downgrading, reload the dump file using `mysql` or `mysqlimport` to re-create your tables. For examples, see Section 2.10.3, "Copying MySQL Databases to Another Machine."

The normal symptom of a downward-incompatible table format change when you downgrade is that you can't open tables. In that case, use the following procedure:

1. Stop the older MySQL server that you are downgrading to.
2. Restart the newer MySQL server you are downgrading from.
3. Dump any tables that were inaccessible to the older server by using `mysqldump` to create a dump file.
4. Stop the newer MySQL server and restart the older one.
5. Reload the dump file into the older server. Your tables should be accessible.

2.11.1 Downgrading to MySQL 4.1

After downgrading from MySQL 5.0, you may see the following information in the `mysql.err` file:

```
Incorrect information in file: './mysql/user.frm'
```

In this case, you can do the following:

1. Start MySQL 5.0.4 (or newer).
2. Run `mysql_fix_privilege_tables`, which will change the `mysql.user` table to a format that both MySQL 4.1 and 5.0 can use.
3. Stop the MySQL server.
4. Start MySQL 4.1.

If the preceding procedure fails, you should be able to do the following instead:

1. Start MySQL 5.0.4 (or newer).
2. Run `mysqldump --opt --add-drop-table mysql > /tmp/mysql.dump`.
3. Stop the MySQL server.
4. Start MySQL 4.1 with the `--skip-grant` option.
5. Run `mysql mysql < /tmp/mysql.dump`.
6. Run `mysqladmin flush-privileges`.

2.12 Operating System–Specific Notes

For information about operating system-related issues, see the section in the online "MySQL Reference Manual" at `http://dev.mysql.com/doc/mysql/en/operating-system-specific-notes.html`.

2.13 Perl Installation Notes

Perl support for MySQL is provided by means of the `DBI/DBD` client interface. The interface requires Perl 5.6.1 or later. It *does not work* if you have an older version of Perl.

If you want to use transactions with Perl DBI, you need to have `DBD::mysql` version 1.2216 or newer. `DBD::mysql` 2.9003 or newer is recommended.

If you are using the MySQL 4.1 or newer client library, you must use `DBD::mysql` 2.9003 or newer.

Perl support is not included with MySQL distributions. You can obtain the necessary modules from `http://search.cpan.org` for Unix, or by using the ActiveState `ppm` program on Windows. The following sections describe how to do this.

Perl support for MySQL must be installed if you want to run the MySQL benchmark scripts. See Section 6.1.4, "The MySQL Benchmark Suite."

2.13.1 Installing Perl on Unix

MySQL Perl support requires that you have installed MySQL client programming support (libraries and header files). Most installation methods install the necessary files. However, if you installed MySQL from RPM files on Linux, be sure that you've installed the developer RPM. The client programs are in the client RPM, but client programming support is in the developer RPM.

If you want to install Perl support, the files you need can be obtained from the CPAN (Comprehensive Perl Archive Network) at http://search.cpan.org.

The easiest way to install Perl modules on Unix is to use the CPAN module. For example:

```
shell> perl -MCPAN -e shell
cpan> install DBI
cpan> install DBD::mysql
```

The DBD::mysql installation runs a number of tests. These tests attempt to connect to the local MySQL server using the default username and password. (The default username is your login name on Unix, and ODBC on Windows. The default password is "no password.") If you cannot connect to the server with those values (for example, if your account has a password), the tests fail. You can use force install DBD::mysql to ignore the failed tests.

DBI requires the Data::Dumper module. It may be installed; if not, you should install it before installing DBI.

It is also possible to download the module distributions in the form of compressed tar archives and build the modules manually. For example, to unpack and build a DBI distribution, use a procedure such as this:

1. Unpack the distribution into the current directory:

   ```
   shell> gunzip < DBI-VERSION.tar.gz | tar xvf -
   ```

   This command creates a directory named DBI-VERSION.

2. Change location into the top-level directory of the unpacked distribution:

   ```
   shell> cd DBI-VERSION
   ```

3. Build the distribution and compile everything:

   ```
   shell> perl Makefile.PL
   shell> make
   shell> make test
   shell> make install
   ```

The make test command is important because it verifies that the module is working. Note that when you run that command during the DBD::mysql installation to exercise the interface code, the MySQL server must be running or the test fails.

It is a good idea to rebuild and reinstall the `DBD::mysql` distribution whenever you install a new release of MySQL, particularly if you notice symptoms such as that all your `DBI` scripts fail after you upgrade MySQL.

If you don't have access rights to install Perl modules in the system directory or if you want to install local Perl modules, the following reference may be useful: `http://servers.digitaldaze.com/extensions/perl/modules.html#modules`.

Look under the heading "Installing New Modules that Require Locally Installed Modules."

2.13.2 Installing ActiveState Perl on Windows

On Windows, you should do the following to install the MySQL `DBD` module with ActiveState Perl:

1. Get ActiveState Perl from `http://www.activestate.com/Products/ActivePerl/` and install it.

2. Open a console window ("DOS window").

3. If necessary, set the `HTTP_proxy` variable. For example, you might try a setting like this:

   ```
   set HTTP_proxy=my.proxy.com:3128
   ```

4. Start the PPM program:

   ```
   C:\> C:\perl\bin\ppm.pl
   ```

5. If you have not previously done so, install `DBI`:

   ```
   ppm> install DBI
   ```

6. If this succeeds, run the following command:

   ```
   install \
   ftp://ftp.de.uu.net/pub/CPAN/authors/id/JWIED/DBD-mysql-1.2212.x86.ppd
   ```

This procedure should work with ActiveState Perl 5.6 or newer.

If you cannot get the procedure to work, you should install the MyODBC driver instead and connect to the MySQL server through ODBC:

```
use DBI;
$dbh= DBI->connect("DBI:ODBC:$dsn",$user,$password) ||
  die "Got error $DBI::errstr when connecting to $dsn\n";
```

2.13.3 Problems Using the Perl DBI/DBD Interface

If Perl reports that it cannot find the `../mysql/mysql.so` module, the problem is probably that Perl cannot locate the `libmysqlclient.so` shared library. You should be able to fix this problem by one of the following methods:

- Compile the `DBD::mysql` distribution with `perl Makefile.PL -static -config` rather than `perl Makefile.PL`.

- Copy `libmysqlclient.so` to the directory where your other shared libraries are located (probably `/usr/lib` or `/lib`).
- Modify the `-L` options used to compile `DBD::mysql` to reflect the actual location of `libmysqlclient.so`.
- On Linux, you can add the pathname of the directory where `libmysqlclient.so` is located to the `/etc/ld.so.conf` file.
- Add the pathname of the directory where `libmysqlclient.so` is located to the `LD_RUN_PATH` environment variable. Some systems use `LD_LIBRARY_PATH` instead.

Note that you may also need to modify the `-L` options if there are other libraries that the linker fails to find. For example, if the linker cannot find `libc` because it is in `/lib` and the link command specifies `-L/usr/lib`, change the `-L` option to `-L/lib` or add `-L/lib` to the existing link command.

If you get the following errors from `DBD::mysql`, you are probably using `gcc` (or using an old binary compiled with `gcc`):

```
/usr/bin/perl: can't resolve symbol '__moddi3'
/usr/bin/perl: can't resolve symbol '__divdi3'
```

Add `-L/usr/lib/gcc-lib/... -lgcc` to the link command when the `mysql.so` library gets built (check the output from `make` for `mysql.so` when you compile the Perl client). The `-L` option should specify the pathname of the directory where `libgcc.a` is located on your system.

Another cause of this problem may be that Perl and MySQL aren't both compiled with `gcc`. In this case, you can solve the mismatch by compiling both with `gcc`.

You may see the following error from `DBD::mysql` when you run the tests:

```
t/00base...........install_driver(mysql) failed:
Can't load '../blib/arch/auto/DBD/mysql/mysql.so' for module DBD::mysql:
../blib/arch/auto/DBD/mysql/mysql.so: undefined symbol:
uncompress at /usr/lib/perl5/5.00503/i586-linux/DynaLoader.pm line 169.
```

This means that you need to include the `-lz` compression library on the link line. That can be done by changing the following line in the file `lib/DBD/mysql/Install.pm`:

```
$sysliblist .= " -lm";
```

Change that line to:

```
$sysliblist .= " -lm -lz";
```

After this, you *must* run `make realclean` and then proceed with the installation from the beginning.

If you want to install DBI on SCO, you have to edit the `Makefile` in DBI-*xxx* and each subdirectory. Note that the following assumes `gcc` 2.95.2 or newer:

```
OLD:                                       NEW:
CC = cc                                    CC = gcc
CCCDLFLAGS = -KPIC -W1,-Bexport            CCCDLFLAGS = -fpic
CCDLFLAGS = -wl,-Bexport                   CCDLFLAGS =

LD = ld                                    LD = gcc -G -fpic
LDDLFLAGS = -G -L/usr/local/lib            LDDLFLAGS = -L/usr/local/lib
LDFLAGS = -belf -L/usr/local/lib           LDFLAGS = -L/usr/local/lib

LD = ld                                    LD = gcc -G -fpic
OPTIMISE = -Od                             OPTIMISE = -O1

OLD:
CCCFLAGS = -belf -dy -w0 -U M_XENIX -DPERL_SCO5 -I/usr/local/include

NEW:
CCFLAGS = -U M_XENIX -DPERL_SCO5 -I/usr/local/include
```

These changes are necessary because the Perl dynaloader does not load the DBI modules if they were compiled with icc or cc.

If you want to use the Perl module on a system that doesn't support dynamic linking (such as SCO), you can generate a static version of Perl that includes DBI and DBD::mysql. The way this works is that you generate a version of Perl with the DBI code linked in and install it on top of your current Perl. Then you use that to build a version of Perl that additionally has the DBD code linked in, and install that.

On SCO, you must have the following environment variables set:

```
LD_LIBRARY_PATH=/lib:/usr/lib:/usr/local/lib:/usr/progressive/lib
```

Or:

```
LD_LIBRARY_PATH=/usr/lib:/lib:/usr/local/lib:/usr/ccs/lib:\
    /usr/progressive/lib:/usr/skunk/lib
LIBPATH=/usr/lib:/lib:/usr/local/lib:/usr/ccs/lib:\
    /usr/progressive/lib:/usr/skunk/lib
MANPATH=scohelp:/usr/man:/usr/local1/man:/usr/local/man:\
    /usr/skunk/man:
```

First, create a Perl that includes a statically linked DBI module by running these commands in the directory where your DBI distribution is located:

```
shell> perl Makefile.PL -static -config
shell> make
shell> make install
shell> make perl
```

Then you must install the new Perl. The output of make perl indicates the exact make command you need to execute to perform the installation. On SCO, this is make -f Makefile.aperl inst_perl MAP_TARGET=perl.

Next, use the just-created Perl to create another Perl that also includes a statically linked DBD::mysql by running these commands in the directory where your DBD::mysql distribution is located:

```
shell> perl Makefile.PL -static -config
shell> make
shell> make install
shell> make perl
```

Finally, you should install this new Perl. Again, the output of make perl indicates the command to use.

Using MySQL Programs

This chapter provides a brief overview of the command-line programs provided by MySQL AB and discusses the general syntax for specifying options when you run these programs. Most programs have options that are specific to their own operation, but the option syntax is similar for all of them. Later chapters provide more detailed descriptions of individual programs, including which options they recognize.

MySQL AB also provides three GUI client programs for use with MySQL Server:

- MySQL Administrator: This tool is used for administering MySQL servers, databases, tables, and user accounts.
- MySQL Query Browser: This graphical tool is provided by MySQL AB for creating, executing, and optimizing queries on MySQL databases.
- MySQL Migration Toolkit: This tool helps you migrate schemas and data from other relational database management systems for use with MySQL.

These GUI programs each have their own manuals that you can access at `http://dev.mysql.com/doc/`.

3.1 Overview of MySQL Programs

MySQL AB provides several types of programs:

- The MySQL server and server startup scripts:
  - `mysqld` is the MySQL server.
  - `mysqld_safe`, `mysql.server`, and `mysqld_multi` are server startup scripts.
  - `mysql_install_db` initializes the data directory and the initial databases.
  - MySQL Instance Manager monitors and manages MySQL Server instances.

  Chapter 4, "Database Administration," discusses these programs further.

- Client programs that access the server:
  - `mysql` is a command-line client for executing SQL statements interactively or in batch mode.
  - `mysqladmin` is an administrative client.
  - `mysqlcheck` performs table maintenance operations.
  - `mysqldump` and `mysqlhotcopy` make database backups.
  - `mysqlimport` imports data files.
  - `mysqlshow` displays information about databases and tables.

  Chapter 7, "Client and Utility Programs," discusses these programs further.
- Utility programs that operate independently of the server:
  - `myisamchk` performs table maintenance operations.
  - `myisampack` produces compressed, read-only tables.
  - `mysqlbinlog` is a tool for processing binary log files.
  - `perror` displays the meaning of error codes.

  Chapter 7, "Client and Utility Programs," discusses these programs further.

Most MySQL distributions include all of these programs, except for those programs that are platform-specific. (For example, the server startup scripts are not used on Windows.) The exception is that RPM distributions are more specialized. There is one RPM for the server, another for client programs, and so forth. If you appear to be missing one or more programs, see Chapter 2, "Installing and Upgrading MySQL," for information on types of distributions and what they contain. It may be that you have a distribution that does not include all programs and you need to install something else.

3.2 Invoking MySQL Programs

To invoke a MySQL program from the command line (that is, from your shell or command prompt), enter the program name followed by any options or other arguments needed to instruct the program what you want it to do. The following commands show some sample program invocations. "`shell>`" represents the prompt for your command interpreter; it is not part of what you type. The particular prompt you see depends on your command interpreter. Typical prompts are `$` for `sh` or `bash`, `%` for `csh` or `tcsh`, and `C:\>` for the Windows `command.com` or `cmd.exe` command interpreters.

```
shell> mysql -u root test
shell> mysqladmin extended-status variables
shell> mysqlshow --help
shell> mysqldump --user=root personnel
```

Arguments that begin with a single or double dash ('-', '--') are option arguments. Options typically specify the type of connection a program should make to the server or affect its operational mode. Option syntax is described in Section 3.3, "Specifying Program Options."

Non-option arguments (arguments with no leading dash) provide additional information to the program. For example, the `mysql` program interprets the first non-option argument as a database name, so the command `mysql -u root test` indicates that you want to use the `test` database.

Later sections that describe individual programs indicate which options a program understands and describe the meaning of any additional non-option arguments.

Some options are common to a number of programs. The most common of these are the `--host` (or `-h`), `--user` (or `-u`), and `--password` (or `-p`) options that specify connection parameters. They indicate the host where the MySQL server is running, and the username and password of your MySQL account. All MySQL client programs understand these options; they allow you to specify which server to connect to and the account to use on that server.

You may find it necessary to invoke MySQL programs using the pathname to the `bin` directory in which they are installed. This is likely to be the case if you get a "program not found" error whenever you attempt to run a MySQL program from any directory other than the `bin` directory. To make it more convenient to use MySQL, you can add the pathname of the `bin` directory to your `PATH` environment variable setting. That enables you to run a program by typing only its name, not its entire pathname. For example, if `mysql` is installed in `/usr/local/mysql/bin`, you'll be able to run it by invoking it as `mysql`; it will not be necessary to invoke it as `/usr/local/mysql/bin/mysql`.

Consult the documentation for your command interpreter for instructions on setting your `PATH` variable. The syntax for setting environment variables is interpreter-specific.

3.3 Specifying Program Options

There are several ways to specify options for MySQL programs:

- List the options on the command line following the program name. This is most common for options that apply to a specific invocation of the program.

- List the options in an option file that the program reads when it starts. This is common for options that you want the program to use each time it runs.

- List the options in environment variables. This method is useful for options that you want to apply each time the program runs. In practice, option files are used more commonly for this purpose. However, Section 4.13.2, "Running Multiple Servers on Unix," discusses one situation in which environment variables can be very helpful. It describes a handy technique that uses such variables to specify the TCP/IP port number and Unix socket file for both the server and client programs.

MySQL programs determine which options are given first by examining environment variables, then by reading option files, and then by checking the command line. If an option is specified multiple times, the last occurrence takes precedence. This means that environment variables have the lowest precedence and command-line options the highest.

You can take advantage of the way that MySQL programs process options by specifying default values for a program's options in an option file. That enables you to avoid typing them each time you run the program, but also allows you to override the defaults if necessary by using command-line options.

3.3.1 Using Options on the Command Line

Program options specified on the command line follow these rules:

- Options are given after the command name.
- An option argument begins with one dash or two dashes, depending on whether it has a short name or a long name. Many options have both forms. For example, `-?` and `--help` are the short and long forms of the option that instructs a MySQL program to display a help message.
- Option names are case sensitive. `-v` and `-V` are both legal and have different meanings. (They are the corresponding short forms of the `--verbose` and `--version` options.)
- Some options take a value following the option name. For example, `-h localhost` or `--host=localhost` indicate the MySQL server host to a client program. The option value tells the program the name of the host where the MySQL server is running.
- For a long option that takes a value, separate the option name and the value by an '=' sign. For a short option that takes a value, the option value can immediately follow the option letter, or there can be a space between: `-hlocalhost` and `-h localhost` are equivalent. An exception to this rule is the option for specifying your MySQL password. This option can be given in long form as `--password=pass_val` or as `--password`. In the latter case (with no password value given), the program prompts you for the password. The password option also may be given in short form as `-ppass_val` or as `-p`. However, for the short form, if the password value is given, it must follow the option letter with *no intervening space*. The reason for this is that if a space follows the option letter, the program has no way to tell whether a following argument is supposed to be the password value or some other kind of argument. Consequently, the following two commands have two completely different meanings:

  ```
  shell> mysql -ptest
  shell> mysql -p test
  ```

  The first command instructs mysql to use a password value of test, but specifies no default database. The second instructs mysql to prompt for the password value and to use test as the default database.

Some options control behavior that can be turned on or off. For example, the mysql client supports a `--column-names` option that determines whether or not to display a row of column names at the beginning of query results. By default, this option is enabled. However, you may want to disable it in some instances, such as when sending the output of `mysql` into another program that expects to see only data and not an initial header line.

To disable column names, you can specify the option using any of these forms:

```
--disable-column-names
--skip-column-names
--column-names=0
```

The `--disable` and `--skip` prefixes and the `=0` suffix all have the same effect: They turn the option off.

The "enabled" form of the option may be specified in any of these ways:

```
--column-names
--enable-column-names
--column-names=1
```

If an option is prefixed by `--loose`, a program does not exit with an error if it does not recognize the option, but instead issues only a warning:

```
shell> mysql --loose-no-such-option
mysql: WARNING: unknown option '--no-such-option'
```

The `--loose` prefix can be useful when you run programs from multiple installations of MySQL on the same machine and list options in an option file. An option that may not be recognized by all versions of a program can be given using the `--loose` prefix (or `loose` in an option file). Versions of the program that recognize the option process it normally, and versions that do not recognize it issue a warning and ignore it.

Another option that may occasionally be useful with `mysql` is the `--execute` or `-e` option, which can be used to pass SQL statements to the server. The statements must be enclosed by single or double quotation marks. If you wish to use quoted values within a statement, you should use double quotes for the statement, and single quotes for any quoted values within the statement. When this option is used, `mysql` executes the statements and exits.

For example, you can use the following command to obtain a list of user accounts:

```
shell> mysql -u root -p --execute="SELECT User, Host FROM user" mysql
Enter password: ******
+------+-----------+
| User | Host      |
+------+-----------+
|      | gigan     |
| root | gigan     |
|      | localhost |
| jon  | localhost |
| root | localhost |
+------+-----------+
shell>
```

Note that the long form (`--execute`) is followed by an equal sign (`=`).

In the preceding example, the name of the `mysql` database was passed as a separate argument. However, the same statement could have been executed using this command, which specifies no default database:

```
mysql> mysql -u root -p --execute="SELECT User, Host FROM mysql.user"
```

Multiple SQL statements may be passed on the command line, separated by semicolons:

```
shell> mysql -u root -p -e "SELECT VERSION();SELECT NOW()"
Enter password: ******
+------------+
| VERSION()  |
+------------+
| 5.0.19-log |
+------------+
+---------------------+
| NOW()               |
+---------------------+
| 2006-01-05 21:19:04 |
+---------------------+
```

The `--execute` or `-e` option may also be used to pass commands in an analogous fashion to the `ndb_mgm` management client for MySQL Cluster. See Section 9.3.6, "Safe Shutdown and Restart," for an example.

3.3.2 Using Option Files

Most MySQL programs can read startup options from option files (also sometimes called "configuration files"). Option files provide a convenient way to specify commonly used options so that they need not be entered on the command line each time you run a program.

To determine whether a program reads option files, invoke it with the `--help` option (`--verbose` and `--help` for `mysqld`). If the program reads option files, the help message indicates which files it looks for and which option groups it recognizes.

Note: Option files used with MySQL Cluster programs are covered in Section 9.4, "MySQL Cluster Configuration."

On Windows, MySQL programs read startup options from the following files:

Filename	Purpose
WINDIR\my.ini	Global options
C:\my.cnf	Global options
INSTALLDIR\my.ini	Global options
defaults-extra-file	The file specified with --defaults-extra-file=*path*, if any

WINDIR represents the location of your Windows directory. This is commonly C:\WINDOWS or C:\WINNT. You can determine its exact location from the value of the WINDIR environment variable using the following command:

C:\> **echo %WINDIR%**

INSTALLDIR represents the installation directory of MySQL. This is typically C:*PROGRAMDIR*\ MySQL\MySQL 5.0 Server where *PROGRAMDIR* represents the programs directory (usually Program Files on English-language versions of Windows), when MySQL 5.0 has been installed using the installation and configuration wizards. See Section 2.3.4.14, "The Location of the my.ini File."

On Unix, MySQL programs read startup options from the following files:

Filename	Purpose
/etc/my.cnf	Global options
$MYSQL_HOME/my.cnf	Server-specific options
defaults-extra-file	The file specified with --defaults-extra-file=*path*, if any
~/.my.cnf	User-specific options

MYSQL_HOME is an environment variable containing the path to the directory in which the server-specific my.cnf file resides. (This was *DATADIR* prior to MySQL version 5.0.3.)

If MYSQL_HOME is not set and you start the server using the mysqld_safe program, mysqld_safe attempts to set MYSQL_HOME as follows:

- Let *BASEDIR* and *DATADIR* represent the pathnames of the MySQL base directory and data directory, respectively.
- If there is a my.cnf file in *DATADIR* but not in *BASEDIR*, mysqld_safe sets MYSQL_HOME to *DATADIR*.
- Otherwise, if MYSQL_HOME is not set and there is no my.cnf file in *DATADIR*, mysqld_safe sets MYSQL_HOME to *BASEDIR*.

Typically, *DATADIR* is /usr/local/mysql/data for a binary installation or /usr/local/var for a source installation. Note that this is the data directory location that was specified at configuration time, not the one specified with the --datadir option when mysqld starts. Use of --datadir at runtime has no effect on where the server looks for option files, because it looks for them before processing any options.

MySQL looks for option files in the order just described and reads any that exist. If an option file that you want to use does not exist, create it with a plain text editor.

If multiple instances of a given option are found, the last instance takes precedence. There is one exception: For mysqld, the *first* instance of the --user option is used as a security precaution, to prevent a user specified in an option file from being overridden on the command line.

Note: On Unix platforms, MySQL ignores configuration files that are world-writable. This is intentional, and acts as a security measure.

Any long option that may be given on the command line when running a MySQL program can be given in an option file as well. To get the list of available options for a program, run it with the --help option.

The syntax for specifying options in an option file is similar to command-line syntax, except that you omit the leading two dashes. For example, --quick or --host=localhost on the command line should be specified as quick or host=localhost in an option file. To specify an option of the form --loose-*opt_name* in an option file, write it as loose-*opt_name*.

Empty lines in option files are ignored. Non-empty lines can take any of the following forms:

- #*comment*, ;*comment*

  Comment lines start with '#' or ';'. A '#' comment can start in the middle of a line as well.

- [*group*]

  group is the name of the program or group for which you want to set options. After a group line, any option-setting lines apply to the named group until the end of the option file or another group line is given.

- *opt_name*

  This is equivalent to --*opt_name* on the command line.

- *opt_name=value*

  This is equivalent to --*opt_name=value* on the command line. In an option file, you can have spaces around the '=' character, something that is not true on the command line. You can enclose the value within single quotes or double quotes, which is useful if the value contains a '#' comment character or whitespace.

For options that take a numeric value, the value can be given with a suffix of K, M, or G (either uppercase or lowercase) to indicate a multiplier of 1024, 1024^2 or 1024^3. For example, the following command tells mysqladmin to ping the server 1024 times, sleeping 10 seconds between each ping:

```
mysql> mysqladmin --count=1K --sleep=10 ping
```

Leading and trailing blanks are automatically deleted from option names and values. You may use the escape sequences '\b', '\t', '\n', '\r', '\\', and '\s' in option values to represent the backspace, tab, newline, carriage return, backslash, and space characters, respectively.

Because the '\\' escape sequence represents a single backslash, you must write each '\' as '\\'. Alternatively, you can specify the value using '/' rather than '\' as the pathname separator.

If an option group name is the same as a program name, options in the group apply specifically to that program. For example, the [mysqld] and [mysql] groups apply to the mysqld server and the mysql client program, respectively.

The [client] option group is read by all client programs (but *not* by mysqld). This allows you to specify options that apply to all clients. For example, [client] is the perfect group to use to specify the password that you use to connect to the server. (But make sure that the option file is readable and writable only by yourself, so that other people cannot find out your password.) Be sure not to put an option in the [client] group unless it is recognized by *all* client programs that you use. Programs that do not understand the option quit after displaying an error message if you try to run them.

Here is a typical global option file:

```
[client]
port=3306
socket=/tmp/mysql.sock

[mysqld]
port=3306
socket=/tmp/mysql.sock
key_buffer_size=16M
max_allowed_packet=8M

[mysqldump]
quick
```

The preceding option file uses *var_name=value* syntax for the lines that set the key_buffer_size and max_allowed_packet variables.

Here is a typical user option file:

```
[client]
# The following password will be sent to all standard MySQL clients
password="my_password"

[mysql]
no-auto-rehash
connect_timeout=2

[mysqlhotcopy]
interactive-timeout
```

If you want to create option groups that should be read by mysqld servers from a specific MySQL release series only, you can do this by using groups with names of [mysqld-4.1], [mysqld-5.0], and so forth. The following group indicates that the --new option should be used only by MySQL servers with 5.0.x version numbers:

```
[mysqld-5.0]
new
```

Beginning with MySQL 5.0.4, it is possible to use `!include` directives in option files to include other option files and `!includedir` to search specific directories for option files. For example, to include the `/home/mydir/myopt.cnf` file, you can use the following directive:

```
!include /home/me/myopt.cnf
```

To search the `/home/mydir` directory and read option files found there, you would use this directive:

```
!includedir /home/mydir
```

Note: Currently, any files to be found and included using the `!includedir` directive on Unix operating systems *must* have filenames ending in `.cnf`. On Windows, this directive checks for files with the `.ini` or `.cnf` extension.

Note that options read from included files are applied in the context of the current option group. Suppose that you were to write the following lines in `my.cnf`:

```
[mysqld]
!include /home/mydir/myopt.cnf
```

In this case, the `myopt.cnf` file is processed only for the server, and the `!include` directive is ignored by any client applications. However, if you were to use the following lines, the directory `/home/mydir/my-dump-options` is checked for option files by `mysqldump` only, and not by the server or by any other client applications:

```
[mysqldump]
!includedir /home/mydir/my-dump-options
```

If you have a source distribution, you can find sample option files named `my-xxxx.cnf` in the `support-files` directory. If you have a binary distribution, look in the `support-files` directory under your MySQL installation directory. On Windows, the sample option files may be located in the MySQL installation directory (see earlier in this section or Chapter 2, "Installing and Upgrading MySQL," if you do not know where this is). Currently, there are sample option files for small, medium, large, and very large systems. To experiment with one of these files, copy it to `C:\my.cnf` on Windows or to `.my.cnf` in your home directory on Unix.

Note: On Windows, the `.cnf` option file extension might not be displayed.

All MySQL programs that support option files handle the following options. They affect option-file handling, so they must be given on the command line and not in an option file. To work properly, each of these options must immediately follow the command name, with the exception that `--print-defaults` may be used immediately after `--defaults-file` or `--defaults-extra-file`.

- `--no-defaults`

  Don't read any option files.

- `--print-defaults`

  Print the program name and all options that it gets from option files.

- `--defaults-file=file_name`

  Use only the given option file. *file_name* is the full pathname to the file.

- `--defaults-extra-file=file_name`

  Read this option file after the global option file but (on Unix) before the user option file. *file_name* is the full pathname to the file.

In shell scripts, you can use the `my_print_defaults` program to parse option files and see what options would be used by a given program. The following example shows the output that `my_print_defaults` might produce when asked to show the options found in the `[client]` and `[mysql]` groups:

```
shell> my_print_defaults client mysql
--port=3306
--socket=/tmp/mysql.sock
--no-auto-rehash
```

Note for developers: Option file handling is implemented in the C client library simply by processing all options in the appropriate group or groups before any command-line arguments. This works well for programs that use the last instance of an option that is specified multiple times. If you have a C or C++ program that handles multiply specified options this way but that doesn't read option files, you need add only two lines to give it that capability. Check the source code of any of the standard MySQL clients to see how to do this.

Several other language interfaces to MySQL are based on the C client library, and some of them provide a way to access option file contents. These include Perl and Python. For details, see the documentation for your preferred interface.

3.3.3 Using Environment Variables to Specify Options

To specify an option using an environment variable, set the variable using the syntax appropriate for your command processor. For example, on Windows or NetWare, you can set the USER variable to specify your MySQL account name. To do so, use this syntax:

```
SET USER=your_name
```

The syntax on Unix depends on your shell. Suppose that you want to specify the TCP/IP port number using the `MYSQL_TCP_PORT` variable. Typical syntax (such as for sh, bash, zsh, and so on) is as follows:

```
MYSQL_TCP_PORT=3306
export MYSQL_TCP_PORT
```

The first command sets the variable, and the `export` command exports the variable to the shell environment so that its value becomes accessible to MySQL and other processes.

For csh and tcsh, use `setenv` to make the shell variable available to the environment:

```
setenv MYSQL_TCP_PORT 3306
```

The commands to set environment variables can be executed at your command prompt to take effect immediately, but the settings persist only until you log out. To have the settings take effect each time you log in, place the appropriate command or commands in a startup file that your command interpreter reads each time it starts. Typical startup files are AUTOEXEC.BAT for Windows, .bash_profile for bash, or .tcshrc for tcsh. Consult the documentation for your command interpreter for specific details.

3.3.4 Using Options to Set Program Variables

Many MySQL programs have internal variables that can be set at runtime. Program variables are set the same way as any other long option that takes a value. For example, mysql has a max_allowed_packet variable that controls the maximum size of its communication buffer. To set the max_allowed_packet variable for mysql to a value of 16MB, use either of the following commands:

```
shell> mysql --max_allowed_packet=16777216
shell> mysql --max_allowed_packet=16M
```

The first command specifies the value in bytes. The second specifies the value in megabytes. For variables that take a numeric value, the value can be given with a suffix of K, M, or G (either uppercase or lowercase) to indicate a multiplier of 1024, 1024^2 or 1024^3. (For example, when used to set max_allowed_packet, the suffixes indicate units of kilobytes, megabytes, or gigabytes.)

In an option file, variable settings are given without the leading dashes:

```
[mysql]
max_allowed_packet=16777216
```

Or:

```
[mysql]
max_allowed_packet=16M
```

If you like, underscores in a variable name can be specified as dashes. The following option groups are equivalent. Both set the size of the server's key buffer to 512MB:

```
[mysqld]
key_buffer_size=512M
```

```
[mysqld]
key-buffer-size=512M
```

Note: Before MySQL 4.0.2, the only syntax for setting program variables was --set-variable=*option*=*value* (or set-variable=*option*=*value* in option files). This syntax still is recognized, but is deprecated as of MySQL 4.0.2.

Many server system variables can also be set at runtime. For details, see Section 4.2.3.2, "Dynamic System Variables."

4

Database Administration

This chapter covers topics that deal with administering a MySQL installation:

- Configuring the server
- Managing user accounts
- Performing backups
- The server log files
- The query cache

4.1 Overview of Server-Side Programs

The MySQL server, `mysqld`, is the main program that does most of the work in a MySQL installation. The server is accompanied by several related scripts that perform setup operations when you install MySQL or that assist you in starting and stopping the server. This section provides an overview of the server and related programs. The following sections provide more detailed information about each of these programs.

Each MySQL program takes many different options. Most programs provide a `--help` option that you can use to get a description of the program's different options. For example, try `mysqld --help`.

You can override default option values for MySQL programs by specifying options on the command line or in an option file. Section 3.3, "Specifying Program Options."

The following list briefly describes the MySQL server and server-related programs:

- `mysqld`

  The SQL daemon (that is, the MySQL server). To use client programs, `mysqld` must be running, because clients gain access to databases by connecting to the server. See Section 4.2, "`mysqld`—The MySQL Server."

- `mysqld-max`

  A version of the server that includes additional features. See Section 4.3, "The `mysqld-max` Extended MySQL Server."

- `mysqld_safe`

  A server startup script. `mysqld_safe` attempts to start `mysqld-max` if it exists, and `mysqld` otherwise. See Section 4.4.1, "`mysqld_safe`—MySQL Server Startup Script."

- `mysql.server`

  A server startup script. This script is used on systems that use System V–style run directories containing scripts that start system services for particular run levels. It invokes `mysqld_safe` to start the MySQL server. See Section 4.4.2, "`mysql.server`—MySQL Server Startup Script."

- `mysqld_multi`

  A server startup script that can start or stop multiple servers installed on the system. See Section 4.4.3, "`mysqld_multi`—Manage Multiple MySQL Servers." As of MySQL 5.0.3 (Unix-like systems) or 5.0.13 (Windows), an alternative to `mysqld_multi` is `mysqlmanager`, the MySQL Instance Manager. See Section 4.5, "`mysqlmanager`—The MySQL Instance Manager."

- `mysql_install_db`

  This script creates the MySQL database and initializes the grant tables with default privileges. It is usually executed only once, when first installing MySQL on a system. See Section 2.9.2, "Unix Post-Installation Procedures."

- `mysql_fix_privilege_tables`

  This program is used after a MySQL upgrade operation. It updates the grant tables with any changes that have been made in newer versions of MySQL. See Section 4.6.1, "`mysql_fix_privilege_tables`—Upgrade MySQL System Tables."

  Note: As of MySQL 5.0.19, this program has been superseded by `mysql_upgrade`.

- `mysql_upgrade`

  This program is used after a MySQL upgrade operation. It checks tables for incompatibilities and repairs them if necessary, and updates the grant tables with any changes that have been made in newer versions of MySQL. See Section 4.6.2, "`mysql_upgrade`—Check Tables for MySQL Upgrade."

- `mysqlmanager`

  The MySQL Instance Manager, a program for monitoring and managing MySQL servers. See Section 4.5, "`mysqlmanager`—The MySQL Instance Manager."

There are several other programs that are run on the server host:

- `make_binary_distribution`

  This program makes a binary release of a compiled MySQL. This could be sent by FTP to `/pub/mysql/upload/` on `ftp.mysql.com` for the convenience of other MySQL users.

4.2 `mysqld`—The MySQL Server

`mysqld` is the MySQL server. The following discussion covers these MySQL server configuration topics:

- Startup options that the server supports
- Server system variables
- Server status variables
- How to set the server SQL mode
- The server shutdown process

4.2.1 `mysqld` Command Options

When you start the `mysqld` server, you can specify program options using any of the methods described in Section 3.3, "Specifying Program Options." The most common methods are to provide options in an option file or on the command line. However, in most cases it is desirable to make sure that the server uses the same options each time it runs. The best way to ensure this is to list them in an option file. See Section 3.3.2, "Using Option Files."

`mysqld` reads options from the `[mysqld]` and `[server]` groups. `mysqld_safe` reads options from the `[mysqld]`, `[server]`, `[mysqld_safe]`, and `[safe_mysqld]` groups. `mysql.server` reads options from the `[mysqld]` and `[mysql.server]` groups.

An embedded MySQL server usually reads options from the `[server]`, `[embedded]`, and `[xxxxx_SERVER]` groups, where *xxxxx* is the name of the application into which the server is embedded.

`mysqld` accepts many command options. For a brief summary, execute `mysqld --help`. To see the full list, use `mysqld --verbose --help`.

The following list shows some of the most common server options. Additional options are described in other sections:

- Options that affect security: See Section 4.7.3, "Security-Related `mysqld` Options."
- SSL-related options: See Section 4.9.7.5, "SSL Command Options."
- Binary log control options: See Section 4.12.3, "The Binary Log."
- Replication-related options: See Section 5.9, "Replication Startup Options."
- Options specific to particular storage engines: See Section 8.1.1, "`MyISAM` Startup Options," Section 8.5.3, "`BDB` Startup Options," Section 8.2.4, "`InnoDB` Startup Options and System Variables," and Section 9.5.5.1, "MySQL Cluster-Related Command Options for `mysqld`."

You can also set the values of server system variables by using variable names as options, as described later in this section.

- `--help, -?`

  Display a short help message and exit. Use both the `--verbose` and `--help` options to see the full message.

- `--allow-suspicious-udfs`

  This option controls whether user-defined functions that have only an xxx symbol for the main function can be loaded. By default, the option is off and only UDFs that have at least one auxiliary symbol can be loaded; this prevents attempts at loading functions from shared object files other than those containing legitimate UDFs. This option was added in version 5.0.3.

- `--ansi`

  Use standard (ANSI) SQL syntax instead of MySQL syntax. For more precise control over the server SQL mode, use the `--sql-mode` option instead. See Section 1.9.3, "Running MySQL in ANSI Mode," and Section 4.2.5, "The Server SQL Mode."

- `--basedir=path, -b path`

  The path to the MySQL installation directory. All paths are usually resolved relative to this directory.

- `--bind-address=IP`

  The IP address to bind to.

- `--binlog-format={row|statement}`

  Specify whether to use row-based or statement-based replication (statement-based is default). See Section 5.3, "Row-Based Replication." This option was added in MySQL 5.1.5.

- `--binlog-row-event-max-size=N`

  Specify the maximum size of a row-based binary log event, in bytes. Rows are grouped into events smaller than this size if possible. The value should be a multiple of 256. The default is 1024. See Section 5.3, "Row-Based Replication." This option was added in MySQL 5.1.5.

- `--bootstrap`

  This option is used by the `mysql_install_db` script to create the MySQL privilege tables without having to start a full MySQL server.

- `--character-sets-dir=path`

  The directory where character sets are installed. See Section 4.11.1, "The Character Set Used for Data and Sorting."

- `--character-set-client-handshake`

  Don't ignore character set information sent by the client. To ignore client information and use the default server character set, use `--skip-character-set-client-handshake`; this makes MySQL behave like MySQL 4.0.

- `--character-set-filesystem=charset_name`

  The filesystem character set. This option sets the `character_set_filesystem` system variable. It was added in MySQL 5.0.19.

- `--character-set-server=charset_name, -C charset_name`

  Use *charset_name* as the default server character set. See Section 4.11.1, "The Character Set Used for Data and Sorting."

- `--chroot=path`

  Put the `mysqld` server in a closed environment during startup by using the `chroot()` system call. This is a recommended security measure. Note that use of this option somewhat limits `LOAD DATA INFILE` and `SELECT ... INTO OUTFILE`.

- `--collation-server=collation_name`

  Use *collation_name* as the default server collation. See Section 4.11.1, "The Character Set Used for Data and Sorting."

- `--console`

  (Windows only.) Write error log messages to `stderr` and `stdout` even if `--log-error` is specified. `mysqld` does not close the console window if this option is used.

- `--core-file`

  Write a core file if `mysqld` dies. For some systems, you must also specify the `--core-file-size` option to `mysqld_safe`. See Section 4.4.1, "`mysqld_safe`—MySQL Server Startup Script." Note that on some systems, such as Solaris, you do not get a core file if you are also using the `--user` option.

- `--datadir=path, -h path`

  The path to the data directory.

- `--debug[=debug_options], -# [debug_options]`

  If MySQL is configured with `--with-debug`, you can use this option to get a trace file of what `mysqld` is doing. The *debug_options* string often is `'d:t:o,file_name'`. The default is `'d:t:i:o,mysqld.trace'`.

- `--default-character-set=charset_name` (*DEPRECATED*)

  Use *charset_name* as the default character set. This option is deprecated in favor of `--character-set-server`. See Section 4.11.1, "The Character Set Used for Data and Sorting."

- `--default-collation=collation_name`

  Use *collation_name* as the default collation. This option is deprecated in favor of `--collation-server`. See Section 4.11.1, "The Character Set Used for Data and Sorting."

- `--default-storage-engine=type`

  Set the default storage engine (table type) for tables. See Chapter 8, "Storage Engines and Table Types."

- `--default-table-type=type`

This option is a synonym for `--default-storage-engine`.

- `--default-time-zone=timezone`

Set the default server time zone. This option sets the global `time_zone` system variable. If this option is not given, the default time zone is the same as the system time zone (given by the value of the `system_time_zone` system variable).

- `--delay-key-write[= OFF | ON | ALL]`

Specify how to use delayed key writes. Delayed key writing causes key buffers not to be flushed between writes for `MyISAM` tables. `OFF` disables delayed key writes. `ON` enables delayed key writes for those tables that were created with the `DELAY_KEY_WRITE` option. `ALL` delays key writes for all `MyISAM` tables. See Section 6.5.2, "Tuning Server Parameters," and Section 8.1.1, "`MyISAM` Startup Options."

Note: If you set this variable to `ALL`, you should not use `MyISAM` tables from within another program (such as another MySQL server or `myisamchk`) when the tables are in use. Doing so leads to index corruption.

- `--des-key-file=file_name`

Read the default DES keys from this file. These keys are used by the `DES_ENCRYPT()` and `DES_DECRYPT()` functions.

- `--enable-named-pipe`

Enable support for named pipes. This option applies only on Windows NT, 2000, XP, and 2003 systems, and can be used only with the `mysqld-nt` and `mysqld-max-nt` servers that support named-pipe connections.

- `--exit-info[=flags], -T [flags]`

This is a bit mask of different flags that you can use for debugging the `mysqld` server. Do not use this option unless you know *exactly* what it does!

- `--external-locking`

Enable external locking (system locking), which is disabled by default as of MySQL 4.0. Note that if you use this option on a system on which `lockd` does not fully work (such as Linux), it is easy for `mysqld` to deadlock. This option previously was named `--enable-locking`.

Note: If you use this option to enable updates to `MyISAM` tables from many MySQL processes, you must ensure that the following conditions are satisfied:

- You should not use the query cache for queries that use tables that are updated by another process.
- You should not use `--delay-key-write=ALL` or `DELAY_KEY_WRITE=1` on any shared tables.

The easiest way to ensure this is to always use `--external-locking` together with `--delay-key-write=OFF` and `--query-cache-size=0`. (This is not done by default because in many setups it is useful to have a mixture of the preceding options.)

- `--flush`

  Flush (synchronize) all changes to disk after each SQL statement. Normally, MySQL does a write of all changes to disk only after each SQL statement and lets the operating system handle the synchronizing to disk.

- `--init-file=file_name`

  Read SQL statements from this file at startup. Each statement must be on a single line and should not include comments.

- `--innodb-safe-binlog`

  Add consistency guarantees between the content of `InnoDB` tables and the binary log. See Section 4.12.3, "The Binary Log." This option was removed in MySQL 5.0.3, having been made obsolete by the introduction of XA transaction support.

- `--innodb-xxx`

  The `InnoDB` options are listed in Section 8.2.4, "`InnoDB` Startup Options and System Variables."

- `--language=lang_name`, `-L lang_name`

  Return client error messages in the given language. `lang_name` can be given as the language name or as the full pathname to the directory where the language files are installed. See Section 4.11.2, "Setting the Error Message Language."

- `--large-pages`

  Some hardware/operating system architectures support memory pages greater than the default (usually 4KB). The actual implementation of this support depends on the underlying hardware and OS. Applications that perform a lot of memory accesses may obtain performance improvements by using large pages due to reduced Translation Lookaside Buffer (TLB) misses.

  Currently, MySQL supports only the Linux implementation of large pages support (which is called "HugeTLB" in Linux). We have plans to extend this support to FreeBSD, Solaris and possibly other platforms.

  Before large pages can be used on Linux, it is necessary to configure the HugeTLB memory pool. For reference, consult the `hugetlbpage.txt` file in the Linux kernel source.

  This option is disabled by default. It was added in MySQL 5.0.3.

- `--log[=file_name]`, `-l [file_name]`

  Log connections and SQL statements received from clients to this file. See Section 4.12.2, "The General Query Log." If you omit the filename, MySQL uses `host_name.log` as the filename.

- `--log-bin[=base_name]`

  Enable binary logging. The server logs all statements that change data to the binary log, which is used for backup and replication. See Section 4.12.3, "The Binary Log."

The option value, if given, is the basename for the log sequence. The server creates binary log files in sequence by adding a numeric suffix to the basename. It is recommended that you specify a basename. Otherwise, MySQL uses *host_name*-bin as the basename.

- `--log-bin-index[=`*file_name*`]`

The index file for binary log filenames. See Section 4.12.3, "The Binary Log." If you omit the filename, and if you didn't specify one with `--log-bin`, MySQL uses *host_name*-bin.index as the filename.

- `--log-bin-trust-function-creators[={0|1}]`

With no argument or an argument of 1, this option sets the `log_bin_trust_function_creators` system variable to 1. With an argument of 0, this option sets the system variable to 0. `log_bin_trust_function_creators` affects how MySQL enforces restrictions on stored function creation.

This option was added in MySQL 5.0.16.

- `--log-bin-trust-routine-creators[={0|1}]`

This is the old name for `--log-bin-trust-function-creators`. Before MySQL 5.0.16, it also applies to stored procedures, not just stored functions and sets the `log_bin_trust_routine_creators` system variable. As of 5.0.16, this option is deprecated. It is recognized for backward compatibility but its use results in a warning.

This option was added in MySQL 5.0.6.

- `--log-error[=`*file_name*`]`

Log errors and startup messages to this file. See Section 4.12.1, "The Error Log." If you omit the filename, MySQL uses *host_name*.err. If the filename has no extension, the server adds an extension of .err.

- `--log-isam[=`*file_name*`]`

Log all `MyISAM` changes to this file (used only when debugging `MyISAM`).

- `--log-long-format` (*DEPRECATED*)

Log extra information to the update log, binary update log, and slow query log, if they have been activated. For example, the username and timestamp are logged for all queries. This option is deprecated, as it now represents the default logging behavior. (See the description for `--log-short-format`.) The `--log-queries-not-using-indexes` option is available for the purpose of logging queries that do not use indexes to the slow query log.

- `--log-queries-not-using-indexes`

If you are using this option with `--log-slow-queries`, queries that do not use indexes are logged to the slow query log. See Section 4.12.4, "The Slow Query Log."

- `--log-short-format`

Log less information to the update log, binary update log, and slow query log, if they have been activated. For example, the username and timestamp are not logged for queries.

- `--log-slow-admin-statements`

Log slow administrative statements such as `OPTIMIZE TABLE`, `ANALYZE TABLE`, and `ALTER TABLE` to the slow query log.

- `--log-slow-queries[=file_name]`

Log all queries that have taken more than `long_query_time` seconds to execute to this file. See Section 4.12.4, "The Slow Query Log." See the descriptions of the `--log-long-format` and `--log-short-format` options for details.

- `--log-warnings[=level]`, `-W [level]`

Print out warnings such as `Aborted connection...` to the error log. Enabling this option is recommended, for example, if you use replication (you get more information about what is happening, such as messages about network failures and reconnections). This option is enabled (1) by default, and the default `level` value if omitted is 1. To disable this option, use `--log-warnings=0`. Aborted connections are not logged to the error log unless the value is greater than 1.

- `--low-priority-updates`

Give table-modifying operations (`INSERT`, `REPLACE`, `DELETE`, `UPDATE`) lower priority than selects. This can also be done via `{INSERT | REPLACE | DELETE | UPDATE} LOW_PRIORITY` ... to lower the priority of only one query, or by `SET LOW_PRIORITY_UPDATES=1` to change the priority in one thread. See Section 6.3.2, "Table Locking Issues."

- `--memlock`

Lock the `mysqld` process in memory. This works on systems such as Solaris that support the `mlockall()` system call. This might help if you have a problem where the operating system is causing `mysqld` to swap on disk. Note that use of this option requires that you run the server as `root`, which is normally not a good idea for security reasons. See Section 4.7.5, "How to Run MySQL As a Normal User."

- `--myisam-recover[=option[,option]...]]`

Set the `MyISAM` storage engine recovery mode. The option value is any combination of the values of `DEFAULT`, `BACKUP`, `FORCE`, or `QUICK`. If you specify multiple values, separate them by commas. You can also use a value of `""` to disable this option. If this option is used, each time `mysqld` opens a `MyISAM` table, it checks whether the table is marked as crashed or wasn't closed properly. (The last option works only if you are running with external locking disabled.) If this is the case, `mysqld` runs a check on the table. If the table was corrupted, `mysqld` attempts to repair it.

The following options affect how the repair works:

Option	Description
DEFAULT	The same as not giving any option to `--myisam-recover`.
BACKUP	If the data file was changed during recovery, save a backup of the `tbl_name`.MYD file as `tbl_name-datetime`.BAK.
FORCE	Run recovery even if we would lose more than one row from the .MYD file.
QUICK	Don't check the rows in the table if there aren't any delete blocks.

Before the server automatically repairs a table, it writes a note about the repair to the error log. If you want to be able to recover from most problems without user intervention, you should use the options `BACKUP,FORCE`. This forces a repair of a table even if some rows would be deleted, but it keeps the old data file as a backup so that you can later examine what happened.

See Section 8.1.1, "`MyISAM` Startup Options."

- `--ndb-connectstring=connect_string`

  When using the `NDB` storage engine, it is possible to point out the management server that distributes the cluster configuration by setting the connect string option. See Section 9.4.4.2, "The MySQL Cluster `connectstring`," for syntax.

- `--ndbcluster`

  If the binary includes support for the `NDB Cluster` storage engine, this option enables the engine, which is disabled by default. See Chapter 9, "MySQL Cluster."

- `--old-passwords`

  Force the server to generate short (pre-4.1) password hashes for new passwords. This is useful for compatibility when the server must support older client programs. See Section 4.8.9, "Password Hashing As of MySQL 4.1."

- `--one-thread`

  Only use one thread (for debugging under Linux). This option is available only if the server is built with debugging enabled.

- `--open-files-limit=count`

  Change the number of file descriptors available to `mysqld`. If this option is not set or is set to 0, `mysqld` uses the value to reserve file descriptors with `setrlimit()`. If the value is 0, `mysqld` reserves `max_connections`×5 or `max_connections` + `table_open_cache`×2 files (whichever is larger). You should try increasing this value if `mysqld` gives you the error `Too many open files`.

- `--pid-file=path`

  The pathname of the process ID file. This file is used by other programs such as `mysqld_safe` to determine the server's process ID.

- `--port=port_num`, `-P port_num`

  The port number to use when listening for TCP/IP connections. The port number must be 1024 or higher unless the server is started by the `root` system user.

- `--port-open-timeout=num`

  On some systems, when the server is stopped, the TCP/IP port might not become available immediately. If the server is restarted quickly afterward, its attempt to reopen the port can fail. This option indicates how many seconds the server should wait for the TCP/IP port to become free if it cannot be opened. The default is not to wait. This option was added in MySQL 5.0.19.

- `--safe-mode`

  Skip some optimization stages.

- `--safe-show-database` (*DEPRECATED*)

  See Section 4.8.3, "Privileges Provided by MySQL."

- `--safe-user-create`

  If this option is enabled, a user cannot create new MySQL users by using the `GRANT` statement, if the user doesn't have the `INSERT` privilege for the `mysql.user` table or any column in the table.

- `--secure-auth`

  Disallow authentication by clients that attempt to use accounts that have old (pre-4.1) passwords.

- `--shared-memory`

  Enable shared-memory connections by local clients. This option is available only on Windows.

- `--shared-memory-base-name=name`

  The name of shared memory to use for shared-memory connections. This option is available only on Windows. The default name is `MYSQL`. The name is case sensitive.

- `--skip-bdb`

  Disable the `BDB` storage engine. This saves memory and might speed up some operations. Do not use this option if you require `BDB` tables.

- `--skip-concurrent-insert`

  Turn off the ability to select and insert at the same time on `MyISAM` tables. (This is to be used only if you think you have found a bug in this feature.)

- `--skip-external-locking`

  Do not use external locking (system locking). With external locking disabled, you must shut down the server to use `myisamchk`. (See Section 1.4.3, "MySQL Stability.") To avoid this requirement, use the `CHECK TABLE` and `REPAIR TABLE` statements to check and repair `MyISAM` tables.

  External locking has been disabled by default since MySQL 4.0.

- `--skip-grant-tables`

  This option causes the server not to use the privilege system at all, which gives anyone with access to the server *unrestricted access to all databases*. You can cause a running server to start using the grant tables again by executing `mysqladmin flush-privileges` or `mysqladmin reload` command from a system shell, or by issuing a MySQL `FLUSH PRIVILEGES` statement after connecting to the server. This option also suppresses loading of user-defined functions (UDFs).

- `--skip-host-cache`

  Do not use the internal hostname cache for faster name-to-IP resolution. Instead, query the DNS server every time a client connects. See Section 6.5.6, "How MySQL Uses DNS."

- `--skip-innodb`

  Disable the InnoDB storage engine. This saves memory and disk space and might speed up some operations. Do not use this option if you require InnoDB tables.

- `--skip-name-resolve`

  Do not resolve hostnames when checking client connections. Use only IP numbers. If you use this option, all Host column values in the grant tables must be IP numbers or localhost. See Section 6.5.6, "How MySQL Uses DNS."

- `--skip-ndbcluster`

  Disable the NDB Cluster storage engine. This is the default for binaries that were built with NDB Cluster storage engine support; the server allocates memory and other resources for this storage engine only if the `--ndbcluster` option is given explicitly. See Section 9.4.3, "Quick Test Setup of MySQL Cluster," for an example of usage.

- `--skip-networking`

  Don't listen for TCP/IP connections at all. All interaction with mysqld must be made via named pipes or shared memory (on Windows) or Unix socket files (on Unix). This option is highly recommended for systems where only local clients are allowed. See Section 6.5.6, "How MySQL Uses DNS."

- `--standalone`

  Available on Windows NT–based systems only; instructs the MySQL server not to run as a service.

- `--symbolic-links, --skip-symbolic-links`

  Enable or disable symbolic link support. This option has different effects on Windows and Unix:

  - On Windows, enabling symbolic links allows you to establish a symbolic link to a database directory by creating a *db_name*.sym file that contains the path to the real directory. See Section 6.6.1.3, "Using Symbolic Links for Databases on Windows."

  - On Unix, enabling symbolic links means that you can link a MyISAM index file or data file to another directory with the INDEX DIRECTORY or DATA DIRECTORY options of the CREATE TABLE statement. If you delete or rename the table, the files that its symbolic links point to also are deleted or renamed. See Section 6.6.1.2, "Using Symbolic Links for Tables on Unix."

- `--skip-safemalloc`

  If MySQL is configured with `--with-debug=full`, all MySQL programs check for memory overruns during each memory allocation and memory freeing operation. This checking is very slow, so for the server you can avoid it when you don't need it by using the `--skip-safemalloc` option.

- `--skip-show-database`

With this option, the SHOW DATABASES statement is allowed only to users who have the SHOW DATABASES privilege, and the statement displays all database names. Without this option, SHOW DATABASES is allowed to all users, but displays each database name only if the user has the SHOW DATABASES privilege or some privilege for the database. Note that *any* global privilege is considered a privilege for the database.

- `--skip-stack-trace`

Don't write stack traces. This option is useful when you are running mysqld under a debugger. On some systems, you also must use this option to get a core file.

- `--skip-thread-priority`

Disable using thread priorities for faster response time.

- `--socket=path`

On Unix, this option specifies the Unix socket file to use when listening for local connections. The default value is /tmp/mysql.sock. On Windows, the option specifies the pipe name to use when listening for local connections that use a named pipe. The default value is MySQL (not case sensitive).

- `--sql-mode=value[,value[,value...]]`

Set the SQL mode. See Section 4.2.5, "The Server SQL Mode."

- `--temp-pool`

This option causes most temporary files created by the server to use a small set of names, rather than a unique name for each new file. This works around a problem in the Linux kernel dealing with creating many new files with different names. With the old behavior, Linux seems to "leak" memory, because it is being allocated to the directory entry cache rather than to the disk cache.

- `--transaction-isolation=level`

Sets the default transaction isolation level. The level value can be READ-UNCOMMITTED, READ-COMMITTED, REPEATABLE-READ, or SERIALIZABLE.

- `--tmpdir=path, -t path`

The path of the directory to use for creating temporary files. It might be useful if your default /tmp directory resides on a partition that is too small to hold temporary tables. This option accepts several paths that are used in round-robin fashion. Paths should be separated by colon characters (':') on Unix and semicolon characters (';') on Windows, NetWare, and OS/2. If the MySQL server is acting as a replication slave, you should not set --tmpdir to point to a directory on a memory-based filesystem or to a directory that is cleared when the server host restarts. A replication slave needs some of its temporary files to survive a machine restart so that it can replicate temporary tables or LOAD DATA INFILE operations. If files in the temporary file directory are lost when the server restarts, replication fails.

- --user={*user_name* | *user_id*}, -u {*user_name* | *user_id*}

  Run the mysqld server as the user having the name *user_name* or the numeric user ID *user_id*. ("User" in this context refers to a system login account, not a MySQL user listed in the grant tables.)

  This option is *mandatory* when starting mysqld as root. The server changes its user ID during its startup sequence, causing it to run as that particular user rather than as root. See Section 4.7.1, "General Security Guidelines."

  To avoid a possible security hole where a user adds a --user=root option to a my.cnf file (thus causing the server to run as root), mysqld uses only the first --user option specified and produces a warning if there are multiple --user options. Options in /etc/my.cnf and $MYSQL_HOME/my.cnf are processed before command-line options, so it is recommended that you put a --user option in /etc/my.cnf and specify a value other than root. The option in /etc/my.cnf is found before any other --user options, which ensures that the server runs as a user other than root, and that a warning results if any other --user option is found.

- --version, -V

  Display version information and exit.

You can assign a value to a server system variable by using an option of the form --*var_name*=*value*. For example, --key_buffer_size=32M sets the key_buffer_size variable to a value of 32MB.

Note that when you assign a value to a variable, MySQL might automatically correct the value to stay within a given range, or adjust the value to the closest allowable value if only certain values are allowed.

If you want to restrict the maximum value to which a variable can be set at runtime with SET, you can define this by using the --maximum-*var_name*=*value* command-line option.

It is also possible to set variables by using --set-variable=*var_name*=*value* or -O *var_name*=*value* syntax. *This syntax is deprecated.*

You can change the values of most system variables for a running server with the SET statement.

Section 4.2.2, "Server System Variables," provides a full description for all variables, and additional information for setting them at server startup and runtime. Section 6.5.2, "Tuning Server Parameters," includes information on optimizing the server by tuning system variables.

4.2.2 Server System Variables

The mysql server maintains many system variables that indicate how it is configured. Each system variable has a default value. System variables can be set at server startup using options on the command line or in an option file. Most of them can be changed dynamically while the server is running by means of the SET statement, which enables you to modify operation of the server without having to stop and restart it. You can refer to system variable values in expressions.

There are several ways to see the names and values of system variables:

- To see the values that a server will use based on its compiled-in defaults and any option files that it reads, use this command:

  ```
  mysqld --verbose --help
  ```

- To see the values that a server will use based on its compiled-in defaults, ignoring the settings in any option files, use this command:

  ```
  mysqld --no-defaults --verbose --help
  ```

- To see the current values used by a running server, use the SHOW VARIABLES statement.

This section provides a description of each system variable. Variables with no version indicated are present in all MySQL 5.0 releases. For historical information concerning their implementation, please see "MySQL 3.23, 4.0, 4.1 Reference Manual."

For additional system variable information, see these sections:

- Section 4.2.3, "Using System Variables," discusses the syntax for setting and displaying system variable values.
- Section 4.2.3.2, "Dynamic System Variables," lists the variables that can be set at run-time.
- Information on tuning system variables can be found in Section 6.5.2, "Tuning Server Parameters."
- Section 8.2.4, "InnoDB Startup Options and System Variables," lists InnoDB system variables.

Note: Some of the following variable descriptions refer to "enabling" or "disabling" a variable. These variables can be enabled with the SET statement by setting them to ON or 1, or disabled by setting them to OFF or 0. However, to set such a variable on the command line or in an option file, you must set it to 1 or 0; setting it to ON or OFF will not work. For example, on the command line, --delay_key_write=1 works but --delay_key_write=ON does not.

Values for buffer sizes, lengths, and stack sizes are given in bytes unless otherwise specified.

- auto_increment_increment

  auto_increment_increment and auto_increment_offset are intended for use with master-to-master replication, and can be used to control the operation of AUTO_INCREMENT columns. Both variables can be set globally or locally, and each can assume an integer value between 1 and 65,535 inclusive. Setting the value of either of these two variables to 0 causes its value to be set to 1 instead. Attempting to set the value of either of these two variables to an integer greater than 65,535 or less than 0 causes its value to be set to 65,535 instead. Attempting to set the value of auto_increment_increment or auto_increment_offset to a non-integer value gives rise to an error, and the actual value of the variable remains unchanged.

These two variables affect AUTO_INCREMENT column behavior as follows:

- auto_increment_increment controls the interval between successive column values. For example:

```
mysql> SHOW VARIABLES LIKE 'auto_inc%';
+--------------------------+-------+
| Variable_name            | Value |
+--------------------------+-------+
| auto_increment_increment | 1     |
| auto_increment_offset    | 1     |
+--------------------------+-------+
2 rows in set (0.00 sec)

mysql> CREATE TABLE autoincl
    -> (col INT NOT NULL AUTO_INCREMENT PRIMARY KEY);
  Query OK, 0 rows affected (0.04 sec)

mysql> SET @@auto_increment_increment=10;
Query OK, 0 rows affected (0.00 sec)

mysql> SHOW VARIABLES LIKE 'auto_inc%';
+--------------------------+-------+
| Variable_name            | Value |
+--------------------------+-------+
| auto_increment_increment | 10    |
| auto_increment_offset    | 1     |
+--------------------------+-------+
2 rows in set (0.01 sec)

mysql> INSERT INTO autoincl VALUES (NULL), (NULL), (NULL), (NULL);
Query OK, 4 rows affected (0.00 sec)
Records: 4  Duplicates: 0  Warnings: 0

mysql> SELECT col FROM autoincl;
+-----+
| col |
+-----+
|   1 |
|  11 |
|  21 |
|  31 |
+-----+
4 rows in set (0.00 sec)
```

(Note how SHOW VARIABLES is used here to obtain the current values for these variables.)

- auto_increment_offset determines the starting point for the AUTO_INCREMENT column value. Consider the following, assuming that these statements are executed during the same session as the example given in the description for auto_increment_increment:

```
mysql> SET @@auto_increment_offset=5;
Query OK, 0 rows affected (0.00 sec)

mysql> SHOW VARIABLES LIKE 'auto_inc%';
+-------------------------+-------+
| Variable_name           | Value |
+-------------------------+-------+
| auto_increment_increment | 10    |
| auto_increment_offset   | 5     |
+-------------------------+-------+
2 rows in set (0.00 sec)

mysql> CREATE TABLE autoinc2
    -> (col INT NOT NULL AUTO_INCREMENT PRIMARY KEY);
Query OK, 0 rows affected (0.06 sec)

mysql> INSERT INTO autoinc2 VALUES (NULL), (NULL), (NULL), (NULL);
Query OK, 4 rows affected (0.00 sec)
Records: 4  Duplicates: 0  Warnings: 0

mysql> SELECT col FROM autoinc2;
+-----+
| col |
+-----+
|   5 |
|  15 |
|  25 |
|  35 |
+-----+
4 rows in set (0.02 sec)
```

If the value of auto_increment_offset is greater than that of auto_increment_increment, the value of auto_increment_offset is ignored.

Should one or both of these variables be changed and then new rows inserted into a table containing an AUTO_INCREMENT column, the results may seem counterintuitive because the series of AUTO_INCREMENT values is calculated without regard to any values already present in the column, and the next value inserted is the least value in the series that is greater than the maximum existing value in the AUTO_INCREMENT column. In other words, the series is calculated like so:

```
auto_increment_offset + N × auto_increment_increment
```

where *N* is a positive integer value in the series [1, 2, 3, ...]. For example:

```
mysql> SHOW VARIABLES LIKE 'auto_inc%';
+--------------------------+-------+
| Variable_name            | Value |
+--------------------------+-------+
| auto_increment_increment | 10    |
| auto_increment_offset    | 5     |
+--------------------------+-------+
2 rows in set (0.00 sec)

mysql> SELECT col FROM autoincl;
+-----+
| col |
+-----+
|   1 |
|  11 |
|  21 |
|  31 |
+-----+
4 rows in set (0.00 sec)

mysql> INSERT INTO autoincl VALUES (NULL), (NULL), (NULL), (NULL);
Query OK, 4 rows affected (0.00 sec)
Records: 4  Duplicates: 0  Warnings: 0

mysql> SELECT col FROM autoincl;
+-----+
| col |
+-----+
|   1 |
|  11 |
|  21 |
|  31 |
|  35 |
|  45 |
|  55 |
|  65 |
+-----+
8 rows in set (0.00 sec)
```

The values shown for auto_increment_increment and auto_increment_offset generate the series $5 + N \times 10$, that is, [5, 15, 25, 35, 45, ...]. The greatest value present in the col column prior to the INSERT is 31, and the next available value in the AUTO_INCREMENT series is 35, so the inserted values for col begin at that point and the results are as shown for the SELECT query.

It is important to remember that it is not possible to confine the effects of these two variables to a single table, and thus they do not take the place of the sequences offered by some other database management systems; these variables control the behavior of all AUTO_INCREMENT columns in *all* tables on the MySQL server. If one of these variables is set globally, its effects persist until the global value is changed or overridden by setting them locally, or until mysqld is restarted. If set locally, the new value affects AUTO_INCREMENT columns for all tables into which new rows are inserted by the current user for the duration of the session, unless the values are changed during that session.

The auto_increment_increment variable was added in MySQL 5.0.2. Its default value is 1. See Section 5.15, "Auto-Increment in Multiple-Master Replication."

- auto_increment_offset

This variable was introduced in MySQL 5.0.2. Its default value is 1. For particulars, see the description for auto_increment_increment.

- back_log

The number of outstanding connection requests MySQL can have. This comes into play when the main MySQL thread gets very many connection requests in a very short time. It then takes some time (although very little) for the main thread to check the connection and start a new thread. The back_log value indicates how many requests can be stacked during this short time before MySQL momentarily stops answering new requests. You need to increase this only if you expect a large number of connections in a short period of time.

In other words, this value is the size of the listen queue for incoming TCP/IP connections. Your operating system has its own limit on the size of this queue. The manual page for the Unix listen() system call should have more details. Check your OS documentation for the maximum value for this variable. back_log cannot be set higher than your operating system limit.

- basedir

The MySQL installation base directory. This variable can be set with the --basedir option.

- bdb_cache_size

The size of the buffer that is allocated for caching indexes and rows for BDB tables. If you don't use BDB tables, you should start mysqld with --skip-bdb to not allocate memory for this cache.

- bdb_home

The base directory for BDB tables. This should be assigned the same value as the datadir variable.

- bdb_log_buffer_size

The size of the buffer that is allocated for caching indexes and rows for BDB tables. If you don't use BDB tables, you should set this to 0 or start mysqld with --skip-bdb to not allocate memory for this cache.

- bdb_logdir

  The directory where the BDB storage engine writes its log files. This variable can be set with the --bdb-logdir option.

- bdb_max_lock

  The maximum number of locks that can be active for a BDB table (10,000 by default). You should increase this value if errors such as the following occur when you perform long transactions or when mysqld has to examine many rows to calculate a query:

  ```
  bdb: Lock table is out of available locks
  Got error 12 from ...
  ```

- bdb_shared_data

  This is ON if you are using --bdb-shared-data to start Berkeley DB in multi-process mode. (Do not use DB_PRIVATE when initializing Berkeley DB.)

- bdb_tmpdir

  The BDB temporary file directory.

- binlog_cache_size

  The size of the cache to hold the SQL statements for the binary log during a transaction. A binary log cache is allocated for each client if the server supports any transactional storage engines and if the server has the binary log enabled (--log-bin option). If you often use large, multiple-statement transactions, you can increase this cache size to get more performance. The Binlog_cache_use and Binlog_cache_disk_use status variables can be useful for tuning the size of this variable. See Section 4.12.3, "The Binary Log."

- binlog_format

  The binary logging format, either STATEMENT or ROW. binlog_format is set by the --binlog-format option. See Section 5.3, "Row-Based Replication." This variable was added in MySQL 5.1.5.

- bulk_insert_buffer_size

  MyISAM uses a special tree-like cache to make bulk inserts faster for INSERT ... SELECT, INSERT ... VALUES (...), (...), ..., and LOAD DATA INFILE when adding data to non-empty tables. This variable limits the size of the cache tree in bytes per thread. Setting it to 0 disables this optimization. The default value is 8MB.

- character_set_client

  The character set for statements that arrive from the client.

- character_set_connection

  The character set used for literals that do not have a character set introducer and for number-to-string conversion.

- `character_set_database`

  The character set used by the default database. The server sets this variable whenever the default database changes. If there is no default database, the variable has the same value as `character_set_server`.

- `character_set_filesystem`

  The filesystem character set. This variable is used to interpret string literals that refer to filenames, such as in the `LOAD DATA INFILE` and `SELECT ... INTO OUTFILE` statements and the `LOAD_FILE()` function. Such filenames are converted from `character_set_client` to `character_set_filesystem` before the file opening attempt occurs. The default value is `binary`, which means that no conversion occurs. For systems on which multi-byte filenames are allowed, a different value may be more appropriate. For example, if the system represents filenames using UTF-8, set `character_set_filesytem` to `'utf8'`. This variable was added in MySQL 5.0.19.

- `character_set_results`

  The character set used for returning query results to the client.

- `character_set_server`

  The server's default character set.

- `character_set_system`

  The character set used by the server for storing identifiers. The value is always `utf8`.

- `character_sets_dir`

  The directory where character sets are installed.

- `collation_connection`

  The collation of the connection character set.

- `collation_database`

  The collation used by the default database. The server sets this variable whenever the default database changes. If there is no default database, the variable has the same value as `collation_server`.

- `collation_server`

  The server's default collation.

- `completion_type`

  The transaction completion type:

  - If the value is 0 (the default), `COMMIT` and `ROLLBACK` are unaffected.
  - If the value is 1, `COMMIT` and `ROLLBACK` are equivalent to `COMMIT AND CHAIN` and `ROLLBACK AND CHAIN`, respectively. (A new transaction starts immediately with the same isolation level as the just-terminated transaction.)
  - If the value is 2, `COMMIT` and `ROLLBACK` are equivalent to `COMMIT RELEASE` and `ROLLBACK RELEASE`, respectively. (The server disconnects after terminating the transaction.)

  This variable was added in MySQL 5.0.3

- concurrent_insert

  If ON (the default), MySQL allows INSERT and SELECT statements to run concurrently for MyISAM tables that have no free blocks in the middle. You can turn this option off by starting mysqld with --safe or --skip-new.

  In MySQL 5.0.6, this variable was changed to take three integer values:

Value	Description
0	Off.
1	(Default) Enables concurrent insert for MyISAM tables that don't have holes.
2	Enables concurrent inserts for all MyISAM tables. If table has a hole and is in use by another thread the new row will be inserted at end of table. If table is not in use, MySQL does a normal read lock and inserts the new row into the hole.

  See also Section 6.3.3, "Concurrent Inserts."

- connect_timeout

  The number of seconds that the mysqld server waits for a connect packet before responding with Bad handshake.

- datadir

  The MySQL data directory. This variable can be set with the --datadir option.

- date_format

  This variable is not implemented.

- datetime_format

  This variable is not implemented.

- default_week_format

  The default mode value to use for the WEEK() function.

- delay_key_write

  This option applies only to MyISAM tables. It can have one of the following values to affect handling of the DELAY_KEY_WRITE table option that can be used in CREATE TABLE statements.

Option	Description
OFF	DELAY_KEY_WRITE is ignored.
ON	MySQL honors any DELAY_KEY_WRITE option specified in CREATE TABLE statements. This is the default value.
ALL	All new opened tables are treated as if they were created with the DELAY_KEY_WRITE option enabled.

  If DELAY_KEY_WRITE is enabled for a table, the key buffer is not flushed for the table on every index update, but only when the table is closed. This speeds up writes on keys a lot, but if you use this feature, you should add automatic checking of all MyISAM tables by starting the server with the --myisam-recover option (for example, --myisam-recover=BACKUP,FORCE). See Section 4.2.1, "mysqld Command Options," and Section 8.1.1, "MyISAM Startup Options."

Note that enabling external locking with --external-locking offers no protection against index corruption for tables that use delayed key writes.

- delayed_insert_limit

  After inserting delayed_insert_limit delayed rows, the INSERT DELAYED handler thread checks whether there are any SELECT statements pending. If so, it allows them to execute before continuing to insert delayed rows.

- delayed_insert_timeout

  How many seconds an INSERT DELAYED handler thread should wait for INSERT statements before terminating.

- delayed_queue_size

  This is a per-table limit on the number of rows to queue when handling INSERT DELAYED statements. If the queue becomes full, any client that issues an INSERT DELAYED statement waits until there is room in the queue again.

- div_precision_increment

  This variable indicates the number of digits of precision by which to increase the result of division operations performed with the / operator. The default value is 4. The minimum and maximum values are 0 and 30, respectively. The following example illustrates the effect of increasing the default value.

  ```
  mysql> SELECT 1/7;
  +--------+
  | 1/7    |
  +--------+
  | 0.1429 |
  +--------+
  mysql> SET div_precision_increment = 12;
  mysql> SELECT 1/7;
  +----------------+
  | 1/7            |
  +----------------+
  | 0.142857142857 |
  +----------------+
  ```

  This variable was added in MySQL 5.0.6.

- engine_condition_pushdown

  This variable applies to NDB. By default it is 0 (OFF): If you execute a query such as SELECT * FROM t WHERE mycol = 42, where mycol is a non-indexed column, the query is executed as a full table scan on every NDB node. Each node sends every row to the MySQL server, which applies the WHERE condition. If engine_condition_pushdown is set to 1 (ON), the condition is "pushed down" to the storage engine and sent to the NDB nodes. Each node uses the condition to perform the scan, and sends back to the MySQL server only the rows that match the condition.

This variable was added in MySQL 5.0.3. Before that, the default NDB behavior is the same as for a value of OFF.

- expire_logs_days

The number of days for automatic binary log removal. The default is 0, which means "no automatic removal." Possible removals happen at startup and at binary log rotation.

- flush

If ON, the server flushes (synchronizes) all changes to disk after each SQL statement. Normally, MySQL does a write of all changes to disk only after each SQL statement and lets the operating system handle the synchronizing to disk. This variable is set to ON if you start mysqld with the --flush option.

- flush_time

If this is set to a non-zero value, all tables are closed every flush_time seconds to free up resources and synchronize unflushed data to disk. We recommend that this option be used only on Windows 9x or Me, or on systems with minimal resources.

- ft_boolean_syntax

The list of operators supported by boolean full-text searches performed using IN BOOLEAN MODE.

The default variable value is '+ -><()~*:""&| '. The rules for changing the value are as follows:

- Operator function is determined by position within the string.
- The replacement value must be 14 characters.
- Each character must be an ASCII non-alphanumeric character.
- Either the first or second character must be a space.
- No duplicates are allowed except the phrase quoting operators in positions 11 and 12. These two characters are not required to be the same, but they are the only two that may be.
- Positions 10, 13, and 14 (which by default are set to ':', '&', and '|') are reserved for future extensions.

- ft_max_word_len

The maximum length of the word to be included in a FULLTEXT index.

Note: FULLTEXT indexes must be rebuilt after changing this variable. Use REPAIR TABLE *tbl_name* QUICK.

- ft_min_word_len

The minimum length of the word to be included in a FULLTEXT index.

Note: FULLTEXT indexes must be rebuilt after changing this variable. Use REPAIR TABLE *tbl_name* QUICK.

- ft_query_expansion_limit

The number of top matches to use for full-text searches performed using WITH QUERY EXPANSION.

- ft_stopword_file

The file from which to read the list of stopwords for full-text searches. All the words from the file are used; comments are *not* honored. By default, a built-in list of stopwords is used (as defined in the myisam/ft_static.c file). Setting this variable to the empty string (' ') disables stopword filtering.

Note: FULLTEXT indexes must be rebuilt after changing this variable or the contents of the stopword file. Use REPAIR TABLE *tbl_name* QUICK.

- group_concat_max_len

The maximum allowed result length for the GROUP_CONCAT() function. The default is 1024.

- have_archive

YES if mysqld supports ARCHIVE tables, NO if not.

- have_bdb

YES if mysqld supports BDB tables. DISABLED if --skip-bdb is used.

- have_blackhole_engine

YES if mysqld supports BLACKHOLE tables, NO if not.

- have_compress

YES if the zlib compression library is available to the server, NO if not. If not, the COMPRESS() and UNCOMPRESS() functions cannot be used.

- have_crypt

YES if the crypt() system call is available to the server, NO if not. If not, the ENCRYPT() function cannot be used.

- have_csv

YES if mysqld supports ARCHIVE tables, NO if not.

- have_example_engine

YES if mysqld supports EXAMPLE tables, NO if not.

- have_federated_engine

YES if mysqld supports FEDERATED tables, NO if not. This variable was added in MySQL 5.0.3.

- have_geometry

YES if the server supports spatial data types, NO if not.

- `have_innodb`

  YES if `mysqld` supports InnoDB tables. DISABLED if `--skip-innodb` is used.

- `have_isam`

  In MySQL 5.0, this variable appears only for reasons of backward compatibility. It is always NO because ISAM tables are no longer supported.

- `have_ndbcluster`

  YES if `mysqld` supports `NDB Cluster` tables. DISABLED if `--skip-ndbcluster` is used.

- `have_openssl`

  YES if `mysqld` supports SSL connections, NO if not.

- `have_query_cache`

  YES if `mysqld` supports the query cache, NO if not.

- `have_raid`

  In MySQL 5.0, this variable appears only for reasons of backward compatibility. It is always NO because RAID tables are no longer supported.

- `have_row_based_replication`

  YES if the server can perform replication using row-based binary logging. If the value is NO, the server can use only statement-based logging. See Section 5.3, "Row-Based Replication." This variable was added in MySQL 5.1.5.

- `have_rtree_keys`

  YES if RTREE indexes are available, NO if not. (These are used for spatial indexes in MyISAM tables.)

- `have_symlink`

  YES if symbolic link support is enabled, NO if not. This is required on Unix for support of the `DATA DIRECTORY` and `INDEX DIRECTORY` table options, and on Windows for support of data directory symlinks.

- `init_connect`

  A string to be executed by the server for each client that connects. The string consists of one or more SQL statements. To specify multiple statements, separate them by semicolon characters. For example, each client begins by default with autocommit mode enabled. There is no global system variable to specify that autocommit should be disabled by default, but `init_connect` can be used to achieve the same effect:

  ```
  SET GLOBAL init_connect='SET AUTOCOMMIT=0';
  ```

  This variable can also be set on the command line or in an option file. To set the variable as just shown using an option file, include these lines:

  ```
  [mysqld]
  init_connect='SET AUTOCOMMIT=0'
  ```

Note that the content of init_connect is not executed for users that have the SUPER privilege. This is done so that an erroneous value for init_connect does not prevent all clients from connecting. For example, the value might contain a statement that has a syntax error, thus causing client connections to fail. Not executing init_connect for users that have the SUPER privilege enables them to open a connection and fix the init_connect value.

- init_file

The name of the file specified with the --init-file option when you start the server. This should be a file containing SQL statements that you want the server to execute when it starts. Each statement must be on a single line and should not include comments.

- init_slave

This variable is similar to init_connect, but is a string to be executed by a slave server each time the SQL thread starts. The format of the string is the same as for the init_connect variable.

- innodb_*xxx*

InnoDB system variables are listed in Section 8.2.4, "InnoDB Startup Options and System Variables."

- interactive_timeout

The number of seconds the server waits for activity on an interactive connection before closing it. An interactive client is defined as a client that uses the CLIENT_INTERACTIVE option to mysql_real_connect(). See also wait_timeout.

- join_buffer_size

The size of the buffer that is used for joins that do not use indexes and thus perform full table scans. Normally, the best way to get fast joins is to add indexes. Increase the value of join_buffer_size to get a faster full join when adding indexes is not possible. One join buffer is allocated for each full join between two tables. For a complex join between several tables for which indexes are not used, multiple join buffers might be necessary.

- key_buffer_size

Index blocks for MyISAM tables are buffered and are shared by all threads. key_buffer_size is the size of the buffer used for index blocks. The key buffer is also known as the key cache.

The maximum allowable setting for key_buffer_size is 4GB. The effective maximum size might be less, depending on your available physical RAM and per-process RAM limits imposed by your operating system or hardware platform.

Increase the value to get better index handling (for all reads and multiple writes) to as much as you can afford. Using a value that is 25% of total memory on a machine that mainly runs MySQL is quite common. However, if you make the value too large (for example, more than 50% of your total memory) your system might start to page and become extremely slow. MySQL relies on the operating system to perform filesystem caching for data reads, so you must leave some room for the filesystem cache. Consider also the memory requirements of other storage engines.

For even more speed when writing many rows at the same time, use LOCK TABLES. See Section 6.2.16, "Speed of INSERT Statements."

You can check the performance of the key buffer by issuing a SHOW STATUS statement and examining the Key_read_requests, Key_reads, Key_write_requests, and Key_writes status variables. The Key_reads/Key_read_requests ratio should normally be less than 0.01. The Key_writes/Key_write_requests ratio is usually near 1 if you are using mostly updates and deletes, but might be much smaller if you tend to do updates that affect many rows at the same time or if you are using the DELAY_KEY_WRITE table option.

The fraction of the key buffer in use can be determined using key_buffer_size in conjunction with the Key_blocks_unused status variable and the buffer block size, which is available from the key_cache_block_size system variable:

```
1 - ((Key_blocks_unused × key_cache_block_size) / key_buffer_size)
```

This value is an approximation because some space in the key buffer may be allocated internally for administrative structures.

It is possible to create multiple MyISAM key caches. The size limit of 4GB applies to each cache individually, not as a group. See Section 6.4.6, "The MyISAM Key Cache."

- key_cache_age_threshold

This value controls the demotion of buffers from the hot sub-chain of a key cache to the warm sub-chain. Lower values cause demotion to happen more quickly. The minimum value is 100. The default value is 300. See Section 6.4.6, "The MyISAM Key Cache."

- key_cache_block_size

The size in bytes of blocks in the key cache. The default value is 1024. See Section 6.4.6, "The MyISAM Key Cache."

- key_cache_division_limit

The division point between the hot and warm sub-chains of the key cache buffer chain. The value is the percentage of the buffer chain to use for the warm sub-chain. Allowable values range from 1 to 100. The default value is 100. See Section 6.4.6, "The MyISAM Key Cache."

- language

The language used for error messages.

- large_file_support

Whether mysqld was compiled with options for large file support.

- `large_pages`

  Whether large page support is enabled. This variable was added in MySQL 5.0.3.

- `license`

  The type of license the server has.

- `local_infile`

  Whether LOCAL is supported for LOAD DATA INFILE statements. See Section 4.7.4, "Security Issues with LOAD DATA LOCAL."

- `locked_in_memory`

  Whether mysqld was locked in memory with --memlock.

- `log`

  Whether logging of all statements to the general query log is enabled. See Section 4.12.2, "The General Query Log."

- `log_bin`

  Whether the binary log is enabled. See Section 4.12.3, "The Binary Log."

- `log_bin_trust_function_creators`

  This variable applies when binary logging is enabled. It controls whether stored function creators can be trusted not to create stored functions that will cause unsafe events to be written to the binary log. If set to 0 (the default), users are not allowed to create or alter stored functions unless they have the SUPER privilege in addition to the CREATE ROUTINE or ALTER ROUTINE privilege. A setting of 0 also enforces the restriction that a function must be declared with the DETERMINISTIC characteristic, or with the READS SQL DATA or NO SQL characteristic. If the variable is set to 1, MySQL does not enforce these restrictions on stored function creation.

  This variable was added in MySQL 5.0.16.

- `log_bin_trust_routine_creators`

  This is the old name for `log_bin_trust_function_creators`. Before MySQL 5.0.16, it also applies to stored procedures, not just stored functions. As of 5.0.16, this variable is deprecated. It is recognized for backward compatibility but its use results in a warning.

  This variable was added in MySQL 5.0.6.

- `log_error`

  The location of the error log.

- `log_slave_updates`

  Whether updates received by a slave server from a master server should be logged to the slave's own binary log. Binary logging must be enabled on the slave for this to have any effect. See Section 5.9, "Replication Startup Options."

- `log_slow_queries`

    Whether slow queries should be logged. "Slow" is determined by the value of the `long_query_time` variable. See Section 4.12.4, "The Slow Query Log."

- `log_warnings`

    Whether to produce additional warning messages. It is enabled (1) by default. Aborted connections are not logged to the error log unless the value is greater than 1.

- `long_query_time`

    If a query takes longer than this many seconds, the server increments the `Slow_queries` status variable. If you are using the `--log-slow-queries` option, the query is logged to the slow query log file. This value is measured in real time, not CPU time, so a query that is under the threshold on a lightly loaded system might be above the threshold on a heavily loaded one. The minimum value is 1. The default is 10. See Section 4.12.4, "The Slow Query Log."

- `low_priority_updates`

    If set to 1, all INSERT, UPDATE, DELETE, and LOCK TABLE WRITE statements wait until there is no pending SELECT or LOCK TABLE READ on the affected table. This variable previously was named `sql_low_priority_updates`.

- `lower_case_file_system`

    This variable describes the case sensitivity of filenames on the filesystem where the data directory is located. OFF means filenames are case sensitive, ON means they are not case sensitive.

- `lower_case_table_names`

    If set to 1, table names are stored in lowercase on disk and table name comparisons are not case sensitive. If set to 2, table names are stored as given but compared in lower-case. This option also applies to database names and table aliases.

    If you are using InnoDB tables, you should set this variable to 1 on all platforms to force names to be converted to lowercase.

    You should *not* set this variable to 0 if you are running MySQL on a system that does not have case-sensitive filenames (such as Windows or Mac OS X). If this variable is not set at startup and the filesystem on which the data directory is located does not have case-sensitive filenames, MySQL automatically sets `lower_case_table_names` to 2.

- `max_allowed_packet`

    The maximum size of one packet or any generated/intermediate string.

    The packet message buffer is initialized to `net_buffer_length` bytes, but can grow up to `max_allowed_packet` bytes when needed. This value by default is small to catch large (possibly incorrect) packets.

    You must increase this value if you are using large BLOB columns or long strings. It should be as big as the biggest BLOB you want to use. The protocol limit for `max_allowed_packet` is 1GB.

- `max_binlog_cache_size`

  If a multiple-statement transaction requires more than this amount of memory, the server generates a `Multi-statement transaction required more than 'max_binlog_cache_size' bytes of storage` error.

- `max_binlog_size`

  If a write to the binary log causes the current log file size to exceed the value of this variable, the server rotates the binary logs (closes the current file and opens the next one). You cannot set this variable to more than 1GB or to less than 4096 bytes. The default value is 1GB.

  A transaction is written in one chunk to the binary log, so it is never split between several binary logs. Therefore, if you have big transactions, you might see binary logs larger than `max_binlog_size`.

  If `max_relay_log_size` is 0, the value of `max_binlog_size` applies to relay logs as well.

- `max_connect_errors`

  If there are more than this number of interrupted connections from a host, that host is blocked from further connections. You can unblock blocked hosts with the FLUSH HOSTS statement.

- `max_connections`

  The number of simultaneous client connections allowed. Increasing this value increases the number of file descriptors that `mysqld` requires. See Section 6.4.8, "How MySQL Opens and Closes Tables," for comments on file descriptor limits.

- `max_delayed_threads`

  Do not start more than this number of threads to handle INSERT DELAYED statements. If you try to insert data into a new table after all INSERT DELAYED threads are in use, the row is inserted as if the DELAYED attribute wasn't specified. If you set this to 0, MySQL never creates a thread to handle DELAYED rows; in effect, this disables DELAYED entirely.

- `max_error_count`

  The maximum number of error, warning, and note messages to be stored for display by the SHOW ERRORS and SHOW WARNINGS statements.

- `max_heap_table_size`

  This variable sets the maximum size to which MEMORY tables are allowed to grow. The value of the variable is used to calculate MEMORY table MAX_ROWS values. Setting this variable has no effect on any existing MEMORY table, unless the table is re-created with a statement such as CREATE TABLE or altered with ALTER TABLE or TRUNCATE TABLE.

- `max_insert_delayed_threads`

  This variable is a synonym for `max_delayed_threads`.

- max_join_size

    Do not allow SELECT statements that probably need to examine more than max_join_size rows (for single-table statements) or row combinations (for multiple-table statements) or that are likely to do more than max_join_size disk seeks. By setting this value, you can catch SELECT statements where keys are not used properly and that would probably take a long time. Set it if your users tend to perform joins that lack a WHERE clause, that take a long time, or that return millions of rows.

    Setting this variable to a value other than DEFAULT resets the value of SQL_BIG_SELECTS to 0. If you set the SQL_BIG_SELECTS value again, the max_join_size variable is ignored.

    If a query result is in the query cache, no result size check is performed, because the result has previously been computed and it does not burden the server to send it to the client.

    This variable previously was named sql_max_join_size.

- max_length_for_sort_data

    The cutoff on the size of index values that determines which filesort algorithm to use. See Section 6.2.12, "ORDER BY Optimization."

- max_relay_log_size

    If a write by a replication slave to its relay log causes the current log file size to exceed the value of this variable, the slave rotates the relay logs (closes the current file and opens the next one). If max_relay_log_size is 0, the server uses max_binlog_size for both the binary log and the relay log. If max_relay_log_size is greater than 0, it constrains the size of the relay log, which enables you to have different sizes for the two logs. You must set max_relay_log_size to between 4096 bytes and 1GB (inclusive), or to 0. The default value is 0. See Section 5.4, "Replication Implementation Details."

- max_seeks_for_key

    Limit the assumed maximum number of seeks when looking up rows based on a key. The MySQL optimizer assumes that no more than this number of key seeks are required when searching for matching rows in a table by scanning an index, regardless of the actual cardinality of the index. By setting this to a low value (say, 100), you can force MySQL to prefer indexes instead of table scans.

- max_sort_length

    The number of bytes to use when sorting BLOB or TEXT values. Only the first max_sort_length bytes of each value are used; the rest are ignored.

- max_tmp_tables

    The maximum number of temporary tables a client can keep open at the same time. (This option does not yet do anything.)

- max_user_connections

    The maximum number of simultaneous connections allowed to any given MySQL account. A value of 0 means "no limit."

Before MySQL 5.0.3, this variable has only global scope. Beginning with MySQL 5.0.3, it also has a read-only session scope. The session variable has the same value as the global variable unless the current account has a non-zero MAX_USER_CONNECTIONS resource limit. In that case, the session value reflects the account limit.

- max_write_lock_count

After this many write locks, allow some pending read lock requests to be processed in between.

- myisam_data_pointer_size

The default pointer size, in bytes, to be used by CREATE TABLE for MyISAM tables when no MAX_ROWS option is specified. This variable cannot be less than 2 or larger than 7. The default value is 6 (4 before MySQL 5.0.6). This variable was added in MySQL 4.1.2.

- myisam_max_extra_sort_file_size (*DEPRECATED*)

If the temporary file used for fast MyISAM index creation would be larger than using the key cache by the amount specified here, prefer the key cache method. This is mainly used to force long character keys in large tables to use the slower key cache method to create the index. The value is given in bytes.

Note: This variable was removed in MySQL 5.0.6.

- myisam_max_sort_file_size

The maximum size of the temporary file MySQL is allowed to use while re-creating a MyISAM index (during REPAIR TABLE, ALTER TABLE, or LOAD DATA INFILE). If the file size would be larger than this value, the index is created using the key cache instead, which is slower. The value is given in bytes.

- myisam_recover_options

The value of the --myisam-recover option. See Section 4.2.1, "mysqld Command Options."

- myisam_repair_threads

If this value is greater than 1, MyISAM table indexes are created in parallel (each index in its own thread) during the Repair by sorting process. The default value is 1. **Note**: Multi-threaded repair is still *beta-quality* code.

- myisam_sort_buffer_size

The size of the buffer that is allocated when sorting MyISAM indexes during a REPAIR TABLE or when creating indexes with CREATE INDEX or ALTER TABLE.

- myisam_stats_method

How the server treats NULL values when collecting statistics about the distribution of index values for MyISAM tables. This variable has two possible values: nulls_equal and nulls_unequal. For nulls_equal, all NULL index values are considered equal and form a single value group that has a size equal to the number of NULL values. For nulls_unequal, NULL values are considered unequal, and each NULL forms a distinct value group of size 1.

The method that is used for generating table statistics influences how the optimizer chooses indexes for query execution, as described in Section 6.4.7, "MyISAM Index Statistics Collection."

This variable was added in MySQL 5.0.14. For older versions, the statistics collection method is equivalent to nulls_equal.

- multi_read_range

Specifies the maximum number of ranges to send to a storage engine during range selects. The default value is 256. Sending multiple ranges to an engine is a feature that can improve the performance of certain selects dramatically, particularly for NDBCLUSTER. This engine needs to send the range requests to all nodes, and sending many of those requests at once reduces the communication costs significantly. This variable was added in MySQL 5.0.3.

- named_pipe

(Windows only.) Indicates whether the server supports connections over named pipes.

- net_buffer_length

The communication buffer is reset to this size between SQL statements. This variable should not normally be changed, but if you have very little memory, you can set it to the expected length of statements sent by clients. If statements exceed this length, the buffer is automatically enlarged, up to max_allowed_packet bytes.

- net_read_timeout

The number of seconds to wait for more data from a connection before aborting the read. This timeout applies only to TCP/IP connections, not to connections made via Unix socket files, named pipes, or shared memory. When the server is reading from the client, net_read_timeout is the timeout value controlling when to abort. When the server is writing to the client, net_write_timeout is the timeout value controlling when to abort. See also slave_net_timeout.

- net_retry_count

If a read on a communication port is interrupted, retry this many times before giving up. This value should be set quite high on FreeBSD because internal interrupts are sent to all threads.

- net_write_timeout

The number of seconds to wait for a block to be written to a connection before aborting the write. This timeout applies only to TCP/IP connections, not to connections made via Unix socket files, named pipes, or shared memory. See also net_read_timeout.

- new

This variable was used in MySQL 4.0 to turn on some 4.1 behaviors, and is retained for backward compatibility. In MySQL 5.0, its value is always OFF.

- `old_passwords`

  Whether the server should use pre-4.1-style passwords for MySQL user accounts.

- `one_shot`

  This is not a variable, but it can be used when setting some variables.

- `open_files_limit`

  The number of files that the operating system allows `mysqld` to open. This is the real value allowed by the system and might be different from the value you gave using the `--open-files-limit` option to `mysqld` or `mysqld_safe`. The value is 0 on systems where MySQL can't change the number of open files.

- `optimizer_prune_level`

  Controls the heuristics applied during query optimization to prune less-promising partial plans from the optimizer search space. A value of 0 disables heuristics so that the optimizer performs an exhaustive search. A value of 1 causes the optimizer to prune plans based on the number of rows retrieved by intermediate plans. This variable was added in MySQL 5.0.1.

- `optimizer_search_depth`

  The maximum depth of search performed by the query optimizer. Values larger than the number of relations in a query result in better query plans, but take longer to generate an execution plan for a query. Values smaller than the number of relations in a query return an execution plan quicker, but the resulting plan may be far from optimal. If set to 0, the system automatically picks a reasonable value. If set to the maximum number of tables used in a query plus 2, the optimizer switches to the algorithm used in MySQL 5.0.0 (and previous versions) for performing searches. This variable was added in MySQL 5.0.1.

- `pid_file`

  The pathname of the process ID (PID) file. This variable can be set with the `--pid-file` option.

- `port`

  The number of the port on which the server listens for TCP/IP connections. This variable can be set with the `--port` option.

- `preload_buffer_size`

  The size of the buffer that is allocated when preloading indexes.

- `protocol_version`

  The version of the client/server protocol used by the MySQL server.

- `query_alloc_block_size`

  The allocation size of memory blocks that are allocated for objects created during statement parsing and execution. If you have problems with memory fragmentation, it might help to increase this a bit.

- `query_cache_limit`

  Don't cache results that are larger than this number of bytes. The default value is 1MB.

- `query_cache_min_res_unit`

  The minimum size (in bytes) for blocks allocated by the query cache. The default value is 4096 (4KB). Tuning information for this variable is given in Section 4.14.3, "Query Cache Configuration."

- `query_cache_size`

  The amount of memory allocated for caching query results. The default value is 0, which disables the query cache. Note that `query_cache_size` bytes of memory are allocated even if `query_cache_type` is set to 0. See Section 4.14.3, "Query Cache Configuration," for more information.

- `query_cache_type`

  Set the query cache type. Setting the GLOBAL value sets the type for all clients that connect thereafter. Individual clients can set the SESSION value to affect their own use of the query cache. Possible values are shown in the following table:

Option	Description
0 or OFF	Don't cache or retrieve results. Note that this does not deallocate the query cache buffer. To do that, you should set `query_cache_size` to 0.
1 or ON	Cache all query results except for those that begin with SELECT SQL_NO_CACHE.
2 or DEMAND	Cache results only for queries that begin with SELECT SQL_CACHE.

  This variable defaults to ON.

- `query_cache_wlock_invalidate`

  Normally, when one client acquires a WRITE lock on a MyISAM table, other clients are not blocked from issuing statements that read from the table if the query results are present in the query cache. Setting this variable to 1 causes acquisition of a WRITE lock for a table to invalidate any queries in the query cache that refer to the table. This forces other clients that attempt to access the table to wait while the lock is in effect.

- `query_prealloc_size`

  The size of the persistent buffer used for statement parsing and execution. This buffer is not freed between statements. If you are running complex queries, a larger `query_prealloc_size` value might be helpful in improving performance, because it can reduce the need for the server to perform memory allocation during query execution operations.

- `range_alloc_block_size`

  The size of blocks that are allocated when doing range optimization.

- `read_buffer_size`

  Each thread that does a sequential scan allocates a buffer of this size (in bytes) for each table it scans. If you do many sequential scans, you might want to increase this value, which defaults to 131072.

- `read_only`

When the variable is set to `ON` for a replication slave server, it causes the slave to allow no updates except from slave threads or from users that have the `SUPER` privilege. This can be useful to ensure that a slave server accepts updates only from its master server and not from clients. As of MySQL 5.0.16, this variable does not apply to `TEMPORARY` tables.

- `relay_log_purge`

Disables or enables automatic purging of relay log files as soon as they are not needed any more. The default value is 1 (`ON`).

- `read_rnd_buffer_size`

When reading rows in sorted order following a key-sorting operation, the rows are read through this buffer to avoid disk seeks. Setting the variable to a large value can improve `ORDER BY` performance by a lot. However, this is a buffer allocated for each client, so you should not set the global variable to a large value. Instead, change the session variable only from within those clients that need to run large queries.

- `secure_auth`

If the MySQL server has been started with the `--secure-auth` option, it blocks connections from all accounts that have passwords stored in the old (pre-4.1) format. In that case, the value of this variable is `ON`, otherwise it is `OFF`.

You should enable this option if you want to prevent all use of passwords employing the old format (and hence insecure communication over the network).

Server startup fails with an error if this option is enabled and the privilege tables are in pre-4.1 format.

- `server_id`

The server ID. This value is set by the `--server-id` option. It is used for replication to enable master and slave servers to identify themselves uniquely.

- `shared_memory`

(Windows only.) Whether the server allows shared-memory connections.

- `shared_memory_base_name`

(Windows only.) The name of shared memory to use for shared-memory connections. This is useful when running multiple MySQL instances on a single physical machine. The default name is `MYSQL`. The name is case sensitive.

- `skip_external_locking`

This is `OFF` if mysqld uses external locking, `ON` if external locking is disabled.

- `skip_networking`

This is `ON` if the server allows only local (non-TCP/IP) connections. On Unix, local connections use a Unix socket file. On Windows, local connections use a named pipe or shared memory. On NetWare, only TCP/IP connections are supported, so do not set this variable to `ON`. This variable can be set to `ON` with the `--skip-networking` option.

- `skip_show_database`

  This prevents people from using the SHOW DATABASES statement if they do not have the SHOW DATABASES privilege. This can improve security if you have concerns about users being able to see databases belonging to other users. Its effect depends on the SHOW DATABASES privilege: If the variable value is ON, the SHOW DATABASES statement is allowed only to users who have the SHOW DATABASES privilege, and the statement displays all database names. If the value is OFF, SHOW DATABASES is allowed to all users, but displays the names of only those databases for which the user has the SHOW DATABASES or other privilege.

- `slave_compressed_protocol`

  Whether to use compression of the slave/master protocol if both the slave and the master support it.

- `slave_load_tmpdir`

  The name of the directory where the slave creates temporary files for replicating LOAD DATA INFILE statements.

- `slave_net_timeout`

  The number of seconds to wait for more data from a master/slave connection before aborting the read. This timeout applies only to TCP/IP connections, not to connections made via Unix socket files, named pipes, or shared memory.

- `slave_skip_errors`

  The replication errors that the slave should skip (ignore).

- `slave_transaction_retries`

  If a replication slave SQL thread fails to execute a transaction because of an InnoDB deadlock or exceeded InnoDB's innodb_lock_wait_timeout or NDBCluster's TransactionDeadlockDetectionTimeout or TransactionInactiveTimeout, it automatically retries slave_transaction_retries times before stopping with an error. The default prior to MySQL 4.0.3 is 0. You must explicitly set the value greater than 0 to enable the "retry" behavior, which is probably a good idea. In MySQL 5.0.3 or newer, the default is 10.

- `slow_launch_time`

  If creating a thread takes longer than this many seconds, the server increments the slow_launch_threads status variable.

- `socket`

  On Unix platforms, this variable is the name of the socket file that is used for local client connections. The default is /tmp/mysql.sock. (For some distribution formats, the directory might be different, such as /var/lib/mysql for RPMs.)

  On Windows, this variable is the name of the named pipe that is used for local client connections. The default value is MySQL (not case sensitive).

- `sort_buffer_size`

  Each thread that needs to do a sort allocates a buffer of this size. Increase this value for faster ORDER BY or GROUP BY operations.

- `sql_mode`

  The current server SQL mode, which can be set dynamically. See Section 4.2.5, "The Server SQL Mode."

- `sql_slave_skip_counter`

  The number of events from the master that a slave server should skip.

- `storage_engine`

  The default storage engine (table type). To set the storage engine at server startup, use the --default-storage-engine option. See Section 4.2.1, "mysqld Command Options."

- `sync_binlog`

  If the value of this variable is positive, the MySQL server synchronizes its binary log to disk (using fdatasync()) after every sync_binlog writes to the binary log. Note that there is one write to the binary log per statement if autocommit is enabled, and one write per transaction otherwise. The default value is 0, which does no synchronizing to disk. A value of 1 is the safest choice, because in the event of a crash you lose at most one statement or transaction from the binary log. However, it is also the slowest choice (unless the disk has a battery-backed cache, which makes synchronization very fast).

  If the value of sync_binlog is 0 (the default), no extra flushing is done. The server relies on the operating system to flush the file contents occasionally as for any other file.

- `sync_frm`

  If this variable is set to 1, when any non-temporary table is created its .frm file is synchronized to disk (using fdatasync()). This is slower but safer in case of a crash. The default is 1.

- `system_time_zone`

  The server system time zone. When the server begins executing, it inherits a time zone setting from the machine defaults, possibly modified by the environment of the account used for running the server or the startup script. The value is used to set system_time_zone. Typically the time zone is specified by the TZ environment variable. It also can be specified using the --timezone option of the mysqld_safe script.

  The system_time_zone variable differs from time_zone. Although they might have the same value, the latter variable is used to initialize the time zone for each client that connects. See Section 4.11.8, "MySQL Server Time Zone Support."

- `table_cache`

  The number of open tables for all threads. Increasing this value increases the number of file descriptors that mysqld requires. You can check whether you need to increase the table cache by checking the Opened_tables status variable. See Section 4.2.4, "Server Status Variables." If the value of Opened_tables is large and you don't do FLUSH TABLES often (which just forces all tables to be closed and reopened), you should increase the value of the `table_cache` variable. For more information about the table cache, see Section 6.4.8, "How MySQL Opens and Closes Tables."

- `table_type`

  This variable is a synonym for `storage_engine`. In MySQL 5.0, `storage_engine` is the preferred name.

- `thread_cache_size`

  How many threads the server should cache for reuse. When a client disconnects, the client's threads are put in the cache if there are fewer than `thread_cache_size` threads there. Requests for threads are satisfied by reusing threads taken from the cache if possible, and only when the cache is empty is a new thread created. This variable can be increased to improve performance if you have a lot of new connections. (Normally, this doesn't provide a notable performance improvement if you have a good thread implementation.) By examining the difference between the `Connections` and `Threads_created` status variables, you can see how efficient the thread cache is. For details, see Section 4.2.4, "Server Status Variables."

- `thread_concurrency`

  On Solaris, `mysqld` calls `thr_setconcurrency()` with this value. This function enables applications to give the threads system a hint about the desired number of threads that should be run at the same time.

- `thread_stack`

  The stack size for each thread. Many of the limits detected by the `crash-me` test are dependent on this value. The default is large enough for normal operation. See Section 6.1.4, "The MySQL Benchmark Suite." The default is 192KB.

- `time_format`

  This variable is not implemented.

- `time_zone`

  The current time zone. This variable is used to initialize the tome zone for each client that connects. By default, the initial value of this is `'SYSTEM'` (which means, "use the value of `system_time_zone`"). The value can be specified explicitly at server startup with the `--default-time-zone` option. See Section 4.11.8, "MySQL Server Time Zone Support."

- `tmp_table_size`

  If an in-memory temporary table exceeds this size, MySQL automatically converts it to an on-disk `MyISAM` table. Increase the value of `tmp_table_size` if you do many advanced `GROUP BY` queries and you have lots of memory.

- `tmpdir`

  The directory used for temporary files and temporary tables. This variable can be set to a list of several paths that are used in round-robin fashion. Paths should be separated by colon characters (':') on Unix and semicolon characters (';') on Windows, NetWare, and OS/2.

The multiple-directory feature can be used to spread the load between several physical disks. If the MySQL server is acting as a replication slave, you should not set `tmpdir` to point to a directory on a memory-based filesystem or to a directory that is cleared when the server host restarts. A replication slave needs some of its temporary files to survive a machine restart so that it can replicate temporary tables or `LOAD DATA INFILE` operations. If files in the temporary file directory are lost when the server restarts, replication fails. However, if you are using MySQL 4.0.0 or later, you can set the slave's temporary directory using the `slave_load_tmpdir` variable. In that case, the slave won't use the general `tmpdir` value and you can set `tmpdir` to a non-permanent location.

- `transaction_alloc_block_size`

The amount in bytes by which to increase a per-transaction memory pool which needs memory. See the description of `transaction_prealloc_size`.

- `transaction_prealloc_size`

There is a per-transaction memory pool from which various transaction-related allocations take memory. The initial size of the pool in bytes is `transaction_prealloc_size`. For every allocation that cannot be satisfied from the pool because it has insufficient memory available, the pool is increased by `transaction_alloc_block_size` bytes. When the transaction ends, the pool is truncated to `transaction_prealloc_size` bytes.

By making `transaction_prealloc_size` sufficiently large to contain all statements within a single transaction, you can avoid many `malloc()` calls.

- `tx_isolation`

The default transaction isolation level. Defaults to `REPEATABLE-READ`.

This variable is set by the `SET TRANSACTION ISOLATION LEVEL` statement. If you set `tx_isolation` directly to an isolation level name that contains a space, the name should be enclosed within quotes, with the space replaced by a dash. For example:

```
SET tx_isolation = 'READ-COMMITTED';
```

- `updatable_views_with_limit`

This variable controls whether updates can be made using a view that does not contain a primary key in the underlying table, if the update contains a `LIMIT` clause. (Such updates often are generated by GUI tools.) An update is an `UPDATE` or `DELETE` statement. Primary key here means a `PRIMARY KEY`, or a `UNIQUE` index in which no column can contain `NULL`.

The variable can have two values:

  - `1` or `YES`: Issue a warning only (not an error message). This is the default value.
  - `0` or `NO`: Prohibit the update.

This variable was added in MySQL 5.0.2.

- version

  The version number for the server.

- version_bdb

  The BDB storage engine version.

- version_comment

  The configure script has a --with-comment option that allows a comment to be specified when building MySQL. This variable contains the value of that comment.

- version_compile_machine

  The type of machine or architecture on which MySQL was built.

- version_compile_os

  The type of operating system on which MySQL was built.

- wait_timeout

  The number of seconds the server waits for activity on a non-interactive connection before closing it. This timeout applies only to TCP/IP connections, not to connections made via Unix socket files, named pipes, or shared memory.

  On thread startup, the session wait_timeout value is initialized from the global wait_timeout value or from the global interactive_timeout value, depending on the type of client (as defined by the CLIENT_INTERACTIVE connect option to mysql_real_connect()). See also interactive_timeout.

4.2.3 Using System Variables

The mysql server maintains many system variables that indicate how it is configured. Section 4.2.2, "Server System Variables," describes the meaning of these variables. Each system variable has a default value. System variables can be set at server startup using options on the command line or in an option file. Most of them can be changed dynamically while the server is running by means of the SET statement, which enables you to modify operation of the server without having to stop and restart it. You can refer to system variable values in expressions.

The server maintains two kinds of system variables. Global variables affect the overall operation of the server. Session variables affect its operation for individual client connections. A given system variable can have both a global and a session value. Global and session system variables are related as follows:

- When the server starts, it initializes all global variables to their default values. These defaults can be changed by options specified on the command line or in an option file. (See Section 3.3, "Specifying Program Options.")

- The server also maintains a set of session variables for each client that connects. The client's session variables are initialized at connect time using the current values of the corresponding global variables. For example, the client's SQL mode is controlled by the session `sql_mode` value, which is initialized when the client connects to the value of the global `sql_mode` value.

System variable values can be set globally at server startup by using options on the command line or in an option file. When you use a startup option to set a variable that takes a numeric value, the value can be given with a suffix of K, M, or G (either uppercase or lowercase) to indicate a multiplier of 1024, 1024^2 or 1024^3; that is, units of kilobytes, megabytes, or gigabytes, respectively. Thus, the following command starts the server with a query cache size of 16 megabytes and a maximum packet size of one gigabyte:

```
mysqld --query_cache_size=16M --max_allowed_packet=1G
```

Within an option file, those variables are set like this:

```
[mysqld]
query_cache_size=16M
max_allowed_packet=1G
```

The lettercase of suffix letters does not matter; 16M and 16m are equivalent, as are 1G and 1g.

If you want to restrict the maximum value to which a system variable can be set at runtime with the SET statement, you can specify this maximum by using an option of the form `--maximum-var_name=value` at server startup. For example, to prevent the value of `query_cache_size` from being increased to more than 32MB at runtime, use the option `--maximum-query_cache_size=32M`.

Many system variables are dynamic and can be changed while the server runs by using the SET statement. For a list, see Section 4.2.3.2, "Dynamic System Variables." To change a system variable with SET, refer to it as `var_name`, optionally preceded by a modifier:

- To indicate explicitly that a variable is a global variable, precede its name by GLOBAL or `@@global.`. The SUPER privilege is required to set global variables.
- To indicate explicitly that a variable is a session variable, precede its name by SESSION, `@@session.`, or `@@`. Setting a session variable requires no special privilege, but a client can change only its own session variables, not those of any other client.
- LOCAL and `@@local.` are synonyms for SESSION and `@@session.`.
- If no modifier is present, SET changes the session variable.

A SET statement can contain multiple variable assignments, separated by commas. If you set several system variables, the most recent GLOBAL or SESSION modifier in the statement is used for following variables that have no modifier specified.

Examples:

```
SET sort_buffer_size=10000;
SET @@local.sort_buffer_size=10000;
SET GLOBAL sort_buffer_size=1000000, SESSION sort_buffer_size=1000000;
```

```
SET @@sort_buffer_size=1000000;
SET @@global.sort_buffer_size=1000000, @@local.sort_buffer_size=1000000;
```

When you assign a value to a system variable with SET, you cannot use suffix letters in the value (as can be done with startup options). However, the value can take the form of an expression:

```
SET sort_buffer_size = 10 * 1024 * 1024;
```

The @@var_name syntax for system variables is supported for compatibility with some other database systems.

If you change a session system variable, the value remains in effect until your session ends or until you change the variable to a different value. The change is not visible to other clients.

If you change a global system variable, the value is remembered and used for new connections until the server restarts. (To make a global system variable setting permanent, you should set it in an option file.) The change is visible to any client that accesses that global variable. However, the change affects the corresponding session variable only for clients that connect after the change. The global variable change does not affect the session variable for any client that is currently connected (not even that of the client that issues the SET GLOBAL statement).

To prevent incorrect usage, MySQL produces an error if you use SET GLOBAL with a variable that can only be used with SET SESSION or if you do not specify GLOBAL (or @@global.) when setting a global variable.

To set a SESSION variable to the GLOBAL value or a GLOBAL value to the compiled-in MySQL default value, use the DEFAULT keyword. For example, the following two statements are identical in setting the session value of max_join_size to the global value:

```
SET max_join_size=DEFAULT;
SET @@session.max_join_size=@@global.max_join_size;
```

Not all system variables can be set to DEFAULT. In such cases, use of DEFAULT results in an error.

You can refer to the values of specific global or session system variables in expressions by using one of the @@-modifiers. For example, you can retrieve values in a SELECT statement like this:

```
SELECT @@global.sql_mode, @@session.sql_mode, @@sql_mode;
```

When you refer to a system variable in an expression as @@var_name (that is, when you do not specify @@global. or @@session.), MySQL returns the session value if it exists and the global value otherwise. (This differs from SET @@var_name = value, which always refers to the session value.)

Note: Some system variables can be enabled with the SET statement by setting them to ON or 1, or disabled by setting them to OFF or 0. However, to set such a variable on the command line or in an option file, you must set it to 1 or 0; setting it to ON or OFF will not work. For example, on the command line, --delay_key_write=1 works but --delay_key_write=ON does not.

To display system variable names and values, use the SHOW VARIABLES statement.

```
mysql> SHOW VARIABLES;
+--------+------------------------------------------------------------+
| Variable_name                  | Value                              |
+--------+------------------------------------------------------------+
| auto_increment_increment       | 1                                  |
| auto_increment_offset          | 1                                  |
| automatic_sp_privileges        | ON                                 |
| back_log                       | 50                                 |
| basedir                        | /                                  |
| bdb_cache_size                 | 8388600                            |
| bdb_home                       | /var/lib/mysql/                    |
| bdb_log_buffer_size            | 32768                              |
| bdb_logdir                     |                                    |
| bdb_max_lock                   | 10000                              |
| bdb_shared_data                | OFF                                |
| bdb_tmpdir                     | /tmp/                              |
| binlog_cache_size              | 32768                              |
| bulk_insert_buffer_size        | 8388608                            |
| character_set_client           | latin1                             |
| character_set_connection       | latin1                             |
| character_set_database         | latin1                             |
| character_set_results          | latin1                             |
| character_set_server           | latin1                             |
| character_set_system           | utf8                               |
| character_sets_dir             | /usr/share/mysql/charsets/         |
| collation_connection           | latin1_swedish_ci                  |
| collation_database             | latin1_swedish_ci                  |
| collation_server               | latin1_swedish_ci                  |
...
| innodb_additional_mem_pool_size | 1048576                           |
| innodb_autoextend_increment    | 8                                  |
| innodb_buffer_pool_awe_mem_mb  | 0                                  |
| innodb_buffer_pool_size        | 8388608                            |
| innodb_checksums               | ON                                 |
| innodb_commit_concurrency      | 0                                  |
| innodb_concurrency_tickets     | 500                                |
| innodb_data_file_path          | ibdata1:10M:autoextend             |
| innodb_data_home_dir           |                                    |
...
```

```
| version                 | 5.0.19-Max                          |
| version_comment         | MySQL Community Edition - Max (GPL)  |
| version_compile_machine | i686                                |
| version_compile_os      | pc-linux-gnu                        |
| wait_timeout            | 28800                               |
+---------+-----------------------------------------------------+
```

With a LIKE clause, the statement displays only those variables that match the pattern. To obtain a specific variable name, use a LIKE clause as shown:

```
SHOW VARIABLES LIKE 'max_join_size';
SHOW SESSION VARIABLES LIKE 'max_join_size';
```

To get a list of variables whose names match a pattern, use the '%' wildcard character in a LIKE clause:

```
SHOW VARIABLES LIKE '%size%';
SHOW GLOBAL VARIABLES LIKE '%size%';
```

Wildcard characters can be used in any position within the pattern to be matched. Strictly speaking, because '_' is a wildcard that matches any single character, you should escape it as '_' to match it literally. In practice, this is rarely necessary.

For SHOW VARIABLES, if you specify neither GLOBAL nor SESSION, MySQL returns SESSION values.

The reason for requiring the GLOBAL keyword when setting GLOBAL-only variables but not when retrieving them is to prevent problems in the future. If we were to remove a SESSION variable that has the same name as a GLOBAL variable, a client with the SUPER privilege might accidentally change the GLOBAL variable rather than just the SESSION variable for its own connection. If we add a SESSION variable with the same name as a GLOBAL variable, a client that intends to change the GLOBAL variable might find only its own SESSION variable changed.

4.2.3.1 Structured System Variables

A structured variable differs from a regular system variable in two respects:

- Its value is a structure with components that specify server parameters considered to be closely related.
- There might be several instances of a given type of structured variable. Each one has a different name and refers to a different resource maintained by the server.

MySQL 5.0 supports one structured variable type, which specifies parameters governing the operation of key caches. A key cache structured variable has these components:

- key_buffer_size
- key_cache_block_size
- key_cache_division_limit
- key_cache_age_threshold

This section describes the syntax for referring to structured variables. Key cache variables are used for syntax examples, but specific details about how key caches operate are found elsewhere, in Section 6.4.6, "The MyISAM Key Cache."

To refer to a component of a structured variable instance, you can use a compound name in *instance_name.component_name* format. Examples:

```
hot_cache.key_buffer_size
hot_cache.key_cache_block_size
cold_cache.key_cache_block_size
```

For each structured system variable, an instance with the name of default is always predefined. If you refer to a component of a structured variable without any instance name, the default instance is used. Thus, default.key_buffer_size and key_buffer_size both refer to the same system variable.

Structured variable instances and components follow these naming rules:

- For a given type of structured variable, each instance must have a name that is unique *within* variables of that type. However, instance names need not be unique *across* structured variable types. For example, each structured variable has an instance named default, so default is not unique across variable types.

- The names of the components of each structured variable type must be unique across all system variable names. If this were not true (that is, if two different types of structured variables could share component member names), it would not be clear which default structured variable to use for references to member names that are not qualified by an instance name.

- If a structured variable instance name is not legal as an unquoted identifier, refer to it as a quoted identifier using backticks. For example, hot-cache is not legal, but `hot-cache` is.

- global, session, and local are not legal instance names. This avoids a conflict with notation such as @@global.*var_name* for referring to non-structured system variables.

Currently, the first two rules have no possibility of being violated because the only structured variable type is the one for key caches. These rules will assume greater significance if some other type of structured variable is created in the future.

With one exception, you can refer to structured variable components using compound names in any context where simple variable names can occur. For example, you can assign a value to a structured variable using a command-line option:

```
shell> mysqld --hot_cache.key_buffer_size=64K
```

In an option file, use this syntax:

```
[mysqld]
hot_cache.key_buffer_size=64K
```

If you start the server with this option, it creates a key cache named hot_cache with a size of 64KB in addition to the default key cache that has a default size of 8MB.

Suppose that you start the server as follows:

```
shell> mysqld --key_buffer_size=256K \
         --extra_cache.key_buffer_size=128K \
         --extra_cache.key_cache_block_size=2048
```

In this case, the server sets the size of the default key cache to 256KB. (You could also have written --default.key_buffer_size=256K.) In addition, the server creates a second key cache named extra_cache that has a size of 128KB, with the size of block buffers for caching table index blocks set to 2048 bytes.

The following example starts the server with three different key caches having sizes in a 3:1:1 ratio:

```
shell> mysqld --key_buffer_size=6M \
         --hot_cache.key_buffer_size=2M \
         --cold_cache.key_buffer_size=2M
```

Structured variable values may be set and retrieved at runtime as well. For example, to set a key cache named hot_cache to a size of 10MB, use either of these statements:

```
mysql> SET GLOBAL hot_cache.key_buffer_size = 10*1024*1024;
mysql> SET @@global.hot_cache.key_buffer_size = 10*1024*1024;
```

To retrieve the cache size, do this:

```
mysql> SELECT @@global.hot_cache.key_buffer_size;
```

However, the following statement does not work. The variable is not interpreted as a compound name, but as a simple string for a LIKE pattern-matching operation:

```
mysql> SHOW GLOBAL VARIABLES LIKE 'hot_cache.key_buffer_size';
```

This is the exception to being able to use structured variable names anywhere a simple variable name may occur.

4.2.3.2 Dynamic System Variables

Many server system variables are dynamic and can be set at runtime using SET GLOBAL or SET SESSION. You can also obtain their values using SELECT. See Section 4.2.3, "Using System Variables."

The following table shows the full list of all dynamic system variables. The last column indicates for each variable whether GLOBAL or SESSION (or both) apply. The table also lists session options that can be set with the SET statement.

Variables that have a type of "string" take a string value. Variables that have a type of "numeric" take a numeric value. Variables that have a type of "boolean" can be set to 0, 1, ON or OFF. (If you set them on the command line or in an option file, use the numeric values.) Variables that are marked as "enumeration" normally should be set to one of the available values for the variable, but can also be set to the number that corresponds to the desired enumeration value. For enumerated system variables, the first enumeration value corresponds to 0. This differs from ENUM columns, for which the first enumeration value corresponds to 1.

Variable Name	Value Type	Type
autocommit	boolean	SESSION
big_tables	boolean	SESSION
binlog_cache_size	numeric	GLOBAL
bulk_insert_buffer_size	numeric	GLOBAL | SESSION
character_set_client	string	GLOBAL | SESSION
character_set_connection	string	GLOBAL | SESSION
character_set_filesystem	string	GLOBAL | SESSION
character_set_results	string	GLOBAL | SESSION
character_set_server	string	GLOBAL | SESSION
collation_connection	string	GLOBAL | SESSION
collation_server	string	GLOBAL | SESSION
completion_type	numeric	GLOBAL | SESSION
concurrent_insert	boolean	GLOBAL
connect_timeout	numeric	GLOBAL
convert_character_set	string	GLOBAL | SESSION
default_week_format	numeric	GLOBAL | SESSION
delay_key_write	OFF | ON | ALL	GLOBAL
delayed_insert_limit	numeric	GLOBAL
delayed_insert_timeout	numeric	GLOBAL
delayed_queue_size	numeric	GLOBAL
div_precision_increment	numeric	GLOBAL | SESSION
engine_condition_pushdown	boolean	GLOBAL | SESSION
error_count	numeric	SESSION
expire_logs_days	numeric	GLOBAL
flush	boolean	GLOBAL
flush_time	numeric	GLOBAL
foreign_key_checks	boolean	SESSION
ft_boolean_syntax	numeric	GLOBAL
group_concat_max_len	numeric	GLOBAL | SESSION
identity	numeric	SESSION
innodb_autoextend_increment	numeric	GLOBAL

Variable Name	Value Type	Type
innodb_commit_concurrency	numeric	GLOBAL
innodb_concurrency_tickets	numeric	GLOBAL
innodb_max_dirty_pages_pct	numeric	GLOBAL
innodb_max_purge_lag	numeric	GLOBAL
innodb_support_xa	boolean	GLOBAL | SESSION
innodb_sync_spin_loops	numeric	GLOBAL
innodb_table_locks	boolean	GLOBAL | SESSION
innodb_thread_concurrency	numeric	GLOBAL
innodb_thread_sleep_delay	numeric	GLOBAL
insert_id	boolean	SESSION
interactive_timeout	numeric	GLOBAL | SESSION
join_buffer_size	numeric	GLOBAL | SESSION
key_buffer_size	numeric	GLOBAL
last_insert_id	numeric	SESSION
local_infile	boolean	GLOBAL
log_warnings	numeric	GLOBAL
long_query_time	numeric	GLOBAL | SESSION
low_priority_updates	boolean	GLOBAL | SESSION
max_allowed_packet	numeric	GLOBAL | SESSION
max_binlog_cache_size	numeric	GLOBAL
max_binlog_size	numeric	GLOBAL
max_connect_errors	numeric	GLOBAL
max_connections	numeric	GLOBAL
max_delayed_threads	numeric	GLOBAL
max_error_count	numeric	GLOBAL | SESSION
max_heap_table_size	numeric	GLOBAL | SESSION
max_insert_delayed_threads	numeric	GLOBAL
max_join_size	numeric	GLOBAL | SESSION
max_relay_log_size	numeric	GLOBAL
max_seeks_for_key	numeric	GLOBAL | SESSION
max_sort_length	numeric	GLOBAL | SESSION
max_tmp_tables	numeric	GLOBAL | SESSION
max_user_connections	numeric	GLOBAL
max_write_lock_count	numeric	GLOBAL
myisam_stats_method	enum	GLOBAL | SESSION
multi_read_range	numeric	GLOBAL | SESSION
myisam_data_pointer_size	numeric	GLOBAL
log_bin_trust_function_creators	boolean	GLOBAL

Variable Name	Value Type	Type
myisam_max_sort_file_size	numeric	GLOBAL | SESSION
myisam_repair_threads	numeric	GLOBAL | SESSION
myisam_sort_buffer_size	numeric	GLOBAL | SESSION
net_buffer_length	numeric	GLOBAL | SESSION
net_read_timeout	numeric	GLOBAL | SESSION
net_retry_count	numeric	GLOBAL | SESSION
net_write_timeout	numeric	GLOBAL | SESSION
old_passwords	numeric	GLOBAL | SESSION
optimizer_prune_level	numeric	GLOBAL | SESSION
optimizer_search_depth	numeric	GLOBAL | SESSION
preload_buffer_size	numeric	GLOBAL | SESSION
query_alloc_block_size	numeric	GLOBAL | SESSION
query_cache_limit	numeric	GLOBAL
query_cache_size	numeric	GLOBAL
query_cache_type	enumeration	GLOBAL | SESSION
query_cache_wlock_invalidate	boolean	GLOBAL | SESSION
query_prealloc_size	numeric	GLOBAL | SESSION
range_alloc_block_size	numeric	GLOBAL | SESSION
read_buffer_size	numeric	GLOBAL | SESSION
read_only	numeric	GLOBAL
read_rnd_buffer_size	numeric	GLOBAL | SESSION
rpl_recovery_rank	numeric	GLOBAL
safe_show_database	boolean	GLOBAL
secure_auth	boolean	GLOBAL
server_id	numeric	GLOBAL
slave_compressed_protocol	boolean	GLOBAL
slave_net_timeout	numeric	GLOBAL
slave_transaction_retries	numeric	GLOBAL
slow_launch_time	numeric	GLOBAL
sort_buffer_size	numeric	GLOBAL | SESSION
sql_auto_is_null	boolean	SESSION
sql_big_selects	boolean	SESSION
sql_big_tables	boolean	SESSION
sql_buffer_result	boolean	SESSION
sql_log_bin	boolean	SESSION
sql_log_off	boolean	SESSION
sql_log_update	boolean	SESSION
sql_low_priority_updates	boolean	GLOBAL | SESSION

Variable Name	Value Type	Type
sql_max_join_size	numeric	GLOBAL | SESSION
sql_mode	enumeration	GLOBAL | SESSION
sql_notes	boolean	SESSION
sql_quote_show_create	boolean	SESSION
sql_safe_updates	boolean	SESSION
sql_select_limit	numeric	SESSION
sql_slave_skip_counter	numeric	GLOBAL
updatable_views_with_limit	enumeration	GLOBAL | SESSION
sql_warnings	boolean	SESSION
sync_binlog	numeric	GLOBAL
sync_frm	boolean	GLOBAL
storage_engine	enumeration	GLOBAL | SESSION
table_cache	numeric	GLOBAL
table_type	enumeration	GLOBAL | SESSION
thread_cache_size	numeric	GLOBAL
time_zone	string	GLOBAL | SESSION
timestamp	boolean	SESSION
tmp_table_size	enumeration	GLOBAL | SESSION
transaction_alloc_block_size	numeric	GLOBAL | SESSION
transaction_prealloc_size	numeric	GLOBAL | SESSION
tx_isolation	enumeration	GLOBAL | SESSION
unique_checks	boolean	SESSION
wait_timeout	numeric	GLOBAL | SESSION
warning_count	numeric	SESSION

4.2.4 Server Status Variables

The server maintains many status variables that provide information about its operation. You can view these variables and their values by using the SHOW STATUS statement:

```
mysql> SHOW STATUS;
+----------------------------------+------------+
| Variable_name                    | Value      |
+----------------------------------+------------+
| Aborted_clients                  | 0          |
| Aborted_connects                 | 0          |
| Bytes_received                   | 155372598  |
| Bytes_sent                       | 1176560426 |
...
| Connections                      | 30023      |
| Created_tmp_disk_tables          | 0          |
```

```
| Created_tmp_files              | 3         |
| Created_tmp_tables             | 2         |
...
| Threads_created                | 217       |
| Threads_running                | 88        |
| Uptime                         | 1389872   |
+-------------------------------+-----------+
```

Many status variables are reset to 0 by the FLUSH STATUS statement.

The status variables have the following meanings. Variables with no version indicated were already present prior to MySQL 5.0. For information regarding their implementation history, see "MySQL 3.23, 4.0, 4.1 Reference Manual."

- Aborted_clients

  The number of connections that were aborted because the client died without closing the connection properly.

- Aborted_connects

  The number of failed attempts to connect to the MySQL server.

- Binlog_cache_disk_use

  The number of transactions that used the temporary binary log cache but that exceeded the value of binlog_cache_size and used a temporary file to store statements from the transaction.

- Binlog_cache_use

  The number of transactions that used the temporary binary log cache.

- Bytes_received

  The number of bytes received from all clients.

- Bytes_sent

  The number of bytes sent to all clients.

- Com_xxx

  The Com_xxx statement counter variables indicate the number of times each xxx statement has been executed. There is one status variable for each type of statement. For example, Com_delete and Com_insert count DELETE and INSERT statements, respectively.

  The Com_stmt_xxx status variables were added in 5.0.8:

  - Com_stmt_prepare

  - Com_stmt_execute

  - Com_stmt_fetch

  - Com_stmt_send_long_data

  - Com_stmt_reset

  - Com_stmt_close

Those variables stand for prepared statement commands. Their names refer to the COM_*xxx* command set used in the network layer. In other words, their values increase whenever prepared statement API calls such as mysql_stmt_prepare(), mysql_stmt_execute(), and so forth are executed. However, Com_stmt_prepare, Com_stmt_execute, and Com_stmt_close also increase for PREPARE, EXECUTE, or DEALLOCATE PREPARE, respectively. Additionally, the values of the older (available since MySQL 4.1.3) statement counter variables Com_prepare_sql, Com_execute_sql, and Com_dealloc_sql increase for the PREPARE, EXECUTE, and DEALLOCATE PREPARE statements. Com_stmt_fetch stands for the total number of network round-trips issued when fetching from cursors.

All of the Com_stmt_*xxx* variables are increased even if a prepared statement argument is unknown or an error occurred during execution. In other words, their values correspond to the number of requests issued, not to the number of requests successfully completed.

- Compression

Whether the client connection uses compression in the client/server protocol. Added in MySQL 5.0.16.

- Connections

The number of connection attempts (successful or not) to the MySQL server.

- Created_tmp_disk_tables

The number of temporary tables on disk created automatically by the server while executing statements.

- Created_tmp_files

How many temporary files mysqld has created.

- Created_tmp_tables

The number of in-memory temporary tables created automatically by the server while executing statements. If Created_tmp_disk_tables is large, you may want to increase the tmp_table_size value to cause temporary tables to be memory-based instead of disk-based.

- Delayed_errors

The number of rows written with INSERT DELAYED for which some error occurred (probably duplicate key).

- Delayed_insert_threads

The number of INSERT DELAYED handler threads in use.

- Delayed_writes

The number of INSERT DELAYED rows written.

- Flush_commands

The number of executed FLUSH statements.

- `Handler_commit`

  The number of internal COMMIT statements.

- `Handler_discover`

  The MySQL server can ask the NDB Cluster storage engine if it knows about a table with a given name. This is called "discovery." `Handler_discover` indicates the number of times that tables have been discovered via this mechanism.

- `Handler_delete`

  The number of times that rows have been deleted from tables.

- `Handler_read_first`

  The number of times the first entry was read from an index. If this value is high, it suggests that the server is doing a lot of full index scans; for example, SELECT col1 FROM foo, assuming that col1 is indexed.

- `Handler_read_key`

  The number of requests to read a row based on a key. If this value is high, it is a good indication that your tables are properly indexed for your queries.

- `Handler_read_next`

  The number of requests to read the next row in key order. This value is incremented if you are querying an index column with a range constraint or if you are doing an index scan.

- `Handler_read_prev`

  The number of requests to read the previous row in key order. This read method is mainly used to optimize ORDER BY ... DESC.

- `Handler_read_rnd`

  The number of requests to read a row based on a fixed position. This value is high if you are doing a lot of queries that require sorting of the result. You probably have a lot of queries that require MySQL to scan entire tables or you have joins that don't use keys properly.

- `Handler_read_rnd_next`

  The number of requests to read the next row in the data file. This value is high if you are doing a lot of table scans. Generally this suggests that your tables are not properly indexed or that your queries are not written to take advantage of the indexes you have.

- `Handler_rollback`

  The number of internal ROLLBACK statements.

- `Handler_update`

  The number of requests to update a row in a table.

- `Handler_write`

  The number of requests to insert a row in a table.

- Innodb_buffer_pool_pages_data

  The number of pages containing data (dirty or clean). Added in MySQL 5.0.2.

- Innodb_buffer_pool_pages_dirty

  The number of pages currently dirty. Added in MySQL 5.0.2.

- Innodb_buffer_pool_pages_flushed

  The number of buffer pool page-flush requests. Added in MySQL 5.0.2.

- Innodb_buffer_pool_pages_free

  The number of free pages. Added in MySQL 5.0.2.

- Innodb_buffer_pool_pages_latched

  The number of latched pages in InnoDB buffer pool. These are pages currently being read or written or that cannot be flushed or removed for some other reason. Added in MySQL 5.0.2.

- Innodb_buffer_pool_pages_misc

  The number of pages that are busy because they have been allocated for administrative overhead such as row locks or the adaptive hash index. This value can also be calculated as Innodb_buffer_pool_pages_total − Innodb_buffer_pool_pages_free − Innodb_buffer_pool_pages_data. Added in MySQL 5.0.2.

- Innodb_buffer_pool_pages_total

  The total size of buffer pool, in pages. Added in MySQL 5.0.2.

- Innodb_buffer_pool_read_ahead_rnd

  The number of "random" read-aheads initiated by InnoDB. This happens when a query scans a large portion of a table but in random order. Added in MySQL 5.0.2.

- Innodb_buffer_pool_read_ahead_seq

  The number of sequential read-aheads initiated by InnoDB. This happens when InnoDB does a sequential full table scan. Added in MySQL 5.0.2.

- Innodb_buffer_pool_read_requests

  The number of logical read requests InnoDB has done. Added in MySQL 5.0.2.

- Innodb_buffer_pool_reads

  The number of logical reads that InnoDB could not satisfy from the buffer pool and had to do a single-page read. Added in MySQL 5.0.2.

- Innodb_buffer_pool_wait_free

  Normally, writes to the InnoDB buffer pool happen in the background. However, if it is necessary to read or create a page and no clean pages are available, it is also necessary to wait for pages to be flushed first. This counter counts instances of these waits. If the buffer pool size has been set properly, this value should be small. Added in MySQL 5.0.2.

- `Innodb_buffer_pool_write_requests`

  The number writes done to the InnoDB buffer pool. Added in MySQL 5.0.2.

- `Innodb_data_fsyncs`

  The number of fsync() operations so far. Added in MySQL 5.0.2.

- `Innodb_data_pending_fsyncs`

  The current number of pending fsync() operations. Added in MySQL 5.0.2.

- `Innodb_data_pending_reads`

  The current number of pending reads. Added in MySQL 5.0.2.

- `Innodb_data_pending_writes`

  The current number of pending writes. Added in MySQL 5.0.2.

- `Innodb_data_read`

  The amount of data read so far, in bytes. Added in MySQL 5.0.2.

- `Innodb_data_reads`

  The total number of data reads. Added in MySQL 5.0.2.

- `Innodb_data_writes`

  The total number of data writes. Added in MySQL 5.0.2.

- `Innodb_data_written`

  The amount of data written so far, in bytes. Added in MySQL 5.0.2.

- `Innodb_dblwr_writes, Innodb_dblwr_pages_written`

  The number of doublewrite operations that have been performed and the number of pages that have been written for this purpose. Added in MySQL 5.0.2. See Section 8.2.14.1, "Disk I/O."

- `Innodb_log_waits`

  The number of times that the log buffer was too small and a wait was required for it to be flushed before continuing. Added in MySQL 5.0.2.

- `Innodb_log_write_requests`

  The number of log write requests. Added in MySQL 5.0.2.

- `Innodb_log_writes`

  The number of physical writes to the log file. Added in MySQL 5.0.2.

- `Innodb_os_log_fsyncs`

  The number of fsync() writes done to the log file. Added in MySQL 5.0.2.

- `Innodb_os_log_pending_fsyncs`

  The number of pending log file fsync() operations. Added in MySQL 5.0.2.

- `Innodb_os_log_pending_writes`

  The number of pending log file writes. Added in MySQL 5.0.2.

- `Innodb_os_log_written`

  The number of bytes written to the log file. Added in MySQL 5.0.2.

- `Innodb_page_size`

  The compiled-in InnoDB page size (default 16KB). Many values are counted in pages; the page size allows them to be easily converted to bytes. Added in MySQL 5.0.2.

- `Innodb_pages_created`

  The number of pages created. Added in MySQL 5.0.2.

- `Innodb_pages_read`

  The number of pages read. Added in MySQL 5.0.2.

- `Innodb_pages_written`

  The number of pages written. Added in MySQL 5.0.2.

- `Innodb_row_lock_current_waits`

  The number of row locks currently being waited for. Added in MySQL 5.0.3.

- `Innodb_row_lock_time`

  The total time spent in acquiring row locks, in milliseconds. Added in MySQL 5.0.3.

- `Innodb_row_lock_time_avg`

  The average time to acquire a row lock, in milliseconds. Added in MySQL 5.0.3.

- `Innodb_row_lock_time_max`

  The maximum time to acquire a row lock, in milliseconds. Added in MySQL 5.0.3.

- `Innodb_row_lock_waits`

  The number of times a row lock had to be waited for. Added in MySQL 5.0.3.

- `Innodb_rows_deleted`

  The number of rows deleted from InnoDB tables. Added in MySQL 5.0.2.

- `Innodb_rows_inserted`

  The number of rows inserted into InnoDB tables. Added in MySQL 5.0.2.

- `Innodb_rows_read`

  The number of rows read from InnoDB tables. Added in MySQL 5.0.2.

- `Innodb_rows_updated`

  The number of rows updated in InnoDB tables. Added in MySQL 5.0.2.

- `Key_blocks_not_flushed`

  The number of key blocks in the key cache that have changed but have not yet been flushed to disk.

- `Key_blocks_unused`

  The number of unused blocks in the key cache. You can use this value to determine how much of the key cache is in use; see the discussion of `key_buffer_size` in Section 4.2.2, "Server System Variables."

- `Key_blocks_used`

  The number of used blocks in the key cache. This value is a high-water mark that indicates the maximum number of blocks that have ever been in use at one time.

- `Key_read_requests`

  The number of requests to read a key block from the cache.

- `Key_reads`

  The number of physical reads of a key block from disk. If `Key_reads` is large, your `key_buffer_size` value is probably too small. The cache miss rate can be calculated as `Key_reads/Key_read_requests`.

- `Key_write_requests`

  The number of requests to write a key block to the cache.

- `Key_writes`

  The number of physical writes of a key block to disk.

- `Last_query_cost`

  The total cost of the last compiled query as computed by the query optimizer. This is useful for comparing the cost of different query plans for the same query. The default value of 0 means that no query has been compiled yet. This variable was added in MySQL 5.0.1, with a default value of –1. In MySQL 5.0.7, the default was changed to 0; also in version 5.0.7, the scope of `Last_query_cost` was changed to session rather than global.

  Prior to MySQL 5.0.16, this variable was not updated for queries served from the query cache.

- `Max_used_connections`

  The maximum number of connections that have been in use simultaneously since the server started.

- `Not_flushed_delayed_rows`

  The number of rows waiting to be written in `INSERT DELAY` queues.

- `Open_files`

  The number of files that are open.

- `Open_streams`

  The number of streams that are open (used mainly for logging).

- `Open_tables`

  The number of tables that are open.

- `Opened_tables`

  The number of tables that have been opened. If `Opened_tables` is big, your `table_cache` value is probably too small.

- Qcache_free_blocks

  The number of free memory blocks in the query cache.

- Qcache_free_memory

  The amount of free memory for the query cache.

- Qcache_hits

  The number of query cache hits.

- Qcache_inserts

  The number of queries added to the query cache.

- Qcache_lowmem_prunes

  The number of queries that were deleted from the query cache because of low memory.

- Qcache_not_cached

  The number of non-cached queries (not cacheable, or not cached due to the
  query_cache_type setting).

- Qcache_queries_in_cache

  The number of queries registered in the query cache.

- Qcache_total_blocks

  The total number of blocks in the query cache.

- Questions

  The number of statements that clients have sent to the server.

- Rpl_status

  The status of fail-safe replication (not yet implemented).

- Select_full_join

  The number of joins that perform table scans because they do not use indexes. If this
  value is not 0, you should carefully check the indexes of your tables.

- Select_full_range_join

  The number of joins that used a range search on a reference table.

- Select_range

  The number of joins that used ranges on the first table. This is normally not a critical
  issue even if the value is quite large.

- Select_range_check

  The number of joins without keys that check for key usage after each row. If this is not
  0, you should carefully check the indexes of your tables.

- Select_scan

  The number of joins that did a full scan of the first table.

- Slave_open_temp_tables

  The number of temporary tables that the slave SQL thread currently has open.

- Slave_running

  This is ON if this server is a slave that is connected to a master.

- Slave_retried_transactions

  The total number of times since startup that the replication slave SQL thread has retried transactions. This variable was added in version 5.0.4.

- Slow_launch_threads

  The number of threads that have taken more than slow_launch_time seconds to create.

- Slow_queries

  The number of queries that have taken more than long_query_time seconds. See Section 4.12.4, "The Slow Query Log."

- Sort_merge_passes

  The number of merge passes that the sort algorithm has had to do. If this value is large, you should consider increasing the value of the sort_buffer_size system variable.

- Sort_range

  The number of sorts that were done using ranges.

- Sort_rows

  The number of sorted rows.

- Sort_scan

  The number of sorts that were done by scanning the table.

- Ssl_xxx

  Variables used for SSL connections.

- Table_locks_immediate

  The number of times that a table lock was acquired immediately.

- Table_locks_waited

  The number of times that a table lock could not be acquired immediately and a wait was needed. If this is high and you have performance problems, you should first optimize your queries, and then either split your table or tables or use replication.

- Threads_cached

  The number of threads in the thread cache.

- Threads_connected

  The number of currently open connections.

- Threads_created

  The number of threads created to handle connections. If Threads_created is big, you may want to increase the thread_cache_size value. The cache hit rate can be calculated as Threads_created/Connections.

- Threads_running

  The number of threads that are not sleeping.

- Uptime

  The number of seconds that the server has been up.

4.2.5 The Server SQL Mode

The MySQL server can operate in different SQL modes, and can apply these modes differently for different clients. This capability enables each application to tailor the server's operating mode to its own requirements.

Modes define what SQL syntax MySQL should support and what kind of data validation checks it should perform. This makes it easier to use MySQL in different environments and to use MySQL together with other database servers.

You can set the default SQL mode by starting mysqld with the --sql-mode="*modes*" option. *modes* is a list of different modes separated by comma (',') characters. The default value is empty (no modes set). The *modes* value also can be empty (--sql-mode="") if you want to clear it explicitly.

You can change the SQL mode at runtime by using a SET [GLOBAL|SESSION] sql_mode='*modes*' statement to set the sql_mode system value. Setting the GLOBAL variable requires the SUPER privilege and affects the operation of all clients that connect from that time on. Setting the SESSION variable affects only the current client. Any client can change its own session sql_mode value at any time.

You can retrieve the current global or session sql_mode value with the following statements:

```
SELECT @@global.sql_mode;
SELECT @@session.sql_mode;
```

The most important sql_mode values are probably these:

- ANSI

  Change syntax and behavior to be more conformant to standard SQL.

- STRICT_TRANS_TABLES

  If a value could not be inserted as given into a transactional table, abort the statement. For a non-transactional table, abort the statement if the value occurs in a single-row statement or the first row of a multiple-row statement. More detail is given later in this section. (Implemented in MySQL 5.0.2.)

- TRADITIONAL

  Make MySQL behave like a "traditional" SQL database system. A simple description of this mode is "give an error instead of a warning" when inserting an incorrect value into a column. **Note**: The INSERT/UPDATE aborts as soon as the error is noticed. This may not be what you want if you are using a non-transactional storage engine, because data changes made prior to the error are not be rolled back, resulting in a "partially done" update. (Added in MySQL 5.0.2.)

When this manual refers to "strict mode," it means a mode where at least one of STRICT_TRANS_TABLES or STRICT_ALL_TABLES is enabled.

The following list describes all supported modes:

- ALLOW_INVALID_DATES

  Don't do full checking of dates. Check only that the month is in the range from 1 to 12 and the day is in the range from 1 to 31. This is very convenient for Web applications where you obtain year, month, and day in three different fields and you want to store exactly what the user inserted (without date validation). This mode applies to DATE and DATETIME columns. It does not apply TIMESTAMP columns, which always require a valid date.

  This mode is implemented in MySQL 5.0.2. Before 5.0.2, this was the default MySQL date-handling mode. As of 5.0.2, the server requires that month and day values be legal, and not merely in the range 1 to 12 and 1 to 31, respectively. With strict mode disabled, invalid dates such as '2004-04-31' are converted to '0000-00-00' and a warning is generated. With strict mode enabled, invalid dates generate an error. To allow such dates, enable ALLOW_INVALID_DATES.

- ANSI_QUOTES

  Treat '"' as an identifier quote character (like the '`' quote character) and not as a string quote character. You can still use '`' to quote identifiers with this mode enabled. With ANSI_QUOTES enabled, you cannot use double quotes to quote literal strings, because it is interpreted as an identifier.

- ERROR_FOR_DIVISION_BY_ZERO

  Produce an error in strict mode (otherwise a warning) when a division by zero (or MOD(X,0)) occurs during an INSERT or UPDATE. If this mode is not enabled, MySQL instead returns NULL for divisions by zero. For INSERT IGNORE or UPDATE IGNORE, MySQL generates a warning for divisions by zero, but the result of the operation is NULL. (Implemented in MySQL 5.0.2.)

- HIGH_NOT_PRECEDENCE

  From MySQL 5.0.2 on, the precedence of the NOT operator is such that expressions such as NOT a BETWEEN b AND c are parsed as NOT (a BETWEEN b AND c). Before MySQL 5.0.2, the expression is parsed as (NOT a) BETWEEN b AND c. The old higher-precedence behavior can be obtained by enabling the HIGH_NOT_PRECEDENCE SQL mode. (Added in MySQL 5.0.2.)

```
mysql> SET sql_mode = '';
mysql> SELECT NOT 1 BETWEEN -5 AND 5;
        -> 0
```

```
mysql> SET sql_mode = 'broken_not';
mysql> SELECT NOT 1 BETWEEN -5 AND 5;
        -> 1
```

- IGNORE_SPACE

  Allow spaces between a function name and the '(' character. This forces all function names to be treated as reserved words. As a result, if you want to access any database, table, or column name that is a reserved word, you must quote it. For example, because there is a USER() function, the name of the user table in the mysql database and the User column in that table become reserved, so you must quote them:

  ```
  SELECT "User" FROM mysql."user";
  ```

  The IGNORE_SPACE SQL mode applies to built-in functions, not to stored routines. It is always allowable to have spaces after a routine name, regardless of whether IGNORE_SPACE is enabled.

- NO_AUTO_CREATE_USER

  Prevent GRANT from automatically creating new users if it would otherwise do so, unless a non-empty password also is specified. (Added in MySQL 5.0.2.)

- NO_AUTO_VALUE_ON_ZERO

  NO_AUTO_VALUE_ON_ZERO affects handling of AUTO_INCREMENT columns. Normally, you generate the next sequence number for the column by inserting either NULL or 0 into it. NO_AUTO_VALUE_ON_ZERO suppresses this behavior for 0 so that only NULL generates the next sequence number.

  This mode can be useful if 0 has been stored in a table's AUTO_INCREMENT column. (Storing 0 is not a recommended practice, by the way.) For example, if you dump the table with mysqldump and then reload it, MySQL normally generates new sequence numbers when it encounters the 0 values, resulting in a table with contents different from the one that was dumped. Enabling NO_AUTO_VALUE_ON_ZERO before reloading the dump file solves this problem. mysqldump now automatically includes in its output a statement that enables NO_AUTO_VALUE_ON_ZERO, to avoid this problem.

- NO_BACKSLASH_ESCAPES

  Disable the use of the backslash character ('\') as an escape character within strings. With this mode enabled, backslash becomes any ordinary character like any other. (Implemented in MySQL 5.0.1.)

- NO_DIR_IN_CREATE

  When creating a table, ignore all INDEX DIRECTORY and DATA DIRECTORY directives. This option is useful on slave replication servers.

- NO_ENGINE_SUBSTITUTION

  Prevents automatic substitution of the default storage engine when a statement such as CREATE TABLE specifies a storage engine that is disabled or not compiled in. (Implemented in MySQL 5.0.8.)

- NO_FIELD_OPTIONS

Do not print MySQL-specific column options in the output of SHOW CREATE TABLE. This mode is used by mysqldump in portability mode.

- NO_KEY_OPTIONS

Do not print MySQL-specific index options in the output of SHOW CREATE TABLE. This mode is used by mysqldump in portability mode.

- NO_TABLE_OPTIONS

Do not print MySQL-specific table options (such as ENGINE) in the output of SHOW CREATE TABLE. This mode is used by mysqldump in portability mode.

- NO_UNSIGNED_SUBTRACTION

In subtraction operations, do not mark the result as UNSIGNED if one of the operands is unsigned. Note that this makes BIGINT UNSIGNED not 100% usable in all contexts.

- NO_ZERO_DATE

In strict mode, don't allow '0000-00-00' as a valid date. You can still insert zero dates with the IGNORE option. When not in strict mode, the date is accepted but a warning is generated. (Added in MySQL 5.0.2.)

- NO_ZERO_IN_DATE

In strict mode, don't accept dates where the month or day part is 0. If used with the IGNORE option, MySQL inserts a '0000-00-00' date for any such date. When not in strict mode, the date is accepted but a warning is generated. (Added in MySQL 5.0.2.)

- ONLY_FULL_GROUP_BY

Do not allow queries for which the GROUP BY clause refers to a column that is not present in the output column list.

- PIPES_AS_CONCAT

Treat || as a string concatenation operator (same as CONCAT()) rather than as a synonym for OR.

- REAL_AS_FLOAT

Treat REAL as a synonym for FLOAT. By default, MySQL treats REAL as a synonym for DOUBLE.

- STRICT_ALL_TABLES

Enable strict mode for all storage engines. Invalid data values are rejected. Additional detail follows. (Added in MySQL 5.0.2.)

- STRICT_TRANS_TABLES

Enable strict mode for transactional storage engines, and when possible for non-transactional storage engines. Additional details follow. (Implemented in MySQL 5.0.2.)

Strict mode controls how MySQL handles input values that are invalid or missing. A value can be invalid for several reasons. For example, it might have the wrong data type for the column, or it might be out of range. A value is missing when a new row to be inserted does not contain a value for a column that has no explicit DEFAULT clause in its definition.

For transactional tables, an error occurs for invalid or missing values in a statement when either of the STRICT_ALL_TABLES or STRICT_TRANS_TABLES modes are enabled. The statement is aborted and rolled back.

For non-transactional tables, the behavior is the same for either mode, if the bad value occurs in the first row to be inserted or updated. The statement is aborted and the table remains unchanged. If the statement inserts or modifies multiple rows and the bad value occurs in the second or later row, the result depends on which strict option is enabled:

- For STRICT_ALL_TABLES, MySQL returns an error and ignores the rest of the rows. However, in this case, the earlier rows still have been inserted or updated. This means that you might get a partial update, which might not be what you want. To avoid this, it's best to use single-row statements because these can be aborted without changing the table.

- For STRICT_TRANS_TABLES, MySQL converts an invalid value to the closest valid value for the column and insert the adjusted value. If a value is missing, MySQL inserts the implicit default value for the column data type. In either case, MySQL generates a warning rather than an error and continues processing the statement. Implicit defaults are described in the "MySQL Language Reference."

Strict mode disallows invalid date values such as '2004-04-31'. It does not disallow dates with zero parts such as '2004-04-00' or "zero" dates. To disallow these as well, enable the NO_ZERO_IN_DATE and NO_ZERO_DATE SQL modes in addition to strict mode.

If you are not using strict mode (that is, neither STRICT_TRANS_TABLES nor STRICT_ALL_TABLES is enabled), MySQL inserts adjusted values for invalid or missing values and produces warnings. In strict mode, you can produce this behavior by using INSERT IGNORE or UPDATE IGNORE.

The following special modes are provided as shorthand for combinations of mode values from the preceding list. All are available in MySQL 5.0 beginning with version 5.0.0, except for TRADITIONAL, which was implemented in MySQL 5.0.2.

The descriptions include all mode values that are available in the most recent version of MySQL. For older versions, a combination mode does not include individual mode values that are not available except in newer versions.

- ANSI

  Equivalent to REAL_AS_FLOAT, PIPES_AS_CONCAT, ANSI_QUOTES, IGNORE_SPACE. Before MySQL 5.0.3, ANSI also includes ONLY_FULL_GROUP_BY. See Section 1.9.3, "Running MySQL in ANSI Mode."

- DB2

  Equivalent to `PIPES_AS_CONCAT`, `ANSI_QUOTES`, `IGNORE_SPACE`, `NO_KEY_OPTIONS`, `NO_TABLE_OPTIONS`, `NO_FIELD_OPTIONS`.

- MAXDB

  Equivalent to `PIPES_AS_CONCAT`, `ANSI_QUOTES`, `IGNORE_SPACE`, `NO_KEY_OPTIONS`, `NO_TABLE_OPTIONS`, `NO_FIELD_OPTIONS`, `NO_AUTO_CREATE_USER`.

- MSSQL

  Equivalent to `PIPES_AS_CONCAT`, `ANSI_QUOTES`, `IGNORE_SPACE`, `NO_KEY_OPTIONS`, `NO_TABLE_OPTIONS`, `NO_FIELD_OPTIONS`.

- MYSQL323

  Equivalent to `NO_FIELD_OPTIONS`, `HIGH_NOT_PRECEDENCE`.

- MYSQL40

  Equivalent to `NO_FIELD_OPTIONS`, `HIGH_NOT_PRECEDENCE`.

- ORACLE

  Equivalent to `PIPES_AS_CONCAT`, `ANSI_QUOTES`, `IGNORE_SPACE`, `NO_KEY_OPTIONS`, `NO_TABLE_OPTIONS`, `NO_FIELD_OPTIONS`, `NO_AUTO_CREATE_USER`.

- POSTGRESQL

  Equivalent to `PIPES_AS_CONCAT`, `ANSI_QUOTES`, `IGNORE_SPACE`, `NO_KEY_OPTIONS`, `NO_TABLE_OPTIONS`, `NO_FIELD_OPTIONS`.

- TRADITIONAL

  Equivalent to `STRICT_TRANS_TABLES`, `STRICT_ALL_TABLES`, `NO_ZERO_IN_DATE`, `NO_ZERO_DATE`, `ERROR_FOR_DIVISION_BY_ZERO`, `NO_AUTO_CREATE_USER`.

4.2.6 The MySQL Server Shutdown Process

The server shutdown process takes place as follows:

1. The shutdown process is initiated.

   Server shutdown can be initiated several ways. For example, a user with the `SHUTDOWN` privilege can execute a `mysqladmin shutdown` command. `mysqladmin` can be used on any platform supported by MySQL. Other operating system–specific shutdown initiation methods are possible as well: The server shuts down on Unix when it receives a `SIGTERM` signal. A server running as a service on Windows shuts down when the services manager tells it to.

2. The server creates a shutdown thread if necessary.

   Depending on how shutdown was initiated, the server might create a thread to handle the shutdown process. If shutdown was requested by a client, a shutdown thread is created. If shutdown is the result of receiving a `SIGTERM` signal, the signal thread might handle shutdown itself, or it might create a separate thread to do so. If the server tries to create a shutdown thread and cannot (for example, if memory is exhausted), it issues a diagnostic message that appears in the error log:

```
Error: Can't create thread to kill server
```

3. The server stops accepting new connections.

To prevent new activity from being initiated during shutdown, the server stops accepting new client connections. It does this by closing the network connections to which it normally listens for connections: the TCP/IP port, the Unix socket file, the Windows named pipe, and shared memory on Windows.

4. The server terminates current activity.

For each thread that is associated with a client connection, the connection to the client is broken and the thread is marked as killed. Threads die when they notice that they are so marked. Threads for idle connections die quickly. Threads that currently are processing statements check their state periodically and take longer to die. For additional information about thread termination, see the description of the KILL statement in the "MySQL Language Reference," in particular for the instructions about killed REPAIR TABLE or OPTIMIZE TABLE operations on MyISAM tables.

For threads that have an open transaction, the transaction is rolled back. Note that if a thread is updating a non-transactional table, an operation such as a multiple-row UPDATE or INSERT may leave the table partially updated, because the operation can terminate before completion.

If the server is a master replication server, threads associated with currently connected slaves are treated like other client threads. That is, each one is marked as killed and exits when it next checks its state.

If the server is a slave replication server, the I/O and SQL threads, if active, are stopped before client threads are marked as killed. The SQL thread is allowed to finish its current statement (to avoid causing replication problems), and then stops. If the SQL thread was in the middle of a transaction at this point, the transaction is rolled back.

5. Storage engines are shut down or closed.

At this stage, the table cache is flushed and all open tables are closed.

Each storage engine performs any actions necessary for tables that it manages. For example, MyISAM flushes any pending index writes for a table. InnoDB flushes its buffer pool to disk (starting from 5.0.5: unless innodb_fast_shutdown is 2), writes the current LSN to the tablespace, and terminates its own internal threads.

6. The server exits.

4.3 The `mysqld-max` Extended MySQL Server

A MySQL-Max server is a version of the `mysqld` MySQL server that has been built to include additional features. The MySQL-Max distribution to use depends on your platform:

- For Windows, MySQL binary distributions include both the standard server (`mysqld.exe`) and the MySQL-Max server (`mysqld-max.exe`), so no special distribution is needed. Just use a regular Windows distribution. See Section 2.3, "Installing MySQL on Windows."

- For Linux, if you install MySQL using RPM distributions, the `MySQL-Max` RPM presupposes that you have already installed the regular server RPM. Use the regular `MySQL-server` RPM first to install a standard server named `mysqld`, and then use the `MySQL-Max` RPM to install a server named `mysqld-max`. See Section 2.4, "Installing MySQL on Linux," for more information on the Linux RPM packages.

- All other MySQL-Max distributions contain a single server that is named `mysqld` but that has the additional features included.

You can find the MySQL-Max binaries on the MySQL AB Web site at `http://dev.mysql.com/downloads/`.

MySQL AB builds the MySQL-Max servers by using the following `configure` options:

- `--with-server-suffix=-max`

  This option adds a `-max` suffix to the `mysqld` version string.

- `--with-innodb`

  This option enables support for the `InnoDB` storage engine. MySQL-Max servers always include `InnoDB` support. From MySQL 4.0 onward, `InnoDB` is included by default in all binary distributions, so a MySQL-Max server is not needed to obtain `InnoDB` support.

- `--with-bdb`

  This option enables support for the Berkeley DB (`BDB`) storage engine on those platforms for which `BDB` is available. (See notes in the following discussion.)

- `--with-blackhole-storage-engine`

  This option enables support for the `BLACKHOLE` storage engine.

- `--with-csv-storage-engine`

  This option enables support for the `CSV` storage engine.

- `--with-example-storage-engine`

  This option enables support for the `EXAMPLE` storage engine.

- `--with-federated-storage-engine`

  This option enables support for the `FEDERATED` storage engine.

- `--with-ndbcluster`

  This option enables support for the `NDB Cluster` storage engine on those platforms for which Cluster is available. (See notes in the following discussion.)

- USE_SYMDIR

  This define is enabled to turn on database symbolic link support for Windows. From MySQL 4.0 onward, symbolic link support is enabled for all Windows servers, so a MySQL-Max server is not needed to take advantage of this feature.

MySQL-Max binary distributions are a convenience for those who wish to install precompiled programs. If you build MySQL using a source distribution, you can build your own Max-like server by enabling the same features at configuration time that the MySQL-Max binary distributions are built with.

MySQL-Max servers include the BerkeleyDB (BDB) storage engine whenever possible, but not all platforms support BDB.

Currently, MySQL Cluster is supported on Linux (on most platforms), Solaris, Mac OS X, and HP-UX only. Some users have reported success in using MySQL Cluster built from source on BSD operating systems, but these are not officially supported at this time. Note that, even for servers compiled with Cluster support, the NDB Cluster storage engine is not enabled by default. You must start the server with the --ndbcluster option to use it as part of a MySQL Cluster. (For details, see Section 9.4, "MySQL Cluster Configuration.")

The following table shows the platforms for which MySQL-Max binaries include support for BDB and NDB Cluster.

System	BDB Support	NDB Support
AIX 5.2	N	N
HP-UX	Y	Y
Linux-IA-64	N	Y
Linux-Intel	Y	Y
Mac OS X	N	Y
NetWare	N	N
SCO 6	N	N
Solaris-SPARC	Y	Y
Solaris-Intel	N	Y
Solaris-AMD 64	Y	Y
Windows NT/2000/XP	Y	N

To find out which storage engines your server supports, use the SHOW ENGINES statement. For example:

```
mysql> SHOW ENGINES\G
*************************** 1. row ***************************
 Engine: MyISAM
Support: DEFAULT
Comment: Default engine as of MySQL 3.23 with great performance
```

```
*************************** 2. row ***************************
 Engine: MEMORY
Support: YES
Comment: Hash based, stored in memory, useful for temporary tables
*************************** 3. row ***************************
 Engine: InnoDB
Support: YES
Comment: Supports transactions, row-level locking, and foreign keys
*************************** 4. row ***************************
 Engine: BerkeleyDB
Support: NO
Comment: Supports transactions and page-level locking
*************************** 5. row ***************************
 Engine: BLACKHOLE
Support: YES
Comment: /dev/null storage engine (anything you write to it disappears)
...
```

The precise output from SHOW ENGINES may vary according to the MySQL version used (and the features that are enabled). The Support values in the output indicate the server's level of support for each feature, as shown here:

Value	Meaning
YES	The feature is supported and is active.
NO	The feature is not supported.
DISABLED	The feature is supported but has been disabled.

A value of NO means that the server was compiled without support for the feature, so it cannot be activated at runtime.

A value of DISABLED occurs either because the server was started with an option that disables the feature, or because not all options required to enable it were given. In the latter case, the error log file should contain a reason indicating why the option is disabled. See Section 4.12.1, "The Error Log."

You might also see DISABLED for a storage engine if the server was compiled to support it, but was started with a --skip-*engine* option. For example, --skip-innodb disables the InnoDB engine. For the NDB Cluster storage engine, DISABLED means the server was compiled with support for MySQL Cluster, but was not started with the --ndb-cluster option.

All MySQL servers support MyISAM tables, because MyISAM is the default storage engine.

4.4 MySQL Server Startup Programs

This section describes several programs that are used to start `mysqld`, the MySQL server.

4.4.1 `mysqld_safe`—MySQL Server Startup Script

`mysqld_safe` is the recommended way to start a `mysqld` server on Unix and NetWare. `mysqld_safe` adds some safety features such as restarting the server when an error occurs and logging runtime information to an error log file. NetWare-specific behaviors are listed later in this section.

Note: To preserve backward compatibility with older versions of MySQL, MySQL binary distributions still include `safe_mysqld` as a symbolic link to `mysqld_safe`. However, you should not rely on this because it is removed as of MySQL 5.1.

By default, `mysqld_safe` tries to start an executable named `mysqld-max` if it exists, and `mysqld` otherwise. Be aware of the implications of this behavior:

- On Linux, the `MySQL-Max` RPM relies on this `mysqld_safe` behavior. The RPM installs an executable named `mysqld-max`, which causes `mysqld_safe` to automatically use that executable rather than `mysqld` from that point on.

- If you install a MySQL-Max distribution that includes a server named `mysqld-max`, and then upgrade later to a non-Max version of MySQL, `mysqld_safe` will still attempt to run the old `mysqld-max` server. If you perform such an upgrade, you should manually remove the old `mysqld-max` server to ensure that `mysqld_safe` runs the new `mysqld` server.

To override the default behavior and specify explicitly the name of the server you want to run, specify a `--mysqld` or `--mysqld-version` option to `mysqld_safe`. You can also use `--ledir` to indicate the directory where `mysqld_safe` should look for the server.

Many of the options to `mysqld_safe` are the same as the options to `mysqld`. See Section 4.2.1, "`mysqld` Command Options."

All options specified to `mysqld_safe` on the command line are passed to `mysqld`. If you want to use any options that are specific to `mysqld_safe` and that `mysqld` doesn't support, do not specify them on the command line. Instead, list them in the `[mysqld_safe]` group of an option file. See Section 3.3.2, "Using Option Files."

`mysqld_safe` reads all options from the `[mysqld]`, `[server]`, and `[mysqld_safe]` sections in option files. For backward compatibility, it also reads `[safe_mysqld]` sections, although you should rename such sections to `[mysqld_safe]` in MySQL 5.0 installations.

`mysqld_safe` supports the following options:

- `--help`

  Display a help message and exit. (Added in MySQL 5.0.3.)

- `--autoclose`

  (NetWare only) On NetWare, `mysqld_safe` provides a screen presence. When you unload (shut down) the `mysqld_safe` NLM, the screen does not by default go away. Instead, it prompts for user input:

  `*<NLM has terminated; Press any key to close the screen>*`

  If you want NetWare to close the screen automatically instead, use the `--autoclose` option to `mysqld_safe`.

- `--basedir=path`

  The path to the MySQL installation directory.

- `--core-file-size=size`

  The size of the core file that `mysqld` should be able to create. The option value is passed to `ulimit -c`.

- `--datadir=path`

  The path to the data directory.

- `--defaults-extra-file=path`

  The name of an option file to be read in addition to the usual option files. This must be the first option on the command line if it is used.

- `--defaults-file=file_name`

  The name of an option file to be read instead of the usual option files. This must be the first option on the command line if it is used.

- `--ledir=path`

  If `mysqld_safe` cannot find the server, use this option to indicate the pathname to the directory where the server is located.

- `--log-error=file_name`

  Write the error log to the given file. See Section 4.12.1, "The Error Log."

- `--mysqld=prog_name`

  The name of the server program (in the `ledir` directory) that you want to start. This option is needed if you use the MySQL binary distribution but have the data directory outside of the binary distribution. If `mysqld_safe` cannot find the server, use the `--ledir` option to indicate the pathname to the directory where the server is located.

- `--mysqld-version=suffix`

  This option is similar to the `--mysqld` option, but you specify only the suffix for the server program name. The basename is assumed to be `mysqld`. For example, if you use `--mysqld-version=max`, `mysqld_safe` starts the `mysqld-max` program in the `ledir` directory. If the argument to `--mysqld-version` is empty, `mysqld_safe` uses `mysqld` in the `ledir` directory.

- `--nice=priority`

  Use the `nice` program to set the server's scheduling priority to the given value.

- `--no-defaults`

  Do not read any option files. This must be the first option on the command line if it is used.

- `--open-files-limit=count`

  The number of files that `mysqld` should be able to open. The option value is passed to `ulimit -n`. Note that you need to start `mysqld_safe` as `root` for this to work properly!

- `--pid-file=file_name`

  The pathname of the process ID file.

- `--port=port_num`

  The port number that the server should use when listening for TCP/IP connections. The port number must be 1024 or higher unless the server is started by the `root` system user.

- `--socket=path`

  The Unix socket file that the server should use when listening for local connections.

- `--timezone=timezone`

  Set the `TZ` time zone environment variable to the given option value. Consult your operating system documentation for legal time zone specification formats.

- `--user={user_name | user_id}`

  Run the `mysqld` server as the user having the name *user_name* or the numeric user ID *user_id*. ("User" in this context refers to a system login account, not a MySQL user listed in the grant tables.)

If you execute `mysqld_safe` with the `--defaults-file` or `--defaults-extra-option` option to name an option file, the option must be the first one given on the command line or the option file will not be used. For example, this command will not use the named option file:

```
mysql> mysqld_safe --port=port_num --defaults-file=file_name
```

Instead, use the following command:

```
mysql> mysqld_safe --defaults-file=file_name --port=port_num
```

The `mysqld_safe` script is written so that it normally can start a server that was installed from either a source or a binary distribution of MySQL, even though these types of distributions typically install the server in slightly different locations. (See Section 2.1.5, "Installation Layouts.") `mysqld_safe` expects one of the following conditions to be true:

- The server and databases can be found relative to the working directory (the directory from which `mysqld_safe` is invoked). For binary distributions, `mysqld_safe` looks under its working directory for `bin` and `data` directories. For source distributions, it looks for `libexec` and `var` directories. This condition should be met if you execute `mysqld_safe` from your MySQL installation directory (for example, `/usr/local/mysql` for a binary distribution).

- If the server and databases cannot be found relative to the working directory, `mysqld_safe` attempts to locate them by absolute pathnames. Typical locations are `/usr/local/libexec` and `/usr/local/var`. The actual locations are determined from the values configured into the distribution at the time it was built. They should be correct if MySQL is installed in the location specified at configuration time.

Because `mysqld_safe` tries to find the server and databases relative to its own working directory, you can install a binary distribution of MySQL anywhere, as long as you run `mysqld_safe` from the MySQL installation directory:

```
shell> cd mysql_installation_directory
shell> bin/mysqld_safe &
```

If `mysqld_safe` fails, even when invoked from the MySQL installation directory, you can specify the `--ledir` and `--datadir` options to indicate the directories in which the server and databases are located on your system.

Normally, you should not edit the `mysqld_safe` script. Instead, configure `mysqld_safe` by using command-line options or options in the `[mysqld_safe]` section of a `my.cnf` option file. In rare cases, it might be necessary to edit `mysqld_safe` to get it to start the server properly. However, if you do this, your modified version of `mysqld_safe` might be overwritten if you upgrade MySQL in the future, so you should make a copy of your edited version that you can reinstall.

On NetWare, `mysqld_safe` is a NetWare Loadable Module (NLM) that is ported from the original Unix shell script. It starts the server as follows:

1. Runs a number of system and option checks.
2. Runs a check on `MyISAM` tables.
3. Provides a screen presence for the MySQL server.
4. Starts `mysqld`, monitors it, and restarts it if it terminates in error.
5. Sends error messages from `mysqld` to the `host_name.err` file in the data directory.
6. Sends `mysqld_safe` screen output to the `host_name.safe` file in the data directory.

4.4.2 `mysql.server`—MySQL Server Startup Script

MySQL distributions on Unix include a script named `mysql.server`. It can be used on systems such as Linux and Solaris that use System V–style run directories to start and stop system services. It is also used by the Mac OS X Startup Item for MySQL.

`mysql.server` can be found in the `support-files` directory under your MySQL installation directory or in a MySQL source distribution.

If you use the Linux server RPM package (`MySQL-server-VERSION.rpm`), the `mysql.server` script will be installed in the `/etc/init.d` directory with the name `mysql`. You need not install it manually. See Section 2.4, "Installing MySQL on Linux," for more information on the Linux RPM packages.

Some vendors provide RPM packages that install a startup script under a different name such as `mysqld`.

If you install MySQL from a source distribution or using a binary distribution format that does not install `mysql.server` automatically, you can install it manually. Instructions are provided in Section 2.9.2.2, "Starting and Stopping MySQL Automatically."

`mysql.server` reads options from the `[mysql.server]` and `[mysqld]` sections of option files. For backward compatibility, it also reads `[mysql_server]` sections, although you should rename such sections to `[mysql.server]` when using MySQL 5.0.

4.4.3 `mysqld_multi`—Manage Multiple MySQL Servers

`mysqld_multi` is designed to manage several `mysqld` processes that listen for connections on different Unix socket files and TCP/IP ports. It can start or stop servers, or report their current status. The MySQL Instance Manager is an alternative means of managing multiple servers (see Section 4.5, "`mysqlmanager`—The MySQL Instance Manager").

`mysqld_multi` searches for groups named `[mysqldN]` in `my.cnf` (or in the file named by the `--config-file` option). *N* can be any positive integer. This number is referred to in the following discussion as the option group number, or *GNR*. Group numbers distinguish option groups from one another and are used as arguments to `mysqld_multi` to specify which servers you want to start, stop, or obtain a status report for. Options listed in these groups are the same that you would use in the `[mysqld]` group used for starting `mysqld`. (See, for example, Section 2.9.2.2, "Starting and Stopping MySQL Automatically.") However, when using multiple servers, it is necessary that each one use its own value for options such as the Unix socket file and TCP/IP port number. For more information on which options must be unique per server in a multiple-server environment, see Section 4.13, "Running Multiple MySQL Servers on the Same Machine."

To invoke `mysqld_multi`, use the following syntax:

```
shell> mysqld_multi [options] {start|stop|report} [GNR[,GNR] ...]
```

`start`, `stop`, and `report` indicate which operation to perform. You can perform the designated operation for a single server or multiple servers, depending on the *GNR* list that follows the option name. If there is no list, `mysqld_multi` performs the operation for all servers in the option file.

Each *GNR* value represents an option group number or range of group numbers. The value should be the number at the end of the group name in the option file. For example, the *GNR* for a group named [mysqld17] is 17. To specify a range of numbers, separate the first and last numbers by a dash. The *GNR* value 10-13 represents groups [mysqld10] through [mysqld13]. Multiple groups or group ranges can be specified on the command line, separated by commas. There must be no whitespace characters (spaces or tabs) in the *GNR* list; anything after a whitespace character is ignored.

This command starts a single server using option group [mysqld17]:

```
shell> mysqld_multi start 17
```

This command stops several servers, using option groups [mysqld8] and [mysqld10] through [mysqld13]:

```
shell> mysqld_multi stop 8,10-13
```

For an example of how you might set up an option file, use this command:

```
shell> mysqld_multi --example
```

mysqld_multi supports the following options:

- --help

  Display a help message and exit.

- --config-file=*file_name*

  Specify the name of an alternative option file. This affects where mysqld_multi looks for [mysqld*N*] option groups. Without this option, all options are read from the usual my.cnf file. The option does not affect where mysqld_multi reads its own options, which are always taken from the [mysqld_multi] group in the usual my.cnf file.

- --example

  Display a sample option file.

- --log=*file_name*

  Specify the name of the log file. If the file exists, log output is appended to it.

- --mysqladmin=*prog_name*

  The mysqladmin binary to be used to stop servers.

- --mysqld=*prog_name*

  The mysqld binary to be used. Note that you can specify mysqld_safe as the value for this option also. If you use mysqld_safe to start the server, you can include the mysqld or ledir options in the corresponding [mysqld*N*] option group. These options indicate the name of the server that mysqld_safe should start and the pathname of the directory where the server is located. (See the descriptions for these options in Section 4.4.1, "mysqld_safe—MySQL Server Startup Script.") Example:

```
[mysqld38]
mysqld = mysqld-max
ledir  = /opt/local/mysql/libexec
```

- `--no-log`

  Print log information to `stdout` rather than to the log file. By default, output goes to the log file.

- `--password=password`

  The password of the MySQL account to use when invoking `mysqladmin`. Note that the password value is not optional for this option, unlike for other MySQL programs.

- `--silent`

  Silent mode; disable warnings.

- `--tcp-ip`

  Connect to each MySQL server via the TCP/IP port instead of the Unix socket file. (If a socket file is missing, the server might still be running, but accessible only via the TCP/IP port.) By default, connections are made using the Unix socket file. This option affects `stop` and `report` operations.

- `--user=user_name`

  The username of the MySQL account to use when invoking `mysqladmin`.

- `--verbose`

  Be more verbose.

- `--version`

  Display version information and exit.

Some notes about `mysqld_multi`:

- **Most important**: Before using `mysqld_multi` be sure that you understand the meanings of the options that are passed to the `mysqld` servers and *why* you would want to have separate `mysqld` processes. Beware of the dangers of using multiple `mysqld` servers with the same data directory. Use separate data directories, unless you *know* what you are doing. Starting multiple servers with the same data directory does *not* give you extra performance in a threaded system. See Section 4.13, "Running Multiple MySQL Servers on the Same Machine."

- **Important**: Make sure that the data directory for each server is fully accessible to the Unix account that the specific `mysqld` process is started as. *Do not* use the Unix `root` account for this, unless you *know* what you are doing. See Section 4.7.5, "How to Run MySQL As a Normal User."

- Make sure that the MySQL account used for stopping the `mysqld` servers (with the `mysqladmin` program) has the same username and password for each server. Also, make sure that the account has the `SHUTDOWN` privilege. If the servers that you want to manage have different usernames or passwords for the administrative accounts, you might want to create an account on each server that has the same username and password. For example, you might set up a common `multi_admin` account by executing the following commands for each server:

```
shell> mysql -u root -S /tmp/mysql.sock -p
Enter password:
mysql> GRANT SHUTDOWN ON *.*
    -> TO 'multi_admin'@'localhost' IDENTIFIED BY 'multipass';
```

See Section 4.8.2, "How the Privilege System Works." You have to do this for each mysqld server. Change the connection parameters appropriately when connecting to each one. Note that the hostname part of the account name must allow you to connect as multi_admin from the host where you want to run mysqld_multi.

- The Unix socket file and the TCP/IP port number must be different for every mysqld.

- The --pid-file option is very important if you are using mysqld_safe to start mysqld (for example, --mysqld=mysqld_safe). Every mysqld should have its own process ID file. The advantage of using mysqld_safe instead of mysqld is that mysqld_safe monitors its mysqld process and restarts it if the process terminates due to a signal sent using kill -9 or for other reasons, such as a segmentation fault. Please note that the mysqld_safe script might require that you start it from a certain place. This means that you might have to change location to a certain directory before running mysqld_multi. If you have problems starting, please see the mysqld_safe script. Check especially the lines:

```
-------------------------------------------------------------
MY_PWD=`pwd`
# Check if we are starting this relative (for the binary release)
if test -d $MY_PWD/data/mysql -a -f ./share/mysql/english/errmsg.sys -a \
 -x ./bin/mysqld
-------------------------------------------------------------
```

The test performed by these lines should be successful, or you might encounter problems. See Section 4.4.1, "mysqld_safe—MySQL Server Startup Script."

- You might want to use the --user option for mysqld, but to do this you need to run the mysqld_multi script as the Unix root user. Having the option in the option file doesn't matter; you just get a warning if you are not the superuser and the mysqld processes are started under your own Unix account.

The following example shows how you might set up an option file for use with mysqld_multi. The order in which the mysqld programs are started or stopped depends on the order in which they appear in the option file. Group numbers need not form an unbroken sequence. The first and fifth [mysqldN] groups were intentionally omitted from the example to illustrate that you can have "gaps" in the option file. This gives you more flexibility.

```
# This file should probably be in your home dir (~/.my.cnf)
# or /etc/my.cnf
# Version 2.1 by Jani Tolonen

[mysqld_multi]
```

```
mysqld      = /usr/local/bin/mysqld_safe
mysqladmin  = /usr/local/bin/mysqladmin
user        = multi_admin
password    = multipass

[mysqld2]
socket    = /tmp/mysql.sock2
port      = 3307
pid-file  = /usr/local/mysql/var2/hostname.pid2
datadir   = /usr/local/mysql/var2
language  = /usr/local/share/mysql/english
user      = john

[mysqld3]
socket    = /tmp/mysql.sock3
port      = 3308
pid-file  = /usr/local/mysql/var3/hostname.pid3
datadir   = /usr/local/mysql/var3
language  = /usr/local/share/mysql/swedish
user      = monty

[mysqld4]
socket    = /tmp/mysql.sock4
port      = 3309
pid-file  = /usr/local/mysql/var4/hostname.pid4
datadir   = /usr/local/mysql/var4
language  = /usr/local/share/mysql/estonia
user      = tonu

[mysqld6]
socket    = /tmp/mysql.sock6
port      = 3311
pid-file  = /usr/local/mysql/var6/hostname.pid6
datadir   = /usr/local/mysql/var6
language  = /usr/local/share/mysql/japanese
user      = jani
```

See Section 3.3.2, "Using Option Files."

4.5 `mysqlmanager`—The MySQL Instance Manager

`mysqlmanager` is the MySQL Instance Manager (IM). This program is a daemon running on a TCP/IP port that serves to monitor and manage MySQL Database Server instances. MySQL Instance Manager is available for Unix-like operating systems, and also on Windows as of MySQL 5.0.13.

MySQL Instance Manager is included in MySQL distributions from version 5.0.3, and can be used in place of the `mysqld_safe` script to start and stop the MySQL Server, *even from a remote host*. MySQL Instance Manager also implements the functionality (and most of the syntax) of the `mysqld_multi` script. A more detailed description of MySQL Instance Manager follows.

4.5.1 Starting the MySQL Server with MySQL Instance Manager

Normally, the `mysqld` MySQL Database Server is started with the `mysql.server` script, which usually resides in the `/etc/init.d/` folder. In MySQL 5.0.3 this script invokes `mysqlmanager` (the MySQL Instance Manager binary) to start MySQL. (In prior versions of MySQL the `mysqld_safe` script is used for this purpose.) Starting from MySQL 5.0.4 the behavior of the startup script was changed again to incorporate both setup schemes. In version 5.0.4, the startup script uses the old scheme (invoking `mysqld_safe`) by default, but you can set the `use_mysqld_safe` variable in the script to 0 (zero) to use the MySQL Instance Manager to start a server.

The Instance Manager's behavior in this case depends on the options given in the MySQL configuration file. If there is no configuration file, the MySQL Instance Manager creates a server instance named `mysqld` and attempts to start it with default (compiled-in) configuration values. This means that the IM cannot guess the placement of `mysqld` if it is not installed in the default location. If you have installed the MySQL server in a non-standard location, you should use a configuration file. See Section 2.1.5, "Installation Layouts."

If there is a configuration file, the IM reads it to find `[mysqld]` sections (for example, `[mysqld]`, `[mysqld1]`, `[mysqld2]`, and so forth). Each such section specifies an instance. When it starts, the Instance Manager attempts to start all server instances that it finds. By default, the Instance Manager stops all server instances when it shuts down.

Note that there is a special `--mysqld-path=path-to-mysqld-binary` option that is recognized only by the IM. Use this variable to let the IM know where the `mysqld` binary resides. You should also set `basedir` and `datadir` options for the server.

The typical startup/shutdown cycle for a MySQL server with the MySQL Instance Manager enabled is as follows:

1. The MySQL Instance Manager is started with `/etc/init.d/mysql` script.
2. The MySQL Instance Manager starts all instances and monitors them.
3. If a server instance fails the MySQL Instance Manager restarts it.
4. If the MySQL Instance Manager is shut down (for instance with the `/etc/init.d/mysql stop` command), all instances are shut down by the MySQL Instance Manager.

4.5.2 Connecting to the MySQL Instance Manager and Creating User Accounts

Communication with the MySQL Instance Manager is handled using the MySQL client-server protocol. As such, you can connect to the IM using the standard mysql client program, as well as the MySQL C API. The IM supports the version of the MySQL client/server protocol used by the client tools and libraries distributed along with MySQL 4.1 or later.

4.5.2.1 Instance Manager Users and Passwords

The Instance Manager stores its user information in a password file. The default name of the password file is /etc/mysqlmanager.passwd.

Password entries have the following format:

```
petr:*35110DC9B4D8140F5DE667E28C72DD2597B5C848
```

If there are no entries in the /etc/mysqlmanager.passwd file, you cannot connect to the Instance Manager.

To generate a new entry, invoke Instance Manager with the --passwd option. Then the output can be appended to the /etc/mysqlmanager.passwd file to add a new user. Here is an example:

```
shell> mysqlmanager --passwd >> /etc/mysqlmanager.passwd
Creating record for new user.
Enter user name: mike
Enter password: password
Re-type password: password
```

The preceding command causes the following line to be added to /etc/mysqlmanager.passwd:

```
mike:*00A51F3F48415C7D4E8908980D443C29C69B60C9
```

4.5.2.2 MySQL Server Accounts for Status Monitoring

To monitor server status, the MySQL Instance Manager will attempt to connect to the MySQL server instance at regular intervals using the MySQL_Instance_Manager@localhost user account with a password of check_connection.

You are *not* required to create a MySQL_Instance_M@localhost user account in order for the MySQL Instance Manager to monitor server status, because a login failure is sufficient to identify that the server is operational. However, if the account does not exist, failed connection attempts are logged by the server to its general query log (see Section 4.12.2, "The General Query Log").

4.5.3 MySQL Instance Manager Command Options

The MySQL Instance Manager supports a number of command line options. For a brief listing, invoke `mysqlmanager` with the `--help` option.

`mysqlmanager` supports the following options:

- `--help, -?`

  Display a help message and exit.

- `--bind-address=IP`

  The IP address to bind to.

- `--default-mysqld-path=path`

  On Unix, the pathname of the MySQL Server binary, if no path was provided in the instance section. Example: `--default-mysqld-path=/usr/sbin/mysqld`

- `--defaults-file=file_name`

  Read Instance Manager and MySQL Server settings from the given file. All configuration changes by the Instance Manager will be made to this file. This must be the first option on the command line if it is used.

- `--install`

  On Windows, install Instance Manager as a Windows service. This option was added in MySQL 5.0.11.

- `--log=file_name`

  The path to the IM log file. This is used with the `--run-as-service` option.

- `--monitoring-interval=seconds`

  The interval in seconds for monitoring instances. The default value is 20 seconds. Instance Manager tries to connect to each monitored instance to check whether it is alive/not hanging. In the case of a failure, IM performs several attempts to restart the instance. The `nonguarded` option in the appropriate instance section disables this behavior for a particular instance.

- `--passwd, -P`

  Prepare an entry for the password file and exit.

- `--password-file=file_name`

  Look for the Instance Manager users and passwords in this file. The default file is `/etc/mysqlmanager.passwd`.

- `--pid-file=file_name`

  The process ID file to use. By default, this file is named `mysqlmanager.pid`.

- `--port=port_num`

  The TCP/IP port number to use for incoming connections. (The default port number assigned by IANA is 2273.)

- `--print-defaults`

  Print the current defaults and exit. This must be the first option on the command line if it is used.

- `--remove`

  On Windows, removes Instance Manager as a Windows service. This assumes that Instance Manager has been run with `--install` previously. This option was added in MySQL 5.0.11.

- `--run-as-service`

  On Unix, daemonize and start the angel process. The angel process is simple and unlikely to crash. It will restart the Instance Manager itself in case of a failure.

- `--socket=path`

  On Unix, the socket file to use for incoming connections. By default, the file is named `/tmp/mysqlmanager.sock`.

- `--standalone`

  On Windows, run Instance Manager in standalone mode. This option was added in MySQL 5.0.13.

- `--user=user_name`

  On Unix, the username to start and run the `mysqlmanager` under. It is recommended to run `mysqlmanager` under the same user account used to run the `mysqld` server. ("User" in this context refers to a system login account, not a MySQL user listed in the grant tables.)

- `--version, -V`

  Output version information and exit.

4.5.4 MySQL Instance Manager Configuration Files

Instance Manager uses the standard `my.cnf` file. It uses the `[manager]` section to read options for itself and the `[mysqld]` sections to create instances. The `[manager]` section contains any of the options listed in Section 4.5.3, "MySQL Instance Manager Command Options." Here is an example `[manager]` section:

```
# MySQL Instance Manager options section
[manager]
default-mysqld-path = /usr/local/mysql/libexec/mysqld
socket=/tmp/manager.sock
pid-file=/tmp/manager.pid
password-file = /home/cps/.mysqlmanager.passwd
monitoring-interval = 2
port = 1999
bind-address = 192.168.1.5
```

Prior to MySQL 5.0.10, the MySQL Instance Manager read the same configuration files as the MySQL Server, including /etc/my.cnf, ~/.my.cnf, etc. As of MySQL 5.0.10, the MySQL Instance Manager reads and manages the /etc/my.cnf file only on Unix. On Windows, MySQL Instance Manager reads the my.ini file in the directory where Instance Manager is installed. The default option file location can be changed with the --defaults-file=*file_name* option.

Instance sections specify options given to each instance at startup. These are mainly common MySQL server options, but there are some IM-specific options:

- mysqld-path = *path*

  The pathname to the mysqld server binary.

- shutdown-delay = *seconds*

  The number of seconds IM should wait for the instance to shut down. The default value is 35 seconds. After the delay expires, the IM assumes that the instance is hanging and attempts to terminate it. If you use InnoDB with large tables, you should increase this value.

- nonguarded

  This option should be specified if you want to disable IM monitoring functionality for a certain instance.

Here are some sample instance sections:

```
[mysqld]
mysqld-path=/usr/local/mysql/libexec/mysqld
socket=/tmp/mysql.sock
port=3307
server_id=1
skip-stack-trace
core-file
skip-bdb
log-bin
log-error
log=mylog
log-slow-queries

[mysqld2]
nonguarded
port=3308
server_id=2
mysqld-path= /home/cps/mysql/trees/mysql-5.0/sql/mysqld
socket     = /tmp/mysql.sock5
pid-file   = /tmp/hostname.pid5
datadir= /home/cps/mysql_data/data_dir1
language=/home/cps/mysql/trees/mysql-5.0/sql/share/english
log-bin
log=/tmp/fordel.log
```

4.5.5 Commands Recognized by the MySQL Instance Manager

Once you've set up a password file for the MySQL Instance Manager and the IM is running, you can connect to it. You can use the `mysql` client tool connect through a standard MySQL API. The following list of commands shows the MySQL Instance Manager currently accepts, with samples.

- START INSTANCE *instance_name*

  This command attempts to start an instance.

  ```
  mysql> START INSTANCE mysqld4;
  Query OK, 0 rows affected (0,00 sec)
  ```

- STOP INSTANCE *instance_name*

  This command attempts to stop an instance.

  ```
  mysql> STOP INSTANCE mysqld4;
  Query OK, 0 rows affected (0,00 sec)
  ```

- SHOW INSTANCES

  Shows the names of all loaded instances.

  ```
  mysql> SHOW INSTANCES;
  +---------------+---------+
  | instance_name | status  |
  +---------------+---------+
  | mysqld3       | offline |
  | mysqld4       | online  |
  | mysqld2       | offline |
  +---------------+---------+
  3 rows in set (0,04 sec)
  ```

- SHOW INSTANCE STATUS *instance_name*

  Shows the status and the version information for an instance.

  ```
  mysql> SHOW INSTANCE STATUS mysqld3;
  +---------------+--------+---------+
  | instance_name | status | version |
  +---------------+--------+---------+
  | mysqld3       | online | unknown |
  +---------------+--------+---------+
  1 row in set (0.00 sec)
  ```

- SHOW INSTANCE OPTIONS *instance_name*

  Shows the options used by an instance.

  ```
  mysql> SHOW INSTANCE OPTIONS mysqld3;
  ```

```
+--------------+---------------------------------------------------+
| option_name  | value                                             |
+--------------+---------------------------------------------------+
| instance_name | mysqld3                                          |
| mysqld-path  | /home/cps/mysql/trees/mysql-4.1/sql/mysqld        |
| port         | 3309                                              |
| socket       | /tmp/mysql.sock3                                  |
| pid-file     | hostname.pid3                                     |
| datadir      | /home/cps/mysql_data/data_dir1/                   |
| language     | /home/cps/mysql/trees/mysql-4.1/sql/share/english |
+--------------+---------------------------------------------------+
7 rows in set (0.01 sec)
```

- SHOW *instance_name* LOG FILES

  The command lists all log files used by the instance. The result set contains the path to the log file and the log file size. If no log file path is specified in the configuration file (for example, log=/var/mysql.log), the Instance Manager tries to guess its placement. If the IM is unable to guess the log file placement you should specify the log file location explicitly by using the appropriate log option in the instance section of the configuration file.

  ```
  mysql> SHOW mysqld LOG FILES;
  +-------------+-------------------------------------+----------+
  | Logfile     | Path                                | Filesize |
  +-------------+-------------------------------------+----------+
  | ERROR LOG   | /home/cps/var/mysql/owlet.err       | 9186     |
  | GENERAL LOG | /home/cps/var/mysql/owlet.log       | 471503   |
  | SLOW LOG    | /home/cps/var/mysql/owlet-slow.log  | 4463     |
  +-------------+-------------------------------------+----------+
  3 rows in set (0.01 sec)
  ```

- SHOW *instance_name* LOG {ERROR | SLOW | GENERAL} *size*[,*offset_from_end*]

  This command retrieves a portion of the specified log file. Because most users are interested in the latest log messages, the *size* parameter defines the number of bytes you would like to retrieve starting from the log end. You can retrieve data from the middle of the log file by specifying the optional *offset_from_end* parameter. The following example retrieves 21 bytes of data, starting 23 bytes from the end of the log file and ending 2 bytes from the end of the log file:

  ```
  mysql> SHOW mysqld LOG GENERAL 21, 2;
  +---------------------+
  | Log                 |
  +---------------------+
  | using password: YES |
  +---------------------+
  1 row in set (0.00 sec)
  ```

- SET *instance_name.option_name=option_value*

  This command edits the specified instance's configuration file to change or add instance options. The IM assumes that the configuration file is located at /etc/my.cnf. You should check that the file exists and has appropriate permissions.

  ```
  mysql> SET mysqld2.port=3322;
  Query OK, 0 rows affected (0.00 sec)
  ```

  Changes made to the configuration file do not take effect until the MySQL server is restarted. In addition, these changes are not stored in the instance manager's local cache of instance settings until a FLUSH INSTANCES command is executed.

- UNSET *instance_name.option_name*

  This command removes an option from an instance's configuration file.

  ```
  mysql> UNSET mysqld2.port;
  Query OK, 0 rows affected (0.00 sec)
  ```

  Changes made to the configuration file do not take effect until the MySQL server is restarted. In addition, these changes are not stored in the instance manager's local cache of instance settings until a FLUSH INSTANCES command is executed.

- FLUSH INSTANCES

  This command forces IM to reread the configuration file and to refresh internal structures. This command should be performed after editing the configuration file. The command does not restart instances.

  ```
  mysql> FLUSH INSTANCES;
  Query OK, 0 rows affected (0.04 sec)
  ```

4.6 Installation-Related Programs

4.6.1 mysql_fix_privilege_tables—Upgrade MySQL System Tables

Some releases of MySQL introduce changes to the structure of the system tables in the mysql database to add new privileges or support new features. When you update to a new version of MySQL, you should update your system tables as well to make sure that their structure is up to date. Otherwise, there might be capabilities that you cannot take advantage of. First, make a backup of your mysql database, and then use the following procedure.

Note: As of MySQL 5.0.19, mysql_fix_privilege_tables is superseded by mysql_upgrade, which should be used instead. See Section 4.6.2, "mysql_upgrade—Check Tables for MySQL Upgrade."

On Unix or Unix-like systems, update the system tables by running the `mysql_fix_privilege_tables` script:

```
shell> mysql_fix_privilege_tables
```

You must run this script while the server is running. It attempts to connect to the server running on the local host as `root`. If your `root` account requires a password, indicate the password on the command line like this:

```
shell> mysql_fix_privilege_tables --password=root_password
```

The `mysql_fix_privilege_tables` script performs any actions necessary to convert your system tables to the current format. You might see some `Duplicate column name` warnings as it runs; you can ignore them.

After running the script, stop the server and restart it.

On Windows systems, MySQL distributions include a `mysql_fix_privilege_tables.sql` SQL script that you can run using the `mysql` client. For example, if your MySQL installation is located at `C:\Program Files\MySQL\MySQL Server 5.0`, the commands look like this:

```
C:\> cd "C:\Program Files\MySQL\MySQL Server 5.0"
C:\> bin\mysql -u root -p mysql
mysql> SOURCE scripts/mysql_fix_privilege_tables.sql
```

The `mysql` command will prompt you for the `root` password; enter it when prompted.

If your installation is located in some other directory, adjust the pathnames appropriately.

As with the Unix procedure, you might see some `Duplicate column name` warnings as `mysql` processes the statements in the `mysql_fix_privilege_tables.sql` script; you can ignore them.

After running the script, stop the server and restart it.

4.6.2 `mysql_upgrade`—Check Tables for MySQL Upgrade

`mysql_upgrade` should be executed each time you upgrade MySQL. It checks all tables in all databases for incompatibilities with the current version of MySQL Server. If a table is found to have a possible incompatibility, it is checked. If any problems are found, the table is repaired. `mysql_upgrade` also upgrades the system tables so that you can take advantage of new privileges or capabilities that might have been added.

All checked and repaired tables are marked with the current MySQL version number. This ensures that next time you run `mysql_upgrade` with the same version of the server, it can tell whether there is any need to check or repair the table again.

`mysql_upgrade` also saves the MySQL version number in a file named `mysql_upgrade.info` in the data directory. This is used to quickly check if all tables have been checked for this release so that table-checking can be skipped. To ignore this file, use the `--force` option.

To check and repair tables and to upgrade the system tables, `mysql_upgrade` executes the following commands:

```
mysqlcheck --check-upgrade --all-databases --auto-repair
mysql_fix_privilege_tables
```

`mysql_upgrade` currently works only on Unix. On Windows, you can execute the `mysqlcheck` command manually, and then upgrade your system tables as described in Section 4.6.1, "`mysql_fix_privilege_tables`—Upgrade MySQL System Tables."

For details about what is checked, see the description of the FOR UPGRADE option of the CHECK TABLE statement.

To use `mysql_upgrade`, make sure that the server is running, and then invoke it like this:

```
shell> mysql_upgrade [options]
```

`mysql_upgrade` reads options from the command line and from the [`mysqld`] and [`mysql_upgrade`] groups in option files. It supports the following options:

- `--basedir=path`

  The path to the MySQL installation directory.

- `--datadir=path`

  The path to the data directory.

- `--force`

  Force execution of `mysqlcheck` even if `mysql_upgrade` has already been executed for the current version of MySQL. (In other words, this option causes the `mysql_upgrade.info` file to be ignored.)

- `--user=user_name`, `-u user_name`

  The MySQL username to use when connecting to the server. The default username is `root`.

- `--verbose`

  Verbose mode. Print more information about what the program does.

Other options are passed to `mysqlcheck` and to `mysql_fix_privilege_tables`. For example, it might be necessary to specify the `--password[=password]` option.

`mysql_upgrade` was added in MySQL 5.0.19. It supersedes the older `mysql_fix_privilege_tables` script.

4.7 General Security Issues

This section describes some general security issues to be aware of and what you can do to make your MySQL installation more secure against attack or misuse. For information specifically about the access control system that MySQL uses for setting up user accounts and checking database access, see Section 4.8, "The MySQL Access Privilege System."

4.7.1 General Security Guidelines

Anyone using MySQL on a computer connected to the Internet should read this section to avoid the most common security mistakes.

In discussing security, we emphasize the necessity of fully protecting the entire server host (not just the MySQL server) against all types of applicable attacks: eavesdropping, altering, playback, and denial of service. We do not cover all aspects of availability and fault tolerance here.

MySQL uses security based on Access Control Lists (ACLs) for all connections, queries, and other operations that users can attempt to perform. There is also support for SSL-encrypted connections between MySQL clients and servers. Many of the concepts discussed here are not specific to MySQL at all; the same general ideas apply to almost all applications.

When running MySQL, follow these guidelines whenever possible:

- **Do not ever give anyone (except MySQL root accounts) access to the user table in the mysql database!** This is critical. **The encrypted password is the real password in MySQL.** Anyone who knows the password that is listed in the user table and has access to the host listed for the account **can easily log in as that user**.

- Learn the MySQL access privilege system. The GRANT and REVOKE statements are used for controlling access to MySQL. Do not grant more privileges than necessary. Never grant privileges to all hosts.

  Checklist:

    - Try mysql -u root. If you are able to connect successfully to the server without being asked for a password, anyone can connect to your MySQL server as the MySQL root user with full privileges! Review the MySQL installation instructions, paying particular attention to the information about setting a root password. See Section 2.9.3, "Securing the Initial MySQL Accounts."

    - Use the SHOW GRANTS statement to check which accounts have access to what. Then use the REVOKE statement to remove those privileges that are not necessary.

- Do not store any plain-text passwords in your database. If your computer becomes compromised, the intruder can take the full list of passwords and use them. Instead, use MD5(), SHA1(), or some other one-way hashing function and store the hash value.

- Do not choose passwords from dictionaries. Special programs exist to break passwords. Even passwords like "xfish98" are very bad. Much better is "duag98" which contains the same word "fish" but typed one key to the left on a standard QWERTY keyboard. Another method is to use a password that is taken from the first characters of each word in a sentence (for example, "Mary had a little lamb" results in a password of "Mhall"). The password is easy to remember and type, but difficult to guess for someone who does not know the sentence.

- Invest in a firewall. This protects you from at least 50% of all types of exploits in any software. Put MySQL behind the firewall or in a demilitarized zone (DMZ).

  Checklist:

  - Try to scan your ports from the Internet using a tool such as nmap. MySQL uses port 3306 by default. This port should not be accessible from untrusted hosts. Another simple way to check whether or not your MySQL port is open is to try the following command from some remote machine, where *server_host* is the hostname or IP number of the host on which your MySQL server runs:

    ```
    shell> telnet server_host 3306
    ```

    If you get a connection and some garbage characters, the port is open, and should be closed on your firewall or router, unless you really have a good reason to keep it open. If telnet hangs or the connection is refused, the port is blocked, which is how you want it to be.

- Do not trust any data entered by users of your applications. They can try to trick your code by entering special or escaped character sequences in Web forms, URLs, or whatever application you have built. Be sure that your application remains secure if a user enters something like "; DROP DATABASE mysql;". This is an extreme example, but large security leaks and data loss might occur as a result of hackers using similar techniques, if you do not prepare for them.

  A common mistake is to protect only string data values. Remember to check numeric data as well. If an application generates a query such as SELECT * FROM table WHERE ID=234 when a user enters the value 234, the user can enter the value 234 OR 1=1 to cause the application to generate the query SELECT * FROM table WHERE ID=234 OR 1=1. As a result, the server retrieves every row in the table. This exposes every row and causes excessive server load. The simplest way to protect from this type of attack is to use single quotes around the numeric constants: SELECT * FROM table WHERE ID='234'. If the user enters extra information, it all becomes part of the string. In a numeric context, MySQL automatically converts this string to a number and strips any trailing non-numeric characters from it.

  Sometimes people think that if a database contains only publicly available data, it need not be protected. This is incorrect. Even if it is allowable to display any row in the database, you should still protect against denial of service attacks (for example, those that are based on the technique in the preceding paragraph that causes the server to waste resources). Otherwise, your server becomes unresponsive to legitimate users.

  Checklist:

  - Try to enter single and double quote marks ("'" and '"') in all of your Web forms. If you get any kind of MySQL error, investigate the problem right away.
  - Try to modify dynamic URLs by adding %22 ('"'), %23 ('#'), and %27 ("'") to them.

- Try to modify data types in dynamic URLs from numeric to character types using the characters shown in the previous examples. Your application should be safe against these and similar attacks.

- Try to enter characters, spaces, and special symbols rather than numbers in numeric fields. Your application should remove them before passing them to MySQL or else generate an error. Passing unchecked values to MySQL is very dangerous!

- Check the size of data before passing it to MySQL.

- Have your application connect to the database using a username different from the one you use for administrative purposes. Do not give your applications any access privileges they do not need.

- Many application programming interfaces provide a means of escaping special characters in data values. Properly used, this prevents application users from entering values that cause the application to generate statements that have a different effect than you intend:

  - MySQL C API: Use the `mysql_real_escape_string()` API call.

  - MySQL++: Use the `escape` and `quote` modifiers for query streams.

  - PHP: Use the `mysql_escape_string()` function, which is based on the function of the same name in the MySQL C API. (Prior to PHP 4.0.3, use `addslashes()` instead.) In PHP 5, you can use the `mysqli` extension, which supports the improved MySQL authentication protocol and passwords, as well as prepared statements with placeholders.

  - Perl DBI: Use the `quote()` method or use placeholders.

  - Ruby DBI: Use placeholders.

  - Java JDBC: Use a `PreparedStatement` object and placeholders.

  Other programming interfaces might have similar capabilities.

- Do not transmit plain (unencrypted) data over the Internet. This information is accessible to everyone who has the time and ability to intercept it and use it for their own purposes. Instead, use an encrypted protocol such as SSL or SSH. MySQL supports internal SSL connections as of version 4.0. Another technique is to use SSH port-forwarding to create an encrypted (and compressed) tunnel for the communication.

- Learn to use the `tcpdump` and `strings` utilities. In most cases, you can check whether MySQL data streams are unencrypted by issuing a command like the following:

```
shell> tcpdump -l -i eth0 -w - src or dst port 3306 | strings
```

(This works under Linux and should work with small modifications under other systems.) **Warning**: If you do not see plaintext data, this doesn't always mean that the information actually is encrypted. If you need high security, you should consult with a security expert.

4.7.2 Making MySQL Secure Against Attackers

When you connect to a MySQL server, you should use a password. The password is not transmitted in clear text over the connection. Password handling during the client connection sequence was upgraded in MySQL 4.1.1 to be very secure. If you are still using pre-4.1.1-style passwords, the encryption algorithm is not as strong as the newer algorithm. With some effort, a clever attacker who can sniff the traffic between the client and the server can crack the password. (See Section 4.8.9, "Password Hashing as of MySQL 4.1," for a discussion of the different password handling methods.)

All other information is transferred as text, and can be read by anyone who is able to watch the connection. If the connection between the client and the server goes through an untrusted network, and you are concerned about this, you can use the compressed protocol to make traffic much more difficult to decipher. You can also use MySQL's internal SSL support to make the connection even more secure. See Section 4.9.7, "Using Secure Connections." Alternatively, use SSH to get an encrypted TCP/IP connection between a MySQL server and a MySQL client. You can find an Open Source SSH client at `http://www.openssh.org/`, and a commercial SSH client at `http://www.ssh.com/`.

To make a MySQL system secure, you should strongly consider the following suggestions:

- Require all MySQL accounts to have a password. A client program does not necessarily know the identity of the person running it. It is common for client/server applications that the user can specify any username to the client program. For example, anyone can use the `mysql` program to connect as any other person simply by invoking it as `mysql -u` *other_user db_name* if *other_user* has no password. If all accounts have a password, connecting using another user's account becomes much more difficult.

  For a discussion of methods for setting passwords, see Section 4.9.5, "Assigning Account Passwords."

- Never run the MySQL server as the Unix `root` user. This is extremely dangerous, because any user with the `FILE` privilege is able to cause the server to create files as `root` (for example, ~`root`/.`bashrc`). To prevent this, `mysqld` refuses to run as `root` unless that is specified explicitly using the `--user=root` option.

  `mysqld` can (and should) be run as an ordinary, unprivileged user instead. You can create a separate Unix account named `mysql` to make everything even more secure. Use this account only for administering MySQL. To start `mysqld` as a different Unix user, add a `user` option that specifies the username in the `[mysqld]` group of the `my.cnf` option file where you specify server options. For example:

  ```
  [mysqld]
  user=mysql
  ```

  This causes the server to start as the designated user whether you start it manually or by using `mysqld_safe` or `mysql.server`. For more details, see Section 4.7.5, "How to Run MySQL As a Normal User."

Running `mysqld` as a Unix user other than `root` does not mean that you need to change the `root` username in the `user` table. *Usernames for MySQL accounts have nothing to do with usernames for Unix accounts.*

- Do not allow the use of symlinks to tables. (This capability can be disabled with the `--skip-symbolic-links` option.) This is especially important if you run `mysqld` as `root`, because anyone that has write access to the server's data directory then could delete any file in the system! See Section 6.6.1.2, "Using Symbolic Links for Tables on Unix."

- Make sure that the only Unix user with read or write privileges in the database directories is the user that `mysqld` runs as.

- Do not grant the `PROCESS` or `SUPER` privilege to non-administrative users. The output of `mysqladmin processlist` and `SHOW PROCESSLIST` shows the text of any statements currently being executed, so any user who is allowed to see the server process list might be able to see statements issued by other users such as `UPDATE user SET password= PASSWORD('not_secure')`.

  `mysqld` reserves an extra connection for users who have the `SUPER` privilege, so that a MySQL `root` user can log in and check server activity even if all normal connections are in use.

  The `SUPER` privilege can be used to terminate client connections, change server operation by changing the value of system variables, and control replication servers.

- Do not grant the `FILE` privilege to non-administrative users. Any user who has this privilege can write a file anywhere in the filesystem with the privileges of the `mysqld` daemon. To make this a bit safer, files generated with `SELECT ... INTO OUTFILE` do not overwrite existing files and are writable by everyone.

  The `FILE` privilege may also be used to read any file that is world-readable or accessible to the Unix user that the server runs as. With this privilege, you can read any file into a database table. This could be abused, for example, by using `LOAD DATA` to load `/etc/passwd` into a table, which then can be displayed with `SELECT`.

- If you do not trust your DNS, you should use IP numbers rather than hostnames in the grant tables. In any case, you should be very careful about creating grant table entries using hostname values that contain wildcards.

- If you want to restrict the number of connections allowed to a single account, you can do so by setting the `max_user_connections` variable in `mysqld`. The `GRANT` statement also supports resource control options for limiting the extent of server use allowed to an account.

4.7.3 Security-Related `mysqld` Options

The following `mysqld` options affect security:

- `--allow-suspicious-udfs`

  This option controls whether user-defined functions that have only an xxx symbol for the main function can be loaded. By default, the option is off and only UDFs that have at least one auxiliary symbol can be loaded; this prevents attempts at loading functions from shared object files other than those containing legitimate UDFs. For MySQL 5.0, this option was added in MySQL 5.0.3.

- `--local-infile[={0|1}]`

  If you start the server with `--local-infile=0`, clients cannot use LOCAL in LOAD DATA statements. See Section 4.7.4, "Security Issues with LOAD DATA LOCAL."

- `--old-passwords`

  Force the server to generate short (pre-4.1) password hashes for new passwords. This is useful for compatibility when the server must support older client programs. See Section 4.8.9, "Password Hashing as of MySQL 4.1."

- `--safe-show-database` (*OBSOLETE*)

  In previous versions of MySQL, this option caused the SHOW DATABASES statement to display the names of only those databases for which the user had some kind of privilege. In MySQL 5.0, this option is no longer available because this is now the default behavior, and there is a SHOW DATABASES privilege that can be used to control access to database names on a per-account basis.

- `--safe-user-create`

  If this option is enabled, a user cannot create new MySQL users by using the GRANT statement unless the user has the INSERT privilege for the mysql.user table. If you want a user to have the ability to create new users that have those privileges that the user has right to grant, you should grant the user the following privilege:

  ```
  GRANT INSERT(user) ON mysql.user TO 'user_name'@'host_name';
  ```

  This ensures that the user cannot change any privilege columns directly, but has to use the GRANT statement to give privileges to other users.

- `--secure-auth`

  Disallow authentication for accounts that have old (pre-4.1) passwords.

  The mysql client also has a `--secure-auth` option, which prevents connections to a server if the server requires a password in old format for the client account.

- `--skip-grant-tables`

  This option causes the server not to use the privilege system at all. This gives anyone with access to the server *unrestricted access* to *all databases*. You can cause a running server to start using the grant tables again by executing mysqladmin flush-privileges or mysqladmin reload command from a system shell, or by issuing a MySQL FLUSH PRIVILEGES statement. This option also suppresses loading of user-defined functions (UDFs).

- `--skip-name-resolve`

  Hostnames are not resolved. All Host column values in the grant tables must be IP numbers or localhost.

- `--skip-networking`

  Do not allow TCP/IP connections over the network. All connections to `mysqld` must be made via Unix socket files.

- `--skip-show-database`

  With this option, the `SHOW DATABASES` statement is allowed only to users who have the `SHOW DATABASES` privilege, and the statement displays all database names. Without this option, `SHOW DATABASES` is allowed to all users, but displays each database name only if the user has the `SHOW DATABASES` privilege or some privilege for the database. Note that any global privilege is a privilege for the database.

4.7.4 Security Issues with LOAD DATA LOCAL

The `LOAD DATA` statement can load a file that is located on the server host, or it can load a file that is located on the client host when the `LOCAL` keyword is specified.

There are two potential security issues with supporting the `LOCAL` version of `LOAD DATA` statements:

- The transfer of the file from the client host to the server host is initiated by the MySQL server. In theory, a patched server could be built that would tell the client program to transfer a file of the server's choosing rather than the file named by the client in the `LOAD DATA` statement. Such a server could access any file on the client host to which the client user has read access.

- In a Web environment where the clients are connecting from a Web server, a user could use `LOAD DATA LOCAL` to read any files that the Web server process has read access to (assuming that a user could run any command against the SQL server). In this environment, the client with respect to the MySQL server actually is the Web server, not the remote program being run by the user who connects to the Web server.

To deal with these problems, we changed how `LOAD DATA LOCAL` is handled as of MySQL 3.23.49 and MySQL 4.0.2 (4.0.13 on Windows):

- By default, all MySQL clients and libraries in binary distributions are compiled with the `--enable-local-infile` option to be compatible with MySQL 3.23.48 and before.

- If you build MySQL from source but do not invoke `configure` with the `--enable-local-infile` option, `LOAD DATA LOCAL` cannot be used by any client unless it is written explicitly to invoke `mysql_options(... MYSQL_OPT_LOCAL_INFILE, 0)`.

- You can disable all `LOAD DATA LOCAL` commands from the server side by starting `mysqld` with the `--local-infile=0` option.

- For the `mysql` command-line client, `LOAD DATA LOCAL` can be enabled by specifying the `--local-infile[=1]` option, or disabled with the `--local-infile=0` option. Similarly, for `mysqlimport`, the `--local` or `-L` option enables local data file loading. In any case, successful use of a local loading operation requires that the server is enabled to allow it.

- If you use LOAD DATA LOCAL in Perl scripts or other programs that read the [client] group from option files, you can add the local-infile=1 option to that group. However, to keep this from causing problems for programs that do not understand local-infile, specify it using the loose- prefix:

```
[client]
loose-local-infile=1
```

- If LOAD DATA LOCAL INFILE is disabled, either in the server or the client, a client that attempts to issue such a statement receives the following error message:

```
ERROR 1148: The used command is not allowed with this MySQL version
```

4.7.5 How to Run MySQL As a Normal User

On Windows, you can run the server as a Windows service using a normal user account.

On Unix, the MySQL server mysqld can be started and run by any user. However, you should avoid running the server as the Unix root user for security reasons. To change mysqld to run as a normal unprivileged Unix user *user_name*, you must do the following:

1. Stop the server if it's running (use mysqladmin shutdown).
2. Change the database directories and files so that *user_name* has privileges to read and write files in them (you might need to do this as the Unix root user):

```
shell> chown -R user_name /path/to/mysql/datadir
```

   If you do not do this, the server will not be able to access databases or tables when it runs as *user_name*.

   If directories or files within the MySQL data directory are symbolic links, you'll also need to follow those links and change the directories and files they point to. chown -R might not follow symbolic links for you.

3. Start the server as user *user_name*. If you are using MySQL 3.22 or later, another alternative is to start mysqld as the Unix root user and use the --user=*user_name* option. mysqld starts up, and then switches to run as the Unix user *user_name* before accepting any connections.

4. To start the server as the given user automatically at system startup time, specify the username by adding a user option to the [mysqld] group of the /etc/my.cnf option file or the my.cnf option file in the server's data directory. For example:

```
[mysqld]
user=user_name
```

If your Unix machine itself isn't secured, you should assign passwords to the MySQL root accounts in the grant tables. Otherwise, any user with a login account on that machine can run the mysql client with a --user=root option and perform any operation. (It is a good idea to assign passwords to MySQL accounts in any case, but especially so when other login accounts exist on the server host.) See Section 2.9, "Post-Installation Setup and Testing."

4.8 The MySQL Access Privilege System

MySQL has an advanced but non-standard security and privilege system. The following discussion describes how it works.

4.8.1 What the Privilege System Does

The primary function of the MySQL privilege system is to authenticate a user who connects from a given host and to associate that user with privileges on a database such as SELECT, INSERT, UPDATE, and DELETE.

Additional functionality includes the capability to have anonymous users and to grant privileges for MySQL-specific functions such as LOAD DATA INFILE and administrative operations.

4.8.2 How the Privilege System Works

The MySQL privilege system ensures that all users may perform only the operations allowed to them. As a user, when you connect to a MySQL server, your identity is determined by *the host from which you connect* and *the username you specify*. When you issue requests after connecting, the system grants privileges according to your identity and *what you want to do*.

MySQL considers both your hostname and username in identifying you because there is little reason to assume that a given username belongs to the same person everywhere on the Internet. For example, the user joe who connects from office.example.com need not be the same person as the user joe who connects from home.example.com. MySQL handles this by allowing you to distinguish users on different hosts that happen to have the same name: You can grant one set of privileges for connections by joe from office.example.com, and a different set of privileges for connections by joe from home.example.com.

MySQL access control involves two stages when you run a client program that connects to the server:

- Stage 1: The server checks whether it should allow you to connect.
- Stage 2: Assuming that you can connect, the server checks each statement you issue to determine whether you have sufficient privileges to perform it. For example, if you try to select rows from a table in a database or drop a table from the database, the server verifies that you have the SELECT privilege for the table or the DROP privilege for the database.

If your privileges are changed (either by yourself or someone else) while you are connected, those changes do not necessarily take effect immediately for the next statement that you issue. See Section 4.8.7, "When Privilege Changes Take Effect," for details.

The server stores privilege information in the grant tables of the mysql database (that is, in the database named mysql). The MySQL server reads the contents of these tables into memory when it starts and re-reads them under the circumstances indicated in Section 4.8.7, "When Privilege Changes Take Effect." Access-control decisions are based on the in-memory copies of the grant tables.

Normally, you manipulate the contents of the grant tables indirectly by using statements such as GRANT and REVOKE to set up accounts and control the privileges available to each one. The discussion here describes the underlying structure of the grant tables and how the server uses their contents when interacting with clients.

The server uses the user, db, and host tables in the mysql database at both stages of access control. The columns in the user and db tables are shown here. The host table is similar to the db table but has a specialized use as described in Section 4.8.6, "Access Control, Stage 2: Request Verification."

Table Name	User	Db
Scope columns	Host	Host
	User	Db
	Password	User
Privilege columns	Select_priv	Select_priv
	Insert_priv	Insert_priv
	Update_priv	Update_priv
	Delete_priv	Delete_priv
	Index_priv	Index_priv
	Alter_priv	Alter_priv
	Create_priv	Create_priv
	Drop_priv	Drop_priv
	Grant_priv	Grant_priv
	Create_view_priv	Create_view_priv
	Show_view_priv	Show_view_priv
	Create_routine_priv	Create_routine_priv
	Alter_routine_priv	Alter_routine_priv
	Execute_priv	Execute_priv
	Create_tmp_table_priv	Create_tmp_table_priv
	Lock_tables_priv	Lock_tables_priv
	References_priv	References_priv
	Reload_priv	
	Shutdown_priv	
	Process_priv	
	File_priv	
	Show_db_priv	
	Super_priv	
	Repl_slave_priv	
	Repl_client_priv	
Security columns	ssl_type	
	ssl_cipher	
	x509_issuer	
	x509_subject	

Table Name	User	Db
Resource control columns	`max_questions`	
	`max_updates`	
	`max_connections`	
	`max_user_connections`	

`Execute_priv` was present in MySQL 5.0.0, but did not become operational until MySQL 5.0.3.

The `Create_view_priv` and `Show_view_priv` columns were added in MySQL 5.0.1.

The `Create_routine_priv`, `Alter_routine_priv`, and `max_user_connections` columns were added in MySQL 5.0.3.

During the second stage of access control, the server performs request verification to make sure that each client has sufficient privileges for each request that it issues. In addition to the user, db, and host grant tables, the server may also consult the `tables_priv` and `columns_priv` tables for requests that involve tables. The `tables_priv` and `columns_priv` tables provide finer privilege control at the table and column levels. They have the following columns:

Table Name	tables_priv	columns_priv
Scope columns	`Host`	`Host`
	`Db`	`Db`
	`User`	`User`
	`Table_name`	`Table_name`
		`Column_name`
Privilege columns	`Table_priv`	`Column_priv`
	`Column_priv`	
Other columns	`Timestamp`	`Timestamp`
	`Grantor`	

The `Timestamp` and `Grantor` columns currently are unused and are discussed no further here.

For verification of requests that involve stored routines, the server may consult the `procs_priv` table. This table has the following columns:

Table Name	procs_priv
Scope columns	`Host`
	`Db`
	`User`
	`Routine_name`
	`Routine_type`
Privilege columns	`Proc_priv`
Other columns	`Timestamp`
	`Grantor`

The procs_priv table exists as of MySQL 5.0.3. The Routine_type column was added in MySQL 5.0.6. It is an ENUM column with values of 'FUNCTION' or 'PROCEDURE' to indicate the type of routine the row refers to. This column allows privileges to be granted separately for a function and a procedure with the same name.

The Timestamp and Grantor columns currently are unused and are discussed no further here.

Each grant table contains scope columns and privilege columns:

- Scope columns determine the scope of each row (entry) in the tables; that is, the context in which the row applies. For example, a user table row with Host and User values of 'thomas.loc.gov' and 'bob' would be used for authenticating connections made to the server from the host thomas.loc.gov by a client that specifies a username of bob. Similarly, a db table row with Host, User, and Db column values of 'thomas.loc.gov', 'bob', and 'reports' would be used when bob connects from the host thomas.loc.gov to access the reports database. The tables_priv and columns_priv tables contain scope columns indicating tables or table/column combinations to which each row applies. The procs_priv scope columns indicate the stored routine to which each row applies.

- Privilege columns indicate which privileges are granted by a table row; that is, what operations can be performed. The server combines the information in the various grant tables to form a complete description of a user's privileges. Section 4.8.6, "Access Control, Stage 2: Request Verification," describes the rules that are used to do this.

Scope columns contain strings. They are declared as shown here; the default value for each is the empty string:

Column Name	Type
Host	CHAR(60)
User	CHAR(16)
Password	CHAR(16)
Db	CHAR(64)
Table_name	CHAR(64)
Column_name	CHAR(64)
Routine_name	CHAR(64)

For access-checking purposes, comparisons of Host values are case insensitive. User, Password, Db, and Table_name values are case sensitive. Column_name and Routine_name values are case insensitive.

In the user, db, and host tables, each privilege is listed in a separate column that is declared as ENUM('N','Y') DEFAULT 'N'. In other words, each privilege can be disabled or enabled, with the default being disabled.

In the `tables_priv`, `columns_priv`, and `procs_priv` tables, the privilege columns are declared as SET columns. Values in these columns can contain any combination of the privileges controlled by the table:

Table Name	Column Name	Possible Set Elements
tables_priv	Table_priv	'Select', 'Insert', 'Update', 'Delete', 'Create', 'Drop', 'Grant', 'References', 'Index', 'Alter', 'Create View', 'Show view'
tables_priv	Column_priv	'Select', 'Insert', 'Update', 'References'
columns_priv	Column_priv	'Select', 'Insert', 'Update', 'References'
procs_priv	Proc_priv	'Execute', 'Alter Routine', 'Grant'

Briefly, the server uses the grant tables in the following manner:

- The `user` table scope columns determine whether to reject or allow incoming connections. For allowed connections, any privileges granted in the `user` table indicate the user's global (superuser) privileges. Any privilege granted in this table applies to *all* databases on the server.

  Note: Because any global privilege is considered a privilege for all databases, any global privilege enables a user to see all database names with SHOW DATABASES or by examining the SCHEMATA table of INFORMATION_SCHEMA.

- The `db` table scope columns determine which users can access which databases from which hosts. The privilege columns determine which operations are allowed. A privilege granted at the database level applies to the database and to all its tables.

- The `host` table is used in conjunction with the `db` table when you want a given `db` table row to apply to several hosts. For example, if you want a user to be able to use a database from several hosts in your network, leave the `Host` value empty in the user's `db` table row, and then populate the `host` table with a row for each of those hosts. This mechanism is described more detail in Section 4.8.6, "Access Control, Stage 2: Request Verification."

  Note: The `host` table must be modified directly with statements such as INSERT, UPDATE, and DELETE. It is not affected by statements such as GRANT and REVOKE that modify the grant tables indirectly. Most MySQL installations need not use this table at all.

- The `tables_priv` and `columns_priv` tables are similar to the `db` table, but are more fine-grained: They apply at the table and column levels rather than at the database level. A privilege granted at the table level applies to the table and to all its columns. A privilege granted at the column level applies only to a specific column.

- The `procs_priv` table applies to stored routines. A privilege granted at the routine level applies only to a single routine.

Administrative privileges (such as RELOAD or SHUTDOWN) are specified only in the `user` table. The reason for this is that administrative operations are operations on the server itself and are not database-specific, so there is no reason to list these privileges in the other grant tables. In fact, to determine whether you can perform an administrative operation, the server need consult only the user table.

The FILE privilege also is specified only in the user table. It is not an administrative privilege as such, but your ability to read or write files on the server host is independent of the database you are accessing.

The mysqld server reads the contents of the grant tables into memory when it starts. You can tell it to re-read the tables by issuing a FLUSH PRIVILEGES statement or executing a mysqladmin flush-privileges or mysqladmin reload command. Changes to the grant tables take effect as indicated in Section 4.8.7, "When Privilege Changes Take Effect."

When you modify the contents of the grant tables, it is a good idea to make sure that your changes set up privileges the way you want. To check the privileges for a given account, use the SHOW GRANTS statement. For example, to determine the privileges that are granted to an account with Host and User values of pc84.example.com and bob, issue this statement:

```
SHOW GRANTS FOR 'bob'@'pc84.example.com';
```

For general advice on security issues, see Section 4.7, "General Security Issues." For additional help in diagnosing privilege-related problems, see Section 4.8.8, "Causes of Access denied Errors."

4.8.3 Privileges Provided by MySQL

Information about account privileges is stored in the user, db, host, tables_priv, columns_priv, and procs_priv tables in the mysql database. The MySQL server reads the contents of these tables into memory when it starts and re-reads them under the circumstances indicated in Section 4.8.7, "When Privilege Changes Take Effect." Access-control decisions are based on the in-memory copies of the grant tables.

The names used in the GRANT and REVOKE statements to refer to privileges are shown in the following table, along with the column name associated with each privilege in the grant tables and the context in which the privilege applies.

Privilege	Column	Context
CREATE	Create_priv	Databases, tables, or indexes
DROP	Drop_priv	Databases or tables
GRANT OPTION	Grant_priv	Databases, tables, or stored routines
REFERENCES	References_priv	Databases or tables
ALTER	Alter_priv	Tables
DELETE	Delete_priv	Tables
INDEX	Index_priv	Tables
INSERT	Insert_priv	Tables
SELECT	Select_priv	Tables

Privilege	Column	Context
UPDATE	Update_priv	Tables
CREATE VIEW	Create_view_priv	Views
SHOW VIEW	Show_view_priv	Views
ALTER ROUTINE	Alter_routine_priv	Stored routines
CREATE ROUTINE	Create_routine_priv	Stored routines
EXECUTE	Execute_priv	Stored routines
FILE	File_priv	File access on server host
CREATE TEMPORARY TABLES	Create_tmp_table_priv	Server administration
LOCK TABLES	Lock_tables_priv	Server administration
CREATE USER	Create_user_priv	Server administration
PROCESS	Process_priv	Server administration
RELOAD	Reload_priv	Server administration
REPLICATION CLIENT	Repl_client_priv	Server administration
REPLICATION SLAVE	Repl_slave_priv	Server administration
SHOW DATABASES	Show_db_priv	Server administration
SHUTDOWN	Shutdown_priv	Server administration
SUPER	Super_priv	Server administration

Some releases of MySQL introduce changes to the structure of the grant tables to add new privileges or features. Whenever you update to a new version of MySQL, you should update your grant tables to make sure that they have the current structure so that you can take advantage of any new capabilities. See Section 4.6.2, "mysql_upgrade—Check Tables for MySQL Upgrade."

CREATE VIEW and SHOW VIEW were added in MySQL 5.0.1. CREATE USER, CREATE ROUTINE, and ALTER ROUTINE were added in MySQL 5.0.3. Although EXECUTE was present in MySQL 5.0.0, it did not become operational until MySQL 5.0.3.

To create or alter stored routines if binary logging is enabled, you may also need the SUPER privilege.

The CREATE and DROP privileges allow you to create new databases and tables, or to drop (remove) existing databases and tables. *If you grant the DROP privilege for the mysql database to a user, that user can drop the database in which the MySQL access privileges are stored.*

The SELECT, INSERT, UPDATE, and DELETE privileges allow you to perform operations on rows in existing tables in a database.

SELECT statements require the SELECT privilege only if they actually retrieve rows from a table. Some SELECT statements do not access tables and can be executed without permission for any database. For example, you can use the mysql client as a simple calculator to evaluate expressions that make no reference to tables:

```
SELECT 1+1;
SELECT PI()*2;
```

The INDEX privilege enables you to create or drop (remove) indexes. INDEX applies to existing tables. If you have the CREATE privilege for a table, you can include index definitions in the CREATE TABLE statement.

The ALTER privilege enables you to use ALTER TABLE to change the structure of or rename tables.

The CREATE ROUTINE privilege is needed for creating stored routines (functions and procedures). ALTER ROUTINE privilege is needed for altering or dropping stored routines, and EXECUTE is needed for executing stored routines.

The GRANT privilege enables you to give to other users those privileges that you yourself possess. It can be used for databases, tables, and stored routines.

The FILE privilege gives you permission to read and write files on the server host using the LOAD DATA INFILE and SELECT ... INTO OUTFILE statements. A user who has the FILE privilege can read any file on the server host that is either world-readable or readable by the MySQL server. (This implies the user can read any file in any database directory, because the server can access any of those files.) The FILE privilege also enables the user to create new files in any directory where the MySQL server has write access. As a security measure, the server will not overwrite existing files.

The remaining privileges are used for administrative operations. Many of them can be performed by using the mysqladmin program or by issuing SQL statements. The following table shows which mysqladmin commands each administrative privilege enables you to execute:

Privilege	Commands Permitted to Privilege Holders
RELOAD	flush-hosts, flush-logs, flush-privileges, flush-status, flush-tables, flush-threads, refresh, reload
SHUTDOWN	Shutdown
PROCESS	Processlist
SUPER	Kill

The reload command tells the server to re-read the grant tables into memory. flush-privileges is a synonym for reload. The refresh command closes and reopens the log files and flushes all tables. The other flush-xxx commands perform functions similar to refresh, but are more specific and may be preferable in some instances. For example, if you want to flush just the log files, flush-logs is a better choice than refresh.

The shutdown command shuts down the server. There is no corresponding SQL statement.

The processlist command displays information about the threads executing within the server (that is, information about the statements being executed by clients). The kill command terminates server threads. You can always display or kill your own threads, but you need the PROCESS privilege to display threads initiated by other users and the SUPER privilege to kill them.

The CREATE TEMPORARY TABLES privilege enables the use of the keyword TEMPORARY in CREATE TABLE statements.

The LOCK TABLES privilege enables the use of explicit LOCK TABLES statements to lock tables for which you have the SELECT privilege. This includes the use of write locks, which prevents anyone else from reading the locked table.

The REPLICATION CLIENT privilege enables the use of SHOW MASTER STATUS and SHOW SLAVE STATUS.

The REPLICATION SLAVE privilege should be granted to accounts that are used by slave servers to connect to the current server as their master. Without this privilege, the slave cannot request updates that have been made to databases on the master server.

The SHOW DATABASES privilege allows the account to see database names by issuing the SHOW DATABASE statement. Accounts that do not have this privilege see only databases for which they have some privileges, and cannot use the statement at all if the server was started with the --skip-show-database option. Note that *any* global privilege is a privilege for the database.

It is a good idea to grant to an account only those privileges that it needs. You should exercise particular caution in granting the FILE and administrative privileges:

- The FILE privilege can be abused to read into a database table any files that the MySQL server can read on the server host. This includes all world-readable files and files in the server's data directory. The table can then be accessed using SELECT to transfer its contents to the client host.

- The GRANT privilege enables users to give their privileges to other users. Two users that have different privileges and with the GRANT privilege are able to combine privileges.

- The ALTER privilege may be used to subvert the privilege system by renaming tables.

- The SHUTDOWN privilege can be abused to deny service to other users entirely by terminating the server.

- The PROCESS privilege can be used to view the plain text of currently executing statements, including statements that set or change passwords.

- The SUPER privilege can be used to terminate other clients or change how the server operates.

- Privileges granted for the mysql database itself can be used to change passwords and other access privilege information. Passwords are stored encrypted, so a malicious user cannot simply read them to know the plain text password. However, a user with write access to the user table Password column can change an account's password, and then connect to the MySQL server using that account.

There are some things that you cannot do with the MySQL privilege system:

- You cannot explicitly specify that a given user should be denied access. That is, you cannot explicitly match a user and then refuse the connection.

- You cannot specify that a user has privileges to create or drop tables in a database but not to create or drop the database itself.

- A password applies globally to an account. You cannot associate a password with a specific object such as a database, table, or routine.

4.8.4 Connecting to the MySQL Server

MySQL client programs generally expect you to specify certain connection parameters when you want to access a MySQL server:

- The name of the host where the MySQL server is running

- Your username

- Your password

For example, the `mysql` client can be started as follows from a command-line prompt (indicated here by `shell>`):

```
shell> mysql -h host_name -u user_name -pyour_pass
```

Alternative forms of the -h, -u, and -p options are `--host=host_name`, `--user=user_name`, and `--password=your_pass`. Note that there is *no space* between -p or --password= and the password following it.

If you use a -p or --password option but do not specify the password value, the client program prompts you to enter the password. The password is not displayed as you enter it. This is more secure than giving the password on the command line. Any user on your system may be able to see a password specified on the command line by executing a command such as `ps auxww`. See Section 4.9.6, "Keeping Your Password Secure."

MySQL client programs use default values for any connection parameter option that you do not specify:

- The default hostname is `localhost`.

- The default username is `ODBC` on Windows and your Unix login name on Unix.

- No password is supplied if neither -p nor --password is given.

Thus, for a Unix user with a login name of `joe`, all of the following commands are equivalent:

```
shell> mysql -h localhost -u joe
shell> mysql -h localhost
shell> mysql -u joe
shell> mysql
```

Other MySQL clients behave similarly.

You can specify different default values to be used when you make a connection so that you need not enter them on the command line each time you invoke a client program. This can be done in a couple of ways:

- You can specify connection parameters in the [client] section of an option file. The relevant section of the file might look like this:

```
[client]
host=host_name
user=user_name
password=your_pass
```

   Section 3.3.2, "Using Option Files," discusses option files further.

- You can specify some connection parameters using environment variables. The host can be specified for mysql using MYSQL_HOST. The MySQL username can be specified using USER (this is for Windows and NetWare only). The password can be specified using MYSQL_PWD, although this is insecure; see Section 4.9.6, "Keeping Your Password Secure."

4.8.5 Access Control, Stage 1: Connection Verification

When you attempt to connect to a MySQL server, the server accepts or rejects the connection based on your identity and whether you can verify your identity by supplying the correct password. If not, the server denies access to you completely. Otherwise, the server accepts the connection, and then enters Stage 2 and waits for requests.

Your identity is based on two pieces of information:

- The client host from which you connect
- Your MySQL username

Identity checking is performed using the three user table scope columns (Host, User, and Password). The server accepts the connection only if the Host and User columns in some user table row match the client hostname and username and the client supplies the password specified in that row.

Host values in the user table may be specified as follows:

- A Host value may be a hostname or an IP number, or 'localhost' to indicate the local host.
- You can use the wildcard characters '%' and '_' in Host column values. These have the same meaning as for pattern-matching operations performed with the LIKE operator. For example, a Host value of '%' matches any hostname, whereas a value of '%.mysql.com' matches any host in the mysql.com domain.
- For Host values specified as IP numbers, you can specify a netmask indicating how many address bits to use for the network number. For example:

```
GRANT ALL PRIVILEGES ON db.* TO david@'192.58.197.0/255.255.255.0';
```

This allows `david` to connect from any client host having an IP number `client_ip` for which the following condition is true:

```
client_ip & netmask = host_ip
```

That is, for the `GRANT` statement just shown:

```
client_ip & 255.255.255.0 = 192.58.197.0
```

IP numbers that satisfy this condition and can connect to the MySQL server are those in the range from `192.58.197.0` to `192.58.197.255`.

Note: The netmask can only be used to tell the server to use 8, 16, 24, or 32 bits of the address. Examples:

- `192.0.0.0/255.0.0.0`: Anything on the 192 class A network
- `192.168.0.0/255.255.0.0`: Anything on the 192.168 class B network
- `192.168.1.0/255.255.255.0`: Anything on the 192.168.1 class C network
- `192.168.1.1`: Only this specific IP

The following netmask (28 bits) will not work:

```
192.168.0.1/255.255.255.240
```

- A blank `Host` value in a db table row means that its privileges should be combined with those in the row in the `host` table that matches the client hostname. The privileges are combined using an `AND` (intersection) operation, not `OR` (union). Section 4.8.6, "Access Control, Stage 2: Request Verification," discusses use of the `host` table further.

  A blank `Host` value in the other grant tables is the same as `'%'`.

Because you can use IP wildcard values in the `Host` column (for example, `'144.155.166.%'` to match every host on a subnet), someone could try to exploit this capability by naming a host `144.155.166.somewhere.com`. To foil such attempts, MySQL disallows matching on host-names that start with digits and a dot. Thus, if you have a host named something like `1.2.foo.com`, its name never matches the `Host` column of the grant tables. An IP wildcard value can match only IP numbers, not hostnames.

In the `User` column, wildcard characters are not allowed, but you can specify a blank value, which matches any name. If the `user` table row that matches an incoming connection has a blank username, the user is considered to be an anonymous user with no name, not a user with the name that the client actually specified. This means that a blank username is used for all further access checking for the duration of the connection (that is, during Stage 2).

The `Password` column can be blank. This is not a wildcard and does not mean that any password matches. It means that the user must connect without specifying a password.

Non-blank `Password` values in the `user` table represent encrypted passwords. MySQL does not store passwords in plaintext form for anyone to see. Rather, the password supplied by a user who is attempting to connect is encrypted (using the PASSWORD() function). The encrypted password then is used during the connection process when checking whether the password is correct. (This is done without the encrypted password ever traveling over the connection.) From MySQL's point of view, the encrypted password is the *real* password, so you should never give anyone access to it. In particular, *do not give non-administrative users read access to tables in the* mysql *database.*

MySQL 5.0 employs the stronger authentication method (first implemented in MySQL 4.1) that has better password protection during the connection process than in earlier versions. It is secure even if TCP/IP packets are sniffed or the mysql database is captured. Section 4.8.9, "Password Hashing as of MySQL 4.1," discusses password encryption further.

The following table shows how various combinations of Host and User values in the user table apply to incoming connections.

Host Value	User Value	Allowable Connections
'thomas.loc.gov'	'fred'	fred, connecting from thomas.loc.gov
'thomas.loc.gov'	' '	Any user, connecting from thomas.loc.gov
'%'	'fred'	fred, connecting from any host
'%'	' '	Any user, connecting from any host
'%.loc.gov'	'fred'	fred, connecting from any host in the loc.gov domain
'x.y.%'	'fred'	fred, connecting from x.y.net, x.y.com, x.y.edu, and so on (this is probably not useful)
'144.155.166.177'	'fred'	fred, connecting from the host with IP address 144.155.166.177
'144.155.166.%'	'fred'	fred, connecting from any host in the 144.155.166 class C subnet
'144.155.166.0/255.255.255.0'	'fred'	Same as previous example

It is possible for the client hostname and username of an incoming connection to match more than one row in the user table. The preceding set of examples demonstrates this: Several of the entries shown match a connection from thomas.loc.gov by fred.

When multiple matches are possible, the server must determine which of them to use. It resolves this issue as follows:

- Whenever the server reads the user table into memory, it sorts the rows.
- When a client attempts to connect, the server looks through the rows in sorted order.
- The server uses the first row that matches the client hostname and username.

To see how this works, suppose that the user table looks like this:

```
+-----------+----------+-
| Host      | User     | ...
+-----------+----------+-
| %         | root     | ...
| %         | jeffrey  | ...
| localhost | root     | ...
| localhost |          | ...
+-----------+----------+-
```

When the server reads the table into memory, it orders the rows with the most-specific Host values first. Literal hostnames and IP numbers are the most specific. The pattern '%' means "any host" and is least specific. Rows with the same Host value are ordered with the most-specific User values first (a blank User value means "any user" and is least specific). For the user table just shown, the result after sorting looks like this:

```
+-----------+----------+-
| Host      | User     | ...
+-----------+----------+-
| localhost | root     | ...
| localhost |          | ...
| %         | jeffrey  | ...
| %         | root     | ...
+-----------+----------+-
```

When a client attempts to connect, the server looks through the sorted rows and uses the first match found. For a connection from localhost by jeffrey, two of the rows from the table match: the one with Host and User values of 'localhost' and '', and the one with values of '%' and 'jeffrey'. The 'localhost' row appears first in sorted order, so that is the one the server uses.

Here is another example. Suppose that the user table looks like this:

```
+----------------+----------+-
| Host           | User     | ...
+----------------+----------+-
| %              | jeffrey  | ...
| thomas.loc.gov |          | ...
+----------------+----------+-
```

The sorted table looks like this:

```
+----------------+----------+-
| Host           | User     | ...
+----------------+----------+-
| thomas.loc.gov |          | ...
| %              | jeffrey  | ...
+----------------+----------+-
```

A connection by `jeffrey` from `thomas.loc.gov` is matched by the first row, whereas a connection by `jeffrey` from `whitehouse.gov` is matched by the second.

It is a common misconception to think that, for a given username, all rows that explicitly name that user are used first when the server attempts to find a match for the connection. This is simply not true. The previous example illustrates this, where a connection from `thomas.loc.gov` by `jeffrey` is first matched not by the row containing `'jeffrey'` as the `User` column value, but by the row with no username. As a result, `jeffrey` is authenticated as an anonymous user, even though he specified a username when connecting.

If you are able to connect to the server, but your privileges are not what you expect, you probably are being authenticated as some other account. To find out what account the server used to authenticate you, use the `CURRENT_USER()` function. It returns a value in *user_name@host_name* format that indicates the `User` and `Host` values from the matching user table row. Suppose that `jeffrey` connects and issues the following query:

```
mysql> SELECT CURRENT_USER();
+----------------+
| CURRENT_USER() |
+----------------+
| @localhost     |
+----------------+
```

The result shown here indicates that the matching user table row had a blank `User` column value. In other words, the server is treating `jeffrey` as an anonymous user.

Another thing you can do to diagnose authentication problems is to print out the user table and sort it by hand to see where the first match is being made.

4.8.6 Access Control, Stage 2: Request Verification

After you establish a connection, the server enters Stage 2 of access control. For each request that you issue via that connection, the server determines what operation you want to perform, and then checks whether you have sufficient privileges to do so. This is where the privilege columns in the grant tables come into play. These privileges can come from any of the `user`, `db`, `host`, `tables_priv`, `columns_priv`, or `procs_priv` tables. (You may find it helpful to refer to Section 4.8.2, "How the Privilege System Works," which lists the columns present in each of the grant tables.)

The user table grants privileges that are assigned to you on a global basis and that apply no matter what the default database is. For example, if the user table grants you the DELETE privilege, you can delete rows from any table in any database on the server host! In other words, user table privileges are superuser privileges. It is wise to grant privileges in the user table only to superusers such as database administrators. For other users, you should leave all privileges in the user table set to `'N'` and grant privileges at more specific levels only. You can grant privileges for particular databases, tables, columns, or routines.

The db and host tables grant database-specific privileges. Values in the scope columns of these tables can take the following forms:

- The wildcard characters '%' and '_' can be used in the Host and Db columns of either table. These have the same meaning as for pattern-matching operations performed with the LIKE operator. If you want to use either character literally when granting privileges, you must escape it with a backslash. For example, to include the underscore character ('_') as part of a database name, specify it as '_' in the GRANT statement.

- A '%' Host value in the db table means "any host." A blank Host value in the db table means "consult the host table for further information" (a process that is described later in this section).

- A '%' or blank Host value in the host table means "any host."

- A '%' or blank Db value in either table means "any database."

- A blank User value in either table matches the anonymous user.

The server reads the db and host tables into memory and sorts them at the same time that it reads the user table. The server sorts the db table based on the Host, Db, and User scope columns, and sorts the host table based on the Host and Db scope columns. As with the user table, sorting puts the most-specific values first and least-specific values last, and when the server looks for matching entries, it uses the first match that it finds.

The tables_priv, columns_priv, and procs_priv tables grant table-specific, column-specific, and routine-specific privileges. Values in the scope columns of these tables can take the following forms:

- The wildcard characters '%' and '_' can be used in the Host column. These have the same meaning as for pattern-matching operations performed with the LIKE operator.

- A '%' or blank Host value means "any host."

- The Db, Table_name, and Column_name columns cannot contain wildcards or be blank.

The server sorts the tables_priv, columns_priv, and procs_priv tables based on the Host, Db, and User columns. This is similar to db table sorting, but simpler because only the Host column can contain wildcards.

The server uses the sorted tables to verify each request that it receives. For requests that require administrative privileges such as SHUTDOWN or RELOAD, the server checks only the user table row because that is the only table that specifies administrative privileges. The server grants access if the row allows the requested operation and denies access otherwise. For example, if you want to execute mysqladmin shutdown but your user table row doesn't grant the SHUTDOWN privilege to you, the server denies access without even checking the db or host tables. (They contain no Shutdown_priv column, so there is no need to do so.)

For database-related requests (INSERT, UPDATE, and so on), the server first checks the user's global (superuser) privileges by looking in the user table row. If the row allows the requested operation, access is granted. If the global privileges in the user table are insufficient, the server determines the user's database-specific privileges by checking the db and host tables:

1. The server looks in the db table for a match on the Host, Db, and User columns. The Host and User columns are matched to the connecting user's hostname and MySQL username. The Db column is matched to the database that the user wants to access. If there is no row for the Host and User, access is denied.

2. If there is a matching db table row and its Host column is not blank, that row defines the user's database-specific privileges.

3. If the matching db table row's Host column is blank, it signifies that the host table enumerates which hosts should be allowed access to the database. In this case, a further lookup is done in the host table to find a match on the Host and Db columns. If no host table row matches, access is denied. If there is a match, the user's database-specific privileges are computed as the intersection (*not* the union!) of the privileges in the db and host table entries; that is, the privileges that are 'Y' in both entries. (This way you can grant general privileges in the db table row and then selectively restrict them on a host-by-host basis using the host table entries.)

After determining the database-specific privileges granted by the db and host table entries, the server adds them to the global privileges granted by the user table. If the result allows the requested operation, access is granted. Otherwise, the server successively checks the user's table and column privileges in the tables_priv and columns_priv tables, adds those to the user's privileges, and allows or denies access based on the result. For stored routine operations, the server uses the procs_priv table rather than tables_priv and columns_priv.

Expressed in boolean terms, the preceding description of how a user's privileges are calculated may be summarized like this:

```
global privileges
OR (database privileges AND host privileges)
OR table privileges
OR column privileges
OR routine privileges
```

It may not be apparent why, if the global user row privileges are initially found to be insufficient for the requested operation, the server adds those privileges to the database, table, and column privileges later. The reason is that a request might require more than one type of privilege. For example, if you execute an INSERT INTO ... SELECT statement, you need both the INSERT and the SELECT privileges. Your privileges might be such that the user table row grants one privilege and the db table row grants the other. In this case, you have the necessary privileges to perform the request, but the server cannot tell that from either table by itself; the privileges granted by the entries in both tables must be combined.

The host table is not affected by the GRANT or REVOKE statements, so it is unused in most MySQL installations. If you modify it directly, you can use it for some specialized purposes, such as to maintain a list of secure servers. For example, at TcX, the host table contains a list of all machines on the local network. These are granted all privileges.

You can also use the host table to indicate hosts that are *not* secure. Suppose that you have a machine public.your.domain that is located in a public area that you do not consider secure. You can allow access to all hosts on your network except that machine by using host table entries like this:

```
+-------------------+----+-
| Host              | Db | ...
+-------------------+----+-
| public.your.domain | % | ... (all privileges set to 'N')
| %.your.domain     | %  | ... (all privileges set to 'Y')
+-------------------+----+-
```

Naturally, you should always test your changes to the grant tables (for example, by using SHOW GRANTS) to make sure that your access privileges are actually set up the way you think they are.

4.8.7 When Privilege Changes Take Effect

When mysqld starts, it reads all grant table contents into memory. The in-memory tables become effective for access control at that point.

When the server reloads the grant tables, privileges for existing client connections are affected as follows:

- Table and column privilege changes take effect with the client's next request.
- Database privilege changes take effect at the next USE *db_name* statement.
- Changes to global privileges and passwords take effect the next time the client connects.

If you modify the grant tables indirectly using statements such as GRANT, REVOKE, or SET PASSWORD, the server notices these changes and loads the grant tables into memory again immediately.

If you modify the grant tables directly using statements such as INSERT, UPDATE, or DELETE, your changes have no effect on privilege checking until you either restart the server or tell it to reload the tables. To reload the grant tables manually, issue a FLUSH PRIVILEGES statement or execute a mysqladmin flush-privileges or mysqladmin reload command.

If you change the grant tables directly but forget to reload them, your changes have *no effect* until you restart the server. This may leave you wondering why your changes do not seem to make any difference!

4.8.8 Causes of Access denied Errors

If you encounter problems when you try to connect to the MySQL server, the following items describe some courses of action you can take to correct the problem.

- Make sure that the server is running. If it is not running, you cannot connect to it. For example, if you attempt to connect to the server and see a message such as one of those following, one cause might be that the server is not running:

```
shell> mysql
ERROR 2003: Can't connect to MySQL server on 'host_name' (111)
shell> mysql
ERROR 2002: Can't connect to local MySQL server through socket
'/tmp/mysql.sock' (111)
```

It might also be that the server is running, but you are trying to connect using a TCP/IP port, named pipe, or Unix socket file different from the one on which the server is listening. To correct this when you invoke a client program, specify a --port option to indicate the proper port number, or a --socket option to indicate the proper named pipe or Unix socket file. To find out where the socket file is, you can use this command:

```
shell> netstat -ln | grep mysql
```

- The grant tables must be properly set up so that the server can use them for access control. For some distribution types (such as binary distributions on Windows, or RPM distributions on Linux), the installation process initializes the mysql database containing the grant tables. For distributions that do not do this, you must initialize the grant tables manually by running the mysql_install_db script. For details, see Section 2.9.2, "Unix Post-Installation Procedures."

One way to determine whether you need to initialize the grant tables is to look for a mysql directory under the data directory. (The data directory normally is named data or var and is located under your MySQL installation directory.) Make sure that you have a file named user.MYD in the mysql database directory. If you do not, execute the mysql_install_db script. After running this script and starting the server, test the initial privileges by executing this command:

```
shell> mysql -u root test
```

The server should let you connect without error.

- After a fresh installation, you should connect to the server and set up your users and their access permissions:

```
shell> mysql -u root mysql
```

The server should let you connect because the MySQL root user has no password initially. That is also a security risk, so setting the password for the root accounts is something you should do while you're setting up your other MySQL accounts. For instructions on setting the initial passwords, see Section 2.9.3, "Securing the Initial MySQL Accounts."

- If you have updated an existing MySQL installation to a newer version, did you run the `mysql_upgrade` script? If not, do so. The structure of the grant tables changes occasionally when new capabilities are added, so after an upgrade you should always make sure that your tables have the current structure. For instructions, see Section 4.6.2, "mysql_upgrade—Check Tables for MySQL Upgrade."

- If a client program receives the following error message when it tries to connect, it means that the server expects passwords in a newer format than the client is capable of generating:

```
shell> mysql
Client does not support authentication protocol requested
by server; consider upgrading MySQL client
```

  For information on how to deal with this, see Section 4.8.9, "Password Hashing as of MySQL 4.1," and the "MySQL Language Reference."

- If you try to connect as `root` and get the following error, it means that you do not have a row in the `user` table with a `User` column value of `'root'` and that `mysqld` cannot resolve the hostname for your client:

```
Access denied for user ''@'unknown' to database mysql
```

  In this case, you must restart the server with the `--skip-grant-tables` option and edit your /etc/hosts file or \windows\hosts file to add an entry for your host.

- Remember that client programs use connection parameters specified in option files or environment variables. If a client program seems to be sending incorrect default connection parameters when you have not specified them on the command line, check your environment and any applicable option files. For example, if you get `Access denied` when you run a client without any options, make sure that you have not specified an old password in any of your option files!

  You can suppress the use of option files by a client program by invoking it with the `--no-defaults` option. For example:

```
shell> mysqladmin --no-defaults -u root version
```

  The option files that clients use are listed in Section 3.3.2, "Using Option Files."

- If you get the following error, it means that you are using an incorrect `root` password:

```
shell> mysqladmin -u root -pxxxx ver
Access denied for user 'root'@'localhost' (using password: YES)
```

  If the preceding error occurs even when you have not specified a password, it means that you have an incorrect password listed in some option file. Try the `--no-defaults` option as described in the previous item.

  For information on changing passwords, see Section 4.9.5, "Assigning Account Passwords."

If you have lost or forgotten the root password, you can restart mysqld with --skip-grant-tables to change the password.

- If you change a password by using SET PASSWORD, INSERT, or UPDATE, you must encrypt the password using the PASSWORD() function. If you do not use PASSWORD() for these statements, the password will not work. For example, the following statement sets a password, but fails to encrypt it, so the user is not able to connect afterward:

```
SET PASSWORD FOR 'abe'@'host_name' = 'eagle';
```

Instead, set the password like this:

```
SET PASSWORD FOR 'abe'@'host_name' = PASSWORD('eagle');
```

The PASSWORD() function is unnecessary when you specify a password using the GRANT or (beginning with MySQL 5.0.2) CREATE USER statements, or the mysqladmin password command. Each of those automatically uses PASSWORD() to encrypt the password. See Section 4.9.5, "Assigning Account Passwords."

- localhost is a synonym for your local hostname, and is also the default host to which clients try to connect if you specify no host explicitly.

To avoid this problem on such systems, you can use a --host=127.0.0.1 option to name the server host explicitly. This will make a TCP/IP connection to the local mysqld server. You can also use TCP/IP by specifying a --host option that uses the actual hostname of the local host. In this case, the hostname must be specified in a user table row on the server host, even though you are running the client program on the same host as the server.

- If you get an Access denied error when trying to connect to the database with mysql -u user_name, you may have a problem with the user table. Check this by executing mysql -u root mysql and issuing this SQL statement:

```
SELECT * FROM user;
```

The result should include a row with the Host and User columns matching your computer's hostname and your MySQL username.

- The Access denied error message tells you who you are trying to log in as, the client host from which you are trying to connect, and whether you were using a password. Normally, you should have one row in the user table that exactly matches the hostname and username that were given in the error message. For example, if you get an error message that contains using password: NO, it means that you tried to log in without a password.

- If the following error occurs when you try to connect from a host other than the one on which the MySQL server is running, it means that there is no row in the user table with a Host value that matches the client host:

```
Host ... is not allowed to connect to this MySQL server
```

You can fix this by setting up an account for the combination of client hostname and username that you are using when trying to connect.

If you do not know the IP number or hostname of the machine from which you are connecting, you should put a row with '%' as the Host column value in the user table. After trying to connect from the client machine, use a SELECT USER() query to see how you really did connect. (Then change the '%' in the user table row to the actual hostname that shows up in the log. Otherwise, your system is left insecure because it allows connections from any host for the given username.)

On Linux, another reason that this error might occur is that you are using a binary MySQL version that is compiled with a different version of the glibc library than the one you are using. In this case, you should either upgrade your operating system or glibc, or download a source distribution of MySQL version and compile it yourself. A source RPM is normally trivial to compile and install, so this is not a big problem.

- If you specify a hostname when trying to connect, but get an error message where the hostname is not shown or is an IP number, it means that the MySQL server got an error when trying to resolve the IP number of the client host to a name:

```
shell> mysqladmin -u root -pxxxx -h some_hostname ver
Access denied for user 'root'@'' (using password: YES)
```

This indicates a DNS problem. To fix it, execute mysqladmin flush-hosts to reset the internal DNS hostname cache. See Section 6.5.6, "How MySQL Uses DNS."

Some permanent solutions are:

- Determine what is wrong with your DNS server and fix it.
- Specify IP numbers rather than hostnames in the MySQL grant tables.
- Put an entry for the client machine name in /etc/hosts or \windows\hosts.
- Start mysqld with the --skip-name-resolve option.
- Start mysqld with the --skip-host-cache option.
- On Unix, if you are running the server and the client on the same machine, connect to localhost. Unix connections to localhost use a Unix socket file rather than TCP/IP.
- On Windows, if you are running the server and the client on the same machine and the server supports named pipe connections, connect to the hostname . (period). Connections to . use a named pipe rather than TCP/IP.

- If mysql -u root test works but mysql -h your_hostname -u root test results in Access denied (where your_hostname is the actual hostname of the local host), you may not have the correct name for your host in the user table. A common problem here is that the Host value in the user table row specifies an unqualified hostname, but your system's name resolution routines return a fully qualified domain name (or vice versa). For example, if you have an entry with host 'tcx' in the user table, but your DNS tells

MySQL that your hostname is `'tcx.subnet.se'`, the entry does not work. Try adding an entry to the user table that contains the IP number of your host as the Host column value. (Alternatively, you could add an entry to the user table with a Host value that contains a wildcard; for example, `'tcx.%'`. However, use of hostnames ending with '%' is *insecure* and is *not* recommended!)

- If `mysql -u` *user_name* test works but `mysql -u` *user_name* *other_db_name* does not, you have not granted database access for *other_db_name* to the given user.

- If `mysql -u` *user_name* works when executed on the server host, but `mysql -h` *host_name* `-u` *user_name* does not work when executed on a remote client host, you have not enabled access to the server for the given username from the remote host.

- If you cannot figure out why you get Access denied, remove from the user table all entries that have Host values containing wildcards (entries that contain '%' or '_'). A very common error is to insert a new entry with Host='%' and User='*some_user*', thinking that this allows you to specify localhost to connect from the same machine. The reason that this does not work is that the default privileges include an entry with Host='localhost' and User=''. Because that entry has a Host value 'localhost' that is more specific than '%', it is used in preference to the new entry when connecting from localhost! The correct procedure is to insert a second entry with Host='localhost' and User='*some_user*', or to delete the entry with Host='localhost' and User=''. After deleting the entry, remember to issue a FLUSH PRIVILEGES statement to reload the grant tables.

- If you get the following error, you may have a problem with the db or host table:

  `Access to database denied`

  If the entry selected from the db table has an empty value in the Host column, make sure that there are one or more corresponding entries in the host table specifying which hosts the db table entry applies to.

- If you are able to connect to the MySQL server, but get an Access denied message whenever you issue a SELECT ... INTO OUTFILE or LOAD DATA INFILE statement, your entry in the user table does not have the FILE privilege enabled.

- If you change the grant tables directly (for example, by using INSERT, UPDATE, or DELETE statements) and your changes seem to be ignored, remember that you must execute a FLUSH PRIVILEGES statement or a mysqladmin flush-privileges command to cause the server to re-read the privilege tables. Otherwise, your changes have no effect until the next time the server is restarted. Remember that after you change the root password with an UPDATE command, you won't need to specify the new password until after you flush the privileges, because the server won't know you've changed the password yet!

- If your privileges seem to have changed in the middle of a session, it may be that a MySQL administrator has changed them. Reloading the grant tables affects new client connections, but it also affects existing connections as indicated in Section 4.8.7, "When Privilege Changes Take Effect."

- If you have access problems with a Perl, PHP, Python, or ODBC program, try to connect to the server with `mysql -u user_name db_name` or `mysql -u user_name -pyour_pass db_name`. If you are able to connect using the `mysql` client, the problem lies with your program, not with the access privileges. (There is no space between -p and the password; you can also use the `--password=your_pass` syntax to specify the password. If you use the -p --password option with no password value, MySQL prompts you for the password.)

- For testing, start the `mysqld` server with the `--skip-grant-tables` option. Then you can change the MySQL grant tables and use the `mysqlaccess` script to check whether your modifications have the desired effect. When you are satisfied with your changes, execute `mysqladmin flush-privileges` to tell the `mysqld` server to start using the new grant tables. (Reloading the grant tables overrides the `--skip-grant-tables` option. This enables you to tell the server to begin using the grant tables again without stopping and restarting it.)

- If everything else fails, start the `mysqld` server with a debugging option (for example, `--debug=d,general,query`). This prints host and user information about attempted connections, as well as information about each command issued.

- If you have any other problems with the MySQL grant tables and feel you must post the problem to the mailing list, always provide a dump of the MySQL grant tables. You can dump the tables with the `mysqldump mysql` command. To file a bug report, see the instructions in Section 1.8, "How to Report Bugs or Problems." In some cases, you may need to restart `mysqld` with `--skip-grant-tables` to run `mysqldump`.

4.8.9 Password Hashing as of MySQL 4.1

MySQL user accounts are listed in the user table of the `mysql` database. Each MySQL account is assigned a password, although what is stored in the Password column of the user table is not the plaintext version of the password, but a hash value computed from it. Password hash values are computed by the `PASSWORD()` function.

MySQL uses passwords in two phases of client/server communication:

- When a client attempts to connect to the server, there is an initial authentication step in which the client must present a password that has a hash value matching the hash value stored in the user table for the account that the client wants to use.

- After the client connects, it can (if it has sufficient privileges) set or change the password hashes for accounts listed in the user table. The client can do this by using the `PASSWORD()` function to generate a password hash, or by using the `GRANT` or `SET PASSWORD` statements.

In other words, the server *uses* hash values during authentication when a client first attempts to connect. The server *generates* hash values if a connected client invokes the `PASSWORD()` function or uses a `GRANT` or `SET PASSWORD` statement to set or change a password.

The password-hashing mechanism was updated in MySQL 4.1 to provide better security and to reduce the risk of passwords being intercepted. However, this new mechanism is understood only by MySQL 4.1 (and newer) servers and clients, which can result in some compatibility problems. A 4.1 or newer client can connect to a pre-4.1 server, because the client understands both the old and new password-hashing mechanisms. However, a pre-4.1 client that attempts to connect to a 4.1 or newer server may run into difficulties. For example, a 3.23 `mysql` client that attempts to connect to a 5.0 server may fail with the following error message:

```
shell> mysql -h localhost -u root
Client does not support authentication protocol requested
by server; consider upgrading MySQL client
```

Another common example of this phenomenon occurs for attempts to use the older PHP `mysql` extension after upgrading to MySQL 4.1 or newer.

The following discussion describes the differences between the old and new password mechanisms, and what you should do if you upgrade your server but need to maintain backward compatibility with pre-4.1 clients. This information is of particular importance to PHP programmers migrating MySQL databases from version 4.0 or lower to version 4.1 or higher.

Note: This discussion contrasts 4.1 behavior with pre-4.1 behavior, but the 4.1 behavior described here actually begins with 4.1.1. MySQL 4.1.0 is an "odd" release because it has a slightly different mechanism than that implemented in 4.1.1 and up. Differences between 4.1.0 and more recent versions are described further in "MySQL 3.23, 4.0, 4.1 Reference Manual."

Prior to MySQL 4.1, password hashes computed by the PASSWORD() function are 16 bytes long. Such hashes look like this:

```
mysql> SELECT PASSWORD('mypass');
+--------------------+
| PASSWORD('mypass') |
+--------------------+
| 6f8c114b58f2ce9e   |
+--------------------+
```

The `Password` column of the `user` table (in which these hashes are stored) also is 16 bytes long before MySQL 4.1.

As of MySQL 4.1, the PASSWORD() function has been modified to produce a longer 41-byte hash value:

```
mysql> SELECT PASSWORD('mypass');
+-------------------------------------------+
| PASSWORD('mypass')                        |
+-------------------------------------------+
| *6C8989366EAF75BB670AD8EA7A7FC1176A95CEF4 |
+-------------------------------------------+
```

Accordingly, the `Password` column in the `user` table also must be 41 bytes long to store these values:

- If you perform a new installation of MySQL 5.0, the `Password` column is made 41 bytes long automatically.
- Upgrading from MySQL 4.1 (4.1.1 or later in the 4.1 series) to MySQL 5.0 should not give rise to any issues in this regard because both versions use the same password hashing mechanism. If you wish to upgrade an older release of MySQL to version 5.0, you should upgrade to version 4.1 first, and then upgrade the 4.1 installation to 5.0.

A widened `Password` column can store password hashes in both the old and new formats. The format of any given password hash value can be determined two ways:

- The obvious difference is the length (16 bytes versus 41 bytes).
- A second difference is that password hashes in the new format always begin with a '*' character, whereas passwords in the old format never do.

The longer password hash format has better cryptographic properties, and client authentication based on long hashes is more secure than that based on the older short hashes.

The differences between short and long password hashes are relevant both for how the server uses passwords during authentication and for how it generates password hashes for connected clients that perform password-changing operations.

The way in which the server uses password hashes during authentication is affected by the width of the `Password` column:

- If the column is short, only short-hash authentication is used.
- If the column is long, it can hold either short or long hashes, and the server can use either format:
  - Pre-4.1 clients can connect, although because they know only about the old hashing mechanism, they can authenticate only using accounts that have short hashes.
  - 4.1 and later clients can authenticate using accounts that have short or long hashes.

Even for short-hash accounts, the authentication process is actually a bit more secure for 4.1 and later clients than for older clients. In terms of security, the gradient from least to most secure is:

- Pre-4.1 client authenticating with short password hash
- 4.1 or later client authenticating with short password hash
- 4.1 or later client authenticating with long password hash

The way in which the server generates password hashes for connected clients is affected by the width of the `Password` column and by the `--old-passwords` option. A 4.1 or later server generates long hashes only if certain conditions are met: The `Password` column must be wide enough to hold long values and the `--old-passwords` option must not be given. These conditions apply as follows:

- The `Password` column must be wide enough to hold long hashes (41 bytes). If the column has not been updated and still has the pre-4.1 width of 16 bytes, the server notices that long hashes cannot fit into it and generates only short hashes when a client performs password-changing operations using `PASSWORD()`, `GRANT`, or `SET PASSWORD`. This is the behavior that occurs if you have upgraded to 4.1 but have not yet run the `mysql_fix_privilege_tables` script to widen the `Password` column.

- If the `Password` column is wide, it can store either short or long password hashes. In this case, `PASSWORD()`, `GRANT`, and `SET PASSWORD` generate long hashes unless the server was started with the `--old-passwords` option. That option forces the server to generate short password hashes instead.

The purpose of the `--old-passwords` option is to enable you to maintain backward compatibility with pre-4.1 clients under circumstances where the server would otherwise generate long password hashes. The option doesn't affect authentication (4.1 and later clients can still use accounts that have long password hashes), but it does prevent creation of a long password hash in the user table as the result of a password-changing operation. Were that to occur, the account no longer could be used by pre-4.1 clients. Without the `--old-passwords` option, the following undesirable scenario is possible:

- An old client connects to an account that has a short password hash.
- The client changes its own password. Without `--old-passwords`, this results in the account having a long password hash.
- The next time the old client attempts to connect to the account, it cannot, because the account has a long password hash that requires the new hashing mechanism during authentication. (Once an account has a long password hash in the user table, only 4.1 and later clients can authenticate for it, because pre-4.1 clients do not understand long hashes.)

This scenario illustrates that, if you must support older pre-4.1 clients, it is dangerous to run a 4.1 or newer server without using the `--old-passwords` option. By running the server with `--old-passwords`, password-changing operations do not generate long password hashes and thus do not cause accounts to become inaccessible to older clients. (Those clients cannot inadvertently lock themselves out by changing their password and ending up with a long password hash.)

The downside of the `--old-passwords` option is that any passwords you create or change use short hashes, even for 4.1 clients. Thus, you lose the additional security provided by long password hashes. If you want to create an account that has a long hash (for example, for use by 4.1 clients), you must do so while running the server without `--old-passwords`.

The following scenarios are possible for running a 4.1 or later server:

Scenario 1: Short `Password` column in user table:

- Only short hashes can be stored in the Password column.

- The server uses only short hashes during client authentication.

- For connected clients, password hash-generating operations involving PASSWORD(), GRANT, or SET PASSWORD use short hashes exclusively. Any change to an account's password results in that account having a short password hash.

- The --old-passwords option can be used but is superfluous because with a short Password column, the server generates only short password hashes anyway.

Scenario 2: Long Password column; server not started with --old-passwords option:

- Short or long hashes can be stored in the Password column.

- 4.1 and later clients can authenticate using accounts that have short or long hashes.

- Pre-4.1 clients can authenticate only using accounts that have short hashes.

- For connected clients, password hash-generating operations involving PASSWORD(), GRANT, or SET PASSWORD use long hashes exclusively. A change to an account's password results in that account having a long password hash.

As indicated earlier, a danger in this scenario is that it is possible for accounts that have a short password hash to become inaccessible to pre-4.1 clients. A change to such an account's password made via GRANT, PASSWORD(), or SET PASSWORD results in the account being given a long password hash. From that point on, no pre-4.1 client can authenticate to that account until the client upgrades to 4.1.

To deal with this problem, you can change a password in a special way. For example, normally you use SET PASSWORD as follows to change an account password:

```
SET PASSWORD FOR 'some_user'@'some_host' = PASSWORD('mypass');
```

To change the password but create a short hash, use the OLD_PASSWORD() function instead:

```
SET PASSWORD FOR 'some_user'@'some_host' = OLD_PASSWORD('mypass');
```

OLD_PASSWORD() is useful for situations in which you explicitly want to generate a short hash.

Scenario 3: Long Password column; 4.1 or newer server started with --old-passwords option:

- Short or long hashes can be stored in the Password column.

- 4.1 and later clients can authenticate for accounts that have short or long hashes (but note that it is possible to create long hashes only when the server is started without --old-passwords).

- Pre-4.1 clients can authenticate only for accounts that have short hashes.

- For connected clients, password hash-generating operations involving PASSWORD(), GRANT, or SET PASSWORD use short hashes exclusively. Any change to an account's password results in that account having a short password hash.

In this scenario, you cannot create accounts that have long password hashes, because the --old-passwords option prevents generation of long hashes. Also, if you create an account with a long hash before using the --old-passwords option, changing the account's password while --old-passwords is in effect results in the account being given a short password, causing it to lose the security benefits of a longer hash.

The disadvantages for these scenarios may be summarized as follows:

In scenario 1, you cannot take advantage of longer hashes that provide more secure authentication.

In scenario 2, accounts with short hashes become inaccessible to pre-4.1 clients if you change their passwords without explicitly using OLD_PASSWORD().

In scenario 3, --old-passwords prevents accounts with short hashes from becoming inaccessible, but password-changing operations cause accounts with long hashes to revert to short hashes, and you cannot change them back to long hashes while --old-passwords is in effect.

4.8.9.1 Implications of Password Hashing Changes for Application Programs

An upgrade to MySQL version 4.1 or later can cause compatibility issues for applications that use PASSWORD() to generate passwords for their own purposes. Applications really should not do this, because PASSWORD() should be used only to manage passwords for MySQL accounts. But some applications use PASSWORD() for their own purposes anyway.

If you upgrade to 4.1 or later from a pre-4.1 version of MySQL and run the server under conditions where it generates long password hashes, an application using PASSWORD() for its own passwords breaks. The recommended course of action in such cases is to modify the application to use another function, such as SHA1() or MD5(), to produce hashed values. If that is not possible, you can use the OLD_PASSWORD() function, which is provided for generating short hashes in the old format. However, you should note that OLD_PASSWORD() may one day no longer be supported.

If the server is running under circumstances where it generates short hashes, OLD_PASSWORD() is available but is equivalent to PASSWORD().

4.9 MySQL User Account Management

This section describes how to set up accounts for clients of your MySQL server. It discusses the following topics:

- The meaning of account names and passwords as used in MySQL and how that compares to names and passwords used by your operating system
- How to set up new accounts and remove existing accounts
- How to change passwords

- Guidelines for using passwords securely
- How to use secure connections with SSL

4.9.1 MySQL Usernames and Passwords

A MySQL account is defined in terms of a username and the client host or hosts from which the user can connect to the server. The account also has a password. There are several distinctions between the way usernames and passwords are used by MySQL and the way they are used by your operating system:

- Usernames, as used by MySQL for authentication purposes, have nothing to do with usernames (login names) as used by Windows or Unix. On Unix, most MySQL clients by default try to log in using the current Unix username as the MySQL username, but that is for convenience only. The default can be overridden easily, because client programs allow any username to be specified with a -u or --user option. Because this means that anyone can attempt to connect to the server using any username, you cannot make a database secure in any way unless all MySQL accounts have passwords. Anyone who specifies a username for an account that has no password is able to connect successfully to the server.

- MySQL usernames can be up to a maximum of 16 characters long. This limit is hard-coded in the MySQL servers and clients, and trying to circumvent it by modifying the definitions of the tables in the mysql database *does not work.*

  Note: *You should never alter any of the tables in the mysql database in any manner whatsoever except by means of the procedure prescribed by MySQL AB that is described in Section 4.6.2, "mysql_upgrade—Check Tables for MySQL Upgrade." Attempting to redefine MySQL's system tables in any other fashion results in undefined (and unsupported!) behavior.*

  Operating system usernames are completely unrelated to MySQL usernames and may even be of a different maximum length. For example, Unix usernames typically are limited to eight characters.

- MySQL passwords have nothing to do with passwords for logging in to your operating system. There is no necessary connection between the password you use to log in to a Windows or Unix machine and the password you use to access the MySQL server on that machine.

- MySQL encrypts passwords using its own algorithm. This encryption is different from that used during the Unix login process. MySQL password encryption is the same as that implemented by the PASSWORD() SQL function. Unix password encryption is the same as that implemented by the ENCRYPT() SQL function. From version 4.1 on, MySQL employs a stronger authentication method that has better password protection during the connection process than in earlier versions. It is secure even if TCP/IP packets are sniffed or the mysql database is captured. (In earlier versions, even though passwords are stored in encrypted form in the user table, knowledge of the encrypted password value could be used to connect to the MySQL server.)

When you install MySQL, the grant tables are populated with an initial set of accounts. These accounts have names and access privileges that are described in Section 2.9.3, "Securing the Initial MySQL Accounts," which also discusses how to assign passwords to them. Thereafter, you normally set up, modify, and remove MySQL accounts using statements such as GRANT and REVOKE.

When you connect to a MySQL server with a command-line client, you should specify the username and password for the account that you want to use:

```
shell> mysql --user=monty --password=guess db_name
```

If you prefer short options, the command looks like this:

```
shell> mysql -u monty -pguess db_name
```

There must be *no space* between the -p option and the following password value. See Section 4.8.4, "Connecting to the MySQL Server."

The preceding commands include the password value on the command line, which can be a security risk. See Section 4.9.6, "Keeping Your Password Secure." To avoid this problem, specify the --password or -p option without any following password value:

```
shell> mysql --user=monty --password db_name
shell> mysql -u monty -p db_name
```

When the password option has no password value, the client program prints a prompt and waits for you to enter the password. (In these examples, *db_name* is *not* interpreted as a password because it is separated from the preceding password option by a space.)

On some systems, the library routine that MySQL uses to prompt for a password automatically limits the password to eight characters. That is a problem with the system library, not with MySQL. Internally, MySQL doesn't have any limit for the length of the password. To work around the problem, change your MySQL password to a value that is eight or fewer characters long, or put your password in an option file.

4.9.2 Adding New User Accounts to MySQL

You can create MySQL accounts in two ways:

- By using statements intended for creating accounts, such as CREATE USER or GRANT
- By manipulating the MySQL grant tables directly with statements such as INSERT, UPDATE, or DELETE

The preferred method is to use account-creation statements because they are more concise and less error-prone. CREATE USER and GRANT are described in the "MySQL Language Reference."

Another option for creating accounts is to use one of several available third-party programs that offer capabilities for MySQL account administration. phpMyAdmin is one such program.

The following examples show how to use the mysql client program to set up new users. These examples assume that privileges are set up according to the defaults described in Section 2.9.3, "Securing the Initial MySQL Accounts." This means that to make changes, you must connect to the MySQL server as the MySQL root user, and the root account must have the INSERT privilege for the mysql database and the RELOAD administrative privilege.

First, use the mysql program to connect to the server as the MySQL root user:

```
shell> mysql --user=root mysql
```

If you have assigned a password to the root account, you'll also need to supply a --password or -p option for this mysql command and also for those later in this section.

After connecting to the server as root, you can add new accounts. The following statements use GRANT to set up four new accounts:

```
mysql> GRANT ALL PRIVILEGES ON *.* TO 'monty'@'localhost'
    ->     IDENTIFIED BY 'some_pass' WITH GRANT OPTION;
mysql> GRANT ALL PRIVILEGES ON *.* TO 'monty'@'%'
    ->     IDENTIFIED BY 'some_pass' WITH GRANT OPTION;
mysql> GRANT RELOAD,PROCESS ON *.* TO 'admin'@'localhost';
mysql> GRANT USAGE ON *.* TO 'dummy'@'localhost';
```

The accounts created by these GRANT statements have the following properties:

- Two of the accounts have a username of monty and a password of some_pass. Both accounts are superuser accounts with full privileges to do anything. One account ('monty'@'localhost') can be used only when connecting from the local host. The other ('monty'@'%') can be used to connect from any other host. Note that it is necessary to have both accounts for monty to be able to connect from anywhere as monty. Without the localhost account, the anonymous-user account for localhost that is created by mysql_install_db would take precedence when monty connects from the local host. As a result, monty would be treated as an anonymous user. The reason for this is that the anonymous-user account has a more specific Host column value than the 'monty'@'%' account and thus comes earlier in the user table sort order. (user table sorting is discussed in Section 4.8.5, "Access Control, Stage 1: Connection Verification.")

- One account has a username of admin and no password. This account can be used only by connecting from the local host. It is granted the RELOAD and PROCESS administrative privileges. These privileges allow the admin user to execute the mysqladmin reload, mysqladmin refresh, and mysqladmin flush-xxx commands, as well as mysqladmin processlist. No privileges are granted for accessing any databases. You could add such privileges later by issuing additional GRANT statements.

- One account has a username of dummy and no password. This account can be used only by connecting from the local host. No privileges are granted. The USAGE privilege in the

GRANT statement enables you to create an account without giving it any privileges. It has the effect of setting all the global privileges to 'N'. It is assumed that you will grant specific privileges to the account later.

As an alternative to GRANT, you can create the same accounts directly by issuing INSERT statements and then telling the server to reload the grant tables using FLUSH PRIVILEGES:

```
shell> mysql --user=root mysql
mysql> INSERT INTO user
    ->       VALUES('localhost','monty',PASSWORD('some_pass'),
    ->       'Y','Y','Y','Y','Y','Y','Y','Y','Y','Y','Y','Y','Y','Y');
mysql> INSERT INTO user
    ->       VALUES('%','monty',PASSWORD('some_pass'),
    ->       'Y','Y','Y','Y','Y','Y','Y','Y','Y','Y','Y','Y','Y','Y');
mysql> INSERT INTO user SET Host='localhost',User='admin',
    ->       Reload_priv='Y', Process_priv='Y';
mysql> INSERT INTO user (Host,User,Password)
    ->       VALUES('localhost','dummy','');
mysql> FLUSH PRIVILEGES;
```

The reason for using FLUSH PRIVILEGES when you create accounts with INSERT is to tell the server to re-read the grant tables. Otherwise, the changes go unnoticed until you restart the server. With GRANT, FLUSH PRIVILEGES is unnecessary.

The reason for using the PASSWORD() function with INSERT is to encrypt the password. The GRANT statement encrypts the password for you, so PASSWORD() is unnecessary.

The 'Y' values enable privileges for the accounts. Depending on your MySQL version, you may have to use a different number of 'Y' values in the first two INSERT statements. For the admin account, you may also employ the more readable extended INSERT syntax using SET.

In the INSERT statement for the dummy account, only the Host, User, and Password columns in the user table row are assigned values. None of the privilege columns are set explicitly, so MySQL assigns them all the default value of 'N'. This is equivalent to what GRANT USAGE does.

Note that to set up a superuser account, it is necessary only to create a user table entry with the privilege columns set to 'Y'. user table privileges are global, so no entries in any of the other grant tables are needed.

The next examples create three accounts and give them access to specific databases. Each of them has a username of custom and password of obscure.

To create the accounts with GRANT, use the following statements:

```
shell> mysql --user=root mysql
mysql> GRANT SELECT,INSERT,UPDATE,DELETE,CREATE,DROP
    ->       ON bankaccount.*
    ->       TO 'custom'@'localhost'
    ->       IDENTIFIED BY 'obscure';
```

```
mysql> GRANT SELECT,INSERT,UPDATE,DELETE,CREATE,DROP
    ->     ON expenses.*
    ->     TO 'custom'@'whitehouse.gov'
    ->     IDENTIFIED BY 'obscure';
mysql> GRANT SELECT,INSERT,UPDATE,DELETE,CREATE,DROP
    ->     ON customer.*
    ->     TO 'custom'@'server.domain'
    ->     IDENTIFIED BY 'obscure';
```

The three accounts can be used as follows:

- The first account can access the bankaccount database, but only from the local host.
- The second account can access the expenses database, but only from the host white-house.gov.
- The third account can access the customer database, but only from the host server.domain.

To set up the custom accounts without GRANT, use INSERT statements as follows to modify the grant tables directly:

```
shell> mysql --user=root mysql
mysql> INSERT INTO user (Host,User,Password)
    ->     VALUES('localhost','custom',PASSWORD('obscure'));
mysql> INSERT INTO user (Host,User,Password)
    ->     VALUES('whitehouse.gov','custom',PASSWORD('obscure'));
mysql> INSERT INTO user (Host,User,Password)
    ->     VALUES('server.domain','custom',PASSWORD('obscure'));
mysql> INSERT INTO db
    ->     (Host,Db,User,Select_priv,Insert_priv,
    ->     Update_priv,Delete_priv,Create_priv,Drop_priv)
    ->     VALUES('localhost','bankaccount','custom',
    ->     'Y','Y','Y','Y','Y','Y');
mysql> INSERT INTO db
    ->     (Host,Db,User,Select_priv,Insert_priv,
    ->     Update_priv,Delete_priv,Create_priv,Drop_priv)
    ->     VALUES('whitehouse.gov','expenses','custom',
    ->     'Y','Y','Y','Y','Y','Y');
mysql> INSERT INTO db
    ->     (Host,Db,User,Select_priv,Insert_priv,
    ->     Update_priv,Delete_priv,Create_priv,Drop_priv)
    ->     VALUES('server.domain','customer','custom',
    ->     'Y','Y','Y','Y','Y','Y');
mysql> FLUSH PRIVILEGES;
```

The first three INSERT statements add user table entries that allow the user custom to connect from the various hosts with the given password, but grant no global privileges (all privileges are set to the default value of 'N'). The next three INSERT statements add db table entries that grant privileges to custom for the bankaccount, expenses, and customer databases, but only when accessed from the proper hosts. As usual when you modify the grant tables directly, you must tell the server to reload them with FLUSH PRIVILEGES so that the privilege changes take effect.

If you want to give a specific user access from all machines in a given domain (for example, mydomain.com), you can issue a GRANT statement that uses the '%' wildcard character in the host part of the account name:

```
mysql> GRANT ...
    ->     ON *.*
    ->     TO 'myname'@'%.mydomain.com'
    ->     IDENTIFIED BY 'mypass';
```

To do the same thing by modifying the grant tables directly, do this:

```
mysql> INSERT INTO user (Host,User,Password,...)
    ->     VALUES('%.mydomain.com','myname',PASSWORD('mypass'),...);
mysql> FLUSH PRIVILEGES;
```

4.9.3 Removing User Accounts from MySQL

To remove an account, use the DROP USER statement.

4.9.4 Limiting Account Resources

One means of limiting use of MySQL server resources is to set the max_user_connections system variable to a non-zero value. However, this method is strictly global, and does not allow for management of individual accounts. In addition, it limits only the number of simultaneous connections made using a single account, and not what a client can do once connected. Both types of control are interest to many MySQL administrators, particularly those working for Internet service providers.

In MySQL 5.0, you can limit the following server resources for individual accounts:

- The number of queries that an account can issue per hour
- The number of updates that an account can issue per hour
- The number of times an account can connect to the server per hour

Any statement that a client can issue counts against the query limit. Only statements that modify databases or tables count against the update limit.

From MySQL 5.0.3 on, it is also possible to limit the number of simultaneous connections to the server on a per-account basis.

An account in this context is a single row in the user table. Each account is uniquely identified by its User and Host column values.

As a prerequisite for using this feature, the user table in the mysql database must contain the resource-related columns. Resource limits are stored in the max_questions, max_updates, max_connections, and max_user_connections columns. If your user table doesn't have these columns, it must be upgraded; see Section 4.6.2, "mysql_upgrade—Check Tables for MySQL Upgrade."

To set resource limits with a GRANT statement, use a WITH clause that names each resource to be limited and a per-hour count indicating the limit value. For example, to create a new account that can access the customer database, but only in a limited fashion, issue this statement:

```
mysql> GRANT ALL ON customer.* TO 'francis'@'localhost'
    ->      IDENTIFIED BY 'frank'
    ->      WITH MAX_QUERIES_PER_HOUR 20
    ->           MAX_UPDATES_PER_HOUR 10
    ->           MAX_CONNECTIONS_PER_HOUR 5
    ->           MAX_USER_CONNECTIONS 2;
```

The limit types need not all be named in the WITH clause, but those named can be present in any order. The value for each per-hour limit should be an integer representing a count per hour. If the GRANT statement has no WITH clause, the limits are each set to the default value of zero (that is, no limit). For MAX_USER_CONNECTIONS, the limit is an integer indicating the maximum number of simultaneous connections the account can make at any one time. If the limit is set to the default value of 0, the max_user_connections system variable determines the number of simultaneous connections for the account.

To set or change limits for an existing account, use a GRANT USAGE statement at the global level (ON *.*). The following statement changes the query limit for francis to 100:

```
mysql> GRANT USAGE ON *.* TO 'francis'@'localhost'
    ->      WITH MAX_QUERIES_PER_HOUR 100;
```

This statement leaves the account's existing privileges unchanged and modifies only the limit values specified.

To remove an existing limit, set its value to 0. For example, to remove the limit on how many times per hour francis can connect, use this statement:

```
mysql> GRANT USAGE ON *.* TO 'francis'@'localhost'
    ->      WITH MAX_CONNECTIONS_PER_HOUR 0;
```

Resource-use counting takes place when any account has a non-zero limit placed on its use of any of the resources.

As the server runs, it counts the number of times each account uses resources. If an account reaches its limit on number of connections within the last hour, further connections for the account are rejected until that hour is up. Similarly, if the account reaches its limit on the number of queries or updates, further queries or updates are rejected until the hour is up. In all such cases, an appropriate error message is issued.

Resource counting is done per account, not per client. For example, if your account has a query limit of 50, you cannot increase your limit to 100 by making two simultaneous client connections to the server. Queries issued on both connections are counted together.

The current per-hour resource-use counts can be reset globally for all accounts, or individually for a given account:

- To reset the current counts to zero for all accounts, issue a FLUSH USER_RESOURCES statement. The counts also can be reset by reloading the grant tables (for example, with a FLUSH PRIVILEGES statement or a mysqladmin reload command).

- The counts for an individual account can be set to zero by re-granting it any of its limits. To do this, use GRANT USAGE as described earlier and specify a limit value equal to the value that the account currently has.

Counter resets do not affect the MAX_USER_CONNECTIONS limit.

All counts begin at zero when the server starts; counts are not carried over through a restart.

4.9.5 Assigning Account Passwords

Passwords may be assigned from the command line by using the mysqladmin command:

```
shell> mysqladmin -u user_name -h host_name password "newpwd"
```

The account for which this command resets the password is the one with a user table row that matches user_name in the User column and the client host *from which you connect* in the Host column.

Another way to assign a password to an account is to issue a SET PASSWORD statement:

```
mysql> SET PASSWORD FOR 'jeffrey'@'%' = PASSWORD('biscuit');
```

Only users such as root that have update access to the mysql database can change the password for other users. If you are not connected as an anonymous user, you can change your own password by omitting the FOR clause:

```
mysql> SET PASSWORD = PASSWORD('biscuit');
```

You can also use a GRANT USAGE statement at the global level (ON *.*) to assign a password to an account without affecting the account's current privileges:

```
mysql> GRANT USAGE ON *.* TO 'jeffrey'@'%' IDENTIFIED BY 'biscuit';
```

Although it is generally preferable to assign passwords using one of the preceding methods, you can also do so by modifying the user table directly:

- To establish a password when creating a new account, provide a value for the Password column:

```
shell> mysql -u root mysql
mysql> INSERT INTO user (Host,User,Password)
    -> VALUES('%','jeffrey',PASSWORD('biscuit'));
mysql> FLUSH PRIVILEGES;
```

- To change the password for an existing account, use UPDATE to set the Password column value:

```
shell> mysql -u root mysql
mysql> UPDATE user SET Password = PASSWORD('bagel')
    -> WHERE Host = '%' AND User = 'francis';
mysql> FLUSH PRIVILEGES;
```

When you assign an account a non-empty password using SET PASSWORD, INSERT, or UPDATE, you must use the PASSWORD() function to encrypt it. PASSWORD() is necessary because the user table stores passwords in encrypted form, not as plaintext. If you forget that fact, you are likely to set passwords like this:

```
shell> mysql -u root mysql
mysql> INSERT INTO user (Host,User,Password)
    -> VALUES('%','jeffrey','biscuit');
mysql> FLUSH PRIVILEGES;
```

The result is that the literal value 'biscuit' is stored as the password in the user table, not the encrypted value. When jeffrey attempts to connect to the server using this password, the value is encrypted and compared to the value stored in the user table. However, the stored value is the literal string 'biscuit', so the comparison fails and the server rejects the connection:

```
shell> mysql -u jeffrey -pbiscuit test
Access denied
```

If you assign passwords using the GRANT ... IDENTIFIED BY statement or the mysqladmin password command, they both take care of encrypting the password for you. In these cases, using PASSWORD() function is unnecessary.

Note: PASSWORD() encryption is different from Unix password encryption. See Section 4.9.1, "MySQL Usernames and Passwords."

4.9.6 Keeping Your Password Secure

On an administrative level, you should never grant access to the user grant table to any non-administrative accounts.

When you run a client program to connect to the MySQL server, it is inadvisable to specify your password in a way that exposes it to discovery by other users. The methods you can use to specify your password when you run client programs are listed here, along with an assessment of the risks of each method:

- Use a -p*your_pass* or --password=*your_pass* option on the command line. For example:

```
shell> mysql -u francis -pfrank db_name
```

This is convenient *but insecure*, because your password becomes visible to system status programs such as ps that may be invoked by other users to display command lines. MySQL clients typically overwrite the command-line password argument with zeros during their initialization sequence. However, there is still a brief interval during which the value is visible. On some systems this strategy is ineffective, anyway, and the password remains visible to ps. (System V Unix systems and perhaps others are subject to this problem.)

- Use the -p or --password option with no password value specified. In this case, the client program solicits the password from the terminal:

```
shell> mysql -u francis -p db_name
Enter password: ********
```

The '*' characters indicate where you enter your password. The password is not displayed as you enter it.

It is more secure to enter your password this way than to specify it on the command line because it is not visible to other users. However, this method of entering a password is suitable only for programs that you run interactively. If you want to invoke a client from a script that runs non-interactively, there is no opportunity to enter the password from the terminal. On some systems, you may even find that the first line of your script is read and interpreted (incorrectly) as your password.

- Store your password in an option file. For example, on Unix you can list your password in the [client] section of the .my.cnf file in your home directory:

```
[client]
password=your_pass
```

If you store your password in .my.cnf, the file should not be accessible to anyone but yourself. To ensure this, set the file access mode to 400 or 600. For example:

```
shell> chmod 600 .my.cnf
```

Section 3.3.2, "Using Option Files," discusses option files in more detail.

- Store your password in the MYSQL_PWD environment variable. This method of specifying your MySQL password must be considered *extremely insecure* and should not be used. Some versions of ps include an option to display the environment of running processes. If you set MYSQL_PWD, your password is exposed to any other user who runs ps. Even on systems without such a version of ps, it is unwise to assume that there are no other methods by which users can examine process environments.

All in all, the safest methods are to have the client program prompt for the password or to specify the password in a properly protected option file.

4.9.7 Using Secure Connections

MySQL supports secure (encrypted) connections between MySQL clients and the server using the Secure Sockets Layer (SSL) protocol. This section discusses how to use SSL connections. It also describes a way to set up SSH on Windows. For information on requiring users to use SSL connections, see the "MySQL Language Reference."

The standard configuration of MySQL is intended to be as fast as possible, so encrypted connections are not used by default. Doing so would make the client/server protocol much slower. Encrypting data is a CPU-intensive operation that requires the computer to do additional work and can delay other MySQL tasks. For applications that require the security provided by encrypted connections, the extra computation is warranted.

MySQL allows encryption to be enabled on a per-connection basis. You can choose a normal unencrypted connection or a secure encrypted SSL connection according the requirements of individual applications.

4.9.7.1 Basic SSL Concepts

To understand how MySQL uses SSL, it is necessary to explain some basic SSL and X509 concepts. People who are familiar with these can skip this part of the discussion.

By default, MySQL uses unencrypted connections between the client and the server. This means that someone with access to the network could watch all your traffic and look at the data being sent or received. They could even change the data while it is in transit between client and server. To improve security a little, you can compress client/server traffic by using the --compress option when invoking client programs. However, this does not foil a determined attacker.

When you need to move information over a network in a secure fashion, an unencrypted connection is unacceptable. Encryption is the way to make any kind of data unreadable. In fact, today's practice requires many additional security elements from encryption algorithms. They should resist many kind of known attacks such as changing the order of encrypted messages or replaying data twice.

SSL is a protocol that uses different encryption algorithms to ensure that data received over a public network can be trusted. It has mechanisms to detect any data change, loss, or replay. SSL also incorporates algorithms that provide identity verification using the X509 standard.

X509 makes it possible to identify someone on the Internet. It is most commonly used in e-commerce applications. In basic terms, there should be some company called a "Certificate Authority" (or CA) that assigns electronic certificates to anyone who needs them. Certificates rely on asymmetric encryption algorithms that have two encryption keys (a public key and a secret key). A certificate owner can show the certificate to another party as proof of identity. A certificate consists of its owner's public key. Any data encrypted with this public key can be decrypted only using the corresponding secret key, which is held by the owner of the certificate.

If you need more information about SSL, X509, or encryption, use your favorite Internet search engine to search for the keywords in which you are interested.

4.9.7.2 Using SSL Connections with OpenSSL

To use SSL connections between the MySQL server and client programs, your system must support either OpenSSL or (as of MySQL 5.0.10) yaSSL. This section covers OpenSSL. To use yaSSL, read Section 4.9.7.3, "Using SSL Connections with yaSSL," instead.

To get secure connections to work with MySQL and OpenSSL, you must do the following:

1. Install the OpenSSL library if it has not already been installed. We have tested MySQL with OpenSSL 0.9.6. If you need OpenSSL, visit http://www.openssl.org/.

2. When you configure MySQL, invoke the `configure` script with the `--with-vio` and `--with-openssl` options:

   ```
   shell> ./configure --with-vio --with-openssl
   ```

3. Make sure that you have upgraded your grant tables to include the SSL-related columns in the `mysql.user` table. This is necessary if your grant tables date from a version prior to MySQL 4.0.0. The upgrade procedure is described in Section 4.6.2, "mysql_upgrade—Check Tables for MySQL Upgrade."

4. To check whether a running `mysqld` server supports OpenSSL, examine the value of the `have_openssl` system variable:

   ```
   mysql> SHOW VARIABLES LIKE 'have_openssl';
   +---------------+-------+
   | Variable_name | Value |
   +---------------+-------+
   | have_openssl  | YES   |
   +---------------+-------+
   ```

   If the value is YES, the server supports OpenSSL connections.

4.9.7.3 Using SSL Connections with yaSSL

Using MySQL's built-in yaSSL support makes it easier to use secure connections. You don't have to install OpenSSL and perform the other steps described in Section 4.9.7.2, "Using SSL Connections with OpenSSL." Also, both MySQL and yaSSL employ the same licensing model.

Currently, yaSSL support is available for these platforms:

- Linux/x86-64 Red Hat Enterprise 3.0
- Linux RHAS21 Itanium-2 with gcc, statically linked
- Linux Itanium-2 with gcc
- Windows (all builds)

To enable yaSSL when building MySQL from source, you should configure MySQL like this:

```
shell> ./configure --with-yassl
```

Note that yaSSL support on Unix platforms requires that either /dev/urandom or /dev/random be installed to retrieve true random numbers. For additional information (especially regarding yaSSL on Solaris versions prior to 2.8 and HP-UX), see Bug #13164 (http://bugs.mysql.com/13164).

To start the MySQL server with yaSSL support, use the same options as with OpenSSL support and identify the certificates needed to establish a secure connection:

```
shell> mysqld --ssl-ca=cacert.pem \
       --ssl-cert=server-cert.pem \
       --ssl-key=server-key.pem
```

- --ssl-ca identifies the Certificate Authority certificate.
- --ssl-cert identifies the server certificate.
- --ssl-key identifies the client certificate.

To establish a secure connection to a MySQL server with yaSSL support, start a client like this:

```
shell> mysql --ssl-ca=cacert.pem \
       --ssl-cert=server-cert.pem \
       --ssl-key=server-key.pem
```

In other words, the options are the same as for the server, and the Certificate Authority certificate has to be the same.

To establish a secure connection from an application program, use the mysql_ssl_set() API function to set the appropriate certificate options, before calling mysql_real_connect().

4.9.7.4 Setting Up SSL Certificates for MySQL

Here is an example of setting up SSL certificates for MySQL using OpenSSL:

```
DIR=`pwd`/openssl
PRIV=$DIR/private

mkdir $DIR $PRIV $DIR/newcerts
cp /usr/share/ssl/openssl.cnf $DIR
replace ./demoCA $DIR -- $DIR/openssl.cnf

# Create necessary files: $database, $serial and $new_certs_dir
# directory (optional)
```

```
touch $DIR/index.txt
echo "01" > $DIR/serial

#
# Generation of Certificate Authority(CA)
#

openssl req -new -x509 -keyout $PRIV/cakey.pem -out $DIR/cacert.pem \
    -config $DIR/openssl.cnf

# Sample output:
# Using configuration from /home/monty/openssl/openssl.cnf
# Generating a 1024 bit RSA private key
# ................++++++
# .........++++++
# writing new private key to '/home/monty/openssl/private/cakey.pem'
# Enter PEM pass phrase:
# Verifying password - Enter PEM pass phrase:
# -----
# You are about to be asked to enter information that will be
# incorporated into your certificate request.
# What you are about to enter is what is called a Distinguished Name
# or a DN.
# There are quite a few fields but you can leave some blank
# For some fields there will be a default value,
# If you enter '.', the field will be left blank.
# -----
# Country Name (2 letter code) [AU]:FI
# State or Province Name (full name) [Some-State]:.
# Locality Name (eg, city) []:
# Organization Name (eg, company) [Internet Widgits Pty Ltd]:MySQL AB
# Organizational Unit Name (eg, section) []:
# Common Name (eg, YOUR name) []:MySQL admin
# Email Address []:

#
# Create server request and key
#
openssl req -new -keyout $DIR/server-key.pem -out \
    $DIR/server-req.pem -days 3600 -config $DIR/openssl.cnf

# Sample output:
# Using configuration from /home/monty/openssl/openssl.cnf
# Generating a 1024 bit RSA private key
# ..++++++
# ..........++++++
```

```
# writing new private key to '/home/monty/openssl/server-key.pem'
# Enter PEM pass phrase:
# Verifying password - Enter PEM pass phrase:
# -----
# You are about to be asked to enter information that will be
# incorporated into your certificate request.
# What you are about to enter is what is called a Distinguished Name
# or a DN.
# There are quite a few fields but you can leave some blank
# For some fields there will be a default value,
# If you enter '.', the field will be left blank.
# -----
# Country Name (2 letter code) [AU]:FI
# State or Province Name (full name) [Some-State]:.
# Locality Name (eg, city) []:
# Organization Name (eg, company) [Internet Widgits Pty Ltd]:MySQL AB
# Organizational Unit Name (eg, section) []:
# Common Name (eg, YOUR name) []:MySQL server
# Email Address []:
#
# Please enter the following 'extra' attributes
# to be sent with your certificate request
# A challenge password []:
# An optional company name []:

#
# Remove the passphrase from the key (optional)
#

openssl rsa -in $DIR/server-key.pem -out $DIR/server-key.pem

#
# Sign server cert
#
openssl ca  -policy policy_anything -out $DIR/server-cert.pem \
    -config $DIR/openssl.cnf -infiles $DIR/server-req.pem

# Sample output:
# Using configuration from /home/monty/openssl/openssl.cnf
# Enter PEM pass phrase:
# Check that the request matches the signature
# Signature ok
# The Subjects Distinguished Name is as follows
# countryName            :PRINTABLE:'FI'
# organizationName       :PRINTABLE:'MySQL AB'
# commonName             :PRINTABLE:'MySQL admin'
```

```
# Certificate is to be certified until Sep 13 14:22:46 2003 GMT
# (365 days)
# Sign the certificate? [y/n]:y
#
#
# 1 out of 1 certificate requests certified, commit? [y/n]y
# Write out database with 1 new entries
# Data Base Updated


#
# Create client request and key
#
openssl req -new -keyout $DIR/client-key.pem -out \
    $DIR/client-req.pem -days 3600 -config $DIR/openssl.cnf


# Sample output:
# Using configuration from /home/monty/openssl/openssl.cnf
# Generating a 1024 bit RSA private key
# ......................................++++++
# .............................................++++++
# writing new private key to '/home/monty/openssl/client-key.pem'
# Enter PEM pass phrase:
# Verifying password - Enter PEM pass phrase:
# -----
# You are about to be asked to enter information that will be
# incorporated into your certificate request.
# What you are about to enter is what is called a Distinguished Name
# or a DN.
# There are quite a few fields but you can leave some blank
# For some fields there will be a default value,
# If you enter '.', the field will be left blank.
# -----
# Country Name (2 letter code) [AU]:FI
# State or Province Name (full name) [Some-State]:.
# Locality Name (eg, city) []:
# Organization Name (eg, company) [Internet Widgits Pty Ltd]:MySQL AB
# Organizational Unit Name (eg, section) []:
# Common Name (eg, YOUR name) []:MySQL user
# Email Address []:
#
# Please enter the following 'extra' attributes
# to be sent with your certificate request
# A challenge password []:
# An optional company name []:


#
```

```
# Remove a passphrase from the key (optional)
#
openssl rsa -in $DIR/client-key.pem -out $DIR/client-key.pem


#
# Sign client cert
#

openssl ca  -policy policy_anything -out $DIR/client-cert.pem \
    -config $DIR/openssl.cnf -infiles $DIR/client-req.pem

# Sample output:
# Using configuration from /home/monty/openssl/openssl.cnf
# Enter PEM pass phrase:
# Check that the request matches the signature
# Signature ok
# The Subjects Distinguished Name is as follows
# countryName           :PRINTABLE:'FI'
# organizationName      :PRINTABLE:'MySQL AB'
# commonName            :PRINTABLE:'MySQL user'
# Certificate is to be certified until Sep 13 16:45:17 2003 GMT
# (365 days)
# Sign the certificate? [y/n]:y
#
#
# 1 out of 1 certificate requests certified, commit? [y/n]y
# Write out database with 1 new entries
# Data Base Updated


#
# Create a my.cnf file that you can use to test the certificates
#

cnf=""
cnf="$cnf [client]"
cnf="$cnf ssl-ca=$DIR/cacert.pem"
cnf="$cnf ssl-cert=$DIR/client-cert.pem"
cnf="$cnf ssl-key=$DIR/client-key.pem"
cnf="$cnf [mysqld]"
cnf="$cnf ssl-ca=$DIR/cacert.pem"
cnf="$cnf ssl-cert=$DIR/server-cert.pem"
cnf="$cnf ssl-key=$DIR/server-key.pem"
echo $cnf | replace " " '
' > $DIR/my.cnf
```

To test SSL connections, start the server as follows, where `$DIR` is the pathname to the directory where the sample `my.cnf` option file is located:

```
shell> mysqld --defaults-file=$DIR/my.cnf &
```

Then invoke a client program using the same option file:

```
shell> mysql --defaults-file=$DIR/my.cnf
```

If you have a MySQL source distribution, you can also test your setup by modifying the preceding `my.cnf` file to refer to the demonstration certificate and key files in the SSL directory of the distribution.

4.9.7.5 SSL Command Options

The following list describes options that are used for specifying the use of SSL, certificate files, and key files. They may be given on the command line or in an option file.

- `--ssl`

  For the server, this option specifies that the server allows SSL connections. For a client program, it allows the client to connect to the server using SSL. This option is not sufficient in itself to cause an SSL connection to be used. You must also specify the `--ssl-ca`, `--ssl-cert`, and `--ssl-key` options.

  This option is more often used in its opposite form to indicate that SSL should *not* be used. To do this, specify the option as `--skip-ssl` or `--ssl=0`.

  Note that use of `--ssl` does not *require* an SSL connection. For example, if the server or client is compiled without SSL support, a normal unencrypted connection is used.

  The secure way to ensure that an SSL connection is used is to create an account on the server that includes a REQUIRE SSL clause in the GRANT statement. Then use this account to connect to the server, with both a server and client that have SSL support enabled.

- `--ssl-ca=file_name`

  The path to a file with a list of trusted SSL CAs.

- `--ssl-capath=directory_name`

  The path to a directory that contains trusted SSL CA certificates in PEM format.

- `--ssl-cert=file_name`

  The name of the SSL certificate file to use for establishing a secure connection.

- `--ssl-cipher=cipher_list`

  A list of allowable ciphers to use for SSL encryption. `cipher_list` has the same format as the `openssl ciphers` command.

  Example: `--ssl-cipher=ALL:-AES:-EXP`

- `--ssl-key=file_name`

  The name of the SSL key file to use for establishing a secure connection.

4.9.7.6 Connecting to MySQL Remotely from Windows with SSH

Here is a note that describes how to get a secure connection to a remote MySQL server with SSH (by David Carlson dcarlson@mplcomm.com):

1. Install an SSH client on your Windows machine. As a user, the best non-free one I have found is from SecureCRT from http://www.vandyke.com/. Another option is f-secure from http://www.f-secure.com/. You can also find some free ones on Google at http://directory.google.com/Top/Computers/Security/Products_and_Tools/Cryptography/SSH/Clients/Windows/.

2. Start your Windows SSH client. Set Host_Name = yourmysqlserver_URL_or_IP. Set userid=your_userid to log in to your server. This userid value might not be the same as the username of your MySQL account.

3. Set up port forwarding. Either do a remote forward (set local_port: 3306, remote_host: yourmysqlservername_or_ip, remote_port: 3306) or a local forward (set port: 3306, host: localhost, remote port: 3306).

4. Save everything, otherwise you will have to redo it the next time.

5. Log in to your server with the SSH session you just created.

6. On your Windows machine, start some ODBC application (such as Access).

7. Create a new file in Windows and link to MySQL using the ODBC driver the same way you normally do, except type in localhost for the MySQL host server, not yourmysqlservername.

At this point, you should have an ODBC connection to MySQL, encrypted using SSH.

4.10 Backup and Recovery

This section discusses how to make database backups (full and incremental) and how to perform table maintenance. The syntax of the SQL statements described here is given in the "MySQL Language Reference." Much of the information here pertains primarily to MyISAM tables. Additional information about InnoDB backup procedures is given in Section 8.2.8, "Backing Up and Recovering an InnoDB Database."

4.10.1 Database Backups

Because MySQL tables are stored as files, it is easy to do a backup. To get a consistent backup, do a LOCK TABLES on the relevant tables, followed by FLUSH TABLES for the tables. You need only a read lock; this allows other clients to continue to query the tables while you are making a copy of the files in the database directory. The FLUSH TABLES statement is needed to ensure that the all active index pages are written to disk before you start the backup.

To make an SQL-level backup of a table, you can use SELECT INTO ... OUTFILE. For this statement, the output file cannot previously exist because allowing extant files to be overwritten would constitute a security risk.

Another technique for backing up a database is to use the `mysqldump` program or the `mysql-hotcopy` script. See Section 7.10, "`mysqldump`—A Database Backup Program," and Section 7.11, "`mysqlhotcopy`—A Database Backup Program."

1. Create a full backup of your database:

   ```
   shell> mysqldump --tab=/path/to/some/dir --opt db_name
   ```

   Or:

   ```
   shell> mysqlhotcopy db_name /path/to/some/dir
   ```

   You can also create a binary backup simply by copying all table files (`*.frm`, `*.MYD`, and `*.MYI` files), as long as the server isn't updating anything. The `mysqlhotcopy` script uses this method. (But note that these methods do not work if your database contains `InnoDB` tables. `InnoDB` does not store table contents in database directories, and `mysqlhotcopy` works only for `MyISAM` tables.)

2. Stop `mysqld` if it is running, and then start it with the `--log-bin[=file_name]` option. See Section 4.12.3, "The Binary Log." The binary log files provide you with the information you need to replicate changes to the database that are made subsequent to the point at which you executed `mysqldump`.

For `InnoDB` tables, it is possible to perform an online backup that takes no locks on tables; see Section 7.10, "`mysqldump`—A Database Backup Program."

MySQL supports incremental backups: You need to start the server with the `--log-bin` option to enable binary logging; see Section 4.12.3, "The Binary Log." At the moment you want to make an incremental backup (containing all changes that happened since the last full or incremental backup), you should rotate the binary log by using `FLUSH LOGS`. This done, you need to copy to the backup location all binary logs, which range from the one of the moment of the last full or incremental backup to the last but one. These binary logs are the incremental backup; at restore time, you apply them as explained further below. The next time you do a full backup, you should also rotate the binary log using `FLUSH LOGS`, `mysqldump --flush-logs`, or `mysqlhotcopy --flushlog`. See Section 7.10, "`mysqldump`—A Database Backup Program," and Section 7.11, "`mysqlhotcopy`—A Database Backup Program."

If your MySQL server is a slave replication server, then regardless of the backup method you choose, you should also back up the `master.info` and `relay-log.info` files when you back up your slave's data. These files are always needed to resume replication after you restore the slave's data. If your slave is subject to replicating `LOAD DATA INFILE` commands, you should also back up any `SQL_LOAD-*` files that may exist in the directory specified by the `--slave-load-tmpdir` option. (This location defaults to the value of the `tmpdir` variable if not specified.) The slave needs these files to resume replication of any interrupted `LOAD DATA INFILE` operations.

If you have to restore `MyISAM` tables, try to recover them using `REPAIR TABLE` or `myisamchk -r` first. That should work in 99.9% of all cases. If `myisamchk` fails, try the following procedure.

Note that it works only if you have enabled binary logging by starting MySQL with the `--log-bin` option.

1. Restore the original `mysqldump` backup, or binary backup.

2. Execute the following command to re-run the updates in the binary logs:

   ```
   shell> mysqlbinlog binlog.[0-9]* | mysql
   ```

   In some cases, you may want to re-run only certain binary logs, from certain positions (usually you want to re-run all binary logs from the date of the restored backup, excepting possibly some incorrect statements). See Section 7.8, "mysqlbinlog—Utility for Processing Binary Log Files," for more information on the `mysqlbinlog` utility and how to use it.

You can also make selective backups of individual files:

- To dump the table, use `SELECT * INTO OUTFILE 'file_name' FROM tbl_name`.
- To reload the table, use `LOAD DATA INFILE 'file_name' REPLACE ....` To avoid duplicate rows, the table must have a `PRIMARY KEY` or a `UNIQUE` index. The `REPLACE` keyword causes old rows to be replaced with new ones when a new row duplicates an old row on a unique key value.

If you have performance problems with your server while making backups, one strategy that can help is to set up replication and perform backups on the slave rather than on the master. See Section 5.1, "Introduction to Replication."

If you are using a Veritas filesystem, you can make a backup like this:

1. From a client program, execute `FLUSH TABLES WITH READ LOCK`.

2. From another shell, execute `mount vxfs snapshot`.

3. From the first client, execute `UNLOCK TABLES`.

4. Copy files from the snapshot.

5. Unmount the snapshot.

4.10.2 Example Backup and Recovery Strategy

This section discusses a procedure for performing backups that allows you to recover data after several types of crashes:

- Operating system crash
- Power failure
- Filesystem crash
- Hardware problem (hard drive, motherboard, and so forth)

The example commands do not include options such as --user and --password for the mysqldump and mysql programs. You should include such options as necessary so that the MySQL server allows you to connect to it.

We assume that data is stored in the InnoDB storage engine, which has support for transactions and automatic crash recovery. We also assume that the MySQL server is under load at the time of the crash. If it were not, no recovery would ever be needed.

For cases of operating system crashes or power failures, we can assume that MySQL's disk data is available after a restart. The InnoDB data files might not contain consistent data due to the crash, but InnoDB reads its logs and finds in them the list of pending committed and non-committed transactions that have not been flushed to the data files. InnoDB automatically rolls back those transactions that were not committed, and flushes to its data files those that were committed. Information about this recovery process is conveyed to the user through the MySQL error log. The following is an example log excerpt:

```
InnoDB: Database was not shut down normally.
InnoDB: Starting recovery from log files...
InnoDB: Starting log scan based on checkpoint at
InnoDB: log sequence number 0 13674004
InnoDB: Doing recovery: scanned up to log sequence number 0 13739520
InnoDB: Doing recovery: scanned up to log sequence number 0 13805056
InnoDB: Doing recovery: scanned up to log sequence number 0 13870592
InnoDB: Doing recovery: scanned up to log sequence number 0 13936128
...
InnoDB: Doing recovery: scanned up to log sequence number 0 20555264
InnoDB: Doing recovery: scanned up to log sequence number 0 20620800
InnoDB: Doing recovery: scanned up to log sequence number 0 20664692
InnoDB: 1 uncommitted transaction(s) which must be rolled back
InnoDB: Starting rollback of uncommitted transactions
InnoDB: Rolling back trx no 16745
InnoDB: Rolling back of trx no 16745 completed
InnoDB: Rollback of uncommitted transactions completed
InnoDB: Starting an apply batch of log records to the database...
InnoDB: Apply batch completed
InnoDB: Started
mysqld: ready for connections
```

For the cases of filesystem crashes or hardware problems, we can assume that the MySQL disk data is *not* available after a restart. This means that MySQL fails to start successfully because some blocks of disk data are no longer readable. In this case, it is necessary to reformat the disk, install a new one, or otherwise correct the underlying problem. Then it is necessary to recover our MySQL data from backups, which means that we must already have made backups. To make sure that is the case, we should design a backup policy.

4.10.2.1 Backup Policy

We all know that backups must be scheduled periodically. A full backup (a snapshot of the data at a point in time) can be done in MySQL with several tools. For example, InnoDB Hot Backup provides online non-blocking physical backup of the InnoDB data files, and mysqldump provides online logical backup. This discussion uses mysqldump.

Assume that we make a backup on Sunday at 1 p.m., when load is low. The following command makes a full backup of all our InnoDB tables in all databases:

```
shell> mysqldump --single-transaction --all-databases > backup_sunday_1_PM.sql
```

This is an online, non-blocking backup that does not disturb the reads and writes on the tables. We assumed earlier that our tables are InnoDB tables, so --single-transaction uses a consistent read and guarantees that data seen by mysqldump does not change. (Changes made by other clients to InnoDB tables are not seen by the mysqldump process.) If we do have other types of tables, we must assume that they are not changed during the backup. For example, for the MyISAM tables in the mysql database, we must assume that no administrative changes are being made to MySQL accounts during the backup.

The resulting .sql file produced by mysqldump contains a set of SQL INSERT statements that can be used to reload the dumped tables at a later time.

Full backups are necessary, but they are not always convenient. They produce large backup files and take time to generate. They are not optimal in the sense that each successive full backup includes all data, even that part that has not changed since the previous full backup. After we have made the initial full backup, it is more efficient to make incremental backups. They are smaller and take less time to produce. The tradeoff is that, at recovery time, you cannot restore your data just by reloading the full backup. You must also process the incremental backups to recover the incremental changes.

To make incremental backups, we need to save the incremental changes. The MySQL server should always be started with the --log-bin option so that it stores these changes in a file while it updates data. This option enables binary logging, so that the server writes each SQL statement that updates data into a file called a "MySQL binary log." Looking at the data directory of a MySQL server that was started with the --log-bin option and that has been running for some days, we find these MySQL binary log files:

```
-rw-rw---- 1 guilhem  guilhem    1277324 Nov 10 23:59 gbichot2-bin.000001
-rw-rw---- 1 guilhem  guilhem          4 Nov 10 23:59 gbichot2-bin.000002
-rw-rw---- 1 guilhem  guilhem         79 Nov 11 11:06 gbichot2-bin.000003
-rw-rw---- 1 guilhem  guilhem        508 Nov 11 11:08 gbichot2-bin.000004
-rw-rw---- 1 guilhem  guilhem  220047446 Nov 12 16:47 gbichot2-bin.000005
-rw-rw---- 1 guilhem  guilhem     998412 Nov 14 10:08 gbichot2-bin.000006
-rw-rw---- 1 guilhem  guilhem        361 Nov 14 10:07 gbichot2-bin.index
```

Each time it restarts, the MySQL server creates a new binary log file using the next number in the sequence. While the server is running, you can also tell it to close the current binary log file and begin a new one manually by issuing a FLUSH LOGS SQL statement or with a mysqladmin flush-logs command. mysqldump also has an option to flush the logs. The .index file in the data directory contains the list of all MySQL binary logs in the directory. This file is used for replication.

The MySQL binary logs are important for recovery because they form the set of incremental backups. If you make sure to flush the logs when you make your full backup, any binary log files created afterward contain all the data changes made since the backup. Let's modify the previous mysqldump command a bit so that it flushes the MySQL binary logs at the moment of the full backup, and so that the dump file contains the name of the new current binary log:

```
shell> mysqldump --single-transaction --flush-logs --master-data=2 \
       --all-databases > backup_sunday_1_PM.sql
```

After executing this command, the data directory contains a new binary log file, gbichot2-bin.000007. The resulting .sql file includes these lines:

```
-- Position to start replication or point-in-time recovery from
-- CHANGE MASTER TO MASTER_LOG_FILE='gbichot2-bin.000007',MASTER_LOG_POS=4;
```

Because the mysqldump command made a full backup, those lines mean two things:

- The .sql file contains all changes made before any changes written to the gbichot2-bin.000007 binary log file or newer.
- All data changes logged after the backup are not present in the .sql, but are present in the gbichot2-bin.000007 binary log file or newer.

On Monday at 1 p.m., we can create an incremental backup by flushing the logs to begin a new binary log file. For example, executing a mysqladmin flush-logs command creates gbichot2-bin.000008. All changes between the Sunday 1 p.m. full backup and Monday 1 p.m. will be in the gbichot2-bin.000007 file. This incremental backup is important, so it is a good idea to copy it to a safe place. (For example, back it up on tape or DVD, or copy it to another machine.) On Tuesday at 1 p.m., execute another mysqladmin flush-logs command. All changes between Monday 1 p.m. and Tuesday 1 p.m. will be in the gbichot2-bin.000008 file (which also should be copied somewhere safe).

The MySQL binary logs take up disk space. To free up space, purge them from time to time. One way to do this is by deleting the binary logs that are no longer needed, such as when we make a full backup:

```
shell> mysqldump --single-transaction --flush-logs --master-data=2 \
       --all-databases --delete-master-logs > backup_sunday_1_PM.sql
```

Note: Deleting the MySQL binary logs with mysqldump --delete-master-logs can be dangerous if your server is a replication master server, because slave servers might not yet fully have processed the contents of the binary log. The description for the PURGE MASTER LOGS statement explains what should be verified before deleting the MySQL binary logs.

4.10.2.2 Using Backups for Recovery

Now, suppose that we have a catastrophic crash on Wednesday at 8 a.m. that requires recovery from backups. To recover, first we restore the last full backup we have (the one from Sunday 1 p.m.). The full backup file is just a set of SQL statements, so restoring it is very easy:

```
shell> mysql < backup_sunday_1_PM.sql
```

At this point, the data is restored to its state as of Sunday 1 p.m. To restore the changes made since then, we must use the incremental backups; that is, the gbichot2-bin.000007 and gbichot2-bin.000008 binary log files. Fetch the files if necessary from where they were backed up, and then process their contents like this:

```
shell> mysqlbinlog gbichot2-bin.000007 gbichot2-bin.000008 | mysql
```

We now have recovered the data to its state as of Tuesday 1 p.m., but still are missing the changes from that date to the date of the crash. To not lose them, we would have needed to have the MySQL server store its MySQL binary logs into a safe location (RAID disks, SAN, …) different from the place where it stores its data files, so that these logs were not on the destroyed disk. (That is, we can start the server with a --log-bin option that specifies a location on a different physical device from the one on which the data directory resides. That way, the logs are safe even if the device containing the directory is lost.) If we had done this, we would have the gbichot2-bin.000009 file at hand, and we could apply it using mysqlbinlog and mysql to restore the most recent data changes with no loss up to the moment of the crash.

4.10.2.3 Backup Strategy Summary

In case of an operating system crash or power failure, InnoDB itself does all the job of recovering data. But to make sure that you can sleep well, observe the following guidelines:

- Always run the MySQL server with the --log-bin option, or even --log-bin=*log_name*, where the log file name is located on some safe media different from the drive on which the data directory is located. If you have such safe media, this technique can also be good for disk load balancing (which results in a performance improvement).

- Make periodic full backups, using the mysqldump command shown earlier in Section 4.10.2.1, "Backup Policy," that makes an online, non-blocking backup.

- Make periodic incremental backups by flushing the logs with FLUSH LOGS or mysqladmin flush-logs.

4.10.3 Point-in-Time Recovery

If a MySQL server was started with the --log-bin option to enable binary logging, you can use the mysqlbinlog utility to recover data from the binary log files, starting from a specified point in time (for example, since your last backup) until the present or another specified point in time. For information on enabling the binary log and using `mysqlbinlog`, see Section 4.12.3, "The Binary Log," and Section 7.8, "`mysqlbinlog`—Utility for Processing Binary Log Files."

To restore data from a binary log, you must know the location and name of the current binary log file. By default, the server creates binary log files in the data directory, but a pathname can be specified with the `--log-bin` option to place the files in a different location. Typically the option is given in an option file (that is, `my.cnf` or `my.ini`, depending on your system). It can also be given on the command line when the server is started. To determine the name of the current binary log file, issue the following statement:

```
mysql> SHOW BINLOG EVENTS\G
```

If you prefer, you can execute the following command from the command line instead:

```
shell> mysql -u root -p -E -e "SHOW BINLOG EVENTS"
```

Enter the root password for your server when `mysql` prompts you for it.

4.10.3.1 Specifying Times for Recovery

To indicate the start and end times for recovery, specify the `--start-date` and `--stop-date` options for `mysqlbinlog`, in `DATETIME` format. As an example, suppose that exactly at 10:00 a.m. on April 20, 2005 an SQL statement was executed that deleted a large table. To restore the table and data, you could restore the previous night's backup, and then execute the following command:

```
shell> mysqlbinlog --stop-date="2005-04-20 9:59:59" \
       /var/log/mysql/bin.123456 | mysql -u root -p
```

This command recovers all of the data up until the date and time given by the `--stop-date` option. If you did not detect the erroneous SQL statement that was entered until hours later, you will probably also want to recover the activity that occurred afterward. Based on this, you could run `mysqlbinlog` again with a start date and time, like so:

```
shell> mysqlbinlog --start-date="2005-04-20 10:01:00" \
       /var/log/mysql/bin.123456 | mysql -u root -p
```

In this command, the SQL statements logged from 10:01 a.m. on will be re-executed. The combination of restoring of the previous night's dump file and the two `mysqlbinlog` commands restores everything up until one second before 10:00 a.m. and everything from 10:01 a.m. on. You should examine the log to be sure of the exact times to specify for the commands. To display the log file contents without executing them, use this command:

```
shell> mysqlbinlog /var/log/mysql/bin.123456 > /tmp/mysql_restore.sql
```

Then open the file with a text editor to examine it.

4.10.3.2 Specifying Positions for Recovery

Instead of specifying dates and times, the --start-position and --stop-position options for mysqlbinlog can be used for specifying log positions. They work the same as the start and stop date options, except that you specify log position numbers rather than dates. Using positions may enable you to be more precise about which part of the log to recover, especially if many transactions occurred around the same time as a damaging SQL statement. To determine the position numbers, run mysqlbinlog for a range of times near the time when the unwanted transaction was executed, but redirect the results to a text file for examination. This can be done like so:

```
shell> mysqlbinlog --start-date="2005-04-20 9:55:00" \
        --stop-date="2005-04-20 10:05:00" \
        /var/log/mysql/bin.123456 > /tmp/mysql_restore.sql
```

This command creates a small text file in the /tmp directory that contains the SQL statements around the time that the deleterious SQL statement was executed. Open this file with a text editor and look for the statement that you don't want to repeat. Determine the positions in the binary log for stopping and resuming the recovery and make note of them. Positions are labeled as log_pos followed by a number. After restoring the previous backup file, use the position numbers to process the binary log file. For example, you would use commands something like these:

```
shell> mysqlbinlog --stop-position="368312" /var/log/mysql/bin.123456 \
        | mysql -u root -p

shell> mysqlbinlog --start-position="368315" /var/log/mysql/bin.123456 \
        | mysql -u root -p
```

The first command recovers all the transactions up until the stop position given. The second command recovers all transactions from the starting position given until the end of the binary log. Because the output of mysqlbinlog includes SET TIMESTAMP statements before each SQL statement recorded, the recovered data and related MySQL logs will reflect the original times at which the transactions were executed.

4.10.4 Table Maintenance and Crash Recovery

This section discusses how to use myisamchk to check or repair MyISAM tables (tables that have .MYD and .MYI files for storing data and indexes). For general myisamchk background, see Section 7.2, "myisamchk—MyISAM Table-Maintenance Utility."

You can use myisamchk to get information about your database tables or to check, repair, or optimize them. The following sections describe how to perform these operations and how to set up a table maintenance schedule.

Even though table repair with myisamchk is quite secure, it is always a good idea to make a backup *before* doing a repair or any maintenance operation that could make a lot of changes to a table.

myisamchk operations that affect indexes can cause FULLTEXT indexes to be rebuilt with full-text parameters that are incompatible with the values used by the MySQL server. To avoid this problem, follow the guidelines in Section 7.2.1, "myisamchk General Options."

In many cases, you may find it simpler to do MyISAM table maintenance using the SQL statements that perform operations that myisamchk can do:

- To check or repair MyISAM tables, use CHECK TABLE or REPAIR TABLE.
- To optimize MyISAM tables, use OPTIMIZE TABLE.
- To analyze MyISAM tables, use ANALYZE TABLE.

These statements can be used directly or by means of the mysqlcheck client program. One advantage of these statements over myisamchk is that the server does all the work. With myisamchk, you must make sure that the server does not use the tables at the same time so that there is no unwanted interaction between myisamchk and the server.

4.10.4.1 Using myisamchk for Crash Recovery

This section describes how to check for and deal with data corruption in MySQL databases. If your tables become corrupted frequently, you should try to find the reason why.

For an explanation of how MyISAM tables can become corrupted, see Section 8.1.4, "MyISAM Table Problems."

If you run mysqld with external locking disabled (which is the default as of MySQL 4.0), you cannot reliably use myisamchk to check a table when mysqld is using the same table. If you can be certain that no one will access the tables through mysqld while you run myisamchk, you only have to execute mysqladmin flush-tables before you start checking the tables. If you cannot guarantee this, you must stop mysqld while you check the tables. If you run myisamchk to check tables that mysqld is updating at the same time, you may get a warning that a table is corrupt even when it is not.

If the server is run with external locking enabled, you can use myisamchk to check tables at any time. In this case, if the server tries to update a table that myisamchk is using, the server will wait for myisamchk to finish before it continues.

If you use myisamchk to repair or optimize tables, you *must* always ensure that the mysqld server is not using the table (this also applies if external locking is disabled). If you don't stop mysqld, you should at least do a mysqladmin flush-tables before you run myisamchk. Your tables *may become corrupted* if the server and myisamchk access the tables simultaneously.

When performing crash recovery, it is important to understand that each MyISAM table tbl_name in a database corresponds to three files in the database directory:

File	Purpose
tbl_name.frm	Definition (format) file
tbl_name.MYD	Data file
tbl_name.MYI	Index file

Each of these three file types is subject to corruption in various ways, but problems occur most often in data files and index files.

myisamchk works by creating a copy of the .MYD data file row by row. It ends the repair stage by removing the old .MYD file and renaming the new file to the original file name. If you use --quick, myisamchk does not create a temporary .MYD file, but instead assumes that the .MYD file is correct and generates only a new index file without touching the .MYD file. This is safe, because myisamchk automatically detects whether the .MYD file is corrupt and aborts the repair if it is. You can also specify the --quick option twice to myisamchk. In this case, myisamchk does not abort on some errors (such as duplicate-key errors) but instead tries to resolve them by modifying the .MYD file. Normally the use of two --quick options is useful only if you have too little free disk space to perform a normal repair. In this case, you should at least make a backup of the table before running myisamchk.

4.10.4.2 How to Check MyISAM Tables for Errors

To check a MyISAM table, use the following commands:

- myisamchk tbl_name

  This finds 99.99% of all errors. What it cannot find is corruption that involves *only* the data file (which is very unusual). If you want to check a table, you should normally run myisamchk without options or with the -s (silent) option.

- myisamchk -m tbl_name

  This finds 99.999% of all errors. It first checks all index entries for errors and then reads through all rows. It calculates a checksum for all key values in the rows and verifies that the checksum matches the checksum for the keys in the index tree.

- myisamchk -e tbl_name

  This does a complete and thorough check of all data (-e means "extended check"). It does a check-read of every key for each row to verify that they indeed point to the correct row. This may take a long time for a large table that has many indexes. Normally, myisamchk stops after the first error it finds. If you want to obtain more information, you can add the -v (verbose) option. This causes myisamchk to keep going, up through a maximum of 20 errors.

- myisamchk -e -i tbl_name

  This is like the previous command, but the -i option tells myisamchk to print additional statistical information.

In most cases, a simple myisamchk command with no arguments other than the table name is sufficient to check a table.

4.10.4.3 How to Repair Tables

The discussion in this section describes how to use `myisamchk` on MyISAM tables (extensions `.MYI` and `.MYD`).

You can also (and should, if possible) use the CHECK TABLE and REPAIR TABLE statements to check and repair MyISAM tables.

Symptoms of corrupted tables include queries that abort unexpectedly and observable errors such as these:

- *tbl_name*.`frm` is locked against change
- Can't find file *tbl_name*.MYI (Errcode: *nnn*)
- Unexpected end of file
- Record file is crashed
- Got error *nnn* from table handler

To get more information about the error, run `perror nnn`, where *nnn* is the error number. The following example shows how to use `perror` to find the meanings for the most common error numbers that indicate a problem with a table:

```
shell> perror 126 127 132 134 135 136 141 144 145
126 = Index file is crashed / Wrong file format
127 = Record-file is crashed
132 = Old database file
134 = Record was already deleted (or record file crashed)
135 = No more room in record file
136 = No more room in index file
141 = Duplicate unique key or constraint on write or update
144 = Table is crashed and last repair failed
145 = Table was marked as crashed and should be repaired
```

Note that error 135 (no more room in record file) and error 136 (no more room in index file) are not errors that can be fixed by a simple repair. In this case, you must use ALTER TABLE to increase the MAX_ROWS and AVG_ROW_LENGTH table option values:

```
ALTER TABLE tbl_name MAX_ROWS=xxx AVG_ROW_LENGTH=yyy;
```

If you do not know the current table option values, use SHOW CREATE TABLE.

For the other errors, you must repair your tables. `myisamchk` can usually detect and fix most problems that occur.

The repair process involves up to four stages, described here. Before you begin, you should change location to the database directory and check the permissions of the table files. On Unix, make sure that they are readable by the user that `mysqld` runs as (and to you, because you need to access the files you are checking). If it turns out you need to modify files, they must also be writable by you.

This section is for the cases where a table check fails (such as those described in Section 4.10.4.2, "How to Check MyISAM Tables for Errors"), or you want to use the extended features that myisamchk provides.

The options that you can use for table maintenance with myisamchk are described in Section 7.2, "myisamchk—MyISAM Table-Maintenance Utility."

If you are going to repair a table from the command line, you must first stop the mysqld server. Note that when you do mysqladmin shutdown on a remote server, the mysqld server is still alive for a while after mysqladmin returns, until all statement-processing has stopped and all index changes have been flushed to disk.

Stage 1: Checking your tables

Run myisamchk *.MYI or myisamchk -e *.MYI if you have more time. Use the -s (silent) option to suppress unnecessary information.

If the mysqld server is stopped, you should use the --update-state option to tell myisamchk to mark the table as "checked."

You have to repair only those tables for which myisamchk announces an error. For such tables, proceed to Stage 2.

If you get unexpected errors when checking (such as out of memory errors), or if myisamchk crashes, go to Stage 3.

Stage 2: Easy safe repair

First, try myisamchk -r -q tbl_name (-r -q means "quick recovery mode"). This attempts to repair the index file without touching the data file. If the data file contains everything that it should and the delete links point at the correct locations within the data file, this should work, and the table is fixed. Start repairing the next table. Otherwise, use the following procedure:

1. Make a backup of the data file before continuing.

2. Use myisamchk -r tbl_name (-r means "recovery mode"). This removes incorrect rows and deleted rows from the data file and reconstructs the index file.

3. If the preceding step fails, use myisamchk --safe-recover tbl_name. Safe recovery mode uses an old recovery method that handles a few cases that regular recovery mode does not (but is slower).

Note: If you want a repair operation to go much faster, you should set the values of the sort_buffer_size and key_buffer_size variables each to about 25% of your available memory when running myisamchk.

If you get unexpected errors when repairing (such as out of memory errors), or if myisamchk crashes, go to Stage 3.

Stage 3: Difficult repair

You should reach this stage only if the first 16KB block in the index file is destroyed or contains incorrect information, or if the index file is missing. In this case, it is necessary to create a new index file. Do so as follows:

1. Move the data file to a safe place.

2. Use the table description file to create new (empty) data and index files:

```
shell> mysql db_name
mysql> SET AUTOCOMMIT=1;
mysql> TRUNCATE TABLE tbl_name;
mysql> quit
```

3. Copy the old data file back onto the newly created data file. (Do not just move the old file back onto the new file. You want to retain a copy in case something goes wrong.)

Go back to Stage 2. `myisamchk -r -q` should work. (This should not be an endless loop.)

You can also use the `REPAIR TABLE tbl_name USE_FRM` SQL statement, which performs the whole procedure automatically. There is also no possibility of unwanted interaction between a utility and the server, because the server does all the work when you use `REPAIR TABLE`.

Stage 4: Very difficult repair

You should reach this stage only if the `.frm` description file has also crashed. That should never happen, because the description file is not changed after the table is created:

1. Restore the description file from a backup and go back to Stage 3. You can also restore the index file and go back to Stage 2. In the latter case, you should start with `myisamchk -r`.

2. If you do not have a backup but know exactly how the table was created, create a copy of the table in another database. Remove the new data file, and then move the `.frm` description and `.MYI` index files from the other database to your crashed database. This gives you new description and index files, but leaves the `.MYD` data file alone. Go back to Stage 2 and attempt to reconstruct the index file.

4.10.4.4 Table Optimization

To coalesce fragmented rows and eliminate wasted space that results from deleting or updating rows, run `myisamchk` in recovery mode:

```
shell> myisamchk -r tbl_name
```

You can optimize a table in the same way by using the `OPTIMIZE TABLE` SQL statement. `OPTIMIZE TABLE` does a table repair and a key analysis, and also sorts the index tree so that key lookups are faster. There is also no possibility of unwanted interaction between a utility and the server, because the server does all the work when you use `OPTIMIZE TABLE`.

myisamchk has a number of other options that you can use to improve the performance of a table:

- --analyze, -a
- --sort-index, -S
- --sort-records=*index_num*, -R *index_num*

For a full description of all available options, see Section 7.2, "myisamchk—MyISAM Table-Maintenance Utility."

4.10.4.5 Getting Information About a Table

To obtain a description of a table or statistics about it, use the commands shown here. We explain some of the information in more detail later.

- myisamchk -d *tbl_name*

  Runs myisamchk in "describe mode" to produce a description of your table. If you start the MySQL server with external locking disabled, myisamchk may report an error for a table that is updated while it runs. However, because myisamchk does not change the table in describe mode, there is no risk of destroying data.

- myisamchk -d -v *tbl_name*

  Adding -v runs myisamchk in verbose mode so that it produces more information about what it is doing.

- myisamchk -eis *tbl_name*

  Shows only the most important information from a table. This operation is slow because it must read the entire table.

- myisamchk -eiv *tbl_name*

  This is like -eis, but tells you what is being done.

Sample output for some of these commands follows. They are based on a table with these data and index file sizes:

```
-rw-rw-r--   1 monty    tcx       317235748 Jan 12 17:30 company.MYD
-rw-rw-r--   1 davida   tcx        96482304 Jan 12 18:35 company.MYI
```

Example of myisamchk -d output:

```
MyISAM file:     company.MYI
Record format:   Fixed length
Data records:    1403698  Deleted blocks:        0
Recordlength:    226
```

```
table description:
Key Start Len Index   Type
1   2     8   unique  double
2   15    10  multip. text packed stripped
3   219   8   multip. double
4   63    10  multip. text packed stripped
5   167   2   multip. unsigned short
6   177   4   multip. unsigned long
7   155   4   multip. text
8   138   4   multip. unsigned long
9   177   4   multip. unsigned long
    193   1           text
```

Example of `myisamchk -d -v` output:

```
MyISAM file:          company
Record format:        Fixed length
File-version:         1
Creation time:        1999-10-30 12:12:51
Recover time:         1999-10-31 19:13:01
Status:               checked
Data records:            1403698  Deleted blocks:        0
Datafile parts:          1403698  Deleted data:          0
Datafile pointer (bytes):      3  Keyfile pointer (bytes):   3
Max datafile length:  3791650815  Max keyfile length: 4294967294
Recordlength:            226
```

```
table description:
Key Start Len Index   Type                         Rec/key    Root Blocksize
1   2     8   unique  double                             1 15845376     1024
2   15    10  multip. text packed stripped               2 25062400     1024
3   219   8   multip. double                            73 40907776     1024
4   63    10  multip. text packed stripped               5 48097280     1024
5   167   2   multip. unsigned short                  4840 55200768     1024
6   177   4   multip. unsigned long                   1346 65145856     1024
7   155   4   multip. text                            4995 75090944     1024
8   138   4   multip. unsigned long                     87 85036032     1024
9   177   4   multip. unsigned long                    178 96481280     1024
    193   1           text
```

Example of `myisamchk -eis` output:

```
Checking MyISAM file: company
Key:  1:  Keyblocks used:  97%  Packed:    0%  Max levels:  4
Key:  2:  Keyblocks used:  98%  Packed:   50%  Max levels:  4
Key:  3:  Keyblocks used:  97%  Packed:    0%  Max levels:  4
Key:  4:  Keyblocks used:  99%  Packed:   60%  Max levels:  3
Key:  5:  Keyblocks used:  99%  Packed:    0%  Max levels:  3
Key:  6:  Keyblocks used:  99%  Packed:    0%  Max levels:  3
```

```
Key:  7:  Keyblocks used:  99%  Packed:    0%  Max levels:  3
Key:  8:  Keyblocks used:  99%  Packed:    0%  Max levels:  3
Key:  9:  Keyblocks used:  98%  Packed:    0%  Max levels:  4
Total:    Keyblocks used:  98%  Packed:   17%


Records:            1403698    M.recordlength:      226
Packed:             0%
Recordspace used:      100%    Empty space:          0%
Blocks/Record:    1.00
Record blocks:      1403698    Delete blocks:        0
Recorddata:       317235748    Deleted data:         0
Lost space:               0    Linkdata:             0


User time 1626.51, System time 232.36
Maximum resident set size 0, Integral resident set size 0
Non physical pagefaults 0, Physical pagefaults 627, Swaps 0
Blocks in 0 out 0, Messages in 0 out 0, Signals 0
Voluntary context switches 639, Involuntary context switches 28966
```

Example of myisamchk -eiv output:

```
Checking MyISAM file: company
Data records: 1403698   Deleted blocks:        0
- check file-size
- check delete-chain
block_size 1024:
index  1:
index  2:
index  3:
index  4:
index  5:
index  6:
index  7:
index  8:
index  9:
No recordlinks
- check index reference
- check data record references index: 1
Key:  1:  Keyblocks used:  97%  Packed:    0%  Max levels:  4
- check data record references index: 2
Key:  2:  Keyblocks used:  98%  Packed:   50%  Max levels:  4
- check data record references index: 3
Key:  3:  Keyblocks used:  97%  Packed:    0%  Max levels:  4
- check data record references index: 4
Key:  4:  Keyblocks used:  99%  Packed:   60%  Max levels:  3
- check data record references index: 5
Key:  5:  Keyblocks used:  99%  Packed:    0%  Max levels:  3
- check data record references index: 6
```

```
Key:  6:  Keyblocks used:  99%  Packed:    0%  Max levels:  3
- check data record references index: 7
Key:  7:  Keyblocks used:  99%  Packed:    0%  Max levels:  3
- check data record references index: 8
Key:  8:  Keyblocks used:  99%  Packed:    0%  Max levels:  3
- check data record references index: 9
Key:  9:  Keyblocks used:  98%  Packed:    0%  Max levels:  4
Total:    Keyblocks used:   9%  Packed:   17%


- check records and index references
*** LOTS OF ROW NUMBERS DELETED ***


Records:           1403698  M.recordlength:  226  Packed:          0%
Recordspace used:     100%  Empty space:       0%  Blocks/Record: 1.00
Record blocks:     1403698  Delete blocks:     0
Recorddata:      317235748  Deleted data:      0
Lost space:              0  Linkdata:          0

User time 1639.63, System time 251.61
Maximum resident set size 0, Integral resident set size 0
Non physical pagefaults 0, Physical pagefaults 10580, Swaps 0
Blocks in 4 out 0, Messages in 0 out 0, Signals 0
Voluntary context switches 10604, Involuntary context switches 122798
```

Explanations for the types of information myisamchk produces are given here. "Keyfile" refers to the index file. "Record" and "row" are synonymous.

- MyISAM file

  Name of the MyISAM (index) file.

- File-version

  Version of MyISAM format. Currently always 2.

- Creation time

  When the data file was created.

- Recover time

  When the index/data file was last reconstructed.

- Data records

  How many rows are in the table.

- Deleted blocks

  How many deleted blocks still have reserved space. You can optimize your table to minimize this space. See Section 4.10.4.4, "Table Optimization."

- Datafile parts

  For dynamic-row format, this indicates how many data blocks there are. For an optimized table without fragmented rows, this is the same as Data records.

- Deleted data

  How many bytes of unreclaimed deleted data there are. You can optimize your table to minimize this space. See Section 4.10.4.4, "Table Optimization."

- Datafile pointer

  The size of the data file pointer, in bytes. It is usually 2, 3, 4, or 5 bytes. Most tables manage with 2 bytes, but this cannot be controlled from MySQL yet. For fixed tables, this is a row address. For dynamic tables, this is a byte address.

- Keyfile pointer

  The size of the index file pointer, in bytes. It is usually 1, 2, or 3 bytes. Most tables manage with 2 bytes, but this is calculated automatically by MySQL. It is always a block address.

- Max datafile length

  How long the table data file can become, in bytes.

- Max keyfile length

  How long the table index file can become, in bytes.

- Recordlength

  How much space each row takes, in bytes.

- Record format

  The format used to store table rows. The preceding examples use Fixed length. Other possible values are Compressed and Packed.

- table description

  A list of all keys in the table. For each key, myisamchk displays some low-level information:

  - Key

    This key's number.

  - Start

    Where in the row this portion of the index starts.

  - Len

    How long this portion of the index is. For packed numbers, this should always be the full length of the column. For strings, it may be shorter than the full length of the indexed column, because you can index a prefix of a string column.

  - Index

    Whether a key value can exist multiple times in the index. Possible values are unique or multip. (multiple).

  - Type

    What data type this portion of the index has. This is a MyISAM data type with the possible values packed, stripped, or empty.

- Root

  Address of the root index block.

- Blocksize

  The size of each index block. By default this is 1024, but the value may be changed at compile time when MySQL is built from source.

- Rec/key

  This is a statistical value used by the optimizer. It tells how many rows there are per value for this index. A unique index always has a value of 1. This may be updated after a table is loaded (or greatly changed) with myisamchk -a. If this is not updated at all, a default value of 30 is given.

  For the table shown in the examples, there are two table description lines for the ninth index. This indicates that it is a multiple-part index with two parts.

- Keyblocks used

  What percentage of the keyblocks are used. When a table has just been reorganized with myisamchk, as for the table in the examples, the values are very high (very near the theoretical maximum).

- Packed

  MySQL tries to pack key values that have a common suffix. This can only be used for indexes on CHAR and VARCHAR columns. For long indexed strings that have similar left-most parts, this can significantly reduce the space used. In the third of the preceding examples, the fourth key is 10 characters long and a 60% reduction in space is achieved.

- Max levels

  How deep the B-tree for this key is. Large tables with long key values get high values.

- Records

  How many rows are in the table.

- M.recordlength

  The average row length. This is the exact row length for tables with fixed-length rows, because all rows have the same length.

- Packed

  MySQL strips spaces from the end of strings. The Packed value indicates the percentage of savings achieved by doing this.

- Recordspace used

  What percentage of the data file is used.

- Empty space

  What percentage of the data file is unused.

- Blocks/Record

  Average number of blocks per row (that is, how many links a fragmented row is composed of). This is always 1.0 for fixed-format tables. This value should stay as close to 1.0 as possible. If it gets too large, you can reorganize the table. See Section 4.10.4.4, "Table Optimization."

- Recordblocks

  How many blocks (links) are used. For fixed-format tables, this is the same as the number of rows.

- Deleteblocks

  How many blocks (links) are deleted.

- Recorddata

  How many bytes in the data file are used.

- Deleted data

  How many bytes in the data file are deleted (unused).

- Lost space

  If a row is updated to a shorter length, some space is lost. This is the sum of all such losses, in bytes.

- Linkdata

  When the dynamic table format is used, row fragments are linked with pointers (4 to 7 bytes each). Linkdata is the sum of the amount of storage used by all such pointers.

If a table has been compressed with myisampack, myisamchk -d prints additional information about each table column. See Section 7.4, "myisampack—Generate Compressed, Read-Only MyISAM Tables," for an example of this information and a description of what it means.

4.10.4.6 Setting Up a Table Maintenance Schedule

It is a good idea to perform table checks on a regular basis rather than waiting for problems to occur. One way to check and repair MyISAM tables is with the CHECK TABLE and REPAIR TABLE statements.

Another way to check tables is to use myisamchk. For maintenance purposes, you can use myisamchk -s. The -s option (short for --silent) causes myisamchk to run in silent mode, printing messages only when errors occur.

It is also a good idea to enable automatic MyISAM table checking. For example, whenever the machine has done a restart in the middle of an update, you usually need to check each table that could have been affected before it is used further. (These are "expected crashed tables.") To check MyISAM tables automatically, start the server with the --myisam-recover option. See Section 4.2.1, "mysqld Command Options."

You should also check your tables regularly during normal system operation. At MySQL AB, we run a cron job to check all our important tables once a week, using a line like this in a crontab file:

```
35 0 * * 0 /path/to/myisamchk --fast --silent /path/to/datadir/*/*.MYI
```

This prints out information about crashed tables so that we can examine and repair them when needed.

Because we have not had any unexpectedly crashed tables (tables that become corrupted for reasons other than hardware trouble) for several years, once a week is more than sufficient for us.

We recommend that to start with, you execute myisamchk -s each night on all tables that have been updated during the last 24 hours, until you come to trust MySQL as much as we do.

Normally, MySQL tables need little maintenance. If you are performing many updates to MyISAM tables with dynamic-sized rows (tables with VARCHAR, BLOB, or TEXT columns) or have tables with many deleted rows you may want to defragment/reclaim space from the tables from time to time. You can do this by using OPTIMIZE TABLE on the tables in question. Alternatively, if you can stop the mysqld server for a while, change location into the data directory and use this command while the server is stopped:

```
shell> myisamchk -r -s --sort-index --sort_buffer_size=16M */*.MYI
```

4.11 MySQL Localization and International Usage

This section describes how to configure the server to use different character sets. It also discusses how to set the server's time zone and enable per-connection time zone support.

4.11.1 The Character Set Used for Data and Sorting

By default, MySQL uses the latin1 (cp1252 West European) character set and the latin1_swedish_ci collation that sorts according to Swedish/Finnish rules. These defaults are suitable for the United States and most of Western Europe.

All MySQL binary distributions are compiled with --with-extra-charsets=complex. This adds code to all standard programs that enables them to handle latin1 and all multi-byte character sets within the binary. Other character sets are loaded from a character-set definition file when needed.

The character set determines what characters are allowed in identifiers. The collation determines how strings are sorted by the ORDER BY and GROUP BY clauses of the SELECT statement.

You can change the default server character set and collation with the --character-set-server and --collation-server options when you start the server. The collation must be a legal collation for the default character set. (Use the SHOW COLLATION statement to determine which collations are available for each character set.) See Section 4.2.1, "mysqld Command Options."

The character sets available depend on the --with-charset=*charset_name* and --with-extra-charsets=*list-of-charsets* | complex | all | none options to configure, and the character set configuration files listed in *SHAREDIR*/charsets/Index. See Section 2.8.2, "Typical configure Options."

If you change the character set when running MySQL, that may also change the sort order. Consequently, you must run myisamchk -r -q --set-collation=*collation_name* on all MyISAM tables, or your indexes may not be ordered correctly.

When a client connects to a MySQL server, the server indicates to the client what the server's default character set is. The client switches to this character set for this connection.

You should use mysql_real_escape_string() when escaping strings for an SQL query. mysql_real_escape_string() is identical to the old mysql_escape_string() function, except that it takes the MYSQL connection handle as the first parameter so that the appropriate character set can be taken into account when escaping characters.

If the client is compiled with paths that differ from where the server is installed and the user who configured MySQL didn't include all character sets in the MySQL binary, you must tell the client where it can find the additional character sets it needs if the server runs with a different character set from the client. You can do this by specifying a --character-sets-dir option to indicate the path to the directory in which the dynamic MySQL character sets are stored. For example, you can put the following in an option file:

```
[client]
character-sets-dir=/usr/local/mysql/share/mysql/charsets
```

You can force the client to use specific character set as follows:

```
[client]
default-character-set=charset_name
```

This is normally unnecessary, however.

4.11.1.1 Using the German Character Set

In MySQL 5.0, character set and collation are specified separately. This means that if you want German sort order, you should select the latin1 character set and either the latin1_german1_ci or latin1_german2_ci collation. For example, to start the server with the latin1_german1_ci collation, use the --character-set-server=latin1 and --collation-server=latin1_german1_ci options.

4.11.2 Setting the Error Message Language

By default, `mysqld` produces error messages in English, but they can also be displayed in any of these other languages: Czech, Danish, Dutch, Estonian, French, German, Greek, Hungarian, Italian, Japanese, Korean, Norwegian, Norwegian-ny, Polish, Portuguese, Romanian, Russian, Slovak, Spanish, or Swedish.

To start `mysqld` with a particular language for error messages, use the `--language` or `-L` option. The option value can be a language name or the full path to the error message file. For example:

```
shell> mysqld --language=swedish
```

Or:

```
shell> mysqld --language=/usr/local/share/swedish
```

The language name should be specified in lowercase.

By default, the language files are located in the `share/LANGUAGE` directory under the MySQL base directory.

You can also change the content of the error messages produced by the server. Details can be found in the MySQL Internals manual, available at `http://dev.mysql.com/doc/`. If you upgrade to a newer version of MySQL after changing the error messages, remember to repeat your changes after the upgrade.

4.11.3 Adding a New Character Set

This section discusses the procedure for adding a new character set to MySQL. You must have a MySQL source distribution to use these instructions. To choose the proper procedure, determine whether the character set is simple or complex:

- If the character set does not need to use special string collating routines for sorting and does not need multi-byte character support, it is simple.
- If it needs either of those features, it is complex.

For example, `latin1` and `danish` are simple character sets, whereas `big5` and `czech` are complex character sets.

In the following instructions, the name of the character set is represented by *MYSET*.

For a simple character set, do the following:

1. Add *MYSET* to the end of the `sql/share/charsets/Index` file. Assign a unique number to it.
2. Create the file `sql/share/charsets/MYSET.conf`. (You can use a copy of `sql/share/charsets/latin1.conf` as the basis for this file.)

The syntax for the file is very simple:

- Comments start with a '#' character and continue to the end of the line.
- Words are separated by arbitrary amounts of whitespace.
- When defining the character set, every word must be a number in hexadecimal format.
- The ctype array takes up the first 257 words. The to_lower[], to_upper[], and sort_order[] arrays take up 256 words each after that.

See Section 4.11.4, "The Character Definition Arrays."

3. Add the character set name to the CHARSETS_AVAILABLE and COMPILED_CHARSETS lists in configure.in.

4. Reconfigure, recompile, and test.

For a complex character set, do the following:

1. Create the file strings/ctype-*MYSET*.c in the MySQL source distribution.

2. Add *MYSET* to the end of the sql/share/charsets/Index file. Assign a unique number to it.

3. Look at one of the existing ctype-*.c files (such as strings/ctype-big5.c) to see what needs to be defined. Note that the arrays in your file must have names like ctype_*MYSET*, to_lower_*MYSET*, and so on. These correspond to the arrays for a simple character set. See Section 4.11.4, "The Character Definition Arrays."

4. Near the top of the file, place a special comment like this:

```
/*
 * This comment is parsed by configure to create ctype.c,
 * so don't change it unless you know what you are doing.
 *
 * .configure. number_MYSET=MYNUMBER
 * .configure. strxfrm_multiply_MYSET=N
 * .configure. mbmaxlen_MYSET=N
 */
```

The configure program uses this comment to include the character set into the MySQL library automatically.

The strxfrm_multiply and mbmaxlen lines are explained in the following sections. You need include them only if you need the string collating functions or the multi-byte character set functions, respectively.

5. You should then create some of the following functions:

- my_strncoll_*MYSET*()
- my_strcoll_*MYSET*()
- my_strxfrm_*MYSET*()
- my_like_range_*MYSET*()

See Section 4.11.5, "String Collating Support."

6. Add the character set name to the CHARSETS_AVAILABLE and COMPILED_CHARSETS lists in configure.in.

7. Reconfigure, recompile, and test.

The sql/share/charsets/README file includes additional instructions.

If you want to have the character set included in the MySQL distribution, mail a patch to the MySQL internals mailing list. See Section 1.7.1, "MySQL Mailing Lists."

4.11.4 The Character Definition Arrays

to_lower[] and to_upper[] are simple arrays that hold the lowercase and uppercase characters corresponding to each member of the character set. For example:

```
to_lower['A'] should contain 'a'
to_upper['a'] should contain 'A'
```

sort_order[] is a map indicating how characters should be ordered for comparison and sorting purposes. Quite often (but not for all character sets) this is the same as to_upper[], which means that sorting is case-insensitive. MySQL sorts characters based on the values of sort_order[] elements. For more complicated sorting rules, see the discussion of string collating in Section 4.11.5, "String Collating Support."

ctype[] is an array of bit values, with one element for one character. (Note that to_lower[], to_upper[], and sort_order[] are indexed by character value, but ctype[] is indexed by character value + 1. This is an old legacy convention for handling EOF.)

You can find the following bitmask definitions in m_ctype.h:

```
#define _U     01       /* Uppercase */
#define _L     02       /* Lowercase */
#define _N     04       /* Numeral (digit) */
#define _S     010      /* Spacing character */
#define _P     020      /* Punctuation */
#define _C     040      /* Control character */
#define _B     0100     /* Blank */
#define _X     0200     /* heXadecimal digit */
```

The ctype[] entry for each character should be the union of the applicable bitmask values that describe the character. For example, 'A' is an uppercase character (_U) as well as a hexadecimal digit (_X), so ctype['A'+1] should contain the value:

```
_U + _X = 01 + 0200 = 0201
```

4.11.5 String Collating Support

If the sorting rules for your language are too complex to be handled with the simple sort_order[] table, you need to use the string collating functions.

The best documentation for this is the existing character sets. Look at the big5, czech, gbk, sjis, and tis160 character sets for examples.

You must specify the strxfrm_multiply_*MYSET*=N value in the special comment at the top of the file. *N* should be set to the maximum ratio the strings may grow during my_strxfrm_*MYSET* (it must be a positive integer).

4.11.6 Multi-Byte Character Support

If you want to add support for a new character set that includes multi-byte characters, you need to use the multi-byte character functions.

The best documentation for this is the existing character sets. Look at the euc_kr, gb2312, gbk, sjis, and ujis character sets for examples. These are implemented in the ctype-*charset_name*.c files in the strings directory.

You must specify the mbmaxlen_*MYSET*=N value in the special comment at the top of the source file. *N* should be set to the size in bytes of the largest character in the set.

4.11.7 Problems with Character Sets

If you try to use a character set that is not compiled into your binary, you might run into the following problems:

- Your program uses an incorrect path to determine where the character sets are stored. (Default /usr/local/mysql/share/mysql/charsets.) This can be fixed by using the --character-sets-dir option when you run the program in question.

- The character set is a multi-byte character set that cannot be loaded dynamically. In this case, you must recompile the program with support for the character set.

- The character set is a dynamic character set, but you do not have a configure file for it. In this case, you should install the configure file for the character set from a new MySQL distribution.

- If your Index file does not contain the name for the character set, your program displays the following error message:
  ```
  ERROR 1105: File '/usr/local/share/mysql/charsets/?.conf'
  not found (Errcode: 2)
  ```

  In this case, you should either get a new Index file or manually add the name of any missing character sets to the current file.

For MyISAM tables, you can check the character set name and number for a table with myisamchk -dvv *tbl_name*.

4.11.8 MySQL Server Time Zone Support

The MySQL server maintains several time zone settings:

- The system time zone. When the server starts, it attempts to determine the time zone of the host machine and uses it to set the `system_time_zone` system variable. The value does not change thereafter.

- The server's current time zone. The global `time_zone` system variable indicates the time zone the server currently is operating in. The initial value for `time_zone` is `'SYSTEM'`, which indicates that the server time zone is the same as the system time zone. The initial value can be specified explicitly with the `--default-time-zone=timezone` option. If you have the `SUPER` privilege, you can set the global value at runtime with this statement:

  ```
  mysql> SET GLOBAL time_zone = timezone;
  ```

- Per-connection time zones. Each client that connects has its own time zone setting, given by the session `time_zone` variable. Initially, the session variable takes its value from the global `time_zone` variable, but the client can change its own time zone with this statement:

  ```
  mysql> SET time_zone = timezone;
  ```

The current values of the global and client-specific time zones can be retrieved like this:

```
mysql> SELECT @@global.time_zone, @@session.time_zone;
```

timezone values can be given as strings indicating an offset from UTC, such as `'+10:00'` or `'-6:00'`. If the time zone information tables in the `mysql` database have been created and populated, you can also use named time zones, such as `'Europe/Helsinki'`, `'US/Eastern'`, or `'MET'`. The value `'SYSTEM'` can be used to indicate that the time zone should be the same as the system time zone. Time zone names are not case sensitive.

The MySQL installation procedure creates the time zone tables in the `mysql` database, but does not load them. You must do so manually. (If you are upgrading to MySQL 4.1.3 or later from an earlier version, you should create the tables by upgrading your `mysql` database. Use the instructions in Section 4.6.2, "`mysql_upgrade`—Check Tables for MySQL Upgrade.")

If your system has its own *zoneinfo* database (the set of files describing time zones), you should use the `mysql_tzinfo_to_sql` program for filling the time zone tables. Examples of such systems are Linux, FreeBSD, Sun Solaris, and Mac OS X. One likely location for these files is the `/usr/share/zoneinfo` directory. If your system does not have a zoneinfo database, you can use the downloadable package described later in this section.

The `mysql_tzinfo_to_sql` program is used to load the time zone tables. On the command line, pass the zoneinfo directory pathname to `mysql_tzinfo_to_sql` and send the output into the `mysql` program. For example:

```
shell> mysql_tzinfo_to_sql /usr/share/zoneinfo | mysql -u root mysql
```

mysql_tzinfo_to_sql reads your system's time zone files and generates SQL statements from them. mysql processes those statements to load the time zone tables.

mysql_tzinfo_to_sql also can be used to load a single time zone file, and to generate leap second information:

- To load a single time zone file *tz_file* that corresponds to a time zone name *tz_name*, invoke mysql_tzinfo_to_sql like this:

  ```
  shell> mysql_tzinfo_to_sql tz_file tz_name | mysql -u root mysql
  ```

- If your time zone needs to account for leap seconds, initialize the leap second information like this, where *tz_file* is the name of your time zone file:

  ```
  shell> mysql_tzinfo_to_sql --leap tz_file | mysql -u root mysql
  ```

If your system doesn't have a zoneinfo database (for example, Windows or HP-UX), you can use the package of pre-built time zone tables that is available for download at http://dev.mysql.com/downloads/timezones.html. This package contains .frm, .MYD, and .MYI files for the MyISAM time zone tables. These tables should be part of the mysql database, so you should place the files in the mysql subdirectory of your MySQL server's data directory. The server should be stopped while you do this.

Warning: Please don't use the downloadable package if your system has a zoneinfo database. Use the mysql_tzinfo_to_sql utility instead. Otherwise, you may cause a difference in date-time handling between MySQL and other applications on your system.

For information about time zone settings in replication setup, please see Section 5.8, "Replication Features and Known Problems."

4.12 MySQL Server Logs

MySQL has several different log files that can help you find out what is going on inside mysqld:

Log Type	Information Written to Log
The error log	Problems encountered starting, running, or stopping mysqld
The general query log	Established client connections and statements received from clients
The binary log	All statements that change data (also used for replication)
The slow log	All queries that took more than long_query_time seconds to execute or didn't use indexes

By default, all log files are created in the mysqld data directory. You can force mysqld to close and reopen the log files (or in some cases switch to a new log) by flushing the logs. Log flushing occurs when you issue a FLUSH LOGS statement or execute mysqladmin flush-logs or mysqladmin refresh.

If you are using MySQL replication capabilities, slave replication servers maintain additional log files called relay logs. These are discussed in Chapter 5, "Replication."

4.12.1 The Error Log

The error log file contains information indicating when `mysqld` was started and stopped and also any critical errors that occur while the server is running. If `mysqld` notices a table that needs to be automatically checked or repaired, it writes a message to the error log.

On some operating systems, the error log contains a stack trace if `mysqld` dies. The trace can be used to determine where `mysqld` died.

If `mysqld` dies unexpectedly and `mysqld_safe` needs to restart it, `mysqld_safe` writes a `restarted mysqld` message to the error log.

You can specify where `mysqld` stores the error log file with the `--log-error[=file_name]` option. If no `file_name` value is given, `mysqld` uses the name `host_name.err` and writes the file in the data directory. If you execute `FLUSH LOGS`, the error log is renamed with the suffix `-old` and `mysqld` creates a new empty log file. (No renaming occurs if the `--log-error` option was not given.)

If you do not specify `--log-error`, or (on Windows) if you use the `--console` option, errors are written to `stderr`, the standard error output. Usually this is your terminal.

On Windows, error output is always written to the `.err` file if `--console` is not given.

4.12.2 The General Query Log

The general query log is a general record of what `mysqld` is doing. The server writes information to this log when clients connect or disconnect, and it logs each SQL statement received from clients. The general query log can be very useful when you suspect an error in a client and want to know exactly what the client sent to `mysqld`.

`mysqld` writes statements to the query log in the order that it receives them. This may be different from the order in which they are executed. This is in contrast to the binary log, for which statements are written after they are executed, but before any locks are released. (Also, the query log contains all statements, whereas the binary log does not contain statements that only select data.)

To enable the general query log, start `mysqld` with the `--log[=file_name]` or `-l [file_name]` option. If no `file_name` value is given, the default name is `host_name.log` in the data directory.

Server restarts and log flushing do not cause a new general query log file to be generated (although flushing closes and reopens it). On Unix, you can rename the file and create a new one by using the following commands:

```
shell> mv host_name.log host_name-old.log
shell> mysqladmin flush-logs
shell> cp host_name-old.log backup-directory
shell> rm host_name-old.log
```

On Windows, you cannot rename the log file while the server has it open. You must stop the server and rename the file, and then restart the server to create a new log file.

4.12.3 The Binary Log

The binary log contains all statements that update data or potentially could have updated it (for example, a DELETE which matched no rows). Statements are stored in the form of "events" that describe the modifications. The binary log also contains information about how long each statement took that updated data.

Note: The binary log has replaced the old update log, which is no longer available as of MySQL 5.0. The binary log contains all information that is available in the update log in a more efficient format and in a manner that is transaction-safe. If you are using transactions, you must use the MySQL binary log for backups instead of the old update log.

The binary log does not contain statements that do not modify any data. If you want to log all statements (for example, to identify a problem query), use the general query log. See Section 4.12.2, "The General Query Log."

The primary purpose of the binary log is to be able to update databases during a restore operation as fully as possible, because the binary log contains all updates done after a backup was made. The binary log is also used on master replication servers as a record of the statements to be sent to slave servers. See Chapter 5, "Replication."

Running the server with the binary log enabled makes performance about 1% slower. However, the benefits of the binary log for restore operations and in allowing you to set up replication generally outweigh this minor performance decrement.

When started with the `--log-bin[=base_name]` option, mysqld writes a log file containing all SQL commands that update data. If no *base_name* value is given, the default name is the name of the host machine followed by -bin. If the basename is given, but not as an absolute pathname, the server writes the file in the data directory. It is recommended that you specify a basename.

If you supply an extension in the log name (for example, `--log-bin=base_name.extension`), the extension is silently removed and ignored.

mysqld appends a numeric extension to the binary log basename. The number increases each time the server creates a new log file, thus creating an ordered series of files. The server creates a new binary log file each time it starts or flushes the logs. The server also creates a new binary log file automatically when the current log's size reaches max_binlog_size. A binary log file may become larger than max_binlog_size if you are using large transactions because a transaction is written to the file in one piece, never split between files.

To keep track of which binary log files have been used, mysqld also creates a binary log index file that contains the names of all used binary log files. By default this has the same basename as the binary log file, with the extension '.index'. You can change the name of the binary log index file with the `--log-bin-index[=file_name]` option. You should not manually edit this file while `mysqld` is running; doing so would confuse `mysqld`.

Writes to the binary log file and binary log index file are handled in the same way as writes to `MyISAM` tables.

You can delete all binary log files with the `RESET MASTER` statement, or a subset of them with `PURGE MASTER LOGS`.

The binary log format has some known limitations that can affect recovery from backups. See Section 5.8, "Replication Features and Known Problems."

Binary logging for stored routines and triggers is done as described in the "MySQL Language Reference."

You can use the following options to `mysqld` to affect what is logged to the binary log. See also the discussion that follows this option list.

If you are using replication, the options described here affect which statements are sent by a master server to its slaves. There are also options for slave servers that control which statements received from the master to execute or ignore. For details, see Section 5.9, "Replication Startup Options."

- `--binlog-do-db=db_name`

  Tell the server to restrict binary logging to updates for which the default database is *db_name* (that is, the database selected by `USE`). All other databases that are not explicitly mentioned are ignored. If you use this option, you should ensure that you do updates only in the default database.

  There is an exception to this for `CREATE DATABASE`, `ALTER DATABASE`, and `DROP DATABASE` statements. The server uses the database named in the statement (not the default database) to decide whether it should log the statement.

  An example of what does not work as you might expect: If the server is started with `binlog-do-db=sales`, and you run `USE prices; UPDATE sales.january SET amount=amount+1000;`, this statement is *not* written into the binary log.

  To log multiple databases, use multiple options, specifying the option once for each database.

- `--binlog-ignore-db=db_name`

  Tell the server to suppress binary logging of updates for which the default database is *db_name* (that is, the database selected by `USE`). If you use this option, you should ensure that you do updates only in the default database.

  As with the `--binlog-do-db` option, there is an exception for the `CREATE DATABASE`, `ALTER DATABASE`, and `DROP DATABASE` statements. The server uses the database named in the statement (not the default database) to decide whether it should log the statement.

  An example of what does not work as you might expect: If the server is started with `binlog-ignore-db=sales`, and you run `USE prices; UPDATE sales.january SET amount=amount+1000;`, this statement *is* written into the binary log.

To ignore multiple databases, use multiple options, specifying the option once for each database.

The server evaluates the options for logging or ignoring updates to the binary log according to the following rules. As described previously, there is an exception for the CREATE DATABASE, ALTER DATABASE, and DROP DATABASE statements. In those cases, the database being *created*, *altered*, *or dropped* replaces the default database in the following rules.

1. Are there --binlog-do-db or --binlog-ignore-db rules?
   - No: Write the statement to the binary log and exit.
   - Yes: Go to the next step.

2. There are some rules (--binlog-do-db, --binlog-ignore-db, or both). Is there a default database (has any database been selected by USE?)?
   - No: Do *not* write the statement, and exit.
   - Yes: Go to the next step.

3. There is a default database. Are there some --binlog-do-db rules?
   - Yes: Does the default database match any of the --binlog-do-db rules?
     - Yes: Write the statement and exit.
     - No: Do *not* write the statement, and exit.
   - No: Go to the next step.

4. There are some --binlog-ignore-db rules. Does the default database match any of the --binlog-ignore-db rules?

   - Yes: Do not write the statement, and exit.
   - No: Write the query and exit.

For example, a slave running with only --binlog-do-db=sales does not write to the binary log any statement for which the default database is different from sales (in other words, --binlog-do-db can sometimes mean "ignore other databases").

If you are using replication, you should not delete old binary log files until you are sure that no slave still needs to use them. For example, if your slaves never run more than three days behind, once a day you can execute mysqladmin flush-logs on the master and then remove any logs that are more than three days old. You can remove the files manually, but it is preferable to use PURGE MASTER LOGS, which also safely updates the binary log index file for you (and which can take a date argument).

A client that has the SUPER privilege can disable binary logging of its own statements by using a SET SQL_LOG_BIN=0 statement.

You can display the contents of binary log files with the mysqlbinlog utility. This can be useful when you want to reprocess statements in the log. For example, you can update a MySQL server from the binary log as follows:

```
shell> mysqlbinlog log_file | mysql -h server_name
```

See Section 7.8, "mysqlbinlog—Utility for Processing Binary Log Files," for more information on the mysqlbinlog utility and how to use it. mysqlbinlog also can be used with relay log files because they are written using the same format as binary log files.

Binary logging is done immediately after a statement completes but before any locks are released or any commit is done. This ensures that the log is logged in execution order.

Updates to non-transactional tables are stored in the binary log immediately after execution. Within an uncommitted transaction, all updates (UPDATE, DELETE, or INSERT) that change transactional tables such as BDB or InnoDB tables are cached until a COMMIT statement is received by the server. At that point, mysqld writes the entire transaction to the binary log before the COMMIT is executed. When the thread that handles the transaction starts, it allocates a buffer of binlog_cache_size to buffer statements. If a statement is bigger than this, the thread opens a temporary file to store the transaction. The temporary file is deleted when the thread ends.

Modifications to non-transactional tables cannot be rolled back. If a transaction that is rolled back includes modifications to non-transactional tables, the entire transaction is logged with a ROLLBACK statement at the end to ensure that the modifications to those tables are replicated.

The Binlog_cache_use status variable shows the number of transactions that used this buffer (and possibly a temporary file) for storing statements. The Binlog_cache_disk_use status variable shows how many of those transactions actually had to use a temporary file. These two variables can be used for tuning binlog_cache_size to a large enough value that avoids the use of temporary files.

The max_binlog_cache_size system variable (default 4GB) can be used to restrict the total size used to cache a multiple-statement transaction. If a transaction is larger than this, it fails and rolls back.

If you are using the binary log, concurrent inserts are converted to normal inserts for CREATE ... SELECT or INSERT ... SELECT statement. This is done to ensure that you can re-create an exact copy of your tables by applying the log during a backup operation.

Note that the binary log format is different in MySQL 5.0 from previous versions of MySQL, due to enhancements in replication. See Section 5.6, "Replication Compatibility Between MySQL Versions."

By default, the binary log is not synchronized to disk at each write. So if the operating system or machine (not only the MySQL server) crashes, there is a chance that the last statements of the binary log are lost. To prevent this, you can make the binary log be synchronized to disk after every N writes to the binary log, with the sync_binlog system variable. See Section 4.2.2, "Server System Variables." 1 is the safest value for sync_binlog, but also the slowest. Even with sync_binlog set to 1, there is still the chance of an inconsistency between the table content and binary log content in case of a crash. For example, if you are using InnoDB tables and the MySQL server processes a COMMIT statement, it writes the whole transaction to the binary log and then commits this transaction into InnoDB. If the server crashes between those two operations, the transaction is rolled back by InnoDB at restart but still exists in the binary log. This problem can be solved with the `--innodb-safe-binlog` option, which adds consistency between the content of InnoDB tables and the binary log. (Note: `--innodb-safe-binlog` is unneeded as of MySQL 5.0; it was made obsolete by the introduction of XA transaction support.)

For this option to provide a greater degree of safety, the MySQL server should also be configured to synchronize the binary log and the InnoDB logs to disk at every transaction. The InnoDB logs are synchronized by default, and `sync_binlog=1` can be used to synchronize the binary log. The effect of this option is that at restart after a crash, after doing a rollback of transactions, the MySQL server cuts rolled back InnoDB transactions from the binary log. This ensures that the binary log reflects the exact data of InnoDB tables, and so, the slave remains in synchrony with the master (not receiving a statement that has been rolled back).

Note that `--innodb-safe-binlog` can be used even if the MySQL server updates other storage engines than InnoDB. Only statements and transactions that affect InnoDB tables are subject to removal from the binary log at InnoDB's crash recovery. If the MySQL server discovers at crash recovery that the binary log is shorter than it should have been, it lacks at least one successfully committed InnoDB transaction. This should not happen if `sync_binlog=1` and the disk/filesystem do an actual sync when they are requested to (some don't), so the server prints an error message `The binary log <name> is shorter than its expected size`. In this case, this binary log is not correct and replication should be restarted from a fresh snapshot of the master's data.

4.12.4 The Slow Query Log

The slow query log consists of all SQL statements that took more than `long_query_time` seconds to execute. The time to acquire the initial table locks is not counted as execution time. The minimum and default values of `long_query_time` are 1 and 10, respectively.

`mysqld` writes a statement to the slow query log after it has been executed and after all locks have been released. Log order may be different from execution order.

To enable the slow query log, start `mysqld` with the `--log-slow-queries[=file_name]` option.

If no `file_name` value is given, the default is the name of the host machine with a suffix of `-slow.log`. If a filename is given, but not as an absolute pathname, the server writes the file in the data directory.

The slow query log can be used to find queries that take a long time to execute and are therefore candidates for optimization. However, examining a long slow query log can become a difficult task. To make this easier, you can process the slow query log using the `mysqldumpslow` command to summarize the queries that appear in the log. Use `mysqldumpslow --help` to see the options that this command supports.

In MySQL 5.0, queries that do not use indexes are logged in the slow query log if the `--log-queries-not-using-indexes` option is specified. To prevent queries that do not use indexes from being logged in the slow query log, use the `--log-queries-not-using-indexes` option. See Section 4.2.1, "mysqld Command Options."

In MySQL 5.0, the `--log-slow-admin-statements` server option enables you to request logging of slow administrative statements such as OPTIMIZE TABLE, ANALYZE TABLE, and ALTER TABLE to the slow query log.

Queries handled by the query cache are not added to the slow query log, nor are queries that would not benefit from the presence of an index because the table has zero rows or one row.

4.12.5 Server Log Maintenance

MySQL Server can create a number of different log files that make it easy to see what is going on. See Section 4.12, "MySQL Server Logs." However, you must clean up these files regularly to ensure that the logs do not take up too much disk space.

When using MySQL with logging enabled, you may want to back up and remove old log files from time to time and tell MySQL to start logging to new files. See Section 4.10.1, "Database Backups."

On a Linux (Red Hat) installation, you can use the `mysql-log-rotate` script for this. If you installed MySQL from an RPM distribution, this script should have been installed automatically. You should be careful with this script if you are using the binary log for replication. You should not remove binary logs until you are certain that their contents have been processed by all slaves.

On other systems, you must install a short script yourself that you start from `cron` (or its equivalent) for handling log files.

You can force MySQL to start using new log files by using `mysqladmin flush-logs` or by using the SQL statement FLUSH LOGS.

A log-flushing operation does the following:

- If general query logging (`--log`) or slow query logging (`--log-slow-queries`) is used, the server closes and reopens the general query log file or slow query log file.
- If binary logging (`--log-bin`) is used, the server closes the current log file and opens a new log file with the next sequence number.

The server creates a new binary log file when you flush the logs. However, it just closes and reopens the general and slow query log files. To cause new files to be created on Unix, rename the current logs before flushing them. At flush time, the server will open new logs with the original names. For example, if the general and slow query logs are named `mysql.log` and `mysql-slow.log`, you can use a series of commands like this:

```
shell> cd mysql-data-directory
shell> mv mysql.log mysql.old
shell> mv mysql-slow.log mysql-slow.old
shell> mysqladmin flush-logs
```

At this point, you can make a backup of `mysql.old` and `mysql-slow.log` and then remove them from disk.

On Windows, you cannot rename log files while the server has them open. You must stop the server and rename them, and then restart the server to create new logs.

4.13 Running Multiple MySQL Servers on the Same Machine

In some cases, you might want to run multiple `mysqld` servers on the same machine. You might want to test a new MySQL release while leaving your existing production setup undisturbed. Or you might want to give different users access to different `mysqld` servers that they manage themselves. (For example, you might be an Internet service provider that wants to provide independent MySQL installations for different customers.)

To run multiple servers on a single machine, each server must have unique values for several operating parameters. These can be set on the command line or in option files. See Section 3.3, "Specifying Program Options."

At least the following options must be different for each server:

- `--port=port_num`

  `--port` controls the port number for TCP/IP connections.

- `--socket=path`

  `--socket` controls the Unix socket file path on Unix and the name of the named pipe on Windows. On Windows, it is necessary to specify distinct pipe names only for those servers that support named-pipe connections.

- `--shared-memory-base-name=name`

  This option currently is used only on Windows. It designates the shared-memory name used by a Windows server to allow clients to connect via shared memory. It is necessary to specify distinct shared-memory names only for those servers that support shared-memory connections.

- `--pid-file=file_name`

  This option is used only on Unix. It indicates the pathname of the file in which the server writes its process ID.

If you use the following log file options, they must be different for each server:

- `--log=file_name`
- `--log-bin=file_name`
- `--log-update=file_name`
- `--log-error=file_name`
- `--bdb-logdir=file_name`

Section 4.12.5, "Server Log Maintenance," discusses the log file options further.

For better performance, you can specify the following options differently for each server, to spread the load between several physical disks:

- `--tmpdir=path`
- `--bdb-tmpdir=path`

Having different temporary directories is also recommended to make it easier to determine which MySQL server created any given temporary file.

With very limited exceptions, each server should use a different data directory, which is specified using the `--datadir=path` option.

Warning: Normally, you should never have two servers that update data in the same databases. This may lead to unpleasant surprises if your operating system does not support fault-free system locking. If (despite this warning) you run multiple servers using the same data directory and they have logging enabled, you must use the appropriate options to specify log file names that are unique to each server. Otherwise, the servers try to log to the same files. Please note that this kind of setup only works with `MyISAM` and `MERGE` tables, and not with any of the other storage engines.

The warning against sharing a data directory among servers also applies in an NFS environment. Allowing multiple MySQL servers to access a common data directory over NFS is a *very bad idea*.

- The primary problem is that NFS is the speed bottleneck. It is not meant for such use.
- Another risk with NFS is that you must devise a way to ensure that two or more servers do not interfere with each other. Usually NFS file locking is handled by the `lockd` daemon, but at the moment there is no platform that performs locking 100% reliably in every situation.

Make it easy for yourself: Forget about sharing a data directory among servers over NFS. A better solution is to have one computer that contains several CPUs and use an operating system that handles threads efficiently.

If you have multiple MySQL installations in different locations, you can specify the base installation directory for each server with the `--basedir=path` option to cause each server to use a different data directory, log files, and PID file. (The defaults for all these values are determined relative to the base directory.) In that case, the only other options you need to specify are the `--socket` and `--port` options. For example, suppose that you install different versions of MySQL using `tar` file binary distributions. These install in different locations, so you can start the server for each installation using the command `bin/mysqld_safe` under its corresponding base directory. `mysqld_safe` determines the proper `--basedir` option to pass to `mysqld`, and you need specify only the `--socket` and `--port` options to `mysqld_safe`.

As discussed in the following sections, it is possible to start additional servers by setting environment variables or by specifying appropriate command-line options. However, if you need to run multiple servers on a more permanent basis, it is more convenient to use option files to specify for each server those option values that must be unique to it. The `--defaults-file` option is useful for this purpose.

4.13.1 Running Multiple Servers on Windows

You can run multiple servers on Windows by starting them manually from the command line, each with appropriate operating parameters. On Windows NT–based systems, you also have the option of installing several servers as Windows services and running them that way. General instructions for running MySQL servers from the command line or as services are given in Section 2.3, "Installing MySQL on Windows." This section describes how to make sure that you start each server with different values for those startup options that must be unique per server, such as the data directory. These options are described in Section 4.13, "Running Multiple MySQL Servers on the Same Machine."

4.13.1.1 Starting Multiple Windows Servers at the Command Line

To start multiple servers manually from the command line, you can specify the appropriate options on the command line or in an option file. It is more convenient to place the options in an option file, but it is necessary to make sure that each server gets its own set of options. To do this, create an option file for each server and tell the server the filename with a `--defaults-file` option when you run it.

Suppose that you want to run `mysqld` on port 3307 with a data directory of `C:\mydata1`, and `mysqld-max` on port 3308 with a data directory of `C:\mydata2`. (To do this, make sure that before you start the servers, each data directory exists and has its own copy of the `mysql` database that contains the grant tables.) Then create two option files. For example, create one file named `C:\my-opts1.cnf` that looks like this:

```
[mysqld]
datadir = C:/mydata1
port = 3307
```

Create a second file named `C:\my-opts2.cnf` that looks like this:

```
[mysqld]
datadir = C:/mydata2
port = 3308
```

Then start each server with its own option file:

```
C:\> C:\mysql\bin\mysqld --defaults-file=C:\my-opts1.cnf
C:\> C:\mysql\bin\mysqld-max --defaults-file=C:\my-opts2.cnf
```

On NT, each server starts in the foreground (no new prompt appears until the server exits later), so you will need to issue those two commands in separate console windows.

To shut down the servers, you must connect to each using the appropriate port number:

```
C:\> C:\mysql\bin\mysqladmin --port=3307 shutdown
C:\> C:\mysql\bin\mysqladmin --port=3308 shutdown
```

Servers configured as just described allow clients to connect over TCP/IP. If your version of Windows supports named pipes and you also want to allow named-pipe connections, use the `mysqld-nt` or `mysqld-max-nt` servers and specify options that enable the named pipe and specify its name. Each server that supports named-pipe connections must use a unique pipe name. For example, the `C:\my-opts1.cnf` file might be written like this:

```
[mysqld]
datadir = C:/mydata1
port = 3307
enable-named-pipe
socket = mypipe1
```

Then start the server this way:

```
C:\> C:\mysql\bin\mysqld-nt --defaults-file=C:\my-opts1.cnf
```

Modify `C:\my-opts2.cnf` similarly for use by the second server.

A similar procedure applies for servers that you want to support shared-memory connections. Enable such connections with the `--shared-memory` option and specify a unique shared-memory name for each server with the `--shared-memory-base-name` option.

4.13.1.2 Starting Multiple Windows Servers As Services

On NT-based systems, a MySQL server can run as a Windows service. The procedures for installing, controlling, and removing a single MySQL service are described in Section 2.3.11, "Starting MySQL As a Windows Service."

You can also install multiple MySQL servers as services. In this case, you must make sure that each server uses a different service name in addition to all the other parameters that must be unique for each server.

For the following instructions, assume that you want to run the `mysqld-nt` server from two different versions of MySQL that are installed at `C:\mysql-4.1.8` and `C:\mysql-5.0.19`, respectively. (This might be the case if you're running 4.1.8 as your production server, but also want to conduct tests using 5.0.19.)

The following principles apply when installing a MySQL service with the `--install` or `--install-manual` option:

- If you specify no service name, the server uses the default service name of `MySQL` and the server reads options from the `[mysqld]` group in the standard option files.

- If you specify a service name after the `--install` option, the server ignores the `[mysqld]` option group and instead reads options from the group that has the same name as the service. The server reads options from the standard option files.

- If you specify a `--defaults-file` option after the service name, the server ignores the standard option files and reads options only from the `[mysqld]` group of the named file.

Note: Before MySQL 4.0.17, only a server installed using the default service name (`MySQL`) or one installed explicitly with a service name of `mysqld` read the `[mysqld]` group in the standard option files. As of 4.0.17, all servers read the `[mysqld]` group if they read the standard option files, even if they are installed using another service name. This allows you to use the `[mysqld]` group for options that should be used by all MySQL services, and an option group named after each service for use by the server installed with that service name.

Based on the preceding information, you have several ways to set up multiple services. The following instructions describe some examples. Before trying any of them, be sure that you shut down and remove any existing MySQL services first.

- **Approach 1**: Specify the options for all services in one of the standard option files. To do this, use a different service name for each server. Suppose that you want to run the 4.1.8 `mysqld-nt` using the service name of `mysqld1` and the 5.0.19 `mysqld-nt` using the service name `mysqld2`. In this case, you can use the `[mysqld1]` group for 4.1.8 and the `[mysqld2]` group for 5.0.19. For example, you can set up `C:\my.cnf` like this:

```
# options for mysqld1 service
[mysqld1]
basedir = C:/mysql-4.1.8
port = 3307
enable-named-pipe
socket = mypipe1

# options for mysqld2 service
[mysqld2]
basedir = C:/mysql-5.0.19
port = 3308
enable-named-pipe
socket = mypipe2
```

Install the services as follows, using the full server pathnames to ensure that Windows registers the correct executable program for each service:

```
C:\> C:\mysql-4.1.8\bin\mysqld-nt --install mysqld1
C:\> C:\mysql-5.0.19\bin\mysqld-nt --install mysqld2
```

To start the services, use the services manager, or use NET START with the appropriate service names:

```
C:\> NET START mysqld1
C:\> NET START mysqld2
```

To stop the services, use the services manager, or use NET STOP with the appropriate service names:

```
C:\> NET STOP mysqld1
C:\> NET STOP mysqld2
```

- **Approach 2**: Specify options for each server in separate files and use --defaults-file when you install the services to tell each server what file to use. In this case, each file should list options using a [mysqld] group.

  With this approach, to specify options for the 4.1.8 mysqld-nt, create a file C:\my-opts1.cnf that looks like this:

  ```
  [mysqld]
  basedir = C:/mysql-4.1.8
  port = 3307
  enable-named-pipe
  socket = mypipe1
  ```

  For the 5.0.19 mysqld-nt, create a file C:\my-opts2.cnf that looks like this:

  ```
  [mysqld]
  basedir = C:/mysql-5.0.19
  port = 3308
  enable-named-pipe
  socket = mypipe2
  ```

  Install the services as follows (enter each command on a single line):

  ```
  C:\> C:\mysql-4.1.8\bin\mysqld-nt --install mysqld1
          --defaults-file=C:\my-opts1.cnf
  C:\> C:\mysql-5.0.19\bin\mysqld-nt --install mysqld2
          --defaults-file=C:\my-opts2.cnf
  ```

  To use a --defaults-file option when you install a MySQL server as a service, you must precede the option with the service name.

  After installing the services, start and stop them the same way as in the preceding example.

To remove multiple services, use mysqld --remove for each one, specifying a service name following the --remove option. If the service name is the default (MySQL), you can omit it.

4.13.2 Running Multiple Servers on Unix

The easiest way is to run multiple servers on Unix is to compile them with different TCP/IP ports and Unix socket files so that each one is listening on different network interfaces. Compiling in different base directories for each installation also results automatically in a separate, compiled-in data directory, log file, and PID file location for each server.

Assume that an existing 4.1.8 server is configured for the default TCP/IP port number (3306) and Unix socket file (/tmp/mysql.sock). To configure a new 5.0.19 server to have different operating parameters, use a configure command something like this:

```
shell> ./configure --with-tcp-port=port_number \
            --with-unix-socket-path=file_name \
            --prefix=/usr/local/mysql-5.0.19
```

Here, port_number and file_name must be different from the default TCP/IP port number and Unix socket file pathname, and the --prefix value should specify an installation directory different from the one under which the existing MySQL installation is located.

If you have a MySQL server listening on a given port number, you can use the following command to find out what operating parameters it is using for several important configurable variables, including the base directory and Unix socket filename:

```
shell> mysqladmin --host=host_name --port=port_number variables
```

With the information displayed by that command, you can tell what option values *not* to use when configuring an additional server.

Note that if you specify localhost as a hostname, mysqladmin defaults to using a Unix socket file connection rather than TCP/IP. From MySQL 4.1 onward, you can explicitly specify the connection protocol to use by using the --protocol={TCP|SOCKET|PIPE|MEMORY} option.

You don't have to compile a new MySQL server just to start with a different Unix socket file and TCP/IP port number. It is also possible to use the same server binary and start each invocation of it with different parameter values at runtime. One way to do so is by using command-line options:

```
shell> mysqld_safe --socket=file_name --port=port_number
```

To start a second server, provide different --socket and --port option values, and pass a --datadir=path option to mysqld_safe so that the server uses a different data directory.

Another way to achieve a similar effect is to use environment variables to set the Unix socket filename and TCP/IP port number:

```
shell> MYSQL_UNIX_PORT=/tmp/mysqld-new.sock
shell> MYSQL_TCP_PORT=3307
shell> export MYSQL_UNIX_PORT MYSQL_TCP_PORT
shell> mysql_install_db --user=mysql
shell> mysqld_safe --datadir=/path/to/datadir &
```

This is a quick way of starting a second server to use for testing. The nice thing about this method is that the environment variable settings apply to any client programs that you invoke from the same shell. Thus, connections for those clients are automatically directed to the second server.

For automatic server execution, the startup script that is executed at boot time should execute the following command once for each server with an appropriate option file path for each command:

```
shell> mysqld_safe --defaults-file=file_name
```

Each option file should contain option values specific to a given server.

On Unix, the `mysqld_multi` script is another way to start multiple servers. See Section 4.4.3, "`mysqld_multi`—Manage Multiple MySQL Servers."

4.13.3 Using Client Programs in a Multiple-Server Environment

To connect with a client program to a MySQL server that is listening to different network interfaces from those compiled into your client, you can use one of the following methods:

- Start the client with `--host=host_name --port=port_number` to connect via TCP/IP to a remote server, with `--host=127.0.0.1 --port=port_number` to connect via TCP/IP to a local server, or with `--host=localhost --socket=file_name` to connect to a local server via a Unix socket file or a Windows named pipe.

- As of MySQL 4.1, start the client with `--protocol=tcp` to connect via TCP/IP, `--protocol=socket` to connect via a Unix socket file, `--protocol=pipe` to connect via a named pipe, or `--protocol=memory` to connect via shared memory. For TCP/IP connections, you may also need to specify `--host` and `--port` options. For the other types of connections, you may need to specify a `--socket` option to specify a Unix socket file or Windows named-pipe name, or a `--shared-memory-base-name` option to specify the shared-memory name. Shared-memory connections are supported only on Windows.

- On Unix, set the `MYSQL_UNIX_PORT` and `MYSQL_TCP_PORT` environment variables to point to the Unix socket file and TCP/IP port number before you start your clients. If you normally use a specific socket file or port number, you can place commands to set these environment variables in your `.login` file so that they apply each time you log in.

- Specify the default Unix socket file and TCP/IP port number in the `[client]` group of an option file. For example, you can use `C:\my.cnf` on Windows, or the `.my.cnf` file in your home directory on Unix. See Section 3.3.2, "Using Option Files."

- In a C program, you can specify the socket file or port number arguments in the `mysql_real_connect()` call. You can also have the program read option files by calling `mysql_options()`.

- If you are using the Perl `DBD::mysql` module, you can read options from MySQL option files. For example:

```
$dsn = "DBI:mysql:test;mysql_read_default_group=client;"
        . "mysql_read_default_file=/usr/local/mysql/data/my.cnf";
$dbh = DBI->connect($dsn, $user, $password);
```

Other programming interfaces may provide similar capabilities for reading option files.

4.14 The MySQL Query Cache

The query cache stores the text of a SELECT statement together with the corresponding result that was sent to the client. If an identical statement is received later, the server retrieves the results from the query cache rather than parsing and executing the statement again.

The query cache is extremely useful in an environment where you have tables that do not change very often and for which the server receives many identical queries. This is a typical situation for many Web servers that generate many dynamic pages based on database content.

Note: The query cache does not return stale data. When tables are modified, any relevant entries in the query cache are flushed.

Note: The query cache does not work in an environment where you have multiple mysqld servers updating the same MyISAM tables.

Note: The query cache is not used for server-side prepared statements. If you're using server-side prepared statements consider that these statement won't be satisfied by the query cache.

Some performance data for the query cache follows. These results were generated by running the MySQL benchmark suite on a Linux Alpha 2 × 500MHz system with 2GB RAM and a 64MB query cache.

- If all the queries you are performing are simple (such as selecting a row from a table with one row), but still differ so that the queries cannot be cached, the overhead for having the query cache active is 13%. This could be regarded as the worst-case scenario. In real life, queries tend to be much more complicated, so the overhead normally is significantly lower.

- Searches for a single row in a single-row table are 238% faster with the query cache than without it. This can be regarded as close to the minimum speedup to be expected for a query that is cached.

To disable the query cache at server startup, set the query_cache_size system variable to 0. By disabling the query cache code, there is no noticeable overhead. If you build MySQL from source, query cache capabilities can be excluded from the server entirely by invoking configure with the --without-query-cache option.

4.14.1 How the Query Cache Operates

This section describes how the query cache works when it is operational. Section 4.14.3, "Query Cache Configuration," describes how to control whether it is operational.

Incoming queries are compared to those in the query cache before parsing, so the following two queries are regarded as different by the query cache:

```
SELECT * FROM tbl_name
Select * from tbl_name
```

Queries must be *exactly* the same (byte for byte) to be seen as identical. In addition, query strings that are identical may be treated as different for other reasons. Queries that use different databases, different protocol versions, or different default character sets are considered different queries and are cached separately.

Before a query result is fetched from the query cache, MySQL checks that the user has SELECT privilege for all databases and tables involved. If this is not the case, the cached result is not used.

If a query result is returned from query cache, the server increments the Qcache_hits status variable, not Com_select. See Section 4.14.4, "Query Cache Status and Maintenance."

If a table changes, all cached queries that use the table become invalid and are removed from the cache. This includes queries that use MERGE tables that map to the changed table. A table can be changed by many types of statements, such as INSERT, UPDATE, DELETE, TRUNCATE, ALTER TABLE, DROP TABLE, or DROP DATABASE.

Transactional InnoDB tables that have been changed are invalidated when a COMMIT is performed.

The query cache also works within transactions when using InnoDB tables, making use of the table version number to detect whether its contents are still current.

In MySQL 5.0, queries generated by views are cached.

Before MySQL 5.0, a query that began with a leading comment could be cached, but could not be fetched from the cache. This problem is fixed in MySQL 5.0.

The query cache works for SELECT SQL_CALC_FOUND_ROWS ... and SELECT FOUND_ROWS() type queries. FOUND_ROWS() returns the correct value even if the preceding query was fetched from the cache because the number of found rows is also stored in the cache.

A query cannot be cached if it contains any of the functions shown in the following table.

BENCHMARK()	CONNECTION_ID()	CURDATE()
CURRENT_DATE()	CURRENT_TIME()	CURRENT_TIMESTAMP()
CURTIME()	DATABASE()	ENCRYPT() with one parameter
FOUND_ROWS()	GET_LOCK()	LAST_INSERT_ID()
LOAD_FILE()	MASTER_POS_WAIT()	NOW()
RAND()	RELEASE_LOCK()	SYSDATE()
UNIX_TIMESTAMP() with no parameters	USER()	

A query also is not cached under these conditions:

- It refers to user-defined functions (UDFs).
- It refers to user variables.
- It refers to tables in the mysql system database.

- It is of any of the following forms:

```
SELECT ... IN SHARE MODE
SELECT ... FOR UPDATE
SELECT ... INTO OUTFILE ...
SELECT ... INTO DUMPFILE ...
SELECT * FROM ... WHERE autoincrement_col IS NULL
```

  The last form is not cached because it is used as the ODBC workaround for obtaining the last insert ID value.

- It was issued as a prepared statement, even if no placeholders were employed. For example, the query used here is not cached:

```
char *my_sql_stmt = "SELECT a, b FROM table_c";
/* ... */
mysql_stmt_prepare(stmt, my_sql_stmt, strlen(my_sql_stmt));
```

- It uses TEMPORARY tables.

- It does not use any tables.

- The user has a column-level privilege for any of the involved tables.

4.14.2 Query Cache SELECT Options

Two query cache-related options may be specified in SELECT statements:

- SQL_CACHE

  The query result is cached if the value of the query_cache_type system variable is ON or DEMAND.

- SQL_NO_CACHE

  The query result is not cached.

Examples:

```
SELECT SQL_CACHE id, name FROM customer;
SELECT SQL_NO_CACHE id, name FROM customer;
```

4.14.3 Query Cache Configuration

The have_query_cache server system variable indicates whether the query cache is available:

```
mysql> SHOW VARIABLES LIKE 'have_query_cache';
+------------------+-------+
| Variable_name    | Value |
+------------------+-------+
| have_query_cache | YES   |
+------------------+-------+
```

When using a standard MySQL binary, this value is always YES, even if query caching is disabled.

Several other system variables control query cache operation. These can be set in an option file or on the command line when starting mysqld. The query cache system variables all have names that begin with query_cache_. They are described briefly in Section 4.2.2, "Server System Variables," with additional configuration information given here.

To set the size of the query cache, set the query_cache_size system variable. Setting it to 0 disables the query cache. The default size is 0, so the query cache is disabled by default.

When you set query_cache_size to a non-zero value, keep in mind that the query cache needs a minimum size of about 40KB to allocate its structures. (The exact size depends on system architecture.) If you set the value too small, you'll get a warning, as in this example:

```
mysql> SET GLOBAL query_cache_size = 40000;
Query OK, 0 rows affected, 1 warning (0.00 sec)

mysql> SHOW WARNINGS\G
*************************** 1. row ***************************
  Level: Warning
   Code: 1282
Message: Query cache failed to set size 39936; new query cache size is 0

mysql> SET GLOBAL query_cache_size = 41984;
Query OK, 0 rows affected (0.00 sec)

mysql> SHOW VARIABLES LIKE 'query_cache_size';
+------------------+-------+
| Variable_name    | Value |
+------------------+-------+
| query_cache_size | 41984 |
+------------------+-------+
```

If the query cache size is greater than 0, the query_cache_type variable influences how it works. This variable can be set to the following values:

- A value of 0 or OFF prevents caching or retrieval of cached results.
- A value of 1 or ON allows caching except of those statements that begin with SELECT SQL_NO_CACHE.
- A value of 2 or DEMAND causes caching of only those statements that begin with SELECT SQL_CACHE.

Setting the GLOBAL query_cache_type value determines query cache behavior for all clients that connect after the change is made. Individual clients can control cache behavior for their own connection by setting the SESSION query_cache_type value. For example, a client can disable use of the query cache for its own queries like this:

```
mysql> SET SESSION query_cache_type = OFF;
```

To control the maximum size of individual query results that can be cached, set the query_cache_limit system variable. The default value is 1MB.

When a query that is to be cached, its result (the data sent to the client) is stored in the query cache during result retrieval. Therefore the data usually is not handled in one big chunk. The query cache allocates blocks for storing this data on demand, so when one block is filled, a new block is allocated. Because memory allocation operation is costly (timewise), the query cache allocates blocks with a minimum size given by the query_cache_min_res_unit system variable. When a query is executed, the last result block is trimmed to the actual data size so that unused memory is freed. Depending on the types of queries your server executes, you might find it helpful to tune the value of query_cache_min_res_unit:

- The default value of query_cache_min_res_unit is 4KB. This should be adequate for most cases.

- If you have a lot of queries with small results, the default block size may lead to memory fragmentation, as indicated by a large number of free blocks. Fragmentation can force the query cache to prune (delete) queries from the cache due to lack of memory. In this case, you should decrease the value of query_cache_min_res_unit. The number of free blocks and queries removed due to pruning are given by the values of the Qcache_free_blocks and Qcache_lowmem_prunes status variables.

- If most of your queries have large results (check the Qcache_total_blocks and Qcache_queries_in_cache status variables), you can increase performance by increasing query_cache_min_res_unit. However, be careful to not make it too large (see the previous item).

4.14.4 Query Cache Status and Maintenance

You can check whether the query cache is present in your MySQL server using the following statement:

```
mysql> SHOW VARIABLES LIKE 'have_query_cache';
+------------------+-------+
| Variable_name    | Value |
+------------------+-------+
| have_query_cache | YES   |
+------------------+-------+
```

You can defragment the query cache to better utilize its memory with the FLUSH QUERY CACHE statement. The statement does not remove any queries from the cache.

The RESET QUERY CACHE statement removes all query results from the query cache. The FLUSH TABLES statement also does this.

To monitor query cache performance, use SHOW STATUS to view the cache status variables:

```
mysql> SHOW STATUS LIKE 'Qcache%';
+-------------------------+--------+
| Variable_name           | Value  |
+-------------------------+--------+
| Qcache_free_blocks      | 36     |
| Qcache_free_memory      | 138488 |
| Qcache_hits             | 79570  |
| Qcache_inserts          | 27087  |
| Qcache_lowmem_prunes    | 3114   |
| Qcache_not_cached       | 22989  |
| Qcache_queries_in_cache | 415    |
| Qcache_total_blocks     | 912    |
+-------------------------+--------+
```

Descriptions of each of these variables are given in Section 4.2.4, "Server Status Variables." Some uses for them are described here.

The total number of SELECT queries is given by this formula:

```
  Com_select
+ Qcache_hits
+ queries with errors found by parser
```

The Com_select value is given by this formula:

```
  Qcache_inserts
+ Qcache_not_cached
+ queries with errors found during the column-privileges check
```

The query cache uses variable-length blocks, so Qcache_total_blocks and Qcache_free_blocks may indicate query cache memory fragmentation. After FLUSH QUERY CACHE, only a single free block remains.

Every cached query requires a minimum of two blocks (one for the query text and one or more for the query results). Also, every table that is used by a query requires one block. However, if two or more queries use the same table, only one table block needs to be allocated.

The information provided by the Qcache_lowmem_prunes status variable can help you tune the query cache size. It counts the number of queries that have been removed from the cache to free up memory for caching new queries. The query cache uses a least recently used (LRU) strategy to decide which queries to remove from the cache. Tuning information is given in Section 4.14.3, "Query Cache Configuration."

Replication

This chapter describes the various replication features provided by MySQL. It introduces replication concepts, shows how to set up replication servers, and serves as a reference to the available replication options. It also provides a list of frequently asked questions (with answers), and troubleshooting advice for solving replication problems.

For a description of the syntax of replication-related SQL statements, see the "MySQL Language Reference."

5.1 Introduction to Replication

MySQL features support for one-way, asynchronous replication, in which one server acts as the master, while one or more other servers act as slaves. This is in contrast to the *synchronous* replication which is a characteristic of MySQL Cluster (see Chapter 9, "MySQL Cluster").

In single-master replication, the master server writes updates to its binary log files and maintains an index of those files to keep track of log rotation. The binary log files serve as a record of updates to be sent to any slave servers. When a slave connects to its master, it informs the master of the position up to which the slave read the logs at its last successful update. The slave receives any updates that have taken place since that time, and then blocks and waits for the master to notify it of new updates.

A slave server can itself serve as a master if you want to set up chained replication servers.

Multiple-master replication is possible, but raises issues not present in single-master replication. See Section 5.15, "Auto-Increment in Multiple-Master Replication."

When you are using replication, all updates to the tables that are replicated should be performed on the master server. Otherwise, you must always be careful to avoid conflicts between updates that users make to tables on the master and updates that they make to tables on the slave. Keep in mind as well that updates on the slave side might be affected differently depending on whether you are using statement-based or row-based replication. Consider the following scenario, where a row is inserted on the slave, followed by a statement on the master side that should empty the table:

```
slave> INSERT INTO tbl VALUES (1);
master> DELETE FROM tbl;
```

The master doesn't know about the INSERT operation on the slave server. With statement-based replication, tbl will be empty on both master and slave as soon as the slave catches up with the master, because the master sends its DELETE statement to the slave. As a result, tbl has the same contents on both servers. With row-based replication, the effect of the DELETE on the slave is different. The master writes to its binary log each row to be deleted from the table. The slave deletes only those rows, and not the row that was inserted on the slave side. As a result, the table has different contents on the master and server, which may cause replication problems.

For information about row-based replication, see Section 5.3, "Row-Based Replication."

Replication offers benefits for robustness, speed, and system administration:

- Robustness is increased with a master/slave setup. In the event of problems with the master, you can switch to the slave as a backup.

- Better response time for clients can be achieved by splitting the load for processing client queries between the master and slave servers. SELECT queries may be sent to the slave to reduce the query processing load of the master. Statements that modify data should still be sent to the master so that the master and slave do not get out of synchrony. This load-balancing strategy is effective if non-updating queries dominate, but that is the normal case.

- Another benefit of using replication is that you can perform database backups using a slave server without disturbing the master. The master continues to process updates while the backup is being made. See Section 4.10.1, "Database Backups."

5.2 Replication Implementation Overview

MySQL replication is based on the master server keeping track of all changes to your databases (updates, deletes, and so on) in its binary logs. Therefore, to use replication, you must enable binary logging on the master server. See Section 4.12.3, "The Binary Log."

Each slave server receives from the master the saved updates that the master has recorded in its binary log, so that the slave can execute the same updates on its copy of the data.

It is *extremely* important to realize that the binary log is simply a record starting from the fixed point in time at which you enable binary logging. Any slaves that you set up need copies of the databases on your master *as they existed at the moment you enabled binary logging on the master*. If you start your slaves with databases that are not in the same state as those on the master when the binary log was started, your slaves are quite likely to fail.

One way to copy the master's data to the slave is to use the LOAD DATA FROM MASTER statement. However, LOAD DATA FROM MASTER works only if all the tables on the master use the MyISAM storage engine. In addition, this statement acquires a global read lock, so no updates on the master are possible while the tables are being transferred to the slave. When we implement lock-free hot table backup, this global read lock will no longer be necessary.

Due to these limitations, we recommend that at this point you use LOAD DATA FROM MASTER only if the dataset on the master is relatively small, or if a prolonged read lock on the master is acceptable. Although the actual speed of LOAD DATA FROM MASTER may vary from system to system, a good rule of thumb for how long it takes is 1 second per 1MB of data. This is a rough estimate, but you should find it fairly accurate if both master and slave are equivalent to 700MHz Pentium CPUs in performance and are connected through a 100Mbps network.

After the slave has been set up with a copy of the master's data, it connects to the master and waits for updates to process. If the master fails, or the slave loses connectivity with your master, the slave keeps trying to connect periodically until it is able to resume listening for updates. The --master-connect-retry option controls the retry interval. The default is 60 seconds.

Each slave keeps track of where it left off when it last read from its master server. The master has no knowledge of how many slaves it has or which ones are up to date at any given time.

5.3 Row-Based Replication

Replication capabilities in MySQL originally were based on propagation of SQL statements from master to slave. This is called *statement-based replication* (SBR). As of MySQL 5.1.5, another basis for replication is available. This is called *row-based replication* (RBR). Instead of sending SQL statements to the slave, the master writes events to its binary log that indicate how individual table rows are affected.

For a comparison that shows the advantages and disadvantages of SBR and RBR, see Section 5.12, "Comparison of Statement-Based Versus Row-Based Replication."

With MySQL's classic statement-based replication, there may be issues with replicating stored routines or triggers. You can avoid these issues by using MySQL's row-based replication instead.

If you build MySQL from source, row-based replication is unavailable unless you invoke configure with the --with-row-based-replication option.

MySQL Server use statement-based replication by default, even if it has been configured with support for row-based replication. To cause row-based replication to be used, start the server with the --binlog-format=row option to enable row-based replication globally (for all client connections). The option also automatically turns on innodb_locks_unsafe_for_binlog, which is safe when row-based replication is used.

Statement-based replication can be chosen at server startup either by specifying --binlog-format=statement or by not using the --binlog-format option at all.

Row-based replication causes *most* changes to be written to the binary log using the row-based format. Some changes, however, must be written to the binary log as statements:

- ANALYZE TABLE
- REPAIR TABLE
- OPTIMIZE TABLE

The `--binlog-row-event-max-size` is available for servers that are capable of row-based replication. Rows are stored into the binary log in chunks having a size in bytes not exceeding the value of this option. The value must be a multiple of 256. The default value is 1024.

5.4 Replication Implementation Details

MySQL replication capabilities are implemented using three threads (one on the master server and two on the slave). When a START SLAVE statement is issued on a slave server, the slave creates an I/O thread, which connects to the master and asks it to send the updates recorded in its binary logs. The master creates a thread to send the binary log contents to the slave. This thread can be identified as the Binlog Dump thread in the output of SHOW PROCESSLIST on the master. The slave I/O thread reads the updates that the master Binlog Dump thread sends and copies them to local files, known as *relay logs*, in the slave's data directory. The third thread is the SQL thread, which the slave creates to read the relay logs and to execute the updates they contain.

In the preceding description, there are three threads per master/slave connection. A master that has multiple slaves creates one thread for each currently-connected slave, and each slave has its own I/O and SQL threads.

The slave uses two threads so that reading updates from the master and executing them can be separated into two independent tasks. Thus, the task of reading statements is not slowed down if statement execution is slow. For example, if the slave server has not been running for a while, its I/O thread can quickly fetch all the binary log contents from the master when the slave starts, even if the SQL thread lags far behind. If the slave stops before the SQL thread has executed all the fetched statements, the I/O thread has at least fetched everything so that a safe copy of the statements is stored locally in the slave's relay logs, ready for execution the next time that the slave starts. This enables the master server to purge its binary logs sooner because it no longer needs to wait for the slave to fetch their contents.

The SHOW PROCESSLIST statement provides information that tells you what is happening on the master and on the slave regarding replication. The following example illustrates how the three threads show up in the output from SHOW PROCESSLIST.

On the master server, the output from SHOW PROCESSLIST looks like this:

```
mysql> SHOW PROCESSLIST\G
*************************** 1. row ***************************
     Id: 2
   User: root
   Host: localhost:32931
     db: NULL
Command: Binlog Dump
   Time: 94
  State: Has sent all binlog to slave; waiting for binlog to
         be updated
   Info: NULL
```

Here, thread 2 is a `Binlog Dump` replication thread for a connected slave. The `State` information indicates that all outstanding updates have been sent to the slave and that the master is waiting for more updates to occur. If you see no `Binlog Dump` threads on a master server, this means that replication is not running—that is, that no slaves are currently connected.

On the slave server, the output from `SHOW PROCESSLIST` looks like this:

```
mysql> SHOW PROCESSLIST\G
*************************** 1. row ***************************
     Id: 10
   User: system user
   Host:
     db: NULL
Command: Connect
   Time: 11
  State: Waiting for master to send event
   Info: NULL
*************************** 2. row ***************************
     Id: 11
   User: system user
   Host:
     db: NULL
Command: Connect
   Time: 11
  State: Has read all relay log; waiting for the slave I/O
         thread to update it
   Info: NULL
```

This information indicates that thread 10 is the I/O thread that is communicating with the master server, and thread 11 is the SQL thread that is processing the updates stored in the relay logs. At the time that the `SHOW PROCESSLIST` was run, both threads were idle, waiting for further updates.

The value in the `Time` column can show how late the slave is compared to the master. See Section 5.11, "Replication FAQ."

5.4.1 Replication Master Thread States

The following list shows the most common states you may see in the `State` column for the master's `Binlog Dump` thread. If you see no `Binlog Dump` threads on a master server, this means that replication is not running—that is, that no slaves are currently connected.

- `Sending binlog event to slave`

  Binary logs consist of *events*, where an event is usually an update plus some other information. The thread has read an event from the binary log and is now sending it to the slave.

- `Finished reading one binlog; switching to next binlog`

  The thread has finished reading a binary log file and is opening the next one to send to the slave.

- Has sent all binlog to slave; waiting for binlog to be updated

  The thread has read all outstanding updates from the binary logs and sent them to the slave. The thread is now idle, waiting for new events to appear in the binary log resulting from new updates occurring on the master.

- Waiting to finalize termination

  A very brief state that occurs as the thread is stopping.

5.4.2 Replication Slave I/O Thread States

The following list shows the most common states you see in the State column for a slave server I/O thread. This state also appears in the Slave_IO_State column displayed by SHOW SLAVE STATUS, so by using that statement, you can get a good view of what is happening.

- Connecting to master

  The thread is attempting to connect to the master.

- Checking master version

  A state that occurs very briefly, after the connection to the master is established.

- Registering slave on master

  A state that occurs very briefly, after the connection to the master is established.

- Requesting binlog dump

  A state that occurs very briefly, after the connection to the master is established. The thread sends to the master a request for the contents of its binary logs, starting from the requested binary log filename and position.

- Waiting to reconnect after a failed binlog dump request

  If the binary log dump request failed (due to disconnection), the thread goes into this state while it sleeps, and then tries to reconnect periodically. The interval between retries can be specified using the --master-connect-retry option.

- Reconnecting after a failed binlog dump request

  The thread is trying to reconnect to the master.

- Waiting for master to send event

  The thread has connected to the master and is waiting for binary log events to arrive. This can last for a long time if the master is idle. If the wait lasts for slave_read_timeout seconds, a timeout occurs. At that point, the thread considers the connection to be broken and makes an attempt to reconnect.

- Queueing master event to the relay log

  The thread has read an event and is copying it to the relay log so that the SQL thread can process it.

- Waiting to reconnect after a failed master event read

  An error occurred while reading (due to disconnection). The thread is sleeping for master-connect-retry seconds before attempting to reconnect.

- Reconnecting after a failed master event read

  The thread is trying to reconnect to the master. When connection is established again, the state becomes `Waiting for master to send event`.

- Waiting for the slave SQL thread to free enough relay log space

  You are using a non-zero `relay_log_space_limit` value, and the relay logs have grown large enough that their combined size exceeds this value. The I/O thread is waiting until the SQL thread frees enough space by processing relay log contents so that it can delete some relay log files.

- Waiting for slave mutex on exit

  A state that occurs briefly as the thread is stopping.

5.4.3 Replication Slave SQL Thread States

The following list shows the most common states you may see in the `State` column for a slave server SQL thread:

- Reading event from the relay log

  The thread has read an event from the relay log so that the event can be processed.

- Has read all relay log; waiting for the slave I/O thread to update it

  The thread has processed all events in the relay log files, and is now waiting for the I/O thread to write new events to the relay log.

- Waiting for slave mutex on exit

  A very brief state that occurs as the thread is stopping.

The `State` column for the I/O thread may also show the text of a statement. This indicates that the thread has read an event from the relay log, extracted the statement from it, and is executing it.

5.4.4 Replication Relay and Status Files

By default, relay logs filenames have the form *host_name*-`relay-bin.`*nnnnnn*, where *host_name* is the name of the slave server host and *nnnnnn* is a sequence number. Successive relay log files are created using successive sequence numbers, beginning with `000001`. The slave uses an index file to track the relay log files currently in use. The default relay log index filename is *host_name*-`relay-bin.index`. By default, the slave server creates relay log files in its data directory. The default filenames can be overridden with the `--relay-log` and `--relay-log-index` server options. See Section 5.9, "Replication Startup Options."

Relay logs have the same format as binary logs and can be read using `mysqlbinlog`. The SQL thread automatically deletes each relay log file as soon as it has executed all events in the file and no longer needs it. There is no explicit mechanism for deleting relay logs because the SQL thread takes care of doing so. However, `FLUSH LOGS` rotates relay logs, which influences when the SQL thread deletes them.

A slave server creates a new relay log file under the following conditions:

- Each time the I/O thread starts.
- When the logs are flushed; for example, with FLUSH LOGS or mysqladmin flush-logs.
- When the size of the current relay log file becomes too large. The meaning of "too large" is determined as follows:
  - If the value of max_relay_log_size is greater than 0, that is the maximum relay log file size.
  - If the value of max_relay_log_size is 0, max_binlog_size determines the maximum relay log file size.

A slave replication server creates two additional small files in the data directory. These *status files* are named master.info and relay-log.info by default. Their names can be changed by using the --master-info-file and --relay-log-info-file options. See Section 5.9, "Replication Startup Options."

The two status files contain information like that shown in the output of the SHOW SLAVE STATUS statement. Because the status files are stored on disk, they survive a slave server's shutdown. The next time the slave starts up, it reads the two files to determine how far it has proceeded in reading binary logs from the master and in processing its own relay logs.

The I/O thread updates the master.info file. The following table shows the correspondence between the lines in the file and the columns displayed by SHOW SLAVE STATUS.

Line	Description
1	Number of lines in the file
2	Master_Log_File
3	Read_Master_Log_Pos
4	Master_Host
5	Master_User
6	Password (not shown by SHOW SLAVE STATUS)
7	Master_Port
8	Connect_Retry
9	Master_SSL_Allowed
10	Master_SSL_CA_File
11	Master_SSL_CA_Path
12	Master_SSL_Cert
13	Master_SSL_Cipher
14	Master_SSL_Key

The SQL thread updates the relay-log.info file. The following table shows the correspondence between the lines in the file and the columns displayed by SHOW SLAVE STATUS.

Line	Description
1	`Relay_Log_File`
2	`Relay_Log_Pos`
3	`Relay_Master_Log_File`
4	`Exec_Master_Log_Pos`

When you back up the slave's data, you should back up these two status files as well, along with the relay log files. They are needed to resume replication after you restore the slave's data. If you lose the relay logs but still have the `relay-log.info` file, you can check it to determine how far the SQL thread has executed in the master binary logs. Then you can use `CHANGE MASTER TO` with the `MASTER_LOG_FILE` and `MASTER_LOG_POS` options to tell the slave to re-read the binary logs from that point. Of course, this requires that the binary logs still exist on the master server.

If your slave is subject to replicating `LOAD DATA INFILE` statements, you should also back up any `SQL_LOAD-*` files that exist in the directory that the slave uses for this purpose. The slave needs these files to resume replication of any interrupted `LOAD DATA INFILE` operations. The directory location is specified using the `--slave-load-tmpdir` option. If this option is not specified, the directory location is the value of the `tmpdir` system variable.

5.5 How to Set Up Replication

This section briefly describes how to set up complete replication of a MySQL server. It assumes that you want to replicate all databases on the master and have not previously configured replication. You must shut down your master server briefly to complete the steps outlined here.

This procedure is written in terms of setting up a single slave, but you can repeat it to set up multiple slaves.

Although this method is the most straightforward way to set up a slave, it is not the only one. For example, if you have a snapshot of the master's data, and the master already has its server ID set and binary logging enabled, you can set up a slave without shutting down the master or even blocking updates to it. For more details, please see Section 5.11, "Replication FAQ."

If you want to administer a MySQL replication setup, we suggest that you read this entire chapter through and try all replication-related SQL statements mentioned in the "MySQL Language Reference." You should also familiarize yourself with the replication startup options described in Section 5.9, "Replication Startup Options."

Note: This procedure and some of the replication SQL statements shown in later sections require the SUPER privilege.

1. Make sure that the versions of MySQL installed on the master and slave are compatible according to the table shown in Section 5.6, "Replication Compatibility Between MySQL Versions." Ideally, you should use the most recent version of MySQL on both master and slave.

If you encounter a problem, please do not report it as a bug until you have verified that the problem is present in the latest MySQL release.

2. Set up an account on the master server that the slave server can use to connect. This account must be given the REPLICATION SLAVE privilege. If the account is used only for replication (which is recommended), you don't need to grant any additional privileges.

Suppose that your domain is mydomain.com and that you want to create an account with a username of repl such that slave servers can use the account to access the master server from any host in your domain using a password of slavepass. To create the account, use this GRANT statement:

```
mysql> GRANT REPLICATION SLAVE ON *.*
    -> TO 'repl'@'%.mydomain.com' IDENTIFIED BY 'slavepass';
```

If you plan to use the LOAD TABLE FROM MASTER or LOAD DATA FROM MASTER statements from the slave host, you must grant this account additional privileges:

- Grant the account the SUPER and RELOAD global privileges.
- Grant the SELECT privilege for all tables that you want to load. Any master tables from which the account cannot SELECT will be ignored by LOAD DATA FROM MASTER.

For additional information about setting up user accounts and privileges, see Section 4.9, "MySQL User Account Management."

3. Flush all the tables and block write statements by executing a FLUSH TABLES WITH READ LOCK statement:

```
mysql> FLUSH TABLES WITH READ LOCK;
```

For InnoDB tables, note that FLUSH TABLES WITH READ LOCK also blocks COMMIT operations. When you have acquired a global read lock, you can start a filesystem snapshot of your InnoDB tables. Internally (inside the InnoDB storage engine) the snapshot won't be consistent (because the InnoDB caches are not flushed), but this is not a cause for concern, because InnoDB resolves this at startup and delivers a consistent result. This means that InnoDB can perform crash recovery when started on this snapshot, without corruption. However, there is no way to stop the MySQL server while ensuring a consistent snapshot of your InnoDB tables.

Leave running the client from which you issue the FLUSH TABLES statement so that the read lock remains in effect. (If you exit the client, the lock is released.) Then take a snapshot of the data on your master server.

The easiest way to create a snapshot is to use an archiving program to make a binary backup of the databases in your master's data directory. For example, use tar on Unix, or PowerArchiver, WinRAR, WinZip, or any similar software on Windows. To use tar to create an archive that includes all databases, change location into the master server's data directory, and then execute this command:

```
shell> tar -cvf /tmp/mysql-snapshot.tar .
```

If you want the archive to include only a database called `this_db`, use this command instead:

```
shell> tar -cvf /tmp/mysql-snapshot.tar ./this_db
```

Then copy the archive file to the `/tmp` directory on the slave server host. On that machine, change location into the slave's data directory, and unpack the archive file using this command:

```
shell> tar -xvf /tmp/mysql-snapshot.tar
```

You may not want to replicate the `mysql` database if the slave server has a different set of user accounts from those that exist on the master. In this case, you should exclude it from the archive. You also need not include any log files in the archive, or the `master.info` or `relay-log.info` files.

While the read lock placed by FLUSH TABLES WITH READ LOCK is in effect, read the value of the current binary log name and offset on the master:

```
mysql > SHOW MASTER STATUS;
+---------------+----------+--------------+------------------+
| File          | Position | Binlog_Do_DB | Binlog_Ignore_DB |
+---------------+----------+--------------+------------------+
| mysql-bin.003 | 73       | test         | manual,mysql     |
+---------------+----------+--------------+------------------+
```

The `File` column shows the name of the log and `Position` shows the offset within the file. In this example, the binary log file is `mysql-bin.003` and the offset is 73. Record these values. You need them later when you are setting up the slave. They represent the replication coordinates at which the slave should begin processing new updates from the master.

If the master has been running previously without binary logging enabled, the log name and position values displayed by SHOW MASTER STATUS or `mysqldump --master-data` will be empty. In that case, the values that you need to use later when specifying the slave's log file and position are the empty string (`' '`) and 4.

After you have taken the snapshot and recorded the log name and offset, you can re-enable write activity on the master:

```
mysql> UNLOCK TABLES;
```

If you are using `InnoDB` tables, ideally you should use the `InnoDB Hot Backup` tool, which takes a consistent snapshot without acquiring any locks on the master server, and records the log name and offset corresponding to the snapshot to be later used on the slave. `Hot Backup` is an additional non-free (commercial) tool that is not included in the standard MySQL distribution. See the `InnoDB Hot Backup` home page at `http://www.innodb.com/manual.php` for detailed information.

Without the `Hot Backup` tool, the quickest way to take a binary snapshot of `InnoDB` tables is to shut down the master server and copy the `InnoDB` data files, log files, and table format files (.frm files). To record the current log file name and offset, you should issue the following statements before you shut down the server:

```
mysql> FLUSH TABLES WITH READ LOCK;
mysql> SHOW MASTER STATUS;
```

Then record the log name and the offset from the output of SHOW MASTER STATUS as was shown earlier. After recording the log name and the offset, shut down the server *without* unlocking the tables to make sure that the server goes down with the snapshot corresponding to the current log file and offset:

```
shell> mysqladmin -u root shutdown
```

An alternative that works for both MyISAM and InnoDB tables is to take an SQL dump of the master instead of a binary copy as described in the preceding discussion. For this, you can use mysqldump --master-data on your master and later load the SQL dump file into your slave. However, this is slower than doing a binary copy.

4. Make sure that the [mysqld] section of the my.cnf file on the master host includes a log-bin option. The section should also have a server-id=*master_id* option, where *master_id* must be a positive integer value from 1 to $2^{32} - 1$. For example:

```
[mysqld]
log-bin=mysql-bin
server-id=1
```

If those options are not present, add them and restart the server. The server cannot act as a replication master unless binary logging is enabled.

Note: For the greatest possible durability and consistency in a replication setup using InnoDB with transactions, you should use innodb_flush_log_at_trx_commit=1, sync_binlog=1, and, before MySQL 5.0.3, innodb_safe_binlog, in the master my.cnf file. (innodb_safe_binlog is not needed from 5.0.3 on.)

5. Stop the server that is to be used as a slave and add the following lines to its my.cnf file:

```
[mysqld]
server-id=slave_id
```

The *slave_id* value, like the *master_id* value, must be a positive integer value from 1 to $2^{32} - 1$. In addition, it is necessary that the ID of the slave be different from the ID of the master. For example:

```
[mysqld]
server-id=2
```

If you are setting up multiple slaves, each one must have a unique server-id value that differs from that of the master and from each of the other slaves. Think of server-id values as something similar to IP addresses: These IDs uniquely identify each server instance in the community of replication partners.

If you do not specify a server-id value, it is set to 1 if you have not defined master-host; otherwise it is set to 2. Note that in the case of server-id omission, a master refuses connections from all slaves, and a slave refuses to connect to a master. Thus, omitting `server-id` is good only for backup with a binary log.

6. If you made a binary backup of the master server's data, copy it to the slave server's data directory before starting the slave. Make sure that the privileges on the files and directories are correct. The system account that you use to run the slave server must be able to read and write the files, just as on the master.

   If you made a backup using `mysqldump`, start the slave first. The dump file is loaded in a later step.

7. Start the slave server. If it has been replicating previously, start the slave server with the `--skip-slave-start` option so that it doesn't immediately try to connect to its master. You also may want to start the slave server with the `--log-warnings` option to get more messages in the error log about problems (for example, network or connection problems). The option is enabled by default, but aborted connections are not logged to the error log unless the option value is greater than 1.

8. If you made a backup of the master server's data using `mysqldump`, load the dump file into the slave server:

   ```
   shell> mysql -u root -p < dump_file.sql
   ```

9. Execute the following statement on the slave, replacing the option values with the actual values relevant to your system:

   ```
   mysql> CHANGE MASTER TO
       ->        MASTER_HOST='master_host_name',
       ->        MASTER_USER='replication_user_name',
       ->        MASTER_PASSWORD='replication_password',
       ->        MASTER_LOG_FILE='recorded_log_file_name',
       ->        MASTER_LOG_POS=recorded_log_position;
   ```

   The following table shows the maximum allowable length for the string-valued options:

MASTER_HOST	60
MASTER_USER	16
MASTER_PASSWORD	32
MASTER_LOG_FILE	255

10. Start the slave threads:

    ```
    mysql> START SLAVE;
    ```

After you have performed this procedure, the slave should connect to the master and catch up on any updates that have occurred since the snapshot was taken.

If you have forgotten to set the `server-id` option for the master, slaves cannot connect to it.

If you have forgotten to set the `server-id` option for the slave, you get the following error in the slave's error log:

```
Warning: You should set server-id to a non-0 value if master_host
is set; we will force server id to 2, but this MySQL server will
not act as a slave.
```

You also find error messages in the slave's error log if it is not able to replicate for any other reason.

Once a slave is replicating, you can find in its data directory one file named `master.info` and another named `relay-log.info`. The slave uses these two files to keep track of how much of the master's binary log it has processed. Do *not* remove or edit these files unless you know exactly what you are doing and fully understand the implications. Even in that case, it is preferred that you use the `CHANGE MASTER TO` statement to change replication parameters. The slave will use the values specified in the statement to update the status files automatically.

Note: The content of `master.info` overrides some of the server options specified on the command line or in `my.cnf`. See Section 5.9, "Replication Startup Options," for more details.

Once you have a snapshot of the master, you can use it to set up other slaves by following the slave portion of the procedure just described. You do not need to take another snapshot of the master; you can use the same one for each slave.

5.6 Replication Compatibility Between MySQL Versions

The binary log format as implemented in MySQL 5.0 is considerably different from that used in previous versions. Major changes were made in MySQL 5.0.3 (for improvements to handling of character sets and `LOAD DATA INFILE`) and 5.0.4 (for improvements to handling of time zones).

We recommend using the most recent MySQL version available because replication capabilities are continually being improved. We also recommend using the same version for both the master and the slave. We recommend upgrading masters and slaves running alpha or beta versions to new (production) versions. Replication from a 5.0.3 master to a 5.0.2 slave will fail; from a 5.0.4 master to a 5.0.3 slave will also fail. In general, slaves running MySQL 5.0.x can be used with older masters (even those running MySQL 3.23, 4.0, or 4.1), but not the reverse.

Note: You *cannot* replicate from a master that uses a newer binary log format to a slave that uses an older format (for example, from MySQL 5.0 to MySQL 4.1). This has significant implications for upgrading replication servers, as described in Section 5.7, "Upgrading a Replication Setup."

The preceding information pertains to replication compatibility at the protocol level. However, there can be other constraints, such as SQL-level compatibility issues. For example, a 5.0 master cannot replicate to a 4.1 slave if the replicated statements use SQL features available in 5.0 but not in 4.1. These and other issues are discussed in Section 5.8, "Replication Features and Known Problems."

5.7 Upgrading a Replication Setup

When you upgrade servers that participate in a replication setup, the procedure for upgrading depends on the current server versions and the version to which you are upgrading.

5.7.1 Upgrading Replication to 5.0

This section applies to upgrading replication from MySQL 3.23, 4.0, or 4.1 to MySQL 5.0. A 4.0 server should be 4.0.3 or newer.

When you upgrade a master to 5.0 from an earlier MySQL release series, you should first ensure that all the slaves of this master are using the same 5.0.x release. If this is not the case, you should first upgrade the slaves. To upgrade each slave, shut it down, upgrade it to the appropriate 5.0.x version, restart it, and restart replication. The 5.0 slave is able to read the old relay logs written prior to the upgrade and to execute the statements they contain. Relay logs created by the slave after the upgrade are in 5.0 format.

After the slaves have been upgraded, shut down the master, upgrade it to the same 5.0.x release as the slaves, and restart it. The 5.0 master is able to read the old binary logs written prior to the upgrade and to send them to the 5.0 slaves. The slaves recognize the old format and handle it properly. Binary logs created by the master following the upgrade are in 5.0 format. These too are recognized by the 5.0 slaves.

In other words, there are no measures to take when upgrading to MySQL 5.0, except that the slaves must be MySQL 5.0 before you can upgrade the master to 5.0. Note that downgrading from 5.0 to older versions does not work so simply: You must ensure that any 5.0 binary logs or relay logs have been fully processed, so that you can remove them before proceeding with the downgrade.

Downgrading a replication setup to a previous version cannot be done once you've switched from statement-based to row-based replication, and after the first row-based statement has been written to the binlog. See Section 5.3, "Row-Based Replication."

5.8 Replication Features and Known Problems

In general, replication compatibility at the SQL level requires that any features used be supported by both the master and the slave servers. If you use a feature on a master server that is available only as of a given version of MySQL, you cannot replicate to a slave that is older than that version. Such incompatibilities are likely to occur between series, so that, for example, you cannot replicate from MySQL 5.0 to 4.1. However, these incompatibilities also can occur for within-series replication. For example, the SLEEP() function is available in MySQL 5.0.12 and up. If you use this function on the master server, you cannot replicate to a slave server that is older than MySQL 5.0.12.

If you are planning to use replication between 5.0 and a previous version of MySQL you should consult the edition of the "MySQL Reference Manual" corresponding to the earlier release series for information regarding the replication characteristics of that series.

The following list provides details about what is supported and what is not. Additional InnoDB-specific information about replication is given in Section 8.2.6.5, "InnoDB and MySQL Replication."

With MySQL's classic statement-based replication, there may be issues with replicating stored routines or triggers. You can avoid these issues by using MySQL's row-based replication (RBR) instead. For a description of row-based replication, see Section 5.3, "Row-Based Replication."

- **Known issue**: In MySQL 5.0.17, the syntax for CREATE TRIGGER changed to include a DEFINER clause for specifying which access privileges to check at trigger invocation time. However, if you attempt to replicate from a master server older than MySQL 5.0.17 to a slave running MySQL 5.0.17 through 5.0.19, replication of CREATE TRIGGER statements fails on the slave with a Definer not fully qualified error. A workaround is to create triggers on the master using a version-specific comment embedded in each CREATE TRIGGER statement:

  ```
  CREATE /*!50017 DEFINER = 'root'@'localhost' */ TRIGGER ... ;
  ```

  CREATE TRIGGER statements written this way will replicate to newer slaves, which pick up the DEFINER clause from the comment and execute successfully. This slave problem is fixed as of MySQL 5.0.20.

- Replication of AUTO_INCREMENT, LAST_INSERT_ID(), and TIMESTAMP values is done correctly.

- The USER(), UUID(), and LOAD_FILE() functions are replicated without change and thus do not work reliably on the slave unless row-based replication is enabled. (See Section 5.3, "Row-Based Replication.")

- User privileges are replicated only if the mysql database is replicated. That is, the GRANT, REVOKE, SET PASSWORD, CREATE USER, and DROP USER statements take effect on the slave only if the replication setup includes the mysql database.

  If you're replicating all databases, but don't want statements that affect user privileges to be replicated, set up the slave to not replicate the mysql database, using the --replicate-wild-ignore-table=mysql.% option. The slave will recognize that issuing privilege-related SQL statements won't have an effect, and thus not execute those statements.

- *The following restriction applies to statement-based replication only, not to row-based replication.* The GET_LOCK(), RELEASE_LOCK(), IS_FREE_LOCK(), and IS_USED_LOCK() functions that handle user-level locks are replicated without the slave knowing the concurrency context on master. Therefore, these functions should not be used to insert into a master's table because the content on the slave would differ. (For example, do not issue a statement such as INSERT INTO mytable VALUES(GET_LOCK(...)).)

- The FOREIGN_KEY_CHECKS, SQL_MODE, UNIQUE_CHECKS, and SQL_AUTO_IS_NULL variables are all replicated in MySQL 5.0. The storage_engine system variable (also known as table_type) is not yet replicated, which is a good thing for replication between different storage engines.

- Starting from MySQL 5.0.3 (master and slave), replication works even if the master and slave have different global character set variables. Starting from MySQL 5.0.4 (master and slave), replication works even if the master and slave have different global time zone variables.

- The following applies to replication between MySQL servers that use different character sets:

  1. If the master uses MySQL 4.1, you must *always* use the same *global* character set and collation on the master and the slave, regardless of the MySQL version running on the slave. (These are controlled by the `--character-set-server` and `--collation-server` options.) Otherwise, you may get duplicate-key errors on the slave, because a key that is unique in the master character set might not be unique in the slave character set. Note that this is not a cause for concern when master and slave are both MySQL 5.0 or later.

  2. If the master is older than MySQL 4.1.3, the character set of any client should never be made different from its global value because this character set change is not known to the slave. In other words, clients should not use `SET NAMES`, `SET CHARACTER SET`, and so forth. If both the master and the slave are 4.1.3 or newer, clients can freely set session values for character set variables because these settings are written to the binary log and so are known to the slave. That is, clients can use `SET NAMES` or `SET CHARACTER SET` or can set variables such as `collation_client` or `collation_server`. However, clients are prevented from changing the *global* value of these variables; as stated previously, the master and slave must always have identical global character set values.

  3. If you have databases on the master with character sets that differ from the global `character_set_server` value, you should design your `CREATE TABLE` statements so that tables in those databases do not implicitly rely on the database default character set (see Bug #2326 at `http://bugs.mysql.com/2326`). A good workaround is to state the character set and collation explicitly in `CREATE TABLE`.

- If the master uses MySQL 4.1, the same system time zone should be set for both master and slave. Otherwise some statements will not be replicated properly, such as statements that use the `NOW()` or `FROM_UNIXTIME()` functions. You can set the time zone in which MySQL server runs by using the `--timezone=`*timezone_name* option of the `mysqld_safe` script or by setting the `TZ` environment variable. Both master and slave should also have the same default connection time zone setting; that is, the `--default-time-zone` parameter should have the same value for both master and slave. Note that this is not necessary when the master is MySQL 5.0 or later.

- `CONVERT_TZ(...,...,@@global.time_zone)` is not properly replicated. `CONVERT_TZ(...,...,@@session.time_zone)` is properly replicated only if the master and slave are from MySQL 5.0.4 or newer.

- Session variables are not replicated properly when used in statements that update tables. For example, `SET MAX_JOIN_SIZE=1000` followed by `INSERT INTO mytable VALUES(@@MAX_JOIN_SIZE)` will not insert the same data on the master and the slave. This does not apply to the common sequence of `SET TIME_ZONE=...` followed by `INSERT INTO mytable VALUES(CONVERT_TZ(...,...,@@time_zone))`, which replicates correctly as of MySQL 5.0.4.

Replication of session variables is not a problem when row-based replication is being used. See Section 5.3, "Row-Based Replication."

- It is possible to replicate transactional tables on the master using non-transactional tables on the slave. For example, you can replicate an `InnoDB` master table as a `MyISAM` slave table. However, if you do this, there are problems if the slave is stopped in the middle of a `BEGIN/COMMIT` block because the slave restarts at the beginning of the `BEGIN` block.

- Update statements that refer to user-defined variables (that is, variables of the form `@var_name`) are replicated correctly in MySQL 5.0. However, this is not true for versions prior to 4.1. Note that user variable names are case insensitive starting in MySQL 5.0. You should take this into account when setting up replication between MySQL 5.0 and older versions.

- Slaves can connect to masters using SSL.

- In MySQL 5.0 (starting from 5.0.3), there is a global system variable `slave_transaction_retries`: If the replication slave SQL thread fails to execute a transaction because of an `InnoDB` deadlock or because it exceeded the `InnoDB` `innodb_lock_wait_timeout` or the NDBCluster `TransactionDeadlockDetectionTimeout` or `TransactionInactiveTimeout` value, the transaction automatically retries `slave_transaction_retries` times before stopping with an error. The default value is 10. Starting from MySQL 5.0.4, the total retry count can be seen in the output of `SHOW STATUS`; see Section 4.2.4, "Server Status Variables."

- If a `DATA DIRECTORY` or `INDEX DIRECTORY` table option is used in a `CREATE TABLE` statement on the master server, the table option is also used on the slave. This can cause problems if no corresponding directory exists in the slave host filesystem or if it exists but is not accessible to the slave server. MySQL supports an `sql_mode` option called `NO_DIR_IN_CREATE`. If the slave server is run with this SQL mode enabled, it ignores the `DATA DIRECTORY` and `INDEX DIRECTORY` table options when replicating `CREATE TABLE` statements. The result is that `MyISAM` data and index files are created in the table's database directory.

- *The following restriction applies to statement-based replication only, not to row-based replication*: It is possible for the data on the master and slave to become different if a statement is designed in such a way that the data modification is *non-deterministic*; that is, it is left to the will of the query optimizer. (This is in general not a good practice, even outside of replication.)

- *The following applies only if either the master or the slave is running MySQL version 5.0.3 or older*: If on the master a `LOAD DATA INFILE` is interrupted (integrity constraint violation, killed connection, and so on), the slave skips the `LOAD DATA INFILE` entirely. This means that if this command permanently inserted or updated table records before being interrupted, these modifications are not replicated to the slave.

- Some forms of the `FLUSH` statement are not logged because they could cause problems if replicated to a slave: `FLUSH LOGS`, `FLUSH MASTER`, `FLUSH SLAVE`, and `FLUSH TABLES WITH READ LOCK`. The `FLUSH TABLES`, `ANALYZE TABLE`, `OPTIMIZE TABLE`, and `REPAIR TABLE` statements are written to the binary log and thus replicated to slaves. This is not normally a problem because these statements do not modify table data. However, this can cause difficulties under certain circumstances. If you replicate the privilege tables in the `mysql` database and update those tables directly without using `GRANT`, you must issue a `FLUSH PRIVILEGES` on the slaves to put the new privileges into effect. In addition, if you use `FLUSH TABLES` when renaming a `MyISAM` table that is part of a `MERGE` table, you must issue `FLUSH TABLES` manually on the slaves. These statements are written to the binary log unless you specify `NO_WRITE_TO_BINLOG` or its alias `LOCAL`.

- MySQL supports only one master and many slaves. In the future we plan to add a voting algorithm for changing the master automatically in the event of problems with the current master. We also plan to introduce agent processes to help perform load balancing by sending `SELECT` queries to different slaves.

- When a server shuts down and restarts, its `MEMORY` (`HEAP`) tables become empty. The master replicates this effect to slaves as follows: The first time that the master uses each `MEMORY` table after startup, it logs an event that notifies the slaves that the table needs to be emptied by writing a `DELETE` statement for that table to the binary log. See Section 8.4, "The `MEMORY` (`HEAP`) Storage Engine," for more information.

- Note that this item does not apply when row-based replication is in use because row-based replication does not require that temporary tables be replicated at all. (See Section 5.3, "Row-Based Replication.")

Temporary tables are replicated except in the case where you shut down the slave server (not just the slave threads) and you have replicated temporary tables that are used in updates that have not yet been executed on the slave. If you shut down the slave server, the temporary tables needed by those updates are no longer available when the slave is restarted. To avoid this problem, do not shut down the slave while it has temporary tables open. Instead, use the following procedure:

1. Issue a `STOP SLAVE` statement.

2. Use `SHOW STATUS` to check the value of the `Slave_open_temp_tables` variable.

3. If the value is 0, issue a `mysqladmin shutdown` command to stop the slave.

4. If the value is not 0, restart the slave threads with `START SLAVE`.

5. Repeat the procedure later until the `Slave_open_temp_tables` variable is 0 and you can stop the slave.

- The syntax for multiple-table `DELETE` statements that use table aliases changed between MySQL 4.0 and 4.1. In MySQL 4.0, you should use the true table name to refer to any table from which rows should be deleted:

```
DELETE test FROM test AS t1, test2 WHERE ...
```

In MySQL 4.1, you must use the alias:

```
DELETE t1 FROM test AS t1, test2 WHERE ...
```

If you use such `DELETE` statements, the change in syntax means that a 4.0 master cannot replicate to slaves from 4.1 or higher.

- It is safe to connect servers in a circular master/slave relationship if you use the `--log-slave-updates` option. That means that you can create a setup such as this:

  `A -> B -> C -> A`

  However, many statements do not work correctly in this kind of setup unless your client code is written to take care of the potential problems that can occur from updates that occur in different sequence on different servers.

  Server IDs are encoded in binary log events, so server A knows when an event that it reads was originally created by itself and does not execute the event (unless server A was started with the `--replicate-same-server-id` option, which is meaningful only in rare cases). Thus, there are no infinite loops. This type of circular setup works only if you perform no conflicting updates between the tables. In other words, if you insert data in both A and C, you should never insert a row in A that may have a key that conflicts with a row inserted in C. You should also not update the same rows on two servers if the order in which the updates are applied is significant.

- If a statement on a slave produces an error, the slave SQL thread terminates, and the slave writes a message to its error log. You should then connect to the slave manually and determine the cause of the problem. (`SHOW SLAVE STATUS` is useful for this.) Then fix the problem (for example, you might need to create a non-existent table) and run `START SLAVE`.

- It is safe to shut down a master server and restart it later. When a slave loses its connection to the master, the slave tries to reconnect immediately and retries periodically if that fails. The default is to retry every 60 seconds. This may be changed with the `--master-connect-retry` option. A slave also is able to deal with network connectivity outages. However, the slave notices the network outage only after receiving no data from the master for `slave_net_timeout` seconds. If your outages are short, you may want to decrease `slave_net_timeout`. See Section 4.2.2, "Server System Variables."

- Shutting down the slave (cleanly) is also safe because it keeps track of where it left off. Unclean shutdowns might produce problems, especially if the disk cache was not flushed to disk before the system went down. Your system fault tolerance is greatly increased if you have a good uninterruptible power supply. Unclean shutdowns of the master may cause inconsistencies between the content of tables and the binary log in master; this can be avoided by using `InnoDB` tables and the `--innodb-safe-binlog` option on the master. See Section 4.12.3, "The Binary Log."

  Note: `--innodb-safe-binlog` is unneeded as of MySQL 5.0.3, having been made obsolete by the introduction of XA transaction support.

- Due to the non-transactional nature of `MyISAM` tables, it is possible to have a statement that only partially updates a table and returns an error code. This can happen, for example, on a multiple-row insert that has one row violating a key constraint, or if a long update statement is killed after updating some of the rows. If that happens on the master, the slave thread exits and waits for the database administrator to decide what to do about it unless the error code is legitimate and execution of the statement results in the same error code on the slave. If this error code validation behavior is not desirable, some or all errors can be masked out (ignored) with the `--slave-skip-errors` option.

- If you update transactional tables from non-transactional tables inside a `BEGIN/COMMIT` sequence, updates to the binary log may be out of synchrony with table states if the non-transactional table is updated before the transaction commits. This occurs because the transaction is written to the binary log only when it is committed.

- In situations where transactions mix updates to transactional and non-transactional tables, the order of statements in the binary log is correct, and all needed statements are written to the binary log even in case of a `ROLLBACK`. However, when a second connection updates the non-transactional table before the first connection's transaction is complete, statements can be logged out of order, because the second connection's update is written immediately after it is performed, regardless of the state of the transaction being performed by the first connection.

5.9 Replication Startup Options

This section describes the options that you can use on slave replication servers. You can specify these options either on the command line or in an option file.

On the master and each slave, you must use the `server-id` option to establish a unique replication ID. For each server, you should pick a unique positive integer in the range from 1 to $2^{32} - 1$, and each ID must be different from every other ID. Example: `server-id=3`

Options that you can use on the master server for controlling binary logging are described in Section 4.12.3, "The Binary Log."

Some slave server replication options are handled in a special way, in the sense that each is ignored if a `master.info` file exists when the slave starts and contains a value for the option. The following options are handled this way:

- `--master-host`
- `--master-user`
- `--master-password`
- `--master-port`
- `--master-connect-retry`
- `--master-ssl`
- `--master-ssl-ca`
- `--master-ssl-capath`
- `--master-ssl-cert`
- `--master-ssl-cipher`
- `--master-ssl-key`

The `master.info` file format in MySQL 5.0 includes values corresponding to the SSL options. In addition, the file format includes as its first line the number of lines in the file. If you upgrade an older server (before MySQL 4.1.1) to a newer version, the new server upgrades the `master.info` file to the new format automatically when it starts. However, if you downgrade a newer server to an older version, you should remove the first line manually before starting the older server for the first time.

If no master.info file exists when the slave server starts, it uses the values for those options that are specified in option files or on the command line. This occurs when you start the server as a replication slave for the very first time, or when you have run RESET SLAVE and then have shut down and restarted the slave.

If the master.info file exists when the slave server starts, the server uses its contents and ignores any options that correspond to the values listed in the file. Thus, if you start the slave server with different values of the startup options that correspond to values in the master.info file, the different values have no effect, because the server continues to use the master.info file. To use different values, you must either restart after removing the master.info file or (preferably) use the CHANGE MASTER TO statement to reset the values while the slave is running.

Suppose that you specify this option in your my.cnf file:

```
[mysqld]
master-host=some_host
```

The first time you start the server as a replication slave, it reads and uses that option from the my.cnf file. The server then records the value in the master.info file. The next time you start the server, it reads the master host value from the master.info file only and ignores the value in the option file. If you modify the my.cnf file to specify a different master host of some_other_host, the change still has no effect. You should use CHANGE MASTER TO instead.

Because the server gives an existing master.info file precedence over the startup options just described, you might prefer not to use startup options for these values at all, and instead specify them by using the CHANGE MASTER TO statement.

This example shows a more extensive use of startup options to configure a slave server:

```
[mysqld]
server-id=2
master-host=db-master.mycompany.com
master-port=3306
master-user=pertinax
master-password=freitag
master-connect-retry=60
report-host=db-slave.mycompany.com
```

The following list describes startup options for controlling replication. Many of these options can be reset while the server is running by using the CHANGE MASTER TO statement. Others, such as the --replicate-* options, can be set only when the slave server starts.

- --log-slave-updates

   Normally, a slave does not log to its own binary log any updates that are received from a master server. This option tells the slave to log the updates performed by its SQL thread to its own binary log. For this option to have any effect, the slave must also be started with the `--log-bin` option to enable binary logging. `--log-slave-updates` is used when you want to chain replication servers. For example, you might want to set up replication servers using this arrangement:

```
A -> B -> C
```

Here, A serves as the master for the slave B, and B serves as the master for the slave C. For this to work, B must be both a master *and* a slave. You must start both A and B with `--log-bin` to enable binary logging, and B with the `--log-slave-updates` option so that updates received from A are logged by B to its binary log.

- `--log-warnings[=level]`

This option causes a server to print more messages to the error log about what it is doing. With respect to replication, the server generates warnings that it succeeded in reconnecting after a network/connection failure, and informs you as to how each slave thread started. This option is enabled by default; to disable it, use `--skip-log-warnings`. Aborted connections are not logged to the error log unless the value is greater than 1.

- `--master-connect-retry=seconds`

The number of seconds that the slave thread sleeps before trying to reconnect to the master in case the master goes down or the connection is lost. The value in the `master.info` file takes precedence if it can be read. If not set, the default is 60.

- `--master-host=host_name`

The hostname or IP number of the master replication server. The value in `master.info` takes precedence if it can be read. If no master host is specified, the slave thread does not start.

- `--master-info-file=file_name`

The name to use for the file in which the slave records information about the master. The default name is `master.info` in the data directory.

- `--master-password=password`

The password of the account that the slave thread uses for authentication when it connects to the master. The value in the `master.info` file takes precedence if it can be read. If not set, an empty password is assumed.

- `--master-port=port_number`

The TCP/IP port number that the master is listening on. The value in the `master.info` file takes precedence if it can be read. If not set, the compiled-in setting is assumed (normally 3306).

- `--master-retry-count=count`

The number of times that the slave tries to connect to the master before giving up.

- `--master-ssl, --master-ssl-ca=file_name, --master-ssl-capath=directory_name, --master-ssl-cert=file_name, --master-ssl-cipher=cipher_list, --master-ssl-key=file_name`

These options are used for setting up a secure replication connection to the master server using SSL. Their meanings are the same as the corresponding `--ssl`, `--ssl-ca`, `--ssl-capath`, `--ssl-cert`, `--ssl-cipher`, `--ssl-key` options that are described in Section 4.9.7.5, "SSL Command Options." The values in the `master.info` file take precedence if they can be read.

- `--master-user=user_name`

The username of the account that the slave thread uses for authentication when it connects to the master. This account must have the REPLICATION SLAVE privilege. The value in the `master.info` file, if it can be read, takes precedence. If the master username is not set, the name `test` is assumed.

- `--max-relay-log-size=size`

The size at which the server rotates relay log files automatically. For more information, see Section 5.4.4, "Replication Relay and Status Files."

- `--read-only`

Causes the slave to allow no updates except from slave threads or from users having the SUPER privilege. This enables you to ensure that a slave server accepts no updates from clients. As of MySQL 5.0.16, this option does not apply to TEMPORARY tables.

- `--relay-log=file_name`

The name for the relay log. The default name is `host_name-relay-bin.nnnnnn`, where `host_name` is the name of the slave server host and `nnnnnn` indicates that relay logs are created in numbered sequence. You can specify the option to create hostname-independent relay log names, or if your relay logs tend to be big (and you don't want to decrease `max_relay_log_size`) and you need to put them in some area different from the data directory, or if you want to increase speed by balancing load between disks.

- `--relay-log-index=file_name`

The name to use for the relay log index file. The default name is `host_name-relay-bin.index` in the data directory, where `host_name` is the name of the slave server.

- `--relay-log-info-file=file_name`

The name to use for the file in which the slave records information about the relay logs. The default name is `relay-log.info` in the data directory.

- `--relay-log-purge={0|1}`

Disables or enables automatic purging of relay logs as soon as they are not needed any more. The default value is 1 (enabled). This is a global variable that can be changed dynamically with SET GLOBAL `relay_log_purge = N`.

- `--relay-log-space-limit=size`

This option places an upper limit on the total size in bytes of all relay logs on the slave. A value of 0 means "no limit." This is useful for a slave server host that has limited disk space. When the limit is reached, the I/O thread stops reading binary log events from the master server until the SQL thread has caught up and deleted some unused relay logs. Note that this limit is not absolute: There are cases where the SQL thread needs more events before it can delete relay logs. In that case, the I/O thread exceeds the limit until it becomes possible for the SQL thread to delete some relay logs, because not doing so would cause a deadlock. You should not set `--relay-log-space-limit` to less than twice the value of `--max-relay-log-size` (or `--max-binlog-size` if `--max-relay-log-size` is 0). In that case, there is a chance that the I/O thread waits for free space because `--relay-log-space-limit` is exceeded, but the SQL thread has no relay log to purge and is unable to satisfy the I/O thread. This forces the I/O thread to temporarily ignore `--relay-log-space-limit`.

- `--replicate-do-db=`*db_name*

Tells the slave to restrict replication to statements where the default database (that is, the one selected by USE) is *db_name*. To specify more than one database, use this option multiple times, once for each database. Note that this does not replicate cross-database statements such as UPDATE *some_db.some_table* SET foo='bar' while having selected a different database or no database.

An example of what does not work as you might expect: If the slave is started with `--replicate-do-db=sales` and you issue the following statements on the master, the UPDATE statement is *not* replicated:

```
USE prices;
UPDATE sales.january SET amount=amount+1000;
```

The main reason for this "just check the default database" behavior is that it is difficult from the statement alone to know whether it should be replicated (for example, if you are using multiple-table DELETE statements or multiple-table UPDATE statements that act across multiple databases). It is also faster to check only the default database rather than all databases if there is no need.

If you need cross-database updates to work, use `--replicate-wild-do-table=`*db_name.%* instead. See Section 5.10, "How Servers Evaluate Replication Rules."

- `--replicate-do-table=`*db_name.tbl_name*

Tells the slave thread to restrict replication to the specified table. To specify more than one table, use this option multiple times, once for each table. This works for cross-database updates, in contrast to `--replicate-do-db`. See Section 5.10, "How Servers Evaluate Replication Rules."

- `--replicate-ignore-db=`*db_name*

Tells the slave to not replicate any statement where the default database (that is, the one selected by USE) is *db_name*. To specify more than one database to ignore, use this option multiple times, once for each database. You should not use this option if you are using cross-database updates and you do not want these updates to be replicated. See Section 5.10, "How Servers Evaluate Replication Rules."

An example of what does not work as you might expect: If the slave is started with `--replicate-ignore-db=sales` and you issue the following statements on the master, the UPDATE statement is *not* replicated:

```
USE prices;
UPDATE sales.january SET amount=amount+1000;
```

If you need cross-database updates to work, use `--replicate-wild-ignore-table=db_name.%` instead. See Section 5.10, "How Servers Evaluate Replication Rules."

- `--replicate-ignore-table=db_name.tbl_name`

Tells the slave thread to not replicate any statement that updates the specified table, even if any other tables might be updated by the same statement. To specify more than one table to ignore, use this option multiple times, once for each table. This works for cross-database updates, in contrast to `--replicate-ignore-db`. See Section 5.10, "How Servers Evaluate Replication Rules."

- `--replicate-rewrite-db=from_name->to_name`

Tells the slave to translate the default database (that is, the one selected by USE) to *to_name* if it was *from_name* on the master. Only statements involving tables are affected (not statements such as CREATE DATABASE, DROP DATABASE, and ALTER DATABASE), and only if *from_name* is the default database on the master. This does not work for cross-database updates. The database name translation is done *before* the `--replicate-*` rules are tested.

If you use this option on the command line and the '>' character is special to your command interpreter, quote the option value. For example:

```
shell> mysqld --replicate-rewrite-db="olddb->newdb"
```

- `--replicate-same-server-id`

To be used on slave servers. Usually you should use the default setting of 0, to prevent infinite loops caused by circular replication. If set to 1, the slave does not skip events having its own server ID. Normally, this is useful only in rare configurations. Cannot be set to 1 if `--log-slave-updates` is used. Note that by default the slave I/O thread does not even write binary log events to the relay log if they have the slave's server ID (this optimization helps save disk usage). So if you want to use `--replicate-same-server-id`, be sure to start the slave with this option before you make the slave read its own events that you want the slave SQL thread to execute.

- `--replicate-wild-do-table=db_name.tbl_name`

Tells the slave thread to restrict replication to statements where any of the updated tables match the specified database and table name patterns. Patterns can contain the '%' and '_' wildcard characters, which have the same meaning as for the LIKE pattern-matching operator. To specify more than one table, use this option multiple times, once for each table. This works for cross-database updates. See Section 5.10, "How Servers Evaluate Replication Rules."

Example: `--replicate-wild-do-table=foo%.bar%` replicates only updates that use a table where the database name starts with foo and the table name starts with bar.

If the table name pattern is %, it matches any table name and the option also applies to database-level statements (CREATE DATABASE, DROP DATABASE, and ALTER DATABASE). For example, if you use `--replicate-wild-do-table=foo%.%`, database-level statements are replicated if the database name matches the pattern foo%.

To include literal wildcard characters in the database or table name patterns, escape them with a backslash. For example, to replicate all tables of a database that is named my_own%db, but not replicate tables from the my1ownAABCdb database, you should escape the '_' and '%' characters like this: `--replicate-wild-do-table=my\_own\%db`. If you're using the option on the command line, you might need to double the backslashes or quote the option value, depending on your command interpreter. For example, with the bash shell, you would need to type `--replicate-wild-do-table=my\\_own\\%db`.

- `--replicate-wild-ignore-table=`*db_name.tbl_name*

Tells the slave thread not to replicate a statement where any table matches the given wildcard pattern. To specify more than one table to ignore, use this option multiple times, once for each table. This works for cross-database updates. See Section 5.10, "How Servers Evaluate Replication Rules."

Example: `--replicate-wild-ignore-table=foo%.bar%` does not replicate updates that use a table where the database name starts with foo and the table name starts with bar.

For information about how matching works, see the description of the `--replicate-wild-do-table` option. The rules for including literal wildcard characters in the option value are the same as for `--replicate-wild-ignore-table` as well.

- `--report-host=`*slave_name*

The hostname or IP number of the slave to be reported to the master during slave registration. This value appears in the output of SHOW SLAVE HOSTS on the master server. Leave the value unset if you do not want the slave to register itself with the master. Note that it is not sufficient for the master to simply read the IP number of the slave from the TCP/IP socket after the slave connects. Due to NAT and other routing issues, that IP may not be valid for connecting to the slave from the master or other hosts.

- `--report-port=`*slave_port_num*

The TCP/IP port number for connecting to the slave, to be reported to the master during slave registration. Set this only if the slave is listening on a non-default port or if you have a special tunnel from the master or other clients to the slave. If you are not sure, do not use this option.

- `--skip-slave-start`

Tells the slave server not to start the slave threads when the server starts. To start the threads later, use a START SLAVE statement.

- `--slave_compressed_protocol={0|1}`

If this option is set to 1, use compression for the slave/master protocol if both the slave and the master support it.

- `--slave-load-tmpdir=`*file_name*

The name of the directory where the slave creates temporary files. This option is by default equal to the value of the tmpdir system variable. When the slave SQL thread replicates a LOAD DATA INFILE statement, it extracts the file to be loaded from the relay log into temporary files, and then loads these into the table. If the file loaded on the master is huge, the temporary files on the slave are huge, too. Therefore, it might be advisable to use this option to tell the slave to put temporary files in a directory located in some filesystem that has a lot of available space. In that case, the relay logs are huge as well, so you might also want to use the `--relay-log` option to place the relay logs in that filesystem.

The directory specified by this option should be located in a disk-based filesystem (not a memory-based filesystem) because the temporary files used to replicate LOAD DATA INFILE must survive machine restarts. The directory also should not be one that is cleared by the operating system during the system startup process.

- `--slave-net-timeout=seconds`

The number of seconds to wait for more data from the master before the slave considers the connection broken, aborts the read, and tries to reconnect. The first retry occurs immediately after the timeout. The interval between retries is controlled by the `--master-connect-retry` option.

- `--slave-skip-errors=[err_code1,err_code2,...|all]`

Normally, replication stops when an error occurs on the slave. This gives you the opportunity to resolve the inconsistency in the data manually. This option tells the slave SQL thread to continue replication when a statement returns any of the errors listed in the option value.

Do not use this option unless you fully understand why you are getting errors. If there are no bugs in your replication setup and client programs, and no bugs in MySQL itself, an error that stops replication should never occur. Indiscriminate use of this option results in slaves becoming hopelessly out of synchrony with the master, with you having no idea why this has occurred.

For error codes, you should use the numbers provided by the error message in your slave error log and in the output of SHOW SLAVE STATUS.

You can also (but should not) use the very non-recommended value of all to cause the slave to ignore all error messages and keeps going regardless of what happens. Needless to say, if you use all, there are no guarantees regarding the integrity of your data. Please do not complain (or file bug reports) in this case if the slave's data is not anywhere close to what it is on the master. *You have been warned.*

Examples:

```
--slave-skip-errors=1062,1053
--slave-skip-errors=all
```

5.10 How Servers Evaluate Replication Rules

If a master server does not write a statement to its binary log, the statement is not replicated. If the server does log the statement, the statement is sent to all slaves and each slave determines whether to execute it or ignore it.

On the master side, decisions about which statements to log are based on the `--binlog-do-db` and `--binlog-ignore-db` options that control binary logging. For a description of the rules that servers use in evaluating these options, see Section 4.12.3, "The Binary Log."

On the slave side, decisions about whether to execute or ignore statements received from the master are made according to the `--replicate-*` options that the slave was started with. (See Section 5.9, "Replication Startup Options.") The slave evaluates these options using the following procedure, which first checks the database-level options and then the table-level options.

In the simplest case, when there are no `--replicate-*` options, the procedure yields the result that the slave executes all statements that it receives from the master. Otherwise, the result depends on the particular options given. In general, to make it easier to determine what effect an option set will have, it is recommended that you avoid mixing "do" and "ignore" options, or wildcard and non-wildcard options.

Stage 1. Check the database options.

At this stage, the slave checks whether there are any `--replicate-do-db` or `--replicate-ignore-db` options that specify database-specific conditions:

- *No*: Permit the statement and proceed to the table-checking stage.
- *Yes*: Test the options using the same rules as for the `--binlog-do-db` and `--binlog-ignore-db` options to determine whether to permit or ignore the statement. What is the result of the test?
  - *Permit*: Do not execute the statement immediately. Defer the decision and proceed to the table-checking stage.
  - *Ignore*: Ignore the statement and exit.

This stage can permit a statement for further option-checking, or cause it to be ignored. However, statements that are permitted at this stage are not actually executed yet. Instead, they pass to the following stage that checks the table options.

Stage 2. Check the table options.

First, as a preliminary condition, the slave checks whether statement-based replication is enabled. If so and the statement occurs within a stored function or (prior to MySQL 5.0.12) a stored procedure, execute the statement and exit. (Stored procedures are exempt from this test as of MySQL 5.0.12 because procedure logging occurs at the level of statements that are executed within the routine rather than at the CALL level. If row-based replication is enabled, the slave does not know whether a statement occurred within a stored function on the master, so this condition does not apply.)

Next, the slave checks for table options and evaluates them. If the server reaches this point, it executes all statements if there are no table options. If there are "do" table options, the statement must match one of them if it is to be executed; otherwise, it is ignored. If there are any "ignore" options, all statements are executed except those that match any `ignore` option. The following steps describe how this evaluation occurs in more detail.

1. Are there any `--replicate-*-table` options?

   - *No*: There are no table restrictions, so all statements match. Execute the statement and exit.

   - *Yes*: There are table restrictions. Evaluate the tables to be updated against them. There might be multiple tables to update, so loop through the following steps for each table looking for a matching option. In this case, the behavior depends on whether statement-based replication or row-based replication is enabled:

     - *Statement-based replication*: Proceed to the next step and begin evaluating the table options in the order shown (first the non-wild options, and then the wild options). Only tables that are to be updated are compared to the options. For example, if the statement is `INSERT INTO sales SELECT * FROM prices`, only `sales` is compared to the options. If several tables are to be updated (multiple-table statement), the first table that matches "do" or "ignore" wins. That is, the server checks the first table against the options. If no decision could be made, it checks the second table against the options, and so on.

     - *Row-based replication*: All table row changes are filtered individually. For multiple-table updates, each table is filtered separately according to the options. Some updates may be executed and some not, depending on the options and the changes to be made. Row-based replication correctly handles cases that would not replicate correctly with statement-based replication, as in this example, which assumes that tables in the `foo` database should be replicated:

       ```
       mysql> USE bar;
       mysql> INSERT INTO foo.sometable VALUES (1);
       ```

2. Are there any `--replicate-do-table` options?

   - *No*: Proceed to the next step.

   - *Yes*: Does the table match any of them?

     - *No*: Proceed to the next step.

     - *Yes*: Execute the statement and exit.

3. Are there any `--replicate-ignore-table` options?

   - *No*: Proceed to the next step.

   - *Yes*: Does the table match any of them?

     - *No*: Proceed to the next step.

     - *Yes*: Ignore the statement and exit.

4. Are there any `--replicate-wild-do-table` options?

   - *No*: Proceed to the next step.

   - *Yes*: Does the table match any of them?

     - *No*: Proceed to the next step.

     - *Yes*: Execute the statement and exit.

5. Are there any `--replicate-wild-ignore-table` options?

- *No*: Proceed to the next step.
- *Yes*: Does the table match any of them?
  - *No*: Proceed to the next step.
  - *Yes*: Ignore the statement and exit.

6. No `--replicate-*-table` option was matched. Is there another table to test against these options?

- *No*: We have now tested all tables to be updated and could not match any option. Are there `--replicate-do-table` or `--replicate-wild-do-table` options?
  - *No*: There were no "do" table options, so no explicit "do" match is required. Execute the statement and exit.
  - *Yes*: There were "do" table options, so the statement is executed only with an explicit match to one of them. Ignore the statement and exit.
- *Yes*: Loop.

Examples:

- No `--replicate-*` options at all

  The slave executes all statements that it receives from the master.

- `--replicate-*-db` options, but no table options

  The slave permits or ignores statements using the database options. Then it executes all statements permitted by those options because there are no table restrictions.

- `--replicate-*-table` options, but no database options

  All statements are permitted at the database-checking stage because there are no database conditions. The slave executes or ignores statements based on the table options.

- A mix of database and table options

  The slave permits or ignores statements using the database options. Then it evaluates all statements permitted by those options according to the table options. In some cases, this process can yield what might seem a counterintuitive result. Consider the following set of options:

```
[mysqld]
replicate-do-db    = db1
replicate-do-table = db2.mytbl2
```

  Suppose that db1 is the default database and the slave receives this statement:

```
INSERT INTO mytbl1 VALUES(1,2,3);
```

  The database is db1, which matches the `--replicate-do-db` option at the database-checking stage. The algorithm then proceeds to the table-checking stage. If there were no table options, the statement would be executed. However, because the options include a "do" table option, the statement must match if it is to be executed. The statement does not match, so it is ignored. (The same would happen for any table in db1.)

5.11 Replication FAQ

Q: How do I configure a slave if the master is running and I do not want to stop it?

A: There are several possibilities. If you have taken a snapshot backup of the master at some point and recorded the binary log filename and offset (from the output of SHOW MASTER STATUS) corresponding to the snapshot, use the following procedure:

1. Make sure that the slave is assigned a unique server ID.

2. Execute the following statement on the slave, filling in appropriate values for each option:

```
mysql> CHANGE MASTER TO
    ->        MASTER_HOST='master_host_name',
    ->        MASTER_USER='master_user_name',
    ->        MASTER_PASSWORD='master_pass',
    ->        MASTER_LOG_FILE='recorded_log_file_name',
    ->        MASTER_LOG_POS=recorded_log_position;
```

3. Execute START SLAVE on the slave.

If you do not have a backup of the master server, here is a quick procedure for creating one. All steps should be performed on the master host.

1. Issue this statement to acquire a global read lock:

```
mysql> FLUSH TABLES WITH READ LOCK;
```

2. With the lock still in place, execute this command (or a variation of it):

```
shell> tar zcf /tmp/backup.tar.gz /var/lib/mysql
```

3. Issue this statement and record the output, which you will need later:

```
mysql> SHOW MASTER STATUS;
```

4. Release the lock:

```
mysql> UNLOCK TABLES;
```

An alternative to using the preceding procedure to make a binary copy is to make an SQL dump of the master. To do this, you can use mysqldump --master-data on your master and later load the SQL dump into your slave. However, this is slower than making a binary copy.

Regardless of which of the two methods you use, afterward follow the instructions for the case when you have a snapshot and have recorded the log filename and offset. You can use the same snapshot to set up several slaves. Once you have the snapshot of the master, you can wait to set up a slave as long as the binary logs of the master are left intact. The two practical limitations on the length of time you can wait are the amount of disk space available to retain binary logs on the master and the length of time it takes the slave to catch up.

You can also use LOAD DATA FROM MASTER. This is a convenient statement that transfers a snapshot to the slave and adjusts the log filename and offset all at once. Be warned, however, that it works only for MyISAM tables and it may hold a read lock for a long time. It is not yet implemented as efficiently as we would like. If you have large tables, the preferred method is still to make a binary snapshot on the master server after executing FLUSH TABLES WITH READ LOCK.

Q: Does the slave need to be connected to the master all the time?

A: No, it does not. The slave can go down or stay disconnected for hours or even days, and then reconnect and catch up on updates. For example, you can set up a master/slave relationship over a dial-up link where the link is up only sporadically and for short periods of time. The implication of this is that, at any given time, the slave is not guaranteed to be in synchrony with the master unless you take some special measures.

Q: How do I know how late a slave is compared to the master? In other words, how do I know the date of the last statement replicated by the slave?

A: You can read the Seconds_Behind_Master column in SHOW SLAVE STATUS. See Section 5.4, "Replication Implementation Details."

When the slave SQL thread executes an event read from the master, it modifies its own time to the event timestamp. (This is why TIMESTAMP is well replicated.) In the Time column in the output of SHOW PROCESSLIST, the number of seconds displayed for the slave SQL thread is the number of seconds between the timestamp of the last replicated event and the real time of the slave machine. You can use this to determine the date of the last replicated event. Note that if your slave has been disconnected from the master for one hour, and then reconnects, you may immediately see Time values like 3600 for the slave SQL thread in SHOW PROCESSLIST. This is because the slave is executing statements that are one hour old.

Q: How do I force the master to block updates until the slave catches up?

A: Use the following procedure:

1. On the master, execute these statements:

   ```
   mysql> FLUSH TABLES WITH READ LOCK;
   mysql> SHOW MASTER STATUS;
   ```

   Record the replication coordinates (the log filename and offset) from the output of the SHOW statement.

2. On the slave, issue the following statement, where the arguments to the MASTER_POS_WAIT() function are the replication coordinate values obtained in the previous step:

   ```
   mysql> SELECT MASTER_POS_WAIT('log_name', log_offset);
   ```

   The SELECT statement blocks until the slave reaches the specified log file and offset. At that point, the slave is in synchrony with the master and the statement returns.

3. On the master, issue the following statement to allow the master to begin processing updates again:

   ```
   mysql> UNLOCK TABLES;
   ```

Q: What issues should I be aware of when setting up two-way replication?

A: MySQL replication currently does not support any locking protocol between master and slave to guarantee the atomicity of a distributed (cross-server) update. In other words, it is possible for client A to make an update to co-master 1, and in the meantime, before it propagates to co-master 2, client B could make an update to co-master 2 that makes the update of client A work differently than it did on co-master 1. Thus, when the update of client A makes it to co-master 2, it produces tables that are different from what you have on co-master 1, even after all the updates from co-master 2 have also propagated. This means that you should not chain two servers together in a two-way replication relationship unless you are sure that your updates can safely happen in any order, or unless you take care of mis-ordered updates somehow in the client code.

You should also realize that two-way replication actually does not improve performance very much (if at all) as far as updates are concerned. Each server must do the same number of updates, just as you would have a single server do. The only difference is that there is a little less lock contention, because the updates originating on another server are serialized in one slave thread. Even this benefit might be offset by network delays.

Q: How can I use replication to improve performance of my system?

A: You should set up one server as the master and direct all writes to it. Then configure as many slaves as you have the budget and rackspace for, and distribute the reads among the master and the slaves. You can also start the slaves with the `--skip-innodb`, `--skip-bdb`, `--low-priority-updates`, and `--delay-key-write=ALL` options to get speed improvements on the slave end. In this case, the slave uses non-transactional `MyISAM` tables instead of `InnoDB` and `BDB` tables to get more speed by eliminating transactional overhead.

Q: What should I do to prepare client code in my own applications to use performance-enhancing replication?

A: If the part of your code that is responsible for database access has been properly abstracted/modularized, converting it to run with a replicated setup should be very smooth and easy. Change the implementation of your database access to send all writes to the master, and to send reads to either the master or a slave. If your code does not have this level of abstraction, setting up a replicated system gives you the opportunity and motivation to it clean up. Start by creating a wrapper library or module that implements the following functions:

- `safe_writer_connect()`
- `safe_reader_connect()`
- `safe_reader_statement()`
- `safe_writer_statement()`

`safe_` in each function name means that the function takes care of handling all error conditions. You can use different names for the functions. The important thing is to have a unified interface for connecting for reads, connecting for writes, doing a read, and doing a write.

Then convert your client code to use the wrapper library. This may be a painful and scary process at first, but it pays off in the long run. All applications that use the approach just described are able to take advantage of a master/slave configuration, even one involving multiple slaves. The code is much easier to maintain, and adding troubleshooting options is trivial. You need modify only one or two functions; for example, to log how long each statement took, or which statement among those issued gave you an error.

If you have written a lot of code, you may want to automate the conversion task by using the `replace` utility that comes with standard MySQL distributions, or write your own conversion script. Ideally, your code uses consistent programming style conventions. If not, you are probably better off rewriting it anyway, or at least going through and manually regularizing it to use a consistent style.

Q: When and how much can MySQL replication improve the performance of my system?

A: MySQL replication is most beneficial for a system that processes frequent reads and infrequent writes. In theory, by using a single-master/multiple-slave setup, you can scale the system by adding more slaves until you either run out of network bandwidth, or your update load grows to the point that the master cannot handle it.

To determine how many slaves you can use before the added benefits begin to level out, and how much you can improve performance of your site, you need to know your query patterns, and to determine empirically by benchmarking the relationship between the throughput for reads (reads per second, or `reads`) and for writes (`writes`) on a typical master and a typical slave. The example here shows a rather simplified calculation of what you can get with replication for a hypothetical system.

Let's say that system load consists of 10% writes and 90% reads, and we have determined by benchmarking that reads is $1200 - 2 \times$ `writes`. In other words, the system can do 1,200 reads per second with no writes, the average write is twice as slow as the average read, and the relationship is linear. Let us suppose that the master and each slave have the same capacity, and that we have one master and N slaves. Then we have for each server (master or slave):

`reads = 1200 - 2 X writes`

`reads = 9 X writes / (N + 1)` (reads are split, but writes go to all servers)

`9 X writes / (N + 1) + 2 X writes = 1200`

`writes = 1200 / (2 + 9/(N+1))`

The last equation indicates the maximum number of writes for N slaves, given a maximum possible read rate of 1,200 per minute and a ratio of nine reads per write.

This analysis yields the following conclusions:

- If $N = 0$ (which means we have no replication), our system can handle about 1200/11 = 109 writes per second.
- If $N = 1$, we get up to 184 writes per second.
- If $N = 8$, we get up to 400 writes per second.

- If $N = 17$, we get up to 480 writes per second.
- Eventually, as N approaches infinity (and our budget negative infinity), we can get very close to 600 writes per second, increasing system throughput about 5.5 times. However, with only eight servers, we increase it nearly four times.

Note that these computations assume infinite network bandwidth and neglect several other factors that could be significant on your system. In many cases, you may not be able to perform a computation similar to the one just shown that accurately predicts what will happen on your system if you add N replication slaves. However, answering the following questions should help you decide whether and by how much replication will improve the performance of your system:

- What is the read/write ratio on your system?
- How much more write load can one server handle if you reduce the reads?
- For how many slaves do you have bandwidth available on your network?

Q: How can I use replication to provide redundancy or high availability?

A: With the currently available features, you would have to set up a master and a slave (or several slaves), and to write a script that monitors the master to check whether it is up. Then instruct your applications and the slaves to change master in case of failure. Some suggestions:

- To tell a slave to change its master, use the CHANGE MASTER TO statement.
- A good way to keep your applications informed as to the location of the master is by having a dynamic DNS entry for the master. With bind you can use nsupdate to dynamically update your DNS.
- Run your slaves with the --log-bin option and without --log-slave-updates. In this way, the slave is ready to become a master as soon as you issue STOP SLAVE; RESET MASTER, and CHANGE MASTER TO statement on the other slaves. For example, assume that you have the following setup:

In this diagram, M means the master, S the slaves, WC the clients issuing database writes and reads; clients that issue only database reads are not represented, because they need not switch. S1, S2, and S3 are slaves running with --log-bin and without --log-slave-updates. Because updates received by a slave from the master are not logged in the binary log unless --log-slave-updates is specified, the binary log on each slave is empty initially. If for some reason M becomes unavailable, you can pick one of the slaves to become the new master. For example, if you pick S1, all WC should be redirected to S1, which will log updates to its binary log. S2 and S3 should then replicate from S1.

The reason for running the slave without --log-slave-updates is to prevent slaves from receiving updates twice in case you cause one of the slaves to become the new master. Suppose that S1 has --log-slave-updates enabled. Then it will write updates that it receives from M to its own binary log. When S2 changes from M to S1 as its master, it may receive updates from S1 that it has already received from M.

Make sure that all slaves have processed any statements in their relay log. On each slave, issue STOP SLAVE IO_THREAD, and then check the output of SHOW PROCESSLIST until you see Has read all relay log. When this is true for all slaves, they can be reconfigured to the new setup. On the slave S1 being promoted to become the master, issue STOP SLAVE and RESET MASTER.

On the other slaves S2 and S3, use STOP SLAVE and CHANGE MASTER TO MASTER_HOST='S1' (where 'S1' represents the real hostname of S1). To CHANGE MASTER, add all information about how to connect to S1 from S2 or S3 (*user*, *password*, *port*). In CHANGE MASTER, there is no need to specify the name of S1's binary log or binary log position to read from: We know it is the first binary log and position 4, which are the defaults for CHANGE MASTER. Finally, use START SLAVE on S2 and S3.

Then instruct all WC to direct their statements to S1. From that point on, all update statements sent by WC to S1 are written to the binary log of S1, which then contains every update statement sent to S1 since M died.

The result is this configuration:

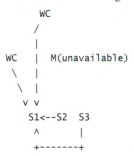

```
      WC
     /
     |
 WC  |   M(unavailable)
  \  |
   \ |
    v v
    S1<--S2   S3
    ^          |
    +-------+
```

When M is up again, you must issue on it the same CHANGE MASTER as that issued on S2 and S3, so that M becomes a slave of S1 and picks up all the WC writes that it missed while it was down. To make M a master again (because it is the most powerful machine, for example), use the preceding procedure as if S1 were unavailable and M is to be the new master. During this procedure, do not forget to run RESET MASTER on M before making S1, S2, and S3 slaves of M. Otherwise, they may pick up old WC writes from before the point at which M became unavailable.

Note that there is no synchronization between the different slaves to a master. Some slaves might be ahead of others. This means that the concept outlined in the previous example might not work. In practice, however, the relay logs of different slaves will most likely not be far behind the master, so it would work, anyway (but there is no guarantee).

Q: How do I tell whether a master server is using statement-based or row-based binary logging format?

A: Check the value of the `binlog_format` system variable:

```
mysql> SHOW VARIABLES LIKE 'binlog_format';
```

The value will be either STATEMENT or ROW.

Q: How do I tell a slave to use row-based replication?

A: Slaves automatically know which format to use.

Q: Does replication work on mixed operating systems (for example, the master runs on Linux while slaves run on Mac OS X and Windows)?

A: Yes.

Q: Does replication work on mixed hardware architectures (for example, the master runs on a 64-bit machine while slaves run on 32-bit machines)?

A: Yes.

5.12 Comparison of Statement-Based Versus Row-Based Replication

Each binary logging format has advantages and disadvantages. This section summarizes them to give you a better basis for choosing the format most appropriate for your situation.

Advantages of statement-based replication:

- Proven technology that has existed in MySQL since 3.23.
- Smaller log files. When updates or deletes affect many rows, *much* smaller log files. Smaller log files require less storage space and are faster to back up.
- Log files contain all statements that made any changes, so they can be used to audit the database.
- Log files can be used for point-in-time recovery, not just for replication purposes. See Section 4.10.3, "Point-in-Time Recovery."
- A slave can be a newer version of MySQL with a different row structure.

Disadvantages of statement-based replication:

- Not all UPDATE statements can be replicated: Any non-deterministic behavior (for example, when using random functions in an SQL statement) is hard to replicate when using statement-based replication. For statements that use a non-deterministic user-defined function (UDF), it is not possible to replicate the result using statement-based replication, whereas row-based replication will just replicate the value returned by the UDF.
- Statements cannot be replicated properly if they use a UDF that is non-deterministic (its value depends on things other than the given parameters).

- Statements that use one of the following functions cannot be replicated properly:
  - `LOAD_FILE()`
  - `UUID()`
  - `USER()`
  - `FOUND_ROWS()`

  All other functions are replicated correctly (including `RAND()`, `NOW()`, `LOAD DATA INFILE`, and so forth).

- `INSERT ... SELECT` requires a greater number of row-level locks than with row-based replication.

- `UPDATE` statements that require a table scan (because no index is used in the `WHERE` clause) must lock a greater number of rows than with row-based replication.

- For `InnoDB`: An `INSERT` statement that uses `AUTO_INCREMENT` blocks other non-conflicting `INSERT` statements.

- Slower to apply data on slave for complex queries.

- Stored functions (not stored procedures) will execute with the same `NOW()` value as the calling statement. (This may be regarded both as a bad thing and a good thing.)

- Deterministic UDFs must be applied on the slaves.

- When getting something wrong on the slave, the difference between master and slave will grow with time.

- Tables have to be (almost) identical on master and slave.

Advantages of row-based replication:

- Everything can be replicated. This is the safest form of replication. Note that currently, DDL (data definition language) statements such as `CREATE TABLE` are replicated using statement-based replication, while DML (data manipulation language) statements, as well as `GRANT` and `REVOKE` statements, are replicated using row-based-replication. For statements like `CREATE ... SELECT`, a `CREATE` statement is generated from the table definition and replicated statement-based, while the row insertions are replicated row-based.

- The technology is the same as most other database management systems; knowledge about other systems transfers to MySQL.

- In many cases, it is faster to apply data on the slave for tables that have primary keys.

- Fewer locks are needed (and thus higher concurrency) on the master for the following types of statements:
  - `INSERT ... SELECT`
  - `INSERT` statements with `AUTO_INCREMENT`
  - `UPDATE` or `DELETE` statements with `WHERE` clauses that don't use keys or don't change most of the examined rows

- Fewer locks on the slave for any INSERT, UPDATE, or DELETE statement.
- It's possible to add multiple threads to apply data on the slave in the future (works better on SMP machines).

Disadvantages of row-based replication:

- Larger log files (much larger in some cases).
- Binary log will contain data for large statements that were rolled back.
- When using row-based replication to replicate a statement (for example, an UPDATE or DELETE statement), each changed row must be written to the binary log. In contrast, when using statement-based replication, only the statement is written to the binary log. If the statement changes many rows, row-based replication may write significantly more data to the binary log. In these cases the binary log will be locked for a longer time to write the data, which may cause concurrency problems.
- Deterministic UDFs that generate large BLOB values will be notably slower to replicate.
- You cannot examine the logs to see what statements were executed.
- You cannot see on the slave what statements were received from the master and executed.
- When making a bulk operation that includes non-transactional storage engines, changes are applied as the statement executes. With row-based replication logging, this means that the binary log is written while the statement is running. On the master, this doesn't provide any problems with concurrency, because tables are locked until the bulk operation terminates. On the slave server, however, tables aren't locked while the slave applies changes, because it doesn't know that those changes are part of a bulk operation.

  In that scenario, if you retrieve data from a table on the master (for example, SELECT * FROM table_name), the server will wait for the bulk operation to complete before executing the SELECT statement, because the table is read-locked. On the slave, the server won't wait (because there is no lock). This means that until the "bulk operation" on the slave has completed you will get different results for the same SELECT query on the master and on the slave.

  This behavior will eventually change, but until it does, you should probably use statement-based replication in a scenario like this.

5.13 Troubleshooting Replication

If you have followed the instructions, and your replication setup is not working, the first thing to do is *check the error log for messages*. Many users have lost time by not doing this soon enough after encountering problems.

If you cannot tell from the error log what the problem was, try the following techniques:

- Verify that the master has binary logging enabled by issuing a SHOW MASTER STATUS statement. If logging is enabled, Position is non-zero. If binary logging is not enabled, verify that you are running the master with the --log-bin and --server-id options.

- Verify that the slave is running. Use SHOW SLAVE STATUS to check whether the Slave_IO_Running and Slave_SQL_Running values are both Yes. If not, verify the options that were used when starting the slave server. For example, --skip-slave-start prevents the slave threads from starting until you issue a START SLAVE statement.

- If the slave is running, check whether it established a connection to the master. Use SHOW PROCESSLIST, find the I/O and SQL threads and check their State column to see what they display. See Section 5.4, "Replication Implementation Details." If the I/O thread state says Connecting to master, verify the privileges for the replication user on the master, the master hostname, your DNS setup, whether the master is actually running, and whether it is reachable from the slave.

- If the slave was running previously but has stopped, the reason usually is that some statement that succeeded on the master failed on the slave. This should never happen if you have taken a proper snapshot of the master, and never modified the data on the slave outside of the slave thread. If the slave stops unexpectedly, it is a bug or you have encountered one of the known replication limitations described in Section 5.8, "Replication Features and Known Problems." If it is a bug, see Section 5.14, "How to Report Replication Bugs or Problems," for instructions on how to report it.

- If a statement that succeeded on the master refuses to run on the slave, try the following procedure if it is not feasible to do a full database resynchronization by deleting the slave's databases and copying a new snapshot from the master:

  1. Determine whether the affected table on the slave is different from the master table. Try to understand how this happened. Then make the slave's table identical to the master's and run START SLAVE.

  2. If the preceding step does not work or does not apply, try to understand whether it would be safe to make the update manually (if needed) and then ignore the next statement from the master.

  3. If you decide that you can skip the next statement from the master, issue the following statements:

     ```
     mysql> SET GLOBAL SQL_SLAVE_SKIP_COUNTER = N;
     mysql> START SLAVE;
     ```

     The value of N should be 1 if the next statement from the master does not use AUTO_INCREMENT or LAST_INSERT_ID(). Otherwise, the value should be 2. The reason for using a value of 2 for statements that use AUTO_INCREMENT or LAST_INSERT_ID() is that they take two events in the binary log of the master.

  4. If you are sure that the slave started out perfectly synchronized with the master, and that no one has updated the tables involved outside of the slave thread, presumably the discrepancy is the result of a bug. If you are running the most recent version of MySQL, please report the problem. If you are running an older version, try upgrading to the latest production release to determine whether the problem persists.

5.14 How to Report Replication Bugs or Problems

When you have determined that there is no user error involved, and replication still either does not work at all or is unstable, it is time to send us a bug report. We need to obtain as much information as possible from you to be able to track down the bug. Please spend some time and effort in preparing a good bug report.

If you have a repeatable test case that demonstrates the bug, please enter it into our bugs database using the instructions given in Section 1.8, "How to Report Bugs or Problems." If you have a "phantom" problem (one that you cannot duplicate at will), use the following procedure:

1. Verify that no user error is involved. For example, if you update the slave outside of the slave thread, the data goes out of synchrony, and you can have unique key violations on updates. In this case, the slave thread stops and waits for you to clean up the tables manually to bring them into synchrony. *This is not a replication problem. It is a problem of outside interference causing replication to fail.*

2. Run the slave with the `--log-slave-updates` and `--log-bin` options. These options cause the slave to log the updates that it receives from the master into its own binary logs.

3. Save all evidence before resetting the replication state. If we have no information or only sketchy information, it becomes difficult or impossible for us to track down the problem. The evidence you should collect is:

   - All binary logs from the master
   - All binary logs from the slave
   - The output of SHOW MASTER STATUS from the master at the time you discovered the problem
   - The output of SHOW SLAVE STATUS from the slave at the time you discovered the problem
   - Error logs from the master and the slave

4. Use `mysqlbinlog` to examine the binary logs. The following should be helpful to find the problem statement. *log_pos* and *log_file* are the `Master_Log_File` and `Read_Master_Log_Pos` values from SHOW SLAVE STATUS.

   ```
   shell> mysqlbinlog -j log_pos log_file | head
   ```

After you have collected the evidence for the problem, try to isolate it as a separate test case first. Then enter the problem with as much information as possible into our bugs database using the instructions at Section 1.8, "How to Report Bugs or Problems."

5.15 Auto-Increment in Multiple-Master Replication

When multiple servers are configured as replication masters, special steps must be taken to prevent key collisions when using AUTO_INCREMENT columns, otherwise multiple masters may attempt to use the same AUTO_INCREMENT value when inserting rows.

The auto_increment_increment and auto_increment_offset system variables help to accommodate multiple-master replication with AUTO_INCREMENT columns. Each of these variables has a default and minimum value of 1, and a maximum value of 65,535. They were introduced in MySQL 5.0.2.

These two variables effect AUTO_INCREMENT column behavior as follows:

- auto_increment_increment controls the increment between successive AUTO_INCREMENT values.
- auto_increment_offset determines the starting point for AUTO_INCREMENT column values.

By choosing non-conflicting values for these variables on different masters, servers in a multiple-master configuration will not use conflicting AUTO_INCREMENT values when inserting new rows into the same table. To set up *N* master servers, set the variables like this:

- Set auto_increment_increment to *N* on each master.
- Set each of the *N* masters to have a different auto_increment_offset, using the values 1, 2, ..., *N*.

For additional information about auto_increment_increment and auto_increment_offset, see Section 4.2.2, "Server System Variables."

6

Optimization

Optimization is a complex task because ultimately it requires understanding of the entire system to be optimized. Although it may be possible to perform some local optimizations with little knowledge of your system or application, the more optimal you want your system to become, the more you must know about it.

This chapter tries to explain and give some examples of different ways to optimize MySQL. Remember, however, that there are always additional ways to make the system even faster, although they may require increasing effort to achieve.

6.1 Optimization Overview

The most important factor in making a system fast is its basic design. You must also know what kinds of processing your system is doing, and what its bottlenecks are. In most cases, system bottlenecks arise from these sources:

- Disk seeks. It takes time for the disk to find a piece of data. With modern disks, the mean time for this is usually lower than 10ms, so we can in theory do about 100 seeks a second. This time improves slowly with new disks and is very hard to optimize for a single table. The way to optimize seek time is to distribute the data onto more than one disk.

- Disk reading and writing. When the disk is at the correct position, we need to read the data. With modern disks, one disk delivers at least 10–20MB/s throughput. This is easier to optimize than seeks because you can read in parallel from multiple disks.

- CPU cycles. When we have the data in main memory, we need to process it to get our result. Having small tables compared to the amount of memory is the most common limiting factor. But with small tables, speed is usually not the problem.

- Memory bandwidth. When the CPU needs more data than can fit in the CPU cache, main memory bandwidth becomes a bottleneck. This is an uncommon bottleneck for most systems, but one to be aware of.

6.1.1 MySQL Design Limitations and Tradeoffs

When using the MyISAM storage engine, MySQL uses extremely fast table locking that allows multiple readers or a single writer. The biggest problem with this storage engine occurs when you have a steady stream of mixed updates and slow selects on a single table. If this is a problem for certain tables, you can use another storage engine for them. See Chapter 8, "Storage Engines and Table Types."

MySQL can work with both transactional and non-transactional tables. To make it easier to work smoothly with non-transactional tables (which cannot roll back if something goes wrong), MySQL has the following rules. Note that these rules apply *only* when not running in strict SQL mode or if you use the IGNORE specifier for INSERT or UPDATE.

- All columns have default values.
- If you insert an inappropriate or out-of-range value into a column, MySQL sets the column to the "best possible value" instead of reporting an error. For numerical values, this is 0, the smallest possible value or the largest possible value. For strings, this is either the empty string or as much of the string as can be stored in the column.
- All calculated expressions return a value that can be used instead of signaling an error condition. For example, 1/0 returns NULL.

To change the preceding behaviors, you can enable stricter data handling by setting the server SQL mode appropriately. For more information about data handling, see Section 1.9.6, "How MySQL Deals with Constraints," and Section 4.2.5, "The Server SQL Mode."

6.1.2 Designing Applications for Portability

Because all SQL servers implement different parts of standard SQL, it takes work to write portable database applications. It is very easy to achieve portability for very simple selects and inserts, but becomes more difficult the more capabilities you require. If you want an application that is fast with many database systems, it becomes even more difficult.

All database systems have some weak points. That is, they have different design compromises that lead to different behavior.

To make a complex application portable, you need to determine which SQL servers it must work with, and then determine what features those servers support. You can use the MySQL crash-me program to find functions, types, and limits that you can use with a selection of database servers. crash-me does not check for every possible feature, but it is still reasonably comprehensive, performing about 450 tests. An example of the type of information crash-me can provide is that you should not use column names that are longer than 18 characters if you want to be able to use Informix or DB2.

The crash-me program and the MySQL benchmarks are all very database independent. By taking a look at how they are written, you can get a feeling for what you must do to make your own applications database independent. The programs can be found in the sql-bench directory of MySQL source distributions. They are written in Perl and use the DBI database interface. Use of DBI in itself solves part of the portability problem because it provides database-independent access methods. See Section 6.1.4, "The MySQL Benchmark Suite."

If you strive for database independence, you need to get a good feeling for each SQL server's bottlenecks. For example, MySQL is very fast in retrieving and updating rows for `MyISAM` tables, but has a problem in mixing slow readers and writers on the same table. Oracle, on the other hand, has a big problem when you try to access rows that you have recently updated (until they are flushed to disk). Transactional database systems in general are not very good at generating summary tables from log tables, because in this case row locking is almost useless.

To make your application *really* database independent, you should define an easily extendable interface through which you manipulate your data. For example, C++ is available on most systems, so it makes sense to use a C++ class-based interface to the databases.

If you use some feature that is specific to a given database system (such as the `REPLACE` statement, which is specific to MySQL), you should implement the same feature for other SQL servers by coding an alternative method. Although the alternative might be slower, it enables the other servers to perform the same tasks.

With MySQL, you can use the `/*! */` syntax to add MySQL-specific keywords to a statement. The code inside `/* */` is treated as a comment (and ignored) by most other SQL servers.

If high performance is more important than exactness, as for some Web applications, it is possible to create an application layer that caches all results to give you even higher performance. By letting old results expire after a while, you can keep the cache reasonably fresh. This provides a method to handle high load spikes, in which case you can dynamically increase the cache size and set the expiration timeout higher until things get back to normal.

In this case, the table creation information should contain information about the initial cache size and how often the table should normally be refreshed.

An attractive alternative to implementing an application cache is to use the MySQL query cache. By enabling the query cache, the server handles the details of determining whether a query result can be reused. This simplifies your application. See Section 4.14, "The MySQL Query Cache."

6.1.3 What We Have Used MySQL For

This section describes an early application for MySQL.

During MySQL initial development, the features of MySQL were made to fit our largest customer, which handled data warehousing for a couple of the largest retailers in Sweden.

From all stores, we got weekly summaries of all bonus card transactions, and were expected to provide useful information for the store owners to help them find how their advertising campaigns were affecting their own customers.

The volume of data was quite huge (about seven million summary transactions per month), and we had data for 4–10 years that we needed to present to the users. We got weekly requests from our customers, who wanted instant access to new reports from this data.

We solved this problem by storing all information per month in compressed "transaction tables." We had a set of simple macros that generated summary tables grouped by different criteria (product group, customer ID, store, and so on) from the tables in which the transactions were stored. The reports were Web pages that were dynamically generated by a small Perl script. This script parsed a Web page, executed the SQL statements in it, and inserted the results. We would have used PHP or mod_perl instead, but they were not available at the time.

For graphical data, we wrote a simple tool in C that could process SQL query results and produce GIF images based on those results. This tool also was dynamically executed from the Perl script that parses the Web pages.

In most cases, a new report could be created simply by copying an existing script and modifying the SQL query that it used. In some cases, we needed to add more columns to an existing summary table or generate a new one. This also was quite simple because we kept all transaction-storage tables on disk. (This amounted to about 50GB of transaction tables and 200GB of other customer data.)

We also let our customers access the summary tables directly with ODBC so that the advanced users could experiment with the data themselves.

This system worked well and we had no problems handling the data with quite modest Sun Ultra SPARCstation hardware (2×200MHz). Eventually the system was migrated to Linux.

6.1.4 The MySQL Benchmark Suite

This benchmark suite is meant to tell any user what operations a given SQL implementation performs well or poorly. You can get a good idea for how the benchmarks work by looking at the code and results in the sql-bench directory in any MySQL source distribution.

Note that this benchmark is single-threaded, so it measures the minimum time for the operations performed. We plan to add multi-threaded tests to the benchmark suite in the future.

To use the benchmark suite, the following requirements must be satisfied:

- The benchmark suite is provided with MySQL source distributions. You can either download a released distribution from http://dev.mysql.com/downloads/, or use the current development source tree. (See Section 2.8.3, "Installing from the Development Source Tree.")

- The benchmark scripts are written in Perl and use the Perl DBI module to access database servers, so DBI must be installed. You also need the server-specific DBD drivers for each of the servers you want to test. For example, to test MySQL, PostgreSQL, and DB2, you must have the DBD::mysql, DBD::Pg, and DBD::DB2 modules installed. See Section 2.13, "Perl Installation Notes."

After you obtain a MySQL source distribution, you can find the benchmark suite located in its sql-bench directory. To run the benchmark tests, build MySQL, and then change location into the sql-bench directory and execute the run-all-tests script:

```
shell> cd sql-bench
shell> perl run-all-tests --server=server_name
```

server_name should be the name of one of the supported servers. To get a list of all options and supported servers, invoke this command:

```
shell> perl run-all-tests --help
```

The crash-me script also is located in the sql-bench directory. crash-me tries to determine what features a database system supports and what its capabilities and limitations are by actually running queries. For example, it determines:

- What data types are supported
- How many indexes are supported
- What functions are supported
- How big a query can be
- How big a VARCHAR column can be

You can find the results from crash-me for many different database servers at http://dev.mysql.com/tech-resources/crash-me.php. For more information about benchmark results, visit http://dev.mysql.com/tech-resources/benchmarks/.

6.1.5 Using Your Own Benchmarks

You should definitely benchmark your application and database to find out where the bottlenecks are. After fixing one bottleneck (or by replacing it with a "dummy" module), you can proceed to identify the next bottleneck. Even if the overall performance for your application currently is acceptable, you should at least make a plan for each bottleneck and decide how to solve it if someday you really need the extra performance.

For examples of portable benchmark programs, look at those in the MySQL benchmark suite. See Section 6.1.4, "The MySQL Benchmark Suite." You can take any program from this suite and modify it for your own needs. By doing this, you can try different solutions to your problem and test which really is fastest for you.

Another free benchmark suite is the Open Source Database Benchmark, available at http://osdb.sourceforge.net/.

It is very common for a problem to occur only when the system is very heavily loaded. We have had many customers who contact us when they have a (tested) system in production and have encountered load problems. In most cases, performance problems turn out to be due to issues of basic database design (for example, table scans are not good under high load) or problems with the operating system or libraries. Most of the time, these problems would be much easier to fix if the systems were not already in production.

To avoid problems like this, you should put some effort into benchmarking your whole application under the worst possible load. You can use Super Smack, available at http://jeremy.zawodny.com/mysql/super-smack/. As suggested by its name, it can bring a system to its knees, so make sure to use it only on your development systems.

6.2 Optimizing SELECT and Other Statements

First, one factor affects all statements: The more complex your permissions setup, the more overhead you have. Using simpler permissions when you issue GRANT statements enables MySQL to reduce permission-checking overhead when clients execute statements. For example, if you do not grant any table-level or column-level privileges, the server need not ever check the contents of the tables_priv and columns_priv tables. Similarly, if you place no resource limits on any accounts, the server does not have to perform resource counting. If you have a very high statement-processing load, it may be worth the time to use a simplified grant structure to reduce permission-checking overhead.

If your problem is with a specific MySQL expression or function, you can perform a timing test by invoking the BENCHMARK() function using the mysql client program. Its syntax is BENCHMARK(loop_count,expression). The return value is always zero, but mysql prints a line displaying approximately how long the statement took to execute. For example:

```
mysql> SELECT BENCHMARK(1000000,1+1);
+------------------------+
| BENCHMARK(1000000,1+1) |
+------------------------+
|                      0 |
+------------------------+
1 row in set (0.32 sec)
```

This result was obtained on a Pentium II 400MHz system. It shows that MySQL can execute 1,000,000 simple addition expressions in 0.32 seconds on that system.

All MySQL functions should be highly optimized, but there may be some exceptions. BENCHMARK() is an excellent tool for finding out if some function is a problem for your queries.

6.2.1 Optimizing Queries with EXPLAIN

EXPLAIN tbl_name

Or:

EXPLAIN [EXTENDED] SELECT select_options

The EXPLAIN statement can be used either as a synonym for DESCRIBE or as a way to obtain information about how MySQL executes a SELECT statement:

- EXPLAIN tbl_name is synonymous with DESCRIBE tbl_name or SHOW COLUMNS FROM tbl_name.
- When you precede a SELECT statement with the keyword EXPLAIN, MySQL displays information from the optimizer about the query execution plan. That is, MySQL explains how it would process the SELECT, including information about how tables are joined and in which order.

This section describes the second use of EXPLAIN for obtaining query execution plan information. For a description of the DESCRIBE and SHOW COLUMNS statements, see the "MySQL Language Reference."

With the help of EXPLAIN, you can see where you should add indexes to tables to get a faster SELECT that uses indexes to find rows. You can also use EXPLAIN to check whether the optimizer joins the tables in an optimal order. To force the optimizer to use a join order corresponding to the order in which the tables are named in the SELECT statement, begin the statement with SELECT STRAIGHT_JOIN rather than just SELECT.

If you have a problem with indexes not being used when you believe that they should be, you should run ANALYZE TABLE to update table statistics, such as cardinality of keys, that can affect the choices the optimizer makes.

EXPLAIN returns a row of information for each table used in the SELECT statement. The tables are listed in the output in the order that MySQL would read them while processing the query. MySQL resolves all joins using a *single-sweep multi-join* method. This means that MySQL reads a row from the first table, and then finds a matching row in the second table, the third table, and so on. When all tables are processed, MySQL outputs the selected columns and backtracks through the table list until a table is found for which there are more matching rows. The next row is read from this table and the process continues with the next table.

When the EXTENDED keyword is used, EXPLAIN produces extra information that can be viewed by issuing a SHOW WARNINGS statement following the EXPLAIN statement. This information displays how the optimizer qualifies table and column names in the SELECT statement, what the SELECT looks like after the application of rewriting and optimization rules, and possibly other notes about the optimization process.

Each output row from EXPLAIN provides information about one table, and each row contains the following columns:

- id

  The SELECT identifier. This is the sequential number of the SELECT within the query.

- select_type

  The type of SELECT, which can be any of those shown in the following table:

SIMPLE	Simple SELECT (not using UNION or subqueries)
PRIMARY	Outermost SELECT
UNION	Second or later SELECT statement in a UNION
DEPENDENT UNION	Second or later SELECT statement in a UNION, dependent on outer query
UNION RESULT	Result of a UNION
SUBQUERY	First SELECT in subquery
DEPENDENT SUBQUERY	First SELECT in subquery, dependent on outer query
DERIVED	Derived table SELECT (subquery in FROM clause)

DEPENDENT typically signifies the use of a correlated subquery.

- table

The table to which the row of output refers.

- type

The join type. The different join types are listed here, ordered from the best type to the worst:

  - system

  The table has only one row (= system table). This is a special case of the const join type.

  - const

  The table has at most one matching row, which is read at the start of the query. Because there is only one row, values from the column in this row can be regarded as constants by the rest of the optimizer. const tables are very fast because they are read only once.

  const is used when you compare all parts of a PRIMARY KEY or UNIQUE index to constant values. In the following queries, *tbl_name* can be used as a const table:

  ```
  SELECT * FROM tbl_name WHERE primary_key=1;
  ```

  ```
  SELECT * FROM tbl_name
    WHERE primary_key_part1=1 AND primary_key_part2=2;
  ```

  - eq_ref

  One row is read from this table for each combination of rows from the previous tables. Other than the system and const types, this is the best possible join type. It is used when all parts of an index are used by the join and the index is a PRIMARY KEY or UNIQUE index.

  eq_ref can be used for indexed columns that are compared using the = operator. The comparison value can be a constant or an expression that uses columns from tables that are read before this table. In the following examples, MySQL can use an eq_ref join to process *ref_table*:

  ```
  SELECT * FROM ref_table,other_table
    WHERE ref_table.key_column=other_table.column;
  ```

  ```
  SELECT * FROM ref_table,other_table
    WHERE ref_table.key_column_part1=other_table.column
    AND ref_table.key_column_part2=1;
  ```

  - ref

  All rows with matching index values are read from this table for each combination of rows from the previous tables. ref is used if the join uses only a leftmost prefix of the key or if the key is not a PRIMARY KEY or UNIQUE index (in other words, if the join cannot select a single row based on the key value). If the key that is used matches only a few rows, this is a good join type.

`ref` can be used for indexed columns that are compared using the = or <=> operator. In the following examples, MySQL can use a `ref` join to process *ref_table*:

```
SELECT * FROM ref_table WHERE key_column=expr;

SELECT * FROM ref_table,other_table
  WHERE ref_table.key_column=other_table.column;

SELECT * FROM ref_table,other_table
  WHERE ref_table.key_column_part1=other_table.column
  AND ref_table.key_column_part2=1;
```

- `ref_or_null`

    This join type is like `ref`, but with the addition that MySQL does an extra search for rows that contain NULL values. This join type optimization is used most often in resolving subqueries. In the following examples, MySQL can use a `ref_or_null` join to process *ref_table*:

    ```
    SELECT * FROM ref_table
      WHERE key_column=expr OR key_column IS NULL;
    ```

    See Section 6.2.7, "IS NULL Optimization."

- `index_merge`

    This join type indicates that the Index Merge optimization is used. In this case, the key column in the output row contains a list of indexes used, and key_len contains a list of the longest key parts for the indexes used. For more information, see Section 6.2.6, "Index Merge Optimization."

- `unique_subquery`

    This type replaces `ref` for some IN subqueries of the following form:

    ```
    value IN (SELECT primary_key FROM single_table WHERE some_expr)
    ```

    `unique_subquery` is just an index lookup function that replaces the subquery completely for better efficiency.

- `index_subquery`

    This join type is similar to `unique_subquery`. It replaces IN subqueries, but it works for non-unique indexes in subqueries of the following form:

    ```
    value IN (SELECT key_column FROM single_table WHERE some_expr)
    ```

- `range`

    Only rows that are in a given range are retrieved, using an index to select the rows. The key column in the output row indicates which index is used. The key_len contains the longest key part that was used. The ref column is NULL for this type.

    `range` can be used when a key column is compared to a constant using any of the =, <>, >, >=, <, <=, IS NULL, <=>, BETWEEN, or IN operators:

    ```
    SELECT * FROM tbl_name
      WHERE key_column = 10;
    ```

```
SELECT * FROM tbl_name
  WHERE key_column BETWEEN 10 and 20;

SELECT * FROM tbl_name
  WHERE key_column IN (10,20,30);

SELECT * FROM tbl_name
  WHERE key_part1= 10 AND key_part2 IN (10,20,30);
```

- index

  This join type is the same as ALL, except that only the index tree is scanned. This usually is faster than ALL because the index file usually is smaller than the data file.

  MySQL can use this join type when the query uses only columns that are part of a single index.

- ALL

  A full table scan is done for each combination of rows from the previous tables. This is normally not good if the table is the first table not marked const, and usually *very* bad in all other cases. Normally, you can avoid ALL by adding indexes that allow row retrieval from the table based on constant values or column values from earlier tables.

- possible_keys

  The possible_keys column indicates which indexes MySQL can choose from to use to find the rows in this table. Note that this column is totally independent of the order of the tables as displayed in the output from EXPLAIN. That means that some of the keys in possible_keys might not be usable in practice with the generated table order.

  If this column is NULL, there are no relevant indexes. In this case, you may be able to improve the performance of your query by examining the WHERE clause to check whether it refers to some column or columns that would be suitable for indexing. If so, create an appropriate index and check the query with EXPLAIN again.

  To see what indexes a table has, use SHOW INDEX FROM tbl_name.

- key

  The key column indicates the key (index) that MySQL actually decided to use. The key is NULL if no index was chosen. To force MySQL to use or ignore an index listed in the possible_keys column, use FORCE INDEX, USE INDEX, or IGNORE INDEX in your query.

  For MyISAM and BDB tables, running ANALYZE TABLE helps the optimizer choose better indexes. For MyISAM tables, myisamchk --analyze does the same. See Section 4.10.4, "Table Maintenance and Crash Recovery."

- key_len

  The key_len column indicates the length of the key that MySQL decided to use. The length is NULL if the key column says NULL. Note that the value of key_len enables you to determine how many parts of a multiple-part key MySQL actually uses.

- ref

The ref column shows which columns or constants are compared to the index named in the key column to select rows from the table.

- rows

The rows column indicates the number of rows MySQL believes it must examine to execute the query.

- Extra

This column contains additional information about how MySQL resolves the query. Here is an explanation of the values that can appear in this column:

- Distinct

MySQL is looking for distinct values, so it stops searching for more rows for the current row combination after it has found the first matching row.

- Not exists

MySQL was able to do a LEFT JOIN optimization on the query and does not examine more rows in this table for the previous row combination after it finds one row that matches the LEFT JOIN criteria. Here is an example of the type of query that can be optimized this way:

```
SELECT * FROM t1 LEFT JOIN t2 ON t1.id=t2.id
  WHERE t2.id IS NULL;
```

Assume that t2.id is defined as NOT NULL. In this case, MySQL scans t1 and looks up the rows in t2 using the values of t1.id. If MySQL finds a matching row in t2, it knows that t2.id can never be NULL, and does not scan through the rest of the rows in t2 that have the same id value. In other words, for each row in t1, MySQL needs to do only a single lookup in t2, regardless of how many rows actually match in t2.

- range checked for each record (index map: *N*)

MySQL found no good index to use, but found that some of the indexes that might be used after column values from preceding tables are known. For each row combination in the preceding tables, MySQL checks whether it is possible to use a range or index_merge access method to retrieve rows. This is not very fast, but is faster than performing a join with no index at all. The applicability criteria are as described in Section 6.2.5, "Range Optimization," and Section 6.2.6, "Index Merge Optimization," with the exception that all column values for the preceding table are known and considered to be constants.

- Using filesort

MySQL must do an extra pass to find out how to retrieve the rows in sorted order. The sort is done by going through all rows according to the join type and storing the sort key and pointer to the row for all rows that match the WHERE clause. The keys then are sorted and the rows are retrieved in sorted order. See Section 6.2.12, "ORDER BY Optimization."

- Using index

  The column information is retrieved from the table using only information in the index tree without having to do an additional seek to read the actual row. This strategy can be used when the query uses only columns that are part of a single index.

- Using temporary

  To resolve the query, MySQL needs to create a temporary table to hold the result. This typically happens if the query contains GROUP BY and ORDER BY clauses that list columns differently.

- Using where

  A WHERE clause is used to restrict which rows to match against the next table or send to the client. Unless you specifically intend to fetch or examine all rows from the table, you may have something wrong in your query if the Extra value is not Using where and the table join type is ALL or index.

  If you want to make your queries as fast as possible, you should look out for Extra values of Using filesort and Using temporary.

- Using sort_union(...), Using union(...), Using intersect(...)

  These indicate how index scans are merged for the index_merge join type. See Section 6.2.6, "Index Merge Optimization," for more information.

- Using index for group-by

  Similar to the Using index way of accessing a table, Using index for group-by indicates that MySQL found an index that can be used to retrieve all columns of a GROUP BY or DISTINCT query without any extra disk access to the actual table. Additionally, the index is used in the most efficient way so that for each group, only a few index entries are read. For details, see Section 6.2.13, "GROUP BY Optimization."

- Using where with pushed condition

  This item applies to NDB Cluster tables *only*. It means that MySQL Cluster is using *condition pushdown* to improve the efficiency of a direct comparison (=) between a non-indexed column and a constant. In such cases, the condition is "pushed down" to the cluster's data nodes where it is evaluated in all partitions simultaneously. This eliminates the need to send non-matching rows over the network, and can speed up such queries by a factor of 5 to 10 times over cases where condition pushdown could be but is not used.

  Suppose that you have a Cluster table defined as follows:

```
CREATE TABLE t1 (
    a INT,
    b INT,
    KEY(a)
) ENGINE=NDBCLUSTER;
```

  In this case, condition pushdown can be used with a query such as this one:

```
SELECT a,b FROM t1 WHERE b = 10;
```

This can be seen in the output of EXPLAIN SELECT, as shown here:

```
mysql> EXPLAIN SELECT a,b FROM t1 WHERE b = 10\G
*************************** 1. row ***************************
           id: 1
  select_type: SIMPLE
        table: t1
         type: ALL
possible_keys: NULL
          key: NULL
      key_len: NULL
          ref: NULL
         rows: 10
        Extra: Using where with pushed condition
```

Condition pushdown *cannot* be used with either of these two queries:

```
SELECT a,b FROM t1 WHERE a = 10;
SELECT a,b FROM t1 WHERE b + 1 = 10;
```

With regard to the first of these two queries, condition pushdown is not applicable because an index exists on column a. In the case of the second query, a condition pushdown cannot be employed because the comparison involving the non-indexed column b is an indirect one. (However, it would apply if you were to reduce b + 1 = 10 to b = 9 in the WHERE clause.)

However, a condition pushdown may also be employed when an indexed column is compared with a constant using a > or < operator:

```
mysql> EXPLAIN SELECT a,b FROM t1 WHERE a<2\G
*************************** 1. row ***************************
           id: 1
  select_type: SIMPLE
        table: t1
         type: range
possible_keys: a
          key: a
      key_len: 5
          ref: NULL
         rows: 2
        Extra: Using where with pushed condition
```

With regard to condition pushdown, keep in mind that:

- Condition pushdown is relevant to MySQL Cluster *only*, and does not occur when executing queries against tables using any other storage engine.
- Condition pushdown capability is not used by default. To enable it, you can start mysqld with the --engine-condition-pushdown option, or execute the following statement:

  ```
  SET engine_condition_pushdown=On;
  ```

Condition pushdown, Using where with pushed condition, and engine_condition_pushdown were all introduced in MySQL 5.0 Cluster.

You can get a good indication of how good a join is by taking the product of the values in the rows column of the EXPLAIN output. This should tell you roughly how many rows MySQL must examine to execute the query. If you restrict queries with the max_join_size system variable, this row product also is used to determine which multiple-table SELECT statements to execute and which to abort. See Section 6.5.2, "Tuning Server Parameters."

The following example shows how a multiple-table join can be optimized progressively based on the information provided by EXPLAIN. Suppose that you have the SELECT statement shown here and that you plan to examine it using EXPLAIN:

```
EXPLAIN SELECT tt.TicketNumber, tt.TimeIn,
               tt.ProjectReference, tt.EstimatedShipDate,
               tt.ActualShipDate, tt.ClientID,
               tt.ServiceCodes, tt.RepetitiveID,
               tt.CurrentProcess, tt.CurrentDPPerson,
               tt.RecordVolume, tt.DPPrinted, et.COUNTRY,
               et_1.COUNTRY, do.CUSTNAME
       FROM tt, et, et AS et_1, do
       WHERE tt.SubmitTime IS NULL
         AND tt.ActualPC = et.EMPLOYID
         AND tt.AssignedPC = et_1.EMPLOYID
         AND tt.ClientID = do.CUSTNMBR;
```

For this example, make the following assumptions:

- The columns being compared have been declared as follows:

Table	Column	Data Type
tt	ActualPC	CHAR(10)
tt	AssignedPC	CHAR(10)
tt	ClientID	CHAR(10)
et	EMPLOYID	CHAR(15)
do	CUSTNMBR	CHAR(15)

- The tables have the following indexes:

Table	Index
tt	ActualPC
tt	AssignedPC
tt	ClientID
et	EMPLOYID (primary key)
do	CUSTNMBR (primary key)

- The tt.ActualPC values are not evenly distributed.

Initially, before any optimizations have been performed, the EXPLAIN statement produces the following information:

```
table type possible_keys key  key_len ref  rows  Extra
et    ALL  PRIMARY       NULL NULL    NULL 74
do    ALL  PRIMARY       NULL NULL    NULL 2135
et_1  ALL  PRIMARY       NULL NULL    NULL 74
tt    ALL  AssignedPC,   NULL NULL    NULL 3872
           ClientID,
           ActualPC
      range checked for each record (key map: 35)
```

Because type is ALL for each table, this output indicates that MySQL is generating a Cartesian product of all the tables; that is, every combination of rows. This takes quite a long time, because the product of the number of rows in each table must be examined. For the case at hand, this product is 74 × 2135 × 74 × 3872 = 45,268,558,720 rows. If the tables were bigger, you can only imagine how long it would take.

One problem here is that MySQL can use indexes on columns more efficiently if they are declared as the same type and size. In this context, VARCHAR and CHAR are considered the same if they are declared as the same size. tt.ActualPC is declared as CHAR(10) and et.EMPLOYID is CHAR(15), so there is a length mismatch.

To fix this disparity between column lengths, use ALTER TABLE to lengthen ActualPC from 10 characters to 15 characters:

```
mysql> ALTER TABLE tt MODIFY ActualPC VARCHAR(15);
```

Now tt.ActualPC and et.EMPLOYID are both VARCHAR(15). Executing the EXPLAIN statement again produces this result:

```
table type   possible_keys key     key_len ref       rows  Extra
tt    ALL    AssignedPC,   NULL    NULL    NULL      3872  Using
             ClientID,                                     where
             ActualPC
do    ALL    PRIMARY       NULL    NULL    NULL      2135
      range checked for each record (key map: 1)
et_1  ALL    PRIMARY       NULL    NULL    NULL      74
      range checked for each record (key map: 1)
et    eq_ref PRIMARY       PRIMARY 15      tt.ActualPC 1
```

This is not perfect, but is much better: The product of the rows values is less by a factor of 74. This version executes in a couple of seconds.

A second alteration can be made to eliminate the column length mismatches for the tt.AssignedPC = et_1.EMPLOYID and tt.ClientID = do.CUSTNMBR comparisons:

```
mysql> ALTER TABLE tt MODIFY AssignedPC VARCHAR(15),
    ->                  MODIFY ClientID  VARCHAR(15);
```

After that modification, EXPLAIN produces the output shown here:

table	type	possible_keys	key	key_len	ref	rows	Extra
et	ALL	PRIMARY	NULL	NULL	NULL	74	
tt	ref	AssignedPC, ClientID, ActualPC	ActualPC	15	et.EMPLOYID	52	Using where
et_1	eq_ref	PRIMARY	PRIMARY	15	tt.AssignedPC	1	
do	eq_ref	PRIMARY	PRIMARY	15	tt.ClientID	1	

At this point, the query is optimized almost as well as possible. The remaining problem is that, by default, MySQL assumes that values in the tt.ActualPC column are evenly distributed, and that is not the case for the tt table. Fortunately, it is easy to tell MySQL to analyze the key distribution:

```
mysql> ANALYZE TABLE tt;
```

With the additional index information, the join is perfect and EXPLAIN produces this result:

table	type	possible_keys	key	key_len	ref	rows	Extra
tt	ALL	AssignedPC ClientID, ActualPC	NULL	NULL	NULL	3872	Using where
et	eq_ref	PRIMARY	PRIMARY	15	tt.ActualPC	1	
et_1	eq_ref	PRIMARY	PRIMARY	15	tt.AssignedPC	1	
do	eq_ref	PRIMARY	PRIMARY	15	tt.ClientID	1	

Note that the rows column in the output from EXPLAIN is an educated guess from the MySQL join optimizer. You should check whether the numbers are even close to the truth by comparing the rows product with the actual number of rows that the query returns. If the numbers are quite different, you might get better performance by using STRAIGHT_JOIN in your SELECT statement and trying to list the tables in a different order in the FROM clause.

6.2.2 Estimating Query Performance

In most cases, you can estimate query performance by counting disk seeks. For small tables, you can usually find a row in one disk seek (because the index is probably cached). For bigger tables, you can estimate that, using B-tree indexes, you need this many seeks to find a row: $\log(row\_count) / \log(index\_block\_length / 3 \times 2 / (index\_length + data\_pointer\_length)) + 1$.

In MySQL, an index block is usually 1,024 bytes and the data pointer is usually 4 bytes. For a 500,000-row table with an index length of three bytes (the size of MEDIUMINT), the formula indicates $\log(500,000)/\log(1024/3*2/(3+7)) + 1 = 4$ seeks.

This index would require storage of about $500,000 \times 7 \times 3/2 = 5.2MB$ (assuming a typical index buffer fill ratio of 2/3), so you probably have much of the index in memory and so need only one or two calls to read data to find the row.

For writes, however, you need four seek requests to find where to place a new index value and normally two seeks to update the index and write the row.

Note that the preceding discussion does not mean that your application performance slowly degenerates by log N. As long as everything is cached by the OS or the MySQL server, things become only marginally slower as the table gets bigger. After the data gets too big to be cached, things start to go much slower until your applications are bound only by disk seeks (which increase by log N). To avoid this, increase the key cache size as the data grows. For MyISAM tables, the key cache size is controlled by the key_buffer_size system variable. See Section 6.5.2, "Tuning Server Parameters."

6.2.3 Speed of SELECT Queries

In general, when you want to make a slow SELECT ... WHERE query faster, the first thing to check is whether you can add an index. All references between different tables should usually be done with indexes. You can use the EXPLAIN statement to determine which indexes are used for a SELECT. See Section 6.2.1, "Optimizing Queries with EXPLAIN," and Section 6.4.5, "How MySQL Uses Indexes."

Some general tips for speeding up queries on MyISAM tables:

- To help MySQL better optimize queries, use ANALYZE TABLE or run myisamchk --analyze on a table after it has been loaded with data. This updates a value for each index part that indicates the average number of rows that have the same value. (For unique indexes, this is always 1.) MySQL uses this to decide which index to choose when you join two tables based on a non-constant expression. You can check the result from the table analysis by using SHOW INDEX FROM *tbl_name* and examining the Cardinality value. myisamchk --description --verbose shows index distribution information.

- To sort an index and data according to an index, use myisamchk --sort-index --sort-records=1 (assuming that you want to sort on index 1). This is a good way to make queries faster if you have a unique index from which you want to read all rows in order according to the index. Note that the first time you sort a large table this way, it may take a long time.

6.2.4 WHERE Clause Optimization

This section discusses optimizations that can be made for processing WHERE clauses. The examples use SELECT statements, but the same optimizations apply for WHERE clauses in DELETE and UPDATE statements.

Work on the MySQL optimizer is ongoing, so this section is incomplete. MySQL performs a great many optimizations, not all of which are documented here.

Some of the optimizations performed by MySQL follow:

- Removal of unnecessary parentheses:

```
   ((a AND b) AND c OR (((a AND b) AND (c AND d))))
-> (a AND b AND c) OR (a AND b AND c AND d)
```

- Constant folding:

```
(a<b AND b=c) AND a=5
-> b>5 AND b=c AND a=5
```

- Constant condition removal (needed because of constant folding):

```
(B>=5 AND B=5) OR (B=6 AND 5=5) OR (B=7 AND 5=6)
-> B=5 OR B=6
```

- Constant expressions used by indexes are evaluated only once.

- COUNT(*) on a single table without a WHERE is retrieved directly from the table information for MyISAM and MEMORY tables. This is also done for any NOT NULL expression when used with only one table.

- Early detection of invalid constant expressions. MySQL quickly detects that some SELECT statements are impossible and returns no rows.

- HAVING is merged with WHERE if you do not use GROUP BY or aggregate functions (COUNT(), MIN(), and so on).

- For each table in a join, a simpler WHERE is constructed to get a fast WHERE evaluation for the table and also to skip rows as soon as possible.

- All constant tables are read first before any other tables in the query. A constant table is any of the following:

  - An empty table or a table with one row.

  - A table that is used with a WHERE clause on a PRIMARY KEY or a UNIQUE index, where all index parts are compared to constant expressions and are defined as NOT NULL.

  All of the following tables are used as constant tables:

```
SELECT * FROM t WHERE primary_key=1;
SELECT * FROM t1,t2
  WHERE t1.primary_key=1 AND t2.primary_key=t1.id;
```

- The best join combination for joining the tables is found by trying all possibilities. If all columns in ORDER BY and GROUP BY clauses come from the same table, that table is preferred first when joining.

- If there is an ORDER BY clause and a different GROUP BY clause, or if the ORDER BY or GROUP BY contains columns from tables other than the first table in the join queue, a temporary table is created.

- If you use the SQL_SMALL_RESULT option, MySQL uses an in-memory temporary table.

- Each table index is queried, and the best index is used unless the optimizer believes that it is more efficient to use a table scan. At one time, a scan was used based on whether the best index spanned more than 30% of the table, but a fixed percentage no longer determines the choice between using an index or a scan. The optimizer now is more complex and bases its estimate on additional factors such as table size, number of rows, and I/O block size.

- In some cases, MySQL can read rows from the index without even consulting the data file. If all columns used from the index are numeric, only the index tree is used to resolve the query.

- Before each row is output, those that do not match the HAVING clause are skipped.

Some examples of queries that are very fast:

```
SELECT COUNT(*) FROM tbl_name;
```

```
SELECT MIN(key_part1),MAX(key_part1) FROM tbl_name;
```

```
SELECT MAX(key_part2) FROM tbl_name
  WHERE key_part1=constant;
```

```
SELECT ... FROM tbl_name
  ORDER BY key_part1,key_part2,... LIMIT 10;
```

```
SELECT ... FROM tbl_name
  ORDER BY key_part1 DESC, key_part2 DESC, ... LIMIT 10;
```

MySQL resolves the following queries using only the index tree, assuming that the indexed columns are numeric:

```
SELECT key_part1,key_part2 FROM tbl_name WHERE key_part1=val;
```

```
SELECT COUNT(*) FROM tbl_name
  WHERE key_part1=val1 AND key_part2=val2;
```

```
SELECT key_part2 FROM tbl_name GROUP BY key_part1;
```

The following queries use indexing to retrieve the rows in sorted order without a separate sorting pass:

```
SELECT ... FROM tbl_name
  ORDER BY key_part1,key_part2,... ;
```

```
SELECT ... FROM tbl_name
  ORDER BY key_part1 DESC, key_part2 DESC, ... ;
```

6.2.5 Range Optimization

The range access method uses a single index to retrieve a subset of table rows that are contained within one or several index value intervals. It can be used for a single-part or multiple-part index. The following sections give a detailed description of how intervals are extracted from the WHERE clause.

6.2.5.1 The Range Access Method for Single-Part Indexes

For a single-part index, index value intervals can be conveniently represented by corresponding conditions in the WHERE clause, so we speak of *range conditions* rather than "intervals."

The definition of a range condition for a single-part index is as follows:

- For both BTREE and HASH indexes, comparison of a key part with a constant value is a range condition when using the =, <=>, IN, IS NULL, or IS NOT NULL operator.

- For BTREE indexes, comparison of a key part with a constant value is a range condition when using the >, <, >=, <=, BETWEEN, !=, or <> operator, or LIKE 'pattern' (where 'pattern' does not start with a wildcard).

- For all types of indexes, multiple range conditions combined with OR or AND form a range condition.

"Constant value" in the preceding descriptions means one of the following:

- A constant from the query string

- A column of a const or system table from the same join

- The result of an uncorrelated subquery

- Any expression composed entirely from subexpressions of the preceding types

Here are some examples of queries with range conditions in the WHERE clause:

```
SELECT * FROM t1
  WHERE key_col > 1
  AND key_col < 10;

SELECT * FROM t1
  WHERE key_col = 1
  OR key_col IN (15,18,20);

SELECT * FROM t1
  WHERE key_col LIKE 'ab%'
  OR key_col BETWEEN 'bar' AND 'foo';
```

Note that some non-constant values may be converted to constants during the constant propagation phase.

MySQL tries to extract range conditions from the WHERE clause for each of the possible indexes. During the extraction process, conditions that cannot be used for constructing the range condition are dropped, conditions that produce overlapping ranges are combined, and conditions that produce empty ranges are removed.

Consider the following statement, where key1 is an indexed column and nonkey is not indexed:

```
SELECT * FROM t1 WHERE
  (key1 < 'abc' AND (key1 LIKE 'abcde%' OR key1 LIKE '%b')) OR
  (key1 < 'bar' AND nonkey = 4) OR
  (key1 < 'uux' AND key1 > 'z');
```

The extraction process for key key1 is as follows:

1. Start with original WHERE clause:

```
(key1 < 'abc' AND (key1 LIKE 'abcde%' OR key1 LIKE '%b')) OR
(key1 < 'bar' AND nonkey = 4) OR
(key1 < 'uux' AND key1 > 'z')
```

2. Remove nonkey = 4 and key1 LIKE '%b' because they cannot be used for a range scan. The correct way to remove them is to replace them with TRUE, so that we do not miss any matching rows when doing the range scan. Having replaced them with TRUE, we get:

```
(key1 < 'abc' AND (key1 LIKE 'abcde%' OR TRUE)) OR
(key1 < 'bar' AND TRUE) OR
(key1 < 'uux' AND key1 > 'z')
```

3. Collapse conditions that are always true or false:

   - (key1 LIKE 'abcde%' OR TRUE) is always true
   - (key1 < 'uux' AND key1 > 'z') is always false

   Replacing these conditions with constants, we get:

   ```
   (key1 < 'abc' AND TRUE) OR (key1 < 'bar' AND TRUE) OR (FALSE)
   ```

   Removing unnecessary TRUE and FALSE constants, we obtain:

   ```
   (key1 < 'abc') OR (key1 < 'bar')
   ```

4. Combining overlapping intervals into one yields the final condition to be used for the range scan:

   ```
   (key1 < 'bar')
   ```

In general (and as demonstrated by the preceding example), the condition used for a range scan is less restrictive than the WHERE clause. MySQL performs an additional check to filter out rows that satisfy the range condition but not the full WHERE clause.

The range condition extraction algorithm can handle nested AND/OR constructs of arbitrary depth, and its output does not depend on the order in which conditions appear in WHERE clause.

6.2.5.2 The Range Access Method for Multiple-Part Indexes

Range conditions on a multiple-part index are an extension of range conditions for a single-part index. A range condition on a multiple-part index restricts index rows to lie within one or several key tuple intervals. Key tuple intervals are defined over a set of key tuples, using ordering from the index.

For example, consider a multiple-part index defined as key1(*key_part1*, *key_part2*, *key_part3*), and the following set of key tuples listed in key order:

key_part1	key_part2	key_part3
NULL	1	'abc'
NULL	1	'xyz'
NULL	2	'foo'
1	1	'abc'
1	1	'xyz'
1	2	'abc'
2	1	'aaa'

The condition *key_part1* = 1 defines this interval:

```
(1,-inf,-inf) <= (key_part1,key_part2,key_part3) < (1,+inf,+inf)
```

The interval covers the 4th, 5th, and 6th tuples in the preceding data set and can be used by the range access method.

By contrast, the condition *key_part3* = 'abc' does not define a single interval and cannot be used by the range access method.

The following descriptions indicate how range conditions work for multiple-part indexes in greater detail.

- For HASH indexes, each interval containing identical values can be used. This means that the interval can be produced only for conditions in the following form:

  ```
      key_part1 cmp const1
  AND key_part2 cmp const2
  AND ...
  AND key_partN cmp constN;
  ```

  Here, *const1*, *const2*, ... are constants, *cmp* is one of the =, <=>, or IS NULL comparison operators, and the conditions cover all index parts. (That is, there are *N* conditions, one for each part of an *N*-part index.) For example, the following is a range condition for a three-part HASH index:

  ```
  key_part1 = 1 AND key_part2 IS NULL AND key_part3 = 'foo'
  ```

  For the definition of what is considered to be a constant, see Section 6.2.5.1, "The Range Access Method for Single-Part Indexes."

- For a BTREE index, an interval might be usable for conditions combined with AND, where each condition compares a key part with a constant value using =, <=>, IS NULL, >, <, >=, <=, !=, <>, BETWEEN, or LIKE '*pattern*' (where '*pattern*' does not start with a wildcard). An interval can be used as long as it is possible to determine a single key tuple containing all rows that match the condition (or two intervals if <> or != is used). For example, for this condition:

  ```
  key_part1 = 'foo' AND key_part2 >= 10 AND key_part3 > 10
  ```

The single interval is:

```
('foo',10,10) < (key_part1,key_part2,key_part3) < ('foo',+inf,+inf)
```

It is possible that the created interval contains more rows than the initial condition. For example, the preceding interval includes the value (`'foo'`, 11, 0), which does not satisfy the original condition.

- If conditions that cover sets of rows contained within intervals are combined with OR, they form a condition that covers a set of rows contained within the union of their intervals. If the conditions are combined with AND, they form a condition that covers a set of rows contained within the intersection of their intervals. For example, for this condition on a two-part index:

```
(key_part1 = 1 AND key_part2 < 2) OR (key_part1 > 5)
```

The intervals are:

```
(1,-inf) < (key_part1,key_part2) < (1,2)
(5,-inf) < (key_part1,key_part2)
```

In this example, the interval on the first line uses one key part for the left bound and two key parts for the right bound. The interval on the second line uses only one key part. The key_len column in the EXPLAIN output indicates the maximum length of the key prefix used.

In some cases, key_len may indicate that a key part was used, but that might be not what you would expect. Suppose that *key_part1* and *key_part2* can be NULL. Then the key_len column displays two key part lengths for the following condition:

```
key_part1 >= 1 AND key_part2 < 2
```

But, in fact, the condition is converted to this:

```
key_part1 >= 1 AND key_part2 IS NOT NULL
```

Section 6.2.5.1, "The Range Access Method for Single-Part Indexes," describes how optimizations are performed to combine or eliminate intervals for range conditions on a single-part index. Analogous steps are performed for range conditions on multiple-part indexes.

6.2.6 Index Merge Optimization

The *Index Merge* method is used to retrieve rows with several range scans and to merge their results into one. The merge can produce unions, intersections, or unions-of-intersections of its underlying scans.

Note: If you have upgraded from a previous version of MySQL, you should be aware that this type of join optimization is first introduced in MySQL 5.0, and represents a significant change in behavior with regard to indexes. (Formerly, MySQL was able to use at most only one index for each referenced table.)

In EXPLAIN output, the Index Merge method appears as `index_merge` in the `type` column. In this case, the `key` column contains a list of indexes used, and `key_len` contains a list of the longest key parts for those indexes.

Examples:

```
SELECT * FROM tbl_name WHERE key_part1 = 10 OR key_part2 = 20;

SELECT * FROM tbl_name
  WHERE (key_part1 = 10 OR key_part2 = 20) AND non_key_part=30;

SELECT * FROM t1, t2
  WHERE (t1.key1 IN (1,2) OR t1.key2 LIKE 'value%')
  AND t2.key1=t1.some_col;

SELECT * FROM t1, t2
  WHERE t1.key1=1
  AND (t2.key1=t1.some_col OR t2.key2=t1.some_col2);
```

The Index Merge method has several access algorithms (seen in the Extra field of EXPLAIN output):

- `Using intersect(...)`
- `Using union(...)`
- `Using sort_union(...)`

The following sections describe these methods in greater detail.

Note: The Index Merge optimization algorithm has the following known deficiencies:

- If a range scan is possible on some key, an Index Merge is not considered. For example, consider this query:

  ```
  SELECT * FROM t1 WHERE (goodkey1 < 10 OR goodkey2 < 20) AND badkey < 30;
  ```

  For this query, two plans are possible:

  - An Index Merge scan using the (`goodkey1 < 10 OR goodkey2 < 20`) condition.
  - A range scan using the `badkey < 30` condition.

However, the optimizer considers only the second plan. If that is not what you want, you can make the optimizer consider Index Merge by using IGNORE INDEX or FORCE INDEX. The following queries are executed using Index Merge:

```
SELECT * FROM t1 FORCE INDEX(goodkey1,goodkey2)
  WHERE (goodkey1 < 10 OR goodkey2 < 20) AND badkey < 30;

SELECT * FROM t1 IGNORE INDEX(badkey)
  WHERE (goodkey1 < 10 OR goodkey2 < 20) AND badkey < 30;
```

- If your query has a complex WHERE clause with deep AND/OR nesting and MySQL doesn't choose the optimal plan, try distributing terms using the following identity laws:

  (x AND y) OR z = (x OR z) AND (y OR z)
  (x OR y) AND z = (x AND z) OR (y AND z)

- Index Merge is not applicable to fulltext indexes. We plan to extend it to cover these in a future MySQL release.

The choice between different possible variants of the Index Merge access method and other access methods is based on cost estimates of various available options.

6.2.6.1 The Index Merge Intersection Access Algorithm

This access algorithm can be employed when a WHERE clause was converted to several range conditions on different keys combined with AND, and each condition is one of the following:

- In this form, where the index has exactly N parts (that is, all index parts are covered):

  key_part1=const1 AND key_part2=const2 ... AND key_partN=constN

- Any range condition over a primary key of an InnoDB or BDB table.

Examples:

```
SELECT * FROM innodb_table WHERE primary_key < 10 AND key_col1=20;

SELECT * FROM tbl_name
  WHERE (key1_part1=1 AND key1_part2=2) AND key2=2;
```

The Index Merge intersection algorithm performs simultaneous scans on all used indexes and produces the intersection of row sequences that it receives from the merged index scans.

If all columns used in the query are covered by the used indexes, full table rows are not retrieved (EXPLAIN output contains Using index in Extra field in this case). Here is an example of such a query:

```
SELECT COUNT(*) FROM t1 WHERE key1=1 AND key2=1;
```

If the used indexes don't cover all columns used in the query, full rows are retrieved only when the range conditions for all used keys are satisfied.

If one of the merged conditions is a condition over a primary key of an InnoDB or BDB table, it is not used for row retrieval, but is used to filter out rows retrieved using other conditions.

6.2.6.2 The Index Merge Union Access Algorithm

The applicability criteria for this algorithm are similar to those for the Index Merge method intersection algorithm. The algorithm can be employed when the table's WHERE clause was converted to several range conditions on different keys combined with OR, and each condition is one of the following:

- In this form, where the index has exactly *N* parts (that is, all index parts are covered):

  `key_part1=const1 AND key_part2=const2 ... AND key_partN=constN`

- Any range condition over a primary key of an `InnoDB` or `BDB` table.

- A condition for which the Index Merge method intersection algorithm is applicable.

Examples:

```
SELECT * FROM t1 WHERE key1=1 OR key2=2 OR key3=3;

SELECT * FROM innodb_table WHERE (key1=1 AND key2=2) OR
  (key3='foo' AND key4='bar') AND key5=5;
```

6.2.6.3 The Index Merge Sort-Union Access Algorithm

This access algorithm is employed when the `WHERE` clause was converted to several range conditions combined by `OR`, but for which the Index Merge method union algorithm is not applicable.

Examples:

```
SELECT * FROM tbl_name WHERE key_col1 < 10 OR key_col2 < 20;

SELECT * FROM tbl_name
  WHERE (key_col1 > 10 OR key_col2 = 20) AND nonkey_col=30;
```

The difference between the sort-union algorithm and the union algorithm is that the sort-union algorithm must first fetch row IDs for all rows and sort them before returning any rows.

6.2.7 IS NULL Optimization

MySQL can perform the same optimization on *col_name* `IS NULL` that it can use for *col_name* = *constant_value*. For example, MySQL can use indexes and ranges to search for `NULL` with `IS NULL`.

Examples:

```
SELECT * FROM tbl_name WHERE key_col IS NULL;

SELECT * FROM tbl_name WHERE key_col <=> NULL;

SELECT * FROM tbl_name
  WHERE key_col=const1 OR key_col=const2 OR key_col IS NULL;
```

If a `WHERE` clause includes a *col_name* `IS NULL` condition for a column that is declared as `NOT NULL`, that expression is optimized away. This optimization does not occur in cases when the column might produce `NULL` anyway; for example, if it comes from a table on the right side of a `LEFT JOIN`.

MySQL can also optimize the combination *col_name* = *expr* `AND` *col_name* `IS NULL`, a form that is common in resolved subqueries. `EXPLAIN` shows `ref_or_null` when this optimization is used.

This optimization can handle one IS NULL for any key part.

Some examples of queries that are optimized, assuming that there is an index on columns a and b of table t2:

```
SELECT * FROM t1 WHERE t1.a=expr OR t1.a IS NULL;

SELECT * FROM t1, t2 WHERE t1.a=t2.a OR t2.a IS NULL;

SELECT * FROM t1, t2
  WHERE (t1.a=t2.a OR t2.a IS NULL) AND t2.b=t1.b;

SELECT * FROM t1, t2
  WHERE t1.a=t2.a AND (t2.b=t1.b OR t2.b IS NULL);

SELECT * FROM t1, t2
  WHERE (t1.a=t2.a AND t2.a IS NULL AND ...)
  OR (t1.a=t2.a AND t2.a IS NULL AND ...);
```

ref_or_null works by first doing a read on the reference key, and then a separate search for rows with a NULL key value.

Note that the optimization can handle only one IS NULL level. In the following query, MySQL uses key lookups only on the expression (t1.a=t2.a AND t2.a IS NULL) and is not able to use the key part on b:

```
SELECT * FROM t1, t2
  WHERE (t1.a=t2.a AND t2.a IS NULL)
  OR (t1.b=t2.b AND t2.b IS NULL);
```

6.2.8 DISTINCT Optimization

DISTINCT combined with ORDER BY needs a temporary table in many cases.

Because DISTINCT may use GROUP BY, you should be aware of how MySQL works with columns in ORDER BY or HAVING clauses that are not part of the selected columns.

In most cases, a DISTINCT clause can be considered as a special case of GROUP BY. For example, the following two queries are equivalent:

```
SELECT DISTINCT c1, c2, c3 FROM t1 WHERE c1 > const;

SELECT c1, c2, c3 FROM t1 WHERE c1 > const GROUP BY c1, c2, c3;
```

Due to this equivalence, the optimizations applicable to GROUP BY queries can be also applied to queries with a DISTINCT clause. Thus, for more details on the optimization possibilities for DISTINCT queries, see Section 6.2.13, "GROUP BY Optimization."

When combining LIMIT row_count with DISTINCT, MySQL stops as soon as it finds row_count unique rows.

If you do not use columns from all tables named in a query, MySQL stops scanning any unused tables as soon as it finds the first match. In the following case, assuming that t1 is used before t2 (which you can check with EXPLAIN), MySQL stops reading from t2 (for any particular row in t1) when it finds the first row in t2:

```
SELECT DISTINCT t1.a FROM t1, t2 where t1.a=t2.a;
```

6.2.9 LEFT JOIN and RIGHT JOIN Optimization

MySQL implements an A LEFT JOIN B join_condition as follows:

- Table B is set to depend on table A and all tables on which A depends.
- Table A is set to depend on all tables (except B) that are used in the LEFT JOIN condition.
- The LEFT JOIN condition is used to decide how to retrieve rows from table B. (In other words, any condition in the WHERE clause is not used.)
- All standard join optimizations are performed, with the exception that a table is always read after all tables on which it depends. If there is a circular dependence, MySQL issues an error.
- All standard WHERE optimizations are performed.
- If there is a row in A that matches the WHERE clause, but there is no row in B that matches the ON condition, an extra B row is generated with all columns set to NULL.
- If you use LEFT JOIN to find rows that do not exist in some table and you have the following test: col_name IS NULL in the WHERE part, where col_name is a column that is declared as NOT NULL, MySQL stops searching for more rows (for a particular key combination) after it has found one row that matches the LEFT JOIN condition.

The implementation of RIGHT JOIN is analogous to that of LEFT JOIN with the roles of the tables reversed.

The join optimizer calculates the order in which tables should be joined. The table read order forced by LEFT JOIN or STRAIGHT_JOIN helps the join optimizer do its work much more quickly, because there are fewer table permutations to check. Note that this means that if you do a query of the following type, MySQL does a full scan on b because the LEFT JOIN forces it to be read before d:

```
SELECT *
  FROM a JOIN b LEFT JOIN c ON (c.key=a.key) LEFT JOIN d ON (d.key=a.key)
  WHERE b.key=d.key;
```

The fix in this case is to reverse the order in which a and b are listed in the FROM clause:

```
SELECT *
  FROM a JOIN b LEFT JOIN c ON (c.key=a.key) LEFT JOIN d ON (d.key=a.key)
  WHERE b.key=d.key;
```

For a LEFT JOIN, if the WHERE condition is always false for the generated NULL row, the LEFT JOIN is changed to a normal join. For example, the WHERE clause would be false in the following query if t2.column1 were NULL:

```
SELECT * FROM t1 LEFT JOIN t2 ON (column1) WHERE t2.column2=5;
```

Therefore, it is safe to convert the query to a normal join:

```
SELECT * FROM t1, t2 WHERE t2.column2=5 AND t1.column1=t2.column1;
```

This can be made faster because MySQL can use table t2 before table t1 if doing so would result in a better query plan. To force a specific table order, use STRAIGHT_JOIN.

6.2.10 Nested Join Optimization

As of MySQL 5.0.1, the syntax for expressing joins allows nested joins.

The syntax of *table_factor* is extended in comparison with the SQL Standard. The latter accepts only *table_reference*, not a list of them inside a pair of parentheses. This is a conservative extension if we consider each comma in a list of *table_reference* items as equivalent to an inner join. For example:

```
SELECT * FROM t1 LEFT JOIN (t2, t3, t4)
              ON (t2.a=t1.a AND t3.b=t1.b AND t4.c=t1.c)
```

is equivalent to:

```
SELECT * FROM t1 LEFT JOIN (t2 CROSS JOIN t3 CROSS JOIN t4)
              ON (t2.a=t1.a AND t3.b=t1.b AND t4.c=t1.c)
```

In MySQL, CROSS JOIN is a syntactic equivalent to INNER JOIN (they can replace each other). In standard SQL, they are not equivalent. INNER JOIN is used with an ON clause; CROSS JOIN is used otherwise.

In versions of MySQL prior to 5.0.1, parentheses in *table_references* were just omitted and all join operations were grouped to the left. In general, parentheses can be ignored in join expressions containing only inner join operations.

After removing parentheses and grouping operations to the left, the join expression:

```
t1 LEFT JOIN (t2 LEFT JOIN t3 ON t2.b=t3.b OR t2.b IS NULL)
   ON t1.a=t2.a
```

transforms into the expression:

```
(t1 LEFT JOIN t2 ON t1.a=t2.a) LEFT JOIN t3
   ON t2.b=t3.b OR t2.b IS NULL
```

Yet, the two expressions are not equivalent. To see this, suppose that the tables t1, t2, and t3 have the following state:

- Table t1 contains rows (1), (2)
- Table t2 contains row (1,101)
- Table t3 contains row (101)

In this case, the first expression returns a result set including the rows (1,1,101,101), (2,NULL,NULL,NULL), whereas the second expression returns the rows (1,1,101,101), (2,NULL,NULL,101):

```
mysql> SELECT *
    -> FROM t1
    ->     LEFT JOIN
    ->     (t2 LEFT JOIN t3 ON t2.b=t3.b OR t2.b IS NULL)
    ->     ON t1.a=t2.a;
+------+------+------+------+
| a    | a    | b    | b    |
+------+------+------+------+
|    1 |    1 |  101 |  101 |
|    2 | NULL | NULL | NULL |
+------+------+------+------+

mysql> SELECT *
    -> FROM (t1 LEFT JOIN t2 ON t1.a=t2.a)
    ->     LEFT JOIN t3
    ->     ON t2.b=t3.b OR t2.b IS NULL;
+------+------+------+------+
| a    | a    | b    | b    |
+------+------+------+------+
|    1 |    1 |  101 |  101 |
|    2 | NULL | NULL |  101 |
+------+------+------+------+
```

In the following example, an outer join operation is used together with an inner join operation:

```
t1 LEFT JOIN (t2, t3) ON t1.a=t2.a
```

That expression cannot be transformed into the following expression:

```
t1 LEFT JOIN t2 ON t1.a=t2.a, t3.
```

For the given table states, the two expressions return different sets of rows:

```
mysql> SELECT *
    -> FROM t1 LEFT JOIN (t2, t3) ON t1.a=t2.a;
+------+------+------+------+
| a    | a    | b    | b    |
+------+------+------+------+
|    1 |    1 |  101 |  101 |
|    2 | NULL | NULL | NULL |
+------+------+------+------+

mysql> SELECT *
    -> FROM t1 LEFT JOIN t2 ON t1.a=t2.a, t3;
+------+------+------+------+
| a    | a    | b    | b    |
+------+------+------+------+
|    1 |    1 |  101 |  101 |
|    2 | NULL | NULL |  101 |
+------+------+------+------+
```

Therefore, if we omit parentheses in a join expression with outer join operators, we might change the result set for the original expression.

More exactly, we cannot ignore parentheses in the right operand of the left outer join operation and in the left operand of a right join operation. In other words, we cannot ignore parentheses for the inner table expressions of outer join operations. Parentheses for the other operand (operand for the outer table) can be ignored.

The following expression:

```
(t1,t2) LEFT JOIN t3 ON P(t2.b,t3.b)
```

is equivalent to this expression:

```
t1, t2 LEFT JOIN t3 ON P(t2.b,t3.b)
```

for any tables t1,t2,t3 and any condition P over attributes t2.b and t3.b.

Whenever the order of execution of the join operations in a join expression (*join_table*) is not from left to right, we talk about nested joins. Consider the following queries:

```
SELECT * FROM t1 LEFT JOIN (t2 LEFT JOIN t3 ON t2.b=t3.b) ON t1.a=t2.a
    WHERE t1.a > 1

SELECT * FROM t1 LEFT JOIN (t2, t3) ON t1.a=t2.a
    WHERE (t2.b=t3.b OR t2.b IS NULL) AND t1.a > 1
```

Those queries are considered to contain these nested joins:

```
t2 LEFT JOIN t3 ON t2.b=t3.b
t2, t3
```

The nested join is formed in the first query with a left join operation, whereas in the second query it is formed with an inner join operation.

In the first query, the parentheses can be omitted: The grammatical structure of the join expression will dictate the same order of execution for join operations. For the second query, the parentheses cannot be omitted, although the join expression here can be interpreted unambiguously without them. (In our extended syntax the parentheses in (t2, t3) of the second query are required, although theoretically the query could be parsed without them: We still would have unambiguous syntactical structure for the query because LEFT JOIN and ON would play the role of the left and right delimiters for the expression (t2,t3).)

The preceding examples demonstrate these points:

- For join expressions involving only inner joins (and not outer joins), parentheses can be removed. You can remove parentheses and evaluate left to right (or, in fact, you can evaluate the tables in any order).

- The same is not true, in general, for outer joins or for outer joins mixed with inner joins. Removal of parentheses may change the result.

Queries with nested outer joins are executed in the same pipeline manner as queries with inner joins. More exactly, a variation of the nested-loop join algorithm is exploited. Recall by what algorithmic schema the nested-loop join executes a query. Suppose that we have a join query over 3 tables T1,T2,T3 of the form:

```
SELECT * FROM T1 INNER JOIN T2 ON P1(T1,T2)
                    INNER JOIN T3 ON P2(T2,T3)
  WHERE P(T1,T2,T3).
```

Here, P1(T1,T2) and P2(T3,T3) are some join conditions (on expressions), whereas P(t1,t2,t3) is a condition over columns of tables T1,T2,T3.

The nested-loop join algorithm would execute this query in the following manner:

```
FOR each row t1 in T1 {
  FOR each row t2 in T2 such that P1(t1,t2) {
    FOR each row t3 in T3 such that P2(t2,t3) {
      IF P(t1,t2,t3) {
        t:=t1||t2||t3; OUTPUT t;
      }
    }
  }
}
```

The notation t1||t2||t3 means "a row constructed by concatenating the columns of rows t1, t2, and t3." In some of the following examples, NULL where a row name appears means that NULL is used for each column of that row. For example, t1||t2||NULL means "a row constructed by concatenating the columns of rows t1 and t2, and NULL for each column of t3."

Now let's consider a query with nested outer joins:

```
SELECT * FROM T1 LEFT JOIN
                (T2 LEFT JOIN T3 ON P2(T2,T3))
                ON P1(T1,T2)
  WHERE P(T1,T2,T3).
```

For this query, we modify the nested-loop pattern to get:

```
FOR each row t1 in T1 {
  BOOL f1:=FALSE;
  FOR each row t2 in T2 such that P1(t1,t2) {
    BOOL f2:=FALSE;
    FOR each row t3 in T3 such that P2(t2,t3) {
      IF P(t1,t2,t3) {
        t:=t1||t2||t3; OUTPUT t;
      }
      f2=TRUE;
      f1=TRUE;
    }
    IF (!f2) {
      IF P(t1,t2,NULL) {
        t:=t1||t2||NULL; OUTPUT t;
      }
      f1=TRUE;
    }
```

```
    }
    IF (!f1) {
      IF P(t1,NULL,NULL) {
        t:=t1||NULL||NULL; OUTPUT t;
      }
    }
  }
}
```

In general, for any nested loop for the first inner table in an outer join operation, a flag is introduced that is turned off before the loop and is checked after the loop. The flag is turned on when for the current row from the outer table a match from the table representing the inner operand is found. If at the end of the loop cycle the flag is still off, no match has been found for the current row of the outer table. In this case, the row is complemented by NULL values for the columns of the inner tables. The result row is passed to the final check for the output or into the next nested loop, but only if the row satisfies the join condition of all embedded outer joins.

In our example, the outer join table expressed by the following expression is embedded:

```
(T2 LEFT JOIN T3 ON P2(T2,T3))
```

Note that for the query with inner joins, the optimizer could choose a different order of nested loops, such as this one:

```
FOR each row t3 in T3 {
  FOR each row t2 in T2 such that P2(t2,t3) {
    FOR each row t1 in T1 such that P1(t1,t2) {
      IF P(t1,t2,t3) {
        t:=t1||t2||t3; OUTPUT t;
      }
    }
  }
}
```

For the queries with outer joins, the optimizer can choose only such an order where loops for outer tables precede loops for inner tables. Thus, for our query with outer joins, only one nesting order is possible. For the following query, the optimizer will evaluate two different nestings:

```
SELECT * T1 LEFT JOIN (T2,T3) ON P1(T1,T2) AND P2(T1,T3)
  WHERE P(T1,T2,T3)
```

The nestings are these:

```
FOR each row t1 in T1 {
  BOOL f1:=FALSE;
  FOR each row t2 in T2 such that P1(t1,t2) {
    FOR each row t3 in T3 such that P2(t1,t3) {
      IF P(t1,t2,t3) {
        t:=t1||t2||t3; OUTPUT t;
      }
      f1:=TRUE
    }
```

```
    }
  IF (!f1) {
    IF P(t1,NULL,NULL) {
      t:=t1||NULL||NULL; OUTPUT t;
    }
  }
}
```

and:

```
FOR each row t1 in T1 {
  BOOL f1:=FALSE;
  FOR each row t3 in T3 such that P2(t1,t3) {
    FOR each row t2 in T2 such that P1(t1,t2) {
      IF P(t1,t2,t3) {
        t:=t1||t2||t3; OUTPUT t;
      }
      f1:=TRUE
    }
  }
  IF (!f1) {
    IF P(t1,NULL,NULL) {
      t:=t1||NULL||NULL; OUTPUT t;
    }
  }
}
```

In both nestings, T1 must be processed in the outer loop because it is used in an outer join. T2 and T3 are used in an inner join, so that join must be processed in the inner loop. However, because the join is an inner join, T2 and T3 can be processed in either order.

When discussing the nested-loop algorithm for inner joins, we omitted some details whose impact on the performance of query execution may be huge. We did not mention so-called "pushed-down" conditions. Suppose that our WHERE condition P(T1,T2,T3) can be represented by a conjunctive formula:

```
P(T1,T2,T2) = C1(T1) AND C2(T2) AND C3(T3).
```

In this case, MySQL actually uses the following nested-loop schema for the execution of the query with inner joins:

```
FOR each row t1 in T1 such that C1(t1) {
  FOR each row t2 in T2 such that P1(t1,t2) AND C2(t2)  {
    FOR each row t3 in T3 such that P2(t2,t3) AND C3(t3) {
      IF P(t1,t2,t3) {
        t:=t1||t2||t3; OUTPUT t;
      }
    }
  }
}
```

You see that each of the conjuncts C1(T1), C2(T2), C3(T3) is pushed out of the most inner loop to the most outer loop where it can be evaluated. If C1(T1) is a very restrictive condition, this condition pushdown may greatly reduce the number of rows from table T1 passed to the inner loops. As a result, the execution time for the query may improve immensely.

For a query with outer joins, the WHERE condition is to be checked only after it has been found that the current row from the outer table has a match in the inner tables. Thus, the optimization of pushing conditions out of the inner nested loops cannot be applied directly to queries with outer joins. Here we have to introduce conditional pushed-down predicates guarded by the flags that are turned on when a match has been encountered.

For our example with outer joins with:

```
P(T1,T2,T3)=C1(T1) AND C(T2) AND C3(T3)
```

the nested-loop schema using guarded pushed-down conditions looks like this:

```
FOR each row t1 in T1 such that C1(t1) {
  BOOL f1:=FALSE;
  FOR each row t2 in T2
      such that P1(t1,t2) AND (f1?C2(t2):TRUE) {
    BOOL f2:=FALSE;
    FOR each row t3 in T3
        such that P2(t2,t3) AND (f1&&f2?C3(t3):TRUE) {
      IF (f1&&f2?TRUE:(C2(t2) AND C3(t3))) {
        t:=t1||t2||t3; OUTPUT t;
      }
      f2=TRUE;
      f1=TRUE;
    }
    IF (!f2) {
      IF (f1?TRUE:C2(t2) && P(t1,t2,NULL)) {
        t:=t1||t2||NULL; OUTPUT t;
      }
      f1=TRUE;
    }
  }
  IF (!f1 && P(t1,NULL,NULL)) {
      t:=t1||NULL||NULL; OUTPUT t;
  }
}
```

In general, pushed-down predicates can be extracted from join conditions such as P1(T1,T2) and P(T2,T3). In this case, a pushed-down predicate is guarded also by a flag that prevents checking the predicate for the NULL-complemented row generated by the corresponding outer join operation.

Note that access by key from one inner table to another in the same nested join is prohibited if it is induced by a predicate from the WHERE condition. (We could use conditional key access in this case, but this technique is not employed yet in MySQL 5.0.)

6.2.11 Outer Join Simplification

Table expressions in the FROM clause of a query are simplified in many cases.

At the parser stage, queries with right outer join operations are converted to equivalent queries containing only left join operations. In the general case, the conversion is performed according to the following rule:

```
(T1, ...) RIGHT JOIN (T2,...) ON P(T1,...,T2,...) =
(T2, ...) LEFT JOIN (T1,...) ON P(T1,...,T2,...)
```

All inner join expressions of the form T1 INNER JOIN T2 ON P(T1,T2) are replaced by the list T1,T2, P(T1,T2) being joined as a conjunct to the WHERE condition (or to the join condition of the embedding join, if there is any).

When the optimizer evaluates plans for join queries with outer join operation, it takes into consideration only the plans where, for each such operation, the outer tables are accessed before the inner tables. The optimizer options are limited because only such plans enable us to execute queries with outer joins operations by the nested loop schema.

Suppose that we have a query of the form:

```
SELECT * T1 LEFT JOIN T2 ON P1(T1,T2)
  WHERE P(T1,T2) AND R(T2)
```

with R(T2) narrowing greatly the number of matching rows from table T2. If we executed the query as it is, the optimizer would have no other choice than to access table T1 before table T2, which may lead to a very inefficient execution plan.

Fortunately, MySQL converts such a query into a query without an outer join operation if the WHERE condition is null-rejected. A condition is called null-rejected for an outer join operation if it evaluates to FALSE or to UNKNOWN for any NULL-complemented row built for the operation.

Thus, for this outer join:

```
T1 LEFT JOIN T2 ON T1.A=T2.A
```

Conditions such as these are null-rejected:

```
T2.B IS NOT NULL,
T2.B > 3,
T2.C <= T1.C,
T2.B < 2 OR T2.C > 1
```

Conditions such as these are not null-rejected:

```
T2.B IS NULL,
T1.B < 3 OR T2.B IS NOT NULL,
T1.B < 3 OR T2.B > 3
```

The general rules for checking whether a condition is null-rejected for an outer join operation are simple. A condition is null-rejected in the following cases:

- If it is of the form A IS NOT NULL, where A is an attribute of any of the inner tables
- If it is a predicate containing a reference to an inner table that evaluates to UNKNOWN when one of its arguments is NULL
- If it is a conjunction containing a null-rejected condition as a conjunct
- If it is a disjunction of null-rejected conditions

A condition can be null-rejected for one outer join operation in a query and not null-rejected for another. In the query:

```
SELECT * FROM T1 LEFT JOIN T2 ON T2.A=T1.A
                LEFT JOIN T3 ON T3.B=T1.B
  WHERE T3.C > 0
```

the WHERE condition is null-rejected for the second outer join operation but is not null-rejected for the first one.

If the WHERE condition is null-rejected for an outer join operation in a query, the outer join operation is replaced by an inner join operation.

For example, the preceding query is replaced with the query:

```
SELECT * FROM T1 LEFT JOIN T2 ON T2.A=T1.A
                INNER JOIN T3 ON T3.B=T1.B
  WHERE T3.C > 0
```

For the original query, the optimizer would evaluate plans compatible with only one access order T1,T2,T3. For the replacing query, it additionally considers the access sequence T3,T1,T2.

A conversion of one outer join operation may trigger a conversion of another. Thus, the query:

```
SELECT * FROM T1 LEFT JOIN T2 ON T2.A=T1.A
                LEFT JOIN T3 ON T3.B=T2.B
  WHERE T3.C > 0
```

will be first converted to the query:

```
SELECT * FROM T1 LEFT JOIN T2 ON T2.A=T1.A
                INNER JOIN T3 ON T3.B=T2.B
  WHERE T3.C > 0
```

which is equivalent to the query:

```
SELECT * FROM (T1 LEFT JOIN T2 ON T2.A=T1.A), T3
  WHERE T3.C > 0 AND T3.B=T2.B
```

Now the remaining outer join operation can be replaced by an inner join, too, because the condition T3.B=T2.B is null-rejected and we get a query without outer joins at all:

```
SELECT * FROM (T1 INNER JOIN T2 ON T2.A=T1.A), T3
  WHERE T3.C > 0 AND T3.B=T2.B
```

Sometimes we succeed in replacing an embedded outer join operation, but cannot convert the embedding outer join. The following query:

```
SELECT * FROM T1 LEFT JOIN
              (T2 LEFT JOIN T3 ON T3.B=T2.B)
              ON T2.A=T1.A
  WHERE T3.C > 0
```

is converted to:

```
SELECT * FROM T1 LEFT JOIN
              (T2 INNER JOIN T3 ON T3.B=T2.B)
              ON T2.A=T1.A
  WHERE T3.C > 0,
```

That can be rewritten only to the form still containing the embedding outer join operation:

```
SELECT * FROM T1 LEFT JOIN
              (T2,T3)
              ON (T2.A=T1.A AND T3.B=T2.B)
  WHERE T3.C > 0.
```

When trying to convert an embedded outer join operation in a query, we must take into account the join condition for the embedding outer join together with the WHERE condition. In the query:

```
SELECT * FROM T1 LEFT JOIN
              (T2 LEFT JOIN T3 ON T3.B=T2.B)
              ON T2.A=T1.A AND T3.C=T1.C
  WHERE T3.D > 0 OR T1.D > 0
```

the WHERE condition is not null-rejected for the embedded outer join, but the join condition of the embedding outer join T2.A=T1.A AND T3.C=T1.C is null-rejected. So the query can be converted to:

```
SELECT * FROM T1 LEFT JOIN
              (T2, T3)
              ON T2.A=T1.A AND T3.C=T1.C AND T3.B=T2.B
  WHERE T3.D > 0 OR T1.D > 0
```

The algorithm that converts outer join operations into inner joins was implemented in full measure, as it has been described here, in MySQL 5.0.1. MySQL 4.1 performs only some simple conversions.

6.2.12 ORDER BY **Optimization**

In some cases, MySQL can use an index to satisfy an ORDER BY clause without doing any extra sorting.

The index can also be used even if the ORDER BY does not match the index exactly, as long as all of the unused portions of the index and all the extra ORDER BY columns are constants in the WHERE clause. The following queries use the index to resolve the ORDER BY part:

```
SELECT * FROM t1
  ORDER BY key_part1,key_part2,... ;

SELECT * FROM t1
  WHERE key_part1=constant
  ORDER BY key_part2;

SELECT * FROM t1
  ORDER BY key_part1 DESC, key_part2 DESC;

SELECT * FROM t1
  WHERE key_part1=1
  ORDER BY key_part1 DESC, key_part2 DESC;
```

In some cases, MySQL *cannot* use indexes to resolve the ORDER BY, although it still uses indexes to find the rows that match the WHERE clause. These cases include the following:

- You use ORDER BY on different keys:

  ```
  SELECT * FROM t1 ORDER BY key1, key2;
  ```

- You use ORDER BY on non-consecutive parts of a key:

  ```
  SELECT * FROM t1 WHERE key2=constant ORDER BY key_part2;
  ```

- You mix ASC and DESC:

  ```
  SELECT * FROM t1 ORDER BY key_part1 DESC, key_part2 ASC;
  ```

- The key used to fetch the rows is not the same as the one used in the ORDER BY:

  ```
  SELECT * FROM t1 WHERE key2=constant ORDER BY key1;
  ```

- You are joining many tables, and the columns in the ORDER BY are not all from the first non-constant table that is used to retrieve rows. (This is the first table in the EXPLAIN output that does not have a const join type.)

- You have different ORDER BY and GROUP BY expressions.

- The type of table index used does not store rows in order. For example, this is true for a HASH index in a MEMORY table.

With EXPLAIN SELECT ... ORDER BY, you can check whether MySQL can use indexes to resolve the query. It cannot if you see Using filesort in the Extra column. See Section 6.2.1, "Optimizing Queries with EXPLAIN."

A filesort optimization is used that records not only the sort key value and row position, but the columns required for the query as well. This avoids reading the rows twice. The filesort algorithm works like this:

1. Read the rows that match the WHERE clause.

2. For each row, record a tuple of values consisting of the sort key value and row position, and also the columns required for the query.

3. Sort the tuples by sort key value.

4. Retrieve the rows in sorted order, but read the required columns directly from the sorted tuples rather than by accessing the table a second time.

This algorithm represents a significant improvement over that used in some older versions of MySQL.

To avoid a slowdown, this optimization is used only if the total size of the extra columns in the sort tuple does not exceed the value of the `max_length_for_sort_data` system variable. (A symptom of setting the value of this variable too high is that you should see high disk activity and low CPU activity.)

If you want to increase `ORDER BY` speed, check whether you can get MySQL to use indexes rather than an extra sorting phase. If this is not possible, you can try the following strategies:

- Increase the size of the `sort_buffer_size` variable.
- Increase the size of the `read_rnd_buffer_size` variable.
- Change `tmpdir` to point to a dedicated filesystem with large amounts of empty space. This option accepts several paths that are used in round-robin fashion. Paths should be separated by colon characters (':') on Unix and semicolon characters (';') on Windows, NetWare, and OS/2. You can use this feature to spread the load across several directories. *Note*: The paths should be for directories in filesystems that are located on different *physical* disks, not different partitions on the same disk.

By default, MySQL sorts all `GROUP BY` *col1, col2, ...* queries as if you specified `ORDER BY` *col1, col2, ...* in the query as well. If you include an `ORDER BY` clause explicitly that contains the same column list, MySQL optimizes it away without any speed penalty, although the sorting still occurs. If a query includes `GROUP BY` but you want to avoid the overhead of sorting the result, you can suppress sorting by specifying `ORDER BY NULL`. For example:

```
INSERT INTO foo
SELECT a, COUNT(*) FROM bar GROUP BY a ORDER BY NULL;
```

6.2.13 GROUP BY Optimization

The most general way to satisfy a `GROUP BY` clause is to scan the whole table and create a new temporary table where all rows from each group are consecutive, and then use this temporary table to discover groups and apply aggregate functions (if any). In some cases, MySQL is able to do much better than that and to avoid creation of temporary tables by using index access.

The most important preconditions for using indexes for `GROUP BY` are that all `GROUP BY` columns reference attributes from the same index, and that the index stores its keys in order (for example, this is a `BTREE` index and not a `HASH` index). Whether use of temporary tables can be replaced by index access also depends on which parts of an index are used in a query, the conditions specified for these parts, and the selected aggregate functions.

There are two ways to execute a GROUP BY query via index access, as detailed in the following sections. In the first method, the grouping operation is applied together with all range predicates (if any). The second method first performs a range scan, and then groups the resulting tuples.

6.2.13.1 Loose Index Scan

The most efficient way to process GROUP BY is when the index is used to directly retrieve the group fields. With this access method, MySQL uses the property of some index types that the keys are ordered (for example, BTREE). This property enables use of lookup groups in an index without having to consider all keys in the index that satisfy all WHERE conditions. This access method considers only a fraction of the keys in an index, so it is called a *loose index scan*. When there is no WHERE clause, a loose index scan reads as many keys as the number of groups, which may be a much smaller number than that of all keys. If the WHERE clause contains range predicates (see the discussion of the range join type in Section 6.2.1, "Optimizing Queries with EXPLAIN"), a loose index scan looks up the first key of each group that satisfies the range conditions, and again reads the least possible number of keys. This is possible under the following conditions:

- The query is over a single table.
- The GROUP BY includes the first consecutive parts of the index. (If, instead of GROUP BY, the query has a DISTINCT clause, all distinct attributes refer to the beginning of the index.)
- The only aggregate functions used (if any) are MIN() and MAX(), and all of them refer to the same column.
- Any other parts of the index than those from the GROUP BY referenced in the query must be constants (that is, they must be referenced in equalities with constants), except for the argument of MIN() or MAX() functions.

The EXPLAIN output for such queries shows Using index for group-by in the Extra column.

The following queries fall into this category, assuming that there is an index idx(c1,c2,c3) on table t1(c1,c2,c3,c4):

```
SELECT c1, c2 FROM t1 GROUP BY c1, c2;
SELECT DISTINCT c1, c2 FROM t1;
SELECT c1, MIN(c2) FROM t1 GROUP BY c1;
SELECT c1, c2 FROM t1 WHERE c1 < const GROUP BY c1, c2;
SELECT MAX(c3), MIN(c3), c1, c2 FROM t1 WHERE c2 > const GROUP BY c1, c2;
SELECT c2 FROM t1 WHERE c1 < const GROUP BY c1, c2;
SELECT c1, c2 FROM t1 WHERE c3 = const GROUP BY c1, c2;
```

The following queries cannot be executed with this quick select method, for the reasons given:

- There are aggregate functions other than MIN() or MAX(), for example:
  ```
  SELECT c1, SUM(c2) FROM t1 GROUP BY c1;
  ```

- The fields in the GROUP BY clause do not refer to the beginning of the index, as shown here:

```
SELECT c1,c2 FROM t1 GROUP BY c2, c3;
```

- The query refers to a part of a key that comes after the GROUP BY part, and for which there is no equality with a constant, an example being:

```
SELECT c1,c3 FROM t1 GROUP BY c1, c2;
```

6.2.13.2 Tight Index Scan

A tight index scan may be either a full index scan or a range index scan, depending on the query conditions.

When the conditions for a loose index scan are not met, it is still possible to avoid creation of temporary tables for GROUP BY queries. If there are range conditions in the WHERE clause, this method reads only the keys that satisfy these conditions. Otherwise, it performs an index scan. Because this method reads all keys in each range defined by the WHERE clause, or scans the whole index if there are no range conditions, we term it a *tight index scan*. Notice that with a tight index scan, the grouping operation is performed only after all keys that satisfy the range conditions have been found.

For this method to work, it is sufficient that there is a constant equality condition for all columns in a query referring to parts of the key coming before or in between parts of the GROUP BY key. The constants from the equality conditions fill in any "gaps" in the search keys so that it is possible to form complete prefixes of the index. These index prefixes then can be used for index lookups. If we require sorting of the GROUP BY result, and it is possible to form search keys that are prefixes of the index, MySQL also avoids extra sorting operations because searching with prefixes in an ordered index already retrieves all the keys in order.

The following queries do not work with the loose index scan access method described earlier, but still work with the tight index scan access method (assuming that there is an index idx(c1,c2,c3) on table t1(c1,c2,c3,c4)).

- There is a gap in the GROUP BY, but it is covered by the condition c2 = 'a':

```
SELECT c1, c2, c3 FROM t1 WHERE c2 = 'a' GROUP BY c1, c3;
```

- The GROUP BY does not begin with the first part of the key, but there is a condition that provides a constant for that part:

```
SELECT c1, c2, c3 FROM t1 WHERE c1 = 'a' GROUP BY c2, c3;
```

6.2.14 LIMIT Optimization

In some cases, MySQL handles a query differently when you are using LIMIT *row_count* and not using HAVING:

- If you are selecting only a few rows with LIMIT, MySQL uses indexes in some cases when normally it would prefer to do a full table scan.

- If you use LIMIT *row_count* with ORDER BY, MySQL ends the sorting as soon as it has found the first *row_count* rows of the sorted result, rather than sorting the entire result. If ordering is done by using an index, this is very fast. If a filesort must be done, all rows that match the query without the LIMIT clause must be selected, and most or all of them must be sorted, before it can be ascertained that the first *row_count* rows have been found. In either case, after the initial rows have been found, there is no need to sort any remainder of the result set, and MySQL does not do so.

- When combining LIMIT *row_count* with DISTINCT, MySQL stops as soon as it finds *row_count* unique rows.

- In some cases, a GROUP BY can be resolved by reading the key in order (or doing a sort on the key) and then calculating summaries until the key value changes. In this case, LIMIT *row_count* does not calculate any unnecessary GROUP BY values.

- As soon as MySQL has sent the required number of rows to the client, it aborts the query unless you are using SQL_CALC_FOUND_ROWS.

- LIMIT 0 quickly returns an empty set. This can be useful for checking the validity of a query. When using one of the MySQL APIs, it can also be employed for obtaining the types of the result columns. (This trick does not work in the MySQL Monitor, which merely displays Empty set in such cases; you should instead use SHOW COLUMNS or DESCRIBE for this purpose.)

- When the server uses temporary tables to resolve the query, it uses the LIMIT *row_count* clause to calculate how much space is required.

6.2.15 How to Avoid Table Scans

The output from EXPLAIN shows ALL in the type column when MySQL uses a table scan to resolve a query. This usually happens under the following conditions:

- The table is so small that it is faster to perform a table scan than to bother with a key lookup. This is common for tables with fewer than 10 rows and a short row length.

- There are no usable restrictions in the ON or WHERE clause for indexed columns.

- You are comparing indexed columns with constant values and MySQL has calculated (based on the index tree) that the constants cover too large a part of the table and that a table scan would be faster. See Section 6.2.4, "WHERE Clause Optimization."

- You are using a key with low cardinality (many rows match the key value) through another column. In this case, MySQL assumes that by using the key it probably will do many key lookups and that a table scan would be faster.

For small tables, a table scan often is appropriate and the performance impact is negligible. For large tables, try the following techniques to avoid having the optimizer incorrectly choose a table scan:

- Use ANALYZE TABLE *tbl_name* to update the key distributions for the scanned table.

- Use FORCE INDEX for the scanned table to tell MySQL that table scans are very expensive compared to using the given index:

```
SELECT * FROM t1, t2 FORCE INDEX (index_for_column)
  WHERE t1.col_name=t2.col_name;
```

- Start mysqld with the --max-seeks-for-key=1000 option or use SET max_seeks_for_key=1000 to tell the optimizer to assume that no key scan causes more than 1,000 key seeks. See Section 4.2.2, "Server System Variables."

6.2.16 Speed of INSERT Statements

The time required for inserting a row is determined by the following factors, where the numbers indicate approximate proportions:

- Connecting: (3)
- Sending query to server: (2)
- Parsing query: (2)
- Inserting row: (1 × size of row)
- Inserting indexes: (1 × number of indexes)
- Closing: (1)

This does not take into consideration the initial overhead to open tables, which is done once for each concurrently running query.

The size of the table slows down the insertion of indexes by log N, assuming B-tree indexes.

You can use the following methods to speed up inserts:

- If you are inserting many rows from the same client at the same time, use INSERT statements with multiple VALUES lists to insert several rows at a time. This is considerably faster (many times faster in some cases) than using separate single-row INSERT statements. If you are adding data to a non-empty table, you can tune the bulk_insert_buffer_size variable to make data insertion even faster. See Section 4.2.2, "Server System Variables."

- If you are inserting a lot of rows from different clients, you can get higher speed by using the INSERT DELAYED statement.

- For a MyISAM table, you can use concurrent inserts to add rows at the same time that SELECT statements are running if there are no deleted rows in middle of the table. See Section 6.3.3, "Concurrent Inserts."

- When loading a table from a text file, use LOAD DATA INFILE. This is usually 20 times faster than using INSERT statements.

- With some extra work, it is possible to make LOAD DATA INFILE run even faster for a MyISAM table when the table has many indexes. Use the following procedure:

  1. Optionally create the table with CREATE TABLE.

  2. Execute a FLUSH TABLES statement or a mysqladmin flush-tables command.

3. Use myisamchk --keys-used=0 -rq */path/to/db/tbl_name*. This removes all use of indexes for the table.

4. Insert data into the table with LOAD DATA INFILE. This does not update any indexes and therefore is very fast.

5. If you intend only to read from the table in the future, use myisampack to compress it. See Section 8.1.3.3, "Compressed Table Characteristics."

6. Re-create the indexes with myisamchk -rq */path/to/db/tbl_name*. This creates the index tree in memory before writing it to disk, which is much faster than updating the index during LOAD DATA INFILE because it avoids lots of disk seeks. The resulting index tree is also perfectly balanced.

7. Execute a FLUSH TABLES statement or a mysqladmin flush-tables command.

Note that LOAD DATA INFILE performs the preceding optimization automatically if the MyISAM table into which you insert data is empty. The main difference is that you can let myisamchk allocate much more temporary memory for the index creation than you might want the server to allocate for index re-creation when it executes the LOAD DATA INFILE statement.

You can also disable or enable the indexes for a MyISAM table by using the following statements rather than myisamchk. If you use these statements, you can skip the FLUSH TABLE operations:

```
ALTER TABLE tbl_name DISABLE KEYS;
ALTER TABLE tbl_name ENABLE KEYS;
```

- To speed up INSERT operations that are performed with multiple statements, lock your tables:

```
LOCK TABLES a WRITE;
INSERT INTO a VALUES (1,23),(2,34),(4,33);
INSERT INTO a VALUES (8,26),(6,29);
UNLOCK TABLES;
```

This benefits performance because the index buffer is flushed to disk only once, after all INSERT statements have completed. Normally, there would be as many index buffer flushes as there are INSERT statements. Explicit locking statements are not needed if you can insert all rows with a single INSERT.

For transactional tables, you should use START TRANSACTION and COMMIT instead of LOCK TABLES to obtain faster insertions.

Locking also lowers the total time for multiple-connection tests, although the maximum wait time for individual connections might go up because they wait for locks. For example:

1. Connection 1 does 1000 inserts

2. Connections 2, 3, and 4 do 1 insert

3. Connection 5 does 1000 inserts

If you do not use locking, connections 2, 3, and 4 finish before 1 and 5. If you use locking, connections 2, 3, and 4 probably do not finish before 1 or 5, but the total time should be about 40% faster.

INSERT, UPDATE, and DELETE operations are very fast in MySQL, but you can obtain better overall performance by adding locks around everything that does more than about five inserts or updates in a row. If you do very many inserts in a row, you could do a LOCK TABLES followed by an UNLOCK TABLES once in a while (each 1,000 rows or so) to allow other threads access to the table. This would still result in a nice performance gain.

INSERT is still much slower for loading data than LOAD DATA INFILE, even when using the strategies just outlined.

- To increase performance for MyISAM tables, for both LOAD DATA INFILE and INSERT, enlarge the key cache by increasing the key_buffer_size system variable. See Section 6.5.2, "Tuning Server Parameters."

6.2.17 Speed of UPDATE Statements

An update statement is optimized like a SELECT query with the additional overhead of a write. The speed of the write depends on the amount of data being updated and the number of indexes that are updated. Indexes that are not changed do not get updated.

Another way to get fast updates is to delay updates and then do many updates in a row later. Performing multiple updates together is much quicker than doing one at a time if you lock the table.

For a MyISAM table that uses dynamic row format, updating a row to a longer total length may split the row. If you do this often, it is very important to use OPTIMIZE TABLE occasionally.

6.2.18 Speed of DELETE Statements

The time required to delete individual rows is exactly proportional to the number of indexes. To delete rows more quickly, you can increase the size of the key cache by increasing the key_buffer_size system variable. See Section 6.5.2, "Tuning Server Parameters."

To delete all rows from a table, TRUNCATE TABLE tbl_name is faster than DELETE FROM tbl_name.

6.2.19 Other Optimization Tips

This section lists a number of miscellaneous tips for improving query processing speed:

- Use persistent connections to the database to avoid connection overhead. If you cannot use persistent connections and you are initiating many new connections to the database, you may want to change the value of the thread_cache_size variable. See Section 6.5.2, "Tuning Server Parameters."
- Always check whether all your queries really use the indexes that you have created in the tables. In MySQL, you can do this with the EXPLAIN statement. See Section 6.2.1, "Optimizing Queries with EXPLAIN."

- Try to avoid complex SELECT queries on MyISAM tables that are updated frequently, to avoid problems with table locking that occur due to contention between readers and writers.

- With MyISAM tables that have no deleted rows in the middle, you can insert rows at the end at the same time that another query is reading from the table. If it is important to be able to do this, you should consider using the table in ways that avoid deleting rows. Another possibility is to run OPTIMIZE TABLE to defragment the table after you have deleted a lot of rows from it. See Section 8.1, "The MyISAM Storage Engine."

- To fix any compression issues that may have occurred with ARCHIVE tables, you can use OPTIMIZE TABLE. See Section 8.8, "The ARCHIVE Storage Engine."

- Use ALTER TABLE ... ORDER BY expr1, expr2, ... if you usually retrieve rows in expr1, expr2, ... order. By using this option after extensive changes to the table, you may be able to get higher performance.

- In some cases, it may make sense to introduce a column that is "hashed" based on information from other columns. If this column is short and reasonably unique, it may be much faster than a "wide" index on many columns. In MySQL, it is very easy to use this extra column:

```
SELECT * FROM tbl_name
  WHERE hash_col=MD5(CONCAT(col1,col2))
  AND col1='constant' AND col2='constant';
```

- For MyISAM tables that change frequently, you should try to avoid all variable-length columns (VARCHAR, BLOB, and TEXT). The table uses dynamic row format if it includes even a single variable-length column. See Chapter 8, "Storage Engines and Table Types."

- It is normally not useful to split a table into different tables just because the rows become large. In accessing a row, the biggest performance hit is the disk seek needed to find the first byte of the row. After finding the data, most modern disks can read the entire row fast enough for most applications. The only cases where splitting up a table makes an appreciable difference is if it is a MyISAM table using dynamic row format that you can change to a fixed row size, or if you very often need to scan the table but do not need most of the columns. See Chapter 8, "Storage Engines and Table Types."

- If you often need to calculate results such as counts based on information from a lot of rows, it may be preferable to introduce a new table and update the counter in real time. An update of the following form is very fast:

```
UPDATE tbl_name SET count_col=count_col+1 WHERE key_col=constant;
```

This is very important when you use MySQL storage engines such as MyISAM that has only table-level locking (multiple readers with single writers). This also gives better performance with most database systems, because the row locking manager in this case has less to do.

- If you need to collect statistics from large log tables, use summary tables instead of scanning the entire log table. Maintaining the summaries should be much faster than trying to calculate statistics "live." Regenerating new summary tables from the logs when things change (depending on business decisions) is faster than changing the running application.

- If possible, you should classify reports as "live" or as "statistical," where data needed for statistical reports is created only from summary tables that are generated periodically from the live data.

- Take advantage of the fact that columns have default values. Insert values explicitly only when the value to be inserted differs from the default. This reduces the parsing that MySQL must do and improves the insert speed.

- In some cases, it is convenient to pack and store data into a BLOB column. In this case, you must provide code in your application to pack and unpack information, but this may save a lot of accesses at some stage. This is practical when you have data that does not conform well to a rows-and-columns table structure.

- Normally, you should try to keep all data non-redundant (observing what is referred to in database theory as *third normal form*). However, there may be situations in which it can be advantageous to duplicate information or create summary tables to gain more speed.

- Stored routines or UDFs (user-defined functions) may be a good way to gain performance for some tasks.

- You can always gain something by caching queries or answers in your application and then performing many inserts or updates together. If your database system supports table locks (as do MySQL and Oracle), this should help to ensure that the index cache is flushed only once after all updates. You can also take advantage of MySQL's query cache to achieve similar results; see Section 4.14, "The MySQL Query Cache."

- Use INSERT DELAYED when you do not need to know when your data is written. This reduces the overall insertion impact because many rows can be written with a single disk write.

- Use INSERT LOW_PRIORITY when you want to give SELECT statements higher priority than your inserts.

- Use SELECT HIGH_PRIORITY to get retrievals that jump the queue. That is, the SELECT is executed even if there is another client waiting to do a write.

- Use multiple-row INSERT statements to store many rows with one SQL statement. Many SQL servers support this, including MySQL.

- Use LOAD DATA INFILE to load large amounts of data. This is faster than using INSERT statements.

- Use AUTO_INCREMENT columns to generate unique values.

- Use OPTIMIZE TABLE once in a while to avoid fragmentation with dynamic-format MyISAM tables. See Section 8.1.3, "MyISAM Table Storage Formats."

- Use MEMORY (HEAP) tables when possible to get more speed. See Section 8.4, "The MEMORY (HEAP) Storage Engine." MEMORY tables are useful for non-critical data that is accessed often, such as information about the last displayed banner for users who don't have cookies enabled in their Web browser. User sessions are another alternative available in many Web application environments for handling volatile state data.

- With Web servers, images and other binary assets should normally be stored as files. That is, store only a reference to the file rather than the file itself in the database. Most Web servers are better at caching files than database contents, so using files is generally faster.

- Columns with identical information in different tables should be declared to have identical data types so that joins based on the corresponding columns will be faster.

- Try to keep column names simple. For example, in a table named customer, use a column name of name instead of customer_name. To make your names portable to other SQL servers, you should keep them shorter than 18 characters.

- If you need really high speed, you should take a look at the low-level interfaces for data storage that the different SQL servers support. For example, by accessing the MySQL MyISAM storage engine directly, you could get a speed increase of two to five times compared to using the SQL interface. To be able to do this, the data must be on the same server as the application, and usually it should only be accessed by one process (because external file locking is really slow). You could eliminate these problems by introducing low-level MyISAM commands in the MySQL server (this could be one easy way to get more performance if needed). By carefully designing the database interface, it should be quite easy to support this type of optimization.

- If you are using numerical data, it is faster in many cases to access information from a database (using a live connection) than to access a text file. Information in the database is likely to be stored in a more compact format than in the text file, so accessing it involves fewer disk accesses. You also save code in your application because you need not parse your text files to find line and column boundaries.

- Replication can provide a performance benefit for some operations. You can distribute client retrievals among replication servers to split up the load. To avoid slowing down the master while making backups, you can make backups using a slave server. See Chapter 5, "Replication."

- Declaring a MyISAM table with the DELAY_KEY_WRITE=1 table option makes index updates faster because they are not flushed to disk until the table is closed. The downside is that if something kills the server while such a table is open, you should ensure that the table is okay by running the server with the --myisam-recover option, or by running myisamchk before restarting the server. (However, even in this case, you should not lose anything by using DELAY_KEY_WRITE, because the key information can always be generated from the data rows.)

6.3 Locking Issues

6.3.1 Locking Methods

MySQL uses table-level locking for MyISAM and MEMORY tables, page-level locking for BDB tables, and row-level locking for InnoDB tables.

In many cases, you can make an educated guess about which locking type is best for an application, but generally it is difficult to say that a given lock type is better than another. Everything depends on the application and different parts of an application may require different lock types.

To decide whether you want to use a storage engine with row-level locking, you should look at what your application does and what mix of select and update statements it uses. For example, most Web applications perform many selects, relatively few deletes, updates based mainly on key values, and inserts into a few specific tables. The base MySQL MyISAM setup is very well tuned for this.

Table locking in MySQL is deadlock-free for storage engines that use table-level locking. Deadlock avoidance is managed by always requesting all needed locks at once at the beginning of a query and always locking the tables in the same order.

The table-locking method MySQL uses for WRITE locks works as follows:

- If there are no locks on the table, put a write lock on it.
- Otherwise, put the lock request in the write lock queue.

The table-locking method MySQL uses for READ locks works as follows:

- If there are no write locks on the table, put a read lock on it.
- Otherwise, put the lock request in the read lock queue.

When a lock is released, the lock is made available to the threads in the write lock queue and then to the threads in the read lock queue. This means that if you have many updates for a table, SELECT statements wait until there are no more updates.

You can analyze the table lock contention on your system by checking the Table_locks_waited and Table_locks_immediate status variables:

```
mysql> SHOW STATUS LIKE 'Table%';
+-----------------------+---------+
| Variable_name         | Value   |
+-----------------------+---------+
| Table_locks_immediate | 1151552 |
| Table_locks_waited    | 15324   |
+-----------------------+---------+
```

If a MyISAM table contains no free blocks in the middle, rows always are inserted at the end of the data file. In this case, you can freely mix concurrent INSERT and SELECT statements for a MyISAM table without locks. That is, you can insert rows into a MyISAM table at the same time other clients are reading from it. (Holes can result from rows having been deleted from or updated in the middle of the table. If there are holes, concurrent inserts are disabled but are re-enabled automatically when all holes have been filled with new data.)

If you want to perform many INSERT and SELECT operations on a table when concurrent inserts are not possible, you can insert rows in a temporary table and update the real table with the rows from the temporary table once in a while. This can be done with the following code:

```
mysql> LOCK TABLES real_table WRITE, insert_table WRITE;
mysql> INSERT INTO real_table SELECT * FROM insert_table;
mysql> TRUNCATE TABLE insert_table;
mysql> UNLOCK TABLES;
```

InnoDB uses row locks and BDB uses page locks. For these two storage engines, deadlocks are possible because they automatically acquire locks during the processing of SQL statements, not at the start of the transaction.

Advantages of row-level locking:

- Fewer lock conflicts when accessing different rows in many threads.
- Fewer changes for rollbacks.
- Possible to lock a single row for a long time.

Disadvantages of row-level locking:

- Requires more memory than page-level or table-level locks.
- Slower than page-level or table-level locks when used on a large part of the table because you must acquire many more locks.
- Definitely much slower than other locks if you often do GROUP BY operations on a large part of the data or if you must scan the entire table frequently.

Table locks are superior to page-level or row-level locks in the following cases:

- Most statements for the table are reads.
- A mix of reads and writes, where writes are updates or deletes for a single row that can be fetched with one key read:

  ```
  UPDATE tbl_name SET column=value WHERE unique_key_col=key_value;
  DELETE FROM tbl_name WHERE unique_key_col=key_value;
  ```

- SELECT combined with concurrent INSERT statements, and very few UPDATE or DELETE statements.
- Many scans or GROUP BY operations on the entire table without any writers.

With higher-level locks, you can more easily tune applications by supporting locks of different types, because the lock overhead is less than for row-level locks.

Options other than row-level or page-level locking:

- Versioning (such as that used in MySQL for concurrent inserts) where it is possible to have one writer at the same time as many readers. This means that the database or table supports different views for the data depending on when access begins. Other common terms for this are "time travel," "copy on write," or "copy on demand."
- Copy on demand is in many cases superior to page-level or row-level locking. However, in the worst case, it can use much more memory than using normal locks.

- Instead of using row-level locks, you can employ application-level locks, such as GET_LOCK() and RELEASE_LOCK() in MySQL. These are advisory locks, so they work only in well-behaved applications.

6.3.2 Table Locking Issues

To achieve a very high lock speed, MySQL uses table locking (instead of page, row, or column locking) for all storage engines except InnoDB and BDB.

For InnoDB and BDB tables, MySQL uses table locking only if you explicitly lock the table with LOCK TABLES. For these storage engines, we recommend that you not use LOCK TABLES at all, because InnoDB uses automatic row-level locking and BDB uses page-level locking to ensure transaction isolation.

For large tables, table locking is much better than row locking for most applications, but there are some pitfalls:

- Table locking enables many threads to read from a table at the same time, but if a thread wants to write to a table, it must first get exclusive access. During the update, all other threads that want to access this particular table must wait until the update is done.

- Table updates normally are considered to be more important than table retrievals, so they are given higher priority. This should ensure that updates to a table are not "starved" even if there is heavy SELECT activity for the table.

- Table locking causes problems in cases such as when a thread is waiting because the disk is full and free space needs to become available before the thread can proceed. In this case, all threads that want to access the problem table are also put in a waiting state until more disk space is made available.

Table locking is also disadvantageous under the following scenario:

- A client issues a SELECT that takes a long time to run.

- Another client then issues an UPDATE on the same table. This client waits until the SELECT is finished.

- Another client issues another SELECT statement on the same table. Because UPDATE has higher priority than SELECT, this SELECT waits for the UPDATE to finish, *and* for the first SELECT to finish.

The following items describe some ways to avoid or reduce contention caused by table locking:

- Try to get the SELECT statements to run faster so that they lock tables for a shorter time. You might have to create some summary tables to do this.

- Start mysqld with --low-priority-updates. This gives all statements that update (modify) a table lower priority than SELECT statements. In this case, the second SELECT statement in the preceding scenario would execute before the UPDATE statement, and would not need to wait for the first SELECT to finish.

- You can specify that all updates issued in a specific connection should be done with low priority by using the SET LOW_PRIORITY_UPDATES=1 statement.

- You can give a specific INSERT, UPDATE, or DELETE statement lower priority with the LOW_PRIORITY attribute.

- You can give a specific SELECT statement higher priority with the HIGH_PRIORITY attribute.

- You can start mysqld with a low value for the max_write_lock_count system variable to force MySQL to temporarily elevate the priority of all SELECT statements that are waiting for a table after a specific number of inserts to the table occur. This allows READ locks after a certain number of WRITE locks.

- If you have problems with INSERT combined with SELECT, you might want to consider switching to MyISAM tables, which support concurrent SELECT and INSERT statements.

- If you mix inserts and deletes on the same table, INSERT DELAYED may be of great help.

- If you have problems with mixed SELECT and DELETE statements, the LIMIT option to DELETE may help.

- Using SQL_BUFFER_RESULT with SELECT statements can help to make the duration of table locks shorter.

- You could change the locking code in mysys/thr_lock.c to use a single queue. In this case, write locks and read locks would have the same priority, which might help some applications.

Here are some tips concerning table locks in MySQL:

- Concurrent users are not a problem if you do not mix updates with selects that need to examine many rows in the same table.

- You can use LOCK TABLES to increase speed, because many updates within a single lock is much faster than updating without locks. Splitting table contents into separate tables may also help.

- If you encounter speed problems with table locks in MySQL, you may be able to improve performance by converting some of your tables to InnoDB or BDB tables. See Section 8.2, "The InnoDB Storage Engine," and Section 8.5, "The BDB (BerkeleyDB) Storage Engine."

6.3.3 Concurrent Inserts

For a MyISAM table, you can use concurrent inserts to add rows at the same time that SELECT statements are running if there are no deleted rows in middle of the table.

Under circumstances where concurrent inserts can be used, there is seldom any need to use the DELAYED modifier for INSERT statements.

If you are using the binary log, concurrent inserts are converted to normal inserts for CREATE ... SELECT or INSERT ... SELECT statements. This is done to ensure that you can re-create an exact copy of your tables by applying the log during a backup operation.

With LOAD DATA INFILE, if you specify CONCURRENT with a MyISAM table that satisfies the condition for concurrent inserts (that is, it contains no free blocks in the middle), other threads can retrieve data from the table while LOAD DATA is executing. Using this option affects the performance of LOAD DATA a bit, even if no other thread is using the table at the same time.

6.4 Optimizing Database Structure

6.4.1 Design Choices

MySQL keeps row data and index data in separate files. Many (almost all) other database systems mix row and index data in the same file. We believe that the MySQL choice is better for a very wide range of modern systems.

Another way to store the row data is to keep the information for each column in a separate area (examples are SDBM and Focus). This causes a performance hit for every query that accesses more than one column. Because this degenerates so quickly when more than one column is accessed, we believe that this model is not good for general-purpose databases.

The more common case is that the index and data are stored together (as in Oracle/Sybase, et al). In this case, you find the row information at the leaf page of the index. The good thing with this layout is that it, in many cases, depending on how well the index is cached, saves a disk read. The bad things with this layout are:

- Table scanning is much slower because you have to read through the indexes to get at the data.

- You cannot use only the index table to retrieve data for a query.

- You use more space because you must duplicate indexes from the nodes (you cannot store the row in the nodes).

- Deletes degenerate the table over time (because indexes in nodes are usually not updated on delete).

- It is more difficult to cache only the index data.

6.4.2 Make Your Data As Small As Possible

One of the most basic optimizations is to design your tables to take as little space on the disk as possible. This can result in huge improvements because disk reads are faster, and smaller tables normally require less main memory while their contents are being actively processed during query execution. Indexing also is a lesser resource burden if done on smaller columns.

MySQL supports many different storage engines (table types) and row formats. For each table, you can decide which storage and indexing method to use. Choosing the proper table format for your application may give you a big performance gain. See Chapter 8, "Storage Engines and Table Types."

You can get better performance for a table and minimize storage space by using the techniques listed here:

- Use the most efficient (smallest) data types possible. MySQL has many specialized types that save disk space and memory. For example, use the smaller integer types if possible to get smaller tables. MEDIUMINT is often a better choice than INT because a MEDIUMINT column uses 25% less space.

- Declare columns to be NOT NULL if possible. It makes everything faster and you save one bit per column. If you really need NULL in your application, you should definitely use it. Just avoid having it on all columns by default.

- For MyISAM tables, if you do not have any variable-length columns (VARCHAR, TEXT, or BLOB columns), a fixed-size row format is used. This is faster but unfortunately may waste some space. See Section 8.1.3, "MyISAM Table Storage Formats." You can hint that you want to have fixed-length rows even if you have VARCHAR columns with the CREATE TABLE option ROW_FORMAT=FIXED.

- Starting with MySQL 5.0.3, InnoDB tables use a more compact storage format. In earlier versions of MySQL, InnoDB rows contain some redundant information, such as the number of columns and the length of each column, even for fixed-size columns. By default, tables are created in the compact format (ROW_FORMAT=COMPACT). If you wish to downgrade to older versions of MySQL, you can request the old format with ROW_FORMAT=REDUNDANT.

  The compact InnoDB format also changes how CHAR columns containing UTF-8 data are stored. With ROW_FORMAT=REDUNDANT, a UTF-8 CHAR(N) occupies 3 × N bytes, given that the maximum length of a UTF-8 encoded character is three bytes. Many languages can be written primarily using single-byte UTF-8 characters, so a fixed storage length often wastes space. With ROW_FORMAT=COMPACT format, InnoDB allocates a variable amount of storage in the range from N to 3 × N bytes for these columns by stripping trailing spaces if necessary. The minimum storage length is kept as N bytes to facilitate in-place updates in typical cases.

- The primary index of a table should be as short as possible. This makes identification of each row easy and efficient.

- Create only the indexes that you really need. Indexes are good for retrieval but bad when you need to store data quickly. If you access a table mostly by searching on a combination of columns, create an index on them. The first part of the index should be the column most used. If you *always* use many columns when selecting from the table, you should use the column with more duplicates first to obtain better compression of the index.

- If it is very likely that a string column has a unique prefix on the first number of characters, it's better to index only this prefix, using MySQL's support for creating an index on the leftmost part of the column. Shorter indexes are faster, not only because they require less disk space, but also because they give you more hits in the index cache, and thus fewer disk seeks. See Section 6.5.2, "Tuning Server Parameters."

- In some circumstances, it can be beneficial to split into two a table that is scanned very often. This is especially true if it is a dynamic-format table and it is possible to use a smaller static format table that can be used to find the relevant rows when scanning the table.

6.4.3 Column Indexes

All MySQL data types can be indexed. Use of indexes on the relevant columns is the best way to improve the performance of SELECT operations.

The maximum number of indexes per table and the maximum index length is defined per storage engine. See Chapter 8, "Storage Engines and Table Types." All storage engines support at least 16 indexes per table and a total index length of at least 256 bytes. Most storage engines have higher limits.

With *col_name(N)* syntax in an index specification, you can create an index that uses only the first *N* characters of a string column. Indexing only a prefix of column values in this way can make the index file much smaller. When you index a BLOB or TEXT column, you *must* specify a prefix length for the index. For example:

```
CREATE TABLE test (blob_col BLOB, INDEX(blob_col(10)));
```

Prefixes can be up to 1000 bytes long (767 bytes for InnoDB tables). Note that prefix limits are measured in bytes, whereas the prefix length in CREATE TABLE statements is interpreted as number of characters. *Be sure to take this into account when specifying a prefix length for a column that uses a multi-byte character set.*

You can also create FULLTEXT indexes. These are used for full-text searches. Only the MyISAM storage engine supports FULLTEXT indexes and only for CHAR, VARCHAR, and TEXT columns. Indexing always takes place over the entire column and partial (column prefix) indexing is not supported.

You can also create indexes on spatial data types. Currently, only MyISAM supports R-tree indexes on spatial types. As of MySQL 5.0.16, other storage engines use B-trees for indexing spatial types (except for ARCHIVE and NDBCLUSTER, which do not support spatial type indexing).

The MEMORY storage engine uses HASH indexes by default, but also supports BTREE indexes.

6.4.4 Multiple-Column Indexes

MySQL can create composite indexes (that is, indexes on multiple columns). An index may consist of up to 15 columns. For certain data types, you can index a prefix of the column (see Section 6.4.3, "Column Indexes").

A multiple-column index can be considered a sorted array containing values that are created by concatenating the values of the indexed columns.

MySQL uses multiple-column indexes in such a way that queries are fast when you specify a known quantity for the first column of the index in a WHERE clause, even if you do not specify values for the other columns.

Suppose that a table has the following specification:

```
CREATE TABLE test (
    id INT NOT NULL,
    last_name CHAR(30) NOT NULL,
    first_name CHAR(30) NOT NULL,
    PRIMARY KEY (id),
    INDEX name (last_name,first_name)
);
```

The name index is an index over the last_name and first_name columns. The index can be used for queries that specify values in a known range for last_name, or for both last_name and first_name. Therefore, the name index is used in the following queries:

```
SELECT * FROM test WHERE last_name='Widenius';

SELECT * FROM test
  WHERE last_name='Widenius' AND first_name='Michael';

SELECT * FROM test
  WHERE last_name='Widenius'
  AND (first_name='Michael' OR first_name='Monty');

SELECT * FROM test
  WHERE last_name='Widenius'
  AND first_name >='M' AND first_name < 'N';
```

However, the name index is *not* used in the following queries:

```
SELECT * FROM test WHERE first_name='Michael';

SELECT * FROM test
  WHERE last_name='Widenius' OR first_name='Michael';
```

The manner in which MySQL uses indexes to improve query performance is discussed further in Section 6.4.5, "How MySQL Uses Indexes."

6.4.5 How MySQL Uses Indexes

Indexes are used to find rows with specific column values quickly. Without an index, MySQL must begin with the first row and then read through the entire table to find the relevant rows. The larger the table, the more this costs. If the table has an index for the columns in question, MySQL can quickly determine the position to seek to in the middle of the data file without having to look at all the data. If a table has 1,000 rows, this is at least 100 times faster than reading sequentially. If you need to access most of the rows, it is faster to read sequentially, because this minimizes disk seeks.

Most MySQL indexes (PRIMARY KEY, UNIQUE, INDEX, and FULLTEXT) are stored in B-trees. Exceptions are that indexes on spatial data types use R-trees, and that MEMORY tables also support hash indexes.

Strings are automatically prefix- and end-space compressed.

In general, indexes are used as described in the following discussion. Characteristics specific to hash indexes (as used in MEMORY tables) are described at the end of this section.

MySQL uses indexes for these operations:

- To find the rows matching a WHERE clause quickly.

- To eliminate rows from consideration. If there is a choice between multiple indexes, MySQL normally uses the index that finds the smallest number of rows.

- To retrieve rows from other tables when performing joins.

- To find the MIN() or MAX() value for a specific indexed column *key_col*. This is optimized by a preprocessor that checks whether you are using WHERE *key_part_N* = *constant* on all key parts that occur before *key_col* in the index. In this case, MySQL does a single key lookup for each MIN() or MAX() expression and replaces it with a constant. If all expressions are replaced with constants, the query returns at once. For example:

```
SELECT MIN(key_part2),MAX(key_part2)
  FROM tbl_name WHERE key_part1=10;
```

- To sort or group a table if the sorting or grouping is done on a leftmost prefix of a usable key (for example, ORDER BY *key_part1*, *key_part2*). If all key parts are followed by DESC, the key is read in reverse order. See Section 6.2.12, "ORDER BY Optimization."

- In some cases, a query can be optimized to retrieve values without consulting the data rows. If a query uses only columns from a table that are numeric and that form a leftmost prefix for some key, the selected values may be retrieved from the index tree for greater speed:

```
SELECT key_part3 FROM tbl_name
  WHERE key_part1=1
```

Suppose that you issue the following SELECT statement:

```
mysql> SELECT * FROM tbl_name WHERE col1=val1 AND col2=val2;
```

If a multiple-column index exists on col1 and col2, the appropriate rows can be fetched directly. If separate single-column indexes exist on col1 and col2, the optimizer tries to find the most restrictive index by deciding which index finds fewer rows and using that index to fetch the rows.

If the table has a multiple-column index, any leftmost prefix of the index can be used by the optimizer to find rows. For example, if you have a three-column index on (col1, col2, col3), you have indexed search capabilities on (col1), (col1, col2), and (col1, col2, col3).

MySQL cannot use a partial index if the columns do not form a leftmost prefix of the index. Suppose that you have the SELECT statements shown here:

```
SELECT * FROM tbl_name WHERE col1=val1;
SELECT * FROM tbl_name WHERE col1=val1 AND col2=val2;

SELECT * FROM tbl_name WHERE col2=val2;
SELECT * FROM tbl_name WHERE col2=val2 AND col3=val3;
```

If an index exists on (col1, col2, col3), only the first two queries use the index. The third and fourth queries do involve indexed columns, but (col2) and (col2, col3) are not leftmost prefixes of (col1, col2, col3).

A B-tree index can be used for column comparisons in expressions that use the =, >, >=, <, <=, or BETWEEN operators. The index also can be used for LIKE comparisons if the argument to LIKE is a constant string that does not start with a wildcard character. For example, the following SELECT statements use indexes:

```
SELECT * FROM tbl_name WHERE key_col LIKE 'Patrick%';
SELECT * FROM tbl_name WHERE key_col LIKE 'Pat%_ck%';
```

In the first statement, only rows with 'Patrick' <= key_col < 'Patricl' are considered. In the second statement, only rows with 'Pat' <= key_col < 'Pau' are considered.

The following SELECT statements do not use indexes:

```
SELECT * FROM tbl_name WHERE key_col LIKE '%Patrick%';
SELECT * FROM tbl_name WHERE key_col LIKE other_col;
```

In the first statement, the LIKE value begins with a wildcard character. In the second statement, the LIKE value is not a constant.

If you use ... LIKE '%string%' and string is longer than three characters, MySQL uses the Turbo Boyer-Moore algorithm to initialize the pattern for the string and then uses this pattern to perform the search more quickly.

A search using col_name IS NULL employs indexes if col_name is indexed.

Any index that does not span all AND levels in the WHERE clause is not used to optimize the query. In other words, to be able to use an index, a prefix of the index must be used in every AND group.

The following WHERE clauses use indexes:

```
... WHERE index_part1=1 AND index_part2=2 AND other_column=3
    /* index = 1 OR index = 2 */
... WHERE index=1 OR A=10 AND index=2
    /* optimized like "index_part1='hello'" */
... WHERE index_part1='hello' AND index_part3=5
    /* Can use index on index1 but not on index2 or index3 */
... WHERE index1=1 AND index2=2 OR index1=3 AND index3=3;
```

These WHERE clauses do *not* use indexes:

```
    /* index_part1 is not used */
... WHERE index_part2=1 AND index_part3=2

    /*  Index is not used in both parts of the WHERE clause  */
... WHERE index=1 OR A=10

    /* No index spans all rows  */
... WHERE index_part1=1 OR index_part2=10
```

Sometimes MySQL does not use an index, even if one is available. One circumstance under which this occurs is when the optimizer estimates that using the index would require MySQL to access a very large percentage of the rows in the table. (In this case, a table scan is likely to be much faster because it requires fewer seeks.) However, if such a query uses LIMIT to retrieve only some of the rows, MySQL uses an index anyway, because it can much more quickly find the few rows to return in the result.

Hash indexes have somewhat different characteristics from those just discussed:

- They are used only for equality comparisons that use the = or <=> operators (but are *very* fast). They are not used for comparison operators such as < that find a range of values.

- The optimizer cannot use a hash index to speed up ORDER BY operations. (This type of index cannot be used to search for the next entry in order.)

- MySQL cannot determine approximately how many rows there are between two values (this is used by the range optimizer to decide which index to use). This may affect some queries if you change a MyISAM table to a hash-indexed MEMORY table.

- Only whole keys can be used to search for a row. (With a B-tree index, any leftmost prefix of the key can be used to find rows.)

6.4.6 The MyISAM Key Cache

To minimize disk I/O, the MyISAM storage engine exploits a strategy that is used by many database management systems. It employs a cache mechanism to keep the most frequently accessed table blocks in memory:

- For index blocks, a special structure called the *key cache* (or *key buffer*) is maintained. The structure contains a number of block buffers where the most-used index blocks are placed.

- For data blocks, MySQL uses no special cache. Instead it relies on the native operating system filesystem cache.

This section first describes the basic operation of the MyISAM key cache. Then it discusses features that improve key cache performance and that enable you to better control cache operation:

- Access to the key cache no longer is serialized among threads. Multiple threads can access the cache concurrently.
- You can set up multiple key caches and assign table indexes to specific caches.

To control the size of the key cache, use the `key_buffer_size` system variable. If this variable is set equal to zero, no key cache is used. The key cache also is not used if the `key_buffer_size` value is too small to allocate the minimal number of block buffers (8).

When the key cache is not operational, index files are accessed using only the native filesystem buffering provided by the operating system. (In other words, table index blocks are accessed using the same strategy as that employed for table data blocks.)

An index block is a contiguous unit of access to the `MyISAM` index files. Usually the size of an index block is equal to the size of nodes of the index B-tree. (Indexes are represented on disk using a B-tree data structure. Nodes at the bottom of the tree are leaf nodes. Nodes above the leaf nodes are non-leaf nodes.)

All block buffers in a key cache structure are the same size. This size can be equal to, greater than, or less than the size of a table index block. Usually one of these two values is a multiple of the other.

When data from any table index block must be accessed, the server first checks whether it is available in some block buffer of the key cache. If it is, the server accesses data in the key cache rather than on disk. That is, it reads from the cache or writes into it rather than reading from or writing to disk. Otherwise, the server chooses a cache block buffer containing a different table index block (or blocks) and replaces the data there with a copy of the required table index block. As soon as the new index block is in the cache, the index data can be accessed.

If it happens that a block selected for replacement has been modified, the block is considered "dirty." In this case, prior to being replaced, its contents are flushed to the table index from which it came.

Usually the server follows an *LRU (Least Recently Used)* strategy: When choosing a block for replacement, it selects the least recently used index block. To make this choice easier, the key cache module maintains a special queue (*LRU chain*) of all used blocks. When a block is accessed, it is placed at the end of the queue. When blocks need to be replaced, blocks at the beginning of the queue are the least recently used and become the first candidates for eviction.

6.4.6.1 Shared Key Cache Access

Threads can access key cache buffers simultaneously, subject to the following conditions:

- A buffer that is not being updated can be accessed by multiple threads.
- A buffer that is being updated causes threads that need to use it to wait until the update is complete.
- Multiple threads can initiate requests that result in cache block replacements, as long as they do not interfere with each other (that is, as long as they need different index blocks, and thus cause different cache blocks to be replaced).

Shared access to the key cache enables the server to improve throughput significantly.

6.4.6.2 Multiple Key Caches

Shared access to the key cache improves performance but does not eliminate contention among threads entirely. They still compete for control structures that manage access to the key cache buffers. To reduce key cache access contention further, MySQL also provides multiple key caches. This feature enables you to assign different table indexes to different key caches.

Where there are multiple key caches, the server must know which cache to use when processing queries for a given MyISAM table. By default, all MyISAM table indexes are cached in the default key cache. To assign table indexes to a specific key cache, use the CACHE INDEX statement. For example, the following statement assigns indexes from the tables t1, t2, and t3 to the key cache named hot_cache:

```
mysql> CACHE INDEX t1, t2, t3 IN hot_cache;
+---------+--------------------+----------+----------+
| Table   | Op                 | Msg_type | Msg_text |
+---------+--------------------+----------+----------+
| test.t1 | assign_to_keycache | status   | OK       |
| test.t2 | assign_to_keycache | status   | OK       |
| test.t3 | assign_to_keycache | status   | OK       |
+---------+--------------------+----------+----------+
```

The key cache referred to in a CACHE INDEX statement can be created by setting its size with a SET GLOBAL parameter setting statement or by using server startup options. For example:

```
mysql> SET GLOBAL keycache1.key_buffer_size=128*1024;
```

To destroy a key cache, set its size to zero:

```
mysql> SET GLOBAL keycache1.key_buffer_size=0;
```

Note that you cannot destroy the default key cache. Any attempt to do this will be ignored:

```
mysql> SET GLOBAL key_buffer_size = 0;

mysql> SHOW VARIABLES LIKE 'key_buffer_size';
+-----------------+---------+
| Variable_name   | Value   |
+-----------------+---------+
| key_buffer_size | 8384512 |
+-----------------+---------+
```

Key cache variables are structured system variables that have a name and components. For keycache1.key_buffer_size, keycache1 is the cache variable name and key_buffer_size is the cache component. See Section 4.2.3.1, "Structured System Variables," for a description of the syntax used for referring to structured key cache system variables.

By default, table indexes are assigned to the main (default) key cache created at the server startup. When a key cache is destroyed, all indexes assigned to it are reassigned to the default key cache.

For a busy server, we recommend a strategy that uses three key caches:

- A "hot" key cache that takes up 20% of the space allocated for all key caches. Use this for tables that are heavily used for searches but that are not updated.

- A "cold" key cache that takes up 20% of the space allocated for all key caches. Use this cache for medium-sized, intensively modified tables, such as temporary tables.

- A "warm" key cache that takes up 60% of the key cache space. Employ this as the default key cache, to be used by default for all other tables.

One reason the use of three key caches is beneficial is that access to one key cache structure does not block access to the others. Statements that access tables assigned to one cache do not compete with statements that access tables assigned to another cache. Performance gains occur for other reasons as well:

- The hot cache is used only for retrieval queries, so its contents are never modified. Consequently, whenever an index block needs to be pulled in from disk, the contents of the cache block chosen for replacement need not be flushed first.

- For an index assigned to the hot cache, if there are no queries requiring an index scan, there is a high probability that the index blocks corresponding to non-leaf nodes of the index B-tree remain in the cache.

- An update operation most frequently executed for temporary tables is performed much faster when the updated node is in the cache and need not be read in from disk first. If the size of the indexes of the temporary tables are comparable with the size of the cold key cache, the probability is very high that the updated node is in the cache.

CACHE INDEX sets up an association between a table and a key cache, but the association is lost each time the server restarts. If you want the association to take effect each time the server starts, one way to accomplish this is to use an option file: Include variable settings that configure your key caches, and an init-file option that names a file containing CACHE INDEX statements to be executed. For example:

```
key_buffer_size = 4G
hot_cache.key_buffer_size = 2G
cold_cache.key_buffer_size = 2G
init_file=/path/to/data-directory/mysqld_init.sql
```

The statements in mysqld_init.sql are executed each time the server starts. The file should contain one SQL statement per line. The following example assigns several tables each to hot_cache and cold_cache:

```
CACHE INDEX db1.t1, db1.t2, db2.t3 IN hot_cache
CACHE INDEX db1.t4, db2.t5, db2.t6 IN cold_cache
```

6.4.6.3 Midpoint Insertion Strategy

By default, the key cache management system uses the LRU strategy for choosing key cache blocks to be evicted, but it also supports a more sophisticated method called the *midpoint insertion strategy*.

When using the midpoint insertion strategy, the LRU chain is divided into two parts: a hot sub-chain and a warm sub-chain. The division point between two parts is not fixed, but the key cache management system takes care that the warm part is not "too short," always containing at least `key_cache_division_limit` percent of the key cache blocks. `key_cache_division_limit` is a component of structured key cache variables, so its value is a parameter that can be set per cache.

When an index block is read from a table into the key cache, it is placed at the end of the warm sub-chain. After a certain number of hits (accesses of the block), it is promoted to the hot sub-chain. At present, the number of hits required to promote a block (3) is the same for all index blocks.

A block promoted into the hot sub-chain is placed at the end of the chain. The block then circulates within this sub-chain. If the block stays at the beginning of the sub-chain for a long enough time, it is demoted to the warm chain. This time is determined by the value of the `key_cache_age_threshold` component of the key cache.

The threshold value prescribes that, for a key cache containing N blocks, the block at the beginning of the hot sub-chain not accessed within the last $N \times$ `key_cache_age_threshold` $/$ 100 hits is to be moved to the beginning of the warm sub-chain. It then becomes the first candidate for eviction, because blocks for replacement always are taken from the beginning of the warm sub-chain.

The midpoint insertion strategy allows you to keep more-valued blocks always in the cache. If you prefer to use the plain LRU strategy, leave the `key_cache_division_limit` value set to its default of 100.

The midpoint insertion strategy helps to improve performance when execution of a query that requires an index scan effectively pushes out of the cache all the index blocks corresponding to valuable high-level B-tree nodes. To avoid this, you must use a midpoint insertion strategy with the `key_cache_division_limit` set to much less than 100. Then valuable frequently hit nodes are preserved in the hot sub-chain during an index scan operation as well.

6.4.6.4 Index Preloading

If there are enough blocks in a key cache to hold blocks of an entire index, or at least the blocks corresponding to its non-leaf nodes, it makes sense to preload the key cache with index blocks before starting to use it. Preloading allows you to put the table index blocks into a key cache buffer in the most efficient way: by reading the index blocks from disk sequentially.

Without preloading, the blocks are still placed into the key cache as needed by queries. Although the blocks will stay in the cache, because there are enough buffers for all of them, they are fetched from disk in random order, and not sequentially.

To preload an index into a cache, use the LOAD INDEX INTO CACHE statement. For example, the following statement preloads nodes (index blocks) of indexes of the tables t1 and t2:

```
mysql> LOAD INDEX INTO CACHE t1, t2 IGNORE LEAVES;
+---------+--------------+----------+----------+
| Table   | Op           | Msg_type | Msg_text |
+---------+--------------+----------+----------+
| test.t1 | preload_keys | status   | OK       |
| test.t2 | preload_keys | status   | OK       |
+---------+--------------+----------+----------+
```

The IGNORE LEAVES modifier causes only blocks for the non-leaf nodes of the index to be preloaded. Thus, the statement shown preloads all index blocks from t1, but only blocks for the non-leaf nodes from t2.

If an index has been assigned to a key cache using a CACHE INDEX statement, preloading places index blocks into that cache. Otherwise, the index is loaded into the default key cache.

6.4.6.5 Key Cache Block Size

It is possible to specify the size of the block buffers for an individual key cache using the key_cache_block_size variable. This permits tuning of the performance of I/O operations for index files.

The best performance for I/O operations is achieved when the size of read buffers is equal to the size of the native operating system I/O buffers. But setting the size of key nodes equal to the size of the I/O buffer does not always ensure the best overall performance. When reading the big leaf nodes, the server pulls in a lot of unnecessary data, effectively preventing reading other leaf nodes.

Currently, you cannot control the size of the index blocks in a table. This size is set by the server when the .MYI index file is created, depending on the size of the keys in the indexes present in the table definition. In most cases, it is set equal to the I/O buffer size.

6.4.6.6 Restructuring a Key Cache

A key cache can be restructured at any time by updating its parameter values. For example:

```
mysql> SET GLOBAL cold_cache.key_buffer_size=4*1024*1024;
```

If you assign to either the key_buffer_size or key_cache_block_size key cache component a value that differs from the component's current value, the server destroys the cache's old structure and creates a new one based on the new values. If the cache contains any dirty blocks, the server saves them to disk before destroying and re-creating the cache. Restructuring does not occur if you change other key cache parameters.

When restructuring a key cache, the server first flushes the contents of any dirty buffers to disk. After that, the cache contents become unavailable. However, restructuring does not block queries that need to use indexes assigned to the cache. Instead, the server directly accesses the table indexes using native filesystem caching. Filesystem caching is not as efficient as using a key cache, so although queries execute, a slowdown can be anticipated. After the cache has been restructured, it becomes available again for caching indexes assigned to it, and the use of filesystem caching for the indexes ceases.

6.4.7 MyISAM **Index Statistics Collection**

Storage engines collect statistics about tables for use by the optimizer. Table statistics are based on value groups, where a value group is a set of rows with the same key prefix value. For optimizer purposes, an important statistic is the average value group size.

MySQL uses the average value group size in the following ways:

- To estimate how many rows must be read for each ref access
- To estimate how many rows a partial join will produce; that is, the number of rows that an operation of this form will produce:

  (...) JOIN *tbl_name* ON *tbl_name.key* = *expr*

As the average value group size for an index increases, the index is less useful for those two purposes because the average number of rows per lookup increases. For the index to be good for optimization purposes, it is best that each index value target a small number of rows in the table. When a given index value yields a large number of rows, the index is less useful and MySQL is less likely to use it.

The average value group size is related to table cardinality, which is the number of value groups. The SHOW INDEX statement displays a cardinality value based on N/S, where N is the number of rows in the table and S is the average value group size. That ratio yields an approximate number of value groups in the table.

For a join based on the <=> comparison operator, NULL is not treated differently from any other value: NULL <=> NULL, just as N <=> N for any other N.

However, for a join based on the = operator, NULL is different from non-NULL values: *expr1* = *expr2* is not true when *expr1* or *expr2* (or both) is NULL. This affects ref accesses for comparisons of the form *tbl_name.key* = *expr*: MySQL will not access the table if the current value of *expr* is NULL, because the comparison cannot be true.

For = comparisons, it does not matter how many NULL values are in the table. For optimization purposes, the relevant value is the average size of the non-NULL value groups. However, MySQL does not currently allow that average size to be collected or used.

For MyISAM tables, you have some control over collection of table statistics by means of the myisam_stats_method system variable. This variable has two possible values, which differ as follows:

- When myisam_stats_method is nulls_equal, all NULL values are treated as identical (that is, they all form a single value group).

  If the NULL value group size is much higher than the average non-NULL value group size, this method skews the average value group size upward. This makes the index appear to the optimizer to be less useful than it really is for joins that look for non-NULL values. Consequently, the nulls_equal method may cause the optimizer not to use the index for ref accesses when it should.

- When myisam_stats_method is nulls_unequal, NULL values are not considered the same. Instead, each NULL value forms a separate value group of size 1.

If you have many NULL values, this method skews the average value group size downward. If the average non-NULL value group size is large, counting NULL values each as a group of size 1 causes the optimizer to overestimate the value of the index for joins that look for non-NULL values. Consequently, the nulls_unequal method may cause the optimizer to use this index for ref lookups when other methods may be better.

If you tend to use many joins that use <=> rather than =, NULL values are not special in comparisons and one NULL is equal to another. In this case, nulls_equal is the appropriate statistics method.

The myisam_stats_method system variable has global and session values. Setting the global value affects MyISAM statistics collection for all MyISAM tables. Setting the session value affects statistics collection only for the current client connection. This means that you can force a table's statistics to be regenerated with a given method without affecting other clients by setting the session value of myisam_stats_method.

To regenerate table statistics, you can use any of the following methods:

- Set myisam_stats_method, and then issue a CHECK TABLE statement
- Execute myisamchk --stats_method=*method_name* --analyze
- Change the table to cause its statistics to go out of date (for example, insert a row and then delete it), and then set myisam_stats_method and issue an ANALYZE TABLE statement

Some caveats regarding the use of myisam_stats_method:

You can force table statistics to be collected explicitly, as just described. However, MySQL may also collect statistics automatically. For example, if during the course of executing statements for a table, some of those statements modify the table, MySQL may collect statistics. (This may occur for bulk inserts or deletes, or some ALTER TABLE statements, for example.) If this happens, the statistics are collected using whatever value myisam_stats_method has at the time. Thus, if you collect statistics using one method, but myisam_stats_method is set to the other method when a table's statistics are collected automatically later, the other method will be used.

There is no way to tell which method was used to generate statistics for a given MyISAM table.

myisam_stats_method applies only to MyISAM tables. Other storage engines have only one method for collecting table statistics. Usually it is closer to the nulls_equal method.

6.4.8 How MySQL Opens and Closes Tables

When you execute a mysqladmin status command, you should see something like this:

```
Uptime: 426 Running threads: 1 Questions: 11082
Reloads: 1 Open tables: 12
```

The Open tables value of 12 can be somewhat puzzling if you have only six tables.

MySQL is multi-threaded, so there may be many clients issuing queries for a given table simultaneously. To minimize the problem with multiple client threads having different states on the same table, the table is opened independently by each concurrent thread. This uses additional memory but normally increases performance. With MyISAM tables, one extra file descriptor is required for the data file for each client that has the table open. (By contrast, the index file descriptor is shared among all threads.)

The table_cache, max_connections, and max_tmp_tables system variables affect the maximum number of files the server keeps open. If you increase one or more of these values, you may run up against a limit imposed by your operating system on the per-process number of open file descriptors. Many operating systems allow you to increase the open-files limit, although the method varies widely from system to system. Consult your operating system documentation to determine whether it is possible to increase the limit and how to do so.

table_cache is related to max_connections. For example, for 200 concurrent running connections, you should have a table cache size of at least $200 \times N$, where N is the maximum number of tables per join in any of the queries which you execute. You must also reserve some extra file descriptors for temporary tables and files.

Make sure that your operating system can handle the number of open file descriptors implied by the table_cache setting. If table_cache is set too high, MySQL may run out of file descriptors and refuse connections, fail to perform queries, and be very unreliable. You also have to take into account that the MyISAM storage engine needs two file descriptors for each unique open table. You can increase the number of file descriptors available to MySQL using the --open-files-limit startup option to mysqld.

The cache of open tables is kept at a level of table_cache entries. The default value is 64; this can be changed with the --table_cache option to mysqld. Note that MySQL may temporarily open more tables than this to execute queries.

MySQL closes an unused table and removes it from the table cache under the following circumstances:

- When the cache is full and a thread tries to open a table that is not in the cache.
- When the cache contains more than table_cache entries and a table in the cache is no longer being used by any threads.
- When a table flushing operation occurs. This happens when someone issues a FLUSH TABLES statement or executes a mysqladmin flush-tables or mysqladmin refresh command.

When the table cache fills up, the server uses the following procedure to locate a cache entry to use:

- Tables that are not currently in use are released, beginning with the table least recently used.
- If a new table needs to be opened, but the cache is full and no tables can be released, the cache is temporarily extended as necessary.

When the cache is in a temporarily extended state and a table goes from a used to unused state, the table is closed and released from the cache.

A table is opened for each concurrent access. This means the table needs to be opened twice if two threads access the same table or if a thread accesses the table twice in the same query (for example, by joining the table to itself). Each concurrent open requires an entry in the table cache. The first open of any `MyISAM` table takes two file descriptors: one for the data file and one for the index file. Each additional use of the table takes only one file descriptor for the data file. The index file descriptor is shared among all threads.

If you are opening a table with the `HANDLER` *tbl_name* `OPEN` statement, a dedicated table object is allocated for the thread. This table object is not shared by other threads and is not closed until the thread calls `HANDLER` *tbl_name* `CLOSE` or the thread terminates. When this happens, the table is put back in the table cache (if the cache is not full).

You can determine whether your table cache is too small by checking the `mysqld` status variable `Opened_tables`:

```
mysql> SHOW STATUS LIKE 'Opened_tables';
+---------------+-------+
| Variable_name | Value |
+---------------+-------+
| Opened_tables | 2741  |
+---------------+-------+
```

If the value is very large, even when you have not issued many `FLUSH TABLES` statements, you should increase the table cache size. See Section 4.2.2, "Server System Variables," and Section 4.2.4, "Server Status Variables."

6.4.9 Drawbacks to Creating Many Tables in the Same Database

If you have many `MyISAM` tables in the same database directory, open, close, and create operations are slow. If you execute `SELECT` statements on many different tables, there is a little overhead when the table cache is full, because for every table that has to be opened, another must be closed. You can reduce this overhead by making the table cache larger.

6.5 Optimizing the MySQL Server

6.5.1 System Factors and Startup Parameter Tuning

We start with system-level factors, because some of these decisions must be made very early to achieve large performance gains. In other cases, a quick look at this section may suffice. However, it is always nice to have a sense of how much can be gained by changing factors that apply at this level.

The operating system to use is very important. To get the best use of multiple-CPU machines, you should use Solaris (because its threads implementation works well) or Linux (because the 2.4 and later kernels have good SMP support). Note that older Linux kernels have a 2GB filesize limit by default. If you have such a kernel and a need for files larger than

2GB, you should get the Large File Support (LFS) patch for the ext2 filesystem. Other filesystems such as ReiserFS and XFS do not have this 2GB limitation.

Before using MySQL in production, we advise you to test it on your intended platform.

Other tips:

- If you have enough RAM, you could remove all swap devices. Some operating systems use a swap device in some contexts even if you have free memory.

- Avoid external locking. Since MySQL 4.0, the default has been for external locking to be disabled on all systems. The --external-locking and --skip-external-locking options explicitly enable and disable external locking.

  Note that disabling external locking does not affect MySQL's functionality as long as you run only one server. Just remember to take down the server (or lock and flush the relevant tables) before you run myisamchk. On some systems it is mandatory to disable external locking because it does not work, anyway.

  The only case in which you cannot disable external locking is when you run multiple MySQL *servers* (not clients) on the same data, or if you run myisamchk to check (not repair) a table without telling the server to flush and lock the tables first. Note that using multiple MySQL servers to access the same data concurrently is generally *not* recommended, except when using MySQL Cluster.

  The LOCK TABLES and UNLOCK TABLES statements use internal locking, so you can use them even if external locking is disabled.

6.5.2 Tuning Server Parameters

You can determine the default buffer sizes used by the mysqld server using this command:

```
shell> mysqld --verbose --help
```

This command produces a list of all mysqld options and configurable system variables. The output includes the default variable values and looks something like this:

```
back_log                    50
binlog_cache_size           32768
bulk_insert_buffer_size     8388608
connect_timeout             5
date_format                 (No default value)
datetime_format             (No default value)
default_week_format         0
delayed_insert_limit        100
delayed_insert_timeout      300
delayed_queue_size          1000
expire_logs_days            0
flush_time                  1800
ft_max_word_len             84
ft_min_word_len             4
ft_query_expansion_limit    20
```

```
ft_stopword_file                    (No default value)
group_concat_max_len                1024
innodb_additional_mem_pool_size     1048576
innodb_autoextend_increment         8
innodb_buffer_pool_awe_mem_mb       0
innodb_buffer_pool_size             8388608
innodb_concurrency_tickets          500
innodb_file_io_threads              4
innodb_force_recovery               0
innodb_lock_wait_timeout            50
innodb_log_buffer_size              1048576
innodb_log_file_size                5242880
innodb_log_files_in_group           2
innodb_mirrored_log_groups          1
innodb_open_files                   300
innodb_sync_spin_loops              20
innodb_thread_concurrency           8
innodb_thread_sleep_delay           10000
interactive_timeout                 28800
join_buffer_size                    131072
key_buffer_size                     8388600
key_cache_age_threshold             300
key_cache_block_size                1024
key_cache_division_limit            100
long_query_time                     10
lower_case_table_names              1
max_allowed_packet                  1048576
max_binlog_cache_size               4294967295
max_binlog_size                     1073741824
max_connect_errors                  10
max_connections                     100
max_delayed_threads                 20
max_error_count                     64
max_heap_table_size                 16777216
max_join_size                       4294967295
max_length_for_sort_data            1024
max_relay_log_size                  0
max_seeks_for_key                   4294967295
max_sort_length                     1024
max_tmp_tables                      32
max_user_connections                0
max_write_lock_count                4294967295
multi_range_count                   256
myisam_block_size                   1024
myisam_data_pointer_size            6
myisam_max_extra_sort_file_size     2147483648
myisam_max_sort_file_size           2147483647
myisam_repair_threads               1
myisam_sort_buffer_size             8388608
```

net_buffer_length	16384
net_read_timeout	30
net_retry_count	10
net_write_timeout	60
open_files_limit	0
optimizer_prune_level	1
optimizer_search_depth	62
preload_buffer_size	32768
query_alloc_block_size	8192
query_cache_limit	1048576
query_cache_min_res_unit	4096
query_cache_size	0
query_cache_type	1
query_cache_wlock_invalidate	FALSE
query_prealloc_size	8192
range_alloc_block_size	2048
read_buffer_size	131072
read_only	FALSE
read_rnd_buffer_size	262144
div_precision_increment	4
record_buffer	131072
relay_log_purge	TRUE
relay_log_space_limit	0
slave_compressed_protocol	FALSE
slave_net_timeout	3600
slave_transaction_retries	10
slow_launch_time	2
sort_buffer_size	2097144
sync-binlog	0
sync-frm	TRUE
sync-replication	0
sync-replication-slave-id	0
sync-replication-timeout	10
table_cache	64
thread_cache_size	0
thread_concurrency	10
thread_stack	196608
time_format	(No default value)
tmp_table_size	33554432
transaction_alloc_block_size	8192
transaction_prealloc_size	4096
updatable_views_with_limit	1
wait_timeout	28800

If there is a mysqld server currently running, you can see the current values of its system variables by connecting to it and issuing this statement:

```
mysql> SHOW VARIABLES;
```

You can also see some statistical and status indicators for a running server by issuing this statement:

```
mysql> SHOW STATUS;
```

System variable and status information also can be obtained using `mysqladmin`:

```
shell> mysqladmin variables
shell> mysqladmin extended-status
```

For a full description for all system and status variables, see Section 4.2.2, "Server System Variables," and Section 4.2.4, "Server Status Variables."

MySQL uses algorithms that are very scalable, so you can usually run with very little memory. However, normally you get better performance by giving MySQL more memory.

When tuning a MySQL server, the two most important variables to configure are `key_buffer_size` and `table_cache`. You should first feel confident that you have these set appropriately before trying to change any other variables.

The following examples indicate some typical variable values for different runtime configurations.

- If you have at least 256MB of memory and many tables and want maximum performance with a moderate number of clients, you should use something like this:

```
shell> mysqld_safe --key_buffer_size=64M --table_cache=256 \
           --sort_buffer_size=4M --read_buffer_size=1M &
```

- If you have only 128MB of memory and only a few tables, but you still do a lot of sorting, you can use something like this:

```
shell> mysqld_safe --key_buffer_size=16M --sort_buffer_size=1M
```

If there are very many simultaneous connections, swapping problems may occur unless `mysqld` has been configured to use very little memory for each connection. `mysqld` performs better if you have enough memory for all connections.

- With little memory and lots of connections, use something like this:

```
shell> mysqld_safe --key_buffer_size=512K --sort_buffer_size=100K \
           --read_buffer_size=100K &
```

Or even this:

```
shell> mysqld_safe --key_buffer_size=512K --sort_buffer_size=16K \
           --table_cache=32 --read_buffer_size=8K \
           --net_buffer_length=1K &
```

If you are performing GROUP BY or ORDER BY operations on tables that are much larger than your available memory, you should increase the value of `read_rnd_buffer_size` to speed up the reading of rows following sorting operations.

When you have installed MySQL, the support-files directory contains some different my.cnf sample files: my-huge.cnf, my-large.cnf, my-medium.cnf, and my-small.cnf. You can use these as a basis for optimizing your system. (On Windows, look in the MySQL installation directory.)

If you specify an option on the command line for mysqld or mysqld_safe, it remains in effect only for that invocation of the server. To use the option every time the server runs, put it in an option file.

To see the effects of a parameter change, do something like this:

```
shell> mysqld --key_buffer_size=32M --verbose --help
```

The variable values are listed near the end of the output. Make sure that the --verbose and --help options are last. Otherwise, the effect of any options listed after them on the command line are not reflected in the output.

For information on tuning the InnoDB storage engine, see Section 8.2.11, "InnoDB Performance Tuning Tips."

6.5.3 Controlling Query Optimizer Performance

The task of the query optimizer is to find an optimal plan for executing an SQL query. Because the difference in performance between "good" and "bad" plans can be orders of magnitude (that is, seconds versus hours or even days), most query optimizers, including that of MySQL, perform a more or less exhaustive search for an optimal plan among all possible query evaluation plans. For join queries, the number of possible plans investigated by the MySQL optimizer grows exponentially with the number of tables referenced in a query. For small numbers of tables (typically less than 7–10) this is not a problem. However, when bigger queries are submitted, the time spent in query optimization may easily become the major bottleneck in the server's performance.

MySQL 5.0.1 introduces a more flexible method for query optimization that allows the user to control how exhaustive the optimizer is in its search for an optimal query evaluation plan. The general idea is that the fewer plans that are investigated by the optimizer, the less time it spends in compiling a query. On the other hand, because the optimizer skips some plans, it may miss finding an optimal plan.

The behavior of the optimizer with respect to the number of plans it evaluates can be controlled via two system variables:

- The optimizer_prune_level variable tells the optimizer to skip certain plans based on estimates of the number of rows accessed for each table. Our experience shows that this kind of "educated guess" rarely misses optimal plans, and may dramatically reduce query compilation times. That is why this option is on (optimizer_prune_level=1) by default. However, if you believe that the optimizer missed a better query plan, this option can be switched off (optimizer_prune_level=0) with the risk that query compilation may take much longer. Note that, even with the use of this heuristic, the optimizer still explores a roughly exponential number of plans.

- The `optimizer_search_depth` variable tells how far into the "future" of each incomplete plan the optimizer should look to evaluate whether it should be expanded further. Smaller values of `optimizer_search_depth` may result in orders of magnitude smaller query compilation times. For example, queries with 12, 13, or more tables may easily require hours and even days to compile if `optimizer_search_depth` is close to the number of tables in the query. At the same time, if compiled with `optimizer_search_depth` equal to 3 or 4, the optimizer may compile in less than a minute for the same query. If you are unsure of what a reasonable value is for `optimizer_search_depth`, this variable can be set to 0 to tell the optimizer to determine the value automatically.

6.5.4 How Compiling and Linking Affects the Speed of MySQL

Most of the following tests were performed on Linux with the MySQL benchmarks, but they should give some indication for other operating systems and workloads.

You obtain the fastest executables when you link with `-static`.

On Linux, it is best to compile the server with `pgcc` and `-03`. You need about 200MB memory to compile `sql_yacc.cc` with these options, because `gcc` or `pgcc` needs a great deal of memory to make all functions inline. You should also set `CXX=gcc` when configuring MySQL to avoid inclusion of the `libstdc++` library, which is not needed. Note that with some versions of `pgcc`, the resulting binary runs only on true Pentium processors, even if you use the compiler option indicating that you want the resulting code to work on all x586-type processors (such as AMD).

By using a better compiler and compilation options, you can obtain a 10–30% speed increase in applications. This is particularly important if you compile the MySQL server yourself.

When we tested both the Cygnus CodeFusion and Fujitsu compilers, neither was sufficiently bug-free to allow MySQL to be compiled with optimizations enabled.

The standard MySQL binary distributions are compiled with support for all character sets. When you compile MySQL yourself, you should include support only for the character sets that you are going to use. This is controlled by the `--with-charset` option to `configure`.

Here is a list of some measurements that we have made:

- If you use `pgcc` and compile everything with `-06`, the `mysqld` server is 1% faster than with `gcc` 2.95.2.
- If you link dynamically (without `-static`), the result is 13% slower on Linux. Note that you still can use a dynamically linked MySQL library for your client applications. It is the server that is most critical for performance.
- For a connection from a client to a server running on the same host, if you connect using TCP/IP rather than a Unix socket file, performance is 7.5% slower. (On Unix, if you connect to the hostname `localhost`, MySQL uses a socket file by default.)

- For TCP/IP connections from a client to a server, connecting to a remote server on another host is 8–11% slower than connecting to a server on the same host, even for connections over 100Mb/s Ethernet.

- When running our benchmark tests using secure connections (all data encrypted with internal SSL support) performance was 55% slower than with unencrypted connections.

- If you compile with `--with-debug=full`, most queries are 20% slower. Some queries may take substantially longer; for example, the MySQL benchmarks run 35% slower. If you use `--with-debug` (without `=full`), the speed decrease is only 15%. For a version of `mysqld` that has been compiled with `--with-debug=full`, you can disable memory checking at runtime by starting it with the `--skip-safemalloc` option. The execution speed should then be close to that obtained when configuring with `--with-debug`.

- On a Sun UltraSPARC-IIe, a server compiled with Forte 5.0 is 4% faster than one compiled with `gcc` 3.2.

- On a Sun UltraSPARC-IIe, a server compiled with Forte 5.0 is 4% faster in 32-bit mode than in 64-bit mode.

- Compiling with `gcc` 2.95.2 for UltraSPARC with the `-mcpu=v8 -Wa,-xarch=v8plusa` options gives 4% more performance.

- On Solaris 2.5.1, MIT-pthreads is 8–12% slower than Solaris native threads on a single processor. With greater loads or more CPUs, the difference should be larger.

- Compiling on Linux-x86 using `gcc` without frame pointers (`-fomit-frame-pointer` or `-fomit-frame-pointer -ffixed-ebp`) makes `mysqld` 1–4% faster.

Binary MySQL distributions for Linux that are provided by MySQL AB used to be compiled with `pgcc`. We had to go back to regular `gcc` due to a bug in `pgcc` that would generate binaries that do not run on AMD. We will continue using `gcc` until that bug is resolved. In the meantime, if you have a non-AMD machine, you can build a faster binary by compiling with `pgcc`. The standard MySQL Linux binary is linked statically to make it faster and more portable.

6.5.5 How MySQL Uses Memory

The following list indicates some of the ways that the `mysqld` server uses memory. Where applicable, the name of the system variable relevant to the memory use is given:

- The key buffer (variable `key_buffer_size`) is shared by all threads; other buffers used by the server are allocated as needed. See Section 6.5.2, "Tuning Server Parameters."

- Each connection uses some thread-specific space:
  - A stack (default 192KB, variable `thread_stack`)
  - A connection buffer (variable `net_buffer_length`)
  - A result buffer (variable `net_buffer_length`)

The connection buffer and result buffer are dynamically enlarged up to `max_allowed_packet` when needed. While a query is running, a copy of the current query string is also allocated.

- All threads share the same base memory.

- When a thread is no longer needed, the memory allocated to it is released and returned to the system unless the thread goes back into the thread cache. In that case, the memory remains allocated.

- Only compressed `MyISAM` tables are memory mapped. This is because the 32-bit memory space of 4GB is not large enough for most big tables. When systems with a 64-bit address space become more common, we may add general support for memory mapping.

- Each request that performs a sequential scan of a table allocates a *read buffer* (variable `read_buffer_size`).

- When reading rows in an arbitrary sequence (for example, following a sort), a *random-read buffer* (variable `read_rnd_buffer_size`) may be allocated in order to avoid disk seeks.

- All joins are executed in a single pass, and most joins can be done without even using a temporary table. Most temporary tables are memory-based hash tables. Temporary tables with a large row length (calculated as the sum of all column lengths) or that contain `BLOB` columns are stored on disk.

  If an internal heap table exceeds the size of `tmp_table_size`, MySQL handles this automatically by changing the in-memory heap table to a disk-based `MyISAM` table as necessary. You can also increase the temporary table size by setting the `tmp_table_size` option to `mysqld`, or by setting the SQL option `SQL_BIG_TABLES` in the client program.

- Most requests that perform a sort allocate a sort buffer and zero to two temporary files depending on the result set size.

- Almost all parsing and calculating is done in a local memory store. No memory overhead is needed for small items, so the normal slow memory allocation and freeing is avoided. Memory is allocated only for unexpectedly large strings. This is done with `malloc()` and `free()`.

- For each `MyISAM` table that is opened, the index file is opened once; the data file is opened once for each concurrently running thread. For each concurrent thread, a table structure, column structures for each column, and a buffer of size $3 \times N$ are allocated (where N is the maximum row length, not counting `BLOB` columns). A `BLOB` column requires five to eight bytes plus the length of the `BLOB` data. The `MyISAM` storage engine maintains one extra row buffer for internal use.

- For each table having `BLOB` columns, a buffer is enlarged dynamically to read in larger `BLOB` values. If you scan a table, a buffer as large as the largest `BLOB` value is allocated.

- Handler structures for all in-use tables are saved in a cache and managed as a FIFO. By default, the cache has 64 entries. If a table has been used by two running threads at the same time, the cache contains two entries for the table. See Section 6.4.8, "How MySQL Opens and Closes Tables."

- A FLUSH TABLES statement or mysqladmin flush-tables command closes all tables that are not in use at once and marks all in-use tables to be closed when the currently executing thread finishes. This effectively frees most in-use memory. FLUSH TABLES does not return until all tables have been closed.

ps and other system status programs may report that mysqld uses a lot of memory. This may be caused by thread stacks on different memory addresses. For example, the Solaris version of ps counts the unused memory between stacks as used memory. You can verify this by checking available swap with swap -s. We test mysqld with several memory-leakage detectors (both commercial and Open Source), so there should be no memory leaks.

6.5.6 How MySQL Uses DNS

When a new client connects to mysqld, mysqld spawns a new thread to handle the request. This thread first checks whether the hostname is in the hostname cache. If not, the thread attempts to resolve the hostname:

- If the operating system supports the thread-safe gethostbyaddr_r() and gethostbyname_r() calls, the thread uses them to perform hostname resolution.
- If the operating system does not support the thread-safe calls, the thread locks a mutex and calls gethostbyaddr() and gethostbyname() instead. In this case, no other thread can resolve hostnames that are not in the hostname cache until the first thread unlocks the mutex.

You can disable DNS hostname lookups by starting mysqld with the --skip-name-resolve option. However, in this case, you can use only IP numbers in the MySQL grant tables.

If you have a very slow DNS and many hosts, you can get more performance by either disabling DNS lookups with --skip-name-resolve or by increasing the HOST_CACHE_SIZE define (default value: 128) and recompiling mysqld.

You can disable the hostname cache by starting the server with the --skip-host-cache option. To clear the hostname cache, issue a FLUSH HOSTS statement or execute the mysqladmin flush-hosts command.

To disallow TCP/IP connections entirely, start mysqld with the --skip-networking option.

6.6 Disk Issues

- Disk seeks are a huge performance bottleneck. This problem becomes more apparent when the amount of data starts to grow so large that effective caching becomes impossible. For large databases where you access data more or less randomly, you can be sure that you need at least one disk seek to read and a couple of disk seeks to write things. To minimize this problem, use disks with low seek times.

- Increase the number of available disk spindles (and thereby reduce the seek overhead) by either symlinking files to different disks or striping the disks:

  - Using symbolic links

    This means that, for `MyISAM` tables, you symlink the index file and data files from their usual location in the data directory to another disk (that may also be striped). This makes both the seek and read times better, assuming that the disk is not used for other purposes as well. See Section 6.6.1, "Using Symbolic Links."

  - Striping

    Striping means that you have many disks and put the first block on the first disk, the second block on the second disk, and the N-th block on the (N `MOD` `number_of_disks`) disk, and so on. This means if your normal data size is less than the stripe size (or perfectly aligned), you get much better performance. Striping is very dependent on the operating system and the stripe size, so benchmark your application with different stripe sizes. See Section 6.1.5, "Using Your Own Benchmarks."

    The speed difference for striping is *very* dependent on the parameters. Depending on how you set the striping parameters and number of disks, you may get differences measured in orders of magnitude. You have to choose to optimize for random or sequential access.

- For reliability, you may want to use RAID 0+1 (striping plus mirroring), but in this case, you need $2 \times N$ drives to hold N drives of data. This is probably the best option if you have the money for it. However, you may also have to invest in some volume-management software to handle it efficiently.

- A good option is to vary the RAID level according to how critical a type of data is. For example, store semi-important data that can be regenerated on a RAID 0 disk, but store really important data such as host information and logs on a RAID 0+1 or RAID N disk. RAID N can be a problem if you have many writes, due to the time required to update the parity bits.

- On Linux, you can get much more performance by using `hdparm` to configure your disk's interface. (Up to 100% under load is not uncommon.) The following `hdparm` options should be quite good for MySQL, and probably for many other applications:

  ```
  hdparm -m 16 -d 1
  ```

  Note that performance and reliability when using this command depend on your hardware, so we strongly suggest that you test your system thoroughly after using `hdparm`. Please consult the `hdparm` manual page for more information. If `hdparm` is not used wisely, filesystem corruption may result, so back up everything before experimenting!

- You can also set the parameters for the filesystem that the database uses:

  If you do not need to know when files were last accessed (which is not really useful on a database server), you can mount your filesystems with the `-o noatime` option. That skips updates to the last access time in inodes on the filesystem, which avoids some disk seeks.

On many operating systems, you can set a filesystem to be updated asynchronously by mounting it with the -o async option. If your computer is reasonably stable, this should give you more performance without sacrificing too much reliability. (This flag is on by default on Linux.)

6.6.1 Using Symbolic Links

You can move tables and databases from the database directory to other locations and replace them with symbolic links to the new locations. You might want to do this, for example, to move a database to a filesystem with more free space or increase the speed of your system by spreading your tables to different disk.

The recommended way to do this is simply to symlink databases to a different disk. Symlink tables only as a last resort.

6.6.1.1 Using Symbolic Links for Databases on Unix

On Unix, the way to symlink a database is first to create a directory on some disk where you have free space and then to create a symlink to it from the MySQL data directory.

```
shell> mkdir /dr1/databases/test
shell> ln -s /dr1/databases/test /path/to/datadir
```

MySQL does not support linking one directory to multiple databases. Replacing a database directory with a symbolic link works as long as you do not make a symbolic link between databases. Suppose that you have a database db1 under the MySQL data directory, and then make a symlink db2 that points to db1:

```
shell> cd /path/to/datadir
shell> ln -s db1 db2
```

The result is that, for any table tbl_a in db1, there also appears to be a table tbl_a in db2. If one client updates db1.tbl_a and another client updates db2.tbl_a, problems are likely to occur.

However, if you really need to do this, it is possible by altering the source file mysys/my_symlink.c, in which you should look for the following statement:

```
if (!(MyFlags & MY_RESOLVE_LINK) ||
    (!lstat(filename,&stat_buff) && S_ISLNK(stat_buff.st_mode)))
```

Change the statement to this:

```
if (1)
```

6.6.1.2 Using Symbolic Links for Tables on Unix

You should not symlink tables on systems that do not have a fully operational realpath() call. (Linux and Solaris support realpath().) You can check whether your system supports symbolic links by issuing a SHOW VARIABLES LIKE 'have_symlink' statement.

Symlinks are fully supported only for MyISAM tables. For files used by tables for other storage engines, you may get strange problems if you try to use symbolic links.

The handling of symbolic links for MyISAM tables works as follows:

- In the data directory, you always have the table format (.frm) file, the data (.MYD) file, and the index (.MYI) file. The data file and index file can be moved elsewhere and replaced in the data directory by symlinks. The format file cannot.

- You can symlink the data file and the index file independently to different directories.

- You can instruct a running MySQL server to perform the symlinking by using the DATA DIRECTORY and INDEX DIRECTORY options to CREATE TABLE. Alternatively, symlinking can be accomplished manually from the command line using ln -s if mysqld is not running.

- myisamchk does not replace a symlink with the data file or index file. It works directly on the file to which the symlink points. Any temporary files are created in the directory where the data file or index file is located.

- **Note**: When you drop a table that is using symlinks, *both the symlink and the file to which the symlink points are dropped*. This is an extremely good reason why you should *not* run mysqld as the system root or allow system users to have write access to MySQL database directories.

- If you rename a table with ALTER TABLE ... RENAME and you do not move the table to another database, the symlinks in the database directory are renamed to the new names and the data file and index file are renamed accordingly.

- If you use ALTER TABLE ... RENAME to move a table to another database, the table is moved to the other database directory. The old symlinks and the files to which they pointed are deleted. In other words, the new table is not symlinked.

- If you are not using symlinks, you should use the --skip-symbolic-links option to mysqld to ensure that no one can use mysqld to drop or rename a file outside of the data directory.

Table symlink operations that are not yet supported:

- ALTER TABLE ignores the DATA DIRECTORY and INDEX DIRECTORY table options.

- BACKUP TABLE and RESTORE TABLE do not respect symbolic links.

- The .frm file must *never* be a symbolic link (as indicated previously, only the data and index files can be symbolic links). Attempting to do this (for example, to make synonyms) produces incorrect results. Suppose that you have a database db1 under the MySQL data directory, a table tbl1 in this database, and in the db1 directory you make a symlink tbl2 that points to tbl1:

```
shell> cd /path/to/datadir/db1
shell> ln -s tbl1.frm tbl2.frm
shell> ln -s tbl1.MYD tbl2.MYD
shell> ln -s tbl1.MYI tbl2.MYI
```

Problems result if one thread reads db1.tbl1 and another thread updates db1.tbl2:

- The query cache is "fooled" (it has no way of knowing that tbl1 has not been updated, so it returns outdated results).
- ALTER statements on tbl2 fail.

6.6.1.3 Using Symbolic Links for Databases on Windows

Symbolic links are enabled by default for all Windows servers. This enables you to put a database directory on a different disk by setting up a symbolic link to it. This is similar to the way that database symbolic links work on Unix, although the procedure for setting up the link is different. If you do not need symbolic links, you can disable them using the --skip-symbolic-links option.

On Windows, you create a symbolic link to a MySQL database by creating a file in the data directory that contains the path to the destination directory. The file should be named *db_name*.sym, where *db_name* is the database name.

Suppose that the MySQL data directory is C:\mysql\data and you want to have database foo located at D:\data\foo. Set up a symlink using this procedure:

1. Make sure that the D:\data\foo directory exists by creating it if necessary. If you already have a database directory named foo in the data directory, you should move it to D:\data. Otherwise, the symbolic link will be ineffective. To avoid problems, make sure that the server is not running when you move the database directory.

2. Create a text file C:\mysql\data\foo.sym that contains the pathname D:\data\foo\.

After this, all tables created in the database foo are created in D:\data\foo. *Note that the symbolic link is not used if a directory with the same name as the database exists in the MySQL data directory.*

Client and Utility Programs

There are many different MySQL client programs that connect to the server to access databases or perform administrative tasks. Other utilities are available as well. These do not establish a client connection with the server but perform MySQL-related operations.

This chapter provides a brief overview of these programs and then a more detailed description of each one. Each program's description indicates its invocation syntax and the options that it understands. See Chapter 3, "Using MySQL Programs," for general information on invoking programs and specifying program options.

7.1 Overview of Client and Utility Programs

The following list briefly describes the MySQL client programs and utilities:

- myisamchk

  A utility to describe, check, optimize, and repair MyISAM tables. See Section 7.2, "myisamchk—MyISAM Table-Maintenance Utility."

- myisamlog

  A utility that processes the contents of a MyISAM log file. See Section 7.3, "myisamlog—Display MyISAM Log File Contents."

- myisampack

  A utility that compresses MyISAM tables to produce smaller read-only tables. See Section 7.4, "myisampack—Generate Compressed, Read-Only MyISAM Tables."

- mysql

  The command-line tool for interactively entering SQL statements or executing them from a file in batch mode. See Section 7.5, "mysql—The MySQL Command-Line Tool."

- mysqlaccess

  A script that checks the access privileges for a hostname, username, and database combination. See Section 7.6, "mysqlaccess—Client for Checking Access Privileges."

- mysqladmin

  A client that performs administrative operations, such as creating or dropping databases, reloading the grant tables, flushing tables to disk, and reopening log files. mysqladmin can also be used to retrieve version, process, and status information from the server. See Section 7.7, "mysqladmin—Client for Administering a MySQL Server."

- mysqlbinlog

  A utility for reading statements from a binary log. The log of executed statements contained in the binary log files can be used to help recover from a crash. See Section 7.8, "mysqlbinlog—Utility for Processing Binary Log Files."

- mysqlcheck

  A table-maintenance client that checks, repairs, analyzes, and optimizes tables. See Section 7.9, "mysqlcheck—A Table Maintenance and Repair Program."

- mysqldump

  A client that dumps a MySQL database into a file as SQL statements or as tab-separated text files. See Section 7.10, "mysqldump—A Database Backup Program."

- mysqlhotcopy

  A utility that quickly makes backups of MyISAM tables while the server is running. See Section 7.11, "mysqlhotcopy—A Database Backup Program."

- mysqlimport

  A client that imports text files into their respective tables using LOAD DATA INFILE. See Section 7.12, "mysqlimport—A Data Import Program."

- mysqlshow

  A client that displays information about databases, tables, columns, and indexes. See Section 7.13, "mysqlshow—Display Database, Table, and Column Information."

- mysql_zap

  A utility that kills processes that match a pattern. Section 7.14, "mysql_zap—Kill Processes That Match a Pattern."

- perror

  A utility that displays the meaning of system or MySQL error codes. See Section 7.15, "perror—Explain Error Codes."

- replace

  A utility program that performs string replacement in the input text. See Section 7.16, "replace—A String-Replacement Utility."

MySQL AB also provides a number of GUI tools for administering and otherwise working with MySQL servers. For basic information about these, see Chapter 3, "Using MySQL Programs."

Each MySQL program takes many different options. Most programs provide a --help option that you can use to get a full description of the program's different options. For example, try mysql --help.

MySQL client programs that communicate with the server using the MySQL client/server library use the following environment variables:

MYSQL_UNIX_PORT	The default Unix socket file; used for connections to localhost
MYSQL_TCP_PORT	The default port number; used for TCP/IP connections
MYSQL_PWD	The default password
MYSQL_DEBUG	Debug trace options when debugging
TMPDIR	The directory where temporary tables and files are created

Use of MYSQL_PWD is insecure. See Section 4.9.6, "Keeping Your Password Secure."

You can override the default option values or values specified in environment variables for all standard programs by specifying options in an option file or on the command line. See Section 3.3, "Specifying Program Options."

7.2 myisamchk—MyISAM Table-Maintenance Utility

The myisamchk utility gets information about your database tables or checks, repairs, or optimizes them. myisamchk works with MyISAM tables (tables that have .MYD and .MYI files for storing data and indexes).

Invoke myisamchk like this:

```
shell> myisamchk [options] tbl_name ...
```

The options specify what you want myisamchk to do. They are described in the following sections. You can also get a list of options by invoking myisamchk --help.

With no options, myisamchk simply checks your table as the default operation. To get more information or to tell myisamchk to take corrective action, specify options as described in the following discussion.

tbl_name is the database table you want to check or repair. If you run myisamchk somewhere other than in the database directory, you must specify the path to the database directory, because myisamchk has no idea where the database is located. In fact, myisamchk doesn't actually care whether the files you are working on are located in a database directory. You can copy the files that correspond to a database table into some other location and perform recovery operations on them there.

You can name several tables on the myisamchk command line if you wish. You can also specify a table by naming its index file (the file with the .MYI suffix). This allows you to specify all tables in a directory by using the pattern *.MYI. For example, if you are in a database directory, you can check all the MyISAM tables in that directory like this:

```
shell> myisamchk *.MYI
```

If you are not in the database directory, you can check all the tables there by specifying the path to the directory:

```
shell> myisamchk /path/to/database_dir/*.MYI
```

You can even check all tables in all databases by specifying a wildcard with the path to the MySQL data directory:

```
shell> myisamchk /path/to/datadir/*/*.MYI
```

The recommended way to quickly check all MyISAM tables is:

```
shell> myisamchk --silent --fast /path/to/datadir/*/*.MYI
```

If you want to check all MyISAM tables and repair any that are corrupted, you can use the following command:

```
shell> myisamchk --silent --force --fast --update-state \
          --key_buffer_size=64M --sort_buffer_size=64M \
          --read_buffer_size=1M --write_buffer_size=1M \
          /path/to/datadir/*/*.MYI
```

This command assumes that you have more than 64MB free. For more information about memory allocation with myisamchk, see Section 7.2.5, "myisamchk Memory Usage."

You must ensure that no other program is using the tables while you are running myisamchk. Otherwise, when you run myisamchk, it may display the following error message:

```
warning: clients are using or haven't closed the table properly
```

This means that you are trying to check a table that has been updated by another program (such as the mysqld server) that hasn't yet closed the file or that has died without closing the file properly.

If mysqld is running, you must force it to flush any table modifications that are still buffered in memory by using FLUSH TABLES. You should then ensure that no one is using the tables while you are running myisamchk. The easiest way to avoid this problem is to use CHECK TABLE instead of myisamchk to check tables.

7.2.1 myisamchk **General Options**

The options described in this section can be used for any type of table maintenance operation performed by myisamchk. The sections following this one describe options that pertain only to specific operations, such as table checking or repairing.

- --help, -?

  Display a help message and exit.

- --debug=*debug_options*, -# *debug_options*

  Write a debugging log. The *debug_options* string often is 'd:t:o,*file_name*'.

- `--silent`, `-s`

  Silent mode. Write output only when errors occur. You can use `-s` twice (`-ss`) to make myisamchk very silent.

- `--verbose`, `-v`

  Verbose mode. Print more information about what the program does. This can be used with `-d` and `-e`. Use `-v` multiple times (`-vv`, `-vvv`) for even more output.

- `--version`, `-V`

  Display version information and exit.

- `--wait`, `-w`

  Instead of terminating with an error if the table is locked, wait until the table is unlocked before continuing. Note that if you are running mysqld with external locking disabled, the table can be locked only by another myisamchk command.

You can also set the following variables by using `--var_name=value` syntax:

Variable	Default Value
decode_bits	9
ft_max_word_len	version-dependent
ft_min_word_len	4
ft_stopword_file	built-in list
key_buffer_size	523264
myisam_block_size	1024
read_buffer_size	262136
sort_buffer_size	2097144
sort_key_blocks	16
stats_method	nulls_unequal
write_buffer_size	262136

The possible myisamchk variables and their default values can be examined with myisamchk `--help`:

sort_buffer_size is used when the keys are repaired by sorting keys, which is the normal case when you use `--recover`.

key_buffer_size is used when you are checking the table with `--extend-check` or when the keys are repaired by inserting keys row by row into the table (like when doing normal inserts). Repairing through the key buffer is used in the following cases:

- You use `--safe-recover`.
- The temporary files needed to sort the keys would be more than twice as big as when creating the key file directly. This is often the case when you have large key values for CHAR, VARCHAR, or TEXT columns, because the sort operation needs to store the complete key values as it proceeds. If you have lots of temporary space and you can force myisamchk to repair by sorting, you can use the `--sort-recover` option.

Repairing through the key buffer takes much less disk space than using sorting, but is also much slower.

If you want a faster repair, set the key_buffer_size and sort_buffer_size variables to about 25% of your available memory. You can set both variables to large values, because only one of them is used at a time.

myisam_block_size is the size used for index blocks.

stats_method influences how NULL values are treated for index statistics collection when the --analyze option is given. It acts like the myisam_stats_method system variable. For more information, see the description of myisam_stats_method in Section 4.2.2, "Server System Variables," and Section 6.4.7, "MyISAM Index Statistics Collection." For MySQL 5.0, stats_method was added in MySQL 5.0.14. For older versions, the statistics collection method is equivalent to nulls_equal.

ft_min_word_len and ft_max_word_len indicate the minimum and maximum word length for FULLTEXT indexes. ft_stopword_file names the stopword file. These need to be set under the following circumstances.

If you use myisamchk to perform an operation that modifies table indexes (such as repair or analyze), the FULLTEXT indexes are rebuilt using the default full-text parameter values for minimum and maximum word length and the stopword file unless you specify otherwise. This can result in queries failing.

The problem occurs because these parameters are known only by the server. They are not stored in MyISAM index files. To avoid the problem if you have modified the minimum or maximum word length or the stopword file in the server, specify the same ft_min_word_len, ft_max_word_len, and ft_stopword_file values to myisamchk that you use for mysqld. For example, if you have set the minimum word length to 3, you can repair a table with myisamchk like this:

```
shell> myisamchk --recover --ft_min_word_len=3 tbl_name.MYI
```

To ensure that myisamchk and the server use the same values for full-text parameters, you can place each one in both the [mysqld] and [myisamchk] sections of an option file:

```
[mysqld]
ft_min_word_len=3

[myisamchk]
ft_min_word_len=3
```

An alternative to using myisamchk is to use REPAIR TABLE, ANALYZE TABLE, OPTIMIZE TABLE, or ALTER TABLE. These statements are performed by the server, which knows the proper full-text parameter values to use.

7.2.2 `myisamchk` Check Options

`myisamchk` supports the following options for table checking operations:

- `--check, -c`

  Check the table for errors. This is the default operation if you specify no option that selects an operation type explicitly.

- `--check-only-changed, -C`

  Check only tables that have changed since the last check.

- `--extend-check, -e`

  Check the table very thoroughly. This is quite slow if the table has many indexes. This option should only be used in extreme cases. Normally, `myisamchk` or `myisamchk --medium-check` should be able to determine whether there are any errors in the table.

  If you are using `--extend-check` and have plenty of memory, setting the `key_buffer_size` variable to a large value helps the repair operation run faster.

- `--fast, -F`

  Check only tables that haven't been closed properly.

- `--force, -f`

  Do a repair operation automatically if `myisamchk` finds any errors in the table. The repair type is the same as that specified with the `--recover` or `-r` option.

- `--information, -i`

  Print informational statistics about the table that is checked.

- `--medium-check, -m`

  Do a check that is faster than an `--extend-check` operation. This finds only 99.99% of all errors, which should be good enough in most cases.

- `--read-only, -T`

  Don't mark the table as checked. This is useful if you use `myisamchk` to check a table that is in use by some other application that doesn't use locking, such as `mysqld` when run with external locking disabled.

- `--update-state, -U`

  Store information in the `.MYI` file to indicate when the table was checked and whether the table crashed. This should be used to get full benefit of the `--check-only-changed` option, but you shouldn't use this option if the `mysqld` server is using the table and you are running it with external locking disabled.

7.2.3 `myisamchk` Repair Options

`myisamchk` supports the following options for table repair operations:

- `--backup, -B`

  Make a backup of the `.MYD` file as *file_name-time*.BAK

- `--character-sets-dir=`*`path`*

  The directory where character sets are installed. See Section 4.11.1, "The Character Set Used for Data and Sorting."

- `--correct-checksum`

  Correct the checksum information for the table.

- `--data-file-length=`*`len`*`, -D `*`len`*

  Maximum length of the data file (when re-creating data file when it is "full").

- `--extend-check, -e`

  Do a repair that tries to recover every possible row from the data file. Normally, this also finds a lot of garbage rows. Don't use this option unless you are desperate.

- `--force, -f`

  Overwrite old intermediate files (files with names like *`tbl_name`*`.TMD`) instead of aborting.

- `--keys-used=`*`val`*`, -k `*`val`*

  For `myisamchk`, the option value is a bit-value that indicates which indexes to update. Each binary bit of the option value corresponds to a table index, where the first index is bit 0. An option value of 0 disables updates to all indexes, which can be used to get faster inserts. Deactivated indexes can be reactivated by using `myisamchk -r`.

- `--max-record-length=`*`len`*

  Skip rows larger than the given length if `myisamchk` cannot allocate memory to hold them.

- `--parallel-recover, -p`

  Use the same technique as `-r` and `-n`, but create all the keys in parallel, using different threads. *This is beta-quality code. Use at your own risk!*

- `--quick, -q`

  Achieve a faster repair by not modifying the data file. You can specify this option twice to force `myisamchk` to modify the original data file in case of duplicate keys.

- `--recover, -r`

  Do a repair that can fix almost any problem except unique keys that aren't unique (which is an extremely unlikely error with `MyISAM` tables). If you want to recover a table, this is the option to try first. You should try `--safe-recover` only if `myisamchk` reports that the table can't be recovered using `--recover`. (In the unlikely case that `--recover` fails, the data file remains intact.)

  If you have lots of memory, you should increase the value of `sort_buffer_size`.

- `--safe-recover, -o`

  Do a repair using an old recovery method that reads through all rows in order and updates all index trees based on the rows found. This is an order of magnitude slower than `--recover`, but can handle a couple of very unlikely cases that `--recover` cannot.

This recovery method also uses much less disk space than `--recover`. Normally, you should repair first with `--recover`, and then with `--safe-recover` only if `--recover` fails.

If you have lots of memory, you should increase the value of `key_buffer_size`.

- `--set-character-set=`*name*

    Change the character set used by the table indexes. This option was replaced by `--set-collation` in MySQL 5.0.3.

- `--set-collation=`*name*

    Specify the collation to use for sorting table indexes. The character set name is implied by the first part of the collation name. This option was added in MySQL 5.0.3.

- `--sort-recover, -n`

    Force `myisamchk` to use sorting to resolve the keys even if the temporary files would be very large.

- `--tmpdir=`*path*, `-t` *path*

    Path of the directory to be used for storing temporary files. If this is not set, `myisamchk` uses the value of the `TMPDIR` environment variable. `tmpdir` can be set to a list of directory paths that are used successively in round-robin fashion for creating temporary files. The separator character between directory names is the colon (':') on Unix and the semicolon (';') on Windows, NetWare, and OS/2.

- `--unpack, -u`

    Unpack a table that was packed with `myisampack`.

7.2.4 Other `myisamchk` Options

`myisamchk` supports the following options for actions other than table checks and repairs:

- `--analyze, -a`

    Analyze the distribution of key values. This improves join performance by enabling the join optimizer to better choose the order in which to join the tables and which indexes it should use. To obtain information about the key distribution, use a `myisamchk` `--description --verbose` *tbl_name* command or the `SHOW INDEX FROM` *tbl_name* statement.

- `--block-search=`*offset*, `-b` *offset*

    Find the record that a block at the given offset belongs to.

- `--description, -d`

    Print some descriptive information about the table.

- `--set-auto-increment[=`*value*`], -A[`*value*`]`

    Force `AUTO_INCREMENT` numbering for new records to start at the given value (or higher, if there are existing records with `AUTO_INCREMENT` values this large). If *value* is not specified, `AUTO_INCREMENT` numbers for new records begin with the largest value currently in the table, plus one.

- `--sort-index, -S`

  Sort the index tree blocks in high-low order. This optimizes seeks and makes table scans that use indexes faster.

- `--sort-records=N, -R N`

  Sort records according to a particular index. This makes your data much more localized and may speed up range-based SELECT and ORDER BY operations that use this index. (The first time you use this option to sort a table, it may be very slow.) To determine a table's index numbers, use SHOW INDEX, which displays a table's indexes in the same order that myisamchk sees them. Indexes are numbered beginning with 1.

  If keys are not packed (PACK_KEYS=0), they have the same length, so when myisamchk sorts and moves records, it just overwrites record offsets in the index. If keys are packed (PACK_KEYS=1), myisamchk must unpack key blocks first, and then re-create indexes and pack the key blocks again. (In this case, re-creating indexes is faster than updating offsets for each index.)

7.2.5 `myisamchk` Memory Usage

Memory allocation is important when you run myisamchk. myisamchk uses no more memory than its memory-related variables are set to. If you are going to use myisamchk on very large tables, you should first decide how much memory you want it to use. The default is to use only about 3MB to perform repairs. By using larger values, you can get myisamchk to operate faster. For example, if you have more than 32MB RAM, you could use options such as these (in addition to any other options you might specify):

```
shell> myisamchk --sort_buffer_size=16M --key_buffer_size=16M \
          --read_buffer_size=1M --write_buffer_size=1M ...
```

Using --sort_buffer_size=16M should probably be enough for most cases.

Be aware that myisamchk uses temporary files in TMPDIR. If TMPDIR points to a memory filesystem, you may easily get out-of-memory errors. If this happens, run myisamchk with the --tmpdir=path option to specify some directory located on a filesystem that has more space.

When repairing, myisamchk also needs a lot of disk space:

- Double the size of the data file (the original file and a copy). This space is not needed if you do a repair with --quick; in this case, only the index file is re-created. This space is needed on the same filesystem as the original data file! (The copy is created in the same directory as the original.)

- Space for the new index file that replaces the old one. The old index file is truncated at the start of the repair operation, so you usually ignore this space. This space is needed on the same filesystem as the original index file!

- When using --recover or --sort-recover (but not when using --safe-recover), you need space for a sort buffer. The following formula yields the amount of space required:

  $(largest\_key + row\_pointer\_length) \times number\_of\_rows \times 2$

You can check the length of the keys and the `row_pointer_length` with `myisamchk -dv` *tbl_name*. This space is allocated in the temporary directory (specified by `TMPDIR` or `--tmpdir=`*path*).

If you have a problem with disk space during repair, you can try `--safe-recover` instead of `--recover`.

7.3 `myisamlog`—Display `MyISAM` Log File Contents

`myisamlog` processes the contents of a `MyISAM` log file.

Invoke `myisamlog` like this:

```
shell> myisamlog [options] [log_file [tbl_name] ...]
```

The default operation is update (-u). If a recovery is done (-r), all writes and possibly updates and deletes are done and errors are only counted. The default log file name is `myisam.log` if no *log_file* argument is given, If tables are named on the command line, only those tables are updated.

`myisamlog` understands the following options:

- `-?`, `-I`

  Display a help message and exit.

- `-c` *N*

  Execute only *N* commands.

- `-f` *N*

  Specify the maximum number of open files.

- `-i`

  Display extra information before exiting.

- `-o` *offset*

  Specify the starting offset.

- `-p` *N*

  Remove *N* components from path.

- `-r`

  Perform a recovery operation.

- `-R` *record_pos_file record_pos*

  Specify record position file and record position.

- `-u`

  Perform an update operation.

- `-v`

  Verbose mode. Print more output about what the program does. This option can be given multiple times to produce more and more output.

- -w *write_file*

  Specify the write file.

- -V

  Display version information.

7.4 `myisampack`—Generate Compressed, Read-Only `MyISAM` Tables

The myisampack utility compresses MyISAM tables. myisampack works by compressing each column in the table separately. Usually, myisampack packs the data file 40%–70%.

When the table is used later, the server reads into memory the information needed to decompress columns. This results in much better performance when accessing individual rows, because you only have to uncompress exactly one row.

MySQL uses mmap() when possible to perform memory mapping on compressed tables. If mmap() does not work, MySQL falls back to normal read/write file operations.

Please note the following:

- If the mysqld server was invoked with external locking disabled, it is not a good idea to invoke myisampack if the table might be updated by the server during the packing process. It is safest to compress tables with the server stopped.

- After packing a table, it becomes read-only. This is generally intended (such as when accessing packed tables on a CD). Allowing writes to a packed table is on our TODO list, but with low priority.

- myisampack can pack BLOB or TEXT columns. (The older pack_isam program for ISAM tables did not have this capability.)

Invoke myisampack like this:

```
shell> myisampack [options] file_name ...
```

Each filename argument should be the name of an index (.MYI) file. If you are not in the database directory, you should specify the pathname to the file. It is permissible to omit the .MYI extension.

After you compress a table with myisampack, you should use myisamchk -rq to rebuild its indexes. See Section 7.2, "myisamchk—MyISAM Table-Maintenance Utility."

myisampack supports the following options:

- --help, -?

  Display a help message and exit.

- --backup, -b

  Make a backup of each table's data file using the name *tbl_name*.OLD.

- `--character-sets-dir=path`

  The directory where character sets are installed. See Section 4.11.1, "The Character Set Used for Data and Sorting."

- `--debug[=debug_options], -# [debug_options]`

  Write a debugging log. The *debug_options* string often is `'d:t:o,file_name'`.

- `--force, -f`

  Produce a packed table even if it becomes larger than the original or if the intermediate file from an earlier invocation of `myisampack` exists. (`myisampack` creates an intermediate file named *tbl_name*.`TMD` in the database directory while it compresses the table. If you kill `myisampack`, the .`TMD` file might not be deleted.) Normally, `myisampack` exits with an error if it finds that *tbl_name*.`TMD` exists. With `--force`, `myisampack` packs the table anyway.

- `--join=big_tbl_name, -j big_tbl_name`

  Join all tables named on the command line into a single table *big_tbl_name*. All tables that are to be combined *must* have identical structure (same column names and types, same indexes, and so forth).

- `--packlength=len, -p len`

  Specify the row length storage size, in bytes. The value should be 1, 2, or 3. `myisampack` stores all rows with length pointers of 1, 2, or 3 bytes. In most normal cases, `myisampack` can determine the correct length value before it begins packing the file, but it may notice during the packing process that it could have used a shorter length. In this case, `myisampack` prints a note that you could use a shorter row length the next time you pack the same file.

- `--silent, -s`

  Silent mode. Write output only when errors occur.

- `--test, -t`

  Do not actually pack the table, just test packing it.

- `--tmpdir=path, -T path`

  Use the named directory as the location where `myisamchk` creates temporary files.

- `--verbose, -v`

  Verbose mode. Write information about the progress of the packing operation and its result.

- `--version, -V`

  Display version information and exit.

- `--wait, -w`

  Wait and retry if the table is in use. If the `mysqld` server was invoked with external locking disabled, it is not a good idea to invoke `myisampack` if the table might be updated by the server during the packing process.

The following sequence of commands illustrates a typical table compression session:

```
shell> ls -l station.*
-rw-rw-r--   1 monty     my           994128 Apr 17 19:00 station.MYD
-rw-rw-r--   1 monty     my            53248 Apr 17 19:00 station.MYI
-rw-rw-r--   1 monty     my             5767 Apr 17 19:00 station.frm

shell> myisamchk -dvv station

MyISAM file:       station
Isam-version:   2
Creation time: 1996-03-13 10:08:58
Recover time:   1997-02-02  3:06:43
Data records:                 1192 Deleted blocks:          0
Datafile parts:               1192 Deleted data:            0
Datafile pointer (bytes):     2 Keyfile pointer (bytes):   2
Max datafile length:   54657023 Max keyfile length:   33554431
Recordlength:                 834
Record format: Fixed length

table description:
Key Start Len Index   Type              Root   Blocksize   Rec/key
1    2     4   unique  unsigned long     1024    1024          1
2    32    30  multip. text              10240   1024          1

Field Start Length Type
1     1      1
2     2      4
3     6      4
4     10     1
5     11     20
6     31     1
7     32     30
8     62     35
9     97     35
10    132    35
11    167    4
12    171    16
13    187    35
14    222    4
15    226    16
16    242    20
17    262    20
18    282    20
19    302    30
20    332    4
21    336    4
22    340    1
23    341    8
```

```
24    349    8
25    357    8
26    365    2
27    367    2
28    369    4
29    373    4
30    377    1
31    378    2
32    380    8
33    388    4
34    392    4
35    396    4
36    400    4
37    404    1
38    405    4
39    409    4
40    413    4
41    417    4
42    421    4
43    425    4
44    429    20
45    449    30
46    479    1
47    480    1
48    481    79
49    560    79
50    639    79
51    718    79
52    797    8
53    805    1
54    806    1
55    807    20
56    827    4
57    831    4
```

```
shell> myisampack station.MYI
Compressing station.MYI: (1192 records)
- Calculating statistics

normal:      20  empty-space:   16  empty-zero:    12  empty-fill:  11
pre-space:    0  end-space:     12  table-lookups:  5  zero:         7
Original trees:  57  After join: 17
- Compressing file
87.14%
Remember to run myisamchk -rq on compressed tables

shell> ls -l station.*
-rw-rw-r--   1 monty    my         127874 Apr 17 19:00 station.MYD
```

```
-rw-rw-r--    1 monty    my              55296 Apr 17 19:04 station.MYI
-rw-rw-r--    1 monty    my               5767 Apr 17 19:00 station.frm

shell> myisamchk -dvv station

MyISAM file:      station
Isam-version:  2
Creation time: 1996-03-13 10:08:58
Recover time:  1997-04-17 19:04:26
Data records:               1192  Deleted blocks:            0
Datafile parts:             1192  Deleted data:              0
Datafile pointer (bytes):      3  Keyfile pointer (bytes):   1
Max datafile length:    16777215  Max keyfile length:   131071
Recordlength:                834
Record format: Compressed


table description:
Key Start Len Index    Type                  Root  Blocksize    Rec/key
1   2     4   unique   unsigned long        10240       1024          1
2   32    30  multip.  text                 54272       1024          1


Field Start Length Type                            Huff tree  Bits
1     1     1      constant                            1       0
2     2     4      zerofill(1)                         2       9
3     6     4      no zeros, zerofill(1)               2       9
4     10    1                                          3       9
5     11    20     table-lookup                        4       0
6     31    1                                          3       9
7     32    30     no endspace, not_always             5       9
8     62    35     no endspace, not_always, no empty   6       9
9     97    35     no empty                            7       9
10    132   35     no endspace, not_always, no empty   6       9
11    167   4      zerofill(1)                         2       9
12    171   16     no endspace, not_always, no empty   5       9
13    187   35     no endspace, not_always, no empty   6       9
14    222   4      zerofill(1)                         2       9
15    226   16     no endspace, not_always, no empty   5       9
16    242   20     no endspace, not_always             8       9
17    262   20     no endspace, no empty               8       9
18    282   20     no endspace, no empty               5       9
19    302   30     no endspace, no empty               6       9
20    332   4      always zero                         2       9
21    336   4      always zero                         2       9
22    340   1                                          3       9
23    341   8      table-lookup                        9       0
24    349   8      table-lookup                       10       0
25    357   8      always zero                         2       9
26    365   2                                          2       9
27    367   2      no zeros, zerofill(1)               2       9
```

28	369	4	no zeros, zerofill(1)	2	9
29	373	4	table-lookup	11	0
30	377	1		3	9
31	378	2	no zeros, zerofill(1)	2	9
32	380	8	no zeros	2	9
33	388	4	always zero	2	9
34	392	4	table-lookup	12	0
35	396	4	no zeros, zerofill(1)	13	9
36	400	4	no zeros, zerofill(1)	2	9
37	404	1		2	9
38	405	4	no zeros	2	9
39	409	4	always zero	2	9
40	413	4	no zeros	2	9
41	417	4	always zero	2	9
42	421	4	no zeros	2	9
43	425	4	always zero	2	9
44	429	20	no empty	3	9
45	449	30	no empty	3	9
46	479	1		14	4
47	480	1		14	4
48	481	79	no endspace, no empty	15	9
49	560	79	no empty	2	9
50	639	79	no empty	2	9
51	718	79	no endspace	16	9
52	797	8	no empty	2	9
53	805	1		17	1
54	806	1		3	9
55	807	20	no empty	3	9
56	827	4	no zeros, zerofill(2)	2	9
57	831	4	no zeros, zerofill(1)	2	9

myisampack displays the following kinds of information:

- normal

    The number of columns for which no extra packing is used.

- empty-space

    The number of columns containing values that are only spaces. These occupy one bit.

- empty-zero

    The number of columns containing values that are only binary zeros. These occupy one bit.

- empty-fill

    The number of integer columns that do not occupy the full byte range of their type. These are changed to a smaller type. For example, a BIGINT column (eight bytes) can be stored as a TINYINT column (one byte) if all its values are in the range from -128 to 127.

- `pre-space`

  The number of decimal columns that are stored with leading spaces. In this case, each value contains a count for the number of leading spaces.

- `end-space`

  The number of columns that have a lot of trailing spaces. In this case, each value contains a count for the number of trailing spaces.

- `table-lookup`

  The column had only a small number of different values, which were converted to an ENUM before Huffman compression.

- `zero`

  The number of columns for which all values are zero.

- `Original trees`

  The initial number of Huffman trees.

- `After join`

  The number of distinct Huffman trees left after joining trees to save some header space.

After a table has been compressed, `myisamchk -dvv` prints additional information about each column:

- `Type`

  The data type. The value may contain any of the following descriptors:

  - `constant`

    All rows have the same value.

  - `no endspace`

    Do not store endspace.

  - `no endspace, not_always`

    Do not store endspace and do not do endspace compression for all values.

  - `no endspace, no empty`

    Do not store endspace. Do not store empty values.

  - `table-lookup`

    The column was converted to an ENUM.

  - `zerofill(N)`

    The most significant N bytes in the value are always 0 and are not stored.

  - `no zeros`

    Do not store zeros.

  - `always zero`

    Zero values are stored using one bit.

- `Huff tree`

  The number of the Huffman tree associated with the column.

- `Bits`

  The number of bits used in the Huffman tree.

After you run `myisampack`, you must run `myisamchk` to re-create any indexes. At this time, you can also sort the index blocks and create statistics needed for the MySQL optimizer to work more efficiently:

```
shell> myisamchk -rq --sort-index --analyze tbl_name.MYI
```

After you have installed the packed table into the MySQL database directory, you should execute `mysqladmin flush-tables` to force `mysqld` to start using the new table.

To unpack a packed table, use the `--unpack` option to `myisamchk`.

7.5 `mysql`—The MySQL Command-Line Tool

`mysql` is a simple SQL shell (with GNU `readline` capabilities). It supports interactive and non-interactive use. When used interactively, query results are presented in an ASCII-table format. When used non-interactively (for example, as a filter), the result is presented in tab-separated format. The output format can be changed using command options.

If you have problems due to insufficient memory for large result sets, use the `--quick` option. This forces `mysql` to retrieve results from the server a row at a time rather than retrieving the entire result set and buffering it in memory before displaying it. This is done by returning the result set using the `mysql_use_result()` C API function in the client/server library rather than `mysql_store_result()`.

Using `mysql` is very easy. Invoke it from the prompt of your command interpreter as follows:

```
shell> mysql db_name
```

Or:

```
shell> mysql --user=user_name --password=your_password db_name
```

Then type an SQL statement, end it with ';', \g, or \G and press Enter.

You can execute SQL statements in a script file (batch file) like this:

```
shell> mysql db_name < script.sql > output.tab
```

7.5.1 `mysql` Options

`mysql` supports the following options:

- `--help, -?`

  Display a help message and exit.

- `--auto-rehash`

  Enable automatic rehashing. This option is on by default, which enables table and column name completion. Use `--skip-auto-rehash` to disable rehashing. That causes `mysql` to start faster, but you must issue the `rehash` command if you want to use table and column name completion.

- `--batch, -B`

  Print results using tab as the column separator, with each row on a new line. With this option, `mysql` does not use the history file.

- `--character-sets-dir=path`

  The directory where character sets are installed. See Section 4.11.1, "The Character Set Used for Data and Sorting."

- `--column-names`

  Write column names in results.

- `--compress, -C`

  Compress all information sent between the client and the server if both support compression.

- `--database=db_name, -D db_name`

  The database to use. This is useful primarily in an option file.

- `--debug[=debug_options], -# [debug_options]`

  Write a debugging log. The `debug_options` string often is `'d:t:o,file_name'`. The default is `'d:t:o,/tmp/mysql.trace'`.

- `--debug-info, -T`

  Print some debugging information when the program exits.

- `--default-character-set=charset_name`

  Use `charset_name` as the default character set. See Section 4.11.1, "The Character Set Used for Data and Sorting."

- `--delimiter=str`

  Set the statement delimiter. The default is the semicolon character (';').

- `--execute=statement, -e statement`

  Execute the statement and quit. The default output format is like that produced with `--batch`. See Section 3.3.1, "Using Options on the Command Line," for some examples.

- `--force, -f`

  Continue even if an SQL error occurs.

- `--host=host_name, -h host_name`

  Connect to the MySQL server on the given host.

- `--html, -H`

  Produce HTML output.

- `--ignore-spaces, -i`

  Ignore spaces after function names. The effect of this is described in the discussion for the `IGNORE_SPACE` SQL mode (see Section 4.2.5, "The Server SQL Mode").

- `--line-numbers`

  Write line numbers for errors. Disable this with `--skip-line-numbers`.

- `--local-infile[={0|1}]`

  Enable or disable `LOCAL` capability for `LOAD DATA INFILE`. With no value, the option enables `LOCAL`. The option may be given as `--local-infile=0` or `--local-infile=1` to explicitly disable or enable `LOCAL`. Enabling `LOCAL` has no effect if the server does not also support it.

- `--named-commands, -G`

  Enable named `mysql` commands. Long-format commands are allowed, not just short-format commands. For example, `quit` and `\q` both are recognized. Use `--skip-named-commands` to disable named commands. See Section 7.5.2, "mysql Commands."

- `--no-auto-rehash, -A`

  Deprecated form of `-skip-auto-rehash`. See the description for `--auto-rehash`.

- `--no-beep, -b`

  Do not beep when errors occur.

- `--no-named-commands, -g`

  Disable named commands. Use the `\*` form only, or use named commands only at the beginning of a line ending with a semicolon (';'). `mysql` starts with this option *enabled* by default. However, even with this option, long-format commands still work from the first line. See Section 7.5.2, "mysql Commands."

- `--no-pager`

  Deprecated form of `--skip-pager`. See the `--pager` option.

- `--no-tee`

  Do not copy output to a file. Section 7.5.2, "mysql Commands," discusses tee files further.

- `--one-database, -o`

  Ignore statements except those for the default database named on the command line. This is useful for skipping updates to other databases in the binary log.

- `--pager[=command]`

  Use the given command for paging query output. If the command is omitted, the default pager is the value of your `PAGER` environment variable. Valid pagers are `less`, `more`, `cat [> filename]`, and so forth. This option works only on Unix. It does not work in batch mode. To disable paging, use `--skip-pager`. Section 7.5.2, "mysql Commands," discusses output paging further.

- `--password[=password]`, `-p[password]`

  The password to use when connecting to the server. If you use the short option form (`-p`), you *cannot* have a space between the option and the password. If you omit the `password` value following the `--password` or `-p` option on the command line, you are prompted for one.

  Specifying a password on the command line should be considered insecure. See Section 4.9.6, "Keeping Your Password Secure."

- `--port=port_num`, `-P port_num`

  The TCP/IP port number to use for the connection.

- `--prompt=format_str`

  Set the prompt to the specified format. The default is `mysql>`. The special sequences that the prompt can contain are described in Section 7.5.2, "mysql Commands."

- `--protocol={TCP|SOCKET|PIPE|MEMORY}`

  The connection protocol to use.

- `--quick, -q`

  Do not cache each query result, print each row as it is received. This may slow down the server if the output is suspended. With this option, `mysql` does not use the history file.

- `--raw, -r`

  Write column values without escape conversion. Often used with the `--batch` option.

- `--reconnect`

  If the connection to the server is lost, automatically try to reconnect. A single reconnect attempt is made each time the connection is lost. To suppress reconnection behavior, use `--skip-reconnect`.

- `--safe-updates, --i-am-a-dummy, -U`

  Allow only those UPDATE and DELETE statements that specify which rows to modify by using key values. If you have set this option in an option file, you can override it by using `--safe-updates` on the command line. See Section 7.5.4, "mysql Tips," for more information about this option.

- `--secure-auth`

  Do not send passwords to the server in old (pre-4.1.1) format. This prevents connections except for servers that use the newer password format.

- `--show-warnings`

  Cause warnings to be shown after each statement if there are any. This option applies to interactive and batch mode. This option was added in MySQL 5.0.6.

- `--sigint-ignore`

  Ignore SIGINT signals (typically the result of typing Control-C).

- `--silent, -s`

  Silent mode. Produce less output. This option can be given multiple times to produce less and less output.

- `--skip-column-names, -N`

  Do not write column names in results.

- `--skip-line-numbers, -L`

  Do not write line numbers for errors. Useful when you want to compare result files that include error messages.

- `--socket=path, -S path`

  For connections to `localhost`, the Unix socket file to use, or, on Windows, the name of the named pipe to use.

- `--table, -t`

  Display output in table format. This is the default for interactive use, but can be used to produce table output in batch mode.

- `--tee=file_name`

  Append a copy of output to the given file. This option does not work in batch mode. Section 7.5.2, "mysql Commands," discusses tee files further.

- `--unbuffered, -n`

  Flush the buffer after each query.

- `--user=user_name, -u user_name`

  The MySQL username to use when connecting to the server.

- `--verbose, -v`

  Verbose mode. Produce more output about what the program does. This option can be given multiple times to produce more and more output. (For example, -v -v -v produces table output format even in batch mode.)

- `--version, -V`

  Display version information and exit.

- `--vertical, -E`

  Print query output rows vertically (one line per column value). Without this option, you can specify vertical output for individual statements by terminating them with \G.

- `--wait, -w`

  If the connection cannot be established, wait and retry instead of aborting.

- `--xml, -X`

  Produce XML output.

You can also set the following variables by using `--var_name=value` syntax:

- `connect_timeout`

  The number of seconds before connection timeout. (Default value is 0.)

- `max_allowed_packet`

  The maximum packet length to send to or receive from the server. (Default value is 16MB.)

- `max_join_size`

  The automatic limit for rows in a join when using `--safe-updates`. (Default value is 1,000,000.)

- `net_buffer_length`

  The buffer size for TCP/IP and socket communication. (Default value is 16KB.)

- `select_limit`

  The automatic limit for SELECT statements when using `--safe-updates`. (Default value is 1,000.)

It is also possible to set variables by using `--set-variable=`*var_name*`=`*value* or `-O` *var_name*`=`*value* syntax. *This syntax is deprecated.*

On Unix, the `mysql` client writes a record of executed statements to a history file. By default, the history file is named `.mysql_history` and is created in your home directory. To specify a different file, set the value of the `MYSQL_HISTFILE` environment variable.

If you do not want to maintain a history file, first remove `.mysql_history` if it exists, and then use either of the following techniques:

- Set the `MYSQL_HISTFILE` variable to `/dev/null`. To cause this setting to take effect each time you log in, put the setting in one of your shell's startup files.
- Create `.mysql_history` as a symbolic link to `/dev/null`:

  ```
  shell> ln -s /dev/null $HOME/.mysql_history
  ```

  You need do this only once.

7.5.2 `mysql` Commands

`mysql` sends each SQL statement that you issue to the server to be executed. There is also a set of commands that `mysql` itself interprets. For a list of these commands, type `help` or `\h` at the `mysql>` prompt:

```
mysql> help

List of all MySQL commands:
Note that all text commands must be first on line and end with ';'
?          (\?) Synonym for `help'.
clear      (\c) Clear command.
connect    (\r) Reconnect to the server. Optional arguments are db and host.
delimiter  (\d) Set statement delimiter. NOTE: Takes the rest of the line as
                new delimiter.
edit       (\e) Edit command with $EDITOR.
ego        (\G) Send command to mysql server, display result vertically.
```

```
exit       (\q) Exit mysql. Same as quit.
go         (\g) Send command to mysql server.
help       (\h) Display this help.
nopager    (\n) Disable pager, print to stdout.
notee      (\t) Don't write into outfile.
pager      (\P) Set PAGER [to_pager]. Print the query results via PAGER.
print      (\p) Print current command.
prompt     (\R) Change your mysql prompt.
quit       (\q) Quit mysql.
rehash     (\#) Rebuild completion hash.
source     (\.) Execute an SQL script file. Takes a file name as an argument.
status     (\s) Get status information from the server.
system     (\!) Execute a system shell command.
tee        (\T) Set outfile [to_outfile]. Append everything into given
                outfile.
use        (\u) Use another database. Takes database name as argument.
warnings   (\W) Show warnings after every statement.
nowarning  (\w) Don't show warnings after every statement.
```

Each command has both a long and short form. The long form is not case sensitive; the short form is. The long form can be followed by an optional semicolon terminator, but the short form should not.

In the delimiter command, you should avoid the use of the backslash ('\') character because that is the escape character for MySQL.

The edit, nopager, pager, and system commands work only in Unix.

The status command provides some information about the connection and the server you are using. If you are running in --safe-updates mode, status also prints the values for the mysql variables that affect your queries.

To log queries and their output, use the tee command. All the data displayed on the screen is appended into a given file. This can be very useful for debugging purposes also. You can enable this feature on the command line with the --tee option, or interactively with the tee command. The tee file can be disabled interactively with the notee command. Executing tee again re-enables logging. Without a parameter, the previous file is used. Note that tee flushes query results to the file after each statement, just before mysql prints its next prompt.

By using the --pager option, it is possible to browse or search query results in interactive mode with Unix programs such as less, more, or any other similar program. If you specify no value for the option, mysql checks the value of the PAGER environment variable and sets the pager to that. Output paging can be enabled interactively with the pager command and disabled with nopager. The command takes an optional argument; if given, the paging program is set to that. With no argument, the pager is set to the pager that was set on the command line, or stdout if no pager was specified.

Output paging works only in Unix because it uses the popen() function, which does not exist on Windows. For Windows, the tee option can be used instead to save query output, although this is not as convenient as pager for browsing output in some situations.

Here are a few tips about the `pager` command:

- You can use it to write to a file and the results go only to the file:

```
mysql> pager cat > /tmp/log.txt
```

You can also pass any options for the program that you want to use as your pager:

```
mysql> pager less -n -i -S
```

- In the preceding example, note the -S option. You may find it very useful for browsing wide query results. Sometimes a very wide result set is difficult to read on the screen. The -S option to less can make the result set much more readable because you can scroll it horizontally using the left-arrow and right-arrow keys. You can also use -S interactively within less to switch the horizontal-browse mode on and off. For more information, read the less manual page:

```
shell> man less
```

- You can specify very complex pager commands for handling query output:

```
mysql> pager cat | tee /dr1/tmp/res.txt \
          | tee /dr2/tmp/res2.txt | less -n -i -S
```

In this example, the command would send query results to two files in two different directories on two different filesystems mounted on /dr1 and /dr2, yet still display the results onscreen via less.

You can also combine the tee and pager functions. Have a tee file enabled and pager set to less, and you are able to browse the results using the less program and still have everything appended into a file the same time. The difference between the Unix tee used with the pager command and the mysql built-in tee command is that the built-in tee works even if you do not have the Unix tee available. The built-in tee also logs everything that is printed on the screen, whereas the Unix tee used with pager does not log quite that much. Additionally, tee file logging can be turned on and off interactively from within mysql. This is useful when you want to log some queries to a file, but not others.

The default mysql> prompt can be reconfigured. The string for defining the prompt can contain the following special sequences:

Option	Description
\v	The server version
\d	The default database
\h	The server host
\p	The current TCP/IP port or socket file
\u	Your username
\U	Your full *user_name@host_name* account name
\\	A literal '\' backslash character
\n	A newline character

Option	Description
\t	A tab character
\	A space (a space follows the backslash)
_	A space
\R	The current time, in 24-hour military time (0–23)
\r	The current time, standard 12-hour time (1–12)
\m	Minutes of the current time
\y	The current year, two digits
\Y	The current year, four digits
\D	The full current date
\s	Seconds of the current time
\w	The current day of the week in three-letter format (Mon, Tue, ...)
\P	am/pm
\o	The current month in numeric format
\O	The current month in three-letter format (Jan, Feb, ...)
\c	A counter that increments for each statement you issue
\S	Semicolon
\'	Single quote
\"	Double quote

'\' followed by any other letter just becomes that letter.

If you specify the `prompt` command with no argument, `mysql` resets the prompt to the default of `mysql>`.

You can set the prompt in several ways:

- *Use an environment variable.* You can set the `MYSQL_PS1` environment variable to a prompt string. For example:

```
shell> export MYSQL_PS1="(\u@\h) [\d]> "
```

- *Use a command-line option.* You can set the `--prompt` option on the command line to `mysql`. For example:

```
shell> mysql --prompt="(\u@\h) [\d]> "
(user@host) [database]>
```

- *Use an option file.* You can set the `prompt` option in the `[mysql]` group of any MySQL option file, such as `/etc/my.cnf` or the `.my.cnf` file in your home directory. For example:

```
[mysql]
prompt=(\\u@\\h) [\\d]>\\_
```

In this example, note that the backslashes are doubled. If you set the prompt using the `prompt` option in an option file, it is advisable to double the backslashes when using the special prompt options. There is some overlap in the set of allowable prompt options and the set of special escape sequences that are recognized in option files. (These sequences are listed in Section 3.3.2, "Using Option Files.") The overlap may cause you problems if you use single backslashes. For example, \s is interpreted as a space rather than as the current seconds value. The following example shows how to define a prompt within an option file to include the current time in HH:MM:SS> format:

```
[mysql]
prompt="\\r:\\m:\\s> "
```

- *Set the prompt interactively.* You can change your prompt interactively by using the prompt (or \R) command. For example:

```
mysql> prompt (\u@\h) [\d]>\_
PROMPT set to '(\u@\h) [\d]>\_'
(user@host) [database]>
(user@host) [database]> prompt
Returning to default PROMPT of mysql>
mysql>
```

7.5.3 Executing SQL Statements from a Text File

The mysql client typically is used interactively, like this:

```
shell> mysql db_name
```

However, it is also possible to put your SQL statements in a file and then tell mysql to read its input from that file. To do so, create a text file *text_file* that contains the statements you wish to execute. Then invoke mysql as shown here:

```
shell> mysql db_name < text_file
```

If you place a USE *db_name* statement as the first statement in the file, it is unnecessary to specify the database name on the command line:

```
shell> mysql < text_file
```

If you are already running mysql, you can execute an SQL script file using the source or \. command:

```
mysql> source file_name
mysql> \. file_name
```

Sometimes you may want your script to display progress information to the user. For this you can insert statements like this:

```
SELECT '<info_to_display>' AS ' ';
```

The statement shown outputs <info_to_display>.

7.5.4 mysql Tips

This section describes some techniques that can help you use mysql more effectively.

7.5.4.1 Displaying Query Results Vertically

Some query results are much more readable when displayed vertically, instead of in the usual horizontal table format. Queries can be displayed vertically by terminating the query with \G instead of a semicolon. For example, longer text values that include newlines often are much easier to read with vertical output:

```
mysql> SELECT * FROM mails WHERE LENGTH(txt) < 300 LIMIT 300,1\G
*************************** 1. row ***************************
  msg_nro: 3068
     date: 2000-03-01 23:29:50
time_zone: +0200
mail_from: Monty
    reply: monty@no.spam.com
  mail_to: "Thimble Smith" <tim@no.spam.com>
      sbj: UTF-8
      txt: >>>>> "Thimble" == Thimble Smith writes:

Thimble> Hi.  I think this is a good idea.  Is anyone familiar
Thimble> with UTF-8 or Unicode? Otherwise, I'll put this on my
Thimble> TODO list and see what happens.

Yes, please do that.

Regards,
Monty
     file: inbox-jani-1
     hash: 190402944
1 row in set (0.09 sec)
```

7.5.4.2 Using the --safe-updates Option

For beginners, a useful startup option is --safe-updates (or --i-am-a-dummy, which has the same effect). It is helpful for cases when you might have issued a DELETE FROM tbl_name statement but forgotten the WHERE clause. Normally, such a statement deletes all rows from the table. With --safe-updates, you can delete rows only by specifying the key values that identify them. This helps prevent accidents.

When you use the --safe-updates option, mysql issues the following statement when it connects to the MySQL server:

```
SET SQL_SAFE_UPDATES=1,SQL_SELECT_LIMIT=1000, SQL_MAX_JOIN_SIZE=1000000;
```

The SET statement has the following effects:

- You are not allowed to execute an UPDATE or DELETE statement unless you specify a key constraint in the WHERE clause or provide a LIMIT clause (or both). For example:

```
UPDATE tbl_name SET not_key_column=val WHERE key_column=val;

UPDATE tbl_name SET not_key_column=val LIMIT 1;
```

- The server limits all large SELECT results to 1,000 rows unless the statement includes a LIMIT clause.
- The server aborts multiple-table SELECT statements that probably need to examine more than 1,000,000 row combinations.

To specify limits different from 1,000 and 1,000,000, you can override the defaults by using the --select_limit and --max_join_size options:

```
shell> mysql --safe-updates --select_limit=500 --max_join_size=10000
```

7.5.4.3 Disabling mysql Auto-Reconnect

If the mysql client loses its connection to the server while sending a query, it immediately and automatically tries to reconnect once to the server and send the query again. However, even if mysql succeeds in reconnecting, your first connection has ended and all your previous session objects and settings are lost: temporary tables, the autocommit mode, and user-defined and session variables. Also, any current transaction rolls back. This behavior may be dangerous for you, as in the following example where the server was shut down and restarted without you knowing it:

```
mysql> SET @a=1;
Query OK, 0 rows affected (0.05 sec)

mysql> INSERT INTO t VALUES(@a);
ERROR 2006: MySQL server has gone away
No connection. Trying to reconnect...
Connection id:     1
Current database: test

Query OK, 1 row affected (1.30 sec)

mysql> SELECT * FROM t;
+------+
| a    |
+------+
| NULL |
+------+
1 row in set (0.05 sec)
```

The @a user variable has been lost with the connection, and after the reconnection it is undefined. If it is important to have mysql terminate with an error if the connection has been lost, you can start the mysql client with the --skip-reconnect option.

7.6 mysqlaccess—Client for Checking Access Privileges

mysqlaccess is a diagnostic tool that Yves Carlier has provided for the MySQL distribution. It checks the access privileges for a hostname, username, and database combination. Note that `mysqlaccess` checks access using only the user, db, and host tables. It does not check table, column, or routine privileges specified in the `tables_priv`, `columns_priv`, or `procs_priv` tables.

Invoke `mysqlaccess` like this:

```
shell> mysqlaccess [host_name [user_name [db_name]]] [options]
```

`mysqlaccess` understands the following options:

- `--help, -?`

  Display a help message and exit.

- `--brief, -b`

  Generate reports in single-line tabular format.

- `--commit`

  Copy the new access privileges from the temporary tables to the original grant tables. The grant tables must be flushed for the new privileges to take effect. (For example, execute a `mysqladmin reload` command.)

- `--copy`

  Reload the temporary grant tables from original ones.

- `--db=db_name, -d db_name`

  Specify the database name.

- `--debug=N`

  Specify the debug level. N can be an integer from 0 to 3.

- `--host=host_name, -h host_name`

  The hostname to use in the access privileges.

- `--howto`

  Display some examples that show how to use `mysqlaccess`.

- `--old_server`

  Assume that the server is an old MySQL server (before MySQL 3.21) that does not yet know how to handle full WHERE clauses.

- `--password[=password], -p[password]`

  The password to use when connecting to the server. If you omit the *password* value following the `--password` or `-p` option on the command line, you are prompted for one.

  Specifying a password on the command line should be considered insecure. See Section 4.9.6, "Keeping Your Password Secure."

- `--plan`

  Display suggestions and ideas for future releases.

- `--preview`

  Show the privilege differences after making changes to the temporary grant tables.

- `--relnotes`

  Display the release notes.

- `--rhost=host_name, -H host_name`

  Connect to the MySQL server on the given host.

- `--rollback`

  Undo the most recent changes to the temporary grant tables.

- `--spassword[=password], -P[password]`

  The password to use when connecting to the server as the superuser. If you omit the *password* value following the `--password` or `-p` option on the command line, you are prompted for one.

  Specifying a password on the command line should be considered insecure. See Section 4.9.6, "Keeping Your Password Secure."

- `--superuser=user_name, -U user_name`

  Specify the username for connecting as the superuser.

- `--table, -t`

  Generate reports in table format.

- `--user=user_name, -u user_name`

  The username to use in the access privileges.

- `--version, -v`

  Display version information and exit.

If your MySQL distribution is installed in some non-standard location, you must change the location where `mysqlaccess` expects to find the `mysql` client. Edit the `mysqlaccess` script at approximately line 18. Search for a line that looks like this:

```
$MYSQL     = '/usr/local/bin/mysql';    # path to mysql executable
```

Change the path to reflect the location where `mysql` actually is stored on your system. If you do not do this, a `Broken pipe` error will occur when you run `mysqlaccess`.

7.7 `mysqladmin`—Client for Administering a MySQL Server

`mysqladmin` is a client for performing administrative operations. You can use it to check the server's configuration and current status, to create and drop databases, and more.

Invoke `mysqladmin` like this:

```
shell> mysqladmin [options] command [command-arg] [command [command-arg]] ...
```

`mysqladmin` supports the commands described in the following list. Some of the commands take an argument following the command name.

- create *db_name*

  Create a new database named *db_name*.

- debug

  Tell the server to write debug information to the error log.

- drop *db_name*

  Delete the database named *db_name* and all its tables.

- extended-status

  Display the server status variables and their values.

- flush-hosts

  Flush all information in the host cache.

- flush-logs

  Flush all logs.

- flush-privileges

  Reload the grant tables (same as reload).

- flush-status

  Clear status variables.

- flush-tables

  Flush all tables.

- flush-threads

  Flush the thread cache.

- kill *id,id,...*

  Kill server threads. If multiple thread ID values are given, there must be no spaces in the list.

- old-password *new-password*

  This is like the password command but stores the password using the old (pre-4.1) password-hashing format. (See Section 4.8.9, "Password Hashing as of MySQL 4.1.")

- password *new-password*

  Set a new password. This changes the password to *new-password* for the account that you use with mysqladmin for connecting to the server. Thus, the next time you invoke mysqladmin (or any other client program) using the same account, you will need to specify the new password.

  If the *new-password* value contains spaces or other characters that are special to your command interpreter, you need to enclose it within quotes. On Windows, be sure to use double quotes rather than single quotes; single quotes are not stripped from the password, but rather are interpreted as part of the password. For example:

```
shell> mysqladmin password "my new password"
```

- ping

  Check whether the server is alive. The return status from mysqladmin is 0 if the server is running, 1 if it is not. This is 0 even in case of an error such as Access denied, because this means that the server is running but refused the connection, which is different from the server not running.

- processlist

  Show a list of active server threads. This is like the output of the SHOW PROCESSLIST statement. If the --verbose option is given, the output is like that of SHOW FULL PROCESSLIST.

- reload

  Reload the grant tables.

- refresh

  Flush all tables and close and open log files.

- shutdown

  Stop the server.

- start-slave

  Start replication on a slave server.

- status

  Display a short server status message.

- stop-slave

  Stop replication on a slave server.

- variables

  Display the server system variables and their values.

- version

  Display version information from the server.

All commands can be shortened to any unique prefix. For example:

```
shell> mysqladmin proc stat
+----+-------+-----------+----+---------+------+-------+------------------+
| Id | User  | Host      | db | Command | Time | State | Info             |
+----+-------+-----------+----+---------+------+-------+------------------+
| 51 | monty | localhost |    | Query   | 0    |       | show processlist |
+----+-------+-----------+----+---------+------+-------+------------------+
Uptime: 1473624  Threads: 1  Questions: 39487
Slow queries: 0  Opens: 541  Flush tables: 1
Open tables: 19  Queries per second avg: 0.0268
```

The mysqladmin status command result displays the following values:

- Uptime

  The number of seconds the MySQL server has been running.

- Threads

  The number of active threads (clients).

- Questions

  The number of questions (queries) from clients since the server was started.

- Slow queries

  The number of queries that have taken more than long_query_time seconds. See Section 4.12.4, "The Slow Query Log."

- Opens

  The number of tables the server has opened.

- Flush tables

  The number of flush-*, refresh, and reload commands the server has executed.

- Open tables

  The number of tables that currently are open.

- Memory in use

  The amount of memory allocated directly by mysqld. This value is displayed only when MySQL has been compiled with --with-debug=full.

- Maximum memory used

  The maximum amount of memory allocated directly by mysqld. This value is displayed only when MySQL has been compiled with --with-debug=full.

If you execute mysqladmin shutdown when connecting to a local server using a Unix socket file, mysqladmin waits until the server's process ID file has been removed, to ensure that the server has stopped properly.

mysqladmin supports the following options:

- --help, -?

  Display a help message and exit.

- --character-sets-dir=path

  The directory where character sets are installed. See Section 4.11.1, "The Character Set Used for Data and Sorting."

- --compress, -C

  Compress all information sent between the client and the server if both support compression.

- --count=N, -c N

  The number of iterations to make for repeated command execution. This works only with the --sleep option.

- --debug[=debug_options], -# [debug_options]

  Write a debugging log. The debug_options string often is 'd:t:o,file_name'. The default is 'd:t:o,/tmp/mysqladmin.trace'.

- `--default-character-set=charset_name`

  Use *charset_name* as the default character set. See Section 4.11.1, "The Character Set Used for Data and Sorting."

- `--force, -f`

  Do not ask for confirmation for the drop *db_name* command. With multiple commands, continue even if an error occurs.

- `--host=host_name, -h host_name`

  Connect to the MySQL server on the given host.

- `--password[=password], -p[password]`

  The password to use when connecting to the server. If you use the short option form (-p), you *cannot* have a space between the option and the password. If you omit the *password* value following the --password or -p option on the command line, you are prompted for one.

  Specifying a password on the command line should be considered insecure. See Section 4.9.6, "Keeping Your Password Secure."

- `--port=port_num, -P port_num`

  The TCP/IP port number to use for the connection.

- `--protocol={TCP|SOCKET|PIPE|MEMORY}`

  The connection protocol to use.

- `--relative, -r`

  Show the difference between the current and previous values when used with the --sleep option. Currently, this option works only with the extended-status command.

- `--silent, -s`

  Exit silently if a connection to the server cannot be established.

- `--sleep=delay, -i delay`

  Execute commands repeatedly, sleeping for *delay* seconds in between. The --count option determines the number of iterations.

- `--socket=path, -S path`

  For connections to localhost, the Unix socket file to use, or, on Windows, the name of the named pipe to use.

- `--user=user_name, -u user_name`

  The MySQL username to use when connecting to the server.

- `--verbose, -v`

  Verbose mode. Print more information about what the program does.

- `--version, -V`

  Display version information and exit.

- `--vertical, -E`

  Print output vertically. This is similar to --relative, but prints output vertically.

- `--wait[=`*count*`]`, `-w[`*count*`]`

    If the connection cannot be established, wait and retry instead of aborting. If a *count* value is given, it indicates the number of times to retry. The default is one time.

You can also set the following variables by using `--`*var_name*`=`*value* syntax:

- `connect_timeout`

    The maximum number of seconds before connection timeout. The default value is 43200 (12 hours).

- `shutdown_timeout`

    The maximum number of seconds to wait for server shutdown. The default value is 3600 (1 hour).

It is also possible to set variables by using `--set-variable=`*var_name*`=`*value* or `-O `*var_name*`=`*value* syntax. *This syntax is deprecated.*

7.8 `mysqlbinlog`—Utility for Processing Binary Log Files

The binary log files that the server generates are written in binary format. To examine these files in text format, use the `mysqlbinlog` utility.

Invoke `mysqlbinlog` like this:

```
shell> mysqlbinlog [options] log_file ...
```

For example, to display the contents of the binary log file named `binlog.000003`, use this command:

```
shell> mysqlbinlog binlog.0000003
```

The output includes all events contained in `binlog.000003`. Event information includes the statement executed, the time the statement took, the thread ID of the client that issued it, the timestamp when it was executed, and so forth.

The output from `mysqlbinlog` can be re-executed (for example, by using it as input to `mysql`) to reapply the statements in the log. This is useful for recovery operations after a server crash. For other usage examples, see the discussion later in this section.

Normally, you use `mysqlbinlog` to read binary log files directly and apply them to the local MySQL server. It is also possible to read binary logs from a remote server by using the `--read-from-remote-server` option. When you read remote binary logs, the connection parameter options can be given to indicate how to connect to the server. These options are `--host`, `--password`, `--port`, `--protocol`, `--socket`, and `--user`; they are ignored except when you also use the `--read-from-remote-server` option.

You can also use `mysqlbinlog` to read relay log files written by a slave server in a replication setup. Relay logs have the same format as binary log files.

Binary logs and relay logs are discussed further in Section 4.12.3, "The Binary Log," and Section 5.4.4, "Replication Relay and Status Files."

`mysqlbinlog` supports the following options:

- `--help, -?`

    Display a help message and exit.

- `--character-sets-dir=path`

    The directory where character sets are installed. See Section 4.11.1, "The Character Set Used for Data and Sorting."

- `--database=db_name, -d db_name`

    List entries for just this database (local log only).

- `--debug[=debug_options], -# [debug_options]`

    Write a debugging log. A typical *debug_options* string is often `'d:t:o,file_name'`.

- `--disable-log-bin, -D`

    Disable binary logging. This is useful for avoiding an endless loop if you use the `--to-last-log` option and are sending the output to the same MySQL server. This option also is useful when restoring after a crash to avoid duplication of the statements you have logged.

    This option requires that you have the SUPER privilege. It causes `mysqlbinlog` to include a `SET SQL_LOG_BIN=0` statement in its output to disable binary logging of the remaining output. The SET statement is ineffective unless you have the SUPER privilege.

- `--force-read, -f`

    With this option, if `mysqlbinlog` reads a binary log event that it does not recognize, it prints a warning, ignores the event, and continues. Without this option, `mysqlbinlog` stops if it reads such an event.

- `--hexdump, -H`

    Display a hex dump of the log in comments. This output can be helpful for replication debugging. Hex dump format is discussed later in this section. This option was added in MySQL 5.0.16.

- `--host=host_name, -h host_name`

    Get the binary log from the MySQL server on the given host.

- `--local-load=path, -l path`

    Prepare local temporary files for LOAD DATA INFILE in the specified directory.

- `--offset=N, -o N`

    Skip the first *N* entries in the log.

- `--password[=password], -p[password]`

    The password to use when connecting to the server. If you use the short option form (-p), you *cannot* have a space between the option and the password. If you omit the *password* value following the `--password` or `-p` option on the command line, you are prompted for one.

Specifying a password on the command line should be considered insecure. See Section 4.9.6, "Keeping Your Password Secure."

- `--port=port_num`, `-P port_num`

The TCP/IP port number to use for connecting to a remote server.

- `--position=N`, `-j N`

Deprecated. Use `--start-position` instead.

- `--protocol={TCP|SOCKET|PIPE|MEMORY}`

The connection protocol to use.

- `--read-from-remote-server`, `-R`

Read the binary log from a MySQL server rather than reading a local log file. Any connection parameter options are ignored unless this option is given as well. These options are `--host`, `--password`, `--port`, `--protocol`, `--socket`, and `--user`.

- `--result-file=name`, `-r name`

Direct output to the given file.

- `--short-form`, `-s`

Display only the statements contained in the log, without any extra information.

- `--socket=path`, `-S path`

For connections to `localhost`, the Unix socket file to use, or, on Windows, the name of the named pipe to use.

- `--start-datetime=datetime`

Start reading the binary log at the first event having a timestamp equal to or later than the *datetime* argument. The *datetime* value is relative to the local time zone on the machine where you run `mysqlbinlog`. The value should be in a format accepted for the `DATETIME` or `TIMESTAMP` data types. For example:

```
shell> mysqlbinlog --start-datetime="2005-12-25 11:25:56" binlog.000003
```

This option is useful for point-in-time recovery. See Section 4.10.2, "Example Backup and Recovery Strategy."

- `--stop-datetime=datetime`

Stop reading the binary log at the first event having a timestamp equal or posterior to the *datetime* argument. This option is useful for point-in-time recovery. See the description of the `--start-datetime` option for information about the *datetime* value.

- `--start-position=N`

Start reading the binary log at the first event having a position equal to the *N* argument.

- `--stop-position=N`

Stop reading the binary log at the first event having a position equal or greater than the *N* argument.

- --to-last-log, -t

  Do not stop at the end of the requested binary log from a MySQL server, but rather continue printing until the end of the last binary log. If you send the output to the same MySQL server, this may lead to an endless loop. This option requires --read-from-remote-server.

- --user=*user_name*, -u *user_name*

  The MySQL username to use when connecting to a remote server.

- --version, -V

  Display version information and exit.

You can also set the following variable by using --*var_name*=*value* syntax:

- open_files_limit

  Specify the number of open file descriptors to reserve.

It is also possible to set variables by using --set-variable=*var_name*=*value* or -O *var_name*=*value* syntax. *This syntax is deprecated.*

You can pipe the output of mysqlbinlog into the mysql client to execute the statements contained in the binary log. This is used to recover from a crash when you have an old backup (see Section 4.10.1, "Database Backups"). For example:

```
shell> mysqlbinlog binlog.000001 | mysql
```

Or:

```
shell> mysqlbinlog binlog.[0-9]* | mysql
```

You can also redirect the output of mysqlbinlog to a text file instead, if you need to modify the statement log first (for example, to remove statements that you do not want to execute for some reason). After editing the file, execute the statements that it contains by using it as input to the mysql program.

mysqlbinlog has the --start-position option, which prints only those statements with an offset in the binary log greater than or equal to a given position (the given position must match the start of one event). It also has options to stop and start when it sees an event with a given date and time. This enables you to perform point-in-time recovery using the --stop-datetime option (to be able to say, for example, "roll forward my databases to how they were today at 10:30 a.m.").

If you have more than one binary log to execute on the MySQL server, the safe method is to process them all using a single connection to the server. Here is an example that demonstrates what may be *unsafe*:

```
shell> mysqlbinlog binlog.000001 | mysql # DANGER!!
shell> mysqlbinlog binlog.000002 | mysql # DANGER!!
```

Processing binary logs this way using different connections to the server causes problems if the first log file contains a CREATE TEMPORARY TABLE statement and the second log contains a statement that uses the temporary table. When the first mysql process terminates, the server drops the temporary table. When the second mysql process attempts to use the table, the server reports "unknown table."

To avoid problems like this, use a *single* connection to execute the contents of all binary logs that you want to process. Here is one way to do so:

```
shell> mysqlbinlog binlog.000001 binlog.000002 | mysql
```

Another approach is to write all the logs to a single file and then process the file:

```
shell> mysqlbinlog binlog.000001 >  /tmp/statements.sql
shell> mysqlbinlog binlog.000002 >> /tmp/statements.sql
shell> mysql -e "source /tmp/statements.sql"
```

mysqlbinlog can produce output that reproduces a LOAD DATA INFILE operation without the original data file. mysqlbinlog copies the data to a temporary file and writes a LOAD DATA LOCAL INFILE statement that refers to the file. The default location of the directory where these files are written is system-specific. To specify a directory explicitly, use the --local-load option.

Because mysqlbinlog converts LOAD DATA INFILE statements to LOAD DATA LOCAL INFILE statements (that is, it adds LOCAL), both the client and the server that you use to process the statements must be configured to allow LOCAL capability. See Section 4.7.4, "Security Issues with LOAD DATA LOCAL."

Warning: The temporary files created for LOAD DATA LOCAL statements are *not* automatically deleted because they are needed until you actually execute those statements. You should delete the temporary files yourself after you no longer need the statement log. The files can be found in the temporary file directory and have names like *original_file_name-#-#*.

The --hexdump option produces a hex dump of the log contents in comments:

```
shell> mysqlbinlog --hexdump master-bin.000001
```

With the preceding command, the output might look like this:

```
/*!40019 SET @@session.max_insert_delayed_threads=0*/;
/*!50003 SET @OLD_COMPLETION_TYPE=@@COMPLETION_TYPE,COMPLETION_TYPE=0*/;
# at 4
#051024 17:24:13 server id 1  end_log_pos 98
# Position Timestamp   Type   Master ID        Size       Master Pos    Flags
# 00000004 9d fc 5c 43   0f   01 00 00 00   5e 00 00 00   62 00 00 00   00 00
# 00000017 04 00 35 2e 30 2e 31 35  2d 64 65 62 75 67 2d 6c |..5.0.15.debug.1|
# 00000027 6f 67 00 00 00 00 00 00  00 00 00 00 00 00 00 00 |og..............|
# 00000037 00 00 00 00 00 00 00 00  00 00 00 00 00 00 00 00 |................|
# 00000047 00 00 00 00 9d fc 5c 43  13 38 0d 00 08 00 12 00 |......C.8......|
# 00000057 04 04 04 04 12 00 00 4b  00 04 1a               |.......K...|
#       Start: binlog v 4, server v 5.0.15-debug-log created 051024 17:24:13
#       at startup
ROLLBACK;
```

Hex dump output currently contains the following elements. This format might change in the future.

- `Position`: The byte position within the log file.
- `Timestamp`: The event timestamp. In the example shown, `'9d fc 5c 43'` is the representation of `'051024 17:24:13'` in hexadecimal.
- `Type`: The type of the log event. In the example shown, `'0f'` means that the example event is a `FORMAT_DESCRIPTION_EVENT`. The following table lists the possible types.

Type	Name	Meaning
00	UNKNOWN_EVENT	This event should never be present in the log.
01	START_EVENT_V3	This indicates the start of a log file written by MySQL 4 or earlier.
02	QUERY_EVENT	The most common type of events. These contain statements executed on the master.
03	STOP_EVENT	Indicates that master has stopped.
04	ROTATE_EVENT	Written when the master switches to a new log file.
05	INTVAR_EVENT	Used mainly for AUTO_INCREMENT values and when the LAST_INSERT_ID() function is used in the statement.
06	LOAD_EVENT	Used for LOAD DATA INFILE in MySQL 3.23.
07	SLAVE_EVENT	Reserved for future use.
08	CREATE_FILE_EVENT	Used for LOAD DATA INFILE statements. This indicates the start of execution of such a statement. A temporary file is created on the slave. Used in MySQL 4 only.
09	APPEND_BLOCK_EVENT	Contains data for use in a LOAD DATA INFILE statement. The data is stored in the temporary file on the slave.
0a	EXEC_LOAD_EVENT	Used for LOAD DATA INFILE statements. The contents of the temporary file is stored in the table on the slave. Used in MySQL 4 only.
0b	DELETE_FILE_EVENT	Rollback of a LOAD DATA INFILE statement. The temporary file should be deleted on the slave.
0c	NEW_LOAD_EVENT	Used for LOAD DATA INFILE in MySQL 4 and earlier.
0d	RAND_EVENT	Used to send information about random values if the RAND() function is used in the statement.
0e	USER_VAR_EVENT	Used to replicate user variables.
0f	FORMAT_DESCRIPTION_EVENT	This indicates the start of a log file written by MySQL 5 or later.
10	XID_EVENT	Event indicating commit of an XA transaction.
11	BEGIN_LOAD_QUERY_EVENT	Used for LOAD DATA INFILE statements in MySQL 5 and later.
12	EXECUTE_LOAD_QUERY_EVENT	Used for LOAD DATA INFILE statements in MySQL 5 and later.
13	TABLE_MAP_EVENT	Reserved for future use.
14	WRITE_ROWS_EVENT	Reserved for future use.
15	UPDATE_ROWS_EVENT	Reserved for future use.
16	DELETE_ROWS_EVENT	Reserved for future use.

- `Master ID`: The server ID of the master that created the event.
- `Size`: The size in bytes of the event.
- `Master Pos`: The position of the event in the original master log file.
- `Flags`: 16 flags. Currently, the following flags are used. The others are reserved for the future.

Flag	Name	Meaning
01	LOG_EVENT_BINLOG_IN_USE_F	Log file correctly closed. (Used only in FORMAT_ DESCRIPTION_EVENT.) If this flag is set (if the flags are, for example, '01 00') in a FORMAT_DESCRIPTION_EVENT, the log file has not been properly closed. Most probably this is because of a master crash (for example, due to power failure).
02		Reserved for future use.
04	LOG_EVENT_THREAD_SPECIFIC_F	Set if the event is dependent on the connection it was executed in (for example, '04 00'); for example, if the event uses temporary tables.
08	LOG_EVENT_SUPPRESS_USE_F	Set in some circumstances when the event is not dependent on the default database.

The other flags are reserved for future use.

7.9 `mysqlcheck`—A Table Maintenance and Repair Program

The `mysqlcheck` client checks, repairs, optimizes, and analyzes tables.

`mysqlcheck` is similar in function to `myisamchk`, but works differently. The main operational difference is that `mysqlcheck` must be used when the `mysqld` server is running, whereas `myisamchk` should be used when it is not. The benefit of using `mysqlcheck` is that you do not have to stop the server to check or repair your tables.

`mysqlcheck` uses the SQL statements CHECK TABLE, REPAIR TABLE, ANALYZE TABLE, and OPTIMIZE TABLE in a convenient way for the user. It determines which statements to use for the operation you want to perform, and then sends the statements to the server to be executed. For details about which storage engines each statement works with, see the descriptions for those statements in the "MySQL Language Reference."

The MyISAM storage engine supports all four statements, so `mysqlcheck` can be used to perform all four operations on MyISAM tables. Other storage engines do not necessarily support all operations. In such cases, an error message is displayed. For example, if `test.t` is a MEMORY table, an attempt to check it produces this result:

```
shell> mysqlcheck test t
test.t
note     : The storage engine for the table doesn't support check
```

There are three general ways to invoke mysqlcheck:

```
shell> mysqlcheck [options] db_name [tables]
shell> mysqlcheck [options] --databases db_name1 [db_name2 db_name3...]
shell> mysqlcheck [options] --all-databases
```

If you do not name any tables following *db_name* or if you use the --databases or --all-databases option, entire databases are checked.

mysqlcheck has a special feature compared to other client programs. The default behavior of checking tables (--check) can be changed by renaming the binary. If you want to have a tool that repairs tables by default, you should just make a copy of mysqlcheck named mysqlrepair, or make a symbolic link to mysqlcheck named mysqlrepair. If you invoke mysqlrepair, it repairs tables on command.

The following names can be used to change mysqlcheck default behavior:

mysqlrepair	The default option is –repair
mysqlanalyze	The default option is –analyze
mysqloptimize	The default option is –optimize

mysqlcheck supports the following options:

- --help, -?

  Display a help message and exit.

- --all-databases, -A

  Check all tables in all databases. This is the same as using the --databases option and naming all the databases on the command line.

- --all-in-1, -1

  Instead of issuing a statement for each table, execute a single statement for each database that names all the tables from that database to be processed.

- --analyze, -a

  Analyze the tables.

- --auto-repair

  If a checked table is corrupted, automatically fix it. Any necessary repairs are done after all tables have been checked.

- --character-sets-dir=*path*

  The directory where character sets are installed. See Section 4.11.1, "The Character Set Used for Data and Sorting."

- --check, -c

  Check the tables for errors. This is the default operation.

- --check-only-changed, -C

  Check only tables that have changed since the last check or that have not been closed properly.

- `--check-upgrade, -g`

  Invoke CHECK TABLE with the FOR UPGRADE option to check tables for incompatibilities with the current version of the server. This option was added in MySQL 5.0.19.

- `--compress`

  Compress all information sent between the client and the server if both support compression.

- `--databases, -B`

  Process all tables in the named databases. Normally, mysqlcheck treats the first name argument on the command line as a database name and following names as table names. With this option, it treats all name arguments as database names.

- `--debug[=debug_options], -# [debug_options]`

  Write a debugging log. A typical *debug_options* string is often `'d:t:o,file_name'`.

- `--default-character-set=charset_name`

  Use *charset_name* as the default character set. See Section 4.11.1, "The Character Set Used for Data and Sorting."

- `--extended, -e`

  If you are using this option to check tables, it ensures that they are 100% consistent but takes a long time.

  If you are using this option to repair tables, it runs an extended repair that may not only take a long time to execute, but may produce a lot of garbage rows also!

- `--fast, -F`

  Check only tables that have not been closed properly.

- `--force, -f`

  Continue even if an SQL error occurs.

- `--host=host_name, -h host_name`

  Connect to the MySQL server on the given host.

- `--medium-check, -m`

  Do a check that is faster than an --extended operation. This finds only 99.99% of all errors, which should be good enough in most cases.

- `--optimize, -o`

  Optimize the tables.

- `--password[=password], -p[password]`

  The password to use when connecting to the server. If you use the short option form (-p), you *cannot* have a space between the option and the password. If you omit the *password* value following the --password or -p option on the command line, you are prompted for one.

  Specifying a password on the command line should be considered insecure. See Section 4.9.6, "Keeping Your Password Secure."

- --port=*port_num*, -P *port_num*

  The TCP/IP port number to use for the connection.

- --protocol={TCP|SOCKET|PIPE|MEMORY}

  The connection protocol to use.

- --quick, -q

  If you are using this option to check tables, it prevents the check from scanning the rows to check for incorrect links. This is the fastest check method.

  If you are using this option to repair tables, it tries to repair only the index tree. This is the fastest repair method.

- --repair, -r

  Perform a repair that can fix almost anything except unique keys that are not unique.

- --silent, -s

  Silent mode. Print only error messages.

- --socket=*path*, -S *path*

  For connections to localhost, the Unix socket file to use, or, on Windows, the name of the named pipe to use.

- --tables

  Override the --databases or -B option. All name arguments following the option are regarded as table names.

- --use-frm

  For repair operations on MyISAM tables, get the table structure from the .frm file so that the table can be repaired even if the .MYI header is corrupted.

- --user=*user_name*, -u *user_name*

  The MySQL username to use when connecting to the server.

- --verbose, -v

  Verbose mode. Print information about the various stages of program operation.

- --version, -V

  Display version information and exit.

7.10 mysqldump—A Database Backup Program

The mysqldump client is a backup program originally written by Igor Romanenko. It can be used to dump a database or a collection of databases for backup or for transferring the data to another SQL server (not necessarily a MySQL server). The dump contains SQL statements to create the table or populate it, or both.

If you are doing a backup on the server, and your tables all are MyISAM tables, consider using the mysqlhotcopy instead because it can accomplish faster backups and faster restores. See Section 7.11, "mysqlhotcopy—A Database Backup Program."

There are three general ways to invoke `mysqldump`:

```
shell> mysqldump [options] db_name [tables]
shell> mysqldump [options] --databases db_name1 [db_name2 db_name3...]
shell> mysqldump [options] --all-databases
```

If you do not name any tables following *db_name* or if you use the `--databases` or `--all-databases` option, entire databases are dumped.

To get a list of the options your version of `mysqldump` supports, execute `mysqldump --help`.

If you run `mysqldump` without the `--quick` or `--opt` option, `mysqldump` loads the whole result set into memory before dumping the result. This can be a problem if you are dumping a big database. The `--opt` option is enabled by default, but can be disabled with `--skip-opt`.

If you are using a recent copy of the `mysqldump` program to generate a dump to be reloaded into a very old MySQL server, you should not use the `--opt` or `--extended-insert` option. Use `--skip-opt` instead.

`mysqldump` supports the following options:

- `--help, -?`

  Display a help message and exit.

- `--add-drop-database`

  Add a DROP DATABASE statement before each CREATE DATABASE statement.

- `--add-drop-table`

  Add a DROP TABLE statement before each CREATE TABLE statement.

- `--add-locks`

  Surround each table dump with LOCK TABLES and UNLOCK TABLES statements. This results in faster inserts when the dump file is reloaded. See Section 6.2.16, "Speed of INSERT Statements."

- `--all-databases, -A`

  Dump all tables in all databases. This is the same as using the `--databases` option and naming all the databases on the command line.

- `--allow-keywords`

  Allow creation of column names that are keywords. This works by prefixing each column name with the table name.

- `--character-sets-dir=path`

  The directory where character sets are installed. See Section 4.11.1, "The Character Set Used for Data and Sorting."

- `--comments, -i`

  Write additional information in the dump file such as program version, server version, and host. This option is enabled by default. To suppress additional, use `--skip-comments`.

- --compact

  Produce less verbose output. This option suppresses comments and enables the --skip-add-drop-table, --no-set-names, --skip-disable-keys, and --skip-add-locks options.

- --compatible=*name*

  Produce output that is more compatible with other database systems or with older MySQL servers. The value of name can be ansi, mysql323, mysql40, postgresql, oracle, mssql, db2, maxdb, no_key_options, no_table_options, or no_field_options. To use several values, separate them by commas. These values have the same meaning as the corresponding options for setting the server SQL mode. See Section 4.2.5, "The Server SQL Mode."

  This option does not guarantee compatibility with other servers. It only enables those SQL mode values that are currently available for making dump output more compatible. For example, --compatible=oracle does not map data types to Oracle types or use Oracle comment syntax.

- --complete-insert, -c

  Use complete INSERT statements that include column names.

- --compress, -C

  Compress all information sent between the client and the server if both support compression.

- --create-options

  Include all MySQL-specific table options in the CREATE TABLE statements.

- --databases, -B

  Dump several databases. Normally, mysqldump treats the first name argument on the command line as a database name and following names as table names. With this option, it treats all name arguments as database names. CREATE DATABASE and USE statements are included in the output before each new database.

- --debug[=*debug_options*], -# [*debug_options*]

  Write a debugging log. The *debug_options* string is often 'd:t:o,*file_name*'. The default is 'd:t:o,/tmp/mysqldump.trace'.

- --default-character-set=*charset_name*

  Use *charset_name* as the default character set. See Section 4.11.1, "The Character Set Used for Data and Sorting." If not specified, mysqldump uses utf8.

- --delayed-insert

  Write INSERT DELAYED statements rather than INSERT statements.

- --delete-master-logs

  On a master replication server, delete the binary logs after performing the dump operation. This option automatically enables --master-data.

- `--disable-keys, -K`

  For each table, surround the `INSERT` statements with `/*!40000 ALTER TABLE tbl_name DISABLE KEYS */;` and `/*!40000 ALTER TABLE tbl_name ENABLE KEYS */;` statements. This makes loading the dump file faster because the indexes are created after all rows are inserted. This option is effective for `MyISAM` tables only.

- `--extended-insert, -e`

  Use multiple-row `INSERT` syntax that include several `VALUES` lists. This results in a smaller dump file and speeds up inserts when the file is reloaded.

- `--fields-terminated-by=..., --fields-enclosed-by=..., --fields-optionally-enclosed-by=..., --fields-escaped-by=..., --lines-terminated-by=...`

  These options are used with the `-T` option and have the same meaning as the corresponding clauses for `LOAD DATA INFILE`.

- `--first-slave, -x`

  Deprecated. Now renamed to `--lock-all-tables`.

- `--flush-logs, -F`

  Flush the MySQL server log files before starting the dump. This option requires the `RELOAD` privilege. Note that if you use this option in combination with the `--all-databases` (or `-A`) option, the logs are flushed *for each database dumped*. The exception is when using `--lock-all-tables` or `--master-data`: In this case, the logs are flushed only once, corresponding to the moment that all tables are locked. If you want your dump and the log flush to happen at exactly the same moment, you should use `--flush-logs` together with either `--lock-all-tables` or `--master-data`.

- `--force, -f`

  Continue even if an SQL error occurs during a table dump.

- `--host=host_name, -h host_name`

  Dump data from the MySQL server on the given host. The default host is `localhost`.

- `--hex-blob`

  Dump binary columns using hexadecimal notation (for example, `'abc'` becomes `0x616263`). The affected data types are `BINARY`, `VARBINARY`, and `BLOB`. As of MySQL 5.0.13, `BIT` columns are affected as well.

- `--ignore-table=db_name.tbl_name`

  Do not dump the given table, which must be specified using both the database and table names. To ignore multiple tables, use this option multiple times.

- `--insert-ignore`

  Write `INSERT` statements with the `IGNORE` option.

- `--lock-all-tables, -x`

  Lock all tables across all databases. This is achieved by acquiring a global read lock for the duration of the whole dump. This option automatically turns off `--single-transaction` and `--lock-tables`.

- `--lock-tables, -l`

  Lock all tables before starting the dump. The tables are locked with READ LOCAL to allow concurrent inserts in the case of MyISAM tables. For transactional tables such as InnoDB and BDB, `--single-transaction` is a much better option, because it does not need to lock the tables at all.

  Please note that when dumping multiple databases, `--lock-tables` locks tables for each database separately. So, this option does not guarantee that the tables in the dump file are logically consistent between databases. Tables in different databases may be dumped in completely different states.

- `--master-data[=value]`

  Write the binary log filename and position to the output. This option requires the RELOAD privilege and the binary log must be enabled. If the option value is equal to 1, the position and filename are written to the dump output in the form of a CHANGE MASTER statement that makes a slave server start from the correct position in the master's binary logs if you use this SQL dump of the master to set up a slave. If the option value is equal to 2, the CHANGE MASTER statement is written as an SQL comment. This is the default action if *value* is omitted.

  The `--master-data` option turns on `--lock-all-tables`, unless `--single-transaction` also is specified (in which case, a global read lock is only acquired a short time at the beginning of the dump). See also the description for `--single-transaction`. In all cases, any action on logs happens at the exact moment of the dump. This option automatically turns off `--lock-tables`.

- `--no-autocommit`

  Enclose the INSERT statements for each dumped table within SET AUTOCOMMIT=0 and COMMIT statements.

- `--no-create-db, -n`

  This option suppresses the CREATE DATABASE statements that are otherwise included in the output if the `--databases` or `--all-databases` option is given.

- `--no-create-info, -t`

  Do not write CREATE TABLE statements that re-create each dumped table.

- `--no-data, -d`

  Do not write any row information for the table. This is very useful if you want to dump only the CREATE TABLE statement for the table.

- `--opt`

  This option is shorthand; it is the same as specifying `--add-drop-table --add-locks --create-options --disable-keys --extended-insert --lock-tables --quick --set-charset`. It should give you a fast dump operation and produce a dump file that can be reloaded into a MySQL server quickly.

  This option is enabled by default, but can be disabled with `--skip-opt`. To disable only certain of the options enabled by `--opt`, use their `--skip` forms; for example, `--skip-add-drop-table` or `--skip-quick`.

- `--order-by-primary`

  Sorts each table's rows by its primary key, or its first unique index, if such an index exists. This is useful when dumping a `MyISAM` table to be loaded into an `InnoDB` table, but will make the dump itself take considerably longer.

- `--password[=password]`, `-p[password]`

  The password to use when connecting to the server. If you use the short option form (`-p`), you *cannot* have a space between the option and the password. If you omit the *password* value following the `--password` or `-p` option on the command line, you are prompted for one.

  Specifying a password on the command line should be considered insecure. See Section 4.9.6, "Keeping Your Password Secure."

- `--port=port_num`, `-P port_num`

  The TCP/IP port number to use for the connection.

- `--protocol={TCP|SOCKET|PIPE|MEMORY}`

  The connection protocol to use.

- `--quick`, `-q`

  This option is useful for dumping large tables. It forces `mysqldump` to retrieve rows for a table from the server a row at a time rather than retrieving the entire row set and buffering it in memory before writing it out.

- `--quote-names`, `-Q`

  Quote database, table, and column names within '`' characters. If the `ANSI_QUOTES` SQL mode is enabled, names are quoted within '"' characters. This option is enabled by default. It can be disabled with `--skip-quote-names`, but this option should be given after any option such as `--compatible` that may enable `--quote-names`.

- `--result-file=file`, `-r file`

  Direct output to a given file. This option should be used on Windows to prevent newline '\n' characters from being converted to '\r\n' carriage return/newline sequences.

- `--routines`, `-R`

  Dump stored routines (functions and procedures) from the dumped databases. The output generated by using `--routines` contains `CREATE PROCEDURE` and `CREATE FUNCTION` statements to re-create the routines. However, these statements do not include attributes such as the routine definer or the creation and modification timestamps. This means that when the routines are reloaded, they will be created with the definer set to the reloading user and timestamps equal to the reload time.

  If you require routines to be re-created with their original definer and timestamp attributes, do not use `--routines`. Instead, dump and reload the contents of the `mysql.proc` table directly, using a MySQL account that has appropriate privileges for the `mysql` database.

  This option was added in MySQL 5.0.13. Before that, stored routines are not dumped.

- `--set-charset`

  Add SET NAMES *default_character_set* to the output. This option is enabled by default. To suppress the SET NAMES statement, use `--skip-set-charset`.

- `--single-transaction`

  This option issues a BEGIN SQL statement before dumping data from the server. It is useful only with transactional tables such as InnoDB and BDB, because then it dumps the consistent state of the database at the time when BEGIN was issued without blocking any applications.

  When using this option, you should keep in mind that only InnoDB tables are dumped in a consistent state. For example, any MyISAM or MEMORY tables dumped while using this option may still change state.

  The `--single-transaction` option and the `--lock-tables` option are mutually exclusive, because LOCK TABLES causes any pending transactions to be committed implicitly.

  To dump big tables, you should combine this option with `--quick`.

- `--socket=`*path*, `-S` *path*

  For connections to localhost, the Unix socket file to use, or, on Windows, the name of the named pipe to use.

- `--skip-comments`

  See the description for the `--comments` option.

- `--tab=`*path*, `-T` *path*

  Produce tab-separated data files. For each dumped table, mysqldump creates a *tbl_name*.sql file that contains the CREATE TABLE statement that creates the table, and a *tbl_name*.txt file that contains its data. The option value is the directory in which to write the files.

  By default, the .txt data files are formatted using tab characters between column values and a newline at the end of each line. The format can be specified explicitly using the `--fields-`*xxx* and `--lines--`*xxx* options.

  Note: This option should be used only when mysqldump is run on the same machine as the mysqld server. You must have the FILE privilege, and the server must have permission to write files in the directory that you specify.

- `--tables`

  Override the `--databases` or `-B` option. All name arguments following the option are regarded as table names.

- `--triggers`

  Dump triggers for each dumped table. This option is enabled by default; disable it with `--skip-triggers`. This option was added in MySQL 5.0.11. Before that, triggers are not dumped.

- `--tz-utc`

  Add SET TIME_ZONE='+00:00' to the dump file so that TIMESTAMP columns can be dumped and reloaded between servers in different time zones. Without this option,

TIMESTAMP columns are dumped and reloaded in the time zones local to the source and destination servers, which can cause the values to change. --tz-utc also protects against changes due to daylight saving time. --tz-utc is enabled by default. To disable it, use --skip-tz-utc. This option was added in MySQL 5.0.15.

- --user=*user_name*, -u *user_name*

  The MySQL username to use when connecting to the server.

- --verbose, -v

  Verbose mode. Print more information about what the program does.

- --version, -V

  Display version information and exit.

- --where='*where_condition*', -w '*where_condition*'

  Dump only rows selected by the given WHERE condition. Note that quotes around the condition are mandatory if it contains spaces or other characters that are special to your command interpreter.

  Examples:

  ```
  --where="user='jimf'"
  -w"userid>1"
  -w"userid<1"
  ```

- --xml, -X

  Write dump output as well-formed XML.

You can also set the following variables by using --*var_name*=*value* syntax:

- max_allowed_packet

  The maximum size of the buffer for client/server communication. The maximum is 1GB.

- net_buffer_length

  The initial size of the buffer for client/server communication. When creating multiple-row-insert statements (as with option --extended-insert or --opt), mysqldump creates rows up to net_buffer_length length. If you increase this variable, you should also ensure that the net_buffer_length variable in the MySQL server is at least this large.

It is also possible to set variables by using --set-variable=*var_name*=*value* or -O *var_name*=*value* syntax. *This syntax is deprecated.*

The most common use of mysqldump is probably for making a backup of an entire database:

```
shell> mysqldump --opt db_name > backup-file.sql
```

You can read the dump file back into the server like this:

```
shell> mysql db_name < backup-file.sql
```

Or like this:

```
shell> mysql -e "source /path-to-backup/backup-file.sql" db_name
```

mysqldump is also very useful for populating databases by copying data from one MySQL server to another:

```
shell> mysqldump --opt db_name | mysql --host=remote_host -C db_name
```

It is possible to dump several databases with one command:

```
shell> mysqldump --databases db_name1 [db_name2 ...] > my_databases.sql
```

To dump all databases, use the --all-databases option:

```
shell> mysqldump --all-databases > all_databases.sql
```

For InnoDB tables, mysqldump provides a way of making an online backup:

```
shell> mysqldump --all-databases --single-transaction > all_databases.sql
```

This backup just needs to acquire a global read lock on all tables (using FLUSH TABLES WITH READ LOCK) at the beginning of the dump. As soon as this lock has been acquired, the binary log coordinates are read and the lock is released. If and only if one long updating statement is running when the FLUSH statement is issued, the MySQL server may get stalled until that long statement finishes, and then the dump becomes lock-free. If the update statements that the MySQL server receives are short (in terms of execution time), the initial lock period should not be noticeable, even with many updates.

For point-in-time recovery (also known as "roll-forward," when you need to restore an old backup and replay the changes that happened since that backup), it is often useful to rotate the binary log (see Section 4.12.3, "The Binary Log") or at least know the binary log coordinates to which the dump corresponds:

```
shell> mysqldump --all-databases --master-data=2 > all_databases.sql
```

Or:

```
shell> mysqldump --all-databases --flush-logs --master-data=2
            > all_databases.sql
```

The simultaneous use of --master-data and --single-transaction provides a convenient way to make an online backup suitable for point-in-time recovery if tables are stored in the InnoDB storage engine.

For more information on making backups, see Section 4.10.1, "Database Backups," and Section 4.10.2, "Example Backup and Recovery Strategy."

7.11 mysqlhotcopy—A Database Backup Program

mysqlhotcopy is a Perl script that was originally written and contributed by Tim Bunce. It uses LOCK TABLES, FLUSH TABLES, and cp or scp to make a database backup quickly. It is the fastest way to make a backup of the database or single tables, but it can be run only on the same machine where the database directories are located. `mysqlhotcopy` works only for backing up `MyISAM` and `ARCHIVE` tables. It runs on Unix and NetWare.

```
shell> mysqlhotcopy db_name [/path/to/new_directory]
```

```
shell> mysqlhotcopy db_name_1 ... db_name_n /path/to/new_directory
```

Back up tables in the given database that match a regular expression:

```
shell> mysqlhotcopy db_name./regex/
```

The regular expression for the table name can be negated by prefixing it with a tilde ('~'):

```
shell> mysqlhotcopy db_name./~regex/
```

mysqlhotcopy supports the following options:

- `--help, -?`

  Display a help message and exit.

- `--addtodest`

  Do not rename target directory (if it exists); merely add files to it.

- `--allowold`

  Do not abort if a target exists; rename it by adding an _old suffix.

- `--checkpoint=db_name.tbl_name`

  Insert checkpoint entries into the specified database db_name and table tbl_name.

- `--chroot=path`

  Base directory of the `chroot` jail in which `mysqld` operates. The path value should match that of the `--chroot` option given to `mysqld`.

- `--debug`

  Enable debug output.

- `--dryrun, -n`

  Report actions without performing them.

- `--flushlog`

  Flush logs after all tables are locked.

- `--host=host_name, -h host_name`

  The hostname of the local host to use for making a TCP/IP connection to the local server. By default, the connection is made to `localhost` using a Unix socket file.

- `--keepold`

  Do not delete previous (renamed) target when done.

- `--method=command`

  The method for copying files (`cp` or `scp`).

- `--noindices`

  Do not include full index files in the backup. This makes the backup smaller and faster. The indexes for reloaded tables can be reconstructed later with `myisamchk -rq`.

- `--password=password, -ppassword`

  The password to use when connecting to the server. Note that the password value is not optional for this option, unlike for other MySQL programs. You can use an option file to avoid giving the password on the command line.

  Specifying a password on the command line should be considered insecure. See Section 4.9.6, "Keeping Your Password Secure."

- `--port=port_num, -P port_num`

  The TCP/IP port number to use when connecting to the local server.

- `--quiet, -q`

  Be silent except for errors.

- `--record_log_pos=db_name.tbl_name`

  Record master and slave status in the specified database *db_name* and table *tbl_name*.

- `--regexp=expr`

  Copy all databases with names that match the given regular expression.

- `--resetmaster`

  Reset the binary log after locking all the tables.

- `--resetslave`

  Reset the `master.info` file after locking all the tables.

- `--socket=path, -S path`

  The Unix socket file to use for the connection.

- `--suffix=str`

  The suffix for names of copied databases.

- `--tmpdir=path`

  The temporary directory. The default is `/tmp`.

- `--user=user_name, -u user_name`

  The MySQL username to use when connecting to the server.

`mysqlhotcopy` reads the `[client]` and `[mysqlhotcopy]` option groups from option files.

To execute `mysqlhotcopy`, you must have access to the files for the tables that you are backing up, the SELECT privilege for those tables, and the RELOAD privilege (to be able to execute FLUSH TABLES).

Use `perldoc` for additional `mysqlhotcopy` documentation, including information about the structure of the tables needed for the `--checkpoint` and `--record_log_pos` options:

```
shell> perldoc mysqlhotcopy
```

7.12 `mysqlimport`—A Data Import Program

The `mysqlimport` client provides a command-line interface to the `LOAD DATA INFILE` SQL statement. Most options to `mysqlimport` correspond directly to clauses of `LOAD DATA INFILE` syntax.

Invoke `mysqlimport` like this:

```
shell> mysqlimport [options] db_name textfile1 [textfile2 ...]
```

For each text file named on the command line, `mysqlimport` strips any extension from the filename and uses the result to determine the name of the table into which to import the file's contents. For example, files named `patient.txt`, `patient.text`, and `patient` all would be imported into a table named `patient`.

`mysqlimport` supports the following options:

- `--help, -?`

  Display a help message and exit.

- `--character-sets-dir=path`

  The directory where character sets are installed. See Section 4.11.1, "The Character Set Used for Data and Sorting."

- `--columns=column_list, -c column_list`

  This option takes a comma-separated list of column names as its value. The order of the column names indicates how to match data file columns with table columns.

- `--compress, -C`

  Compress all information sent between the client and the server if both support compression.

- `--debug[=debug_options], -# [debug_options]`

  Write a debugging log. The `debug_options` string often is `'d:t:o,file_name'`.

- `--default-character-set=charset_name`

  Use `charset_name` as the default character set. See Section 4.11.1, "The Character Set Used for Data and Sorting."

- `--delete, -D`

  Empty the table before importing the text file.

- `--fields-terminated-by=..., --fields-enclosed-by=..., --fields-optionally-enclosed-by=..., --fields-escaped-by=..., --lines-terminated-by=...`

  These options have the same meaning as the corresponding clauses for `LOAD DATA INFILE`.

- `--force, -f`

  Ignore errors. For example, if a table for a text file does not exist, continue processing any remaining files. Without `--force`, `mysqlimport` exits if a table does not exist.

- `--host=host_name, -h host_name`

  Import data to the MySQL server on the given host. The default host is localhost.

- `--ignore, -i`

  See the description for the `--replace` option.

- `--ignore-lines=N`

  Ignore the first N lines of the data file.

- `--local, -L`

  Read input files locally from the client host.

- `--lock-tables, -l`

  Lock *all* tables for writing before processing any text files. This ensures that all tables are synchronized on the server.

- `--low-priority`

  Use LOW_PRIORITY when loading the table.

- `--password[=password], -p[password]`

  The password to use when connecting to the server. If you use the short option form (-p), you *cannot* have a space between the option and the password. If you omit the *password* value following the `--password` or `-p` option on the command line, you are prompted for one.

  Specifying a password on the command line should be considered insecure. See Section 4.9.6, "Keeping Your Password Secure."

- `--port=port_num, -P port_num`

  The TCP/IP port number to use for the connection.

- `--protocol={TCP|SOCKET|PIPE|MEMORY}`

  The connection protocol to use.

- `--replace, -r`

  The `--replace` and `--ignore` options control handling of input rows that duplicate existing rows on unique key values. If you specify `--replace`, new rows replace existing rows that have the same unique key value. If you specify `--ignore`, input rows that duplicate an existing row on a unique key value are skipped. If you do not specify either option, an error occurs when a duplicate key value is found, and the rest of the text file is ignored.

- `--silent, -s`

  Silent mode. Produce output only when errors occur.

- `--socket=path, -S path`

  For connections to localhost, the Unix socket file to use, or, on Windows, the name of the named pipe to use.

- `--user=user_name, -u user_name`

  The MySQL username to use when connecting to the server.

- --verbose, -v

    Verbose mode. Print more information about what the program does.

- --version, -V

    Display version information and exit.

Here is a sample session that demonstrates use of mysqlimport:

```
shell> mysql -e 'CREATE TABLE imptest(id INT, n VARCHAR(30))' test
shell> ed
a
100      Max Sydow
101      Count Dracula
.
w imptest.txt
32
q
shell> od -c imptest.txt
0000000   1   0   0  \t   M   a   x       S   y   d   o   w  \n   1   0
0000020   1  \t   C   o   u   n   t       D   r   a   c   u   l   a  \n
0000040
shell> mysqlimport --local test imptest.txt
test.imptest: Records: 2  Deleted: 0  Skipped: 0  Warnings: 0
shell> mysql -e 'SELECT * FROM imptest' test
+------+--------------+
| id   | n            |
+------+--------------+
|  100 | Max Sydow    |
|  101 | Count Dracula |
+------+--------------+
```

7.13 mysqlshow—Display Database, Table, and Column Information

The mysqlshow client can be used to quickly see which databases exist, their tables, or a table's columns or indexes.

mysqlshow provides a command-line interface to several SQL SHOW statements. The same information can be obtained by using those statements directly. For example, you can issue them from the mysql client program.

Invoke mysqlshow like this:

```
shell> mysqlshow [options] [db_name [tbl_name [col_name]]]
```

- If no database is given, a list of database names is shown.
- If no table is given, all matching tables in the database are shown.
- If no column is given, all matching columns and column types in the table are shown.

The output displays only the names of those databases, tables, or columns for which you have some privileges.

If the last argument contains shell or SQL wildcard characters ('*', '?', '%', or '_'), only those names that are matched by the wildcard are shown. If a database name contains any under-scores, those should be escaped with a backslash (some Unix shells require two) to get a list of the proper tables or columns. '*' and '?' characters are converted into SQL '%' and '_' wildcard characters. This might cause some confusion when you try to display the columns for a table with a '_' in the name, because in this case, mysqlshow shows you only the table names that match the pattern. This is easily fixed by adding an extra '%' last on the command line as a separate argument.

mysqlshow supports the following options:

- --help, -?

  Display a help message and exit.

- --character-sets-dir=*path*

  The directory where character sets are installed. See Section 4.11.1, "The Character Set Used for Data and Sorting."

- --compress, -C

  Compress all information sent between the client and the server if both support com-pression.

- --count

  Show the number of rows per table. This can be slow for non-MyISAM tables. This option was added in MySQL 5.0.6.

- --debug[=*debug_options*], -# [*debug_options*]

  Write a debugging log. The *debug_options* string often is 'd:t:o,*file_name*'.

- --default-character-set=*charset_name*

  Use *charset_name* as the default character set. See Section 4.11.1, "The Character Set Used for Data and Sorting."

- --host=*host_name*, -h *host_name*

  Connect to the MySQL server on the given host.

- --keys, -k

  Show table indexes.

- --password[=*password*], -p[*password*]

  The password to use when connecting to the server. If you use the short option form (-p), you *cannot* have a space between the option and the password. If you omit the *password* value following the --password or -p option on the command line, you are prompted for one.

  Specifying a password on the command line should be considered insecure. See Section 4.9.6, "Keeping Your Password Secure."

- --port=*port_num*, -P *port_num*

  The TCP/IP port number to use for the connection.

- `--protocol={TCP|SOCKET|PIPE|MEMORY}`

  The connection protocol to use.

- `--show-table-type, -t`

  Show a column indicating the table type, as in SHOW FULL TABLES. The type is BASE TABLE or VIEW. This option was added in MySQL 5.0.4.

- `--socket=path, -S path`

  For connections to localhost, the Unix socket file to use, or, on Windows, the name of the named pipe to use.

- `--status, -i`

  Display extra information about each table.

- `--user=user_name, -u user_name`

  The MySQL username to use when connecting to the server.

- `--verbose, -v`

  Verbose mode. Print more information about what the program does. This option can be used multiple times to increase the amount of information.

- `--version, -V`

  Display version information and exit.

7.14 `mysql_zap`—Kill Processes That Match a Pattern

`mysql_zap` kills processes that match a pattern. It uses the `ps` command and Unix signals, so it runs on Unix and Unix-like systems.

Invoke `mysql_zap` like this:

```
shell> mysql_zap [-signal] [-?Ift] pattern
```

A process matches if its output line from the `ps` command contains the pattern. By default, `mysql_zap` asks for confirmation for each process. Respond y to kill the process, or q to exit `mysql_zap`. For any other response, `mysql_zap` does not attempt to kill the process.

If the `-signal` option is given, it specifies the name or number of the signal to send to each process. Otherwise, `mysql_zap` tries first with TERM (signal 15) and then with KILL (signal 9).

`mysql_zap` understands the following additional options:

- `--help, -?, -I`

  Display a help message and exit.

- `-f`

  Force mode. `mysql_zap` attempts to kill each process without confirmation.

- `-t`

  Test mode. Display information about each process but do not kill it.

7.15 `perror`—Explain Error Codes

For most system errors, MySQL displays, in addition to an internal text message, the system error code in one of the following styles:

```
message ... (errno: #)
message ... (Errcode: #)
```

You can find out what the error code means by examining the documentation for your system or by using the `perror` utility.

`perror` prints a description for a system error code or for a storage engine (table handler) error code.

Invoke `perror` like this:

```
shell> perror [options] errorcode ...
```

Example:

```
shell> perror 13 64
Error code  13:  Permission denied
Error code  64:  Machine is not on the network
```

To obtain the error message for a MySQL Cluster error code, invoke `perror` with the `--ndb` option:

```
shell> perror --ndb errorcode
```

Note that the meaning of system error messages may be dependent on your operating system. A given error code may mean different things on different operating systems.

`perror` supports the following options:

- `--help, --info, -I, -?`

  Display a help message and exit.

- `--ndb`

  Print the error message for a MySQL Cluster error code.

- `--silent, -s`

  Silent mode. Print only the error message.

- `--verbose, -v`

  Verbose mode. Print error code and message. This is the default behavior.

- `--version, -V`

  Display version information and exit.

7.16 `replace`—A String-Replacement Utility

The `replace` utility program changes strings in place in files or on the standard input.

Invoke `replace` in one of the following ways:

```
shell> replace from to [from to] ... -- file [file] ...
shell> replace from to [from to] ... < file
```

from represents a string to look for and *to* represents its replacement. There can be one or more pairs of strings.

Use the -- option to indicate where the string-replacement list ends and the filenames begin. In this case, any file named on the command line is modified in place, so you may want to make a copy of the original before converting it. `replace` prints a message indicating which of the input files it actually modifies.

If the -- option is not given, `replace` reads the standard input and writes to the standard output.

`replace` uses a finite state machine to match longer strings first. It can be used to swap strings. For example, the following command swaps a and b in the given files, `file1` and `file2`:

```
shell> replace a b b a -- file1 file2 ...
```

`replace` supports the following options:

- `-?, -I`

  Display a help message and exit.

- `-# debug_options`

  Write a debugging log. The *debug_options* string often is `'d:t:o,file_name'`.

- `-s`

  Silent mode. Print less information what the program does.

- `-v`

  Verbose mode. Print more information about what the program does.

- `-V`

  Display version information and exit.

Storage Engines and Table Types

MySQL supports several storage engines that act as handlers for different table types. MySQL storage engines include both those that handle transaction-safe tables and those that handle non-transaction-safe tables:

- MyISAM manages non-transactional tables. It provides high-speed storage and retrieval, as well as fulltext searching capabilities. MyISAM is supported in all MySQL configurations, and is the default storage engine unless you have configured MySQL to use a different one by default.

- The MEMORY storage engine provides in-memory tables. The MERGE storage engine allows a collection of identical MyISAM tables to be handled as a single table. Like MyISAM, the MEMORY and MERGE storage engines handle non-transactional tables, and both are also included in MySQL by default.

  Note: The MEMORY storage engine formerly was known as the HEAP engine.

- The InnoDB and BDB storage engines provide transaction-safe tables. BDB is included in MySQL-Max binary distributions on those operating systems that support it. InnoDB is also included by default in all MySQL 5.0 binary distributions. In source distributions, you can enable or disable either engine by configuring MySQL as you like.

- The EXAMPLE storage engine is a "stub" engine that does nothing. You can create tables with this engine, but no data can be stored in them or retrieved from them. The purpose of this engine is to serve as an example in the MySQL source code that illustrates how to begin writing new storage engines. As such, it is primarily of interest to developers.

- NDB Cluster is the storage engine used by MySQL Cluster to implement tables that are partitioned over many computers. It is available in MySQL-Max 5.0 binary distributions. This storage engine is currently supported on Linux, Solaris, and Mac OS X only. We intend to add support for this engine on other platforms, including Windows, in future MySQL releases.

- The ARCHIVE storage engine is used for storing large amounts of data without indexes with a very small footprint.

- The CSV storage engine stores data in text files using comma-separated values format.

- The BLACKHOLE storage engine accepts but does not store data and retrievals always return an empty set.

- The FEDERATED storage engine was added in MySQL 5.0.3. This engine stores data in a remote database. Currently, it works with MySQL only, using the MySQL C Client API. In future releases, we intend to enable it to connect to other data sources using other drivers or client connection methods.

This chapter describes each of the MySQL storage engines except for NDB Cluster, which is covered in Chapter 9, "MySQL Cluster."

When you create a new table, you can specify which storage engine to use by adding an ENGINE or TYPE table option to the CREATE TABLE statement:

```
CREATE TABLE t (i INT) ENGINE = INNODB;
CREATE TABLE t (i INT) TYPE = MEMORY;
```

The older term TYPE is supported as a synonym for ENGINE for backward compatibility, but ENGINE is the preferred term and TYPE is deprecated.

If you omit the ENGINE or TYPE option, the default storage engine is used. Normally, this is MyISAM, but you can change it by using the --default-storage-engine or --default-table-type server startup option, or by setting the storage_engine or table_type system variable.

When MySQL is installed on Windows using the MySQL Configuration Wizard, the InnoDB storage engine can be selected as the default instead of MyISAM. See Section 2.3.4.6, "The Database Usage Dialog."

To convert a table from one storage engine to another, use an ALTER TABLE statement that indicates the new engine:

```
ALTER TABLE t ENGINE = MYISAM;
ALTER TABLE t TYPE = BDB;
```

If you try to use a storage engine that is not compiled in or that is compiled in but deactivated, MySQL instead creates a table using the default storage engine, usually MyISAM. This behavior is convenient when you want to copy tables between MySQL servers that support different storage engines. (For example, in a replication setup, perhaps your master server supports transactional storage engines for increased safety, but the slave servers use only non-transactional storage engines for greater speed.)

This automatic substitution of the default storage engine for unavailable engines can be confusing for new MySQL users. A warning is generated whenever a storage engine is automatically changed.

For new tables, MySQL always creates an .frm file to hold the table and column definitions. The table's index and data may be stored in one or more other files, depending on the storage engine. The server creates the .frm file above the storage engine level. Individual storage engines create any additional files required for the tables that they manage.

A database may contain tables of different types. That is, tables need not all be created with the same storage engine.

Transaction-safe tables (TSTs) have several advantages over non-transaction-safe tables (NTSTs):

- They are safer. Even if MySQL crashes or you get hardware problems, you can get your data back, either by automatic recovery or from a backup plus the transaction log.
- You can combine many statements and accept them all at the same time with the COMMIT statement (if autocommit is disabled).
- You can execute ROLLBACK to ignore your changes (if autocommit is disabled).
- If an update fails, all of your changes are reverted. (With non-transaction-safe tables, all changes that have taken place are permanent.)
- Transaction-safe storage engines can provide better concurrency for tables that get many updates concurrently with reads.

You can combine transaction-safe and non-transaction-safe tables in the same statements to get the best of both worlds. However, although MySQL supports several transaction-safe storage engines, for best results, you should not mix different storage engines within a transaction with autocommit disabled. For example, if you do this, changes to non-transaction-safe tables still are committed immediately and cannot be rolled back.

Non-transaction-safe tables have several advantages of their own, all of which occur because there is no transaction overhead:

- Much faster
- Lower disk space requirements
- Less memory required to perform updates

8.1 The MyISAM Storage Engine

MyISAM is the default storage engine. It is based on the older ISAM code but has many useful extensions. (Note that MySQL 5.0 does *not* support ISAM.)

Each MyISAM table is stored on disk in three files. The files have names that begin with the table name and have an extension to indicate the file type. An .frm file stores the table format. The data file has an .MYD (MYData) extension. The index file has an .MYI (MYIndex) extension.

To specify explicitly that you want a MyISAM table, indicate that with an ENGINE table option:

```
CREATE TABLE t (i INT) ENGINE = MYISAM;
```

The older term TYPE is supported as a synonym for ENGINE for backward compatibility, but ENGINE is the preferred term and TYPE is deprecated.

Normally, it is unnecessary to use ENGINE to specify the MyISAM storage engine. MyISAM is the default engine unless the default has been changed. To ensure that MyISAM is used in situations where the default might have been changed, include the ENGINE option explicitly.

You can check or repair MyISAM tables with the mysqlcheck client or myisamchk utility. You can also compress MyISAM tables with myisampack to take up much less space. See Section 4.10.4.1, "Using myisamchk for Crash Recovery," Section 7.4, "myisampack—Generate Compressed, Read-Only MyISAM Tables," and Section 7.9, "mysqlcheck—A Table Maintenance and Repair Program."

MyISAM tables have the following characteristics:

- All data values are stored with the low byte first. This makes the data machine and operating system independent. The only requirements for binary portability are that the machine uses two's-complement signed integers and IEEE floating-point format. These requirements are widely used among mainstream machines. Binary compatibility might not be applicable to embedded systems, which sometimes have peculiar processors.

  There is no significant speed penalty for storing data low byte first; the bytes in a table row normally are unaligned and it takes little more processing to read an unaligned byte in order than in reverse order. Also, the code in the server that fetches column values is not time critical compared to other code.

- All numeric key values are stored with the high byte first to allow better index compression.

- Large files (up to 63-bit file length) are supported on filesystems and operating systems that support large files.

- Dynamic-sized rows are much less fragmented when mixing deletes with updates and inserts. This is done by automatically combining adjacent deleted blocks and by extending blocks if the next block is deleted.

- The maximum number of indexes per MyISAM table is 64. This can be changed by recompiling. Beginning with MySQL 5.0.18, you can configure the build by invoking configure with the --with-max-indexes=N option, where N is the maximum number of indexes to permit per MyISAM table. N must be less than or equal to 128. Before MySQL 5.0.18, you must change the source.

  The maximum number of columns per index is 16.

- The maximum key length is 1000 bytes. This can also be changed by changing the source and recompiling. For the case of a key longer than 250 bytes, a larger key block size than the default of 1024 bytes is used.

- When rows are inserted in sorted order (as when you are using an AUTO_INCREMENT column), the index tree is split so that the high node contains only one key. This improves space utilization in the index tree.

- Internal handling of one AUTO_INCREMENT column per table is supported. MyISAM automatically updates this column for INSERT and UPDATE operations. This makes AUTO_INCREMENT columns faster (at least 10%). Values at the top of the sequence are not reused after being deleted. (When an AUTO_INCREMENT column is defined as the last column of a multiple-column index, reuse of values deleted from the top of a sequence does occur.) The AUTO_INCREMENT value can be reset with ALTER TABLE or myisamchk.

- Dynamic-sized rows are much less fragmented when mixing deletes with updates and inserts. This is done by automatically combining adjacent deleted blocks and by extending blocks if the next block is deleted.

- If a table has no free blocks in the middle of the data file, you can INSERT new rows into it at the same time that other threads are reading from the table. (These are known as "concurrent inserts.") A free block can occur as a result of deleting rows or an update of a dynamic length row with more data than its current contents. When all free blocks are used up (filled in), future inserts become concurrent again. See Section 6.3.3, "Concurrent Inserts."

- You can put the data file and index file on different directories to get more speed with the DATA DIRECTORY and INDEX DIRECTORY table options to CREATE TABLE.

- BLOB and TEXT columns can be indexed.

- NULL values are allowed in indexed columns. This takes 0–1 bytes per key.

- Each character column can have a different character set.

- There is a flag in the MyISAM index file that indicates whether the table was closed correctly. If mysqld is started with the --myisam-recover option, MyISAM tables are automatically checked when opened, and are repaired if the table wasn't closed properly.

- myisamchk marks tables as checked if you run it with the --update-state option. myisamchk --fast checks only those tables that don't have this mark.

- myisamchk --analyze stores statistics for portions of keys, as well as for entire keys.

- myisampack can pack BLOB and VARCHAR columns.

MyISAM also supports the following features:

- Support for a true VARCHAR type; a VARCHAR column starts with a length stored in one or two bytes.

- Tables with VARCHAR columns may have fixed or dynamic row length.

- The sum of the lengths of the VARCHAR and CHAR columns in a table may be up to 64KB.

- A hashed computed index can be used for UNIQUE. This allows you to have UNIQUE on any combination of columns in a table. (However, you cannot search on a UNIQUE computed index.)

Additional resources

- A forum dedicated to the MyISAM storage engine is available at http://forums.mysql.com/list.php?21.

8.1.1 MyISAM Startup Options

The following options to mysqld can be used to change the behavior of MyISAM tables. For additional information, see Section 4.2.1, "mysqld Command Options."

- `--myisam-recover=`*mode*

  Set the mode for automatic recovery of crashed `MyISAM` tables.

- `--delay-key-write=ALL`

  Don't flush key buffers between writes for any `MyISAM` table.

  Note: If you do this, you should not access `MyISAM` tables from another program (such as from another MySQL server or with `myisamchk`) when the tables are in use. Doing so risks index corruption. Using `--external-locking` does not eliminate this risk.

The following system variables affect the behavior of `MyISAM` tables. For additional information, see Section 4.2.2, "Server System Variables."

- `bulk_insert_buffer_size`

  The size of the tree cache used in bulk insert optimization. **Note**: This is a limit *per thread*!

- `myisam_max_extra_sort_file_size`

  Used to help MySQL to decide when to use the slow but safe key cache index creation method. **Note**: This parameter was given in bytes before MySQL 5.0.6, when it was removed.

- `myisam_max_sort_file_size`

  Don't use the fast sort index method to create an index if the temporary file would become larger than this. **Note**: This parameter is given in bytes.

- `myisam_sort_buffer_size`

  Set the size of the buffer used when recovering tables.

Automatic recovery is activated if you start `mysqld` with the `--myisam-recover` option. In this case, when the server opens a `MyISAM` table, it checks whether the table is marked as crashed or whether the open count variable for the table is not 0 and you are running the server with external locking disabled. If either of these conditions is true, the following happens:

- The server checks the table for errors.
- If the server finds an error, it tries to do a fast table repair (with sorting and without re-creating the data file).
- If the repair fails because of an error in the data file (for example, a duplicate-key error), the server tries again, this time re-creating the data file.
- If the repair still fails, the server tries once more with the old repair option method (write row by row without sorting). This method should be able to repair any type of error and has low disk space requirements.

If the recovery wouldn't be able to recover all rows from previously completed statements and you didn't specify `FORCE` in the value of the `--myisam-recover` option, automatic repair aborts with an error message in the error log:

```
Error: Couldn't repair table: test.g00pages
```

If you specify FORCE, a warning like this is written instead:

```
Warning: Found 344 of 354 rows when repairing ./test/g00pages
```

Note that if the automatic recovery value includes BACKUP, the recovery process creates files with names of the form *tbl_name-datetime*.BAK. You should have a cron script that automatically moves these files from the database directories to backup media.

8.1.2 Space Needed for Keys

MyISAM tables use B-tree indexes. You can roughly calculate the size for the index file as (key_length+4)/0.67, summed over all keys. This is for the worst case when all keys are inserted in sorted order and the table doesn't have any compressed keys.

String indexes are space compressed. If the first index part is a string, it is also prefix compressed. Space compression makes the index file smaller than the worst-case figure if a string column has a lot of trailing space or is a VARCHAR column that is not always used to the full length. Prefix compression is used on keys that start with a string. Prefix compression helps if there are many strings with an identical prefix.

In MyISAM tables, you can also prefix compress numbers by specifying the PACK_KEYS=1 table option when you create the table. Numbers are stored with the high byte first, so this helps when you have many integer keys that have an identical prefix.

8.1.3 MyISAM Table Storage Formats

MyISAM supports three different storage formats. Two of them, fixed and dynamic format, are chosen automatically depending on the type of columns you are using. The third, compressed format, can be created only with the myisampack utility.

When you use CREATE TABLE or ALTER TABLE for a table that has no BLOB or TEXT columns, you can force the table format to FIXED or DYNAMIC with the ROW_FORMAT table option. This causes CHAR and VARCHAR columns to become CHAR for FIXED format, or VARCHAR for DYNAMIC format.

You can decompress tables by specifying ROW_FORMAT=DEFAULT with ALTER TABLE.

8.1.3.1 Static (Fixed-Length) Table Characteristics

Static format is the default for MyISAM tables. It is used when the table contains no variable-length columns (VARCHAR, VARBINARY, BLOB, or TEXT). Each row is stored using a fixed number of bytes.

Of the three MyISAM storage formats, static format is the simplest and most secure (least subject to corruption). It is also the fastest of the on-disk formats due to the ease with which rows in the data file can be found on disk: To look up a row based on a row number in the index, multiply the row number by the row length to calculate the row position. Also, when scanning a table, it is very easy to read a constant number of rows with each disk read operation.

The security is evidenced if your computer crashes while the MySQL server is writing to a fixed-format MyISAM file. In this case, myisamchk can easily determine where each row starts and ends, so it can usually reclaim all rows except the partially written one. Note that MyISAM table indexes can always be reconstructed based on the data rows.

Static-format tables have these characteristics:

- CHAR columns are space-padded to the column width. This is also true for NUMERIC and DECIMAL columns created before MySQL 5.0.3. BINARY columns are space-padded to the column width before MySQL 5.0.15. As of 5.0.15, BINARY columns are padded with 0x00 bytes.
- Very quick.
- Easy to cache.
- Easy to reconstruct after a crash, because rows are located in fixed positions.
- Reorganization is unnecessary unless you delete a huge number of rows and want to return free disk space to the operating system. To do this, use OPTIMIZE TABLE or myisamchk -r.
- Usually require more disk space than dynamic-format tables.

8.1.3.2 Dynamic Table Characteristics

Dynamic storage format is used if a MyISAM table contains any variable-length columns (VARCHAR, VARBINARY, BLOB, or TEXT), or if the table was created with the ROW_FORMAT=DYNAMIC table option.

Dynamic format is a little more complex than static format because each row has a header that indicates how long it is. A row can become fragmented (stored in non-contiguous pieces) when it is made longer as a result of an update.

You can use OPTIMIZE TABLE or myisamchk -r to defragment a table. If you have fixed-length columns that you access or change frequently in a table that also contains some variable-length columns, it might be a good idea to move the variable-length columns to other tables just to avoid fragmentation.

Dynamic-format tables have these characteristics:

- All string columns are dynamic except those with a length less than four.
- Each row is preceded by a bitmap that indicates which columns contain the empty string (for string columns) or zero (for numeric columns). Note that this does not include columns that contain NULL values. If a string column has a length of zero after trailing space removal, or a numeric column has a value of zero, it is marked in the bitmap and not saved to disk. Non-empty strings are saved as a length byte plus the string contents.
- Much less disk space usually is required than for fixed-length tables.
- Each row uses only as much space as is required. However, if a row becomes larger, it is split into as many pieces as are required, resulting in row fragmentation. For example, if

you update a row with information that extends the row length, the row becomes fragmented. In this case, you may have to run OPTIMIZE TABLE or myisamchk -r from time to time to improve performance. Use myisamchk -ei to obtain table statistics.

- More difficult than static-format tables to reconstruct after a crash, because rows may be fragmented into many pieces and links (fragments) may be missing.
- The expected row length for dynamic-sized rows is calculated using the following expression:

```
3
+ (number of columns + 7) / 8
+ (number of char columns)
+ (packed size of numeric columns)
+ (length of strings)
+ (number of NULL columns + 7) / 8
```

There is a penalty of 6 bytes for each link. A dynamic row is linked whenever an update causes an enlargement of the row. Each new link is at least 20 bytes, so the next enlargement probably goes in the same link. If not, another link is created. You can find the number of links using myisamchk -ed. All links may be removed with OPTIMIZE TABLE or myisamchk -r.

8.1.3.3 Compressed Table Characteristics

Compressed storage format is a read-only format that is generated with the myisampack tool. Compressed tables can be uncompressed with myisamchk.

Compressed tables have the following characteristics:

- Compressed tables take very little disk space. This minimizes disk usage, which is helpful when using slow disks (such as CD-ROMs).
- Each row is compressed separately, so there is very little access overhead. The header for a row takes up one to three bytes depending on the biggest row in the table. Each column is compressed differently. There is usually a different Huffman tree for each column. Some of the compression types are:
  - Suffix space compression.
  - Prefix space compression.
  - Numbers with a value of zero are stored using one bit.
  - If values in an integer column have a small range, the column is stored using the smallest possible type. For example, a BIGINT column (eight bytes) can be stored as a TINYINT column (one byte) if all its values are in the range from –128 to 127.
  - If a column has only a small set of possible values, the data type is converted to ENUM.
  - A column may use any combination of the preceding compression types.
- Can be used for fixed-length or dynamic-length rows.

8.1.4 MyISAM Table Problems

The file format that MySQL uses to store data has been extensively tested, but there are always circumstances that may cause database tables to become corrupted. The following discussion describes how this can happen and how to handle it.

8.1.4.1 Corrupted MyISAM Tables

Even though the MyISAM table format is very reliable (all changes to a table made by an SQL statement are written before the statement returns), you can still get corrupted tables if any of the following events occur:

- The mysqld process is killed in the middle of a write.
- An unexpected computer shutdown occurs (for example, the computer is turned off).
- Hardware failures.
- You are using an external program (such as myisamchk) to modify a table that is being modified by the server at the same time.
- A software bug in the MySQL or MyISAM code.

Typical symptoms of a corrupt table are:

- You get the following error while selecting data from the table:

  ```
  Incorrect key file for table: '...'. Try to repair it
  ```

- Queries don't find rows in the table or return incomplete results.

You can check the health of a MyISAM table using the CHECK TABLE statement, and repair a corrupted MyISAM table with REPAIR TABLE. When mysqld is not running, you can also check or repair a table with the myisamchk command.

If your tables become corrupted frequently, you should try to determine why this is happening. The most important thing to know is whether the table became corrupted as a result of a server crash. You can verify this easily by looking for a recent restarted mysqld message in the error log. If there is such a message, it is likely that table corruption is a result of the server dying. Otherwise, corruption may have occurred during normal operation. This is a bug. You should try to create a reproducible test case that demonstrates the problem.

8.1.4.2 Problems from Tables Not Being Closed Properly

Each MyISAM index file (.MYI file) has a counter in the header that can be used to check whether a table has been closed properly. If you get the following warning from CHECK TABLE or myisamchk, it means that this counter has gone out of sync:

```
clients are using or haven't closed the table properly
```

This warning doesn't necessarily mean that the table is corrupted, but you should at least check the table.

The counter works as follows:

- The first time a table is updated in MySQL, a counter in the header of the index files is incremented.

- The counter is not changed during further updates.

- When the last instance of a table is closed (because a FLUSH TABLES operation was performed or because there is no room in the table cache), the counter is decremented if the table has been updated at any point.

- When you repair the table or check the table and it is found to be okay, the counter is reset to zero.

- To avoid problems with interaction with other processes that might check the table, the counter is not decremented on close if it was zero.

In other words, the counter can become incorrect only under these conditions:

- A MyISAM table is copied without first issuing LOCK TABLES and FLUSH TABLES.

- MySQL has crashed between an update and the final close. (Note that the table may still be okay, because MySQL always issues writes for everything between each statement.)

- A table was modified by myisamchk --recover or myisamchk --update-state at the same time that it was in use by mysqld.

- Multiple mysqld servers are using the table and one server performed a REPAIR TABLE or CHECK TABLE on the table while it was in use by another server. In this setup, it is safe to use CHECK TABLE, although you might get the warning from other servers. However, REPAIR TABLE should be avoided because when one server replaces the data file with a new one, this is not known to the other servers.

  In general, it is a bad idea to share a data directory among multiple servers. See Section 4.13, "Running Multiple MySQL Servers on the Same Machine," for additional discussion.

8.2 The InnoDB Storage Engine

8.2.1 InnoDB Overview

InnoDB provides MySQL with a transaction-safe (ACID compliant) storage engine that has commit, rollback, and crash recovery capabilities. InnoDB does locking on the row level and also provides an Oracle-style consistent non-locking read in SELECT statements. These features increase multi-user concurrency and performance. There is no need for lock escalation in InnoDB because row-level locks fit in very little space. InnoDB also supports FOREIGN KEY constraints. You can freely mix InnoDB tables with tables from other MySQL storage engines, even within the same statement.

InnoDB has been designed for maximum performance when processing large data volumes. Its CPU efficiency is probably not matched by any other disk-based relational database engine.

Fully integrated with MySQL Server, the InnoDB storage engine maintains its own buffer pool for caching data and indexes in main memory. InnoDB stores its tables and indexes in a tablespace, which may consist of several files (or raw disk partitions). This is different from, for example, MyISAM tables where each table is stored using separate files. InnoDB tables can be of any size even on operating systems where file size is limited to 2GB.

InnoDB is included in binary distributions by default. The Windows Essentials installer makes InnoDB the MySQL default storage engine on Windows.

InnoDB is used in production at numerous large database sites requiring high performance. The famous Internet news site Slashdot.org runs on InnoDB. Mytrix, Inc. stores over 1TB of data in InnoDB, and another site handles an average load of 800 inserts/updates per second in InnoDB.

InnoDB is published under the same GNU GPL License Version 2 (of June 1991) as MySQL. For more information on MySQL licensing, see http://www.mysql.com/company/legal/licensing/.

Additional resources

- A forum dedicated to the InnoDB storage engine is available at http://forums.mysql.com/list.php?22.

8.2.2 InnoDB **Contact Information**

Contact information for Innobase Oy, producer of the InnoDB engine:

```
Web site: http://www.innodb.com/
Email: sales@innodb.com
Phone: +358-9-6969 3250 (office)
       +358-40-5617367 (mobile)


Innobase Oy Inc.
World Trade Center Helsinki
Aleksanterinkatu 17
P.O.Box 800
00101 Helsinki
Finland
```

8.2.3 InnoDB **Configuration**

The InnoDB storage engine is enabled by default. If you don't want to use InnoDB tables, you can add the skip-innodb option to your MySQL option file.

Note: InnoDB provides MySQL with a transaction-safe (ACID compliant) storage engine that has commit, rollback, and crash recovery capabilities. **However, it cannot do so** if the underlying operating system or hardware does not work as advertised. Many operating systems or disk subsystems may delay or reorder write operations to improve performance. On some operating systems, the very system call that should wait until all unwritten data for a file has been flushed—fsync()—might actually return before the data has been flushed to stable storage. Because of this, an operating system crash or a power outage may destroy recently committed data, or in the worst case, even corrupt the database because of write operations having been reordered. If data integrity is important to you, you should perform some "pull-the-plug" tests before using anything in production. On Mac OS X 10.3 and up, InnoDB uses a special fcntl() file flush method. Under Linux, it is advisable to **disable the write-back cache**.

On ATAPI hard disks, a command such hdparm -W0 /dev/hda may work to disable the write-back cache. **Beware that some drives or disk controllers may be unable to disable the write-back cache.**

Two important disk-based resources managed by the InnoDB storage engine are its tablespace data files and its log files.

Note: If you specify no InnoDB configuration options, MySQL creates an auto-extending 10MB data file named ibdata1 and two 5MB log files named ib_logfile0 and ib_logfile1 in the MySQL data directory. To get good performance, you should explicitly provide InnoDB parameters as discussed in the following examples. Naturally, you should edit the settings to suit your hardware and requirements.

The examples shown here are representative. See Section 8.2.4, "InnoDB Startup Options and System Variables," for additional information about InnoDB-related configuration parameters.

To set up the InnoDB tablespace files, use the innodb_data_file_path option in the [mysqld] section of the my.cnf option file. On Windows, you can use my.ini instead. The value of innodb_data_file_path should be a list of one or more data file specifications. If you name more than one data file, separate them by semicolon (';') characters:

```
innodb_data_file_path=datafile_spec1[;datafile_spec2]...
```

For example, a setting that explicitly creates a tablespace having the same characteristics as the default is as follows:

```
[mysqld]
innodb_data_file_path=ibdata1:10M:autoextend
```

This setting configures a single 10MB data file named ibdata1 that is auto-extending. No location for the file is given, so by default, InnoDB creates it in the MySQL data directory.

Sizes are specified using M or G suffix letters to indicate units of MB or GB.

A tablespace containing a fixed-size 50MB data file named ibdata1 and a 50MB auto-extending file named ibdata2 in the data directory can be configured like this:

```
[mysqld]
innodb_data_file_path=ibdata1:50M;ibdata2:50M:autoextend
```

The full syntax for a data file specification includes the filename, its size, and several option-al attributes:

```
file_name:file_size[:autoextend[:max:max_file_size]]
```

The autoextend attribute and those following can be used only for the last data file in the innodb_data_file_path line.

If you specify the autoextend option for the last data file, InnoDB extends the data file if it runs out of free space in the tablespace. The increment is 8MB at a time by default. It can be modified by changing the innodb_autoextend_increment system variable.

If the disk becomes full, you might want to add another data file on another disk. Instructions for reconfiguring an existing tablespace are given in Section 8.2.7, "Adding and Removing InnoDB Data and Log Files."

InnoDB is not aware of the filesystem maximum file size, so be cautious on filesystems where the maximum file size is a small value such as 2GB. To specify a maximum size for an auto-extending data file, use the max attribute. The following configuration allows ibdata1 to grow up to a limit of 500MB:

```
[mysqld]
innodb_data_file_path=ibdata1:10M:autoextend:max:500M
```

InnoDB creates tablespace files in the MySQL data directory by default. To specify a location explicitly, use the innodb_data_home_dir option. For example, to use two files named ibdata1 and ibdata2 but create them in the /ibdata directory, configure InnoDB like this:

```
[mysqld]
innodb_data_home_dir = /ibdata
innodb_data_file_path=ibdata1:50M;ibdata2:50M:autoextend
```

Note: InnoDB does not create directories, so make sure that the /ibdata directory exists before you start the server. This is also true of any log file directories that you configure. Use the Unix or DOS mkdir command to create any necessary directories.

InnoDB forms the directory path for each data file by textually concatenating the value of innodb_data_home_dir to the data file name, adding a pathname separator (slash or back-slash) between values if necessary. If the innodb_data_home_dir option is not mentioned in my.cnf at all, the default value is the "dot" directory ./, which means the MySQL data directory. (The MySQL server changes its current working directory to its data directory when it begins executing.)

If you specify innodb_data_home_dir as an empty string, you can specify absolute paths for the data files listed in the innodb_data_file_path value. The following example is equivalent to the preceding one:

```
[mysqld]
innodb_data_home_dir =
innodb_data_file_path=/ibdata/ibdata1:50M;/ibdata/ibdata2:50M:autoextend
```

A simple `my.cnf` example. Suppose that you have a computer with 128MB RAM and one hard disk. The following example shows possible configuration parameters in `my.cnf` or `my.ini` for `InnoDB`, including the `autoextend` attribute. The example suits most users, both on Unix and Windows, who do not want to distribute `InnoDB` data files and log files onto several disks. It creates an auto-extending data file `ibdata1` and two `InnoDB` log files `ib_logfile0` and `ib_logfile1` in the MySQL data directory. Also, the small archived `InnoDB` log file `ib_arch_log_0000000000` that `InnoDB` creates automatically ends up in the data directory.

```
[mysqld]
# You can write your other MySQL server options here
# ...
# Data files must be able to hold your data and indexes.
# Make sure that you have enough free disk space.
innodb_data_file_path = ibdata1:10M:autoextend
#
# Set buffer pool size to 50-80% of your computer's memory
innodb_buffer_pool_size=70M
innodb_additional_mem_pool_size=10M
#
# Set the log file size to about 25% of the buffer pool size
innodb_log_file_size=20M
innodb_log_buffer_size=8M
#
innodb_flush_log_at_trx_commit=1
```

Make sure that the MySQL server has the proper access rights to create files in the data directory. More generally, the server must have access rights in any directory where it needs to create data files or log files.

Note that data files must be less than 2GB in some filesystems. The combined size of the log files must be less than 4GB. The combined size of data files must be at least 10MB.

When you create an `InnoDB` tablespace for the first time, it is best that you start the MySQL server from the command prompt. `InnoDB` then prints the information about the database creation to the screen, so you can see what is happening. For example, on Windows, if `mysqld` is located in `C:\Program Files\MySQL\MySQL Server 5.0\bin`, you can start it like this:

```
C:\> "C:\Program Files\MySQL\MySQL Server 5.0\bin\mysqld" --console
```

If you do not send server output to the screen, check the server's error log to see what `InnoDB` prints during the startup process.

See Section 8.2.5, "Creating the `InnoDB` Tablespace," for an example of what the information displayed by `InnoDB` should look like.

You can place `InnoDB` options in the `[mysqld]` group of any option file that your server reads when it starts. The locations for option files are described in Section 3.3.2, "Using Option Files."

If you installed MySQL on Windows using the installation and configuration wizards, the option file will be the `my.ini` file located in your MySQL installation directory. See Section 2.3.4.14, "The Location of the `my.ini` File."

If your PC uses a boot loader where the `C:` drive is not the boot drive, your only option is to use the `my.ini` file in your Windows directory (typically `C:\WINDOWS` or `C:\WINNT`). You can use the `SET` command at the command prompt in a console window to print the value of `WINDIR`:

```
C:\> SET WINDIR
windir=C:\WINDOWS
```

If you want to make sure that `mysqld` reads options only from a specific file, you can use the `--defaults-file` option as the first option on the command line when starting the server:

```
mysqld --defaults-file=your_path_to_my_cnf
```

An advanced `my.cnf` example. Suppose that you have a Linux computer with 2GB RAM and three 60GB hard disks at directory paths /, /dr2 and /dr3. The following example shows possible configuration parameters in `my.cnf` for InnoDB:

```
[mysqld]
# You can write your other MySQL server options here
# ...
innodb_data_home_dir =
#
# Data files must be able to hold your data and indexes
innodb_data_file_path = /ibdata/ibdata1:2000M;/dr2/ibdata/ibdata2:2000M:autoextend
#
# Set buffer pool size to 50-80% of your computer's memory,
# but make sure on Linux x86 total memory usage is < 2GB
innodb_buffer_pool_size=1G
innodb_additional_mem_pool_size=20M
innodb_log_group_home_dir = /dr3/iblogs
#
innodb_log_files_in_group = 2
#
# Set the log file size to about 25% of the buffer pool size
innodb_log_file_size=250M
innodb_log_buffer_size=8M
#
innodb_flush_log_at_trx_commit=1
innodb_lock_wait_timeout=50
#
# Uncomment the next lines if you want to use them
#innodb_thread_concurrency=5
```

In some cases, database performance improves if all the data is not placed on the same physical disk. Putting log files on a different disk from data is very often beneficial for performance. The example illustrates how to do this. It places the two data files on different disks and places the log files on the third disk. InnoDB fills the tablespace beginning with the first data file. You can also use raw disk partitions (raw devices) as InnoDB data files, which may speed up I/O. See Section 8.2.3.2, "Using Raw Devices for the Shared Tablespace."

Warning: On 32-bit GNU/Linux x86, you must be careful not to set memory usage too high. glibc may allow the process heap to grow over thread stacks, which crashes your server. It is a risk if the value of the following expression is close to or exceeds 2GB:

```
innodb_buffer_pool_size
+ key_buffer_size
+ max_connections*(sort_buffer_size+read_buffer_size+binlog_cache_size)
+ max_connections*2MB
```

Each thread uses a stack (often 2MB, but only 256KB in MySQL AB binaries) and in the worst case also uses sort_buffer_size + read_buffer_size additional memory.

By compiling MySQL yourself, you can use up to 64GB of physical memory in 32-bit Windows. See the description for innodb_buffer_pool_awe_mem_mb in Section 8.2.4, "InnoDB Startup Options and System Variables."

How to tune other mysqld server parameters? The following values are typical and suit most users:

```
[mysqld]
skip-external-locking
max_connections=200
read_buffer_size=1M
sort_buffer_size=1M
#
# Set key_buffer to 5 - 50% of your RAM depending on how much
# you use MyISAM tables, but keep key_buffer_size + InnoDB
# buffer pool size < 80% of your RAM
key_buffer_size=value
```

8.2.3.1 Using Per-Table Tablespaces

You can store each InnoDB table and its indexes in its own file. This feature is called "multiple tablespaces" because in effect each table has its own tablespace.

Using multiple tablespaces can be beneficial to users who want to move specific tables to separate physical disks or who wish to restore backups of single tables quickly without interrupting the use of the remaining InnoDB tables.

You can enable multiple tablespaces by adding this line to the [mysqld] section of my.cnf:

```
[mysqld]
innodb_file_per_table
```

After restarting the server, InnoDB stores each newly created table into its own file tbl_name.ibd in the database directory where the table belongs. This is similar to what the MyISAM storage engine does, but MyISAM divides the table into a data file tbl_name.MYD and the index file *tbl_name*.MYI. For InnoDB, the data and the indexes are stored together in the .ibd file. The *tbl_name*.frm file is still created as usual.

If you remove the innodb_file_per_table line from my.cnf and restart the server, InnoDB creates tables inside the shared tablespace files again.

innodb_file_per_table affects only table creation, not access to existing tables. If you start the server with this option, new tables are created using .ibd files, but you can still access tables that exist in the shared tablespace. If you remove the option and restart the server, new tables are created in the shared tablespace, but you can still access any tables that were created using multiple tablespaces.

InnoDB always needs the shared tablespace because it puts its internal data dictionary and undo logs there. The .ibd files are not sufficient for InnoDB to operate.

Note: You cannot freely move .ibd files between database directories as you can with MyISAM table files. This is because the table definition that is stored in the InnoDB shared tablespace includes the database name, and because InnoDB must preserve the consistency of transaction IDs and log sequence numbers.

To move an .ibd file and the associated table from one database to another, use a RENAME TABLE statement:

```
RENAME TABLE db1.tbl_name TO db2.tbl_name;
```

If you have a "clean" backup of an .ibd file, you can restore it to the MySQL installation from which it originated as follows:

1. Issue this ALTER TABLE statement:

   ```
   ALTER TABLE tbl_name DISCARD TABLESPACE;
   ```

   Caution: This statement deletes the current .ibd file.

2. Put the backup .ibd file back in the proper database directory.

3. Issue this ALTER TABLE statement:

   ```
   ALTER TABLE tbl_name IMPORT TABLESPACE;
   ```

In this context, a "clean" .ibd file backup means:

- There are no uncommitted modifications by transactions in the .ibd file.
- There are no unmerged insert buffer entries in the .ibd file.
- Purge has removed all delete-marked index records from the .ibd file.
- mysqld has flushed all modified pages of the .ibd file from the buffer pool to the file.

You can make a clean backup .ibd file using the following method:

1. Stop all activity from the mysqld server and commit all transactions.

2. Wait until SHOW ENGINE INNODB STATUS shows that there are no active transactions in the database, and the main thread status of InnoDB is Waiting for server activity. Then you can make a copy of the .ibd file.

Another method for making a clean copy of an .ibd file is to use the commercial InnoDB Hot Backup tool:

1. Use InnoDB Hot Backup to back up the InnoDB installation.

2. Start a second mysqld server on the backup and let it clean up the .ibd files in the backup.

8.2.3.2 Using Raw Devices for the Shared Tablespace

You can use raw disk partitions as data files in the shared tablespace. By using a raw disk, you can perform non-buffered I/O on Windows and on some Unix systems without file-system overhead, which may improve performance.

When you create a new data file, you must put the keyword newraw immediately after the data file size in innodb_data_file_path. The partition must be at least as large as the size that you specify. Note that 1MB in InnoDB is 1024×1024 bytes, whereas 1MB in disk specifications usually means 1,000,000 bytes.

```
[mysqld]
innodb_data_home_dir=
innodb_data_file_path=/dev/hdd1:3Gnewraw;/dev/hdd2:2Gnewraw
```

The next time you start the server, InnoDB notices the newraw keyword and initializes the new partition. However, do not create or change any InnoDB tables yet. Otherwise, when you next restart the server, InnoDB reinitializes the partition and your changes are lost. (As a safety measure InnoDB prevents users from modifying data when any partition with newraw is specified.)

After InnoDB has initialized the new partition, stop the server, change newraw in the data file specification to raw:

```
[mysqld]
innodb_data_home_dir=
innodb_data_file_path=/dev/hdd1:5Graw;/dev/hdd2:2Graw
```

Then restart the server and InnoDB allows changes to be made.

On Windows, you can allocate a disk partition as a data file like this:

```
[mysqld]
innodb_data_home_dir=
innodb_data_file_path=//./D::10Gnewraw
```

The //./ corresponds to the Windows syntax of \\.\ for accessing physical drives.

When you use raw disk partitions, be sure that they have permissions that allow read and write access by the account used for running the MySQL server.

8.2.4 InnoDB Startup Options and System Variables

This section describes the InnoDB-related command options and system variables. System variables that are true or false can be enabled at server startup by naming them, or disabled by using a `skip-` prefix. For example, to enable or disable InnoDB checksums, you can use `--innodb_checksums` or `--skip-innodb_checksums` on the command line, or `innodb_checksums` or `skip-innodb_checksums` in an option file. System variables that take a numeric value can be specified as `--var_name=value` on the command line or as `var_name=value` in option files. For more information on specifying options and system variables, see Section 3.3, "Specifying Program Options." Many of the system variables can be changed at runtime (see Section 4.2.3.2, "Dynamic System Variables").

InnoDB command options:

- `--innodb`

  Enables the InnoDB storage engine, if the server was compiled with InnoDB support. Use `--skip-innodb` to disable InnoDB.

- `--innodb_status_file`

  Causes InnoDB to create a file named `<datadir>/innodb_status.<pid>` in the MySQL data directory. InnoDB periodically writes the output of SHOW ENGINE INNODB STATUS to this file.

InnoDB system variables:

- `innodb_additional_mem_pool_size`

  The size in bytes of a memory pool InnoDB uses to store data dictionary information and other internal data structures. The more tables you have in your application, the more memory you need to allocate here. If InnoDB runs out of memory in this pool, it starts to allocate memory from the operating system and writes warning messages to the MySQL error log. The default value is 1MB.

- `innodb_autoextend_increment`

  The increment size (in MB) for extending the size of an auto-extending tablespace when it becomes full. The default value is 8.

- `innodb_buffer_pool_awe_mem_mb`

  The size of the buffer pool (in MB), if it is placed in the AWE memory. This is relevant only in 32-bit Windows. If your 32-bit Windows operating system supports more than 4GB memory, using so-called "Address Windowing Extensions," you can allocate the InnoDB buffer pool into the AWE physical memory using this variable. The maximum possible value for this variable is 63000. If it is greater than 0, `innodb_buffer_pool_size` is the window in the 32-bit address space of `mysqld` where InnoDB maps that AWE memory. A good value for `innodb_buffer_pool_size` is 500MB.

  To take advantage of AWE memory, you will need to recompile MySQL yourself. The current project settings needed for doing this can be found in the `innobase/os/os0proj.c` source file.

- `innodb_buffer_pool_size`

  The size in bytes of the memory buffer InnoDB uses to cache data and indexes of its tables. The larger you set this value, the less disk I/O is needed to access data in tables. On a dedicated database server, you may set this to up to 80% of the machine physical memory size. However, do not set it too large because competition for physical memory might cause paging in the operating system.

- `innodb_checksums`

  InnoDB can use checksum validation on all pages read from the disk to ensure extra fault tolerance against broken hardware or data files. This validation is enabled by default. However, under some rare circumstances (such as when running benchmarks) this extra safety feature is unneeded and can be disabled with `--skip-innodb_checksums`. This variable was added in MySQL 5.0.3.

- `innodb_commit_concurrency`

  The number of threads that can commit at the same time. A value of 0 disables concurrency control. This variable was added in MySQL 5.0.12.

- `innodb_concurrency_tickets`

  The number of threads that can enter InnoDB concurrently is determined by the `innodb_thread_concurrency` variable. A thread is placed in a queue when it tries to enter InnoDB if the number of threads has already reached the concurrency limit. When a thread is allowed to enter InnoDB, it is given a number of "free tickets" equal to the value of `innodb_concurrency_tickets`, and the thread can enter and leave InnoDB freely until it has used up its tickets. After that point, the thread again becomes subject to the concurrency check (and possible queuing) the next time it tries to enter InnoDB. This variable was added in MySQL 5.0.3.

- `innodb_data_file_path`

  The paths to individual data files and their sizes. The full directory path to each data file is formed by concatenating `innodb_data_home_dir` to each path specified here. The file sizes are specified in MB or GB (1024MB) by appending M or G to the size value. The sum of the sizes of the files must be at least 10MB. If you do not specify `innodb_data_file_path`, the default behavior is to create a single 10MB auto-extending data file named `ibdata1`. The size limit of individual files is determined by your operating system. You can set the file size to more than 4GB on those operating systems that support big files. You can also use raw disk partitions as data files. See Section 8.2.3.2, "Using Raw Devices for the Shared Tablespace."

- `innodb_data_home_dir`

  The common part of the directory path for all InnoDB data files. If you do not set this value, the default is the MySQL data directory. You can specify the value as an empty string, in which case you can use absolute file paths in `innodb_data_file_path`.

- `innodb_doublewrite`

  By default, InnoDB stores all data twice, first to the doublewrite buffer, and then to the actual data files. This variable is enabled by default. It can be turned off with `--skip-innodb_doublewrite` for benchmarks or cases when top performance is needed rather than concern for data integrity or possible failures. This variable was added in MySQL 5.0.3.

- innodb_fast_shutdown

  If you set this variable to 0, InnoDB does a full purge and an insert buffer merge before a shutdown. These operations can take minutes, or even hours in extreme cases. If you set this variable to 1, InnoDB skips these operations at shutdown. The default value is 1. If you set it to 2, InnoDB will just flush its logs and then shut down cold, as if MySQL had crashed; no committed transaction will be lost, but crash recovery will be done at the next startup. The value of 2 can be used as of MySQL 5.0.5, except that it cannot be used on NetWare.

- innodb_file_io_threads

  The number of file I/O threads in InnoDB. Normally, this should be left at the default value of 4, but disk I/O on Windows may benefit from a larger number. On Unix, increasing the number has no effect; InnoDB always uses the default value.

- innodb_file_per_table

  If this variable is enabled, InnoDB creates each new table using its own .ibd file for storing data and indexes, rather than in the shared tablespace. The default is to create tables in the shared tablespace. See Section 8.2.3.1, "Using Per-Table Tablespaces."

- innodb_flush_log_at_trx_commit

  When innodb_flush_log_at_trx_commit is set to 0, the log buffer is written out to the log file once per second and the flush to disk operation is performed on the log file, but nothing is done at a transaction commit. When this value is 1 (the default), the log buffer is written out to the log file at each transaction commit and the flush to disk operation is performed on the log file. When set to 2, the log buffer is written out to the file at each commit, but the flush to disk operation is not performed on it. However, the flushing on the log file takes place once per second also when the value is 2. Note that the once-per-second flushing is not 100% guaranteed to happen every second, due to process scheduling issues.

  The default value of this variable is 1, which is the value that is required for ACID compliance. You can achieve better performance by setting the value different from 1, but then you can lose at most one second worth of transactions in a crash. If you set the value to 0, any mysqld process crash can erase the last second of transactions. If you set the value to 2, only an operating system crash or a power outage can erase the last second of transactions. However, InnoDB's crash recovery is not affected and thus crash recovery does work regardless of the value. Note that many operating systems and some disk hardware fool the flush-to-disk operation. They may tell mysqld that the flush has taken place, even though it has not. Then the durability of transactions is not guaranteed even with the setting 1, and in the worst case a power outage can even corrupt the InnoDB database. Using a battery-backed disk cache in the SCSI disk controller or in the disk itself speeds up file flushes, and makes the operation safer. You can also try using the Unix command hdparm to disable the caching of disk writes in hardware caches, or use some other command specific to the hardware vendor.

- innodb_flush_method

  If set to fdatasync (the default), InnoDB uses fsync() to flush both the data and log files. If set to O_DSYNC, InnoDB uses O_SYNC to open and flush the log files, but uses fsync() to flush the data files. If O_DIRECT is specified (available on some GNU/Linux versions), InnoDB uses O_DIRECT to open the data files, and uses fsync() to flush both the data and log files. Note that InnoDB uses fsync() instead of fdatasync(), and it does not use O_DSYNC by default because there have been problems with it on many varieties of Unix. This variable is relevant only for Unix. On Windows, the flush method is always async_unbuffered and cannot be changed.

- innodb_force_recovery

The crash recovery mode. **Warning**: This variable should be set greater than 0 only in an emergency situation when you want to dump your tables from a corrupt database! Possible values are from 1 to 6. The meanings of these values are described in Section 8.2.8.1, "Forcing InnoDB Recovery." As a safety measure, InnoDB prevents any changes to its data when this variable is greater than 0.

- innodb_lock_wait_timeout

The timeout in seconds an InnoDB transaction may wait for a lock before being rolled back. InnoDB automatically detects transaction deadlocks in its own lock table and rolls back the transaction. InnoDB notices locks set using the LOCK TABLES statement. The default is 50 seconds.

Note: For the greatest possible durability and consistency in a replication setup using InnoDB with transactions, you should use innodb_flush_log_at_trx_commit=1, sync_binlog=1, and, before MySQL 5.0.3, innodb_safe_binlog in your master server my.cnf file. (innodb_safe_binlog is not needed from 5.0.3 on.)

- innodb_locks_unsafe_for_binlog

This variable controls next-key locking in InnoDB searches and index scans. By default, this variable is 0 (disabled), which means that next-key locking is enabled.

Normally, InnoDB uses an algorithm called "next-key locking." InnoDB performs row-level locking in such a way that when it searches or scans a table index, it sets shared or exclusive locks on any index records it encounters. Thus, the row-level locks are actually index record locks. The locks that InnoDB sets on index records also affect the "gap" preceding that index record. If a user has a shared or exclusive lock on record R in an index, another user cannot insert a new index record immediately before R in the order of the index. Enabling this variable causes InnoDB not to use next-key locking in searches or index scans. Next-key locking is still used to ensure foreign key constraints and duplicate key checking. Note that enabling this variable may cause phantom problems: Suppose that you want to read and lock all children from the child table with an identifier value larger than 100, with the intention of updating some column in the selected rows later:

```
SELECT * FROM child WHERE id > 100 FOR UPDATE;
```

Suppose that there is an index on the id column. The query scans that index starting from the first record where id is greater than 100. If the locks set on the index records do not lock out inserts made in the gaps, another client can insert a new row into the table. If you execute the same SELECT within the same transaction, you see a new row in the result set returned by the query. This also means that if new items are added to the database, InnoDB does not guarantee serializability. Therefore, if this variable is enabled InnoDB guarantees at most isolation level READ COMMITTED. (Conflict serializability is still guaranteed.)

Starting from MySQL 5.0.2, this option is even more unsafe. InnoDB in an UPDATE or a DELETE only locks rows that it updates or deletes. This greatly reduces the probability of deadlocks, but they can happen. Note that enabling this variable still does not allow operations such as UPDATE to overtake other similar operations (such as another UPDATE) even in the case when they affect different rows. Consider the following example, beginning with this table:

```
CREATE TABLE A(A INT NOT NULL, B INT) ENGINE = InnoDB;
INSERT INTO A VALUES (1,2),(2,3),(3,2),(4,3),(5,2);
COMMIT;
```

Suppose that one client executes these statements:

```
SET AUTOCOMMIT = 0;
UPDATE A SET B = 5 WHERE B = 3;
```

Then suppose that another client executes these statements following those of the first client:

```
SET AUTOCOMMIT = 0;
UPDATE A SET B = 4 WHERE B = 2;
```

In this case, the second UPDATE must wait for a commit or rollback of the first UPDATE. The first UPDATE has an exclusive lock on row (2,3), and the second UPDATE while scanning rows also tries to acquire an exclusive lock for the same row, which it cannot have. This is because UPDATE two first acquires an exclusive lock on a row and then determines whether the row belongs to the result set. If not, it releases the unnecessary lock, when the innodb_locks_unsafe_for_binlog variable is enabled.

Therefore, InnoDB executes UPDATE one as follows:

```
x-lock(1,2)
unlock(1,2)
x-lock(2,3)
update(2,3) to (2,5)
x-lock(3,2)
unlock(3,2)
x-lock(4,3)
update(4,3) to (4,5)
x-lock(5,2)
unlock(5,2)
```

InnoDB executes UPDATE two as follows:

```
x-lock(1,2)
update(1,2) to (1,4)
x-lock(2,3) - wait for query one to commit or rollback
```

- innodb_log_arch_dir

  The directory where fully written log files would be archived if we used log archiving. If used, the value of this variable should be set the same as innodb_log_group_home_dir. However, it is not required.

- innodb_log_archive

  Whether to log InnoDB archive files. This variable is present for historical reasons, but is unused. Recovery from a backup is done by MySQL using its own log files, so there is no need to archive InnoDB log files. The default for this variable is 0.

- innodb_log_buffer_size

  The size in bytes of the buffer that InnoDB uses to write to the log files on disk. Sensible values range from 1MB to 8MB. The default is 1MB. A large log buffer allows large transactions to run without a need to write the log to disk before the transactions commit. Thus, if you have big transactions, making the log buffer larger saves disk I/O.

- innodb_log_file_size

  The size in bytes of each log file in a log group. The combined size of log files must be less than 4GB on 32-bit computers. The default is 5MB. Sensible values range from 1MB to 1/N-th of the size of the buffer pool, where N is the number of log files in the group. The larger the value, the less checkpoint flush activity is needed in the buffer pool, saving disk I/O. But larger log files also mean that recovery is slower in case of a crash.

- innodb_log_files_in_group

  The number of log files in the log group. InnoDB writes to the files in a circular fashion. The default (and recommended) value is 2.

- innodb_log_group_home_dir

  The directory path to the InnoDB log files. It must have the same value as innodb_log_arch_dir. If you do not specify any InnoDB log variables, the default is to create two 5MB files names ib_logfile0 and ib_logfile1 in the MySQL data directory.

- innodb_max_dirty_pages_pct

  This is an integer in the range from 0 to 100. The default is 90. The main thread in InnoDB tries to write pages from the buffer pool so that the percentage of dirty (not yet written) pages will not exceed this value.

- innodb_max_purge_lag

  This variable controls how to delay INSERT, UPDATE, and DELETE operations when the purge operations are lagging (see Section 8.2.12, "Implementation of Multi-Versioning"). The default value of this variable is 0, meaning that there are no delays.

  The InnoDB transaction system maintains a list of transactions that have delete-marked index records by UPDATE or DELETE operations. Let the length of this list be *purge_lag*. When *purge_lag* exceeds innodb_max_purge_lag, each INSERT, UPDATE and DELETE operation is delayed by (($purge\_lag$/innodb_max_purge_lag)×10)–5 milliseconds. The delay is computed in the beginning of a purge batch, every 10 seconds. The operations are not delayed if purge cannot run because of an old consistent read view that could see the rows to be purged.

A typical setting for a problematic workload might be 1 million, assuming that our transactions are small, only 100 bytes in size, and we can allow 100MB of unpurged rows in our tables.

- `innodb_mirrored_log_groups`

The number of identical copies of log groups to keep for the database. Currently, this should be set to 1.

- `innodb_open_files`

This variable is relevant only if you use multiple tablespaces in `InnoDB`. It specifies the maximum number of `.ibd` files that `InnoDB` can keep open at one time. The minimum value is 10. The default is 300.

The file descriptors used for `.ibd` files are for `InnoDB` only. They are independent of those specified by the `--open-files-limit` server option, and do not affect the operation of the table cache.

- `innodb_safe_binlog`

Adds consistency guarantees between the content of `InnoDB` tables and the binary log. See Section 4.12.3, "The Binary Log." This variable was removed in MySQL 5.0.3, having been made obsolete by the introduction of XA transaction support.

- `innodb_support_xa`

When set to `ON` or 1 (the default), this variable enables `InnoDB` support for two-phase commit in XA transactions. Enabling `innodb_support_xa` causes an extra disk flush for transaction preparation. If you don't care about using XA, you can disable this variable by setting it to `OFF` or 0 to reduce the number of disk flushes and get better `InnoDB` performance. This variable was added in MySQL 5.0.3.

- `innodb_sync_spin_loops`

The number of times a thread waits for an `InnoDB` mutex to be freed before the thread is suspended. This variable was added in MySQL 5.0.3.

- `innodb_table_locks`

`InnoDB` honors `LOCK TABLES`; MySQL does not return from `LOCK TABLE .. WRITE` until all other threads have released all their locks to the table. The default value is 1, which means that `LOCK TABLES` causes `InnoDB` to lock a table internally. In applications using `AUTOCOMMIT=1`, `InnoDB`'s internal table locks can cause deadlocks. You can set `innodb_table_locks=0` in the server option file to remove that problem.

- `innodb_thread_concurrency`

`InnoDB` tries to keep the number of operating system threads concurrently inside `InnoDB` less than or equal to the limit given by this variable. Before MySQL 5.0.8, the default value is 8. If you have performance issues, and `SHOW ENGINE INNODB STATUS` reveals many threads waiting for semaphores, you may have thread "thrashing" and should try setting this variable lower or higher. If you have a computer with many processors and disks, you can try setting the value higher to make better use of your computer's resources. A recommended value is the sum of the number of processors and disks your system has. A value of 500 or greater disables concurrency checking. Starting with MySQL 5.0.8, the default value is 20, and concurrency checking will be disabled if the setting is greater than or equal to 20.

- `innodb_thread_sleep_delay`

  How long `InnoDB` threads sleep before joining the `InnoDB` queue, in microseconds. The default value is 10,000. A value of 0 disables sleep. This variable was added in MySQL 5.0.3.

- `sync_binlog`

  If the value of this variable is positive, the MySQL server synchronizes its binary log to disk (`fdatasync()`) after every `sync_binlog` writes to this binary log. Note that there is one write to the binary log per statement if in autocommit mode, and otherwise one write per transaction. The default value is 0 which does no synchronizing to disk. A value of 1 is the safest choice, because in the event of a crash you lose at most one statement/transaction from the binary log; however, it is also the slowest choice (unless the disk has a battery-backed cache, which makes synchronization very fast).

8.2.5 Creating the `InnoDB` Tablespace

Suppose that you have installed MySQL and have edited your option file so that it contains the necessary `InnoDB` configuration parameters. Before starting MySQL, you should verify that the directories you have specified for `InnoDB` data files and log files exist and that the MySQL server has access rights to those directories. `InnoDB` does not create directories, only files. Check also that you have enough disk space for the data and log files.

It is best to run the MySQL server `mysqld` from the command prompt when you first start the server with `InnoDB` enabled, not from the `mysqld_safe` wrapper or as a Windows service. When you run from a command prompt you see what `mysqld` prints and what is happening. On Unix, just invoke `mysqld`. On Windows, use the `--console` option.

When you start the MySQL server after initially configuring `InnoDB` in your option file, `InnoDB` creates your data files and log files, and prints something like this:

```
InnoDB: The first specified datafile /home/heikki/data/ibdata1
did not exist:
InnoDB: a new database to be created!
InnoDB: Setting file /home/heikki/data/ibdata1 size to 134217728
InnoDB: Database physically writes the file full: wait...
InnoDB: datafile /home/heikki/data/ibdata2 did not exist:
new to be created
InnoDB: Setting file /home/heikki/data/ibdata2 size to 262144000
InnoDB: Database physically writes the file full: wait...
InnoDB: Log file /home/heikki/data/logs/ib_logfile0 did not exist:
new to be created
InnoDB: Setting log file /home/heikki/data/logs/ib_logfile0 size
```

```
to 5242880
InnoDB: Log file /home/heikki/data/logs/ib_logfile1 did not exist:
new to be created
InnoDB: Setting log file /home/heikki/data/logs/ib_logfile1 size
to 5242880
InnoDB: Doublewrite buffer not found: creating new
InnoDB: Doublewrite buffer created
InnoDB: Creating foreign key constraint system tables
InnoDB: Foreign key constraint system tables created
InnoDB: Started
mysqld: ready for connections
```

At this point `InnoDB` has initialized its tablespace and log files. You can connect to the MySQL server with the usual MySQL client programs like `mysql`. When you shut down the MySQL server with `mysqladmin shutdown`, the output is like this:

```
010321 18:33:34  mysqld: Normal shutdown
010321 18:33:34  mysqld: Shutdown Complete
InnoDB: Starting shutdown...
InnoDB: Shutdown completed
```

You can look at the data file and log directories and you see the files created there. The log directory also contains a small file named `ib_arch_log_0000000000`. That file resulted from the database creation, after which `InnoDB` switched off log archiving. When MySQL is started again, the data files and log files have been created already, so the output is much briefer:

```
InnoDB: Started
mysqld: ready for connections
```

If you add the `innodb_file_per_table` option to `my.cnf`, `InnoDB` stores each table in its own `.ibd` file in the same MySQL database directory where the `.frm` file is created. See Section 8.2.3.1, "Using Per-Table Tablespaces."

8.2.5.1 Dealing with InnoDB Initialization Problems

If `InnoDB` prints an operating system error during a file operation, usually the problem has one of the following causes:

- You did not create the `InnoDB` data file directory or the `InnoDB` log directory.
- `mysqld` does not have access rights to create files in those directories.
- `mysqld` cannot read the proper `my.cnf` or `my.ini` option file, and consequently does not see the options that you specified.
- The disk is full or a disk quota is exceeded.
- You have created a subdirectory whose name is equal to a data file that you specified, so the name cannot be used as a filename.
- There is a syntax error in the `innodb_data_home_dir` or `innodb_data_file_path` value.

If something goes wrong when `InnoDB` attempts to initialize its tablespace or its log files, you should delete all files created by `InnoDB`. This means all `ibdata` files and all `ib_logfile` files.

In case you have already created some InnoDB tables, delete the corresponding .frm files for these tables (and any .ibd files if you are using multiple tablespaces) from the MySQL database directories as well. Then you can try the InnoDB database creation again. It is best to start the MySQL server from a command prompt so that you see what is happening.

8.2.6 Creating and Using InnoDB Tables

To create an InnoDB table, specify an ENGINE = InnoDB option in the CREATE TABLE statement:

```
CREATE TABLE customers (a INT, b CHAR (20), INDEX (a)) ENGINE=InnoDB;
```

The older term TYPE is supported as a synonym for ENGINE for backward compatibility, but ENGINE is the preferred term and TYPE is deprecated.

The statement creates a table and an index on column a in the InnoDB tablespace that consists of the data files that you specified in my.cnf. In addition, MySQL creates a file customers.frm in the test directory under the MySQL database directory. Internally, InnoDB adds an entry for the table to its own data dictionary. The entry includes the database name. For example, if test is the database in which the customers table is created, the entry is for 'test/customers'. This means you can create a table of the same name customers in some other database, and the table names do not collide inside InnoDB.

You can query the amount of free space in the InnoDB tablespace by issuing a SHOW TABLE STATUS statement for any InnoDB table. The amount of free space in the tablespace appears in the Comment section in the output of SHOW TABLE STATUS. For example:

```
SHOW TABLE STATUS FROM test LIKE 'customers'
```

Note that the statistics SHOW displays for InnoDB tables are only approximate. They are used in SQL optimization. Table and index reserved sizes in bytes are accurate, though.

8.2.6.1 How to Use Transactions in InnoDB with Different APIs

By default, each client that connects to the MySQL server begins with autocommit mode enabled, which automatically commits every SQL statement as you execute it. To use multiple-statement transactions, you can switch autocommit off with the SQL statement SET AUTOCOMMIT = 0 and use COMMIT and ROLLBACK to commit or roll back your transaction. If you want to leave autocommit on, you can enclose your transactions within START TRANSACTION and either COMMIT or ROLLBACK. The following example shows two transactions. The first is committed; the second is rolled back.

```
shell> mysql test

mysql> CREATE TABLE CUSTOMER (A INT, B CHAR (20), INDEX (A))
    -> ENGINE=InnoDB;
Query OK, 0 rows affected (0.00 sec)
mysql> START TRANSACTION;
Query OK, 0 rows affected (0.00 sec)
mysql> INSERT INTO CUSTOMER VALUES (10, 'Heikki');
```

```
Query OK, 1 row affected (0.00 sec)
mysql> COMMIT;
Query OK, 0 rows affected (0.00 sec)
mysql> SET AUTOCOMMIT=0;
Query OK, 0 rows affected (0.00 sec)
mysql> INSERT INTO CUSTOMER VALUES (15, 'John');
Query OK, 1 row affected (0.00 sec)
mysql> ROLLBACK;
Query OK, 0 rows affected (0.00 sec)
mysql> SELECT * FROM CUSTOMER;
+------+--------+
| A    | B      |
+------+--------+
|   10 | Heikki |
+------+--------+
1 row in set (0.00 sec)
mysql>
```

In APIs such as PHP, Perl DBI, JDBC, ODBC, or the standard C call interface of MySQL, you can send transaction control statements such as COMMIT to the MySQL server as strings just like any other SQL statements such as SELECT or INSERT. Some APIs also offer separate special transaction commit and rollback functions or methods.

8.2.6.2 Converting MyISAM Tables to InnoDB

Important: Do not convert MySQL system tables in the mysql database (such as user or host) to the InnoDB type. This is an unsupported operation. The system tables must always be of the MyISAM type.

If you want all your (non-system) tables to be created as InnoDB tables, you can simply add the line default-storage-engine=innodb to the [mysqld] section of your server option file.

InnoDB does not have a special optimization for separate index creation the way the MyISAM storage engine does. Therefore, it does not pay to export and import the table and create indexes afterward. The fastest way to alter a table to InnoDB is to do the inserts directly to an InnoDB table. That is, use ALTER TABLE ... ENGINE=INNODB, or create an empty InnoDB table with identical definitions and insert the rows with INSERT INTO ... SELECT * FROM .....

If you have UNIQUE constraints on secondary keys, you can speed up a table import by turning off the uniqueness checks temporarily during the import operation:

```
SET UNIQUE_CHECKS=0;
... import operation ...
SET UNIQUE_CHECKS=1;
```

For big tables, this saves a lot of disk I/O because InnoDB can then use its insert buffer to write secondary index records as a batch.

To get better control over the insertion process, it might be good to insert big tables in pieces:

```
INSERT INTO newtable SELECT * FROM oldtable
   WHERE yourkey > something AND yourkey <= somethingelse;
```

After all records have been inserted, you can rename the tables.

During the conversion of big tables, you should increase the size of the InnoDB buffer pool to reduce disk I/O. Do not use more than 80% of the physical memory, though. You can also increase the sizes of the InnoDB log files.

Make sure that you do not fill up the tablespace: InnoDB tables require a lot more disk space than MyISAM tables. If an ALTER TABLE operation runs out of space, it starts a rollback, and that can take hours if it is disk-bound. For inserts, InnoDB uses the insert buffer to merge secondary index records to indexes in batches. That saves a lot of disk I/O. For rollback, no such mechanism is used, and the rollback can take 30 times longer than the insertion.

In the case of a runaway rollback, if you do not have valuable data in your database, it may be advisable to kill the database process rather than wait for millions of disk I/O operations to complete. For the complete procedure, see Section 8.2.8.1, "Forcing InnoDB Recovery."

8.2.6.3 How AUTO_INCREMENT Columns Work in InnoDB

If you specify an AUTO_INCREMENT column for an InnoDB table, the table handle in the InnoDB data dictionary contains a special counter called the auto-increment counter that is used in assigning new values for the column. This counter is stored only in main memory, not on disk.

InnoDB uses the following algorithm to initialize the auto-increment counter for a table T that contains an AUTO_INCREMENT column named ai_col: After a server startup, for the first insert into a table T, InnoDB executes the equivalent of this statement:

```
SELECT MAX(ai_col) FROM T FOR UPDATE;
```

InnoDB increments by one the value retrieved by the statement and assigns it to the column and to the auto-increment counter for the table. If the table is empty, InnoDB uses the value 1. If a user invokes a SHOW TABLE STATUS statement that displays output for the table T and the auto-increment counter has not been initialized, InnoDB initializes but does not increment the value and stores it for use by later inserts. Note that this initialization uses a normal exclusive-locking read on the table and the lock lasts to the end of the transaction.

InnoDB follows the same procedure for initializing the auto-increment counter for a freshly created table.

After the auto-increment counter has been initialized, if a user does not explicitly specify a value for an AUTO_INCREMENT column, InnoDB increments the counter by one and assigns the new value to the column. If the user inserts a row that explicitly specifies the column value, and the value is bigger than the current counter value, the counter is set to the specified column value.

You may see gaps in the sequence of values assigned to the AUTO_INCREMENT column if you roll back transactions that have generated numbers using the counter.

If a user specifies NULL or 0 for the AUTO_INCREMENT column in an INSERT, InnoDB treats the row as if the value had not been specified and generates a new value for it.

The behavior of the auto-increment mechanism is not defined if a user assigns a negative value to the column or if the value becomes bigger than the maximum integer that can be stored in the specified integer type.

When accessing the auto-increment counter, InnoDB uses a special table-level AUTO-INC lock that it keeps to the end of the current SQL statement, not to the end of the transaction. The special lock release strategy was introduced to improve concurrency for inserts into a table containing an AUTO_INCREMENT column. Nevertheless, two transactions cannot have the AUTO-INC lock on the same table simultaneously, which can have a performance impact if the AUTO-INC lock is held for a long time. That might be the case for a statement such as INSERT INTO t1 ... SELECT ... FROM t2 that inserts all rows from one table into another.

InnoDB uses the in-memory auto-increment counter as long as the server runs. When the server is stopped and restarted, InnoDB reinitializes the counter for each table for the first INSERT to the table, as described earlier.

Beginning with MySQL 5.0.3, InnoDB supports the AUTO_INCREMENT = N table option in CREATE TABLE and ALTER TABLE statements, to set the initial counter value or alter the current counter value. The effect of this option is canceled by a server restart, for reasons discussed earlier in this section.

8.2.6.4 FOREIGN KEY Constraints

InnoDB also supports foreign key constraints. The syntax for a foreign key constraint definition in InnoDB looks like this:

```
[CONSTRAINT symbol] FOREIGN KEY ı (index_col_name, ...)
    REFERENCES tbl_name (index_col_name, ...)
    [ON DELETE {RESTRICT | CASCADE | SET NULL | NO ACTION}]
    [ON UPDATE {RESTRICT | CASCADE | SET NULL | NO ACTION}]
```

Foreign keys definitions are subject to the following conditions:

- Both tables must be InnoDB tables and they must not be TEMPORARY tables.

- In the referencing table, there must be an index where the foreign key columns are listed as the *first* columns in the same order. Such an index is created on the referencing table automatically if it does not exist.

- In the referenced table, there must be an index where the referenced columns are listed as the *first* columns in the same order.

- Index prefixes on foreign key columns are not supported. One consequence of this is that BLOB and TEXT columns cannot be included in a foreign key, because indexes on those columns must always include a prefix length.

- If the CONSTRAINT symbol clause is given, the symbol value must be unique in the database. If the clause is not given, InnoDB creates the name automatically.

InnoDB rejects any INSERT or UPDATE operation that attempts to create a foreign key value in a child table if there is no matching candidate key value in the parent table. The action InnoDB takes for any UPDATE or DELETE operation that attempts to update or delete a candidate key value in the parent table that has some matching rows in the child table is dependent on the *referential action* specified using ON UPDATE and ON DELETE subclauses of the FOREIGN KEY clause. When the user attempts to delete or update a row from a parent table, and there are one or more matching rows in the child table, InnoDB supports five options regarding the action to be taken:

- CASCADE: Delete or update the row from the parent table and automatically delete or update the matching rows in the child table. Both ON DELETE CASCADE and ON UPDATE CASCADE are supported. Between two tables, you should not define several ON UPDATE CASCADE clauses that act on the same column in the parent table or in the child table.

- SET NULL: Delete or update the row from the parent table and set the foreign key column or columns in the child table to NULL. This is valid only if the foreign key columns do not have the NOT NULL qualifier specified. Both ON DELETE SET NULL and ON UPDATE SET NULL clauses are supported.

- NO ACTION: In standard SQL, NO ACTION means *no action* in the sense that an attempt to delete or update a primary key value is not allowed to proceed if there is a related foreign key value in the referenced table. InnoDB rejects the delete or update operation for the parent table.

- RESTRICT: Rejects the delete or update operation for the parent table. NO ACTION and RESTRICT are the same as omitting the ON DELETE or ON UPDATE clause. (Some database systems have deferred checks, and NO ACTION is a deferred check. In MySQL, foreign key constraints are checked immediately, so NO ACTION and RESTRICT are the same.)

- SET DEFAULT: This action is recognized by the parser, but InnoDB rejects table definitions containing ON DELETE SET DEFAULT or ON UPDATE SET DEFAULT clauses.

Note that InnoDB supports foreign key references within a table. In these cases, "child table records" really refers to dependent records within the same table.

InnoDB requires indexes on foreign keys and referenced keys so that foreign key checks can be fast and not require a table scan. The index on the foreign key is created automatically. This is in contrast to some older versions, in which indexes had to be created explicitly or the creation of foreign key constraints would fail.

Corresponding columns in the foreign key and the referenced key must have similar internal data types inside InnoDB so that they can be compared without a type conversion. *The size and sign of integer types must be the same.* The length of string types need not be the same. If you specify a SET NULL action, *make sure that you have not declared the columns in the child table as NOT NULL.*

If MySQL reports an error number 1005 from a CREATE TABLE statement, and the error message refers to errno 150, table creation failed because a foreign key constraint was not correctly formed. Similarly, if an ALTER TABLE fails and it refers to errno 150, that means a foreign key definition would be incorrectly formed for the altered table. You can use SHOW ENGINE INNODB STATUS to display a detailed explanation of the most recent InnoDB foreign key error in the server.

Note: InnoDB does not check foreign key constraints on those foreign key or referenced key values that contain a NULL column.

Note: Currently, triggers are not activated by cascaded foreign key actions.

Deviation from SQL standards: If there are several rows in the parent table that have the same referenced key value, InnoDB acts in foreign key checks as if the other parent rows with the same key value do not exist. For example, if you have defined a RESTRICT type constraint, and there is a child row with several parent rows, InnoDB does not allow the deletion of any of those parent rows.

InnoDB performs cascading operations through a depth-first algorithm, based on records in the indexes corresponding to the foreign key constraints.

Deviation from SQL standards: A FOREIGN KEY constraint that references a non-UNIQUE key is not standard SQL. It is an InnoDB extension to standard SQL.

Deviation from SQL standards: If ON UPDATE CASCADE or ON UPDATE SET NULL recurses to update the *same table* it has previously updated during the cascade, it acts like RESTRICT. This means that you cannot use self-referential ON UPDATE CASCADE or ON UPDATE SET NULL operations. This is to prevent infinite loops resulting from cascaded updates. A self-referential ON DELETE SET NULL, on the other hand, is possible, as is a self-referential ON DELETE CASCADE. Cascading operations may not be nested more than 15 levels deep.

Deviation from SQL standards: Like MySQL in general, in an SQL statement that inserts, deletes, or updates many rows, InnoDB checks UNIQUE and FOREIGN KEY constraints row-by-row. According to the SQL standard, the default behavior should be deferred checking. That is, constraints are checked only after the *entire SQL statement* has been processed. Until InnoDB implements deferred constraint checking, some things will be impossible, such as deleting a record that refers to itself via a foreign key.

Here is a simple example that relates parent and child tables through a single-column foreign key:

```
CREATE TABLE parent (id INT NOT NULL,
                     PRIMARY KEY (id)
) ENGINE=INNODB;
CREATE TABLE child (id INT, parent_id INT,
                    INDEX par_ind (parent_id),
                    FOREIGN KEY (parent_id) REFERENCES parent(id)
                      ON DELETE CASCADE
) ENGINE=INNODB;
```

A more complex example in which a product_order table has foreign keys for two other tables. One foreign key references a two-column index in the product table. The other references a single-column index in the customer table:

```
CREATE TABLE product (category INT NOT NULL, id INT NOT NULL,
                      price DECIMAL,
                      PRIMARY KEY(category, id)) ENGINE=INNODB;
CREATE TABLE customer (id INT NOT NULL,
                       PRIMARY KEY (id)) ENGINE=INNODB;
```

```
CREATE TABLE product_order (no INT NOT NULL AUTO_INCREMENT,
                            product_category INT NOT NULL,
                            product_id INT NOT NULL,
                            customer_id INT NOT NULL,
                            PRIMARY KEY(no),
                            INDEX (product_category, product_id),
                            FOREIGN KEY (product_category, product_id)
                              REFERENCES product(category, id)
                              ON UPDATE CASCADE ON DELETE RESTRICT,
                            INDEX (customer_id),
                            FOREIGN KEY (customer_id)
                              REFERENCES customer(id)) ENGINE=INNODB;
```

InnoDB allows you to add a new foreign key constraint to a table by using ALTER TABLE:

```
ALTER TABLE tbl_name
    ADD [CONSTRAINT symbol] FOREIGN KEY ר (index_col_name, ...)
    REFERENCES tbl_name (index_col_name, ...)
    [ON DELETE {RESTRICT | CASCADE | SET NULL | NO ACTION}]
    [ON UPDATE {RESTRICT | CASCADE | SET NULL | NO ACTION}]
```

Remember to create the required indexes first. You can also add a self-referential foreign key constraint to a table using ALTER TABLE.

InnoDB also supports the use of ALTER TABLE to drop foreign keys:

```
ALTER TABLE tbl_name DROP FOREIGN KEY fk_symbol;
```

If the FOREIGN KEY clause included a CONSTRAINT name when you created the foreign key, you can refer to that name to drop the foreign key. Otherwise, the fk_symbol value is internally generated by InnoDB when the foreign key is created. To find out the symbol value when you want to drop a foreign key, use the SHOW CREATE TABLE statement. For example:

```
mysql> SHOW CREATE TABLE ibtest11c\G
*************************** 1. row ***************************
      Table: ibtest11c
Create Table: CREATE TABLE `ibtest11c` (
  `A` int(11) NOT NULL auto_increment,
  `D` int(11) NOT NULL default '0',
  `B` varchar(200) NOT NULL default '',
  `C` varchar(175) default NULL,
  PRIMARY KEY  (`A`,`D`,`B`),
  KEY `B` (`B`,`C`),
  KEY `C` (`C`),
  CONSTRAINT `0_38775` FOREIGN KEY (`A`, `D`)
REFERENCES `ibtest11a` (`A`, `D`)
ON DELETE CASCADE ON UPDATE CASCADE,
  CONSTRAINT `0_38776` FOREIGN KEY (`B`, `C`)
REFERENCES `ibtest11a` (`B`, `C`)
ON DELETE CASCADE ON UPDATE CASCADE
```

```
) ENGINE=INNODB CHARSET=latin1
1 row in set (0.01 sec)
```

```
mysql> ALTER TABLE ibtest11c DROP FOREIGN KEY `0_38775`;
```

You cannot add a foreign key and drop a foreign key in separate clauses of a single ALTER
TABLE statement. Separate statements are required.

The InnoDB parser allows table and column identifiers in a FOREIGN KEY ... REFERENCES ...
clause to be quoted within backticks. (Alternatively, double quotes can be used if the
ANSI_QUOTES SQL mode is enabled.) The InnoDB parser also takes into account the setting of
the lower_case_table_names system variable.

InnoDB returns a table's foreign key definitions as part of the output of the SHOW CREATE
TABLE statement:

```
SHOW CREATE TABLE tbl_name;
```

mysqldump also produces correct definitions of tables to the dump file, and does not forget
about the foreign keys.

You can also display the foreign key constraints for a table like this:

```
SHOW TABLE STATUS FROM db_name LIKE 'tbl_name';
```

The foreign key constraints are listed in the Comment column of the output.

When performing foreign key checks, InnoDB sets shared row-level locks on child or parent
records it has to look at. InnoDB checks foreign key constraints immediately; the check is not
deferred to transaction commit.

To make it easier to reload dump files for tables that have foreign key relationships,
mysqldump automatically includes a statement in the dump output to set FOREIGN_KEY_CHECKS
to 0. This avoids problems with tables having to be reloaded in a particular order when the
dump is reloaded. It is also possible to set this variable manually:

```
mysql> SET FOREIGN_KEY_CHECKS = 0;
mysql> SOURCE dump_file_name;
mysql> SET FOREIGN_KEY_CHECKS = 1;
```

This allows you to import the tables in any order if the dump file contains tables that are
not correctly ordered for foreign keys. It also speeds up the import operation. Setting
FOREIGN_KEY_CHECKS to 0 can also be useful for ignoring foreign key constraints during LOAD
DATA and ALTER TABLE operations.

InnoDB does not allow you to drop a table that is referenced by a FOREIGN KEY constraint,
unless you do SET FOREIGN_KEY_CHECKS=0. When you drop a table, the constraints that were
defined in its create statement are also dropped.

If you re-create a table that was dropped, it must have a definition that conforms to the foreign key constraints referencing it. It must have the right column names and types, and it
must have indexes on the referenced keys, as stated earlier. If these are not satisfied, MySQL
returns error number 1005 and refers to errno 150 in the error message.

8.2.6.5 InnoDB and MySQL Replication

MySQL replication works for InnoDB tables as it does for MyISAM tables. It is also possible to use replication in a way where the storage engine on the slave is not the same as the original storage engine on the master. For example, you can replicate modifications to an InnoDB table on the master to a MyISAM table on the slave.

To set up a new slave for a master, you have to make a copy of the InnoDB tablespace and the log files, as well as the .frm files of the InnoDB tables, and move the copies to the slave. If the innodb_file_per_table variable is enabled, you must also copy the .ibd files as well. For the proper procedure to do this, see Section 8.2.8, "Backing Up and Recovering an InnoDB Database."

If you can shut down the master or an existing slave, you can take a cold backup of the InnoDB tablespace and log files and use that to set up a slave. To make a new slave without taking down any server you can also use the non-free (commercial) InnoDB Hot Backup tool (http://www.innodb.com/order.html).

You cannot set up replication for InnoDB using the LOAD TABLE FROM MASTER statement, which works only for MyISAM tables. There are two possible workarounds:

- Dump the table on the master and import the dump file into the slave.
- Use ALTER TABLE *tbl_name* ENGINE=MyISAM on the master before setting up replication with LOAD TABLE *tbl_name* FROM MASTER, and then use ALTER TABLE to convert the master table back to InnoDB afterward. However, this should not be done for tables that have foreign key definitions because the definitions will be lost.

Transactions that fail on the master do not affect replication at all. MySQL replication is based on the binary log where MySQL writes SQL statements that modify data. A transaction that fails (for example, because of a foreign key violation, or because it is rolled back) is not written to the binary log, so it is not sent to slaves.

8.2.7 Adding and Removing InnoDB Data and Log Files

This section describes what you can do when your InnoDB tablespace runs out of room or when you want to change the size of the log files.

The easiest way to increase the size of the InnoDB tablespace is to configure it from the beginning to be auto-extending. Specify the autoextend attribute for the last data file in the tablespace definition. Then InnoDB increases the size of that file automatically in 8MB increments when it runs out of space. The increment size can be changed by setting the value of the innodb_autoextend_increment system variable, which is measured in MB.

Alternatively, you can increase the size of your tablespace by adding another data file. To do this, you have to shut down the MySQL server, change the tablespace configuration to add a new data file to the end of innodb_data_file_path, and start the server again.

If your last data file was defined with the keyword autoextend, the procedure for reconfiguring the tablespace must take into account the size to which the last data file has grown.

Obtain the size of the data file, round it down to the closest multiple of 1024×1024 bytes (= 1MB), and specify the rounded size explicitly in `innodb_data_file_path`. Then you can add another data file. Remember that only the last data file in the `innodb_data_file_path` can be specified as auto-extending.

As an example, assume that the tablespace has just one auto-extending data file `ibdata1`:

```
innodb_data_home_dir =
innodb_data_file_path = /ibdata/ibdata1:10M:autoextend
```

Suppose that this data file, over time, has grown to 988MB. Here is the configuration line after modifying the original data file to not be auto-extending and adding another auto-extending data file:

```
innodb_data_home_dir =
innodb_data_file_path = /ibdata/ibdata1:988M;/disk2/ibdata2:50M:autoextend
```

When you add a new file to the tablespace configuration, make sure that it does not exist. `InnoDB` will create and initialize the file when you restart the server.

Currently, you cannot remove a data file from the tablespace. To decrease the size of your tablespace, use this procedure:

1. Use `mysqldump` to dump all your `InnoDB` tables.
2. Stop the server.
3. Remove all the existing tablespace files.
4. Configure a new tablespace.
5. Restart the server.
6. Import the dump files.

If you want to change the number or the size of your `InnoDB` log files, you have to stop the MySQL server and make sure that it shuts down without errors (to ensure that there is no information for outstanding transactions in the logs). Then copy the old log files into a safe place just in case something went wrong in the shutdown and you need them to recover the tablespace. Delete the old log files from the log file directory, edit `my.cnf` to change the log file configuration, and start the MySQL server again. `mysqld` sees that no log files exist at startup and tells you that it is creating new ones.

8.2.8 Backing Up and Recovering an `InnoDB` Database

The key to safe database management is making regular backups.

`InnoDB Hot Backup` is an online backup tool you can use to backup your `InnoDB` database while it is running. `InnoDB Hot Backup` does not require you to shut down your database and it does not set any locks or disturb your normal database processing. `InnoDB Hot Backup` is a non-free (commercial) add-on tool with an annual license fee of , 390 per computer on which the MySQL server is run. See the `InnoDB Hot Backup` home page (`http://www.innodb.com/order.html`) for detailed information and screenshots.

If you are able to shut down your MySQL server, you can make a binary backup that consists of all files used by InnoDB to manage its tables. Use the following procedure:

1. Shut down your MySQL server and make sure that it shuts down without errors.
2. Copy all your data files (ibdata files and .ibd files) into a safe place.
3. Copy all your ib_logfile files to a safe place.
4. Copy your my.cnf configuration file or files to a safe place.
5. Copy all the .frm files for your InnoDB tables to a safe place.

Replication works with InnoDB tables, so you can use MySQL replication capabilities to keep a copy of your database at database sites requiring high availability.

In addition to making binary backups as just described, you should also regularly make dumps of your tables with mysqldump. The reason for this is that a binary file might be corrupted without you noticing it. Dumped tables are stored into text files that are human-readable, so spotting table corruption becomes easier. Also, because the format is simpler, the chance for serious data corruption is smaller. mysqldump also has a --single-transaction option that you can use to make a consistent snapshot without locking out other clients.

To be able to recover your InnoDB database to the present from the binary backup just described, you have to run your MySQL server with binary logging turned on. Then you can apply the binary log to the backup database to achieve point-in-time recovery:

```
mysqlbinlog yourhostname-bin.123 | mysql
```

To recover from a crash of your MySQL server, the only requirement is to restart it. InnoDB automatically checks the logs and performs a roll-forward of the database to the present. InnoDB automatically rolls back uncommitted transactions that were present at the time of the crash. During recovery, mysqld displays output something like this:

```
InnoDB: Database was not shut down normally.
InnoDB: Starting recovery from log files...
InnoDB: Starting log scan based on checkpoint at
InnoDB: log sequence number 0 13674004
InnoDB: Doing recovery: scanned up to log sequence number 0 13739520
InnoDB: Doing recovery: scanned up to log sequence number 0 13805056
InnoDB: Doing recovery: scanned up to log sequence number 0 13870592
InnoDB: Doing recovery: scanned up to log sequence number 0 13936128
...
InnoDB: Doing recovery: scanned up to log sequence number 0 20555264
InnoDB: Doing recovery: scanned up to log sequence number 0 20620800
InnoDB: Doing recovery: scanned up to log sequence number 0 20664692
InnoDB: 1 uncommitted transaction(s) which must be rolled back
InnoDB: Starting rollback of uncommitted transactions
InnoDB: Rolling back trx no 16745
InnoDB: Rolling back of trx no 16745 completed
InnoDB: Rollback of uncommitted transactions completed
InnoDB: Starting an apply batch of log records to the database...
```

```
InnoDB: Apply batch completed
InnoDB: Started
mysqld: ready for connections
```

If your database gets corrupted or your disk fails, you have to do the recovery from a back-up. In the case of corruption, you should first find a backup that is not corrupted. After restoring the base backup, do the recovery from the binary log files using `mysqlbinlog` and `mysql` to restore the changes performed after the backup was made.

In some cases of database corruption it is enough just to dump, drop, and re-create one or a few corrupt tables. You can use the `CHECK TABLE` SQL statement to check whether a table is corrupt, although `CHECK TABLE` naturally cannot detect every possible kind of corruption. You can use `innodb_tablespace_monitor` to check the integrity of the file space management inside the tablespace files.

In some cases, apparent database page corruption is actually due to the operating system corrupting its own file cache, and the data on disk may be okay. It is best first to try restart-ing your computer. Doing so may eliminate errors that appeared to be database page cor-ruption.

8.2.8.1 Forcing `InnoDB` Recovery

If there is database page corruption, you may want to dump your tables from the database with `SELECT INTO OUTFILE`. Usually, most of the data obtained in this way is intact. Even so, the corruption may cause `SELECT * FROM` *tbl_name* statements or `InnoDB` background opera-tions to crash or assert, or even to cause `InnoDB` roll-forward recovery to crash. However, you can force the `InnoDB` storage engine to start up while preventing background operations from running, so that you are able to dump your tables. For example, you can add the fol-lowing line to the `[mysqld]` section of your option file before restarting the server:

```
[mysqld]
innodb_force_recovery = 4
```

The allowable non-zero values for `innodb_force_recovery` follow. A larger number includes all precautions of smaller numbers. If you are able to dump your tables with an option value of at most 4, you are relatively safe that only some data on corrupt individual pages is lost. A value of 6 is more drastic because database pages are left in an obsolete state, which in turn may introduce more corruption into B-trees and other database structures.

- 1 (`SRV_FORCE_IGNORE_CORRUPT`)

  Let the server run even if it detects a corrupt page. Try to make `SELECT * FROM` *tbl_name* jump over corrupt index records and pages, which helps in dumping tables.

- 2 (`SRV_FORCE_NO_BACKGROUND`)

  Prevent the main thread from running. If a crash would occur during the purge opera-tion, this recovery value prevents it.

- 3 (`SRV_FORCE_NO_TRX_UNDO`)

  Do not run transaction rollbacks after recovery.

- 4 (SRV_FORCE_NO_IBUF_MERGE)

  Prevent also insert buffer merge operations. If they would cause a crash, do not do them. Do not calculate table statistics.

- 5 (SRV_FORCE_NO_UNDO_LOG_SCAN)

  Do not look at undo logs when starting the database: InnoDB treats even incomplete transactions as committed.

- 6 (SRV_FORCE_NO_LOG_REDO)

  Do not do the log roll-forward in connection with recovery.

You can SELECT from tables to dump them, or DROP or CREATE tables even if forced recovery is used. If you know that a given table is causing a crash on rollback, you can drop it. You can also use this to stop a runaway rollback caused by a failing mass import or ALTER TABLE. You can kill the mysqld process and set innodb_force_recovery to 3 to bring the database up without the rollback, and then DROP the table that is causing the runaway rollback.

The database must not otherwise be used with any non-zero value of innodb_force_recovery. As a safety measure, InnoDB prevents users from performing INSERT, UPDATE, or DELETE operations when innodb_force_recovery is greater than 0.

8.2.8.2 Checkpoints

InnoDB implements a checkpoint mechanism known as "fuzzy" checkpointing. InnoDB flushes modified database pages from the buffer pool in small batches. There is no need to flush the buffer pool in one single batch, which would in practice stop processing of user SQL statements during the checkpointing process.

During crash recovery, InnoDB looks for a checkpoint label written to the log files. It knows that all modifications to the database before the label are present in the disk image of the database. Then InnoDB scans the log files forward from the checkpoint, applying the logged modifications to the database.

InnoDB writes to its log files on a rotating basis. All committed modifications that make the database pages in the buffer pool different from the images on disk must be available in the log files in case InnoDB has to do a recovery. This means that when InnoDB starts to reuse a log file, it has to make sure that the database page images on disk contain the modifications logged in the log file that InnoDB is going to reuse. In other words, InnoDB must create a checkpoint and this often involves flushing of modified database pages to disk.

The preceding description explains why making your log files very large may save disk I/O in checkpointing. It often makes sense to set the total size of the log files as big as the buffer pool or even bigger. The drawback of using large log files is that crash recovery can take longer because there is more logged information to apply to the database.

8.2.9 Moving an InnoDB Database to Another Machine

On Windows, InnoDB always stores database and table names internally in lowercase. To move databases in a binary format from Unix to Windows or from Windows to Unix, you should have all table and database names in lowercase. A convenient way to accomplish this is to add the following line to the [mysqld] section of your my.cnf or my.ini file before creating any databases or tables:

```
[mysqld]
lower_case_table_names=1
```

Like MyISAM data files, InnoDB data and log files are binary-compatible on all platforms having the same floating-point number format. You can move an InnoDB database simply by copying all the relevant files listed in Section 8.2.8, "Backing Up and Recovering an InnoDB Database." If the floating-point formats differ but you have not used FLOAT or DOUBLE data types in your tables, the procedure is the same: simply copy the relevant files. If the formats differ and your tables contain floating-point data, you must use mysqldump to dump your tables on one machine and then import the dump files on the other machine.

One way to increase performance is to switch off autocommit mode when importing data, assuming that the tablespace has enough space for the big rollback segment that the import transactions generate. Do the commit only after importing a whole table or a segment of a table.

8.2.10 InnoDB **Transaction Model and Locking**

In the InnoDB transaction model, the goal is to combine the best properties of a multi-versioning database with traditional two-phase locking. InnoDB does locking on the row level and runs queries as non-locking consistent reads by default, in the style of Oracle. The lock table in InnoDB is stored so space-efficiently that lock escalation is not needed: Typically several users are allowed to lock every row in the database, or any random subset of the rows, without InnoDB running out of memory.

8.2.10.1 InnoDB **Lock Modes**

InnoDB implements standard row-level locking where there are two types of locks:

- A shared (S) lock allows a transaction to read a row (tuple).
- An exclusive (X) lock allows a transaction to update or delete a row.

If transaction T1 holds a shared (S) lock on tuple t:

- A request from some distinct transaction T2 for an S lock on t can be granted immediately. As a result, both T1 and T2 hold an S lock on t.
- A request from some distinct transaction T2 for an X lock on t cannot be granted immediately.

If a transaction T1 holds an exclusive (X) lock on tuple t, a request from some distinct transaction T2 for a lock of either type on t cannot be granted immediately. Instead, transaction T2 has to wait for transaction T1 to release its lock on tuple t.

Additionally, InnoDB supports *multiple granularity locking*, which allows coexistence of record locks and locks on entire tables. To make locking at multiple granularity levels practical, additional types of locks called "intention locks" are used. Intention locks are table locks in InnoDB. The idea behind intention locks is for a transaction to indicate which type of lock (shared or exclusive) it will require later for a row in that table. There are two types of intention locks used in InnoDB (assume that transaction T has requested a lock of the indicated type on table R):

- Intention shared (*IS*): Transaction T intends to set *S* locks on individual rows in table R.
- Intention exclusive (*IX*): Transaction T intends to set *X* locks on those rows.

The intention locking protocol is as follows:

- Before a given transaction can acquire an *S* lock on a given row, it must first acquire an *IS* or stronger lock on the table containing that row.
- Before a given transaction can acquire an *X* lock on a given row, it must first acquire an *IX* lock on the table containing that row.

These rules can be conveniently summarized by means of a *lock type compatibility matrix*:

	X	IX	S	IS
X	Conflict	Conflict	Conflict	Conflict
IX	Conflict	Compatible	Conflict	Compatible
S	Conflict	Conflict	Compatible	Compatible
IS	Conflict	Compatible	Compatible	Compatible

A lock is granted to a requesting transaction if it is compatible with existing locks. A lock is not granted to a requesting transaction if it conflicts with existing locks. A transaction waits until the conflicting existing lock is released. If a lock request conflicts with an existing lock and cannot be granted because it would cause deadlock, an error occurs.

Thus, intention locks do not block anything except full table requests (for example, LOCK TABLES ... WRITE). The main purpose of *IX* and *IS* locks is to show that someone is locking a row, or going to lock a row in the table.

The following example illustrates how an error can occur when a lock request would cause a deadlock. The example involves two clients, A and B.

First, client A creates a table containing one row, and then begins a transaction. Within the transaction, A obtains an *S* lock on the row by selecting it in share mode:

```
mysql> CREATE TABLE t (i INT) ENGINE = InnoDB;
Query OK, 0 rows affected (1.07 sec)

mysql> INSERT INTO t (i) VALUES(1);
Query OK, 1 row affected (0.09 sec)

mysql> START TRANSACTION;
Query OK, 0 rows affected (0.00 sec)
```

```
mysql> SELECT * FROM t WHERE i = 1 LOCK IN SHARE MODE;
+------+
| i    |
+------+
|    1 |
+------+
1 row in set (0.10 sec)
```

Next, client B begins a transaction and attempts to delete the row from the table:

```
mysql> START TRANSACTION;
Query OK, 0 rows affected (0.00 sec)

mysql> DELETE FROM t WHERE i = 1;
```

The delete operation requires an *X* lock. The lock cannot be granted because it is incompatible with the *S* lock that client A holds, so the request goes on the queue of lock requests for the row and client B blocks.

Finally, client A also attempts to delete the row from the table:

```
mysql> DELETE FROM t WHERE i = 1;
ERROR 1213 (40001): Deadlock found when trying to get lock;
try restarting transaction
```

Deadlock occurs here because client A needs an *X* lock to delete the row. However, that lock request cannot be granted because client B is already has a request for an *X* lock and is waiting for client A to release its *S* lock. Nor can the *S* lock held by A be upgraded to an *X* lock because of the prior request by B for an *X* lock. As a result, InnoDB generates an error for client A and releases its locks. At that point, the lock request for client B can be granted and B deletes the row from the table.

8.2.10.2 InnoDB and AUTOCOMMIT

In InnoDB, all user activity occurs inside a transaction. If the autocommit mode is enabled, each SQL statement forms a single transaction on its own. By default, MySQL starts new connections with autocommit enabled.

If the autocommit mode is switched off with SET AUTOCOMMIT = 0, we can consider that a user always has a transaction open. A SQL COMMIT or ROLLBACK statement ends the current transaction and a new one starts. A COMMIT means that the changes made in the current transaction are made permanent and become visible to other users. A ROLLBACK statement, on the other hand, cancels all modifications made by the current transaction. Both statements release all InnoDB locks that were set during the current transaction.

If the connection has autocommit enabled, the user can still perform a multiple-statement transaction by starting it with an explicit START TRANSACTION or BEGIN statement and ending it with COMMIT or ROLLBACK.

8.2.10.3 InnoDB **and** TRANSACTION ISOLATION LEVEL

In terms of the SQL:1992 transaction isolation levels, the InnoDB default is REPEATABLE READ. InnoDB offers all four transaction isolation levels described by the SQL standard. You can set the default isolation level for all connections by using the --transaction-isolation option on the command line or in an option file. For example, you can set the option in the [mysqld] section of an option file like this:

```
[mysqld]
transaction-isolation = {READ-UNCOMMITTED | READ-COMMITTED
                        | REPEATABLE-READ | SERIALIZABLE}
```

A user can change the isolation level for a single session or for all new incoming connections with the SET TRANSACTION statement. Its syntax is as follows:

```
SET [SESSION | GLOBAL] TRANSACTION ISOLATION LEVEL
                    {READ UNCOMMITTED | READ COMMITTED
                    | REPEATABLE READ | SERIALIZABLE}
```

Note that there are hyphens in the level names for the --transaction-isolation option, but not for the SET TRANSACTION statement.

The default behavior is to set the isolation level for the next (not started) transaction. If you use the GLOBAL keyword, the statement sets the default transaction level globally for all new connections created from that point on (but not for existing connections). You need the SUPER privilege to do this. Using the SESSION keyword sets the default transaction level for all future transactions performed on the current connection.

Any client is free to change the session isolation level (even in the middle of a transaction), or the isolation level for the next transaction.

You can determine the global and session transaction isolation levels by checking the value of the tx_isolation system variable with these statements:

```
SELECT @@global.tx_isolation;
SELECT @@tx_isolation;
```

In row-level locking, InnoDB uses next-key locking. That means that besides index records, InnoDB can also lock the "gap" preceding an index record to block insertions by other users immediately before the index record. A "next-key" lock refers to a lock that locks an index record and the gap before it. A "gap" lock refers to a lock that only locks a gap before some index record.

A detailed description of each isolation level in InnoDB follows:

- READ UNCOMMITTED

  SELECT statements are performed in a non-locking fashion, but a possible earlier version of a record might be used. Thus, using this isolation level, such reads are not consistent. This is also called a "dirty read." Otherwise, this isolation level works like READ COMMITTED.

- READ COMMITTED

  A somewhat Oracle-like isolation level. All SELECT ... FOR UPDATE and SELECT ... LOCK IN SHARE MODE statements lock only the index records, not the gaps before them, and thus allow the free insertion of new records next to locked records. UPDATE and DELETE statements using a unique index with a unique search condition lock only the index record found, not the gap before it. In range-type UPDATE and DELETE statements, InnoDB must set next-key or gap locks and block insertions by other users to the gaps covered by the range. This is necessary because "phantom rows" must be blocked for MySQL replication and recovery to work.

  Consistent reads behave as in Oracle: Each consistent read, even within the same transaction, sets and reads its own fresh snapshot. See Section 8.2.10.4, "Consistent Non-Locking Read."

- REPEATABLE READ

  This is the default isolation level of InnoDB. SELECT ... FOR UPDATE, SELECT ... LOCK IN SHARE MODE, UPDATE, and DELETE statements that use a unique index with a unique search condition lock only the index record found, not the gap before it. With other search conditions, these operations employ next-key locking, locking the index range scanned with next-key or gap locks, and block new insertions by other users.

  In consistent reads, there is an important difference from the READ COMMITTED isolation level: All consistent reads within the same transaction read the same snapshot established by the first read. This convention means that if you issue several plain SELECT statements within the same transaction, these SELECT statements are consistent also with respect to each other. See Section 8.2.10.4, "Consistent Non-Locking Read."

- SERIALIZABLE

  This level is like REPEATABLE READ, but InnoDB implicitly commits all plain SELECT statements to SELECT ... LOCK IN SHARE MODE.

8.2.10.4 Consistent Non-Locking Read

A consistent read means that InnoDB uses multi-versioning to present to a query a snapshot of the database at a point in time. The query sees the changes made by those transactions that committed before that point of time, and no changes made by later or uncommitted transactions. The exception to this rule is that the query sees the changes made by earlier statements within the same transaction.

If you are running with the default REPEATABLE READ isolation level, all consistent reads within the same transaction read the snapshot established by the first such read in that transaction. You can get a fresher snapshot for your queries by committing the current transaction and after that issuing new queries.

Consistent read is the default mode in which InnoDB processes SELECT statements in READ COMMITTED and REPEATABLE READ isolation levels. A consistent read does not set any locks on the tables it accesses, and therefore other users are free to modify those tables at the same time a consistent read is being performed on the table.

Note that consistent read does not work over DROP TABLE and over ALTER TABLE. Consistent read does not work over DROP TABLE because MySQL can't use a table that has been dropped and InnoDB destroys the table. Consistent read does not work over ALTER TABLE because it is executed inside of the transaction that creates a new table and inserts rows from the old table to the new table. When you reissue the consistent read, it will not see any rows in the new table, because they were inserted in a transaction that is not visible in the snapshot read by the consistent read.

8.2.10.5 SELECT ... FOR UPDATE and SELECT ... LOCK IN SHARE MODE Locking Reads

In some circumstances, a consistent read is not convenient. For example, you might want to add a new row into your table child, and make sure that the child has a parent in table parent. The following example shows how to implement referential integrity in your application code.

Suppose that you use a consistent read to read the table parent and indeed see the parent of the child in the table. Can you safely add the child row to table child? No, because it may happen that meanwhile some other user deletes the parent row from the table parent without you being aware of it.

The solution is to perform the SELECT in a locking mode using LOCK IN SHARE MODE:

```
SELECT * FROM parent WHERE NAME = 'Jones' LOCK IN SHARE MODE;
```

Performing a read in share mode means that we read the latest available data, and set a shared mode lock on the rows we read. A shared mode lock prevents others from updating or deleting the row we have read. Also, if the latest data belongs to a yet uncommitted transaction of another client connection, we wait until that transaction commits. After we see that the preceding query returns the parent 'Jones', we can safely add the child record to the child table and commit our transaction.

Let us look at another example: We have an integer counter field in a table child_codes that we use to assign a unique identifier to each child added to table child. Obviously, using a consistent read or a shared mode read to read the present value of the counter is not a good idea because two users of the database may then see the same value for the counter, and a duplicate-key error occurs if two users attempt to add children with the same identifier to the table.

Here, LOCK IN SHARE MODE is not a good solution because if two users read the counter at the same time, at least one of them ends up in deadlock when attempting to update the counter.

In this case, there are two good ways to implement the reading and incrementing of the counter: (1) update the counter first by incrementing it by 1 and only after that read it, or (2) read the counter first with a lock mode FOR UPDATE, and increment after that. The latter approach can be implemented as follows:

```
SELECT counter_field FROM child_codes FOR UPDATE;
UPDATE child_codes SET counter_field = counter_field + 1;
```

A SELECT ... FOR UPDATE reads the latest available data, setting exclusive locks on each row it reads. Thus, it sets the same locks a searched SQL UPDATE would set on the rows.

The preceding description is merely an example of how SELECT ... FOR UPDATE works. In MySQL, the specific task of generating a unique identifier actually can be accomplished using only a single access to the table:

```
UPDATE child_codes SET counter_field = LAST_INSERT_ID(counter_field + 1);
SELECT LAST_INSERT_ID();
```

The SELECT statement merely retrieves the identifier information (specific to the current connection). It does not access any table.

Locks set by IN SHARE MODE and FOR UPDATE reads are released when the transaction is committed or rolled back.

8.2.10.6 Next-Key Locking: Avoiding the Phantom Problem

In row-level locking, InnoDB uses an algorithm called *next-key locking*. InnoDB performs the row-level locking in such a way that when it searches or scans an index of a table, it sets shared or exclusive locks on the index records it encounters. Thus, the row-level locks are actually index record locks.

The locks InnoDB sets on index records also affect the "gap" before that index record. If a user has a shared or exclusive lock on record R in an index, another user cannot insert a new index record immediately before R in the index order. This locking of gaps is done to prevent the so-called "phantom problem." Suppose that you want to read and lock all children from the child table having an identifier value greater than 100, with the intention of updating some column in the selected rows later:

```
SELECT * FROM child WHERE id > 100 FOR UPDATE;
```

Suppose that there is an index on the id column. The query scans that index starting from the first record where id is bigger than 100. If the locks set on the index records would not lock out inserts made in the gaps, a new row might meanwhile be inserted to the table. If you execute the same SELECT within the same transaction, you would see a new row in the result set returned by the query. This is contrary to the isolation principle of transactions: A transaction should be able to run so that the data it has read does not change during the transaction. If we regard a set of rows as a data item, the new "phantom" child would violate this isolation principle.

When InnoDB scans an index, it can also lock the gap after the last record in the index. Just that happens in the previous example: The locks set by InnoDB prevent any insert to the table where id would be bigger than 100.

You can use next-key locking to implement a uniqueness check in your application: If you read your data in share mode and do not see a duplicate for a row you are going to insert, you can safely insert your row and know that the next-key lock set on the successor of your row during the read prevents anyone meanwhile inserting a duplicate for your row. Thus, the next-key locking allows you to "lock" the non-existence of something in your table.

8.2.10.7 An Example of Consistent Read in InnoDB

Suppose that you are running in the default REPEATABLE READ isolation level. When you issue a consistent read (that is, an ordinary SELECT statement), InnoDB gives your transaction a timepoint according to which your query sees the database. If another transaction deletes a row and commits after your timepoint was assigned, you do not see the row as having been deleted. Inserts and updates are treated similarly.

You can advance your timepoint by committing your transaction and then doing another SELECT.

This is called "multi-versioned concurrency control."

```
                User A                    User B

              SET AUTOCOMMIT=0;         SET AUTOCOMMIT=0;
time
|             SELECT * FROM t;
|             empty set
|                                       INSERT INTO t VALUES (1, 2);
|
v             SELECT * FROM t;
              empty set
                                        COMMIT;

              SELECT * FROM t;
              empty set

              COMMIT;

              SELECT * FROM t;
              --------------------
              |   1   |   2   |
              --------------------
              1 row in set
```

In this example, user A sees the row inserted by B only when B has committed the insert and A has committed as well, so that the timepoint is advanced past the commit of B.

If you want to see the freshest state of the database, you should use either the READ COMMITTED isolation level or a locking read:

```
SELECT * FROM t LOCK IN SHARE MODE;
```

8.2.10.8 Locks Set by Different SQL Statements in InnoDB

A locking read, an UPDATE, or a DELETE generally set record locks on every index record that is scanned in the processing of the SQL statement. It does not matter if there are WHERE conditions in the statement that would exclude the row. InnoDB does not remember the exact WHERE condition, but only knows which index ranges were scanned. The record locks are normally next-key locks that also block inserts to the "gap" immediately before the record.

If the locks to be set are exclusive, InnoDB always retrieves also the clustered index record and sets a lock on it.

If you do not have indexes suitable for your statement and MySQL has to scan the whole table to process the statement, every row of the table becomes locked, which in turn blocks all inserts by other users to the table. It is important to create good indexes so that your queries do not unnecessarily need to scan many rows.

InnoDB sets specific types of locks as follows:

- SELECT ... FROM is a consistent read, reading a snapshot of the database and setting no locks unless the transaction isolation level is set to SERIALIZABLE. For SERIALIZABLE level, this sets shared next-key locks on the index records it encounters.

- SELECT ... FROM ... LOCK IN SHARE MODE sets shared next-key locks on all index records the read encounters.

- SELECT ... FROM ... FOR UPDATE sets exclusive next-key locks on all index records the read encounters.

- INSERT INTO ... VALUES (...) sets an exclusive lock on the inserted row. Note that this lock is not a next-key lock and does not prevent other users from inserting to the gap before the inserted row. If a duplicate-key error occurs, a shared lock on the duplicate index record is set.

- While initializing a previously specified AUTO_INCREMENT column on a table, InnoDB sets an exclusive lock on the end of the index associated with the AUTO_INCREMENT column. In accessing the auto-increment counter, InnoDB uses a specific table lock mode AUTO-INC where the lock lasts only to the end of the current SQL statement, not to the end of the entire transaction. Note that other clients cannot insert into the table while the AUTO-INC table lock is held; see Section 8.2.10.2, "InnoDB and AUTOCOMMIT."

  InnoDB fetches the value of a previously initialized AUTO_INCREMENT column without setting any locks.

- INSERT INTO T SELECT ... FROM S WHERE ... sets an exclusive (non-next-key) lock on each row inserted into T. InnoDB sets shared next-key locks on S, unless innodb_locks_unsafe_for_binlog is enabled, in which case it does the search on S as a consistent read. InnoDB has to set locks in the latter case: In roll-forward recovery from a backup, every SQL statement has to be executed in exactly the same way it was done originally.

- CREATE TABLE ... SELECT ... performs the SELECT as a consistent read or with shared locks, as in the previous item.

- REPLACE is done like an insert if there is no collision on a unique key. Otherwise, an exclusive next-key lock is placed on the row that has to be updated.

- UPDATE ... WHERE ... sets an exclusive next-key lock on every record the search encounters.

- DELETE FROM ... WHERE ... sets an exclusive next-key lock on every record the search encounters.

- If a FOREIGN KEY constraint is defined on a table, any insert, update, or delete that requires the constraint condition to be checked sets shared record-level locks on the records that it looks at to check the constraint. InnoDB also sets these locks in the case where the constraint fails.

- LOCK TABLES sets table locks, but it is the higher MySQL layer above the InnoDB layer that sets these locks. InnoDB is aware of table locks if innodb_table_locks=1 (the default) and AUTOCOMMIT=0, and the MySQL layer above InnoDB knows about row-level locks. Otherwise, InnoDB's automatic deadlock detection cannot detect deadlocks where such table locks are involved. Also, because the higher MySQL layer does not know about row-level locks, it is possible to get a table lock on a table where another user currently has row-level locks. However, this does not endanger transaction integrity, as discussed in Section 8.2.10.10, "Deadlock Detection and Rollback." See also Section 8.2.16, "Restrictions on InnoDB Tables."

8.2.10.9 Implicit Transaction Commit and Rollback

By default, MySQL begins each client connection with autocommit mode enabled. When autocommit is enabled, MySQL does a commit after each SQL statement if that statement did not return an error. If an SQL statement returns an error, the commit or rollback behavior depends on the error. See Section 8.2.15, "InnoDB Error Handling."

If you have the autocommit mode off and close a connection without explicitly committing the final transaction, MySQL rolls back that transaction.

Each of the following statements (and any synonyms for them) implicitly end a transaction, as if you had done a COMMIT before executing the statement:

- ALTER FUNCTION, ALTER PROCEDURE, ALTER TABLE, BEGIN, CREATE DATABASE, CREATE FUNCTION, CREATE INDEX, CREATE PROCEDURE, CREATE TABLE, DROP DATABASE, DROP FUNCTION, DROP INDEX, DROP PROCEDURE, DROP TABLE, LOAD MASTER DATA, LOCK TABLES, RENAME TABLE, SET AUTOCOMMIT=1, START TRANSACTION, TRUNCATE, UNLOCK TABLES.

- UNLOCK TABLES commits a transaction only if any tables are currently locked.

- The CREATE TABLE, CREATE DATABASE, DROP DATABASE, and TRUNCATE TABLE statements cause an implicit commit beginning with MySQL 5.0.8. The ALTER FUNCTION, ALTER PROCEDURE, CREATE FUNCTION, CREATE PROCEDURE, DROP FUNCTION, and DROP PROCEDURE statements cause an implicit commit beginning with MySQL 5.0.13.

- The CREATE TABLE statement in InnoDB is processed as a single transaction. This means that a ROLLBACK from the user does not undo CREATE TABLE statements the user made during that transaction.

Transactions cannot be nested. This is a consequence of the implicit COMMIT performed for any current transaction when you issue a START TRANSACTION statement or one of its synonyms.

8.2.10.10 Deadlock Detection and Rollback

InnoDB automatically detects a deadlock of transactions and rolls back a transaction or transactions to break the deadlock. InnoDB tries to pick small transactions to roll back, where the size of a transaction is determined by the number of rows inserted, updated, or deleted.

InnoDB is aware of table locks if innodb_table_locks=1 (the default) and AUTOCOMMIT=0, and the MySQL layer above it knows about row-level locks. Otherwise, InnoDB cannot detect deadlocks where a table lock set by a MySQL LOCK TABLES statement or a lock set by a storage engine other than InnoDB is involved. You must resolve these situations by setting the value of the innodb_lock_wait_timeout system variable.

When InnoDB performs a complete rollback of a transaction, all locks set by the transaction are released. However, if just a single SQL statement is rolled back as a result of an error, some of the locks set by the statement may be preserved. This happens because InnoDB stores row locks in a format such that it cannot know afterward which lock was set by which statement.

8.2.10.11 How to Cope with Deadlocks

Deadlocks are a classic problem in transactional databases, but they are not dangerous unless they are so frequent that you cannot run certain transactions at all. Normally, you must write your applications so that they are always prepared to re-issue a transaction if it gets rolled back because of a deadlock.

InnoDB uses automatic row-level locking. You can get deadlocks even in the case of transactions that just insert or delete a single row. That is because these operations are not really "atomic"; they automatically set locks on the (possibly several) index records of the row inserted or deleted.

You can cope with deadlocks and reduce the likelihood of their occurrence with the following techniques:

- Use SHOW ENGINE INNODB STATUS to determine the cause of the latest deadlock. That can help you to tune your application to avoid deadlocks.

- Always be prepared to re-issue a transaction if it fails due to deadlock. Deadlocks are not dangerous. Just try again.

- Commit your transactions often. Small transactions are less prone to collision.

- If you are using locking reads (SELECT ... FOR UPDATE or ... LOCK IN SHARE MODE), try using a lower isolation level such as READ COMMITTED.

- Access your tables and rows in a fixed order. Then transactions form well-defined queues and do not deadlock.

- Add well-chosen indexes to your tables. Then your queries need to scan fewer index records and consequently set fewer locks. Use EXPLAIN SELECT to determine which indexes the MySQL server regards as the most appropriate for your queries.

- Use less locking. If you can afford to allow a SELECT to return data from an old snapshot, do not add the clause FOR UPDATE or LOCK IN SHARE MODE to it. Using the READ

COMMITTED isolation level is good here, because each consistent read within the same transaction reads from its own fresh snapshot.

- If nothing else helps, serialize your transactions with table-level locks. The correct way to use LOCK TABLES with transactional tables, such as InnoDB tables, is to set AUTOCOMMIT = 0 and not to call UNLOCK TABLES until after you commit the transaction explicitly. For example, if you need to write to table t1 and read from table t2, you can do this:

```
SET AUTOCOMMIT=0;
LOCK TABLES t1 WRITE, t2 READ, ...;
... do something with tables t1 and t2 here ...
COMMIT;
UNLOCK TABLES;
```

Table-level locks make your transactions queue nicely, and deadlocks are avoided.

- Another way to serialize transactions is to create an auxiliary "semaphore" table that contains just a single row. Have each transaction update that row before accessing other tables. In that way, all transactions happen in a serial fashion. Note that the InnoDB instant deadlock detection algorithm also works in this case, because the serializing lock is a row-level lock. With MySQL table-level locks, the timeout method must be used to resolve deadlocks.

- In applications that use the LOCK TABLES command, MySQL does not set InnoDB table locks if AUTOCOMMIT=1.

8.2.11 InnoDB Performance Tuning Tips

- If the Unix top tool or the Windows Task Manager shows that the CPU usage percentage with your workload is less than 70%, your workload is probably disk-bound. Maybe you are making too many transaction commits, or the buffer pool is too small. Making the buffer pool bigger can help, but do not set it equal to more than 80% of physical memory.

- Wrap several modifications into one transaction. InnoDB must flush the log to disk at each transaction commit if that transaction made modifications to the database. The rotation speed of a disk is typically at most 167 revolutions/second, which constrains the number of commits to the same 167th of a second if the disk does not "fool" the operating system.

- If you can afford the loss of some of the latest committed transactions if a crash occurs, you can set the innodb_flush_log_at_trx_commit parameter to 0. InnoDB tries to flush the log once per second anyway, although the flush is not guaranteed.

- Make your log files big, even as big as the buffer pool. When InnoDB has written the log files full, it has to write the modified contents of the buffer pool to disk in a checkpoint. Small log files cause many unnecessary disk writes. The drawback of big log files is that the recovery time is longer.

- Make the log buffer quite large as well (on the order of 8MB).

- Use the VARCHAR data type instead of CHAR if you are storing variable-length strings or if the column may contain many NULL values. A CHAR(N) column always takes N characters to store data, even if the string is shorter or its value is NULL. Smaller tables fit better in the buffer pool and reduce disk I/O.

  When using row_format=compact (the default InnoDB record format in MySQL 5.0) and variable-length character sets, such as utf8 or sjis, CHAR(N) will occupy a variable amount of space, at least N bytes.

- In some versions of GNU/Linux and Unix, flushing files to disk with the Unix fsync() call (which InnoDB uses by default) and other similar methods is surprisingly slow. If you are dissatisfied with database write performance, you might try setting the innodb_flush_method parameter to O_DSYNC. Although O_DSYNC seems to be slower on most systems, yours might not be one of them.

- When using the InnoDB storage engine on Solaris 10 for x86_64 architecture (AMD Opteron), it is important to mount any filesystems used for storing InnoDB-related files using the forcedirectio option. (The default on Solaris 10/x86_64 is *not* to use this option.) Failure to use forcedirectio causes a serious degradation of InnoDB's speed and performance on this platform.

  When using the InnoDB storage engine with a large innodb_buffer_pool_size value on any release of Solaris 2.6 and up and any platform (sparc/x86/x64/amd64), a significant performance gain can be achieved by placing InnoDB data files and log files on raw devices or on a separate direct I/O UFS filesystem (using mount option forcedirectio; see mount_ufs(1M)). Users of the Veritas filesystem VxFS should use the mount option convosync=direct.

  Other MySQL data files, such as those for MyISAM tables, should not be placed on a direct I/O filesystem. Executables or libraries *must not* be placed on a direct I/O filesystem.

- When importing data into InnoDB, make sure that MySQL does not have autocommit mode enabled because that requires a log flush to disk for every insert. To disable autocommit during your import operation, surround it with SET AUTOCOMMIT and COMMIT statements:

```
SET AUTOCOMMIT=0;
... SQL import statements ...
COMMIT;
```

  If you use the mysqldump option --opt, you get dump files that are fast to import into an InnoDB table, even without wrapping them with the SET AUTOCOMMIT and COMMIT statements.

- Beware of big rollbacks of mass inserts: InnoDB uses the insert buffer to save disk I/O in inserts, but no such mechanism is used in a corresponding rollback. A disk-bound rollback can take 30 times as long to perform as the corresponding insert. Killing the database process does not help because the rollback starts again on server startup. The only way to get rid of a runaway rollback is to increase the buffer pool so that the rollback becomes CPU-bound and runs fast, or to use a special procedure. See Section 8.2.8.1, "Forcing InnoDB Recovery."

- Beware also of other big disk-bound operations. Use DROP TABLE and CREATE TABLE to empty a table, not DELETE FROM *tbl_name*.

- Use the multiple-row INSERT syntax to reduce communication overhead between the client and the server if you need to insert many rows:

```
INSERT INTO yourtable VALUES (1,2), (5,5), ...;
```

  This tip is valid for inserts into any table, not just InnoDB tables.

- If you have UNIQUE constraints on secondary keys, you can speed up table imports by temporarily turning off the uniqueness checks during the import session:

```
SET UNIQUE_CHECKS=0;
... import operation ...
SET UNIQUE_CHECKS=1;
```

  For big tables, this saves a lot of disk I/O because InnoDB can use its insert buffer to write secondary index records in a batch.

- If you have FOREIGN KEY constraints in your tables, you can speed up table imports by turning the foreign key checks off for the duration of the import session:

```
SET FOREIGN_KEY_CHECKS=0;
... import operation ...
SET FOREIGN_KEY_CHECKS=1;
```

  For big tables, this can save a lot of disk I/O.

- If you often have recurring queries for tables that are not updated frequently, use the query cache:

```
[mysqld]
query_cache_type = ON
query_cache_size = 10M
```

8.2.11.1 SHOW ENGINE INNODB STATUS and the InnoDB Monitors

InnoDB includes InnoDB Monitors that print information about the InnoDB internal state. You can use the SHOW ENGINE INNODB STATUS SQL statement at any time to fetch the output of the standard InnoDB Monitor to your SQL client. This information is useful in performance tuning. (If you are using the mysql interactive SQL client, the output is more readable if you replace the usual semicolon statement terminator with \G.) For a discussion of InnoDB lock modes, see Section 8.2.10.1, "InnoDB Lock Modes."

```
mysql> SHOW ENGINE INNODB STATUS\G
```

Another way to use InnoDB Monitors is to let them periodically write data to the standard output of the mysqld server. In this case, no output is sent to clients. When switched on, InnoDB Monitors print data about every 15 seconds. Server output usually is directed to the .err log in the MySQL data directory. This data is useful in performance tuning. On Windows, you must start the server from a command prompt in a console window with the --console option if you want to direct the output to the window rather than to the error log.

Monitor output includes the following types of information:

- Table and record locks held by each active transaction
- Lock waits of a transactions
- Semaphore waits of threads
- Pending file I/O requests
- Buffer pool statistics
- Purge and insert buffer merge activity of the main InnoDB thread

To cause the standard InnoDB Monitor to write to the standard output of mysqld, use the following SQL statement:

```
CREATE TABLE innodb_monitor (a INT) ENGINE=INNODB;
```

The monitor can be stopped by issuing the following statement:

```
DROP TABLE innodb_monitor;
```

The CREATE TABLE syntax is just a way to pass a command to the InnoDB engine through MySQL's SQL parser: The only things that matter are the table name innodb_monitor and that it be an InnoDB table. The structure of the table is not relevant at all for the InnoDB Monitor. If you shut down the server, the monitor does not restart automatically when you restart the server. You must drop the monitor table and issue a new CREATE TABLE statement to start the monitor. (This syntax may change in a future release.)

You can use innodb_lock_monitor in a similar fashion. This is the same as innodb_monitor, except that it also provides a great deal of lock information. A separate innodb_tablespace_monitor prints a list of created file segments existing in the tablespace and validates the tablespace allocation data structures. In addition, there is innodb_table_monitor with which you can print the contents of the InnoDB internal data dictionary.

A sample of InnoDB Monitor output:

```
mysql> SHOW ENGINE INNODB STATUS\G
*************************** 1. row ***************************
Status:
=====================================
030709 13:00:59 INNODB MONITOR OUTPUT
=====================================
Per second averages calculated from the last 18 seconds
----------
SEMAPHORES
----------
OS WAIT ARRAY INFO: reservation count 413452, signal count 378357
--Thread 32782 has waited at btr0sea.c line 1477 for 0.00 seconds the
semaphore: X-lock on RW-latch at 41a28668 created in file btr0sea.c line 135
a writer (thread id 32782) has reserved it in mode wait exclusive
number of readers 1, waiters flag 1
```

Last time read locked in file btr0sea.c line 731
Last time write locked in file btr0sea.c line 1347
Mutex spin waits 0, rounds 0, OS waits 0
RW-shared spins 108462, OS waits 37964; RW-excl spins 681824, OS waits
375485

LATEST FOREIGN KEY ERROR

030709 13:00:59 Transaction:
TRANSACTION 0 290328284, ACTIVE 0 sec, process no 3195, OS thread id 34831
inserting
15 lock struct(s), heap size 2496, undo log entries 9
MySQL thread id 25, query id 4668733 localhost heikki update
insert into ibtest11a (D, B, C) values (5, 'khDk' ,'khDk')
Foreign key constraint fails for table test/ibtest11a:
,
  CONSTRAINT `0_219242` FOREIGN KEY (`A`, `D`) REFERENCES `ibtest11b` (`A`,
  `D`) ON DELETE CASCADE ON UPDATE CASCADE
Trying to add in child table, in index PRIMARY tuple:
 0: len 4; hex 80000101; asc ....;; 1: len 4; hex 80000005; asc ....;; 2:
 len 4; hex 6b68446b; asc khDk;; 3: len 6; hex 0000114e0edc; asc ...N..;; 4:
 len 7; hex 00000000c3e0a7; asc ....;; 5: len 4; hex 6b68446b; asc khDk;;
But in parent table test/ibtest11b, in index PRIMARY,
the closest match we can find is record:
RECORD: info bits 0 0: len 4; hex 8000015b; asc ...[;; 1: len 4; hex
80000005; asc ....;; 2: len 3; hex 6b6864; asc khd;; 3: len 6; hex
0000111ef3eb; asc ......;; 4: len 7; hex 800001001e0084; asc ....;; 5:
len 3; hex 6b6864; asc khd;;

LATEST DETECTED DEADLOCK

030709 12:59:58
*** (1) TRANSACTION:
TRANSACTION 0 290252780, ACTIVE 1 sec, process no 3185, OS thread id 30733
inserting
LOCK WAIT 3 lock struct(s), heap size 320, undo log entries 146
MySQL thread id 21, query id 4553379 localhost heikki update
INSERT INTO alex1 VALUES(86, 86, 794,'aA35818','bb','c79166','d4766t',
'e187358f','g84586','h794',date_format('2001-04-03 12:54:22','%Y-%m-%d
%H:%i'),7
*** (1) WAITING FOR THIS LOCK TO BE GRANTED:
RECORD LOCKS space id 0 page no 48310 n bits 568 table test/alex1 index
symbole trx id 0 290252780 lock mode S waiting
Record lock, heap no 324 RECORD: info bits 0 0: len 7; hex 61613335383138;
asc aa35818;; 1:
*** (2) TRANSACTION:
TRANSACTION 0 290251546, ACTIVE 2 sec, process no 3190, OS thread id 32782
inserting
130 lock struct(s), heap size 11584, undo log entries 437

```
MySQL thread id 23, query id 4554396 localhost heikki update
REPLACE INTO alex1 VALUES(NULL, 32, NULL,'aa3572','','c3572','d6012t','',
NULL,'h396', NULL, NULL, 7.31,7.31,7.31,200)
*** (2) HOLDS THE LOCK(S):
RECORD LOCKS space id 0 page no 48310 n bits 568 table test/alex1 index
symbole trx id 0 290251546 lock_mode X locks rec but not gap
Record lock, heap no 324 RECORD: info bits 0 0: len 7; hex 61613335383138;
asc aa35818;; 1:
*** (2) WAITING FOR THIS LOCK TO BE GRANTED:
RECORD LOCKS space id 0 page no 48310 n bits 568 table test/alex1 index
symbole trx id 0 290251546 lock_mode X locks gap before rec insert intention
waiting
Record lock, heap no 82 RECORD: info bits 0 0: len 7; hex 61613335373230;
asc aa35720;; 1:
*** WE ROLL BACK TRANSACTION (1)
------------
TRANSACTIONS
------------
Trx id counter 0 290328385
Purge done for trx's n:o < 0 290315608 undo n:o < 0 17
Total number of lock structs in row lock hash table 70
LIST OF TRANSACTIONS FOR EACH SESSION:
---TRANSACTION 0 0, not started, process no 3491, OS thread id 42002
MySQL thread id 32, query id 4668737 localhost heikki
show innodb status
---TRANSACTION 0 290328384, ACTIVE 0 sec, process no 3205, OS thread id
38929 inserting
1 lock struct(s), heap size 320
MySQL thread id 29, query id 4668736 localhost heikki update
insert into speedc values (1519229,1, 'hgjhjgghggjgjgjgjgjggjgjgjgjgjgggjgjg
jlhhgghggggghhjhghggggggghjhghghghghghghhhhghghghjhhjghjghjkghjghjghjghjfhjfh
---TRANSACTION 0 290328383, ACTIVE 0 sec, process no 3180, OS thread id
28684 committing
1 lock struct(s), heap size 320, undo log entries 1
MySQL thread id 19, query id 4668734 localhost heikki update
insert into speedcm values (1603393,1, 'hgjhjgghggjgjgjgjgjggjgjgjgjgjgggjgj
gjlhhgghggggghhjhghggggggghjhghghghghghghhhhghghghjhhjghjghjkghjghjghjghjfhjf
---TRANSACTION 0 290328327, ACTIVE 0 sec, process no 3200, OS thread id
36880 starting index read
LOCK WAIT 2 lock struct(s), heap size 320
MySQL thread id 27, query id 4668644 localhost heikki Searching rows for
update
update ibtest11a set B = 'kHdkkkk' where A = 89572
------- TRX HAS BEEN WAITING 0 SEC FOR THIS LOCK TO BE GRANTED:
RECORD LOCKS space id 0 page no 65556 n bits 232 table test/ibtest11a index
PRIMARY trx id 0 290328327 lock_mode X waiting
Record lock, heap no 1 RECORD: info bits 0 0: len 9; hex 73757072656d756d00;
asc supremum.;;
```

```
------------------
---TRANSACTION 0 290328284, ACTIVE 0 sec, process no 3195, OS thread id
34831 rollback of SQL statement
ROLLING BACK 14 lock struct(s), heap size 2496, undo log entries 9
MySQL thread id 25, query id 4668733 localhost heikki update
insert into ibtest11a (D, B, C) values (5, 'khDk' ,'khDk')
---TRANSACTION 0 290327208, ACTIVE 1 sec, process no 3190, OS thread id
32782
58 lock struct(s), heap size 5504, undo log entries 159
MySQL thread id 23, query id 4668732 localhost heikki update
REPLACE INTO alex1 VALUES(86, 46, 538,'aa95666','bb','c95666','d9486t',
'e200498f','g86814','h538',date_format('2001-04-03 12:54:22','%Y-%m-%d
%H:%i'),
---TRANSACTION 0 290323325, ACTIVE 3 sec, process no 3185, OS thread id
30733 inserting
4 lock struct(s), heap size 1024, undo log entries 165
MySQL thread id 21, query id 4668735 localhost heikki update
INSERT INTO alex1 VALUES(NULL, 49, NULL,'aa42837','','c56319','d1719t','',
NULL,'h321', NULL, NULL, 7.31,7.31,7.31,200)
--------
FILE I/O
--------
I/O thread 0 state: waiting for i/o request (insert buffer thread)
I/O thread 1 state: waiting for i/o request (log thread)
I/O thread 2 state: waiting for i/o request (read thread)
I/O thread 3 state: waiting for i/o request (write thread)
Pending normal aio reads: 0, aio writes: 0,
 ibuf aio reads: 0, log i/o's: 0, sync i/o's: 0
Pending flushes (fsync) log: 0; buffer pool: 0
151671 OS file reads, 94747 OS file writes, 8750 OS fsyncs
25.44 reads/s, 18494 avg bytes/read, 17.55 writes/s, 2.33 fsyncs/s
-------------------------------------
INSERT BUFFER AND ADAPTIVE HASH INDEX
-------------------------------------
Ibuf for space 0: size 1, free list len 19, seg size 21,
85004 inserts, 85004 merged recs, 26669 merges
Hash table size 207619, used cells 14461, node heap has 16 buffer(s)
1877.67 hash searches/s, 5121.10 non-hash searches/s
---
LOG
---
Log sequence number 18 1212842764
Log flushed up to   18 1212665295
Last checkpoint at  18 1135877290
0 pending log writes, 0 pending chkp writes
4341 log i/o's done, 1.22 log i/o's/second
```

```
----------------------
BUFFER POOL AND MEMORY
----------------------
Total memory allocated 84966343; in additional pool allocated 1402624
Buffer pool size    3200
Free buffers        110
Database pages      3074
Modified db pages   2674
Pending reads 0
Pending writes: LRU 0, flush list 0, single page 0
Pages read 171380, created 51968, written 194688
28.72 reads/s, 20.72 creates/s, 47.55 writes/s
Buffer pool hit rate 999 / 1000
--------------
ROW OPERATIONS
--------------
0 queries inside InnoDB, 0 queries in queue
Main thread process no. 3004, id 7176, state: purging
Number of rows inserted 3738558, updated 127415, deleted 33707, read 755779
1586.13 inserts/s, 50.89 updates/s, 28.44 deletes/s, 107.88 reads/s
----------------------------
END OF INNODB MONITOR OUTPUT
============================
```

Some notes on the output:

- If the TRANSACTIONS section reports lock waits, your applications may have lock contention. The output can also help to trace the reasons for transaction deadlocks.

- The SEMAPHORES section reports threads waiting for a semaphore and statistics on how many times threads have needed a spin or a wait on a mutex or a rw-lock semaphore. A large number of threads waiting for semaphores may be a result of disk I/O, or contention problems inside InnoDB. Contention can be due to heavy parallelism of queries or problems in operating system thread scheduling. Setting innodb_thread_concurrency smaller than the default value can help in such situations.

- The BUFFER POOL AND MEMORY section gives you statistics on pages read and written. You can calculate from these numbers how many data file I/O operations your queries currently are doing.

- The ROW OPERATIONS section shows what the main thread is doing.

InnoDB sends diagnostic output to stderr or to files, rather than to stdout or fixed-size memory buffers, to avoid potential buffer overflows. As a side effect, the output of SHOW ENGINE INNODB STATUS is written to a status file in the MySQL data directory every 15 seconds. The name of the file is innodb_status.pid, where pid is the server process ID. InnoDB removes the file for a normal shutdown. If abnormal shutdowns have occurred, instances of these status files may be present and must be removed manually. Before removing them, you might want to examine them to see whether they contain useful information about the cause of abnormal shutdowns. The innodb_status.pid file is created only if the configuration option innodb_status_file=1 is set.

8.2.12 Implementation of Multi-Versioning

Because InnoDB is a multi-versioned storage engine, it must keep information about old versions of rows in the tablespace. This information is stored in a data structure called a "rollback segment" (after an analogous data structure in Oracle).

Internally, InnoDB adds two fields to each row stored in the database. A 6-byte field indicates the transaction identifier for the last transaction that inserted or updated the row. Also, a deletion is treated internally as an update where a special bit in the row is set to mark it as deleted. Each row also contains a 7-byte field called the roll pointer. The roll pointer points to an undo log record written to the rollback segment. If the row was updated, the undo log record contains the information necessary to rebuild the content of the row before it was updated.

InnoDB uses the information in the rollback segment to perform the undo operations needed in a transaction rollback. It also uses the information to build earlier versions of a row for a consistent read.

Undo logs in the rollback segment are divided into insert and update undo logs. Insert undo logs are needed only in transaction rollback and can be discarded as soon as the transaction commits. Update undo logs are used also in consistent reads, but they can be discarded only after there is no transaction present for which InnoDB has assigned a snapshot that in a consistent read could need the information in the update undo log to build an earlier version of a database row.

You must remember to commit your transactions regularly, including those transactions that issue only consistent reads. Otherwise, InnoDB cannot discard data from the update undo logs, and the rollback segment may grow too big, filling up your tablespace.

The physical size of an undo log record in the rollback segment is typically smaller than the corresponding inserted or updated row. You can use this information to calculate the space need for your rollback segment.

In the InnoDB multi-versioning scheme, a row is not physically removed from the database immediately when you delete it with an SQL statement. Only when InnoDB can discard the update undo log record written for the deletion can it also physically remove the corresponding row and its index records from the database. This removal operation is called a "purge," and it is quite fast, usually taking the same order of time as the SQL statement that did the deletion.

In a scenario where the user inserts and deletes rows in smallish batches at about the same rate in the table, it is possible that the purge thread starts to lag behind, and the table grows bigger and bigger, making everything disk-bound and very slow. Even if the table carries just 10MB of useful data, it may grow to occupy 10GB with all the "dead" rows. In such a case, it would be good to throttle new row operations, and allocate more resources to the purge thread. The innodb_max_purge_lag system variable exists for exactly this purpose. See Section 8.2.4, "InnoDB Startup Options and System Variables," for more information.

8.2.13 InnoDB **Table and Index Structures**

MySQL stores its data dictionary information for tables in .frm files in database directories. This is true for all MySQL storage engines. But every InnoDB table also has its own entry in the InnoDB internal data dictionary inside the tablespace. When MySQL drops a table or a database, it has to delete both an .frm file or files, and the corresponding entries inside the InnoDB data dictionary. This is the reason why you cannot move InnoDB tables between databases simply by moving the .frm files.

Every InnoDB table has a special index called the "clustered index" where the data for the rows is stored. If you define a PRIMARY KEY on your table, the index of the primary key is the clustered index.

If you do not define a PRIMARY KEY for your table, MySQL picks the first UNIQUE index that has only NOT NULL columns as the primary key and InnoDB uses it as the clustered index. If there is no such index in the table, InnoDB internally generates a clustered index where the rows are ordered by the row ID that InnoDB assigns to the rows in such a table. The row ID is a 6-byte field that increases monotonically as new rows are inserted. Thus, the rows ordered by the row ID are physically in insertion order.

Accessing a row through the clustered index is fast because the row data is on the same page where the index search leads. If a table is large, the clustered index architecture often saves a disk I/O when compared to the traditional solution. (In many database systems, data storage uses a different page from the index record.)

In InnoDB, the records in non-clustered indexes (also called "secondary" indexes) contain the primary key value for the row. InnoDB uses this primary key value to search for the row from the clustered index. Note that if the primary key is long, the secondary indexes use more space.

InnoDB compares CHAR and VARCHAR strings of different lengths such that the remaining length in the shorter string is treated as if it were padded with spaces.

8.2.13.1 Physical Structure of an Index

All InnoDB indexes are B-trees where the index records are stored in the leaf pages of the tree. The default size of an index page is 16KB. When new records are inserted, InnoDB tries to leave 1/16 of the page free for future insertions and updates of the index records.

If index records are inserted in a sequential order (ascending or descending), the resulting index pages are about 15/16 full. If records are inserted in a random order, the pages are from 1/2 to 15/16 full. If the fill factor of an index page drops below 1/2, InnoDB tries to contract the index tree to free the page.

8.2.13.2 Insert Buffering

It is a common situation in database applications that the primary key is a unique identifier and new rows are inserted in the ascending order of the primary key. Thus, the insertions to the clustered index do not require random reads from a disk.

On the other hand, secondary indexes are usually non-unique, and insertions into secondary indexes happen in a relatively random order. This would cause a lot of random disk I/O operations without a special mechanism used in InnoDB.

If an index record should be inserted to a non-unique secondary index, InnoDB checks whether the secondary index page is in the buffer pool. If that is the case, InnoDB does the insertion directly to the index page. If the index page is not found in the buffer pool, InnoDB inserts the record to a special insert buffer structure. The insert buffer is kept so small that it fits entirely in the buffer pool, and insertions can be done very fast.

Periodically, the insert buffer is merged into the secondary index trees in the database. Often it is possible to merge several insertions to the same page of the index tree, saving disk I/O operations. It has been measured that the insert buffer can speed up insertions into a table up to 15 times.

The insert buffer merging may continue to happen *after* the inserting transaction has been committed. In fact, it may continue to happen after a server shutdown and restart (see Section 8.2.8.1, "Forcing InnoDB Recovery").

The insert buffer merging may take many hours, when many secondary indexes must be updated, and many rows have been inserted. During this time, disk I/O will be increased, which can cause significant slowdown on disk-bound queries. Another significant background I/O operation is the purge thread (see Section 8.2.12, "Implementation of Multi-Versioning").

8.2.13.3 Adaptive Hash Indexes

If a table fits almost entirely in main memory, the fastest way to perform queries on it is to use hash indexes. InnoDB has a mechanism that monitors index searches made to the indexes defined for a table. If InnoDB notices that queries could benefit from building a hash index, it does so automatically.

Note that the hash index is always built based on an existing B-tree index on the table. InnoDB can build a hash index on a prefix of any length of the key defined for the B-tree, depending on the pattern of searches that InnoDB observes for the B-tree index. A hash index can be partial: It is not required that the whole B-tree index is cached in the buffer pool. InnoDB builds hash indexes on demand for those pages of the index that are often accessed.

In a sense, InnoDB tailors itself through the adaptive hash index mechanism to ample main memory, coming closer to the architecture of main-memory databases.

8.2.13.4 Physical Row Structure

Records in InnoDB tables have the following characteristics:

- Each index record contains a six-byte header. The header is used to link together consecutive records, and also in row-level locking.
- Records in the clustered index contain fields for all user-defined columns. In addition, there is a six-byte field for the transaction ID and a seven-byte field for the roll pointer.

- If no primary key was defined for a table, each clustered index record also contains a six-byte row ID field.

- Each secondary index record contains also all the fields defined for the clustered index key.

- A record contains also a pointer to each field of the record. If the total length of the fields in a record is less than 128 bytes, the pointer is one byte; otherwise, two bytes. The array of these pointers is called the "record directory." The area where these pointers point is called the "data part" of the record.

- Internally, InnoDB stores fixed-length character columns such as CHAR(10) in a fixed-length format. InnoDB truncates trailing spaces from VARCHAR columns.

- An SQL NULL value reserves 1 or 2 bytes in the record directory. Besides that, an SQL NULL value reserves zero bytes in the data part of the record if stored in a variable length column. In a fixed-length column, it reserves the fixed length of the column in the data part of the record. The motivation behind reserving the fixed space for NULL values is that it enables an update of the column from NULL to a non-NULL value to be done in place without causing fragmentation of the index page.

8.2.14 InnoDB File Space Management and Disk I/O

8.2.14.1 Disk I/O

InnoDB uses simulated asynchronous disk I/O: InnoDB creates a number of threads to take care of I/O operations, such as read-ahead.

There are two read-ahead heuristics in InnoDB:

- In sequential read-ahead, if InnoDB notices that the access pattern to a segment in the tablespace is sequential, it posts in advance a batch of reads of database pages to the I/O system.

- In random read-ahead, if InnoDB notices that some area in a tablespace seems to be in the process of being fully read into the buffer pool, it posts the remaining reads to the I/O system.

InnoDB uses a novel file flush technique called "doublewrite." It adds safety to recovery following an operating system crash or a power outage, and improves performance on most varieties of Unix by reducing the need for fsync() operations.

Doublewrite means that before writing pages to a data file, InnoDB first writes them to a contiguous tablespace area called the doublewrite buffer. Only after the write and the flush to the doublewrite buffer has completed does InnoDB write the pages to their proper positions in the data file. If the operating system crashes in the middle of a page write, InnoDB can later find a good copy of the page from the doublewrite buffer during recovery.

8.2.14.2 File Space Management

The data files that you define in the configuration file form the tablespace of InnoDB. The files are simply concatenated to form the tablespace. There is no striping in use. Currently, you cannot define where within the tablespace your tables are allocated. However, in a newly created tablespace, InnoDB allocates space starting from the first data file.

The tablespace consists of database pages with a default size of 16KB. The pages are grouped into extents of 64 consecutive pages. The "files" inside a tablespace are called "segments" in InnoDB. The term "rollback segment" is somewhat confusing because it actually contains many tablespace segments.

Two segments are allocated for each index in InnoDB. One is for non-leaf nodes of the B-tree, the other is for the leaf nodes. The idea here is to achieve better sequentiality for the leaf nodes, which contain the data.

When a segment grows inside the tablespace, InnoDB allocates the first 32 pages to it individually. After that InnoDB starts to allocate whole extents to the segment. InnoDB can add to a large segment up to 4 extents at a time to ensure good sequentiality of data.

Some pages in the tablespace contain bitmaps of other pages, and therefore a few extents in an InnoDB tablespace cannot be allocated to segments as a whole, but only as individual pages.

When you ask for available free space in the tablespace by issuing a SHOW TABLE STATUS statement, InnoDB reports the extents that are definitely free in the tablespace. InnoDB always reserves some extents for cleanup and other internal purposes; these reserved extents are not included in the free space.

When you delete data from a table, InnoDB contracts the corresponding B-tree indexes. Whether the freed space becomes available for other users depends on whether the pattern of deletes frees individual pages or extents to the tablespace. Dropping a table or deleting all rows from it is guaranteed to release the space to other users, but remember that deleted rows are physically removed only in an (automatic) purge operation after they are no longer needed for transaction rollbacks or consistent reads. (See Section 8.2.12, "Implementation of Multi-Versioning.")

8.2.14.3 Defragmenting a Table

If there are random insertions into or deletions from the indexes of a table, the indexes may become fragmented. "Fragmentation" means that the physical ordering of the index pages on the disk is not close to the index ordering of the records on the pages, or that there are many unused pages in the 64-page blocks that were allocated to the index.

A symptom of fragmentation is that a table takes more space than it "should" take. How much that is exactly, is difficult to determine. All InnoDB data and indexes are stored in B-trees, and their fill factor may vary from 50% to 100%. Another symptom of fragmentation is that a table scan such as this takes more time than it "should" take:

```
SELECT COUNT(*) FROM t WHERE a_non_indexed_column <> 12345;
```

(In the preceding query, we are "fooling" the SQL optimizer into scanning the clustered index, rather than a secondary index.) Most disks can read 10 to 50MB/s, which can be used to estimate how fast a table scan should run.

It can speed up index scans if you periodically perform a "null" ALTER TABLE operation:

```
ALTER TABLE tbl_name ENGINE=INNODB
```

That causes MySQL to rebuild the table. Another way to perform a defragmentation operation is to use mysqldump to dump the table to a text file, drop the table, and reload it from the dump file.

If the insertions to an index are always ascending and records are deleted only from the end, the InnoDB filespace management algorithm guarantees that fragmentation in the index does not occur.

8.2.15 InnoDB **Error Handling**

Error handling in InnoDB is not always the same as specified in the SQL standard. According to the standard, any error during an SQL statement should cause the rollback of that statement. InnoDB sometimes rolls back only part of the statement, or the whole transaction. The following items describe how InnoDB performs error handling:

- If you run out of file space in the tablespace, a MySQL Table is full error occurs and InnoDB rolls back the SQL statement.

- A transaction deadlock causes InnoDB to roll back the entire transaction. In the case of a lock wait timeout, InnoDB also rolls back the entire transaction before MySQL 5.0.13; as of 5.0.13, InnoDB rolls back only the most recent SQL statement.

  When a transaction rollback occurs due to a deadlock or lock wait timeout, it cancels the effect of the statements within the transaction. But if the start-transaction statement was START TRANSACTION or BEGIN statement, rollback does not cancel that statement. Further SQL statements become part of the transaction until the occurrence of COMMIT, ROLLBACK, or some SQL statement that causes an implicit commit.

- A duplicate-key error rolls back the SQL statement, if you have not specified the IGNORE option in your statement.

- A row too long error rolls back the SQL statement.

- Other errors are mostly detected by the MySQL layer of code (above the InnoDB storage engine level), and they roll back the corresponding SQL statement. Locks are not released in a rollback of a single SQL statement.

During implicit rollbacks, as well as during the execution of an explicit ROLLBACK SQL command, SHOW PROCESSLIST displays Rolling back in the State column for the relevant connection.

8.2.15.1 InnoDB Error Codes

The following is a non-exhaustive list of common InnoDB-specific errors that you may encounter, with information about why each occurs and how to resolve the problem.

- 1005 (ER_CANT_CREATE_TABLE)

  Cannot create table. If the error message refers to errno 150, table creation failed because a foreign key constraint was not correctly formed.

- 1016 (ER_CANT_OPEN_FILE)

  Cannot find the InnoDB table from the InnoDB data files, although the .frm file for the table exists. See Section 8.2.17.1, "Troubleshooting InnoDB Data Dictionary Operations."

- 1114 (ER_RECORD_FILE_FULL)

  InnoDB has run out of free space in the tablespace. You should reconfigure the table-space to add a new data file.

- 1205 (ER_LOCK_WAIT_TIMEOUT)

  Lock wait timeout expired. Transaction was rolled back.

- 1213 (ER_LOCK_DEADLOCK)

  Transaction deadlock. You should rerun the transaction.

- 1216 (ER_NO_REFERENCED_ROW)

  You are trying to add a row but there is no parent row, and a foreign key constraint fails. You should add the parent row first.

- 1217 (ER_ROW_IS_REFERENCED)

  You are trying to delete a parent row that has children, and a foreign key constraint fails. You should delete the children first.

8.2.15.2 Operating System Error Codes

To print the meaning of an operating system error number, use the perror program that comes with the MySQL distribution.

The following table provides a list of some common Linux system error codes. For a more complete list, see Linux source code (http://www.iglu.org.il/lxr/source/include/asm-i386/errno.h).

- 1 (EPERM)

  Operation not permitted

- 2 (ENOENT)

  No such file or directory

- 3 (ESRCH)

  No such process

- 4 (EINTR)

  Interrupted system call

- 5 (EIO)

  I/O error

- 6 (ENXIO)

  No such device or address

- 7 (E2BIG)

  Arg list too long

- 8 (ENOEXEC)

  Exec format error

- 9 (EBADF)

  Bad file number

- 10 (ECHILD)

  No child processes

- 11 (EAGAIN)

  Try again

- 12 (ENOMEM)

  Out of memory

- 13 (EACCES)

  Permission denied

- 14 (EFAULT)

  Bad address

- 15 (ENOTBLK)

  Block device required

- 16 (EBUSY)

  Device or resource busy

- 17 (EEXIST)

  File exists

- 18 (EXDEV)

  Cross-device link

- 19 (ENODEV)

  No such device

- 20 (ENOTDIR)

  Not a directory

- 21 (EISDIR)

  Is a directory

- 22 (EINVAL)

  Invalid argument

- 23 (ENFILE)

  File table overflow

- 24 (EMFILE)

  Too many open files

- 25 (ENOTTY)

  Inappropriate ioctl for device

- 26 (ETXTBSY)

  Text file busy

- 27 (EFBIG)

  File too large

- 28 (ENOSPC)

  No space left on device

- 29 (ESPIPE)

  Illegal seek

- 30 (EROFS)

  Read-only file system

- 31 (EMLINK)

  Too many links

The following table provides a list of some common Windows system error codes. For a complete list see the Microsoft Web site (http://msdn.microsoft.com/library/default.asp?url=/library/en-us/debug/base/system_error_codes.asp).

- 1 (ERROR_INVALID_FUNCTION)

  Incorrect function.

- 2 (ERROR_FILE_NOT_FOUND)

  The system cannot find the file specified.

- 3 (ERROR_PATH_NOT_FOUND)

  The system cannot find the path specified.

- 4 (ERROR_TOO_MANY_OPEN_FILES)

  The system cannot open the file.

- 5 (ERROR_ACCESS_DENIED)

  Access is denied.

- 6 (ERROR_INVALID_HANDLE)

  The handle is invalid.

- 7 (ERROR_ARENA_TRASHED)

  The storage control blocks were destroyed.

- 8 (ERROR_NOT_ENOUGH_MEMORY)

  Not enough storage is available to process this command.

- 9 (ERROR_INVALID_BLOCK)

  The storage control block address is invalid.

- 10 (ERROR_BAD_ENVIRONMENT)

  The environment is incorrect.

- 11 (ERROR_BAD_FORMAT)

  An attempt was made to load a program with an incorrect format.

- 12 (ERROR_INVALID_ACCESS)

  The access code is invalid.

- 13 (ERROR_INVALID_DATA)

  The data is invalid.

- 14 (ERROR_OUTOFMEMORY)

  Not enough storage is available to complete this operation.

- 15 (ERROR_INVALID_DRIVE)

  The system cannot find the drive specified.

- 16 (ERROR_CURRENT_DIRECTORY)

  The directory cannot be removed.

- 17 (ERROR_NOT_SAME_DEVICE)

  The system cannot move the file to a different disk drive.

- 18 (ERROR_NO_MORE_FILES)

  There are no more files.

- 19 (ERROR_WRITE_PROTECT)

  The media is write protected.

- 20 (ERROR_BAD_UNIT)

  The system cannot find the device specified.

- 21 (ERROR_NOT_READY)

  The device is not ready.

- 22 (ERROR_BAD_COMMAND)

  The device does not recognize the command.

- 23 (ERROR_CRC)

  Data error (cyclic redundancy check).

- 24 (ERROR_BAD_LENGTH)

  The program issued a command but the command length is incorrect.

- 25 (ERROR_SEEK)

  The drive cannot locate a specific area or track on the disk.

- 26 (ERROR_NOT_DOS_DISK)

  The specified disk or diskette cannot be accessed.

- 27 (ERROR_SECTOR_NOT_FOUND)

  The drive cannot find the sector requested.

- 28 (ERROR_OUT_OF_PAPER)

  The printer is out of paper.

- 29 (ERROR_WRITE_FAULT)

  The system cannot write to the specified device.

- 30 (ERROR_READ_FAULT)

  The system cannot read from the specified device.

- 31 (ERROR_GEN_FAILURE)

  A device attached to the system is not functioning.

- 32 (ERROR_SHARING_VIOLATION)

  The process cannot access the file because it is being used by another process.

- 33 (ERROR_LOCK_VIOLATION)

  The process cannot access the file because another process has locked a portion of the file.

- 34 (ERROR_WRONG_DISK)

  The wrong diskette is in the drive. Insert %2 (Volume Serial Number: %3) into drive %1.

- 36 (ERROR_SHARING_BUFFER_EXCEEDED)

  Too many files opened for sharing.

- 38 (ERROR_HANDLE_EOF)

  Reached the end of the file.

- 39 (ERROR_HANDLE_DISK_FULL)

  The disk is full.

- 87 (ERROR_INVALID_PARAMETER)

  The parameter is incorrect. (If this error occurs on Windows and you have enabled innodb_file_per_table in a server option file, add the line innodb_flush_method=unbuffered to the file as well.)

- 112 (ERROR_DISK_FULL)

  The disk is full.

- 123 (ERROR_INVALID_NAME)

  The filename, directory name, or volume label syntax is incorrect.

- 1450 (ERROR_NO_SYSTEM_RESOURCES)

  Insufficient system resources exist to complete the requested service.

8.2.16 Restrictions on InnoDB Tables

- **Warning**: Do *not* convert MySQL system tables in the mysql database from MyISAM to InnoDB tables! This is an unsupported operation. If you do this, MySQL does not restart until you restore the old system tables from a backup or re-generate them with the mysql_install_db script.

- A table cannot contain more than 1000 columns.

- The internal maximum key length is 3500 bytes, but MySQL itself restricts this to 1024 bytes.

- The maximum row length, except for VARCHAR, BLOB and TEXT columns, is slightly less than half of a database page. That is, the maximum row length is about 8000 bytes. LONGBLOB and LONGTEXT columns must be less than 4GB, and the total row length, including also BLOB and TEXT columns, must be less than 4GB. InnoDB stores the first 768 bytes of a VARCHAR, BLOB, or TEXT column in the row, and the rest into separate pages.

- Although InnoDB supports row sizes larger than 65535 internally, you cannot define a row containing VARCHAR columns with a combined size larger than 65535:

```
mysql> CREATE TABLE t (a VARCHAR(8000), b VARCHAR(10000),
    -> c VARCHAR(10000), d VARCHAR(10000), e VARCHAR(10000),
    -> f VARCHAR(10000), g VARCHAR(10000)) ENGINE=InnoDB;
ERROR 1118 (42000): Row size too large. The maximum row size for the
used table type, not counting BLOBs, is 65535. You have to change some
columns to TEXT or BLOBs
```

- On some older operating systems, files must be less than 2GB. This is not a limitation of InnoDB itself, but if you require a large tablespace, you will need to configure it using several smaller data files rather than one or a file large data files.

- The combined size of the InnoDB log files must be less than 4GB.

- The minimum tablespace size is 10MB. The maximum tablespace size is four billion database pages (64TB). This is also the maximum size for a table.

- InnoDB tables do not support FULLTEXT indexes.

- InnoDB tables do not support spatial data types before MySQL 5.0.16.

- ANALYZE TABLE determines index cardinality (as displayed in the Cardinality column of SHOW INDEX output) by doing eight random dives to each of the index trees and updating index cardinality estimates accordingly. Note that because these are only estimates, repeated runs of ANALYZE TABLE may produce different numbers. This makes ANALYZE TABLE fast on InnoDB tables but not 100% accurate because it doesn't take all rows into account.

  MySQL uses index cardinality estimates only in join optimization. If some join is not optimized in the right way, you can try using ANALYZE TABLE. In the few cases that ANALYZE TABLE doesn't produce values good enough for your particular tables, you can use FORCE INDEX with your queries to force the use of a particular index, or set the max_seeks_for_key system variable to ensure that MySQL prefers index lookups over table scans. See Section 4.2.2, "Server System Variables."

- SHOW TABLE STATUS does not give accurate statistics on InnoDB tables, except for the physical size reserved by the table. The row count is only a rough estimate used in SQL optimization.

- InnoDB does not keep an internal count of rows in a table. (In practice, this would be somewhat complicated due to multi-versioning.) To process a SELECT COUNT(*) FROM t statement, InnoDB must scan an index of the table, which takes some time if the index is not entirely in the buffer pool. To get a fast count, you have to use a counter table you create yourself and let your application update it according to the inserts and deletes it does. If your table does not change often, using the MySQL query cache is a good solution. SHOW TABLE STATUS also can be used if an approximate row count is sufficient. See Section 8.2.11, "InnoDB Performance Tuning Tips."

- On Windows, InnoDB always stores database and table names internally in lowercase. To move databases in binary format from Unix to Windows or from Windows to Unix, you should always use explicitly lowercase names when creating databases and tables.

- For an AUTO_INCREMENT column, you must always define an index for the table, and that index must contain just the AUTO_INCREMENT column. In MyISAM tables, the AUTO_INCREMENT column may be part of a multi-column index.

- In MySQL 5.0 before MySQL 5.0.3, InnoDB does not support the AUTO_INCREMENT table option for setting the initial sequence value in a CREATE TABLE or ALTER TABLE statement. To set the value with InnoDB, insert a dummy row with a value one less and delete that dummy row, or insert the first row with an explicit value specified.

- While initializing a previously specified AUTO_INCREMENT column on a table, InnoDB sets an exclusive lock on the end of the index associated with the AUTO_INCREMENT column. In accessing the auto-increment counter, InnoDB uses a specific table lock mode AUTO-INC where the lock lasts only to the end of the current SQL statement, not to the end of the entire transaction. Note that other clients cannot insert into the table while the AUTO-INC table lock is held; see Section 8.2.10.2, "InnoDB and AUTOCOMMIT."

- When you restart the MySQL server, InnoDB may reuse an old value that was generated for an AUTO_INCREMENT column but never stored (that is, a value that was generated during an old transaction that was rolled back).

- When an AUTO_INCREMENT column runs out of values, InnoDB wraps a BIGINT to -9223372036854775808 and BIGINT UNSIGNED to 1. However, BIGINT values have 64 bits, so do note that if you were to insert one million rows per second, it would still take nearly three hundred thousand years before BIGINT reached its upper bound. With all other integer type columns, a duplicate-key error results. This is similar to how MyISAM works, because it is mostly general MySQL behavior and not about any storage engine in particular.

- DELETE FROM *tbl_name* does not regenerate the table but instead deletes all rows, one by one.

- Under some conditions, TRUNCATE *tbl_name* for an InnoDB table is mapped to DELETE FROM *tbl_name* and doesn't reset the AUTO_INCREMENT counter.

- In MySQL 5.0, the MySQL LOCK TABLES operation acquires two locks on each table if innodb_table_locks=1 (the default). In addition to a table lock on the MySQL layer, it also acquires an InnoDB table lock. Older versions of MySQL did not acquire InnoDB table locks; the old behavior can be selected by setting innodb_table_locks=0. If no InnoDB table lock is acquired, LOCK TABLES completes even if some records of the tables are being locked by other transactions.

- All InnoDB locks held by a transaction are released when the transaction is committed or aborted. Thus, it does not make much sense to invoke LOCK TABLES on InnoDB tables in AUTOCOMMIT=1 mode, because the acquired InnoDB table locks would be released immediately.

- Sometimes it would be useful to lock further tables in the course of a transaction. Unfortunately, LOCK TABLES in MySQL performs an implicit COMMIT and UNLOCK TABLES. An InnoDB variant of LOCK TABLES has been planned that can be executed in the middle of a transaction.

- The LOAD TABLE FROM MASTER statement for setting up replication slave servers does not work for InnoDB tables. A workaround is to alter the table to MyISAM on the master, do then the load, and after that alter the master table back to InnoDB. Do not do this if the tables use InnoDB-specific features such as foreign keys.

- The default database page size in InnoDB is 16KB. By recompiling the code, you can set it to values ranging from 8KB to 64KB. You must update the values of UNIV_PAGE_SIZE and UNIV_PAGE_SIZE_SHIFT in the univ.i source file.

- Currently, triggers are not activated by cascaded foreign key actions.

- As of MySQL 5.0.19, InnoDB does not ignore trailing spaces when comparing BINARY or VARBINARY column values.

8.2.17 InnoDB **Troubleshooting**

The following general guidelines apply to troubleshooting InnoDB problems:

- When an operation fails or you suspect a bug, you should look at the MySQL server error log, which is the file in the data directory that has a suffix of .err.

- When troubleshooting, it is usually best to run the MySQL server from the command prompt, rather than through the mysqld_safe wrapper or as a Windows service. You can then see what mysqld prints to the console, and so have a better grasp of what is going on. On Windows, you must start the server with the --console option to direct the output to the console window.

- Use the InnoDB Monitors to obtain information about a problem (see Section 8.2.11.1, "SHOW ENGINE INNODB STATUS and the InnoDB Monitors"). If the problem is performance-related, or your server appears to be hung, you should use innodb_monitor to print information about the internal state of InnoDB. If the problem is with locks, use innodb_lock_monitor. If the problem is in creation of tables or other data dictionary operations, use innodb_table_monitor to print the contents of the InnoDB internal data dictionary.

- If you suspect that a table is corrupt, run CHECK TABLE on that table.

8.2.17.1 Troubleshooting InnoDB Data Dictionary Operations

A specific issue with tables is that the MySQL server keeps data dictionary information in .frm files it stores in the database directories, whereas InnoDB also stores the information into its own data dictionary inside the tablespace files. If you move .frm files around, or if the server crashes in the middle of a data dictionary operation, the locations of the .frm files may end up out of synchrony with the locations recorded in the InnoDB internal data dictionary.

A symptom of an out-of-sync data dictionary is that a CREATE TABLE statement fails. If this occurs, you should look in the server's error log. If the log says that the table already exists inside the InnoDB internal data dictionary, you have an orphaned table inside the InnoDB tablespace files that has no corresponding .frm file. The error message looks like this:

```
InnoDB: Error: table test/parent already exists in InnoDB internal
InnoDB: data dictionary. Have you deleted the .frm file
InnoDB: and not used DROP TABLE? Have you used DROP DATABASE
InnoDB: for InnoDB tables in MySQL version <= 3.23.43?
InnoDB: See the Restrictions section of the InnoDB manual.
InnoDB: You can drop the orphaned table inside InnoDB by
InnoDB: creating an InnoDB table with the same name in another
InnoDB: database and moving the .frm file to the current database.
InnoDB: Then MySQL thinks the table exists, and DROP TABLE will
InnoDB: succeed.
```

You can drop the orphaned table by following the instructions given in the error message. If you are still unable to use DROP TABLE successfully, the problem may be due to name completion in the mysql client. To work around this problem, start the mysql client with the --skip-auto-rehash option and try DROP TABLE again. (With name completion on, mysql tries to construct a list of table names, which fails when a problem such as just described exists.)

Another symptom of an out-of-sync data dictionary is that MySQL prints an error that it cannot open a .InnoDB file:

```
ERROR 1016: Can't open file: 'child2.InnoDB'. (errno: 1)
```

In the error log you can find a message like this:

```
InnoDB: Cannot find table test/child2 from the internal data dictionary
InnoDB: of InnoDB though the .frm file for the table exists. Maybe you
InnoDB: have deleted and recreated InnoDB data files but have forgotten
InnoDB: to delete the corresponding .frm files of InnoDB tables?
```

This means that there is an orphaned .frm file without a corresponding table inside InnoDB. You can drop the orphaned .frm file by deleting it manually.

If MySQL crashes in the middle of an ALTER TABLE operation, you may end up with an orphaned temporary table inside the InnoDB tablespace. Using innodb_table_monitor you can see listed a table whose name is #sql-.... You can perform SQL statements on tables whose name contains the character '#' if you enclose the name within backticks. Thus, you can drop such an orphaned table like any other orphaned table using the method described earlier. Note that to copy or rename a file in the Unix shell, you need to put the filename in double quotes if the filename contains '#'.

8.3 The MERGE Storage Engine

The MERGE storage engine, also known as the MRG_MyISAM engine, is a collection of identical MyISAM tables that can be used as one. "Identical" means that all tables have identical column and index information. You cannot merge MyISAM tables in which the columns are listed in a different order, do not have exactly the same columns, or have the indexes in different order. However, any or all of the MyISAM tables can be compressed with myisampack. See Section 7.4, "myisampack—Generate Compressed, Read-Only MyISAM Tables." Differences in table options such as AVG_ROW_LENGTH, MAX_ROWS, or PACK_KEYS do not matter.

When you create a MERGE table, MySQL creates two files on disk. The files have names that begin with the table name and have an extension to indicate the file type. An .frm file stores the table format, and an .MRG file contains the names of the tables that should be used as one. The tables do not have to be in the same database as the MERGE table itself.

You can use SELECT, DELETE, UPDATE, and INSERT on MERGE tables. You must have SELECT, UPDATE, and DELETE privileges on the MyISAM tables that you map to a MERGE table.

If you DROP the MERGE table, you are dropping only the MERGE specification. The underlying tables are not affected.

To create a MERGE table, you must specify a UNION=(list-of-tables) clause that indicates which MyISAM tables you want to use as one. You can optionally specify an INSERT_METHOD option if you want inserts for the MERGE table to take place in the first or last table of the UNION list. Use a value of FIRST or LAST to cause inserts to be made in the first or last table, respectively. If you do not specify an INSERT_METHOD option or if you specify it with a value of NO, attempts to insert rows into the MERGE table result in an error.

The following example shows how to create a MERGE table:

```
mysql> CREATE TABLE t1 (
    ->     a INT NOT NULL AUTO_INCREMENT PRIMARY KEY,
    ->     message CHAR(20)) ENGINE=MyISAM;
mysql> CREATE TABLE t2 (
    ->     a INT NOT NULL AUTO_INCREMENT PRIMARY KEY,
    ->     message CHAR(20)) ENGINE=MyISAM;
mysql> INSERT INTO t1 (message) VALUES ('Testing'),('table'),('t1');
mysql> INSERT INTO t2 (message) VALUES ('Testing'),('table'),('t2');
mysql> CREATE TABLE total (
    ->     a INT NOT NULL AUTO_INCREMENT,
    ->     message CHAR(20), INDEX(a))
    ->     ENGINE=MERGE UNION=(t1,t2) INSERT_METHOD=LAST;
```

The older term TYPE is supported as a synonym for ENGINE for backward compatibility, but ENGINE is the preferred term and TYPE is deprecated.

Note that the a column is indexed as a PRIMARY KEY in the underlying MyISAM tables, but not in the MERGE table. There it is indexed but not as a PRIMARY KEY because a MERGE table cannot enforce uniqueness over the set of underlying tables.

After creating the MERGE table, you can issue queries that operate on the group of tables as a whole:

```
mysql> SELECT * FROM total;
+---+---------+
| a | message |
+---+---------+
| 1 | Testing |
| 2 | table   |
| 3 | t1      |
| 1 | Testing |
| 2 | table   |
| 3 | t2      |
+---+---------+
```

Note that you can also manipulate the .MRG file directly from outside of the MySQL server:

```
shell> cd /mysql-data-directory/current-database
shell> ls -1 t1 t2 > total.MRG
shell> mysqladmin flush-tables
```

To remap a MERGE table to a different collection of MyISAM tables, you can use one of the following methods:

- DROP the MERGE table and re-create it.
- Use ALTER TABLE tbl_name UNION=(...) to change the list of underlying tables.
- Change the .MRG file and issue a FLUSH TABLE statement for the MERGE table and all underlying tables to force the storage engine to read the new definition file.

MERGE tables can help you solve the following problems:

- Easily manage a set of log tables. For example, you can put data from different months into separate tables, compress some of them with myisampack, and then create a MERGE table to use them as one.

- Obtain more speed. You can split a big read-only table based on some criteria, and then put individual tables on different disks. A MERGE table on this could be much faster than using the big table.

- Perform more efficient searches. If you know exactly what you are looking for, you can search in just one of the split tables for some queries and use a MERGE table for others. You can even have many different MERGE tables that use overlapping sets of tables.

- Perform more efficient repairs. It is easier to repair individual tables that are mapped to a MERGE table than to repair a single large table.

- Instantly map many tables as one. A MERGE table need not maintain an index of its own because it uses the indexes of the individual tables. As a result, MERGE table collections are *very* fast to create or remap. (Note that you must still specify the index definitions when you create a MERGE table, even though no indexes are created.)

- If you have a set of tables from which you create a large table on demand, you should instead create a MERGE table on them on demand. This is much faster and saves a lot of disk space.

- Exceed the file size limit for the operating system. Each MyISAM table is bound by this limit, but a collection of MyISAM tables is not.

- You can create an alias or synonym for a MyISAM table by defining a MERGE table that maps to that single table. There should be no really notable performance impact from doing this (only a couple of indirect calls and memcpy() calls for each read).

The disadvantages of MERGE tables are:

- You can use only identical MyISAM tables for a MERGE table.

- You cannot use a number of MyISAM features in MERGE tables. For example, you cannot create FULLTEXT indexes on MERGE tables. (You can, of course, create FULLTEXT indexes on the underlying MyISAM tables, but you cannot search the MERGE table with a full-text search.)

- If the MERGE table is non-temporary, all underlying MyISAM tables must be non-temporary, too. If the MERGE table is temporary, the MyISAM tables can be any mix of temporary and non-temporary.

- MERGE tables use more file descriptors. If 10 clients are using a MERGE table that maps to 10 tables, the server uses $(10 \times 10) + 10$ file descriptors. (10 data file descriptors for each of the 10 clients, and 10 index file descriptors shared among the clients.)

- Key reads are slower. When you read a key, the MERGE storage engine needs to issue a read on all underlying tables to check which one most closely matches the given key. To read the next key, the MERGE storage engine needs to search the read buffers to find the next key. Only when one key buffer is used up does the storage engine need to read the next key block. This makes MERGE keys much slower on eq_ref searches, but not much slower on `ref` searches. See Section 6.2.1, "Optimizing Queries with `EXPLAIN`," for more information about eq_ref and ref.

Additional resources

- A forum dedicated to the `MERGE` storage engine is available at `http://forums.mysql.com/list.php?93`.

8.3.1 MERGE Table Problems

The following are known problems with `MERGE` tables:

- If you use `ALTER TABLE` to change a `MERGE` table to another storage engine, the mapping to the underlying tables is lost. Instead, the rows from the underlying `MyISAM` tables are copied into the altered table, which then uses the specified storage engine.

- `REPLACE` does not work.

- You cannot use `DROP TABLE`, `ALTER TABLE`, `DELETE` without a `WHERE` clause, `REPAIR TABLE`, `TRUNCATE TABLE`, `OPTIMIZE TABLE`, or `ANALYZE TABLE` on any of the tables that are mapped into an open `MERGE` table. If you do so, the `MERGE` table may still refer to the original table, which yields unexpected results. The easiest way to work around this deficiency is to ensure that no `MERGE` tables remain open by issuing a `FLUSH TABLES` statement prior to performing any of those operations.

- `DROP TABLE` on a table that is in use by a `MERGE` table does not work on Windows because the `MERGE` storage engine's table mapping is hidden from the upper layer of MySQL. Windows does not allow open files to be deleted, so you first must flush all `MERGE` tables (with `FLUSH TABLES`) or drop the `MERGE` table before dropping the table.

- A `MERGE` table cannot maintain uniqueness constraints over the entire table. When you perform an `INSERT`, the data goes into the first or last `MyISAM` table (depending on the value of the `INSERT_METHOD` option). MySQL ensures that unique key values remain unique within that `MyISAM` table, but not across all the tables in the collection.

- When you create a `MERGE` table, there is no check to ensure that the underlying tables exist and have identical structures. When the `MERGE` table is used, MySQL checks that the row length for all mapped tables is equal, but this is not foolproof. If you create a `MERGE` table from dissimilar `MyISAM` tables, you are very likely to run into strange problems.

- The order of indexes in the `MERGE` table and its underlying tables should be the same. If you use `ALTER TABLE` to add a `UNIQUE` index to a table used in a `MERGE` table, and then use `ALTER TABLE` to add a non-unique index on the `MERGE` table, the index ordering is different for the tables if there was already a non-unique index in the underlying table. (This happens because `ALTER TABLE` puts `UNIQUE` indexes before non-unique indexes to facilitate rapid detection of duplicate keys.) Consequently, queries on tables with such indexes may return unexpected results.

8.4 The MEMORY (HEAP) Storage Engine

The MEMORY storage engine creates tables with contents that are stored in memory. Formerly, these were known as HEAP tables. MEMORY is the preferred term, although HEAP remains supported for backward compatibility.

Each MEMORY table is associated with one disk file. The filename begins with the table name and has an extension of .frm to indicate that it stores the table definition.

To specify explicitly that you want to create a MEMORY table, indicate that with an ENGINE table option:

```
CREATE TABLE t (i INT) ENGINE = MEMORY;
```

The older term TYPE is supported as a synonym for ENGINE for backward compatibility, but ENGINE is the preferred term and TYPE is deprecated.

As indicated by the name, MEMORY tables are stored in memory. They use hash indexes by default, which makes them very fast, and very useful for creating temporary tables. However, when the server shuts down, all rows stored in MEMORY tables are lost. The tables themselves continue to exist because their definitions are stored in .frm files on disk, but they are empty when the server restarts.

This example shows how you might create, use, and remove a MEMORY table:

```
mysql> CREATE TABLE test ENGINE=MEMORY
    ->      SELECT ip,SUM(downloads) AS down
    ->      FROM log_table GROUP BY ip;
mysql> SELECT COUNT(ip),AVG(down) FROM test;
mysql> DROP TABLE test;
```

MEMORY tables have the following characteristics:

- Space for MEMORY tables is allocated in small blocks. Tables use 100% dynamic hashing for inserts. No overflow area or extra key space is needed. No extra space is needed for free lists. Deleted rows are put in a linked list and are reused when you insert new data into the table. MEMORY tables also have none of the problems commonly associated with deletes plus inserts in hashed tables.

- MEMORY tables can have up to 32 indexes per table, 16 columns per index and a maximum key length of 500 bytes.

- The MEMORY storage engine implements both HASH and BTREE indexes. You can specify one or the other for a given index by adding a USING clause as shown here:

```
CREATE TABLE lookup
    (id INT, INDEX USING HASH (id))
    ENGINE = MEMORY;
CREATE TABLE lookup
    (id INT, INDEX USING BTREE (id))
    ENGINE = MEMORY;
```

General characteristics of B-tree and hash indexes are described in Section 6.4.5, "How MySQL Uses Indexes."

- You can have non-unique keys in a MEMORY table. (This is an uncommon feature for implementations of hash indexes.)

- If you have a hash index on a MEMORY table that has a high degree of key duplication (many index entries containing the same value), updates to the table that affect key values and all deletes are significantly slower. The degree of this slowdown is proportional to the degree of duplication (or, inversely proportional to the index cardinality). You can use a BTREE index to avoid this problem.

- Columns that are indexed can contain NULL values.

- MEMORY tables use a fixed-length row storage format.

- MEMORY tables cannot contain BLOB or TEXT columns.

- MEMORY includes support for AUTO_INCREMENT columns.

- You can use INSERT DELAYED with MEMORY tables.

- MEMORY tables are shared among all clients (just like any other non-TEMPORARY table).

- MEMORY table contents are stored in memory, which is a property that MEMORY tables share with internal tables that the server creates on the fly while processing queries. However, the two types of tables differ in that MEMORY tables are not subject to storage conversion, whereas internal tables are:

  - If an internal table becomes too large, the server automatically converts it to an on-disk table. The size limit is determined by the value of the tmp_table_size system variable.

  - MEMORY tables are never converted to disk tables. To ensure that you don't accidentally do anything foolish, you can set the max_heap_table_size system variable to impose a maximum size on MEMORY tables. For individual tables, you can also specify a MAX_ROWS table option in the CREATE TABLE statement.

- The server needs sufficient memory to maintain all MEMORY tables that are in use at the same time.

- To free memory used by a MEMORY table when you no longer require its contents, you should execute DELETE or TRUNCATE TABLE, or remove the table altogether using DROP TABLE.

- If you want to populate a MEMORY table when the MySQL server starts, you can use the --init-file option. For example, you can put statements such as INSERT INTO ... SELECT or LOAD DATA INFILE into this file to load the table from a persistent data source.

- If you are using replication, the master server's MEMORY tables become empty when it is shut down and restarted. However, a slave is not aware that these tables have become empty, so it returns out-of-date content if you select data from them. When a MEMORY table is used on the master for the first time since the master was started, a DELETE statement is written to the master's binary log automatically, thus synchronizing the slave to the master again. Note that even with this strategy, the slave still has outdated data in the table during the interval between the master's restart and its first use of the table.

However, if you use the `--init-file` option to populate the MEMORY table on the master at startup, it ensures that this time interval is zero.

- The memory needed for one row in a MEMORY table is calculated using the following expression:

```
SUM_OVER_ALL_BTREE_KEYS(max_length_of_key + sizeof(char*) × 4)
+ SUM_OVER_ALL_HASH_KEYS(sizeof(char*) × 2)
+ ALIGN(length_of_row+1, sizeof(char*))
```

ALIGN() represents a round-up factor to cause the row length to be an exact multiple of the `char` pointer size. `sizeof(char*)` is 4 on 32-bit machines and 8 on 64-bit machines.

Additional resources

- A forum dedicated to the MEMORY storage engine is available at `http://forums.mysql.com/list.php?92.`

8.5 The BDB (`BerkeleyDB`) Storage Engine

Sleepycat Software has provided MySQL with the Berkeley DB transactional storage engine. This storage engine typically is called BDB for short. BDB tables may have a greater chance of surviving crashes and are also capable of COMMIT and ROLLBACK operations on transactions.

Support for the BDB storage engine is included in MySQL source distributions and is activated in MySQL-Max binary distributions. The MySQL source distribution comes with a BDB distribution that is patched to make it work with MySQL. You cannot use a non-patched version of BDB with MySQL.

We at MySQL AB work in close cooperation with Sleepycat to keep the quality of the MySQL/BDB interface high. (Even though Berkeley DB is itself very tested and reliable, the MySQL interface is still considered gamma quality. We continue to improve and optimize it.)

When it comes to support for any problems involving BDB tables, we are committed to helping our users locate the problem and create reproducible test cases. Any such test case is forwarded to Sleepycat, which in turn helps us find and fix the problem. Because this is a two-stage operation, any problems with BDB tables may take a little longer for us to fix than for other storage engines. However, we anticipate no significant difficulties with this procedure because the Berkeley DB code itself is used in many applications other than MySQL.

For general information about Berkeley DB, please visit the Sleepycat Web site, `http://www.sleepycat.com/.`

8.5.1 Operating Systems Supported by BDB

Currently, we know that the BDB storage engine works with the following operating systems:

- Linux 2.x Intel
- Sun Solaris (SPARC and x86)
- FreeBSD 4.x/5.x (x86, sparc64)

- IBM AIX 4.3.x
- SCO OpenServer
- SCO UnixWare 7.1.x
- Windows NT/2000/XP

The BDB storage engine does *not* work with the following operating systems:

- Linux 2.x Alpha
- Linux 2.x AMD64
- Linux 2.x IA-64
- Linux 2.x s390
- Mac OS X

Note: The preceding lists are not complete. We update them as we receive more information.

If you build MySQL from source with support for BDB tables, but the following error occurs when you start mysqld, it means that the BDB storage engine is not supported for your architecture:

```
bdb: architecture lacks fast mutexes: applications cannot be threaded
Can't init databases
```

In this case, you must rebuild MySQL without BDB support or start the server with the --skip-bdb option.

8.5.2 Installing BDB

If you have downloaded a binary version of MySQL that includes support for Berkeley DB, simply follow the usual binary distribution installation instructions. (MySQL-Max distributions include BDB support.)

If you build MySQL from source, you can enable BDB support by invoking configure with the --with-berkeley-db option in addition to any other options that you normally use. Download a MySQL 5.0 distribution, change location into its top-level directory, and run this command:

```
shell> ./configure --with-berkeley-db [other-options]
```

For more information, see Section 2.7, "Installing MySQL on Other Unix-Like Systems," Section 2.8, "MySQL Installation Using a Source Distribution," and Section 4.3, "The mysqld-max Extended MySQL Server."

8.5.3 BDB Startup Options

The following options to mysqld can be used to change the behavior of the BDB storage engine. For more information, see Section 4.2.1, "mysqld Command Options."

- `--bdb-home=path`

  The base directory for BDB tables. This should be the same directory that you use for `--datadir`.

- `--bdb-lock-detect=method`

  The BDB lock detection method. The option value should be DEFAULT, OLDEST, RANDOM, or YOUNGEST.

- `--bdb-logdir=file_name`

  The BDB log file directory.

- `--bdb-no-recover`

  Do not start Berkeley DB in recover mode.

- `--bdb-no-sync`

  Don't synchronously flush the BDB logs. This option is deprecated; use `--skip-sync-bdb-logs` instead (see the description for `--sync-bdb-logs`).

- `--bdb-shared-data`

  Start Berkeley DB in multi-process mode. (Do not use DB_PRIVATE when initializing Berkeley DB.)

- `--bdb-tmpdir=path`

  The BDB temporary file directory.

- `--skip-bdb`

  Disable the BDB storage engine.

- `--sync-bdb-logs`

  Synchronously flush the BDB logs. This option is enabled by default. Use `--skip-sync-bdb-logs` to disable it.

If you use the `--skip-bdb` option, MySQL does not initialize the Berkeley DB library and this saves a lot of memory. However, if you use this option, you cannot use BDB tables. If you try to create a BDB table, MySQL uses the default storage engine instead.

Normally, you should start `mysqld` without the `--bdb-no-recover` option if you intend to use BDB tables. However, this may cause problems when you try to start `mysqld` if the BDB log files are corrupted. See Section 2.9.2.3, "Starting and Troubleshooting the MySQL Server."

With the `bdb_max_lock` variable, you can specify the maximum number of locks that can be active on a BDB table. The default is 10,000. You should increase this if errors such as the following occur when you perform long transactions or when `mysqld` has to examine many rows to execute a query:

```
bdb: Lock table is out of available locks
Got error 12 from ...
```

You may also want to change the `binlog_cache_size` and `max_binlog_cache_size` variables if you are using large multiple-statement transactions. See Section 4.12.3, "The Binary Log."

See also Section 4.2.2, "Server System Variables."

8.5.4 Characteristics of BDB Tables

Each BDB table is stored on disk in two files. The files have names that begin with the table name and have an extension to indicate the file type. An .frm file stores the table format, and a .db file contains the table data and indexes.

To specify explicitly that you want a BDB table, indicate that with an ENGINE table option:

```
CREATE TABLE t (i INT) ENGINE = BDB;
```

The older term TYPE is supported as a synonym for ENGINE for backward compatibility, but ENGINE is the preferred term and TYPE is deprecated.

BerkeleyDB is a synonym for BDB in the ENGINE table option.

The BDB storage engine provides transactional tables. The way you use these tables depends on the autocommit mode:

- If you are running with autocommit enabled (which is the default), changes to BDB tables are committed immediately and cannot be rolled back.
- If you are running with autocommit disabled, changes do not become permanent until you execute a COMMIT statement. Instead of committing, you can execute ROLLBACK to forget the changes.

  You can start a transaction with the START TRANSACTION or BEGIN statement to suspend autocommit, or with SET AUTOCOMMIT=0 to disable autocommit explicitly.

The BDB storage engine has the following characteristics:

- BDB tables can have up to 31 indexes per table, 16 columns per index, and a maximum key size of 1024 bytes.
- MySQL requires a primary key in each BDB table so that each row can be uniquely identified. If you don't create one explicitly by declaring a PRIMARY KEY, MySQL creates and maintains a hidden primary key for you. The hidden key has a length of five bytes and is incremented for each insert attempt. This key does not appear in the output of SHOW CREATE TABLE or DESCRIBE.
- The primary key is faster than any other index, because it is stored together with the row data. The other indexes are stored as the key data plus the primary key, so it's important to keep the primary key as short as possible to save disk space and get better speed.

  This behavior is similar to that of InnoDB, where shorter primary keys save space not only in the primary index but in secondary indexes as well.
- If all columns that you access in a BDB table are part of the same index or part of the primary key, MySQL can execute the query without having to access the actual row. In a MyISAM table, this can be done only if the columns are part of the same index.
- Sequential scanning is slower for BDB tables than for MyISAM tables because the data in BDB tables is stored in B-trees and not in a separate data file.
- Key values are not prefix- or suffix-compressed like key values in MyISAM tables. In other words, key information takes a little more space in BDB tables compared to MyISAM tables.

- There are often holes in the BDB table to allow you to insert new rows in the middle of the index tree. This makes BDB tables somewhat larger than MyISAM tables.

- SELECT COUNT(*) FROM *tbl_name* is slow for BDB tables, because no row count is maintained in the table.

- The optimizer needs to know the approximate number of rows in the table. MySQL solves this by counting inserts and maintaining this in a separate segment in each BDB table. If you don't issue a lot of DELETE or ROLLBACK statements, this number should be accurate enough for the MySQL optimizer. However, MySQL stores the number only on close, so it may be incorrect if the server terminates unexpectedly. It should not be fatal even if this number is not 100% correct. You can update the row count by using ANALYZE TABLE or OPTIMIZE TABLE.

- Internal locking in BDB tables is done at the page level.

- LOCK TABLES works on BDB tables as with other tables. If you do not use LOCK TABLES, MySQL issues an internal multiple-write lock on the table (a lock that does not block other writers) to ensure that the table is properly locked if another thread issues a table lock.

- To support transaction rollback, the BDB storage engine maintains log files. For maximum performance, you can use the --bdb-logdir option to place the BDB logs on a different disk than the one where your databases are located.

- MySQL performs a checkpoint each time a new BDB log file is started, and removes any BDB log files that are not needed for current transactions. You can also use FLUSH LOGS at any time to checkpoint the Berkeley DB tables.

  For disaster recovery, you should use table backups plus MySQL's binary log. See Section 4.10.1, "Database Backups."

  Warning: If you delete old log files that are still in use, BDB is not able to do recovery at all and you may lose data if something goes wrong.

- Applications must always be prepared to handle cases where any change of a BDB table may cause an automatic rollback and any read may fail with a deadlock error.

- If you get a full disk with a BDB table, you get an error (probably error 28) and the transaction should roll back. This contrasts with MyISAM tables, for which mysqld waits for sufficient free disk space before continuing.

8.5.5 Things We Need to Fix for BDB

- Opening many BDB tables at the same time may be quite slow. If you are going to use BDB tables, you should not have a very large table cache (for example, with a size larger than 256) and you should use the --no-auto-rehash option when you use the mysql client.

- SHOW TABLE STATUS does not provide some information for BDB tables:

```
mysql> SHOW TABLE STATUS LIKE 'bdbtest'\G
*************************** 1. row ***************************
           Name: bdbtest
         Engine: BerkeleyDB
        Version: 10
     Row_format: Dynamic
           Rows: 154
 Avg_row_length: 0
    Data_length: 0
Max_data_length: 0
   Index_length: 0
      Data_free: 0
 Auto_increment: NULL
    Create_time: NULL
    Update_time: NULL
     Check_time: NULL
      Collation: latin1_swedish_ci
       Checksum: NULL
  Create_options:
        Comment:
```

- Optimize performance.
- Change to use no page locks for table scanning operations.

8.5.6 Restrictions on BDB Tables

The following list indicates restrictions that you must observe when using BDB tables:

- Each BDB table stores in its .db file the path to the file as it was created. This is done to enable detection of locks in a multi-user environment that supports symlinks. As a consequence of this, it is not possible to move BDB table files from one database directory to another.

- When making backups of BDB tables, you must either use mysqldump or else make a backup that includes the files for each BDB table (the .frm and .db files) as well as the BDB log files. The BDB storage engine stores unfinished transactions in its log files and requires them to be present when mysqld starts. The BDB logs are the files in the data directory with names of the form log.NNNNNNNNNN (ten digits).

- If a column that allows NULL values has a unique index, only a single NULL value is allowed. This differs from other storage engines, which allow multiple NULL values in unique indexes.

8.5.7 Errors That May Occur When Using BDB Tables

- If the following error occurs when you start mysqld after upgrading, it means that the current version of BDB doesn't support the old log file format:

```
bdb:  Ignoring log file: .../log.NNNNNNNNNN:
unsupported log version #
```

In this case, you must delete all BDB logs from your data directory (the files that have names of the form log.NNNNNNNNNN) and restart mysqld. We also recommend that you then use mysqldump --opt to dump your BDB tables, drop the tables, and restore them from the dump file.

- If autocommit mode is disabled and you drop a BDB table that is referenced in another transaction, you may get error messages of the following form in your MySQL error log:

```
001119 23:43:56  bdb:  Missing log fileid entry
001119 23:43:56  bdb:  txn_abort: Log undo failed for LSN:
                       1 3644744: Invalid
```

This is not fatal, but the fix is not trivial. Until the problem is fixed, we recommend that you not drop BDB tables except while autocommit mode is enabled.

8.6 The EXAMPLE Storage Engine

The EXAMPLE storage engine is a stub engine that does nothing. Its purpose is to serve as an example in the MySQL source code that illustrates how to begin writing new storage engines. As such, it is primarily of interest to developers.

The EXAMPLE storage engine is included in MySQL-Max binary distributions. To enable this storage engine if you build MySQL from source, invoke configure with the --with-example-storage-engine option.

To examine the source for the EXAMPLE engine, look in the sql/examples directory of a MySQL source distribution.

When you create an EXAMPLE table, the server creates a table format file in the database directory. The file begins with the table name and has an .frm extension. No other files are created. No data can be stored into the table. Retrievals return an empty result.

```
mysql> CREATE TABLE test (i INT) ENGINE = EXAMPLE;
Query OK, 0 rows affected (0.78 sec)

mysql> INSERT INTO test VALUES(1),(2),(3);
ERROR 1031 (HY000): Table storage engine for 'test' doesn't have this option

mysql> SELECT * FROM test;
Empty set (0.31 sec)
```

The EXAMPLE storage engine does not support indexing.

8.7 The FEDERATED Storage Engine

The FEDERATED storage engine is available beginning with MySQL 5.0.3. It is a storage engine that accesses data in tables of remote databases rather than in local tables.

The FEDERATED storage engine is included in MySQL-Max binary distributions. To enable this storage engine if you build MySQL from source, invoke `configure` with the `--with-federated-storage-engine` option.

To examine the source for the FEDERATED engine, look in the `sql` directory of a source distribution for MySQL 5.0.3 or newer.

Additional resources

- A forum dedicated to the FEDERATED storage engine is available at `http://forums.mysql.com/list.php?105`.

8.7.1 Description of the FEDERATED Storage Engine

When you create a FEDERATED table, the server creates a table format file in the database directory. The file begins with the table name and has an `.frm` extension. No other files are created, because the actual data is in a remote table. This differs from the way that storage engines for local tables work.

For local database tables, data files are local. For example, if you create a MyISAM table named users, the MyISAM handler creates a data file named users.MYD. A handler for local tables reads, inserts, deletes, and updates data in local data files, and rows are stored in a format particular to the handler. To read rows, the handler must parse data into columns. To write rows, column values must be converted to the row format used by the handler and written to the local data file.

With the MySQL FEDERATED storage engine, there are no local data files for a table (for example, there is no `.MYD` file). Instead, a remote database stores the data that normally would be in the table. The local server connects to a remote server, and uses the MySQL client API to read, delete, update, and insert data in the remote table. Data retrieval is initiated via a SELECT * FROM `tbl_name` SQL statement. To read the result, rows are fetched one at a time by using the `mysql_fetch_row()` C API function, and then converting the columns in the SELECT result set to the format that the FEDERATED handler expects.

The flow of information is as follows:

1. SQL calls issued locally
2. MySQL handler API (data in handler format)
3. MySQL client API (data converted to SQL calls)
4. Remote database -> MySQL client API
5. Convert result sets (if any) to handler format
6. Handler API -> Result rows or rows-affected count to local

8.7.2 How to Use FEDERATED Tables

The procedure for using FEDERATED tables is very simple. Normally, you have two servers running, either both on the same host or on different hosts. (It is possible for a FEDERATED table to use another table that is managed by the same server, although there is little point in doing so.)

First, you must have a table on the remote server that you want to access by using a FEDERATED table. Suppose that the remote table is in the federated database and is defined like this:

```
CREATE TABLE test_table (
    id     INT(20) NOT NULL AUTO_INCREMENT,
    name   VARCHAR(32) NOT NULL DEFAULT '',
    other  INT(20) NOT NULL DEFAULT '0',
    PRIMARY KEY  (id),
    INDEX name (name),
    INDEX other_key (other)
)
ENGINE=MyISAM
DEFAULT CHARSET=latin1;
```

The example uses a MyISAM table, but the table could use any storage engine.

Next, create a FEDERATED table on the local server for accessing the remote table:

```
CREATE TABLE federated_table (
    id     INT(20) NOT NULL AUTO_INCREMENT,
    name   VARCHAR(32) NOT NULL DEFAULT '',
    other  INT(20) NOT NULL DEFAULT '0',
    PRIMARY KEY  (id),
    INDEX name (name),
    INDEX other_key (other)
)
ENGINE=FEDERATED
DEFAULT CHARSET=latin1
CONNECTION='mysql://root@remote_host:9306/federated/test_table';
```

(Before MySQL 5.0.13, use COMMENT rather than CONNECTION.)

The structure of this table must be exactly the same as that of the remote table, except that the ENGINE table option should be FEDERATED and the CONNECTION table option is a connection string that indicates to the FEDERATED engine how to connect to the remote server.

The FEDERATED engine creates only the test_table.frm file in the federated database.

The remote host information indicates the remote server to which your local server connects, and the database and table information indicates which remote table to use as the data source. In this example, the remote server is indicated to be running as remote_host on port 9306, so there must be a MySQL server running on the remote host and listening to port 9306.

The general form of the connection string in the CONNECTION option is as follows:

```
scheme://user_name[:password]@host_name[:port_num]/db_name/tbl_name
```

Only mysql is supported as the *scheme* value at this point; the password and port number are optional.

Here are some example connection strings:

```
CONNECTION='mysql://username:password@hostname:port/database/tablename'
CONNECTION='mysql://username@hostname/database/tablename'
CONNECTION='mysql://username:password@hostname/database/tablename'
```

The use of CONNECTION for specifying the connection string is non-optimal and is likely to change in future. Keep this in mind for applications that use FEDERATED tables. Such applications are likely to need modification if the format for specifying connection information changes.

Because any password given in the connection string is stored as plain text, it can be seen by any user who can use SHOW CREATE TABLE or SHOW TABLE STATUS for the FEDERATED table, or query the TABLES table in the INFORMATION_SCHEMA database.

8.7.3 Limitations of the FEDERATED Storage Engine

The following items indicate features that the FEDERATED storage engine does and does not support:

- In the first version, the remote server must be a MySQL server. Support by FEDERATED for other database engines may be added in the future.

- The remote table that a FEDERATED table points to *must* exist before you try to access the table through the FEDERATED table.

- It is possible for one FEDERATED table to point to another, but you must be careful not to create a loop.

- There is no support for transactions.

- There is no way for the FEDERATED engine to know if the remote table has changed. The reason for this is that this table must work like a data file that would never be written to by anything other than the database. The integrity of the data in the local table could be breached if there was any change to the remote database.

- The FEDERATED storage engine supports SELECT, INSERT, UPDATE, DELETE, and indexes. It does not support ALTER TABLE, DROP TABLE, or any other Data Definition Language statements. The current implementation does not use prepared statements.

- The implementation uses SELECT, INSERT, UPDATE, and DELETE, but not HANDLER.

- FEDERATED tables do not work with the query cache.

Some of these limitations may be lifted in future versions of the FEDERATED handler.

8.8 The ARCHIVE Storage Engine

The ARCHIVE storage engine is used for storing large amounts of data without indexes in a very small footprint.

The ARCHIVE storage engine is included in MySQL binary distributions. To enable this storage engine if you build MySQL from source, invoke configure with the --with-archive-storage-engine option.

To examine the source for the ARCHIVE engine, look in the sql directory of a MySQL source distribution.

You can check whether the ARCHIVE storage engine is available with this statement:

```
mysql> SHOW VARIABLES LIKE 'have_archive';
```

When you create an ARCHIVE table, the server creates a table format file in the database directory. The file begins with the table name and has an .frm extension. The storage engine creates other files, all having names beginning with the table name. The data and metadata files have extensions of .ARZ and .ARM, respectively. An .ARN file may appear during optimization operations.

The ARCHIVE engine supports INSERT and SELECT, but not DELETE, REPLACE, or UPDATE. It does support ORDER BY operations, BLOB columns, and basically all but spatial data types. The ARCHIVE engine uses row-level locking.

Storage: Rows are compressed as they are inserted. The ARCHIVE engine uses zlib lossless data compression (see http://www.zlib.net/). You can use OPTIMIZE TABLE to analyze the table and pack it into a smaller format (for a reason to use OPTIMIZE TABLE, see later in this section). Beginning with MySQL 5.0.15, the engine also supports CHECK TABLE. There are several types of insertions that are used:

- An INSERT statement just pushes rows into a compression buffer, and that buffer flushes as necessary. The insertion into the buffer is protected by a lock. A SELECT forces a flush to occur, unless the only insertions that have come in were INSERT DELAYED (those flush as necessary).
- A bulk insert is visible only after it completes, unless other inserts occur at the same time, in which case it can be seen partially. A SELECT never causes a flush of a bulk insert unless a normal insert occurs while it is loading.

Retrieval: On retrieval, rows are uncompressed on demand; there is no row cache. A SELECT operation performs a complete table scan: When a SELECT occurs, it finds out how many rows are currently available and reads that number of rows. SELECT is performed as a consistent read. Note that lots of SELECT statements during insertion can deteriorate the compression, unless only bulk or delayed inserts are used. To achieve better compression, you can use OPTIMIZE TABLE or REPAIR TABLE. The number of rows in ARCHIVE tables reported by SHOW TABLE STATUS is always accurate.

Additional resources

- A forum dedicated to the ARCHIVE storage engine is available at http://forums.mysql.com/list.php?112.

8.9 The CSV Storage Engine

The CSV storage engine stores data in text files using comma-separated values format.

To enable this storage engine, use the --with-csv-storage-engine option to configure when you build MySQL.

The CSV storage engine is included in MySQL-Max binary distributions. To enable this storage engine if you build MySQL from source, invoke configure with the --with-csv-storage-engine option.

To examine the source for the CSV engine, look in the sql/examples directory of a MySQL source distribution.

When you create a CSV table, the server creates a table format file in the database directory. The file begins with the table name and has an .frm extension. The storage engine also creates a data file. Its name begins with the table name and has a .CSV extension. The data file is a plain text file. When you store data into the table, the storage engine saves it into the data file in comma-separated values format.

```
mysql> CREATE TABLE test(i INT, c CHAR(10)) ENGINE = CSV;
Query OK, 0 rows affected (0.12 sec)

mysql> INSERT INTO test VALUES(1,'record one'),(2,'record two');
Query OK, 2 rows affected (0.00 sec)
Records: 2  Duplicates: 0  Warnings: 0

mysql> SELECT * FROM test;
+------+------------+
| i    | c          |
+------+------------+
|    1 | record one |
|    2 | record two |
+------+------------+
2 rows in set (0.00 sec)
```

If you examine the test.CSV file in the database directory created by executing the preceding statements, its contents should look like this:

```
"1","record one"
"2","record two"
```

The CSV storage engine does not support indexing.

8.10 The BLACKHOLE Storage Engine

The BLACKHOLE storage engine acts as a "black hole" that accepts data but throws it away and does not store it. Retrievals always return an empty result:

```
mysql> CREATE TABLE test(i INT, c CHAR(10)) ENGINE = BLACKHOLE;
Query OK, 0 rows affected (0.03 sec)
```

```
mysql> INSERT INTO test VALUES(1,'record one'),(2,'record two');
Query OK, 2 rows affected (0.00 sec)
Records: 2  Duplicates: 0  Warnings: 0

mysql> SELECT * FROM test;
Empty set (0.00 sec)
```

The BLACKHOLE storage engine is included in MySQL-Max binary distributions. To enable this storage engine if you build MySQL from source, invoke configure with the --with-blackhole-storage-engine option.

To examine the source for the BLACKHOLE engine, look in the sql directory of a MySQL source distribution.

When you create a BLACKHOLE table, the server creates a table format file in the database directory. The file begins with the table name and has an .frm extension. There are no other files associated with the table.

The BLACKHOLE storage engine supports all kinds of indexes. That is, you can include index declarations in the table definition.

You can check whether the BLACKHOLE storage engine is available with this statement:

```
mysql> SHOW VARIABLES LIKE 'have_blackhole_engine';
```

Inserts into a BLACKHOLE table do not store any data, but if the binary log is enabled, the SQL statements are logged (and replicated to slave servers). This can be useful as a repeater or filter mechanism. For example, suppose that your application requires slave-side filtering rules, but transferring all binary log data to the slave first results in too much traffic. In such a case, it is possible to set up on the master host a "dummy" slave process whose default storage engine is BLACKHOLE, depicted in Figure 8.1.

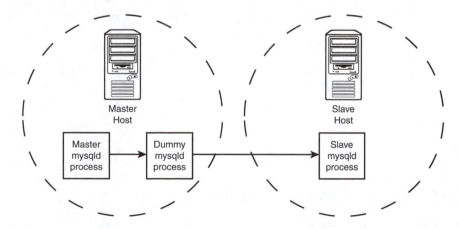

FIGURE 8.1   Replication using BLACKHOLE for filtering.

The master writes to its binary log. The "dummy" mysqld process acts as a slave, applying the desired combination of replicate-do-* and replicate-ignore-* rules, and writes a new, filtered binary log of its own. (See Section 5.9, "Replication Startup Options.") This filtered log is provided to the slave.

The dummy process does not actually store any data, so there is little processing overhead incurred by running the additional mysqld process on the replication master host. This type of setup can be repeated with additional replication slaves.

Other possible uses for the BLACKHOLE storage engine include:

- Verification of dump file syntax.
- Measurement of the overhead from binary logging, by comparing performance using BLACKHOLE with and without binary logging enabled.
- BLACKHOLE is essentially a "no-op" storage engine, so it could be used for finding performance bottlenecks not related to the storage engine itself.

9

MySQL Cluster

MySQL Cluster is a high-availability, high-redundancy version of MySQL adapted for the distributed computing environment. It uses the `NDB Cluster` storage engine to enable running several MySQL servers in a cluster. This storage engine is available in MySQL 5.0 binary releases and in RPMs compatible with most modern Linux distributions. (If you install using RPM files, note that both the `mysql-server` and `mysql-max` RPMs must be installed to have MySQL Cluster capability.)

The operating systems on which MySQL Cluster is currently available are Linux, Mac OS X, and Solaris. (Some users have reported success with running MySQL Cluster on FreeBSD, although this is not yet officially supported by MySQL AB.) We are working to make Cluster run on all operating systems supported by MySQL, including Windows, and will update this page as new platforms are supported.

This chapter represents a work in progress, and its contents are subject to revision as MySQL Cluster continues to evolve. Additional information regarding MySQL Cluster can be found on the MySQL AB Web site at `http://www.mysql.com/products/cluster/`.

Additional resources

- Answers to some commonly asked questions about Cluster may be found in Section 9.11, "MySQL Cluster FAQ."
- The MySQL Cluster mailing list: `http://lists.mysql.com/cluster`.
- The MySQL Cluster Forum: `http://forums.mysql.com/list.php?25`.
- If you are new to MySQL Cluster, you may find our Developer Zone article How to set up a MySQL Cluster for two servers (`http://dev.mysql.com/tech-resources/articles/mysql-cluster-for-two-servers.html`) to be helpful.

9.1 MySQL Cluster Overview

MySQL Cluster is a technology that enables clustering of in-memory databases in a share-nothing system. The share-nothing architecture allows the system to work with very inexpensive hardware, and without any specific requirements on hardware or software. It also does not have any single point of failure because each component has its own memory and disk.

MySQL Cluster integrates the standard MySQL server with an in-memory clustered storage engine called NDB. In our documentation, the term NDB refers to the part of the setup that is specific to the storage engine, whereas "MySQL Cluster" refers to the combination of MySQL and the NDB storage engine.

A MySQL Cluster consists of a set of computers, each running a number of processes including MySQL servers, data nodes for NDB Cluster, management servers, and (possibly) specialized data access programs. The relationship of these components in a cluster is shown in Figure 9.1.

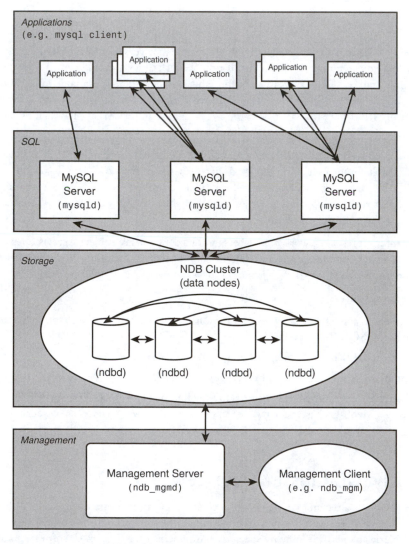

FIGURE 9.1   MySQL Cluster components.

All these programs work together to form a MySQL Cluster. When data is stored in the NDB Cluster storage engine, the tables are stored in the data nodes. Such tables are directly accessible from all other MySQL servers in the cluster. Thus, in a payroll application storing data in a cluster, if one application updates the salary of an employee, all other MySQL servers that query this data can see this change immediately.

The data stored in the data nodes for MySQL Cluster can be mirrored; the cluster can handle failures of individual data nodes with no other impact than that a small number of transactions are aborted due to losing the transaction state. Because transactional applications are expected to handle transaction failure, this should not be a source of problems.

By bringing MySQL Cluster to the Open Source world, MySQL AB makes clustered data management with high availability, high performance, and scalability available to all who need it.

9.2 Basic MySQL Cluster Concepts

NDB is an in-memory storage engine offering high-availability and data-persistence features.

The NDB storage engine can be configured with a range of failover and load-balancing options, but it is easiest to start with the storage engine at the cluster level. MySQL Cluster's NDB storage engine contains a complete set of data, dependent only on other data within the cluster itself.

We will now describe how to set up a MySQL Cluster consisting of an NDB storage engine and some MySQL servers.

The cluster portion of MySQL Cluster is currently configured independently of the MySQL servers. In a MySQL Cluster, each part of the cluster is considered to be a **node**.

Note: In many contexts, the term "node" is used to indicate a computer, but when discussing MySQL Cluster it means a *process*. There can be any number of nodes on a single computer, for which we use the term **cluster host**.

There are three types of cluster nodes, and in a minimal MySQL Cluster configuration, there will be at least three nodes, one of each of these types:

- The **management node** (MGM node): The role of this type of node is to manage the other nodes within the MySQL Cluster, such as providing configuration data, starting and stopping nodes, running backup, and so forth. Because this node type manages the configuration of the other nodes, a node of this type should be started first, before any other node. An MGM node is started with the command ndb_mgmd.

- The **data node**: This is the type of node that stores the cluster's data. There are as many data nodes as there are replicas, times the number of fragments. For example, with two replicas, each having two fragments, you will need four data nodes. It is not necessary to have more than one replica. A data node is started with the command ndbd.

- The **SQL node**: This is the node that accesses the cluster data. In the case of MySQL Cluster, a client node is a traditional MySQL server that uses the NDB Cluster storage engine. An SQL node is typically started with the command `mysqld --ndbcluster` or by using `mysqld` with the `ndbcluster` option added to `my.cnf`.

For a brief introduction to the relationships between nodes, node groups, replicas, and partitions in MySQL Cluster, see Section 9.2.1, "MySQL Cluster Nodes, Node Groups, Replicas, and Partitions."

Configuration of a cluster involves configuring each individual node in the cluster and setting up individual communication links between nodes. MySQL Cluster is currently designed with the intention that storage nodes are homogeneous in terms of processor power, memory space, and bandwidth. In addition, to provide a single point of configuration, all configuration data for the cluster as a whole is located in one configuration file.

The management server (MGM node) manages the cluster configuration file and the cluster log. Each node in the cluster retrieves the configuration data from the management server, and so requires a way to determine where the management server resides. When interesting events occur in the data nodes, the nodes transfer information about these events to the management server, which then writes the information to the cluster log.

In addition, there can be any number of cluster client processes or applications. These are of two types:

- **Standard MySQL clients**: These are no different for MySQL Cluster than they are for standard (non-Cluster) MySQL. In other words, MySQL Cluster can be accessed from existing MySQL applications written in PHP, Perl, C, C++, Java, Python, Ruby, and so on.

- **Management clients**: These clients connect to the management server and provide commands for starting and stopping nodes gracefully, starting and stopping message tracing (debug versions only), showing node versions and status, starting and stopping backups, and so on.

9.2.1 MySQL Cluster Nodes, Node Groups, Replicas, and Partitions

This section discusses the manner in which MySQL Cluster divides and duplicates data for storage.

Central to an understanding of this topic are the following concepts, listed here with brief definitions:

- **(Data) Node**: An `ndbd` process, which stores a *replica*—that is, a copy of the *partition* (see below) assigned to the node group of which the node is a member.

  Each data node is usually located on a separate computer. However, it is also possible to host multiple data nodes on a single computer having more than one processor. In such cases, it is feasible to run one instance of `ndbd` per physical CPU. (Note that a processor with multiple cores is still a single processor.)

  It is common for the terms "node" and "data node" to be used interchangeably when referring to an `ndbd` process; where mentioned, management nodes (`ndb_mgmd` processes) and SQL nodes (`mysqld` processes) are specified as such in this discussion.

- **Node Group**: A node group consists of one or more nodes, and stores a partition, or set of *replicas* (see next item).

  Note: Currently, all node groups in a cluster must have the same number of nodes.

- **Partition**: This is a portion of the data stored by the cluster. There are as many cluster partitions as node groups participating in the cluster, and each node group is responsible for keeping at least one copy of the partition assigned to it (that is, at least one replica) available to the cluster.

- **Replica**: This is a copy of a cluster partition. Each node in a node group stores a replica. Also sometimes known as a *partition replica*.

Figure 9.2 illustrates a MySQL Cluster with four data nodes, arranged in two node groups of two nodes each. Note that no nodes other than data nodes are shown here, although a working cluster requires an ndb_mgm process for cluster management and at least one SQL node to access the data stored by the cluster.

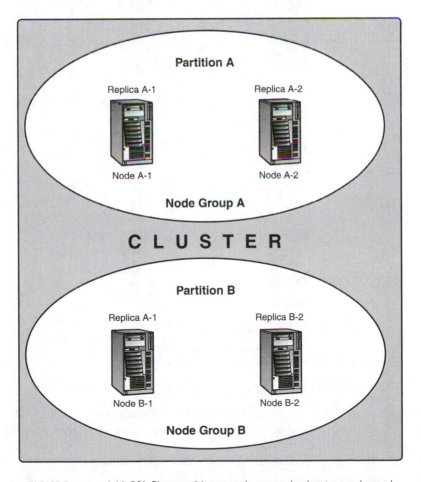

FIGURE 9.2   A MySQL Cluster, with two node groups having two nodes each.

The data stored by the cluster is divided into two partitions, labeled **A** and **B** in the diagram. Each partition is stored—in multiple copies—on a node group. The data making up Partition **A** is stored on Node **A-1**, and this data is identical to that stored by Node **A-2**. The data stored by Nodes **B-1** and **B-2** is also the same—these two nodes store identical copies of the data making up Partition **B**.

What this means so far as the continued operation of a MySQL Cluster is this: so long as each node group participating in the cluster has at least one "live" node, the cluster has a complete copy of all data and remains viable. This is illustrated in Figure 9.3.

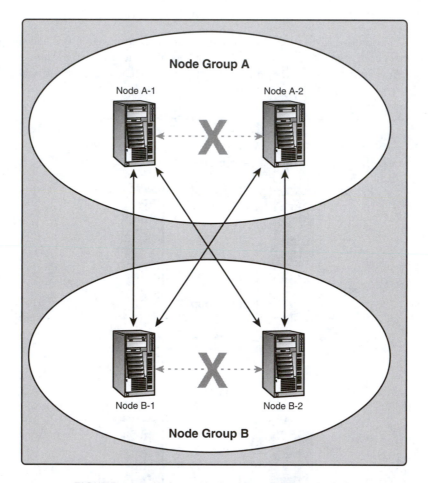

FIGURE 9.3 Nodes required to keep a 2×2 cluster viable.

In this example, where the cluster consists of two node groups of two nodes each, any combination of at least one node in Node Group **A** and at least one node in Node Group **B** is sufficient to keep the cluster "alive" (indicated by arrows in the diagram). However, if both nodes from either node group fail, the remaining two nodes are not sufficient (shown by arrows marked out with an **X**); in either case, the cluster has lost an entire partition and so can no longer provide access to a complete set of all cluster data.

9.3 Simple Multi-Computer How-To

This section is a "How-To" that describes the basics for how to plan, install, configure, and run a MySQL Cluster. Whereas the examples in Section 9.4, "MySQL Cluster Configuration" provide more in-depth information on a variety of clustering options and configuration, the result of following the guidelines and procedures outlined here should be a usable MySQL Cluster that meets the *minimum* requirements for availability and safeguarding of data.

This section covers hardware and software requirements; networking issues; installation of MySQL Cluster; configuration issues; starting, stopping, and restarting the cluster; loading of a sample database; and performing queries.

Basic Assumptions

This How-To makes the following assumptions:

1. The cluster setup has four nodes, each on a separate host, and each with a fixed network address on a typical Ethernet as shown here:

Node	IP Address
Management (MGM) node	192.168.0.10
MySQL server (SQL) node	192.168.0.20
Data (NDBD) node "A"	192.168.0.30
Data (NDBD) node "B"	192.168.0.40

   This may be made clearer in Figure 9.4.

   Note: In the interest of simplicity (and reliability), this How-To uses only numeric IP addresses. However, if DNS resolution is available on your network, it is possible to use hostnames in lieu of IP addresses in configuring Cluster. Alternatively, you can use the /etc/hosts file or your operating system's equivalent for providing a means to do host lookup if such is available.

2. Each host in our scenario is an Intel-based desktop PC running a common, generic Linux distribution installed to disk in a standard configuration, and running no unnecessary services. The core OS with standard TCP/IP networking capabilities should be sufficient. Also for the sake of simplicity, we also assume that the filesystems on all hosts are set up identically. In the event that they are not, you will need to adapt these instructions accordingly.

3. Standard 100 Mbps or 1 gigabit Ethernet cards are installed on each machine, along with the proper drivers for the cards, and that all four hosts are connected via a standard-issue Ethernet networking appliance such as a switch. (All machines should use network cards with the same throughout. That is, all four machines in the cluster should have 100 Mbps cards *or* all four machines should have 1 Gbps cards.) MySQL Cluster will work in a 100 Mbps network; however, gigabit Ethernet will provide better performance.

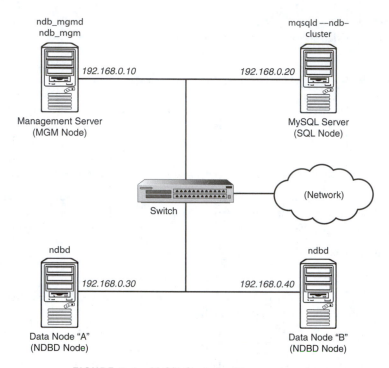

FIGURE 9.4 MySQL Cluster multi-computer setup.

Note that MySQL Cluster is *not* intended for use in a network for which throughput is less than 100 Mbps. For this reason (among others), attempting to run a MySQL Cluster over a public network such as the Internet is not likely to be successful, and is not recommended.

4. For our sample data, we will use the world database, which is available for download from the MySQL AB Web site. Because this database takes up a relatively small amount of space, we assume that each machine has 256MB RAM, which should be sufficient for running the operating system, host NDB process, and (for the data nodes) for storing the database.

Although we refer to a Linux operating system in this How-To, the instructions and procedures that we provide here should be easily adaptable to either Solaris or Mac OS X. We also assume that you already know how to perform a minimal installation and configuration of the operating system with networking capability, or that you are able to obtain assistance in this elsewhere if needed.

We discuss MySQL Cluster hardware, software, and networking requirements in somewhat greater detail in the next section. (See Section 9.3.1, "Hardware, Software, and Networking.")

9.3.1 Hardware, Software, and Networking

One of the strengths of MySQL Cluster is that it can be run on commodity hardware and has no unusual requirements in this regard, other than for large amounts of RAM, due to the fact that all live data storage is done in memory. (Note that this is subject to change, and that we intend to implement disk-based storage in a future MySQL Cluster release.) Naturally, multiple and faster CPUs will enhance performance. Memory requirements for Cluster processes are relatively small.

The software requirements for Cluster are also modest. Host operating systems do not require any unusual modules, services, applications, or configuration to support MySQL Cluster. For Mac OS X or Solaris, the standard installation is sufficient. For Linux, a standard, "out of the box" installation should be all that is necessary. The MySQL software requirements are simple: All that is needed is a production release of MySQL-max 5.0; you must use the -max version of MySQL to have Cluster support. (See Section 4.3, "The mysqld-max Extended MySQL Server.") It is not necessary to compile MySQL yourself merely to be able to use Cluster. In this How-To, we assume that you are using the -max binary appropriate to your Linux, Solaris, or Mac OS X operating system, available via the MySQL software downloads page at http://dev.mysql.com/downloads/.

For inter-node communication, Cluster supports TCP/IP networking in any standard topology, and the minimum expected for each host is a standard 100 Mbps Ethernet card, plus a switch, hub, or router to provide network connectivity for the cluster as a whole. We strongly recommend that a MySQL Cluster be run on its own subnet which is not shared with non-Cluster machines for the following reasons:

- **Security**: Communications between Cluster nodes are not encrypted or shielded in any way. The only means of protecting transmissions within a MySQL Cluster is to run your Cluster on a protected network. If you intend to use MySQL Cluster for Web applications, the cluster should definitely reside behind your firewall and not in your network's De-Militarized Zone (DMZ at http://compnetworking.about.com/cs/networksecurity/g/bldef_dmz.htm) or elsewhere.

- **Efficiency**: Setting up a MySQL Cluster on a private or protected network allows the cluster to make exclusive use of bandwidth between cluster hosts. Using a separate switch for your MySQL Cluster not only helps protect against unauthorized access to Cluster data, it also ensures that Cluster nodes are shielded from interference caused by transmissions between other computers on the network. For enhanced reliability, you can use dual switches and dual cards to remove the network as a single point of failure; many device drivers support failover for such communication links.

It is also possible to use the high-speed Scalable Coherent Interface (SCI) with MySQL Cluster, but this is not a requirement. See Section 9.8, "Using High-Speed Interconnects with MySQL Cluster," for more about this protocol and its use with MySQL Cluster.

9.3.2 Multi-Computer Installation

Each MySQL Cluster host computer running storage or SQL nodes must have installed on it a MySQL-max binary. For management nodes, it is not necessary to install the MySQL server binary, but you do have to install the MGM server daemon and client binaries (ndb_mgmd and ndb_mgm, respectively). This section covers the steps necessary to install the correct binaries for each type of Cluster node.

MySQL AB provides precompiled binaries that support Cluster, and there is generally no need to compile these yourself. Therefore, the first step in the installation process for each cluster host is to download the file mysql-max-5.0.19-pc-linux-gnu-i686.tar.gz from the MySQL downloads area (http://dev.mysql.com/downloads/). We assume that you have placed it in each machine's /var/tmp directory. (If you do require a custom binary, see Section 2.8.3, "Installing from the Development Source Tree.")

RPMs are also available for both 32-bit and 64-bit Linux platforms; as of MySQL 4.1.10a, the -max binaries installed by the RPMs support the NDBCluster storage engine. If you choose to use these rather than the binary files, be aware that you must install *both* the -server and -max packages on all machines that are to host cluster nodes. (See Section 2.4, "Installing MySQL on Linux," for more information about installing MySQL using the RPMs.) After installing from RPM, you will still need to configure the cluster as discussed in Section 9.3.3, "Multi-Computer Configuration."

Note: After completing the installation, do not yet start any of the binaries. We will show you how to do so following the configuration of all nodes.

Storage and SQL Node Installation

On each of the three machines designated to host storage or SQL nodes, perform the following steps as the system root user:

1. Check your /etc/passwd and /etc/group files (or use whatever tools are provided by your operating system for managing users and groups) to see whether there is already a mysql group and mysql user on the system. Some OS distributions create these as part of the operating system installation process. If they are not already present, create a new mysql user group, and then add a mysql user to this group:

    ```
    shell> groupadd mysql
    shell> useradd -g mysql mysql
    ```

    The syntax for useradd and groupadd may differ slightly on different versions of Unix, or they may have different names such as adduser and addgroup.

2. Change location to the directory containing the downloaded file, unpack the archive, and create a symlink to the mysql-max directory named mysql. Note that the actual file and directory names will vary according to the MySQL version number.

    ```
    shell> cd /var/tmp
    shell> tar -xzvf -C /usr/local mysql-max-5.0.19-pc-linux-gnu-i686.tar.gz
    shell> ln -s /usr/local/mysql-max-5.0.19-pc-linux-gnu-i686 /usr/local/mysql
    ```

3. Change location to the `mysql` directory and run the supplied script for creating the system databases:

```
shell> cd mysql
shell> scripts/mysql_install_db --user=mysql
```

4. Set the necessary permissions for the MySQL server and data directories:

```
shell> chown -R root .
shell> chown -R mysql data
shell> chgrp -R mysql .
```

Note that the data directory on each machine hosting a data node is `/usr/local/mysql/data`. We will use this piece of information when we configure the management node. (See Section 9.3.3, "Multi-Computer Configuration.")

5. Copy the MySQL startup script to the appropriate directory, make it executable, and set it to start when the operating system is booted up:

```
shell> cp support-files/mysql.server /etc/rc.d/init.d/
shell> chmod +x /etc/rc.d/init.d/mysql.server
shell> chkconfig --add mysql.server
```

(The startup scripts directory may vary depending on your operating system and version—for example, in some Linux distributions, it is `/etc/init.d`.)

Here we use Red Hat's `chkconfig` for creating links to the startup scripts; use whatever means is appropriate for this purpose on your operating system and distribution, such as `update-rc.d` on Debian.

Remember that the preceding steps must be performed separately for each machine on which a storage or SQL node is to reside.

Management Node Installation

Installation for the management (MGM) node does not require installation of the `mysqld` binary. Only the binaries for the MGM server and client are required, which can be found in the downloaded -max archive. Again, we assume that you have placed this file in `/var/tmp`.

As system `root` (that is, after using `sudo`, `su root`, or your system's equivalent for temporarily assuming the system administrator account's privileges), perform the following steps to install `ndb_mgmd` and `ndb_mgm` on the Cluster management node host:

1. Change location to the `/var/tmp` directory, and extract the `ndb_mgm` and `ndb_mgmd` from the archive into a suitable directory such as `/usr/local`:

```
shell> cd /var/tmp
shell> tar -zxvf mysql-max-5.0.19-pc-linux-gnu-i686.tar.gz \
         /usr/local '*/bin/ndb_mgm*'
```

2. Change location to the directory into which you unpacked the files, and then make both of them executable:

```
shell> cd /usr/local
shell> chmod +x ndb_mgm*
```

In Section 9.3.3, "Multi-Computer Configuration," we will create and write configuration files for all of the nodes in our example Cluster.

9.3.3 Multi-Computer Configuration

For our four-node, four-host MySQL Cluster, we will need to write four configuration files, one per node/host.

- Each data node or SQL node requires a `my.cnf` file that provides two pieces of information: a **connectstring** telling the node where to find the MGM node, and a line telling the MySQL server on this host (the machine hosting the data node) to run in NDB mode.

  For more information on connectstrings, see Section 9.4.4.2, "The MySQL Cluster `connectstring`."

- The management node needs a `config.ini` file telling it how many replicas to maintain, how much memory to allocate for data and indexes on each data node, where to find the data nodes, where to save data to disk on each data node, and where to find any SQL nodes.

Configuring the Storage and SQL Nodes

The `my.cnf` file needed for the data nodes is fairly simple. The configuration file should be located in the `/etc` directory and can be edited using any text editor. (Create the file if it does not exist.) For example:

```
shell> vi /etc/my.cnf
```

We show `vi` being used here to create the file, but any text editor should work just as well.

For each data node and SQL node in our example setup, `my.cnf` should look like this:

```
# Options for mysqld process:
[MYSQLD]
ndbcluster                       # run NDB engine
ndb-connectstring=192.168.0.10   # location of MGM node


# Options for ndbd process:
[MYSQL_CLUSTER]
ndb-connectstring=192.168.0.10   # location of MGM node
```

After entering the preceding information, save this file and exit the text editor. Do this for the machines hosting data node "A", data node "B", and the SQL node.

Configuring the Management Node

The first step in configuring the MGM node is to create the directory in which the configuration file can be found and then to create the file itself. For example (running as `root`):

```
shell> mkdir /var/lib/mysql-cluster
shell> cd /var/lib/mysql-cluster
shell> vi config.ini
```

For our representative setup, the config.ini file should read as follows:

```
# Options affecting ndbd processes on all data nodes:
[NDBD DEFAULT]
NoOfReplicas=2      # Number of replicas
DataMemory=80M      # How much memory to allocate for data storage
IndexMemory=18M     # How much memory to allocate for index storage
                    # For DataMemory and IndexMemory, we have used the
                    # default values. Since the "world" database takes up
                    # only about 500KB, this should be more than enough for
                    # this example Cluster setup.


# TCP/IP options:
[TCP DEFAULT]
portnumber=2202     # This the default; however, you can use any
                    # port that is free for all the hosts in cluster
                    # Note: It is recommended beginning with MySQL 5.0 that
                    # you do not specify the portnumber at all and simply allow
                    # the default value to be used instead


# Management process options:
[NDB_MGMD]
hostname=192.168.0.10            # Hostname or IP address of MGM node
datadir=/var/lib/mysql-cluster   # Directory for MGM node logfiles


# Options for data node "A":
[NDBD]
                                 # (one [NDBD] section per data node)
hostname=192.168.0.30            # Hostname or IP address
datadir=/usr/local/mysql/data    # Directory for this data node's datafiles


# Options for data node "B":
[NDBD]
hostname=192.168.0.40            # Hostname or IP address
datadir=/usr/local/mysql/data    # Directory for this data node's datafiles


# SQL node options:
[MYSQLD]
hostname=192.168.0.20            # Hostname or IP address
                                 # (additional mysqld connections can be
                                 # specified for this node for various
                                 # purposes such as running ndb_restore)
```

(**Note**: The world database can be downloaded from http://dev.mysql.com/doc/, where it can be found listed under "Examples.")

After all the configuration files have been created and these minimal options have been specified, you are ready to proceed with starting the cluster and verifying that all processes are running. We discuss how this is done in Section 9.3.4, "Initial Startup."

For more detailed information about the available MySQL Cluster configuration parameters and their uses, see Section 9.4, "MySQL Cluster Configuration," and Section 9.4.4, "Configuration File." For configuration of MySQL Cluster as relates to making backups, see Section 9.6.5.4, "Configuration for Cluster Backup."

Note: The default port for Cluster management nodes is 1186; the default port for data nodes is 2202. Beginning with MySQL 5.0.3, this restriction is lifted, and the cluster automatically allocates ports for data nodes from those that are already free.

9.3.4 Initial Startup

Starting the cluster is not very difficult after it has been configured. Each cluster node process must be started separately, and on the host where it resides. Although it is possible to start the nodes in any order, it is recommended that the management node be started first, followed by the storage nodes, and then finally by any SQL nodes:

1. On the management host, issue the following command from the system shell to start the MGM node process:

   ```
   shell> ndb_mgmd -f /var/lib/mysql-cluster/config.ini
   ```

   Note that ndb_mgmd must be told where to find its configuration file, using the -f or --config-file option. (See Section 9.5.3, "ndb_mgmd, the Management Server Process," for details.)

2. On each of the data node hosts, run this command to start the ndbd process for the first time:

   ```
   shell> ndbd --initial
   ```

   Note that it is very important to use the --initial parameter *only* when starting ndbd for the first time, or when restarting after a backup/restore operation or a configuration change. This is because the --initial option causes the node to delete any files created by earlier ndbd instances that are needed for recovery, including the recovery log files.

3. If you used RPM files to install MySQL on the cluster host where the SQL node is to reside, you can (and should) use the startup script installed in /etc/init.d to start the MySQL server process on the SQL node. Note that you need to install the -max server RPM *in addition to* the Standard server RPM to run the -max server binary.

If all has gone well, and the cluster has been set up correctly, the cluster should now be operational. You can test this by invoking the ndb_mgm management node client. The output should look like that shown here, although you might see some slight differences in the output depending on the exact version of MySQL that you are using:

```
shell> ndb_mgm
-- NDB Cluster -- Management Client --
ndb_mgm> SHOW
Connected to Management Server at: localhost:1186
Cluster Configuration
```

```
--------------------
[ndbd(NDB)]     2 node(s)
id=2    @192.168.0.30  (Version: 5.0.19, Nodegroup: 0, Master)
id=3    @192.168.0.40  (Version: 5.0.19, Nodegroup: 0)

[ndb_mgmd(MGM)] 1 node(s)
id=1    @192.168.0.10  (Version: 5.0.19)

[mysqld(SQL)]   1 node(s)
id=4    (Version: 5.0.19)
```

Note: If you are using an older version of MySQL, you may see the SQL node referenced as [mysqld(API)]. This reflects an older usage that is now deprecated.

You should now be ready to work with databases, tables, and data in MySQL Cluster. See Section 9.3.5, "Loading Sample Data and Performing Queries," for a brief discussion.

9.3.5 Loading Sample Data and Performing Queries

Working with data in MySQL Cluster is not much different from doing so in MySQL without Cluster. There are two points to keep in mind:

- For a table to be replicated in the cluster, it must use the NDB Cluster storage engine. To specify this, use the ENGINE=NDB or ENGINE=NDBCLUSTER table option. You can add this option when creating the table:

  ```
  CREATE TABLE tbl_name ( ... ) ENGINE=NDBCLUSTER;
  ```

  Alternatively, for an existing table that uses a different storage engine, use ALTER TABLE to change the table to use NDB Cluster:

  ```
  ALTER TABLE tbl_name ENGINE=NDBCLUSTER;
  ```

- Each NDB table *must* have a primary key. If no primary key is defined by the user when a table is created, the NDB Cluster storage engine automatically generates a hidden one. (**Note**: This hidden key takes up space just as does any other table index. It is not uncommon to encounter problems due to insufficient memory for accommodating these automatically created indexes.)

If you are importing tables from an existing database using the output of mysqldump, you can open the SQL script in a text editor and add the ENGINE option to any table creation statements, or replace any existing ENGINE (or TYPE) options. Suppose that you have the world sample database on another MySQL server that does not support MySQL Cluster, and you want to export the City table:

```
shell> mysqldump --add-drop-table world City > city_table.sql
```

The resulting city_table.sql file will contain this table creation statement (and the INSERT statements necessary to import the table data):

```
DROP TABLE IF EXISTS `City`;
CREATE TABLE `City` (
```

```
  `ID` int(11) NOT NULL auto_increment,
  `Name` char(35) NOT NULL default '',
  `CountryCode` char(3) NOT NULL default '',
  `District` char(20) NOT NULL default '',
  `Population` int(11) NOT NULL default '0',
  PRIMARY KEY  (`ID`)
) ENGINE=MyISAM DEFAULT CHARSET=latin1;

INSERT INTO `City` VALUES (1,'Kabul','AFG','Kabol',1780000);
INSERT INTO `City` VALUES (2,'Qandahar','AFG','Qandahar',237500);
INSERT INTO `City` VALUES (3,'Herat','AFG','Herat',186800);
(remaining INSERT statements omitted)
```

You will need to make sure that MySQL uses the NDB storage engine for this table. There
are two ways that this can be accomplished. One of these is to modify the table definition
before importing it into the Cluster database. Using the City table as an example, modify the
ENGINE option of the definition as follows:

```
DROP TABLE IF EXISTS `City`;
CREATE TABLE `City` (
  `ID` int(11) NOT NULL auto_increment,
  `Name` char(35) NOT NULL default '',
  `CountryCode` char(3) NOT NULL default '',
  `District` char(20) NOT NULL default '',
  `Population` int(11) NOT NULL default '0',
  PRIMARY KEY  (`ID`)
) ENGINE=NDBCLUSTER DEFAULT CHARSET=latin1;

INSERT INTO `City` VALUES (1,'Kabul','AFG','Kabol',1780000);
INSERT INTO `City` VALUES (2,'Qandahar','AFG','Qandahar',237500);
INSERT INTO `City` VALUES (3,'Herat','AFG','Herat',186800);
(remaining INSERT statements omitted)
```

This must be done for the definition of each table that is to be part of the clustered database. The easiest way to accomplish this is to do a search-and-replace on the file that contains the definitions and replace all instances of TYPE=*engine_name* or ENGINE=*engine_name*
with ENGINE=NDBCLUSTER. If you do not want to modify the file, you can use the unmodified
file to create the tables, and then use ALTER TABLE to change their storage engine. The particulars are given later in this section.

Assuming that you have already created a database named world on the SQL node of the
cluster, you can then use the mysql command-line client to read city_table.sql, and create
and populate the corresponding table in the usual manner:

```
shell> mysql world < city_table.sql
```

It is very important to keep in mind that the preceding command must be executed on the
host where the SQL node is running (in this case, on the machine with the IP address
192.168.0.20).

To create a copy of the entire `world` database on the SQL node, use `mysqldump` on the non-cluster server to export the database to a file named `world.sql`; for example, in the `/tmp` directory. Then modify the table definitions as just described and import the file into the SQL node of the cluster like this:

```
shell> mysql world < /tmp/world.sql
```

If you save the file to a different location, adjust the preceding instructions accordingly.

It is important to note that `NDB Cluster` in MySQL 5.0 does not support autodiscovery of databases. (See Section 9.9, "Known Limitations of MySQL Cluster.") This means that, once the `world` database and its tables have been created on one data node, you need to issue the `CREATE SCHEMA world` statement (beginning with MySQL 5.0.2, you may use `CREATE SCHEMA world` instead), followed by `FLUSH TABLES` on each SQL node in the cluster. This will cause the node to recognize the database and read its table definitions.

Running `SELECT` queries on the SQL node is no different from running them on any other instance of a MySQL server. To run queries from the command line, you first need to log in to the MySQL Monitor in the usual way (specify the `root` password at the `Enter password:` prompt):

```
shell> mysql -u root -p
Enter password:
Welcome to the MySQL monitor.  Commands end with ; or \g.
Your MySQL connection id is 1 to server version: 5.0.19

Type 'help;' or '\h' for help. Type '\c' to clear the buffer.

mysql>
```

We simply use the MySQL server's root account and assume that you have followed the standard security precautions for installing a MySQL server, including setting a strong root password. For more information, see Section 2.9.3, "Securing the Initial MySQL Accounts."

It is worth taking into account that Cluster nodes do not make use of the MySQL privilege system when accessing one another. Setting or changing MySQL user accounts (including the root account) affects only applications that access the SQL node, not interaction between nodes.

If you did not modify the `ENGINE` clauses in the table definitions prior to importing the SQL script, you should run the following statements at this point:

```
mysql> USE world;
mysql> ALTER TABLE City ENGINE=NDBCLUSTER;
mysql> ALTER TABLE Country ENGINE=NDBCLUSTER;
mysql> ALTER TABLE CountryLanguage ENGINE=NDBCLUSTER;
```

Selecting a database and running a SELECT query against a table in that database is also accomplished in the usual manner, as is exiting the MySQL Monitor:

```
mysql> USE world;
mysql> SELECT Name, Population FROM City ORDER BY Population DESC LIMIT 5;
+-----------+------------+
| Name      | Population |
+-----------+------------+
| Bombay    |   10500000 |
| Seoul     |    9981619 |
| São Paulo |    9968485 |
| Shanghai  |    9696300 |
| Jakarta   |    9604900 |
+-----------+------------+
5 rows in set (0.34 sec)

mysql> \q
Bye

shell>
```

Applications that use MySQL can employ standard APIs to access NDB tables. It is important to remember that your application must access the SQL node, and not the MGM or storage nodes. This brief example shows how we might execute the SELECT statement just shown by using PHP 5's mysqli extension running on a Web server elsewhere on the network:

```php
<!DOCTYPE HTML PUBLIC "-//W3C//DTD HTML 4.01 Transitional//EN"
  "http://www.w3.org/TR/html4/loose.dtd">
<html>
<head>
  <meta http-equiv="Content-Type"
        content="text/html; charset=iso-8859-1">
  <title>SIMPLE mysqli SELECT</title>
</head>
<body>
<?php
  # connect to SQL node:
  $link = new mysqli('192.168.0.20', 'root', 'root_password', 'world');
  # parameters for mysqli constructor are:
  #   host, user, password, database

  if( mysqli_connect_errno() )
    die("Connect failed: " . mysqli_connect_error());

  $query = "SELECT Name, Population
            FROM City
            ORDER BY Population DESC
            LIMIT 5";
```

```
  # if no errors...
  if( $result = $link->query($query) )
  {
?>
<table border="1" width="40%" cellpadding="4" cellspacing ="1">
  <tbody>
  <tr>
    <th width="10%">City</th>
    <th>Population</th>
  </tr>
<?
    # then display the results...
    while($row = $result->fetch_object())
      printf(<tr>\n  <td align=\"center\">%s</td><td>%d</td>\n</tr>\n",
              $row->Name, $row->Population);
?>
  </tbody>
</table>
<?
  # ...and verify the number of rows that were retrieved
    printf("<p>Affected rows: %d</p>\n", $link->affected_rows);
  }
  else
    # otherwise, tell us what went wrong
    echo mysqli_error();

  # free the result set and the mysqli connection object
  $result->close();
  $link->close();
?>
</body>
</html>
```

We assume that the process running on the Web server can reach the IP address of the SQL node.

In a similar fashion, you can use the MySQL C API, Perl-DBI, Python-mysql, or MySQL AB's own Connectors to perform the tasks of data definition and manipulation just as you would normally with MySQL.

9.3.6 Safe Shutdown and Restart

To shut down the cluster, enter the following command in a shell on the machine hosting the MGM node:

```
shell> ndb_mgm -e shutdown
```

The -e option here is used to pass a command to the ndb_mgm client from the shell. See Section 3.3.1, "Using Options on the Command Line." The command causes the ndb_mgm, ndb_mgmd, and any ndbd processes to terminate gracefully. Any SQL nodes can be terminated using mysqladmin shutdown and other means.

To restart the cluster, run these commands:

- On the management host (192.168.0.10 in our example setup):

  ```
  shell> ndb_mgmd -f /var/lib/mysql-cluster/config.ini
  ```

- On each of the data node hosts (192.168.0.30 and 192.168.0.40):

  ```
  shell> ndbd
  ```

  Remember *not* to invoke this command with the --initial option when restarting an NDBD node normally.

- On the SQL host (192.168.0.20):

  ```
  shell> mysqld &
  ```

For information on making Cluster backups, see Section 9.6.5.2, "Using the Management Server to Create a Backup."

To restore the cluster from backup requires the use of the ndb_restore command. This is covered in Section 9.6.5.3, "How to Restore a Cluster Backup."

More information on configuring MySQL Cluster can be found in Section 9.4, "MySQL Cluster Configuration."

9.4 MySQL Cluster Configuration

A MySQL server that is part of a MySQL Cluster differs in only one respect from a normal (non-clustered) MySQL server, in that it employs the NDB Cluster storage engine. This engine is also referred to simply as NDB, and the two forms of the name are synonymous.

To avoid unnecessary allocation of resources, the server is configured by default with the NDB storage engine disabled. To enable NDB, you must modify the server's my.cnf configuration file, or start the server with the --ndbcluster option.

The MySQL server is a part of the cluster, so it also must know how to access an MGM node to obtain the cluster configuration data. The default behavior is to look for the MGM node on localhost. However, should you need to specify that its location is elsewhere, this can be done in my.cnf or on the MySQL server command line. Before the NDB storage engine can be used, at least one MGM node must be operational, as well as any desired data nodes.

9.4.1 Building MySQL Cluster from Source Code

NDB, the Cluster storage engine, is available in binary distributions for Linux, Mac OS X, and Solaris. We are working to make Cluster run on all operating systems supported by MySQL, including Windows.

If you choose to build from a source tarball or the MySQL 5.0 BitKeeper tree, be sure to use the `--with-ndbcluster` option when running `configure`. You can also use the `BUILD/compile-pentium-max` build script. Note that this script includes OpenSSL, so you must either have or obtain OpenSSL to build successfully, or else modify `compile-pentium-max` to exclude this requirement. Of course, you can also just follow the standard instructions for compiling your own binaries, and then perform the usual tests and installation procedure. See Section 2.8.3, "Installing from the Development Source Tree."

9.4.2 Installing the Software

In the next few sections, we assume that you are already familiar with installing MySQL, and here we cover only the differences between configuring MySQL Cluster and configuring MySQL without clustering. (See Chapter 2, "Installing and Upgrading MySQL," if you require more information about the latter.)

You will find Cluster configuration easiest if you have already have all management and data nodes running first; this is likely to be the most time-consuming part of the configuration. Editing the `my.cnf` file is fairly straightforward, and this section will cover only any differences from configuring MySQL without clustering.

9.4.3 Quick Test Setup of MySQL Cluster

To familiarize you with the basics, we will describe the simplest possible configuration for a functional MySQL Cluster. After this, you should be able to design your desired setup from the information provided in the other relevant sections of this chapter.

First, you need to create a configuration directory such as `/var/lib/mysql-cluster`, by executing the following command as the system root user:

```
shell> mkdir /var/lib/mysql-cluster
```

In this directory, create a file named `config.ini` that contains the following information. Substitute appropriate values for `HostName` and `DataDir` as necessary for your system.

```
# file "config.ini" - showing minimal setup consisting of 1 data node,
# 1 management server, and 3 MySQL servers.
# The empty default sections are not required, and are shown only for
# the sake of completeness.
# Data nodes must provide a hostname but MySQL Servers are not required
# to do so.
# If you don't know the hostname for your machine, use localhost.
# The DataDir parameter also has a default value, but it is recommended to
# set it explicitly.
# Note: DB, API, and MGM are aliases for NDBD, MYSQLD, and NDB_MGMD
# respectively. DB and API are deprecated and should not be used in new
# installations.
[NDBD DEFAULT]
NoOfReplicas= 1
```

```
[MYSQLD DEFAULT]
[NDB_MGMD DEFAULT]
[TCP DEFAULT]

[NDB_MGMD]
HostName= myhost.example.com

[NDBD]
HostName= myhost.example.com
DataDir= /var/lib/mysql-cluster

[MYSQLD]
[MYSQLD]
[MYSQLD]
```

You can now start the ndb_mgmd management server. By default, it attempts to read the config.ini file in its current working directory, so change location into the directory where the file is located and then invoke ndb_mgmd:

```
shell> cd /var/lib/mysql-cluster
shell> ndb_mgmd
```

Then start a single DB node by running ndbd. When starting ndbd for a given DB node for the very first time, you should use the --initial option as shown here:

```
shell> ndbd --initial
```

For subsequent ndbd starts, you will generally want to *omit* the --initial option:

```
shell> ndbd
```

The reason for omitting --initial on subsequent restarts is that this option causes ndbd to delete and re-create all existing data and log files (as well as all table metadata) for this data node. One exception to this rule about not using --initial except for the first ndbd invocation is that you use it when restarting the cluster and restoring from backup after adding new data nodes.

By default, ndbd looks for the management server at localhost on port 1186.

Note: If you have installed MySQL from a binary tarball, you will need to specify the path of the ndb_mgmd and ndbd servers explicitly. (Normally, these will be found in /usr/local/mysql/bin.)

Finally, change location to the MySQL data directory (usually /var/lib/mysql or /usr/local/mysql/data), and make sure that the my.cnf file contains the option necessary to enable the NDB storage engine:

```
[mysqld]
ndbcluster
```

You can now start the MySQL server as usual:

```
shell> mysqld_safe --user=mysql &
```

Wait a moment to make sure the MySQL server is running properly. If you see the notice `mysql ended`, check the server's `.err` file to find out what went wrong.

If all has gone well so far, you now can start using the cluster. Connect to the server and verify that the `NDBCLUSTER` storage engine is enabled:

```
shell> mysql
Welcome to the MySQL monitor.  Commands end with ; or \g.
Your MySQL connection id is 1 to server version: 5.0.19-Max

Type 'help;' or '\h' for help. Type '\c' to clear the buffer.

mysql> SHOW ENGINES\G
...
*************************** 12. row ***************************
Engine: NDBCLUSTER
Support: YES
Comment: Clustered, fault-tolerant, memory-based tables
*************************** 13. row ***************************
Engine: NDB
Support: YES
Comment: Alias for NDBCLUSTER
...
```

The row numbers shown in the preceding example output may be different from those shown on your system, depending on how your server is configured.

Try to create an `NDBCLUSTER` table:

```
shell> mysql
mysql> USE test;
Database changed

mysql> CREATE TABLE ctest (i INT) ENGINE=NDBCLUSTER;
Query OK, 0 rows affected (0.09 sec)

mysql> SHOW CREATE TABLE ctest \G
*************************** 1. row ***************************
       Table: ctest
Create Table: CREATE TABLE `ctest` (
  `i` int(11) default NULL
) ENGINE=ndbcluster DEFAULT CHARSET=latin1
1 row in set (0.00 sec)
```

To check that your nodes were set up properly, start the management client:

```
shell> ndb_mgm
```

Use the SHOW command from within the management client to obtain a report on the cluster's status:

```
NDB> SHOW
Cluster Configuration
---------------------
[ndbd(NDB)]     1 node(s)
id=2    @127.0.0.1  (Version: 3.5.3, Nodegroup: 0, Master)

[ndb_mgmd(MGM)] 1 node(s)
id=1    @127.0.0.1  (Version: 3.5.3)

[mysqld(API)]   3 node(s)
id=3    @127.0.0.1  (Version: 3.5.3)
id=4 (not connected, accepting connect from any host)
id=5 (not connected, accepting connect from any host)
```

At this point, you have successfully set up a working MySQL Cluster. You can now store data in the cluster by using any table created with

ENGINE=NDBCLUSTER or its alias ENGINE=NDB.

9.4.4 Configuration File

Configuring MySQL Cluster requires working with two files:

- my.cnf: Specifies options for all MySQL Cluster executables. This file, with which you should be familiar with from previous work with MySQL, must be accessible by each executable running in the cluster.

- config.ini: This file is read only by the MySQL Cluster management server, which then distributes the information contained therein to all processes participating in the cluster. config.ini contains a description of each node involved in the cluster. This includes configuration parameters for data nodes and configuration parameters for connections between all nodes in the cluster.

We are continuously making improvements in Cluster configuration and attempting to simplify this process. Although we strive to maintain backward compatibility, there may be times when introduce an incompatible change. In such cases we will try to let Cluster users know in advance if a change is not backward compatible. If you find such a change and we have not documented it, please report it in the MySQL bugs database using the instructions given in Section 1.8, "How to Report Bugs or Problems."

9.4.4.1 Example Configuration for a MySQL Cluster

To support MySQL Cluster, you will need to update my.cnf as shown in the following example. Note that the options shown here should not be confused with those that are used in config.ini files. You may also specify these parameters on the command line when invoking the executables.

```
# my.cnf
# example additions to my.cnf for MySQL Cluster
# (valid in MySQL 5.0)

# enable ndbcluster storage engine, and provide connectstring for
# management server host (default port is 1186)
[mysqld]
ndbcluster
ndb-connectstring=ndb_mgmd.mysql.com


# provide connectstring for management server host (default port: 1186)
[ndbd]
connect-string=ndb_mgmd.mysql.com

# provide connectstring for management server host (default port: 1186)
[ndb_mgm]
connect-string=ndb_mgmd.mysql.com

# provide location of cluster configuration file
[ndb_mgmd]
config-file=/etc/config.ini
```

(For more information on connectstrings, see Section 9.4.4.2, "The MySQL Cluster connectstring.")

```
# my.cnf
# example additions to my.cnf for MySQL Cluster
# (will work on all versions)

# enable ndbcluster storage engine, and provide connectstring for management
# server host to the default port 1186
[mysqld]
ndbcluster
ndb-connectstring=ndb_mgmd.mysql.com:1186
```

You may also use a separate [mysql_cluster] section in the cluster my.cnf file for settings to be read and used by all executables:

```
# cluster-specific settings
[mysql_cluster]
ndb-connectstring=ndb_mgmd.mysql.com:1186
```

The configuration file is named config.ini by default. It is read by ndb_mgmd at startup and can be placed anywhere. Its location and name are specified by using --config-file=*path_ name* on the ndb_mgmd command line. If the configuration file is not specified, ndb_mgmd by default tries to read a file named config.ini located in the current working directory.

Currently, the configuration file is in INI format, which consists of sections preceded by section headings (surrounded by square brackets), followed by the appropriate parameter names and values. One deviation from the standard INI format is that the parameter name and value can be separated by a colon (':') as well as the equal sign ('='). Another deviation is that sections are not uniquely identified by section name. Instead, unique sections (such as two different nodes of the same type) are identified by a unique ID specified as a parameter within the section.

Default values are defined for most parameters, and can also be specified in config.ini. To create a default value section, simply add the word DEFAULT to the section name. For example, an [NDBD] section contains parameters that apply to a particular data node, whereas an [NDBD DEFAULT] section contains parameters that apply to all data nodes. Suppose that all data nodes should use the same data memory size. To configure them all, create an [NDBD DEFAULT] section that contains a DataMemory line to specify the data memory size.

At a minimum, the configuration file must define the computers and nodes involved in the cluster and on which computers these nodes are located. An example of a simple configuration file for a cluster consisting of one management server, two data nodes, and two MySQL servers is shown here:

```
# file "config.ini" - 2 data nodes and 2 SQL nodes
# This file is placed in the startup directory of ndb_mgmd (the
# management server)
# The first MySQL Server can be started from any host. The second
# can be started only on the host mysqld_5.mysql.com

[NDBD DEFAULT]
NoOfReplicas= 2
DataDir= /var/lib/mysql-cluster

[NDB_MGMD]
Hostname= ndb_mgmd.mysql.com
DataDir= /var/lib/mysql-cluster

[NDBD]
HostName= ndbd_2.mysql.com

[NDBD]
HostName= ndbd_3.mysql.com

[MYSQLD]
[MYSQLD]
HostName= mysqld_5.mysql.com
```

Note that each node has its own section in the config.ini. For instance, this cluster has two data nodes, so the preceding configuration file contains two [NDBD] sections defining these nodes.

There are six different sections that you can use in the config.ini configuration file:

- [COMPUTER]: Defines the cluster hosts.
- [NDBD]: Defines the cluster's data nodes.

- [MYSQLD]: Defines the cluster's MySQL server nodes.
- [MGM] or [NDB_MGMD]: Defines the cluster's management server node.
- [TCP]: Defines TCP/IP connections between nodes in the cluster, with TCP/IP being the default connection protocol.
- [SHM]: Defines shared-memory connections between nodes. Formerly, this type of connection was available only in binaries that were built using the --with-ndb-shm option. In MySQL 5.0-Max, it is enabled by default, but should still be considered experimental.

You can define DEFAULT values for each section. All Cluster parameter names are case-insensitive, which differs from parameters specified in my.cnf or my.ini files.

9.4.4.2 The MySQL Cluster connectstring

With the exception of the MySQL Cluster management server (ndb_mgmd), each node that is part of a MySQL Cluster requires a connectstring that points to the management server's location. This connectstring is used in establishing a connection to the management server as well as in performing other tasks depending on the node's role in the cluster. The syntax for a connectstring is as follows:

```
<connectstring> :=
    [<nodeid-specification>,]<host-specification>[,<host-specification>]

<nodeid-specification> := node_id

<host-specification> := host_name[:port_num]
```

node_id is an integer larger than 1 that identifies a node in config.ini. host_name is a string representing a valid Internet hostname or IP address. port_num is an integer referring to a TCP/IP port number.

```
example 1 (long):     "nodeid=2,myhost1:1100,myhost2:1100,192.168.0.3:1200"
example 2 (short):    "myhost1"
```

All nodes will use localhost:1186 as the default connectstring value if none is provided. If port_num is omitted from the connectstring, the default port is 1186. This port should always be available on the network because it has been assigned by IANA for this purpose (see http://www.iana.org/assignments/port-numbers for details).

By listing multiple <host-specification> values, it is possible to designate several redundant management servers. A cluster node will attempt to contact successive management servers on each host in the order specified, until a successful connection has been established.

There are a number of different ways to specify the connectstring:

- Each executable has its own command-line option that enables specifying the management server at startup. (See the documentation for the respective executable.)
- It is also possible to set the connectstring for all nodes in the cluster at once by placing it in a [mysql_cluster] section in the management server's my.cnf file.

- For backward compatibility, two other options are available, using the same syntax:
    1. Set the NDB_CONNECTSTRING environment variable to contain the connectstring.
    2. Write the connectstring for each executable into a text file named Ndb.cfg and place this file in the executable's startup directory.

    However, these options are now deprecated and should not be used for new installations.

The recommended method for specifying the connectstring is to set it on the command line or in the my.cnf file for each executable.

9.4.4.3 Defining the Computers Making Up a MySQL Cluster

The [COMPUTER] section has no real significance other than serving as a way to avoid the need of defining hostnames for each node in the system. All parameters mentioned here are required.

- Id

    This is an integer value, used to refer to the host computer elsewhere in the configuration file.

- HostName

    This is the computer's hostname or IP address.

9.4.4.4 Defining the MySQL Cluster Management Server

The [NDB_MGMD] section is used to configure the behavior of the management server. [MGM] can be used as an alias; the two section names are equivalent. All parameters in the following list are optional and assume their default values if omitted. **Note**: If neither the ExecuteOnComputer nor the HostName parameter is present, the default value localhost will be assumed for both.

- Id

    Each node in the cluster has a unique identity, which is represented by an integer value in the range 1 to 63 inclusive. This ID is used by all internal cluster messages for addressing the node.

- ExecuteOnComputer

    This refers to one of the computers defined in the [COMPUTER] section.

- PortNumber

    This is the port number on which the management server listens for configuration requests and management commands.

- LogDestination

    This parameter specifies where to send cluster logging information. There are three options in this regard: CONSOLE, SYSLOG, and FILE:

    - CONSOLE outputs the log to stdout:

        CONSOLE

- SYSLOG sends the log to a syslog facility, possible values being one of auth, auth-priv, cron, daemon, ftp, kern, lpr, mail, news, syslog, user, uucp, local0, local1, local2, local3, local4, local5, local6, or local7.

  Note: Not every facility is necessarily supported by every operating system.

  SYSLOG:facility=syslog

- FILE pipes the cluster log output to a regular file on the same machine. The following values can be specified:

  - filename: The name of the logfile.
  - maxsize: The maximum size (in bytes) to which the file can grow before logging rolls over to a new file. When this occurs, the old logfile is renamed by appending .N to the filename, where N is the next number not yet used with this name.
  - maxfiles: The maximum number of logfiles.

  FILE:filename=cluster.log,maxsize=1000000,maxfiles=6

  It is possible to specify multiple log destinations separated by semicolons as shown here:

  CONSOLE;SYSLOG:facility=local0;FILE:filename=/var/log/mgmd

  The default value for the FILE parameter is FILE:filename=ndb_*node_id*_cluster.log,maxsize=1000000,maxfiles=6, where *node_id* is the ID of the node.

- ArbitrationRank

  This parameter is used to define which nodes can act as arbitrators. Only MGM nodes and SQL nodes can be arbitrators. ArbitrationRank can take one of the following values:

  - 0: The node will never be used as an arbitrator.
  - 1: The node has high priority; that is, it will be preferred as an arbitrator over low-priority nodes.
  - 2: Indicates a low-priority node that will be used as an arbitrator only if a node with a higher priority is not available for that purpose.

  Normally, the management server should be configured as an arbitrator by setting its ArbitrationRank to 1 (the default value) and that of all SQL nodes to 0.

- ArbitrationDelay

  An integer value that causes the management server's responses to arbitration requests to be delayed by that number of milliseconds. By default, this value is 0; it is normally not necessary to change it.

- DataDir

  This specifies the directory where output files from the management server will be placed. These files include cluster log files, process output files, and the daemon's process ID (PID) file. (For log files, this location can be overridden by setting the FILE parameter for LogDestination as discussed previously in this section.)

9.4.4.5 Defining MySQL Cluster Data Nodes

The [NDBD] section is used to configure the behavior of the cluster's data nodes. There are many parameters that control buffer sizes, pool sizes, timeouts, and so forth. The only mandatory parameters are:

- Either ExecuteOnComputer or HostName
- The parameter NoOfReplicas

These mandatory parameters must be defined in the [NDBD DEFAULT] section.

Most data node parameters are set in the [NDBD DEFAULT] section. Only those parameters explicitly stated as being able to set local values are allowed to be changed in the [NDBD] section. HostName, Id, and ExecuteOnComputer *must* be defined in the local [NDBD] section.

Identifying Data Nodes

The Id value (that is, the data node identifier) can be allocated on the command line when the node is started or in the configuration file.

For each parameter it is possible to use K, M, or G as a suffix to indicate units of 1024, 1024×1024, or 1024×1024×1024. (For example, 100K means $100 \times 1024 = 102400$.) Parameter names and values are currently case-sensitive.

- Id

    This is the node ID used as the address of the node for all cluster internal messages. This is an integer in the range 1 to 63 inclusive. Each node in the cluster must have a unique identity.

- ExecuteOnComputer

    This refers to one of the computers (hosts) defined in the COMPUTER section.

- HostName

    Specifying this parameter has an effect similar to specifying ExecuteOnComputer. It defines the hostname of the computer on which the storage node is to reside. To specify a hostname other than localhost, either this parameter or ExecuteOnComputer is required.

- ServerPort (*OBSOLETE*)

    Each node in the cluster uses a port to connect to other nodes. This port is used also for non-TCP transporters in the connection setup phase. The default port is allocated dynamically in such a way as to ensure that no two nodes on the same computer receive the same port number, so it should not normally be necessary to specify a value for this parameter.

- NoOfReplicas

    This global parameter can be set only in the [NDBD DEFAULT] section, and defines the number of replicas for each table stored in the cluster. This parameter also specifies the size of node groups. A "node group" is a set of nodes all storing the same information.

    Node groups are formed implicitly. The first node group is formed by the set of data nodes with the lowest node IDs, the next node group by the set of the next lowest node identities, and so on. By way of example, assume that we have 4 data nodes and that NoOfReplicas is set to 2. The four data nodes have node IDs 2, 3, 4 and 5. Then the first node group is formed from nodes 2 and 3, and the second node group by nodes 4 and 5. It is important to configure the cluster in such a manner that nodes in the same node groups are not placed on the same computer because a single hardware failure would cause the entire cluster to crash.

If no node IDs are provided, the order of the data nodes will be the determining factor for the node group. Whether or not explicit assignments are made, they can be viewed in the output of the management client's SHOW statement.

There is no default value for NoOfReplicas; the maximum possible value is 4.

- DataDir

  This parameter specifies the directory where trace files, log files, pid files, and error logs are placed.

- FileSystemPath

  This parameter specifies the directory where all files created for metadata, REDO logs, UNDO logs and data files are placed. The default is the directory specified by DataDir. **Note:** This directory must exist before the ndbd process is initiated.

  The recommended directory hierarchy for MySQL Cluster includes /var/lib/ mysql-cluster, under which a directory for the node's filesystem is created. The name of this subdirectory contains the node ID. For example, if the node ID is 2, this subdirectory is named ndb_2_fs.

- BackupDataDir

  This parameter specifies the directory in which backups are placed. If omitted, the default backup location is the directory named BACKUP under the location specified by the FileSystemPath parameter. (See above.)

Data Memory and Index Memory

DataMemory and IndexMemory are [NDBD] parameters specifying the size of memory segments used to store the actual records and their indexes. In setting values for these, it is important to understand how DataMemory and IndexMemory are used, as they usually need to be updated to reflect actual usage by the cluster:

- DataMemory

  This parameter defines the amount of space (in bytes) available for storing database records. The entire amount specified by this value is allocated in memory, so it is extremely important that the machine has sufficient physical memory to accommodate it.

  The memory allocated by DataMemory is used to store both the actual records and indexes. Each record is currently of fixed size. (Even VARCHAR columns are stored as fixed-width columns.) There is a 16-byte overhead on each record; an additional amount for each record is incurred because it is stored in a 32KB page with 128-byte page overhead (see below). There is also a small amount wasted per page due to the fact that each record is stored in only one page. The maximum record size is currently 8052 bytes.

The memory space defined by DataMemory is also used to store ordered indexes, which use about 10 bytes per record. Each table row is represented in the ordered index. A common error among users is to assume that all indexes are stored in the memory allocated by IndexMemory, but this is not the case: Only primary key and unique hash indexes use this memory; ordered indexes use the memory allocated by DataMemory. However, creating a primary key or unique hash index also creates an ordered index on the same keys, unless you specify USING HASH in the index creation statement. This can be verified by running ndb_desc -d db_name table_name in the management client.

The memory space allocated by DataMemory consists of 32KB pages, which are allocated to table fragments. Each table is normally partitioned into the same number of fragments as there are data nodes in the cluster. Thus, for each node, there are the same number of fragments as are set in NoOfReplicas. Once a page has been allocated, it is currently not possible to return it to the pool of free pages, except by deleting the table. Performing a node recovery also compresses the partition because all records are inserted into empty partitions from other live nodes.

The DataMemory memory space also contains UNDO information: For each update, a copy of the unaltered record is allocated in the DataMemory. There is also a reference to each copy in the ordered table indexes. Unique hash indexes are updated only when the unique index columns are updated, in which case a new entry in the index table is inserted and the old entry is deleted upon commit. For this reason, it is also necessary to allocate enough memory to handle the largest transactions performed by applications using the cluster. In any case, performing a few large transactions holds no advantage over using many smaller ones, for the following reasons:

- Large transactions are not any faster than smaller ones.
- Large transactions increase the number of operations that are lost and must be repeated in event of transaction failure.
- Large transactions use more memory.

The default value for DataMemory is 80MB; the minimum is 1MB. There is no maximum size, but in reality the maximum size has to be adapted so that the process does not start swapping when the limit is reached. This limit is determined by the amount of physical RAM available on the machine and by the amount of memory that the operating system may commit to any one process. 32-bit operating systems are generally limited to 2–4GB per process; 64-bit operating systems can use more. For large databases, it may be preferable to use a 64-bit operating system for this reason. In addition, it is also possible to run more than one ndbd process per machine, and this may prove advantageous on machines with multiple CPUs.

- IndexMemory

This parameter controls the amount of storage used for hash indexes in MySQL Cluster. Hash indexes are always used for primary key indexes, unique indexes, and unique constraints. Note that when defining a primary key and a unique index, two indexes will be created, one of which is a hash index used for all tuple accesses as well as lock handling. It is also used to enforce unique constraints.

The size of the hash index is 25 bytes per record, plus the size of the primary key. For primary keys larger than 32 bytes another 8 bytes is added.

The default value for `IndexMemory` is 18MB. The minimum is 1MB.

The following example illustrates how memory is used for a table. Consider this table definition:

```
CREATE TABLE example (
  a INT NOT NULL,
  b INT NOT NULL,
  c INT NOT NULL,
  PRIMARY KEY(a),
  UNIQUE(b)
) ENGINE=NDBCLUSTER;
```

For each record, there are 12 bytes of data plus 12 bytes overhead. Having no nullable columns saves 4 bytes of overhead. In addition, we have two ordered indexes on columns a and b consuming roughly 10 bytes each per record. There is a primary key hash index on the base table using roughly 29 bytes per record. The unique constraint is implemented by a separate table with b as primary key and a as a column. This other table consumes an additional 29 bytes of index memory per record in the `example` table as well 8 bytes of record data plus 12 bytes of overhead.

Thus, for one million records, we need 58MB for index memory to handle the hash indexes for the primary key and the unique constraint. We also need 64MB for the records of the base table and the unique index table, plus the two ordered index tables.

You can see that hash indexes take up a fair amount of memory space; however, they provide very fast access to the data in return. They are also used in MySQL Cluster to handle uniqueness constraints.

Currently, the only partitioning algorithm is hashing and ordered indexes are local to each node. Thus, ordered indexes cannot be used to handle uniqueness constraints in the general case.

An important point for both `IndexMemory` and `DataMemory` is that the total database size is the sum of all data memory and all index memory for each node group. Each node group is used to store replicated information, so if there are four nodes with two replicas, there will be two node groups. Thus, the total data memory available is 2 × `DataMemory` for each data node.

It is highly recommended that `DataMemory` and `IndexMemory` be set to the same values for all nodes. Data distribution is even over all nodes in the cluster, so the maximum amount of space available for any node can be no greater than that of the smallest node in the cluster.

`DataMemory` and `IndexMemory` can be changed, but decreasing either of these can be risky; doing so can easily lead to a node or even an entire MySQL Cluster that is unable to restart due to there being insufficient memory space. Increasing these values should be acceptable, but it is recommended that such upgrades be performed in the same manner as a software upgrade, beginning with an update of the configuration file, and then restarting the management server followed by restarting each data node in turn.

Updates do not increase the amount of index memory used. Inserts take effect immediately; however, rows are not actually deleted until the transaction is committed.

Transaction Parameters

The next three [NDBD] parameters that we discuss are important because they affect the number of parallel transactions and the sizes of transactions that can be handled by the system. MaxNoOfConcurrentTransactions sets the number of parallel transactions possible in a node. MaxNoOfConcurrentOperations sets the number of records that can be in update phase or locked simultaneously.

Both of these parameters (especially MaxNoOfConcurrentOperations) are likely targets for users setting specific values and not using the default value. The default value is set for systems using small transactions, to ensure that these do not use excessive memory.

- MaxNoOfConcurrentTransactions

  For each active transaction in the cluster there must be a record in one of the cluster nodes. The task of coordinating transactions is spread among the nodes. The total number of transaction records in the cluster is the number of transactions in any given node times the number of nodes in the cluster.

  Transaction records are allocated to individual MySQL servers. Normally, there is at least one transaction record allocated per connection using any table in the cluster. For this reason, you should ensure that there are more transaction records in the cluster than there are concurrent connections to all MySQL servers in the cluster.

  This parameter must be set to the same value for all cluster nodes.

  Changing this parameter is never safe and doing so can cause a cluster to crash. When a node crashes, one of the nodes (actually the oldest surviving node) will build up the transaction state of all transactions ongoing in the crashed node at the time of the crash. It is thus important that this node has as many transaction records as the failed node.

  The default value is 4096.

- MaxNoOfConcurrentOperations

  It is a good idea to adjust the value of this parameter according to the size and number of transactions. When performing transactions of only a few operations each and not involving a great many records, there is no need to set this parameter very high. When performing large transactions involving many records you need to set this parameter higher.

  Records are kept for each transaction updating cluster data, both in the transaction coordinator and in the nodes where the actual updates are performed. These records contain state information needed to find UNDO records for rollback, lock queues, and other purposes.

This parameter should be set to the number of records to be updated simultaneously in transactions, divided by the number of cluster data nodes. For example, in a cluster that has four data nodes and that is expected to handle 1,000,000 concurrent updates using transactions, you should set this value to 1000000 / 4 = 250000.

Read queries that set locks also cause operation records to be created. Some extra space is allocated within individual nodes to accommodate cases where the distribution is not perfect over the nodes.

When queries make use of the unique hash index, there are actually two operation records used per record in the transaction. The first record represents the read in the index table and the second handles the operation on the base table.

The default value is 32768.

This parameter actually handles two values that can be configured separately. The first of these specifies how many operation records are to be placed with the transaction coordinator. The second part specifies how many operation records are to be local to the database.

A very large transaction performed on an eight-node cluster requires as many operation records in the transaction coordinator as there are reads, updates, and deletes involved in the transaction. However, the operation records of the are spread over all eight nodes. Thus, if it is necessary to configure the system for one very large transaction, it is a good idea to configure the two parts separately. MaxNoOfConcurrentOperations will always be used to calculate the number of operation records in the transaction coordinator portion of the node.

It is also important to have an idea of the memory requirements for operation records. These consume about 1KB per record.

- MaxNoOfLocalOperations

By default, this parameter is calculated as 1.1 × MaxNoOfConcurrentOperations. This fits systems with many simultaneous transactions, none of them being very large. If there is a need to handle one very large transaction at a time and there are many nodes, it is a good idea to override the default value by explicitly specifying this parameter.

Transaction Temporary Storage

The next set of [NDBD] parameters is used to determine temporary storage when executing a statement that is part of a Cluster transaction. All records are released when the statement is completed and the cluster is waiting for the commit or rollback.

The default values for these parameters are adequate for most situations. However, users with a need to support transactions involving large numbers of rows or operations may need to increase these values to enable better parallelism in the system, whereas users whose applications require relatively small transactions can decrease the values to save memory.

- MaxNoOfConcurrentIndexOperations

For queries using a unique hash index, another temporary set of operation records is used during a query's execution phase. This parameter sets the size of that pool of records. Thus, this record is allocated only while executing a part of a query. As soon as this part has been executed, the record is released. The state needed to handle aborts and commits is handled by the normal operation records, where the pool size is set by the parameter `MaxNoOfConcurrentOperations`.

The default value of this parameter is 8192. Only in rare cases of extremely high parallelism using unique hash indexes should it be necessary to increase this value. Using a smaller value is possible and can save memory if the DBA is certain that a high degree of parallelism is not required for the cluster.

- `MaxNoOfFiredTriggers`

The default value of `MaxNoOfFiredTriggers` is 4000, which is sufficient for most situations. In some cases it can even be decreased if the DBA feels certain the need for parallelism in the cluster is not high.

A record is created when an operation is performed that affects a unique hash index. Inserting or deleting a record in a table with unique hash indexes or updating a column that is part of a unique hash index fires an insert or a delete in the index table. The resulting record is used to represent this index table operation while waiting for the original operation that fired it to complete. This operation is short-lived but can still require a large number of records in its pool for situations with many parallel write operations on a base table containing a set of unique hash indexes.

- `TransactionBufferMemory`

The memory affected by this parameter is used for tracking operations fired when updating index tables and reading unique indexes. This memory is used to store the key and column information for these operations. It is very rare that the value for this parameter needs to be altered from the default.

Normal read and write operations use a similar buffer, whose usage is even more short-lived. The compile-time parameter `ZATTRBUF_FILESIZE` (found in `ndb/src/kernel/blocks/Dbtc/Dbtc.hpp`) set to 4000×128 bytes (500KB). A similar buffer for key information, `ZDATABUF_FILESIZE` (also in `Dbtc.hpp`) contains $4000 \times 16 = 62.5$KB of buffer space. `Dbtc` is the module that handles transaction coordination.

Scans and Buffering

- `MaxNoOfConcurrentScans`

This parameter is used to control the number of parallel scans that can be performed in the cluster. Each transaction coordinator can handle the number of parallel scans defined for this parameter. Each scan query is performed by scanning all partitions in parallel. Each partition scan uses a scan record in the node where the partition is located, the number of records being the value of this parameter times the number of nodes. The cluster should be able to sustain `MaxNoOfConcurrentScans` scans concurrently from all nodes in the cluster.

Scans are actually performed in two cases. The first of these cases occurs when no hash or ordered indexes exists to handle the query, in which case the query is executed by performing a full table scan. The second case is encountered when there is no hash index to support the query but there is an ordered index. Using the ordered index means executing a parallel range scan. The order is kept on the local partitions only, so it is necessary to perform the index scan on all partitions.

The default value of `MaxNoOfConcurrentScans` is 256. The maximum value is 500.

This parameter specifies the number of scans possible in the transaction coordinator. If the number of local scan records is not provided, it is calculated as the product of `MaxNoOfConcurrentScans` and the number of data nodes in the system.

- `MaxNoOfLocalScans`

Specifies the number of local scan records if many scans are not fully parallelized.

- `BatchSizePerLocalScan`

This parameter is used to calculate the number of lock records that must be there to handle many concurrent scan operations.

The default value is 64; this value has a strong connection to the `ScanBatchSize` defined in the SQL nodes.

- `LongMessageBuffer`

This is an internal buffer used for passing messages within individual nodes and between nodes. Although it is highly unlikely that this would need to be changed, it is configurable. By default, it is set to 1MB.

Logging and Checkpointing

These [NDBD] parameters control log and checkpoint behavior.

- `NoOfFragmentLogFiles`

This parameter sets the size of the node's REDO log files. REDO log files are organized in a ring. It is extremely important that the first and last log files (sometimes referred to as the "head" and "tail" log files, respectively) do not meet. When these files approach one another too closely, the node begins aborting all transactions encompassing updates due to a lack of room for new log records.

A REDO log record is not removed until three local checkpoints have been completed since that log record was inserted. Checkpointing frequency is determined by its own set of configuration parameters discussed elsewhere in this chapter.

The default parameter value is 8, which means 8 sets of 4 16MB files for a total of 512MB. In other words, REDO log space must be allocated in blocks of 64MB. In scenarios requiring a great many updates, the value for `NoOfFragmentLogFiles` may need to be set as high as 300 or even higher to provide sufficient space for REDO logs.

If the checkpointing is slow and there are so many writes to the database that the log files are full and the log tail cannot be cut without jeopardizing recovery, all updating transactions are aborted with internal error code 410 (`Out of log file space temporarily`). This condition prevails until a checkpoint has completed and the log tail can be moved forward.

- MaxNoOfSavedMessages

This parameter sets the maximum number of trace files that are kept before overwriting old ones. Trace files are generated when, for whatever reason, the node crashes.

The default is 25 trace files.

Metadata Objects

The next set of [NDBD] parameters defines pool sizes for metadata objects, used to define the maximum number of attributes, tables, indexes, and trigger objects used by indexes, events, and replication between clusters. Note that these act merely as "suggestions" to the cluster, and any that are not specified revert to the default values shown.

- MaxNoOfAttributes

Defines the number of attributes that can be defined in the cluster.

The default value is 1000, with the minimum possible value being 32. There is no maximum. Each attribute consumes around 200 bytes of storage per node due to the fact that all metadata is fully replicated on the servers.

When setting MaxNoOfAttributes, it is important to prepare in advance for any ALTER TABLE statements that you might want to perform in the future. This is due to the fact that during the execution of ALTER TABLE on a Cluster table, 3 times the number of attributes as in the original table are used. For example, if a table requires 100 attributes, and you want to be able to alter it later, you need to set the value of MaxNoOfAttributes to 300. Assuming that you can create all desired tables without any problems, a good rule of thumb is to add two times the number of attributes in the largest table to MaxNoOfAttributes to be sure. You should also verify that this number is sufficient by trying an actual ALTER TABLE after configuring the parameter. If this is not successful, increase MaxNoOfAttributes by another multiple of the original value and test it again.

- MaxNoOfTables

A table object is allocated for each table, unique hash index, and ordered index. This parameter sets the maximum number of table objects for the cluster as a whole.

For each attribute that has a BLOB data type an extra table is used to store most of the BLOB data. These tables also must be taken into account when defining the total number of tables.

The default value of this parameter is 128. The minimum is 8 and the maximum is 1600. Each table object consumes approximately 20KB per node.

- MaxNoOfOrderedIndexes

For each ordered index in the cluster, an object is allocated describing what is being indexed and its storage segments. By default, each index so defined also defines an ordered index. Each unique index and primary key has both an ordered index and a hash index.

The default value of this parameter is 128. Each object consumes approximately 10KB of data per node.

- `MaxNoOfUniqueHashIndexes`

  For each unique index that is not a primary key, a special table is allocated that maps the unique key to the primary key of the indexed table. By default, an ordered index is also defined for each unique index. To prevent this, you must specify the USING HASH option when defining the unique index.

  The default value is 64. Each index consumes approximately 15KB per node.

- `MaxNoOfTriggers`

  Internal update, insert, and delete triggers are allocated for each unique hash index. (This means that three triggers are created for each unique hash index.) However, an *ordered* index requires only a single trigger object. Backups also use three trigger objects for each normal table in the cluster.

  Note: When replication between clusters is supported, this will also make use of internal triggers.

  This parameter sets the maximum number of trigger objects in the cluster.

  The default value is 768.

- `MaxNoOfIndexes`

  This parameter is deprecated in MySQL 5.0; you should use `MaxNoOfOrderedIndexes` and `MaxNoOfUniqueHashIndexes` instead.

  This parameter is used only by unique hash indexes. There needs to be one record in this pool for each unique hash index defined in the cluster.

  The default value of this parameter is 128.

Boolean Parameters

The behavior of data nodes is also affected by a set of [NDBD] parameters taking on boolean values. These parameters can each be specified as TRUE by setting them equal to 1 or Y, and as FALSE by setting them equal to 0 or N.

- `LockPagesInMainMemory`

  For a number of operating systems, including Solaris and Linux, it is possible to lock a process into memory and so avoid any swapping to disk. This can be used to help guarantee the cluster's real-time characteristics.

  This feature is disabled by default.

- `StopOnError`

  This parameter specifies whether an ndbd process should exit or perform an automatic restart when an error condition is encountered.

  This feature is enabled by default.

- `Diskless`

  It is possible to specify MySQL Cluster tables as *diskless*, meaning that tables are not checkpointed to disk and that no logging occurs. Such tables exist only in main memory. A consequence of using diskless tables is that neither the tables nor the records in those tables survive a crash. However, when operating in diskless mode, it is possible to run `ndbd` on a diskless computer.

Important: This feature causes the *entire* cluster to operate in diskless mode.

When this feature is enabled, backups are performed but backup data is not actually stored.

`Diskless` is disabled by default.

- `RestartOnErrorInsert`

  This feature is accessible only when building the debug version where it is possible to insert errors in the execution of individual blocks of code as part of testing.

  This feature is disabled by default.

Controlling Timeouts, Intervals, and Disk Paging

There are a number of [NDBD] parameters specifying timeouts and intervals between various actions in Cluster data nodes. Most of the timeout values are specified in milliseconds. Any exceptions to this are mentioned where applicable.

- `TimeBetweenWatchDogCheck`

  To prevent the main thread from getting stuck in an endless loop at some point, a "watchdog" thread checks the main thread. This parameter specifies the number of milliseconds between checks. If the process remains in the same state after three checks, the watchdog thread terminates it.

  This parameter can easily be changed for purposes of experimentation or to adapt to local conditions. It can be specified on a per-node basis although there seems to be little reason for doing so.

  The default timeout is 4000 milliseconds (4 seconds).

- `StartPartialTimeout`

  This parameter specifies how long the Cluster waits for all storage nodes to come up before the cluster initialization routine is invoked. This timeout is used to avoid a partial Cluster startup whenever possible.

  The default value is 30000 milliseconds (30 seconds). 0 disables the timeout. In other words, the cluster may start only if all nodes are available.

- `StartPartitionedTimeout`

  If the cluster is ready to start after waiting for `StartPartialTimeout` milliseconds but is still possibly in a partitioned state, the cluster waits until this timeout has also passed.

  The default timeout is 60000 milliseconds (60 seconds).

- `StartFailureTimeout`

  If a data node has not completed its startup sequence within the time specified by this parameter, the node startup fails. Setting this parameter to 0 means that no data node timeout is applied.

  The default value is 60000 milliseconds (60 seconds). For data nodes containing extremely large amounts of data, this parameter should be increased. For example, in the case of a storage node containing several gigabytes of data, a period as long as 10–15 minutes (that is, 600,000 to 1,000,000 milliseconds) might be required to perform a node restart.

- HeartbeatIntervalDbDb

One of the primary methods of discovering failed nodes is by the use of heartbeats. This parameter states how often heartbeat signals are sent and how often to expect to receive them. After missing three heartbeat intervals in a row, the node is declared dead. Thus, the maximum time for discovering a failure through the heartbeat mechanism is four times the heartbeat interval.

The default heartbeat interval is 1500 milliseconds (1.5 seconds). This parameter must not be changed drastically and should not vary widely between nodes. If one node uses 5000 milliseconds and the node watching it uses 1000 milliseconds, obviously the node will be declared dead very quickly. This parameter can be changed during an online software upgrade, but only in small increments.

- HeartbeatIntervalDbApi

Each data node sends heartbeat signals to each MySQL server (SQL node) to ensure that it remains in contact. If a MySQL server fails to send a heartbeat in time it is declared dead, in which case all ongoing transactions are completed and all resources released. The SQL node cannot reconnect until all activities initiated by the previous MySQL instance have been completed. The three-heartbeat criteria for this determination are the same as described for HeartbeatIntervalDbDb.

The default interval is 1500 milliseconds (1.5 seconds). This interval can vary between individual data nodes because each storage node watches the MySQL servers connected to it, independently of all other data nodes.

- TimeBetweenLocalCheckpoints

This parameter is an exception in that it does not specify a time to wait before starting a new local checkpoint; rather, it is used to ensure that local checkpoints are not performed in a cluster where relatively few updates are taking place. In most clusters with high update rates, it is likely that a new local checkpoint is started immediately after the previous one has been completed.

The size of all write operations executed since the start of the previous local checkpoints is added. This parameter is also exceptional in that it is specified as the base-2 logarithm of the number of 4-byte words, so that the default value 20 means 4MB (4×2^{20}) of write operations, 21 would mean 8MB, and so on up to a maximum value of 31, which equates to 8GB of write operations.

All the write operations in the cluster are added together. Setting TimeBetweenLocalCheckpoints to 6 or less means that local checkpoints will be executed continuously without pause, independent of the cluster's workload.

- TimeBetweenGlobalCheckpoints

When a transaction is committed, it is committed in main memory in all nodes on which the data is mirrored. However, transaction log records are not flushed to disk as part of the commit. The reasoning behind this behavior is that having the transaction safely committed on at least two autonomous host machines should meet reasonable standards for durability.

It is also important to ensure that even the worst of cases—a complete crash of the cluster—is handled properly. To guarantee that this happens, all transactions taking place within a given interval are put into a global checkpoint, which can be thought of as a set of committed transactions that has been flushed to disk. In other words, as part of the commit process, a transaction is placed in a global checkpoint group. Later, this group's log records are flushed to disk, and then the entire group of transactions is safely committed to disk on all computers in the cluster.

This parameter defines the interval between global checkpoints. The default is 2000 milliseconds.

- `TimeBetweenInactiveTransactionAbortCheck`

Timeout handling is performed by checking a timer on each transaction once for every interval specified by this parameter. Thus, if this parameter is set to 1000 milliseconds, every transaction will be checked for timing out once per second.

The default value is 1000 milliseconds (1 second).

- `TransactionInactiveTimeout`

This parameter states the maximum time that is permitted to lapse between operations in the same transaction before the transaction is aborted.

The default for this parameter is zero (no timeout). For a real-time database that needs to ensure that no transaction keeps locks for too long, this parameter should be set to a much smaller value. The unit is milliseconds.

- `TransactionDeadlockDetectionTimeout`

When a node executes a query involving a transaction, the node waits for the other nodes in the cluster to respond before continuing. A failure to respond can occur for any of the following reasons:

  - The node is dead.
  - The operation has entered a lock queue.
  - The node requested to perform the action could be heavily overloaded.

This timeout parameter states how long the transaction coordinator waits for query execution by another node before aborting the transaction, and is important for both node failure handling and deadlock detection. Setting it too high can cause an undesirable behavior in situations involving deadlocks and node failure.

The default timeout value is 1200 milliseconds (1.2 seconds).

- `NoOfDiskPagesToDiskAfterRestartTUP`

When executing a local checkpoint, the algorithm flushes all data pages to disk. Merely doing so as quickly as possible without any moderation is likely to impose excessive loads on processors, networks, and disks. To control the write speed, this parameter specifies how many pages per 100 milliseconds are to be written. In this context, a "page" is defined as 8KB. This parameter is specified in units of 80KB per second, so, setting `NoOfDiskPagesToDiskAfterRestartTUP` to a value of 20 entails writing 1.6MB in data pages to disk each second during a local checkpoint. This value includes the writing of UNDO log records for data pages. That is, this parameter handles the limitation of writes from data memory. UNDO log records for index pages are handled by the parameter `NoOfDiskPagesToDiskAfterRestartACC`. (See the entry for `IndexMemory` for information about index pages.)

In short, this parameter specifies how quickly to execute local checkpoints. It operates in conjunction with `NoOfFragmentLogFiles`, `DataMemory`, and `IndexMemory`.

The default value is 40 (3.2MB of data pages per second).

- `NoOfDiskPagesToDiskAfterRestartACC`

This parameter uses the same units as `NoOfDiskPagesToDiskAfterRestartTUP` and acts in a similar fashion, but limits the speed of writing index pages from index memory.

The default value of this parameter is 20 (1.6MB of index memory pages per second).

- `NoOfDiskPagesToDiskDuringRestartTUP`

This parameter is used in a fashion similar to `NoOfDiskPagesToDiskAfterRestartTUP` and `NoOfDiskPagesToDiskAfterRestartACC`, but it does so with regard to local checkpoints executed in the node when a node is restarting. A local checkpoint is always performed as part of all node restarts. During a node restart it is possible to write to disk at a higher speed than at other times, because fewer activities are being performed in the node.

This parameter covers pages written from data memory.

The default value is 40 (3.2MB per second).

- `NoOfDiskPagesToDiskDuringRestartACC`

Controls the number of index memory pages that can be written to disk during the local checkpoint phase of a node restart.

As with `NoOfDiskPagesToDiskAfterRestartTUP` and `NoOfDiskPagesToDiskAfterRestartACC`, values for this parameter are expressed in terms of 8KB pages written per 100 milliseconds (80KB/second).

The default value is 20 (1.6MB per second).

- `ArbitrationTimeout`

This parameter specifies how long data nodes wait for a response from the arbitrator to an arbitration message. If this is exceeded, the network is assumed to have split.

The default value is 1000 milliseconds (1 second).

Buffering and Logging

Several [NDBD] configuration parameters corresponding to former compile-time parameters are also available. These enable the advanced user to have more control over the resources used by node processes and to adjust various buffer sizes at need.

These buffers are used as front ends to the file system when writing log records to disk. If the node is running in diskless mode, these parameters can be set to their minimum values without penalty due to the fact that disk writes are "faked" by the NDB storage engine's filesystem abstraction layer.

- UndoIndexBuffer

  The UNDO index buffer, whose size is set by this parameter, is used during local checkpoints. The NDB storage engine uses a recovery scheme based on checkpoint consistency in conjunction with an operational REDO log. To produce a consistent checkpoint without blocking the entire system for writes, UNDO logging is done while performing the local checkpoint. UNDO logging is activated on a single table fragment at a time. This optimization is possible because tables are stored entirely in main memory.

  The UNDO index buffer is used for the updates on the primary key hash index. Inserts and deletes rearrange the hash index; the NDB storage engine writes UNDO log records that map all physical changes to an index page so that they can be undone at system restart. It also logs all active insert operations for each fragment at the start of a local checkpoint.

  Reads and updates set lock bits and update a header in the hash index entry. These changes are handled by the page-writing algorithm to ensure that these operations need no UNDO logging.

  This buffer is 2MB by default. The minimum value is 1MB, which is sufficient for most applications. For applications doing extremely large or numerous inserts and deletes together with large transactions and large primary keys, it may be necessary to increase the size of this buffer. If this buffer is too small, the NDB storage engine issues internal error code 677 (Index UNDO buffers overloaded).

- UndoDataBuffer

  This parameter sets the size of the UNDO data buffer, which performs a function similar to that of the UNDO index buffer, except the UNDO data buffer is used with regard to data memory rather than index memory. This buffer is used during the local checkpoint phase of a fragment for inserts, deletes, and updates.

  Because UNDO log entries tend to grow larger as more operations are logged, this buffer is also larger than its index memory counterpart, with a default value of 16MB.

  This amount of memory may be unnecessarily large for some applications. In such cases, it is possible to decrease this size to a minimum of 1MB.

  It is rarely necessary to increase the size of this buffer. If there is such a need, it is a good idea to check whether the disks can actually handle the load caused by database update activity. A lack of sufficient disk space cannot be overcome by increasing the size of this buffer.

  If this buffer is too small and gets congested, the NDB storage engine issues internal error code 891 (Data UNDO buffers overloaded).

- RedoBuffer

  All update activities also need to be logged. The REDO log makes it possible to replay these updates whenever the system is restarted. The NDB recovery algorithm uses a "fuzzy" checkpoint of the data together with the UNDO log, and then applies the REDO log to play back all changes up to the restoration point.

  RedoBuffer sets the size of the buffer in which the REDO log is written, and is 8MB by default. The minimum value is 1MB.

If this buffer is too small, the NDB storage engine issues error code 1221 (REDO log buffers overloaded).

In managing the cluster, it is very important to be able to control the number of log messages sent for various event types to stdout. For each event category, there are 16 possible event levels (numbered 0 through 15). Setting event reporting for a given event category to level 15 means all event reports in that category are sent to stdout; setting it to 0 means that there will be no event reports made in that category.

By default, only the startup message is sent to stdout, with the remaining event reporting level defaults being set to 0. The reason for this is that these messages are also sent to the management server's cluster log.

An analogous set of levels can be set for the management client to determine which event levels to record in the cluster log.

- LogLevelStartup

  The reporting level for events generated during startup of the process.

  The default level is 1.

- LogLevelShutdown

  The reporting level for events generated as part of graceful shutdown of a node.

  The default level is 0.

- LogLevelStatistic

  The reporting level for statistical events such as number of primary key reads, number of updates, number of inserts, information relating to buffer usage, and so on.

  The default level is 0.

- LogLevelCheckpoint

  The reporting level for events generated by local and global checkpoints.

  The default level is 0.

- LogLevelNodeRestart

  The reporting level for events generated during node restart.

  The default level is 0.

- LogLevelConnection

  The reporting level for events generated by connections between cluster nodes.

  The default level is 0.

- LogLevelError

  The reporting level for events generated by errors and warnings by the cluster as a whole. These errors do not cause any node failure but are still considered worth reporting.

  The default level is 0.

- LogLevelInfo

  The reporting level for events generated for information about the general state of the cluster.

  The default level is 0.

Backup Parameters

The [NDBD] parameters discussed in this section define memory buffers set aside for execution of online backups.

- BackupDataBufferSize

  In creating a backup, there are two buffers used for sending data to the disk. The backup data buffer is used to fill in data recorded by scanning a node's tables. Once this buffer has been filled to the level specified as BackupWriteSize (see below), the pages are sent to disk. While flushing data to disk, the backup process can continue filling this buffer until it runs out of space. When this happens, the backup process pauses the scan and waits until some disk writes have completed and freed up memory so that scanning may continue.

  The default value is 2MB.

- BackupLogBufferSize

  The backup log buffer fulfills a role similar to that played by the backup data buffer, except that it is used for generating a log of all table writes made during execution of the backup. The same principles apply for writing these pages as with the backup data buffer, except that when there is no more space in the backup log buffer, the backup fails. For that reason, the size of the backup log buffer must be large enough to handle the load caused by write activities while the backup is being made. See Section 9.6.5.4, "Configuration for Cluster Backup."

  The default value for this parameter should be sufficient for most applications. In fact, it is more likely for a backup failure to be caused by insufficient disk write speed than it is for the backup log buffer to become full. If the disk subsystem is not configured for the write load caused by applications, the cluster is unlikely to be able to perform the desired operations.

  It is preferable to configure cluster nodes in such a manner that the processor becomes the bottleneck rather than the disks or the network connections.

  The default value is 2MB.

- BackupMemory

  This parameter is simply the sum of BackupDataBufferSize and BackupLogBufferSize.

  The default value is 2MB + 2MB = 4MB.

- BackupWriteSize

  This parameter specifies the size of messages written to disk by the backup log and backup data buffers.

  The default value is 32KB.

9.4.4.6 Defining the SQL Nodes in a MySQL Cluster

The [MYSQLD] sections in the config.ini file define the behavior of the MySQL servers (SQL nodes) used to access cluster data. None of the parameters shown is required. If no computer or hostname is provided, any host can use this SQL node.

- Id

  The Id value is used to identify the node in all cluster internal messages. It must be an integer in the range 1 to 63 inclusive, and must be unique among all node IDs within the cluster.

- ExecuteOnComputer

  This refers to one of the computers (hosts) defined in a [COMPUTER] section of the configuration file.

- ArbitrationRank

  This parameter defines which nodes can act as arbitrators. Both MGM nodes and SQL nodes can be arbitrators. A value of 0 means that the given node is never used as an arbitrator, a value of 1 gives the node high priority as an arbitrator, and a value of 2 gives it low priority. A normal configuration uses the management server as arbitrator, setting its ArbitrationRank to 1 (the default) and those for all SQL nodes to 0.

- ArbitrationDelay

  Setting this parameter to any other value than 0 (the default) means that responses by the arbitrator to arbitration requests will be delayed by the stated number of milliseconds. It is usually not necessary to change this value.

- BatchByteSize

  For queries that are translated into full table scans or range scans on indexes, it is important for best performance to fetch records in properly sized batches. It is possible to set the proper size both in terms of number of records (BatchSize) and in terms of bytes (BatchByteSize). The actual batch size is limited by both parameters.

  The speed at which queries are performed can vary by more than 40% depending on how this parameter is set. In future releases, MySQL Server will make educated guesses on how to set parameters relating to batch size, based on the query type.

  This parameter is measured in bytes and by default is equal to 32KB.

- BatchSize

  This parameter is measured in number of records and is by default set to 64. The maximum size is 992.

- MaxScanBatchSize

  The batch size is the size of each batch sent from each data node. Most scans are performed in parallel to protect the MySQL Server from receiving too much data from many nodes in parallel; this parameter sets a limit to the total batch size over all nodes.

  The default value of this parameter is set to 256KB. Its maximum size is 16MB.

9.4.4.7 MySQL Cluster TCP/IP Connections

TCP/IP is the default transport mechanism for establishing connections in MySQL Cluster. It is normally not necessary to define connections because Cluster automatically set ups a connection between each of the data nodes, between each data node and all MySQL server nodes, and between each data node and the management server. (For one exception to this rule, see Section 9.4.4.8, "MySQL Cluster TCP/IP Connections Using Direct Connections.") [TCP] sections in the config.ini file explicitly define TCP/IP connections between nodes in the cluster.

It is only necessary to define a connection to override the default connection parameters. In that case, it is necessary to define at least NodeId1, NodeId2, and the parameters to change.

It is also possible to change the default values for these parameters by setting them in the [TCP DEFAULT] section.

- NodeId1, NodeId2

  To identify a connection between two nodes it is necessary to provide their node IDs in the [TCP] section of the configuration file. These are the same unique Id values for each of these nodes as described in Section 9.4.4.6, "Defining the SQL Nodes in a MySQL Cluster."

- SendBufferMemory

  TCP transporters use a buffer to store all messages before performing the send call to the operating system. When this buffer reaches 64KB its contents are sent; these are also sent when a round of messages has been executed. To handle temporary overload situations it is also possible to define a bigger send buffer. The default size of the send buffer is 256KB.

- SendSignalId

  To be able to retrace a distributed message diagram it is necessary to identify each message. When this parameter is set to Y, message IDs are transported over the network. This feature is disabled by default.

- Checksum

  This parameter is a boolean parameter (enabled by setting it to Y or 1, disabled by setting it to N or 0). It is disabled by default. When it is enabled, checksums for all messages are calculated before they placed in the send buffer. This feature ensures that messages are not corrupted while waiting in the send buffer, or by the transport mechanism.

- PortNumber (*OBSOLETE*)

  This formerly specified the port number to be used for listening for connections from other nodes. This parameter should no longer be used.

- ReceiveBufferMemory

  Specifies the size of the buffer used when receiving data from the TCP/IP socket. There is seldom any need to change this parameter from its default value of 64KB, except possibly to save memory.

9.4.4.8 MySQL Cluster TCP/IP Connections Using Direct Connections

Setting up a cluster using direct connections between data nodes requires specifying explicitly the crossover IP addresses of the data nodes so connected in the [TCP] section of the cluster config.ini file.

In the following example, we envision a cluster with at least four hosts, one each for a management server, an SQL node, and two data nodes. The cluster as a whole resides on the 172.23.72.* subnet of a LAN. In addition to the usual network connections, the two data nodes are connected directly using a standard crossover cable, and communicate with one another directly using IP addresses in the 1.1.0.* address range as shown:

```
# Management Server
[NDB_MGMD]
Id=1
HostName=172.23.72.20

# SQL Node
[MYSQLD]
Id=2
HostName=172.23.72.21

# Data Nodes
[NDBD]
Id=3
HostName=172.23.72.22

[NDBD]
Id=4
HostName=172.23.72.23

# TCP/IP Connections
[TCP]
NodeId1=3
NodeId2=4
HostName1=1.1.0.1
HostName2=1.1.0.2
```

The use of direct connections between data nodes can improve the cluster's overall efficiency by allowing the data nodes to bypass an Ethernet device such as a switch, hub, or router, thus cutting down on the cluster's latency. It is important to note that to take the best advantage of direct connections in this fashion with more than two data nodes, you must have a direct connection between each data node and every other data node in the same node group.

9.4.4.9 MySQL Cluster Shared-Memory Connections

MySQL Cluster attempts to use the shared memory transporter and configure it automatically where possible, chiefly where more than one node runs concurrently on the same cluster host. (In very early versions of MySQL Cluster, shared memory segments functioned only when the -max binary was built using --with-ndb-shm.) [SHM] sections in the config.ini file explicitly define shared-memory connections between nodes in the cluster. When explicitly defining shared memory as the connection method, it is necessary to define at least NodeId1, NodeId2, and ShmKey. All other parameters have default values that should work well in most cases.

Important: *SHM functionality is considered experimental only*. It is not officially supported in any MySQL release series up to and including 5.0. This means that you must determine for yourself or by using our free resources (forums, mailing lists) whether it can be made to work correctly in your specific case.

- NodeId1, NodeId2

  To identify a connection between two nodes it is necessary to provide node identifiers for each of them, as NodeId1 and NodeId2.

- ShmKey

  When setting up shared memory segments, a node ID, expressed as an integer, is used to identify uniquely the shared memory segment to use for the communication. There is no default value.

- ShmSize

  Each SHM connection has a shared memory segment where messages between nodes are placed by the sender and read by the reader. The size of this segment is defined by ShmSize. The default value is 1MB.

- SendSignalId

  To retrace the path of a distributed message, it is necessary to provide each message with a unique identifier. Setting this parameter to Y causes these message IDs to be transported over the network as well. This feature is disabled by default.

- Checksum

  This parameter is a boolean (Y/N) parameter, which is disabled by default. When it is enabled, checksums for all messages are calculated before being placed in the send buffer.

  This feature prevents messages from being corrupted while waiting in the send buffer. It also serves as a check against data being corrupted during transport.

9.4.4.10 MySQL Cluster SCI Transport Connections

[SCI] sections in the config.ini file explicitly define SCI (Scalable Coherent Interface) connections between cluster nodes. Using SCI transporters in MySQL Cluster is supported only when the MySQL-Max binaries are built using --with-ndb-sci=*/your/path/to/SCI*. The *path* should point to a directory that contains at a minimum lib and include directories containing SISCI libraries and header files. (See Section 9.8, "Using High-Speed Interconnects with MySQL Cluster," for more information about SCI.)

In addition, SCI requires specialized hardware.

It is strongly recommended to use SCI Transporters only for communication between `ndbd` processes. Note also that using SCI Transporters means that the `ndbd` processes never sleep. For this reason, SCI Transporters should be used only on machines having at least two CPUs dedicated for use by `ndbd` processes. There should be at least one CPU per `ndbd` process, with at least one CPU left in reserve to handle operating system activities.

- `NodeId1, NodeId2`

  To identify a connection between two nodes it is necessary to provide node identifiers for each of them, as `NodeId1` and `NodeId2`.

- `Host1SciId0`

  This identifies the SCI node ID on the first Cluster node (identified by `NodeId1`).

- `Host1SciId1`

  It is possible to set up SCI Transporters for failover between two SCI cards, which then should use separate networks between the nodes. This identifies the node ID and the second SCI card to be used on the first node.

- `Host2SciId0`

  This identifies the SCI node ID on the second Cluster node (identified by `NodeId2`).

- `Host2SciId1`

  When using two SCI cards to provide failover, this parameter identifies the second SCI card to be used on the second node.

- `SharedBufferSize`

  Each SCI transporter has a shared memory segment used for communication between the two nodes. Setting the size of this segment to the default value of 1MB should be sufficient for most applications. Using a smaller value can lead to problems when performing many parallel inserts; if the shared buffer is too small, this can also result in a crash of the `ndbd` process.

- `SendLimit`

  A small buffer in front of the SCI media stores messages before transmitting them over the SCI network. By default, this is set to 8KB. Our benchmarks show that performance is best at 64KB but 16KB reaches within a few percent of this, and there is little if any advantage to increasing it beyond 8KB.

- `SendSignalId`

  To trace a distributed message it is necessary to identify each message uniquely. When this parameter is set to `Y`, message IDs are transported over the network. This feature is disabled by default.

- `Checksum`

  This parameter is a boolean value, and is disabled by default. When `Checksum` is enabled, checksums are calculated for all messages before they are placed in the send buffer. This feature prevents messages from being corrupted while waiting in the send buffer. It also serves as a check against data being corrupted during transport.

9.5 Process Management in MySQL Cluster

Understanding how to manage MySQL Cluster requires a knowledge of four essential processes. In the next few sections of this chapter, we cover the roles played by these processes in a cluster, how to use them, and what startup options are available for each of them:

- Section 9.5.1, "MySQL Server Process Usage for MySQL Cluster"
- Section 9.5.2, "ndbd, the Storage Engine Node Process"
- Section 9.5.3, "ndb_mgmd, the Management Server Process"
- Section 9.5.4, "ndb_mgm, the Management Client Process"

9.5.1 MySQL Server Process Usage for MySQL Cluster

mysqld is the traditional MySQL server process. To be used with MySQL Cluster, mysqld needs to be built with support for the NDB Cluster storage engine, as it is in the precompiled -max binaries available from http://dev.mysql.com/downloads/. If you build MySQL from source, you must invoke configure with the --with-ndbcluster option to enable NDB Cluster storage engine support.

If the mysqld binary has been built with Cluster support, the NDB Cluster storage engine is still disabled by default. You can use either of two possible options to enable this engine:

- Use --ndbcluster as a startup option on the command line when starting mysqld.
- Insert a line containing ndbcluster in the [mysqld] section of your my.cnf file.

An easy way to verify that your server is running with the NDB Cluster storage engine enabled is to issue the SHOW ENGINES statement in the MySQL Monitor (mysql). You should see the value YES as the Support value in the row for NDBCLUSTER. If you see NO in this row or if there is no such row displayed in the output, you are not running an NDB-enabled version of MySQL. If you see DISABLED in this row, you need to enable it in either one of the two ways just described.

To read cluster configuration data, the MySQL server requires at a minimum three pieces of information:

- The MySQL server's own cluster node ID
- The hostname or IP address for the management server (MGM node)
- The number of the TCP/IP port on which it can connect to the management server

Node IDs can be allocated dynamically, so it is not strictly necessary to specify them explicitly.

The mysqld parameter ndb-connectstring is used to specify the connectstring either on the command line when starting mysqld or in my.cnf. The connectstring contains the hostname or IP address where the management server can be found, as well as the TCP/IP port it uses.

In the following example, ndb_mgmd.mysql.com is the host where the management server resides, and the management server listens for cluster messages on port 1186:

```
shell> mysqld --ndb-connectstring=ndb_mgmd.mysql.com:1186
```

See Section 9.4.4.2, "The MySQL Cluster connectstring," for more information on connectstrings.

Given this information, the MySQL server will be a full participant in the cluster. (We sometimes refer to a mysqld process running in this manner as an "SQL node.") It will be fully aware of all cluster data nodes as well as their status, and will establish connections to all data nodes. In this case, it is able to use any data node as a transaction coordinator and to read and update node data.

9.5.2 ndbd, the Storage Engine Node Process

ndbd is the process that is used to handle all the data in tables using the NDB Cluster storage engine. This is the process that empowers a storage node to accomplish distributed transaction handling, node recovery, checkpointing to disk, online backup, and related tasks.

In a MySQL Cluster, a set of ndbd processes cooperate in handling data. These processes can execute on the same computer (host) or on different computers. The correspondences between data nodes and Cluster hosts is completely configurable.

ndbd generates a set of log files that are placed in the directory specified by DataDir in the config.ini configuration file. These log files are listed below. Note that *node_id* represents the node's unique identifier. For example, ndb_2_error.log is the error log generated by the storage node whose node ID is 2.

- ndb_*node_id*_error.log is a file containing records of all crashes that the referenced ndbd process has encountered. Each record in this file contains a brief error string and a reference to a trace file for this crash. A typical entry in this file might appear as shown here:

```
Date/Time: Saturday 30 July 2004 - 00:20:01
Type of error: error
Message: Internal program error (failed ndbrequire)
Fault ID: 2341
Problem data: DbtupFixAlloc.cpp
Object of refer
ence: DBTUP (Line: 173)
ProgramName: NDB Kernel
ProcessID: 14909
TraceFile: ndb_2_trace.log.2
***EOM***
```

Note: *It is very important to be aware that the last entry in the error log file is not necessarily the newest one* (nor is it likely to be). Entries in the error log are *not* listed in chronological order; rather, they correspond to the order of the trace files as determined in the ndb_*node_id*_trace.log.next file (see below). Error log entries are thus overwritten in a cyclical and not sequential fashion.

- ndb_*node_id*_trace.log.*trace_id* is a trace file describing exactly what happened just before the error occurred. This information is useful for analysis by the MySQL Cluster development team.

  It is possible to configure the number of these trace files that will be created before old files are overwritten. *trace_id* is a number which is incremented for each successive trace file.

- ndb_*node_id*_trace.log.next is the file that keeps track of the next trace file number to be assigned.

- ndb_*node_id*_out.log is a file containing any data output by the ndbd process. This file is created only if ndbd is started as a daemon.

- ndb_*node_id*.pid is a file containing the process ID of the ndbd process when started as a daemon. It also functions as a lock file to avoid the starting of nodes with the same identifier.

- ndb_*node_id*_signal.log is a file used only in debug versions of ndbd, where it is possible to trace all incoming, outgoing, and internal messages with their data in the ndbd process.

It is recommended not to use a directory mounted through NFS because in some environments this can cause problems in which the lock on the .pid file remains in effect even after the process has terminated.

To start ndbd, it may also be necessary to specify the hostname of the management server and the port on which it is listening. Optionally, you may also specify the node ID that the process is to use.

```
shell> ndbd --connect-string="nodeid=2;host=ndb_mgmd.mysql.com:1186"
```

See Section 9.4.4.2, "The MySQL Cluster connectstring," for additional information about this issue. Section 9.5.5, "Command Options for MySQL Cluster Processes," describes other options for ndbd.

When ndbd starts, it actually initiates two processes. The first of these is called the "angel process"; its only job is to discover when the execution process has been completed, and then to restart the ndbd process if it is configured to do so. Thus, if you attempt to kill ndbd via the Unix kill command, it is necessary to kill both processes, beginning with the angel process. The preferred method of terminating an ndbd process is to use the management client and stop the process from there.

The execution process uses one thread for reading, writing, and scanning data, as well as all other activities. This thread is implemented asynchronously so that it can easily handle thousands of concurrent activities. In addition, a watch-dog thread supervises the execution thread to make sure that it does not hang in an endless loop. A pool of threads handles file I/O, with each thread able to handle one open file. Threads can also be used for transporter connections by the transporters in the ndbd process. In a system performing a large number of operations, including updates, the ndbd process can consume up to 2 CPUs if permitted to do so. For a machine with many CPUs it is recommended to use several ndbd processes that belong to different node groups.

9.5.3 ndb_mgmd, the Management Server Process

The management server is the process that reads the cluster configuration file and distributes this information to all nodes in the cluster that request it. It also maintains a log of cluster activities. Management clients can connect to the management server and check the cluster's status.

It is not strictly necessary to specify a connectstring when starting the management server. However, if you are using more than one management server, a connectstring should be provided and each node in the cluster should specify its node ID explicitly.

See Section 9.4.4.2, "The MySQL Cluster connectstring," for information about using connectstrings. Section 9.5.5, "Command Options for MySQL Cluster Processes," describes other options for ndb_mgmd.

The following files are created or used by ndb_mgmd in its starting directory, and are placed in the DataDir as specified in the config.ini configuration file. In the list that follows, *node_id* is the unique node identifier.

- config.ini is the configuration file for the cluster as a whole. This file is created by the user and read by the management server. Section 9.4, "MySQL Cluster Configuration," discusses how to set up this file.

- ndb_*node_id*_cluster.log is the cluster events log file. Examples of such events include checkpoint startup and completion, node startup events, node failures, and levels of memory usage. A complete listing of cluster events with descriptions may be found in Section 9.6, "Management of MySQL Cluster."

  When the size of the cluster log reaches one million bytes, the file is renamed to ndb_*node_id*_cluster.log.*seq_id*, where *seq_id* is the sequence number of the cluster log file. (For example: If files with the sequence numbers 1, 2, and 3 already exist, the next log file is named using the number 4.)

- ndb_*node_id*_out.log is the file used for stdout and stderr when running the management server as a daemon.

- ndb_*node_id*.pid is the process ID file used when running the management server as a daemon.

9.5.4 ndb_mgm, the Management Client Process

The management client process is actually not needed to run the cluster. Its value lies in providing a set of commands for checking the cluster's status, starting backups, and performing other administrative functions. The management client accesses the management server using a C API. Advanced users can also employ this API for programming dedicated management processes to perform tasks similar to those performed by ndb_mgm.

To start the management client, it is necessary to supply the hostname and port number of the management server:

```
shell> ndb_mgm [host_name [port_num]]
```

For example:

```
shell> ndb_mgm ndb_mgmd.mysql.com 1186
```

The default hostname and port number are localhost and 1186, respectively.

Additional information about using ndb_mgm can be found in Section 9.5.5.4, "Command Options for ndb_mgm," and Section 9.6.2, "Commands in the Management Client."

9.5.5 Command Options for MySQL Cluster Processes

All MySQL Cluster executables (except for mysqld) take the options described in this section. Users of earlier MySQL Cluster versions should note that some of these options have been changed from those in MySQL 4.1 Cluster to make them consistent with one another as well as with mysqld. You can use the --help option to view a list of supported options.

The following sections describe options specific to individual NDB programs:

- --help --usage, -?

  Prints a short list with descriptions of the available command options.

- --connect-string=connect_string, -c connect_string

  connect_string sets the connectstring to the management server as a command option.

  ```
  shell> ndbd --connect-string="nodeid=2;host=ndb_mgmd.mysql.com:1186"
  ```

- --debug[=options]

  This option can only be used for versions compiled with debugging enabled. It is used to enable output from debug calls in the same manner as for the mysqld process.

- --execute=command -e command

  Can be used to send a command to a Cluster executable from the system shell. For example, either of the following:

  ```
  shell> ndb_mgm -e show
  ```

  or

  ```
  shell> ndb_mgm --execute="SHOW"
  ```

  is equivalent to

  ```
  NDB> SHOW;
  ```

  This is analogous to how the --execute or -e option works with the mysql command-line client. See Section 3.3.1, "Using Options on the Command Line."

- --version, -V

  Prints the version number of the ndbd process. The version number is the MySQL Cluster version number. The version number is relevant because not all versions can be used together, and at startup the MySQL Cluster processes verifies that the versions of the binaries being used can co-exist in the same cluster. This is also important when performing an online software upgrade of MySQL Cluster.

9.5.5.1 MySQL Cluster-Related Command Options for `mysqld`

- `--ndb-connectstring=connect_string`

  When using the `NDB Cluster` storage engine, this option specifies the management server that distributes cluster configuration data.

- `--ndbcluster`

  The `NDB Cluster` storage engine is necessary for using MySQL Cluster. If a `mysqld` binary includes support for the `NDB Cluster` storage engine, the engine is disabled by default. Use the `--ndbcluster` option to enable it. Use `--skip-ndbcluster` to explicitly disable the engine.

9.5.5.2 Command Options for `ndbd`

For options common to NDB programs, see Section 9.5.5, "Command Options for MySQL Cluster Processes."

- `--daemon, -d`

  Instructs `ndbd` to execute as a daemon process. This is the default behavior. `--nodaemon` can be used to not start the process as a daemon.

- `--initial`

  Instructs `ndbd` to perform an initial start. An initial start erases any files created for recovery purposes by earlier instances of `ndbd`. It also re-creates recovery log files. Note that on some operating systems this process can take a substantial amount of time.

  An `--initial` start is to be used only the very first time that the `ndbd` process is started because it removes all files from the Cluster filesystem and re-creates all REDO log files. The exceptions to this rule are:

  - When performing a software upgrade that has changed the contents of any files.
  - When restarting the node with a new version of `ndbd`.
  - As a measure of last resort when for some reason the node restart or system restart repeatedly fails. In this case, be aware that this node can no longer be used to restore data due to the destruction of the datafiles.

  This option does not affect any backup files that have already been created by the affected node.

- `--nodaemon`

  Instructs `ndbd` not to start as a daemon process. This is useful when `ndbd` is being debugged and you want output to be redirected to the screen.

- `--nostart`

  Instructs `ndbd` not to start automatically. When this option is used, `ndbd` connects to the management server, obtains configuration data from it, and initializes communication objects. However, it does not actually start the execution engine until specifically requested to do so by the management server. This can be accomplished by issuing the proper command to the management client.

9.5.5.3 Command Options for ndb_mgmd

For options common to NDB programs, see Section 9.5.5, "Command Options for MySQL Cluster Processes."

- --config-file=*file_name*, -f *file_name*,

  Instructs the management server as to which file it should use for its configuration file. This option must be specified. The filename defaults to config.ini.

  Note: This option also can be given as -c *file_name*, but this shortcut is obsolete and should *not* be used in new installations.

- --daemon, -d

  Instructs ndb_mgmd to start as a daemon process. This is the default behavior.

- --nodaemon

  Instructs ndb_mgmd not to start as a daemon process.

9.5.5.4 Command Options for ndb_mgm

For options common to NDB programs, see Section 9.5.5, "Command Options for MySQL Cluster Processes."

- --try-reconnect=*number*

  If the connection to the management server is broken, the node tries to reconnect to it every 5 seconds until it succeeds. By using this option, it is possible to limit the number of attempts to *number* before giving up and reporting an error instead.

9.6 Management of MySQL Cluster

Managing a MySQL Cluster involves a number of tasks, the first of which is to configure and start MySQL Cluster. This is covered in Section 9.4, "MySQL Cluster Configuration," and Section 9.5, "Process Management in MySQL Cluster."

The following sections cover the management of a running MySQL Cluster.

There are essentially two methods of actively managing a running MySQL Cluster. The first of these is through the use of commands entered into the management client whereby cluster status can be checked, log levels changed, backups started and stopped, and nodes stopped and started. The second method involves studying the contents of the cluster log ndb_*node_id*_cluster.log in the management server's DataDir directory. (Recall that *node_id* represents the unique identifier of the node whose activity is being logged.) The cluster log contains event reports generated by ndbd. It is also possible to send cluster log entries to a Unix system log.

9.6.1 MySQL Cluster Startup Phases

This section describes the steps involved when the cluster is started.

There are several different startup types and modes, as shown here:

- **Initial Start**: The cluster starts with a clean filesystem on all data nodes. This occurs either when the cluster started for the very first time, or when it is restarted using the `--initial` option.
- **System Restart**: The cluster starts and reads data stored in the data nodes. This occurs when the cluster has been shut down after having been in use, when it is desired for the cluster to resume operations from the point where it left off.
- **Node Restart**: This is the online restart of a cluster node while the cluster itself is running.
- **Initial Node Restart**: This is the same as a node restart, except that the node is reinitialized and started with a clean filesystem.

Prior to startup, each data node (`ndbd` process) must be initialized. Initialization consists of the following steps:

1. Obtain a node ID.
2. Fetch configuration data.
3. Allocate ports to be used for inter-node communications.
4. Allocate memory according to settings obtained from the configuration file.

After each data node has been initialized, the cluster startup process can proceed. The stages which the cluster goes through during this process are listed here:

- **Stage 0**

  Clears the cluster filesystem. This stage occurs *only* if the cluster was started with the `--initial` option.

- **Stage 1**

  This stage sets up Cluster connections, establishes inter-node communications, and starts Cluster heartbeats.

- **Stage 2**

  The arbitrator node is elected. If this is a system restart, the cluster determines the latest restorable global checkpoint.

- **Stage 3**

  This stage initializes a number of internal cluster variables.

- **Stage 4**

  For an initial start or initial node restart, the REDO log files are created. The number of these files is equal to `NoOfFragmentLogFiles`.

  For a system restart:

  - Read schema or schemas.
  - Read data from the local checkpoint and undo logs.
  - Apply all redo information until the latest restorable global checkpoint has been reached.

For a node restart, find the tail of the REDO log.

- **Stage 5**

  If this is an initial start, create the SYSTAB_0 and NDB$EVENTS internal system tables.

  For a node restart or an initial node restart:

  1. The node is included in transaction handling operations.

  2. The node schema is compared with that of the master and synchronized with it.

  3. Synchronize data received in the form of INSERT from the other data nodes in this node's node group.

  4. In all cases, wait for complete local checkpoint as determined by the arbitrator.

- **Stage 6**

  Update internal variables.

- **Stage 7**

  Update internal variables.

- **Stage 8**

  In a system restart, rebuild all indexes.

- **Stage 9**

  Update internal variables.

- **Stage 10**

  At this point in a node restart or initial node restart, APIs may connect to the node and begin to receive events.

- **Stage 11**

  At this point in a node restart or initial node restart, event delivery is handed over to the node joining the cluster. The newly-joined node takes over responsibility for delivering its primary data to subscribers.

After this process is completed for an initial start or system restart, transaction handling is enabled. For a node restart or initial node restart, completion of the startup process means that the node may now act as a transaction coordinator.

9.6.2 Commands in the Management Client

In addition to the central configuration file, a cluster may also be controlled through a command-line interface available through the management client ndb_mgm. This is the primary administrative interface to a running cluster.

Commands for the event logs are given in Section 9.6.3, "Event Reports Generated in MySQL Cluster." Commands for creating backups and restoring from backup are provided in Section 9.6.5, "Online Backup of MySQL Cluster."

The management client has the following basic commands. In the listing that follows, *node_id* denotes either a database node ID or the keyword ALL, which indicates that the command should be applied to all of the cluster's data nodes.

- HELP

  Displays information on all available commands.

- SHOW

  Displays information on the cluster's status.

  Note: In a cluster where multiple management nodes are in use, this command displays information only for data nodes that are actually connected to the current management server.

- *node_id* START

  Starts the data node identified by *node_id* (or all data nodes).

- *node_id* STOP

  Stops the data node identified by *node_id* (or all data nodes).

- *node_id* RESTART [-N] [-I]

  Restarts the data node identified by *node_id* (or all data nodes).

- *node_id* STATUS

  Displays status information for the data node identified by *node_id* (or for all data nodes).

- ENTER SINGLE USER MODE *node_id*

  Enters single-user mode, wherein only the MySQL server identified by the node ID *node_id* is allowed to access the database.

- EXIT SINGLE USER MODE

  Exits single-user mode, allowing all SQL nodes (that is, all running mysqld processes) to access the database.

- QUIT

  Terminates the management client.

- SHUTDOWN

  Shuts down all cluster nodes, except for SQL nodes, and exits.

9.6.3 Event Reports Generated in MySQL Cluster

In this section, we discuss the types of event logs provided by MySQL Cluster, and the types of events that are logged.

MySQL Cluster provides two types of event log. These are the **cluster log**, which includes events generated by all cluster nodes, and **node logs**, which are local to each data node.

Output generated by cluster event logging can have multiple destinations including a file, the management server console window, or syslog. Output generated by node event logging is written to the data node's console window.

Both types of event logs can be set to log different subsets of events.

Note: The cluster log is the log recommended for most uses because it provides logging information for an entire cluster in a single file. Node logs are intended to be used only during application development, or for debugging application code.

Each reportable event can be distinguished according to three different criteria:

- *Category*: This can be any one of the following values: STARTUP, SHUTDOWN, STATISTICS, CHECKPOINT, NODERESTART, CONNECTION, ERROR, or INFO.
- *Priority*: This is represented by one of the numbers from 1 to 15 inclusive, where 1 indicates "most important" and 15 "least important."
- *Severity Level*: This can be any one of the following values: ALERT, CRITICAL, ERROR, WARNING, INFO, or DEBUG.

Both the cluster log and the node log can be filtered on these properties.

9.6.3.1 Logging Management Commands

The following management commands are related to the cluster log:

- CLUSTERLOG ON

  Turns the cluster log on.

- CLUSTERLOG OFF

  Turns the cluster log off.

- CLUSTERLOG INFO

  Provides information about cluster log settings.

- *node_id* CLUSTERLOG *category=threshold*

  Logs *category* events with priority less than or equal to *threshold* in the cluster log.

- CLUSTERLOG FILTER *severity_level*

  Toggles cluster logging of events of the specified *severity_level*.

The following table describes the default setting (for all data nodes) of the cluster log category threshold. If an event has a priority with a value lower than or equal to the priority threshold, it is reported in the cluster log.

Note that events are reported per data node, and that the threshold can be set to different values on different nodes.

Category	Default Threshold (All Data Nodes)
STARTUP	7
SHUTDOWN	7
STATISTICS	7
CHECKPOINT	7
NODERESTART	7
CONNECTION	7
ERROR	15
INFO	7

Thresholds are used to filter events within each category. For example, a STARTUP event with a priority of 3 is not logged unless the threshold for STARTUP is changed to 3 or lower. Only events with priority 3 or lower are sent if the threshold is 3.

The following table shows the event severity levels. (**Note**: These correspond to Unix syslog levels, except for LOG_EMERG and LOG_NOTICE, which are not used or mapped.)

1	ALERT	A condition that should be corrected immediately, such as a corrupted system database
2	CRITICAL	Critical conditions, such as device errors or insufficient resources
3	ERROR	Conditions that should be corrected, such as configuration errors
4	WARNING	Conditions that are not errors, but that might require special handling
5	INFO	Informational messages
6	DEBUG	Debugging messages used for NDB Cluster development

Event severity levels can be turned on or off (using CLUSTERLOG FILTER—see above). If a severity level is turned on, all events with a priority less than or equal to the category thresholds are logged. If the severity level is turned off, no events belonging to that severity level are logged.

9.6.3.2 Log Events

An event report reported in the event logs has the following format:

```
datetime [string] severity -- message
```

For example:

```
09:19:30 2005-07-24 [NDB] INFO -- Node 4 Start phase 4 completed
```

This section discusses all reportable events, ordered by category and severity level within each category.

In the event descriptions, GCP and LCP mean "Global Checkpoint" and "Local Checkpoint," respectively.

CONNECTION Events

These events are associated with connections between Cluster nodes.

Event	Priority	Severity Level	Description
DB nodes connected	8	INFO	Data nodes connected
DB nodes disconnected	8	INFO	Data nodes disconnected
Communication closed	8	INFO	SQL node or data node connection closed
Communication opened	8	INFO	SQL node or data node connection opened

CHECKPOINT Events

The logging messages shown here are associated with checkpoints.

Event	Priority	Severity Level	Description
LCP stopped in calc keep GCI	0	ALERT	LCP stopped
Local checkpoint fragment completed	11	INFO	LCP on a fragment has been completed
Global checkpoint completed	10	INFO	GCP finished
Global checkpoint started	9	INFO	Start of GCP: REDO log is written to disk
Local checkpoint completed	8	INFO	LCP completed normally
Local checkpoint started	7	INFO	Start of LCP: data written to disk
Report undo log blocked	7	INFO	UNDO logging blocked; buffer near overflow

STARTUP Events

The following events are generated in response to the startup of a node or of the cluster and of its success or failure. They also provide information relating to the progress of the startup process, including information concerning logging activities.

Event	Priority	Severity Level	Description
Internal start signal received STTORRY	15	INFO	Blocks received after completion of restart
Undo records executed	15	INFO	
New REDO log started	10	INFO	GCI keep X, newest restorable GCI Y
New log started	10	INFO	Log part X, start MB Y, stop MB Z
Node has been refused for inclusion in the cluster	8	INFO	Node cannot be included in cluster due to misconfiguration, inability to establish communication, or other problem
DB node neighbors	8	INFO	Shows neighboring data nodes
DB node start phase X completed	4	INFO	A data node start phase has been completed
Node has been successfully included into the cluster	3	INFO	Displays the node, managing node, and dynamic ID
DB node start phases initiated	1	INFO	NDB Cluster nodes starting
DB node all start phases completed	1	INFO	NDB Cluster nodes started
DB node shutdown initiated	1	INFO	Shutdown of data node has commenced
DB node shutdown aborted	1	INFO	Unable to shut down data node normally

NODERESTART Events

The following events are generated when restarting a node and relate to the success or failure of the node restart process.

Event	Priority	Severity Level	Description
Node failure phase completed	8	ALERT	Reports completion of node failure phases
Node has failed, node state was X	8	ALERT	Reports that a node has failed
Report arbitrator results	2	ALERT	There are eight different possible results for arbitration attempts: • Arbitration check failed—less than 1/2 nodes left • Arbitration check succeeded—node group majority • Arbitration check failed—missing node group • Network partitioning—arbitration required • Arbitration succeeded—affirmative response from node X • Arbitration failed—negative response from node X • Network partitioning—no arbitrator available • Network partitioning—no arbitrator configured
Completed copying a fragment	10	INFO	
Completed copying of dictionary information	8	INFO	
Completed copying distribution information	8	INFO	
Starting to copy fragments	8	INFO	
Completed copying all fragments	8	INFO	
GCP takeover started	7	INFO	
GCP takeover completed	7	INFO	
LCP takeover started	7	INFO	
LCP takeover completed (state = X)	7	INFO	
Report whether an arbitrator is found or not	6	INFO	There are seven different possible outcomes when seeking an arbitrator: • Management server restarts arbitration thread [state=X] • Prepare arbitrator node X [ticket=Y] • Receive arbitrator node X [ticket=Y] • Started arbitrator node X [ticket=Y] • Lost arbitrator node X—process failure [state=Y] • Lost arbitrator node X—process exit [state=Y] • Lost arbitrator node X <error msg> [state=Y]

STATISTICS Events

The following events are of a statistical nature. They provide information such as numbers of transactions and other operations, amount of data sent or received by individual nodes, and memory usage.

Event	Priority	Severity Level	Description
Report job scheduling statistics	9	INFO	Mean internal job scheduling statistics
Sent number of bytes	9	INFO	Mean number of bytes sent to node X
Received number of bytes	9	INFO	Mean number of bytes received from node X
Report transaction statistics	8	INFO	Numbers of transactions, commits, reads, simple reads, writes, concurrent operations, attribute information, and aborts
Report operations	8	INFO	Number of operations
Report table create	7	INFO	
Memory usage	5	INFO	Data and index memory usage (80%, 90%, and 100%)

ERROR Events

These events relate to Cluster errors and warnings. The presence of one or more of these generally indicates that a major malfunction or failure has occurred.

Event	Priority	Severity	Description
Dead due to missed heartbeat	8	ALERT	Node X declared dead due to missed heartbeat
Transporter errors	2	ERROR	
Transporter warnings	8	WARNING	
Missed heartbeats	8	WARNING	Node X missed heartbeat #Y
General warning events	2	WARNING	

INFO Events

These events provide general information about the state of the cluster and activities associated with Cluster maintenance, such as logging and heartbeat transmission.

Event	Priority	Severity	Description
Sent heartbeat	12	INFO	Heartbeat sent to node X
Create log bytes	11	INFO	Log part, log file, MB
General information events	2	INFO	

9.6.4 Single-User Mode

Single-user mode allows the database administrator to restrict access to the database system to a single MySQL server (SQL node). When entering single-user mode, all connections to all other MySQL servers are closed gracefully and all running transactions are aborted. No new transactions are allowed to be started.

Once the cluster has entered single-user mode, only the designated SQL node is granted access to the database.

You can use the ALL STATUS command to see when the cluster has entered single-user mode.

Example:

```
NDB> ENTER SINGLE USER MODE 5
```

After this command has executed and the cluster has entered single-user mode, the SQL node whose node ID is 5 becomes the cluster's only permitted user.

The node specified in the preceding command must be a MySQL Server node; An attempt to specify any other type of node will be rejected.

Note: When the preceding command is invoked, all transactions running on the designated node are aborted, the connection is closed, and the server must be restarted.

The command EXIT SINGLE USER MODE changes the state of the cluster's data nodes from single-user mode to normal mode. MySQL Servers waiting for a connection (that is, for the cluster to become ready and available), are again permitted to connect. The MySQL Server denoted as the single-user SQL node continues to run (if still connected) during and after the state change.

Example:

```
NDB> EXIT SINGLE USER MODE
```

There are two recommended ways to handle a node failure when running in single-user mode:

- Method 1:
    1. Finish all single-user mode transactions
    2. Issue the EXIT SINGLE USER MODE command
    3. Restart the cluster's data nodes
- Method 2:
    Restart database nodes prior to entering single-user mode

9.6.5 Online Backup of MySQL Cluster

This section describes how to create a backup and how to restore the database from a backup at a later time.

9.6.5.1 Cluster Backup Concepts

A backup is a snapshot of the database at a given time. The backup consists of three main parts:

- **Metadata**: The names and definitions of all database tables
- **Table records**: The data actually stored in the database tables at the time that the backup was made
- **Transaction log**: A sequential record telling how and when data was stored in the database

Each of these parts is saved on all nodes participating in the backup. During backup, each node saves these three parts into three files on disk:

- BACKUP-*backup_id.node_id*.ctl

  A control file containing control information and metadata. Each node saves the same table definitions (for all tables in the cluster) to its own version of this file.

- BACKUP-*backup_id*-0.*node_id*.data

  A data file containing the table records, which are saved on a per-fragment basis. That is, different nodes save different fragments during the backup. The file saved by each node starts with a header that states the tables to which the records belong. Following the list of records there is a footer containing a checksum for all records.

- BACKUP-*backup_id.node_id*.log

  A log file containing records of committed transactions. Only transactions on tables stored in the backup are stored in the log. Nodes involved in the backup save different records because different nodes host different database fragments.

In the listing above, *backup_id* stands for the backup identifier and *node_id* is the unique identifier for the node creating the file.

9.6.5.2 Using the Management Server to Create a Backup

Before starting a backup, make sure that the cluster is properly configured for performing one. (See Section 9.6.5.4, "Configuration for Cluster Backup.")

Creating a backup using the management server involves the following steps:

1. Start the management server (ndb_mgm).
2. Execute the command START BACKUP.
3. The management server will reply with the message Start of backup ordered. This means that the management server has submitted the request to the cluster, but has not yet received any response.
4. The management server will reply Backup *backup_id* started, where *backup_id* is the unique identifier for this particular backup. (This identifier will also be saved in the cluster log, if it has not been configured otherwise.) This means that the cluster has received and processed the backup request. It does *not* mean that the backup has finished.

5. The management server will signal that the backup is finished with the message `Backup` *`backup_id`* `completed`.

To abort a backup that is already in progress:

1. Start the management server.

2. Execute the command `ABORT BACKUP` *`backup_id`*. The number *`backup_id`* is the identifier of the backup that was included in the response of the management server when the backup was started (in the message `Backup` *`backup_id`* `started`).

3. The management server will acknowledge the abort request with `Abort of backup` *`backup_id`* `ordered`; note that it has received no actual response to this request yet.

4. After the backup has been aborted, the management server will report `Backup` *`backup_id`* `has been aborted for reason` *`XYZ`*. This means that the cluster has terminated the backup and that all files related to this backup have been removed from the cluster filesystem.

It is also possible to abort a backup in progress from the system shell using this command:

```
shell> ndb_mgm -e "ABORT BACKUP backup_id"
```

Note: If there is no backup with ID *`backup_id`* running when it is aborted, the management server makes no explicit response. However, the fact that an invalid abort command was sent is indicated in the cluster log.

9.6.5.3 How to Restore a Cluster Backup

The cluster restoration program is implemented as a separate command-line utility `ndb_restore`, which reads the files created by the backup and inserts the stored information into the database. The restore program must be executed once for each set of backup files. That is, as many times as there were database nodes running when the backup was created.

The first time you run the `ndb_restore` restoration program, you also need to restore the metadata. In other words, you must re-create the database tables. (Note that the cluster should have an empty database when starting to restore a backup.) The restore program acts as an API to the cluster and therefore requires a free connection to connect to the cluster. This can be verified with the `ndb_mgm` command `SHOW` (you can accomplish this from a system shell using `ndb_mgm -e SHOW`). The `-c` *`connectstring`* option may be used to locate the MGM node (see Section 9.4.4.2, "The MySQL Cluster `connectstring`," for information on connectstrings). The backup files must be present in the directory given as an argument to the restoration program.

It is possible to restore a backup to a database with a different configuration than it was created from. For example, suppose that a backup with backup ID 12, created in a cluster with two database nodes having the node IDs 2 and 3, is to be restored to a cluster with four nodes. Then `ndb_restore` must be run twice—once for each database node in the cluster where the backup was taken.

Note: For rapid restoration, the data may be restored in parallel, provided that there is a sufficient number of cluster connections available. However, the data files must always be applied before the logs.

9.6.5.4 Configuration for Cluster Backup

Four configuration parameters are essential for backup:

- `BackupDataBufferSize`

  The amount of memory used to buffer data before it is written to disk.

- `BackupLogBufferSize`

  The amount of memory used to buffer log records before these are written to disk.

- `BackupMemory`

  The total memory allocated in a database node for backups. This should be the sum of the memory allocated for the backup data buffer and the backup log buffer.

- `BackupWriteSize`

  The size of blocks written to disk. This applies for both the backup data buffer and the backup log buffer.

More detailed information about these parameters can be found in Section 9.4, "MySQL Cluster Configuration."

9.6.5.5 Backup Troubleshooting

If an error code is returned when issuing a backup request, the most likely cause is insufficient memory or insufficient disk space. You should check that there is enough memory allocated for the backup. Also check that there is enough space on the hard drive partition of the backup target.

NDB does not support repeatable reads, which can cause problems with the restoration process. Although the backup process is "hot," restoring a MySQL Cluster from backup is not a 100% "hot" process. This is due to the fact that, for the duration of the restore process, running transactions get non-repeatable reads from the restored data. This means that the state of the data is inconsistent while the restore is in progress.

9.7 MySQL Cluster Replication

Prior to MySQL 5.1.6, asynchronous replication, more usually referred to simply as "replication," was not available when using MySQL Cluster. MySQL 5.1.6 introduces master-slave replication of this type for MySQL Cluster databases. This section explains how to set up and manage a configuration wherein one group of computers operating as a MySQL Cluster replicates to a second computer or group of computers. We assume some familiarity on the part of the reader with standard MySQL replication as discussed elsewhere in this manual. (See Chapter 5, "Replication.")

Normal (non-clustered) replication involves a "master" server and a "slave" server, the master being the source of the operations and data to be replicated and the slave being the recipient of these. In MySQL Cluster, replication is conceptually very similar but can be more complex in practice, because it may be extended to cover a number of different configurations including replicating between two complete clusters. Although a MySQL Cluster itself depends on the NDB Cluster storage engine for clustering functionality, it is not necessary to use the Cluster storage engine on the slave. However, for maximum availability, it is possible to replicate from one MySQL Cluster to another, and it is this type of configuration that we discuss, as shown in Figure 9.5.

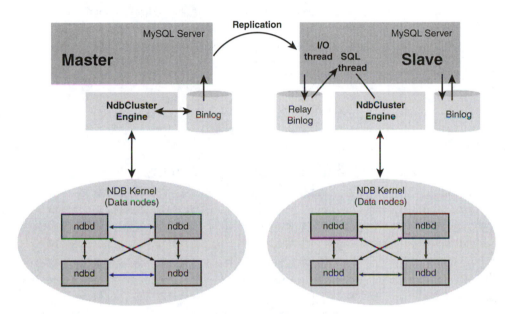

FIGURE 9.5   MySQL Cluster-to-Cluster replication layout.

In this scenario, the replication process is one in which successive states of a master cluster are logged and saved to a slave cluster. This process is accomplished by a special thread known as the NDB binlog injector thread, which runs on each MySQL server and produces a binary log (binlog). This thread ensures that all changes in the cluster producing the binary log—and not just those changes that are effected via the MySQL Server—are inserted into the binary log with the correct serialization order. We refer to the MySQL replication master and replication slave servers as "replication servers" or "replication nodes," and the data flow or line of communication between them as a "replication channel."

9.7.1 Abbreviations and Symbols

Throughout this section, we use the following abbreviations or symbols for referring to the master and slave clusters, and to processes and commands run on the clusters or cluster nodes:

Symbol or Abbreviation	Description (Refers to...)
M	The cluster serving as the (primary) replication master
S	The cluster acting as the (primary) replication slave
shellM>	Shell command to be issued on the master cluster
mysqlM>	MySQL client command issued on a single MySQL server running as an SQL node on the master cluster
mysqlM*>	MySQL client command to be issued on all SQL nodes participating in the replication master cluster
shellS>	Shell command to be issued on the slave cluster
mysqlS>	MySQL client command issued on a single MySQL server running as an SQL node on the slave cluster
mysqlS*>	MySQL client command to be issued on all SQL nodes participating in the replication slave cluster
C	Primary replication channel
C'	Secondary replication channel
M'	Secondary replication master
S'	Secondary replication slave

9.7.2 Assumptions and General Requirements

A replication channel requires two MySQL servers acting as replication servers (one each for the master and slave). For example, this means that in the case of a replication setup with two replication channels (to provide an extra channel for redundancy), there will be a total of four replication nodes, two per cluster.

Each MySQL server used for replication in either cluster must be uniquely identified among all the MySQL replication servers participating in either cluster (you cannot have replication servers on both the master and slave clusters sharing the same ID). This can be done by starting each SQL node using the --server-id=id option, where id is a unique integer. Although it is not strictly necessary, we will assume for purposes of this discussion that all MySQL installations are the same version.

In any event, servers involved in replication must be compatible with one another with respect to both the version of the replication protocol used and the SQL feature sets they support; the simplest and easiest way to assure that this is the case is to use the same MySQL version for all servers involved. Note that in many cases it is not possible to replicate to a slave running a version of MySQL with a lower version number than that of the master—see Section 5.6, "Replication Compatibility Between MySQL Versions," for details.

We assume that the slave server or cluster is dedicated to replication of the master, and that no other data is being stored on it.

9.7.3 Known Issues

The following are known problems or issues when using replication with MySQL Cluster in MySQL 5.1:

- The use of data definition statements, such as CREATE TABLE, DROP TABLE, and ALTER TABLE, are recorded in the binary log for only the MySQL server on which they are issued.

- A MySQL server involved in replication should be started or restarted after using ndb_restore to discover and setup replication of NDB Cluster tables. Alternatively, you can issue a SHOW TABLES statement on all databases in the cluster.

  Similarly, when using CREATE SCHEMA, the new database is not automatically discoverable by the MySQL server. Thus, this statement must be issued on each MySQL server participating in the cluster when creating a new database.

- Restarting the cluster with the --initial option will cause the sequence of GCI and epoch numbers to start over from 0. (This is generally true of MySQL Cluster and not limited to replication scenarios involving Cluster.) The MySQL servers involved in replication should in this case be replicated. After this, you should use the RESET MASTER and RESET SLAVE statements to clear the invalid binlog_index and apply_status tables, respectively.

See Section 9.7.9.2, "Initiating Discovery of Schema Changes," for more information about the first two items listed above, as well as some examples illustrating how to handle applicable situations.

9.7.4 Replication Schema and Tables

Replication in MySQL Cluster makes use of a number of dedicated tables in a separate cluster_replication database on each MySQL Server instance acting as an SQL node in both the cluster being replicated and the replication slave (whether the slave is a single server or a cluster). This database, which is created during the MySQL installation process by the mysql_install_db script, contains a table for storing the binary log's indexing data. Because the binlog_index table is local to each MySQL server and does not participate in clustering, it uses the MyISAM storage engine, and so must be created separately on each mysqld participating in the master cluster. This table is defined as follows:

```
CREATE TABLE `binlog_index` (
         `Position`  BIGINT(20) UNSIGNED NOT NULL,
         `File`      VARCHAR(255) NOT NULL,
         `epoch`     BIGINT(20) UNSIGNED NOT NULL,
         `inserts`   BIGINT(20) UNSIGNED NOT NULL,
         `updates`   BIGINT(20) UNSIGNED NOT NULL,
         `deletes`   BIGINT(20) UNSIGNED NOT NULL,
         `schemaops` BIGNINT(20) UNSIGNED NOT NULL,
         PRIMARY KEY (`epoch`)
) ENGINE=MYISAM  DEFAULT CHARSET=latin1;
```

Figure 9.6 shows the relationship of the MySQL Cluster replication master server, its binlog injector thread, and the cluster_replication.binlog_index table.

MySQL Replication Between Clusters, Injecting into Binlog

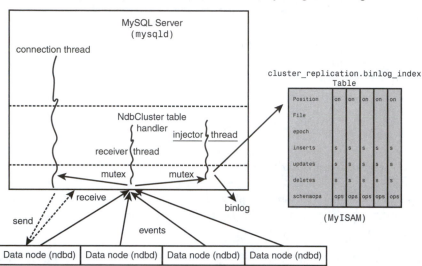

FIGURE 9.6   The replication master cluster, the binlog-injector thread, and
the `binlog_index` table.

An additional table, named `apply_status`, is used to keep a record of the operations that
have been replicated from the master to the slave. Unlike the case with `binlog_index`, the
data in this table is not specific to any one SQL node in the (slave) cluster, and so
`apply_status` can use the `NDB Cluster` storage engine, as shown here:

```
CREATE TABLE `apply_status` (
    `server_id`  INT(10) UNSIGNED NOT NULL,
    `epoch`       BIGINT(20) UNSIGNED NOT NULL,
    PRIMARY KEY  USING HASH (`server_id`)
) ENGINE=NDBCLUSTER  DEFAULT CHARSET=latin1;
```

The `binlog_index` and `apply_status` tables are created in a separate database because they
should not be replicated. No user intervention is normally required to create or maintain
either of them. Both the `binlog_index` and the `apply_status` tables are maintained by the
NDB injector thread. This keeps the master `mysqld` process updated to changes performed
by the NDB storage engine. The NDB *binlog injector thread* receives events directly from the
NDB storage engine. The NDB injector is responsible for capturing all the data events
within the cluster, and ensures that all events changing, inserting, or deleting data are
recorded in the `binlog_index` table. The slave I/O thread will transfer the from the master's
binary log to the slave's relay log.

However, it is advisable to check for the existence and integrity of these tables as an initial
step in preparing a MySQL Cluster for replication. It is possible to view event data recorded
in the binary log by querying the `cluster_replication.binlog_index` table directly on the
master. This can be also be accomplished using the `SHOW BINLOG EVENTS` statement on either
the replication master or slave MySQL servers.

9.7.5 Preparing the Cluster for Replication

Preparing the MySQL Cluster for replication consists of the following steps:

1. Check all MySQL servers for version compatibility (see Section 9.7.2, "Assumptions and General Requirements").

2. Create a slave account on the master Cluster with the appropriate privileges:

```
mysqlM> GRANT REPLICATION SLAVE
    ->     ON *.* TO 'slave_user'@'slave_host'
    ->     IDENTIFIED BY 'slave_password';
```

where *slave_user* is the slave account username, *slave_host* is the hostname or IP address of the replication slave, and *slave_password* is the password to assign to this account.

For example, to create a slave user account with the name "myslave," logging in from the host named "rep-slave," and using the password "53cr37," use the following GRANT statement:

```
mysqlM> GRANT REPLICATION SLAVE
    -> ON *.* TO 'myslave'@'rep-slave'
    -> IDENTIFIED BY '53cr37';
```

For security reasons, it is preferable to use a unique user account—not employed for any other purpose—for the replication slave account.

3. Configure the slave to use the master. Using the MySQL Monitor, this can be accomplished with the CHANGE MASTER TO statement:

```
mysqlS> CHANGE MASTER TO
    -> MASTER_HOST='master_host',
    -> MASTER_PORT=master_port,
    -> MASTER_USER='slave_user',
    -> MASTER_PASSWORD='slave_password';
```

where *master_host* is the hostname or IP address of the replication master, *master_port* is the port for the slave to use for connecting to the master, *slave_user* is the username set up for the slave on the master, and *slave_password* is the password set for that user account in the previous step.

For example, to tell the slave to replicate from the MySQL server whose hostname is "rep-master," using the replication slave account created in the previous step, use the following statement:

```
mysqlS> CHANGE MASTER TO
    -> MASTER_HOST='rep-master'
    -> MASTER_PORT=3306,
    -> MASTER_USER='myslave'
    -> MASTER_PASSWORD='53cr37';
```

You can also configure the slave to use the master by setting the corresponding startup options in the slave server's my.cnf file. To configure the slave in the same way as the preceding example `CHANGE MASTER TO` statement, the following information would need to be included in the slave's `my.cnf` file:

```
[mysqld]
master-host=rep-master
master-port=3306
master-user=myslave
master-password=53cr37
```

See Section 5.9, "Replication Startup Options," for additional options that can be set in `my.cnf` for replication slaves.

Note: To provide replication backup capability, you will also need to add an `ndb-connectstring` option to the slave's `my.cnf` file prior to starting the replication process. See Section 9.7.9, "MySQL Cluster Backups with Replication," for details.

4. If the master cluster is already in use, you can create a backup of the master and load this onto the slave to cut down on the amount of time required for the slave to synchronize itself with the master. If the slave is also running MySQL Cluster, this can be accomplished using the backup and restore procedure described in Section 9.7.9, "MySQL Cluster Backups with Replication."

```
ndb-connectstring=management_host[:port]
```

In the event that you are *not* using MySQL Cluster on the replication slave, you can create a backup with this command on the replication master:

```
shellM> mysqldump --master-data=1
```

Then import the resulting data dump onto the slave by copying the dump file over to the slave. After this, you can use the `mysql` client to import the data from the dumpfile into the slave database as shown here, where *dump_file* is the name of the file that was generated using `mysqldump` on the master, and *db_name* is the name of the database to be replicated:

```
shellS> mysql -u root -p db_name < dump_file
```

For a complete list of options to use with `mysqldump`, see Section 7.10, "mysqldump—A Database Backup Program."

Note that if you copy the data to the slave in this fashion, you should make sure that the slave is started with the `--skip-slave-start` option on the command line, or else include `skip-slave-start` in the slave's `my.cnf` file to keep it from trying to connect to the master to begin replicating before all the data has been loaded. Once the loading of data has completed, follow the additional steps outlined in the next two sections.

5. Ensure that each MySQL server acting as a replication master is configured with a unique server ID, and with binary logging enabled, using the row format. (See Section 5.3, "Row-Based Replication.") These options can be set either in the master server's `my.cnf` file, or on the command line when starting the master `mysqld` process. See Section 9.7.6, "Starting Replication (Single Replication Channel)," for information regarding the latter option.

9.7.6 Starting Replication (Single Replication Channel)

This section outlines the procedure for starting MySQL CLuster replication using a single replication channel.

1. Start the MySQL replication master server by issuing this command:

```
shellM> mysqld --nbdcluster --server-id=id \
        --log-bin --binlog-format=row &
```

where *id* is this server's unique ID (see Section 9.7.2, "Assumptions and General Requirements"). This starts the server's `mysqld` process with binary logging enabled using the proper logging format.

2. Start the MySQL replication slave server as shown here:

```
shellS> mysqld --ndbcluster --server-id=id &
```

where *id* is the slave server's unique ID. It is not necessary to enable logging on the replication slave.

Note that you should use the `--skip-slave-start` option with this command or else you should include `skip-slave-start` in the slave server's `my.cnf` file, unless you want replication to begin immediately. With the use of this option, the start of replication is delayed until the appropriate `START SLAVE` statement has been issued, as explained in Step 4 below.

3. It is necessary to synchronize the slave server with the master server's replication binlog. If binary logging has not previously been running on the master, run the following statement on the slave:

```
mysqlS> CHANGE MASTER TO
    -> MASTER_LOG_FILE='',
    -> MASTER_LOG_POS=4;
```

This instructs the slave to begin reading the master's binary log from the log's starting point. Otherwise—that is, if you are loading data from the master using a backup—see Section 9.7.8, "Implementing Failover with MySQL Cluster," for information on how to obtain the correct values to use for `MASTER_LOG_FILE` and `MASTER_LOG_POS` in such cases.

4. Finally, you must instruct the slave to begin applying replication by issuing this command from the `mysql` client on the replication slave:

```
mysqlS> START SLAVE;
```

This also initiates the transmission of replication data from the master to the slave.

It is also possible to use two replication channels, in a manner similar to the procedure described in the next section; the differences between this and using a single replication channel are covered in Section 9.7.7, "Using Two Replication Channels."

9.7.7 Using Two Replication Channels

In a more complete example scenario, we envision two replication channels to provide redundancy and thereby guard against possible failure of a single replication channel. This requires a total of four replication servers, two masters for the master cluster and two slave servers for the slave cluster. For purposes of the discussion that follows, we assume that unique identifiers are assigned as shown here:

Server ID	Description
1	Master—primary replication channel (M)
2	Master—secondary replication channel (M')
3	Slave—primary replication channel (S)
4	Slave—secondary replication channel (S')

Setting up replication with two channels is not radically different from setting up a single replication channel. First, the mysqld processes for the primary and secondary replication masters must be started, followed by those for the primary and secondary slaves. Then the replication processes may be initiated by issuing the START SLAVE statement on each of the slaves. The commands and the order in which they need to be issued are shown here:

1. Start the primary replication master:

   ```
   shellM> mysqld --ndbcluster --server-id=1 \
                --log-bin --binlog-format=row &
   ```

2. Start the secondary replication master:

   ```
   shellM'> mysqld --ndbcluster --server-id=2 \
                --log-bin --binlog-format=row &
   ```

3. Start the primary replication slave server:

   ```
   shellS> mysqld --ndbcluster --server-id=3 \
                --skip-slave-start &
   ```

4. Start the secondary replication slave:

   ```
   shellS'> mysqld --ndbcluster --server-id=4 \
                --skip-slave-start &
   ```

5. Finally, commence replication on the primary channel by executing the START SLAVE statement on the primary slave as shown here:

   ```
   mysqlS> START SLAVE;
   ```

As mentioned previously, it is not necessary to enable binary logging on replication slaves.

9.7.8 Implementing Failover with MySQL Cluster

In the event that the primary Cluster replication process fails, it is possible to switch over to the secondary replication channel. The following procedure describes the steps required to accomplish this:

1. Obtain the time of the most recent global checkpoint (GCP). That is, you need to determine the most recent epoch from the `apply_status` table on the slave cluster, which can be found using the following query:

```
mysqlS'> SELECT @latest:=MAX(epoch)
    ->         FROM cluster_replication.apply_status;
```

2. Using the information obtained from the query shown in Step 1, obtain the corresponding records from the `binlog_index` table on the master cluster as shown here:

```
mysqlM'> SELECT
    ->     @file:=SUBSTRING_INDEX(File, '/', -1),
    ->     @pos:=Position
    -> FROM cluster_replication.binlog_index
    -> WHERE epoch > @latest
    -> ORDER BY epoch ASC LIMIT 1;
```

These are the records saved on the master since the failure of the primary replication channel. We have employed the user variable `@latest` here to represent the value obtained in Step 1. Of course, it is not possible for one `mysqld` instance to access user variables set on another server instance directly. These values must be "plugged in" to the second query manually or in application code.

3. Now it is possible to synchronize the secondary channel by running the following query on the secondary slave server:

```
mysqlS'> CHANGE MASTER TO
    ->     MASTER_LOG_FILE='@file',
    ->     MASTER_LOG_POS=@pos;
```

Again we have employed user variables (in this case `@file` and `@pos`) to represent the values obtained in Step 2 and applied in Step 3; in practice these values must be inserted manually or using application code that can access both of the servers involved.

Note that `@file` is a string value such as `'/var/log/mysql/replication-master-bin.00001'` and so must be quoted when used in SQL or application code. However, the value represented by `@pos` must *not* be quoted. Although MySQL normally attempts to convert strings to numbers, this case is an exception.

4. You can now initiate replication on the secondary channel by issuing the appropriate command on the secondary slave `mysqld`:

```
mysqlS'> START SLAVE;
```

Once the secondary replication channel is active, you can investigate the failure of the primary and effect repairs. The precise actions required to do this will depend upon the reasons for which the primary channel failed.

If the failure is limited to a single server, it should (in theory) be possible to replicate from M to S', or from M' to S; however, this has not yet been tested.

9.7.9 MySQL Cluster Backups with Replication

This discussion discusses making backups and restoring from them using MySQL Cluster replication. We assume that the replication servers have already been configured as covered previously (see Section 9.7.5, "Preparing the Cluster for Replication," and the sections immediately following). This having been done, the procedure for making a backup and then restoring from it is as follows:

1. There are two different methods by which the backup may be started.

   - **Method A**:

     This method requires that the cluster backup process was previously enabled on the master server, prior to starting the replication process. This can be done by including the line

     ```
     ndb-connectstring=management_host[:port]
     ```

     in a [MYSQL_CLUSTER] section in the my.cnf file, where management_host is the IP address or hostname of the NDB management server for the master cluster, and port is the management server's port number. Note that the port number needs to be specified only if the default port (1186) is not being used. (See Section 9.3.3, "Multi-Computer Configuration," for more information about ports and port allocation in MySQL Cluster.)

     In this case, the backup can be started by executing this statement on the replication master:

     ```
     shellM> ndb_mgm -e "START BACKUP"
     ```

   - **Method B**:

     If the my.cnf file does not specify where to find the management host, you can start the backup process by passing this information to the NDB management client as part of the START BACKUP command, like this:

     ```
     shellM> ndb_mgm management_host:port -e "START BACKUP"
     ```

     where management_host and port are the hostname and port number of the management server. In our scenario as outlined earlier (see Section 9.7.5, "Preparing the Cluster for Replication"), this would be executed as follows:

     ```
     shellM> ndb_mgm rep-master:1186 -e "START BACKUP"
     ```

   In either case, it is highly advisable to allow any pending transactions to be completed before beginning the backup, and then not to permit any new transactions to begin during the backup process.

2. Copy the cluster backup files to the slave that is being brought on line. Each system running an ndbd process for the master cluster will have cluster backup files located on it, and *all* of these files must be copied to the slave to ensure a successful restore. The backup files can be copied into any directory on the computer where the slave management host resides, so long as the MySQL and NDB binaries have read permissions in

that directory. In this case, we will assume that these files have been copied into the directory /var/BACKUPS/BACKUP-1.

It is not necessary that the slave cluster have the same number of ndbd processes (data nodes) as the master; however, it is highly recommended this number be the same. It *is* necessary that the slave be started with the --skip-slave-start option, to prevent premature startup of the replication process.

3. Create any databases on the slave cluster that are present on the master cluster that are to be replicated to the slave. **Important**: A CREATE SCHEMA statement corresponding to each database to be replicated must be executed on each data node in the slave cluster.

4. Reset the slave cluster using this statement in the MySQL Monitor:

```
mysqlS> RESET SLAVE;
```

It is important to make sure that the slave's apply_status table does not contain any records prior to running the restore process. You can accomplish this by running this SQL statement on the slave:

```
mysqlS> DELETE FROM cluster_replication.apply_status;
```

5. You can now start the cluster restoration process on the replication slave using the ndb_restore command for each backup file in turn. For the first of these, it is necessary to include the -m option to restore the cluster metadata:

```
shellS> ndb_restore -c slave_host:port -n node-id \
        -b backup-id -m -r dir
```

dir is the path to the directory where the backup files have been placed on the replication slave. For the ndb_restore commands corresponding to the remaining backup files, the -m option should *not* be used.

For restoring from a master cluster with four data nodes (as shown in Figure 9.5) where the backup files have been copied to the directory /var/BACKUPS/BACKUP-1, the proper sequence of commands to be executed on the slave might look like this:

```
shellS> ndb_restore -c rep-slave:1186 -n 2 -b 1 -m \
        -r ./VAR/BACKUPS/BACKUP-1
shellS> ndb_restore -c rep-slave:1186 -n 3 -b 1 \
        -r ./VAR/BACKUPS/BACKUP-1
shellS> ndb_restore -c rep-slave:1186 -n 4 -b 1 \
        -r ./VAR/BACKUPS/BACKUP-1
shellS> ndb_restore -c rep-slave:1186 -n 5 -b 1 \
        -r ./VAR/BACKUPS/BACKUP-1
```

This sequence of commands causes the most recent epoch records to be written to the slave's apply_status table.

6. Next, it is necessary to make all nodes in the slave cluster aware of the new tables. (This is due to the fact that the NDB Cluster storage engine does not currently support

autodiscovery of schema changes. See Section 9.7.9.2, "Initiating Discovery of Schema Changes.") You can accomplish this using these commands:

```
mysqlS*> USE db_name;
mysqlS*> SHOW TABLES;
```

db_name is the name of the database that was backed up and restored. Where multiple databases have been backed up and then restored, it is necessary to issue the USE and SHOW statements for each database in turn. Note also that these commands must be issued on each host acting as a data node in the slave cluster.

7. Now you need to obtain the most recent epoch from the binlog_index table on the slave (as discussed in Section 9.7.8, "Implementing Failover with MySQL Cluster"):

```
mysqlS> SELECT @latest:=MAX(epoch)
    -> FROM cluster_replication.apply_status;
```

8. Using @latest as the epoch value obtained in the previous step, you can obtain the correct starting position @pos in the correct binary logfile @file from the master's cluster_replication.binlog_index table using the query shown here:

```
mysqlM> SELECT
    ->     @file:=SUBSTRING_INDEX(File, '/', -1),
    ->     @pos:=Position
    -> FROM cluster_replication.binlog_index
    -> WHERE epoch > @latest
    -> ORDER BY epoch ASC LIMIT 1;
```

9. Using the values obtained in the previous step, you can now issue the appropriate CHANGE MASTER TO statement in the slave's mysql client:

```
mysqlS> CHANGE MASTER TO
    ->     MASTER_LOG_FILE='@file',
    ->     MASTER_LOG_POS=@pos;
```

10. Now that the slave "knows" from what point in which binlog file to start reading data from the master, you can cause the slave to begin replicating with this standard MySQL statement:

```
mysqlS> START SLAVE;
```

To perform a backup and restore on a second replication channel, it is necessary only to repeat these steps, substituting the hostnames and IDs of the secondary master and slave for those of the primary master and slave replication servers where appropriate, and running the preceding statements on them.

For additional information on performing Cluster backups and restoring Cluster from backups, see Section 9.6.5, "Online Backup of MySQL Cluster."

9.7.9.1 Automating Synchronization of the Slave to the Master Binlog

It is possible to automate much of the process described in the previous section (see Section 9.7.9, "MySQL Cluster Backups with Replication"). The following Perl script reset-slave.pl serves as an example of how you can do this.

```perl
#!/user/bin/perl -w

#   file: reset-slave.pl

#   Copyright ©2005 MySQL AB

#   This program is free software; you can redistribute it and/or modify
#   it under the terms of the GNU General Public License as published by
#   the Free Software Foundation; either version 2 of the License, or
#   (at your option) any later version.

#   This program is distributed in the hope that it will be useful,
#   but WITHOUT ANY WARRANTY; without even the implied warranty of
#   MERCHANTABILITY or FITNESS FOR A PARTICULAR PURPOSE.  See the
#   GNU General Public License for more details.

#   You should have received a copy of the GNU General Public License
#   along with this program; if not, write to:
#   Free Software Foundation, Inc.
#   59 Temple Place, Suite 330
#   Boston, MA 02111-1307 USA
#
#   Version 1.1


####################### Includes ############################

use DBI;

####################### Globals #############################

my  $m_host='';
my  $m_port='';
my  $m_user='';
my  $m_pass='';
my  $s_host='';
my  $s_port='';
my  $s_user='';
my  $s_pass='';
my  $dbhM='';
my  $dbhS='';
```

```
##################### Sub Prototypes ########################

sub CollectCommandPromptInfo;
sub ConnectToDatabases;
sub DisconnectFromDatabases;
sub GetSlaveEpoch;
sub GetMasterInfo;
sub UpdateSlave;

###################### Program Main ########################

CollectCommandPromptInfo;
ConnectToDatabases;
GetSlaveEpoch;
GetMasterInfo;
UpdateSlave;
DisconnectFromDatabases;

################# Collect Command Prompt Info #################

sub CollectCommandPromptInfo
{
  ### Check that user has supplied correct number of command line args
  die "Usage:\n
      reset-slave >master MySQL host< >master MySQL port< \n
                  >master user< >master pass< >slave MySQL host< \n
                  >slave MySQL port< >slave user< >slave pass< \n
      All 8 arguments must be passed. Use BLANK for NULL passwords\n"
      unless @ARGV == 8;

  $m_host = $ARGV[0];
  $m_port = $ARGV[1];
  $m_user = $ARGV[2];
  $m_pass = $ARGV[3];
  $s_host = $ARGV[4];
  $s_port = $ARGV[5];
  $s_user = $ARGV[6];
  $s_pass = $ARGV[7];

  if ($m_pass eq "BLANK") { $m_pass = '';}
  if ($s_pass eq "BLANK") { $s_pass = '';}
}

############### Make connections to both databases #############

sub ConnectToDatabases
{
  ### Connect to both master and slave cluster databases
```

```perl
  ### Connect to master
  $dbhM
    = DBI->connect(
    "dbi:mysql:database=cluster_replication;host=$m_host;port=$m_port",
    "$m_user", "$m_pass")
      or die "Can't connect to Master Cluster MySQL process!
              Error: $DBI::errstr\n";

  ### Connect to slave
  $dbhS
    = DBI->connect(
          "dbi:mysql:database=cluster_replication;host=$s_host",
          "$s_user", "$s_pass")
    or die "Can't connect to Slave Cluster MySQL process!
            Error: $DBI::errstr\n";
}

##############   Disconnect from both databases ###############

sub DisconnectFromDatabases
{
  ### Disconnect from master

  $dbhM->disconnect
  or warn " Disconnection failed: $DBI::errstr\n";

  ### Disconnect from slave

  $dbhS->disconnect
  or warn " Disconnection failed: $DBI::errstr\n";
}

###################   Find the last good GCI ################

sub GetSlaveEpoch
{
  $sth = $dbhS->prepare("SELECT MAX(epoch)
                         FROM cluster_replication.apply_status;")
      or die "Error while preparing to select epoch from slave: ",
              $dbhS->errstr;

  $sth->execute
      or die "Selecting epoch from slave error: ", $sth->errstr;

  $sth->bind_col (1, \$epoch);
  $sth->fetch;
  print "\tSlave Epoch =  $epoch\n";
  $sth->finish;
}
```

```
####### Find the position of the last GCI in the binlog ########

sub GetMasterInfo
{
  $sth = $dbhM->prepare("SELECT
                            SUBSTRING_INDEX(File, '/', -1), Position
                         FROM cluster_replication.binlog_index
                         WHERE epoch > $epoch
                         ORDER BY epoch ASC LIMIT 1;")
      or die "Prepare to select from master error: ", $dbhM->errstr;

  $sth->execute
      or die "Selecting from master error: ", $sth->errstr;

  $sth->bind_col (1, \$binlog);
  $sth->bind_col (2, \$binpos);
  $sth->fetch;
  print "\tMaster bin log =  $binlog\n";
  print "\tMaster Bin Log position =  $binpos\n";
  $sth->finish;
}


########## Set the slave to process from that location #########

sub UpdateSlave
{
  $sth = $dbhS->prepare("CHANGE MASTER TO
                           MASTER_LOG_FILE='$binlog',
                           MASTER_LOG_POS=$binpos;")
      or die "Prepare to CHANGE MASTER error: ", $dbhS->errstr;

  $sth->execute
        or die "CHNAGE MASTER on slave error: ", $sth->errstr;
  $sth->finish;
  print "\tSlave has been updated. You may now start the slave.\n";
}


# end reset-slave.pl
```

9.7.9.2 Initiating Discovery of Schema Changes

The NDB Cluster storage engine does not at present automatically detect structural changes in databases or tables. When a database or table is created or dropped, or when a table is altered using ALTER TABLE, the cluster must be made aware of the change. When a database is created or dropped, the appropriate CREATE SCHEMA or DROP SCHEMA statement should be issued on each storage node in the cluster to induce discovery of the change, that is:

```
mysqlS*> CREATE SCHEMA db_name;
mysqlS*> DROP SCHEMA db_name;
```

Dropping Tables

When dropping a table that uses the NDB Cluster storage engine, it is necessary to allow any unfinished transactions to be completed and then not to begin any new transactions before performing the DROP operation:

1. Stop performing transactions on the slave.
2. Drop the table:

   ```
   mysqlS> DROP TABLE [db_name.]table_name;
   ```

3. Make all slave mysqld processes aware of the drop:

   ```
   mysqlS*> SHOW TABLES [FROM db_name];
   ```

All of the MySQL slave servers can now "see" that the table has been dropped from the database.

Creating Tables

When creating a new table, you should perform the following steps:

1. Create the table:

   ```
   mysqlS> CREATE TABLE [db_name.]table_name (
       -> #  column and index definitions...
       -> ) ENGINE=NDB;
   ```

2. Make all SQL nodes in the slave cluster aware of the new table:

   ```
   mysqlS*> SHOW TABLES [FROM db_name];
   ```

   You can now start using the table as normal. When creating a new table, note that—unlike the case when dropping tables—it is *not* necessary to stop performing any transactions beforehand.

Altering Tables

When altering tables, you should perform the following steps in the order shown:

1. Ensure that all pending transactions have been completed, and do not initiate any new transactions at this time.
2. Issue any desired ALTER TABLE statements that add or remove columns to or from an existing table. For example:

   ```
   mysqlS> ALTER TABLE table_name /* column definition, ... */;
   ```

3. Force all slave SQL nodes to become aware of the changed table definition. The recommended way to do this is by issuing a "throwaway" SHOW TABLES statement on each slave mysqld:

   ```
   mysqlS*> SHOW TABLES;
   ```

   You may now resume normal operations. These include transactions involving records in the changed table.

Note that when you create a new NDB Cluster table on the master cluster, if you do so using the mysqld that acts as the replication master, you must execute a SHOW TABLES, also on the master mysqld, to initiate discovery properly. Otherwise, the new table and any data it contains cannot be seen by the replication master mysqld, nor by the slave (that is, neither the new table nor its data is replicated). If the table is created on a mysqld that is not acting as the replication master, it does not matter which mysqld issues the SHOW TABLES.

It is also possible to force discovery by issuing a "dummy" SELECT statement using the new or altered table in the statement's FROM clause. Although the statement fails, it causes the change to be recognized by the cluster. However, issuing a SHOW TABLES is the preferred method.

We are working to implement automatic discovery of schema changes in a future MySQL Cluster release. For more information about this and other Cluster issues, see Section 9.9, "Known Limitations of MySQL Cluster."

9.8 Using High-Speed Interconnects with MySQL Cluster

Even before design of NDB Cluster began in 1996, it was evident that one of the major problems to be encountered in building parallel databases would be communication between the nodes in the network. For this reason, NDB Cluster was designed from the very beginning to allow for the use of a number of different data transport mechanisms. In this manual, we use the term "transporter" for these.

Currently, the MySQL Cluster codebase includes support for four different transporters. Most users today employ TCP/IP over Ethernet because it is ubiquitous. TCP/IP is also by far the best-tested transporter in MySQL Cluster.

We are working to make sure that communication with the ndbd process is made in "chunks" that are as large as possible because this benefits all types of data transmission.

For users who desire it, it is also possible to use cluster interconnects to enhance performance even further. There are two ways to achieve this: Either a custom transporter can be designed to handle this case, or you can use socket implementations that bypass the TCP/IP stack to one extent or another. We have experimented with both of these techniques using the SCI (Scalable Coherent Interface) technology developed by Dolphin (http://www.dolphinics.com/).

9.8.1 Configuring MySQL Cluster to Use SCI Sockets

In this section, we show how to adapt a cluster configured for normal TCP/IP communication to use SCI Sockets instead. This documentation is based on SCI Sockets version 2.3.0 as of 01 October, 2004.

Prerequisites

Any machines with which you wish to use SCI Sockets must be equipped with SCI cards.

It is possible to use SCI Sockets with any version of MySQL Cluster. No special builds are needed because it uses normal socket calls which are already available in MySQL Cluster. However, SCI Sockets are currently supported only on the Linux 2.4 and 2.6 kernels. SCI Transporters have been tested successfully on additional operating systems although we have verified these only with Linux 2.4 to date.

There are essentially four requirements for SCI Sockets:

- Building the SCI Socket libraries.
- Installation of the SCI Socket kernel libraries.
- Installation of one or two configuration files.
- The SCI Socket kernel library must enabled either for the entire machine or for the shell where the MySQL Cluster processes are started.

This process needs to be repeated for each machine in the cluster where you plan to use SCI Sockets for inter-node communication.

Two packages need to be retrieved to get SCI Sockets working:

- The source code package containing the DIS support libraries for the SCI Sockets libraries.
- The source code package for the SCI Socket libraries themselves.

Currently, these are available only in source code format. The latest versions of these packages at the time of this writing were available as (respectively) DIS_GPL_2_5_0_SEP_10_2004. tar.gz and SCI_SOCKET_2_3_0_OKT_01_2004.tar.gz. You should be able to find these (or possibly newer versions) at http://www.dolphinics.no/support/downloads.html.

Package Installation

Once you have obtained the library packages, the next step is to unpack them into appropriate directories, with the SCI Sockets library unpacked into a directory below the DIS code. Next, you need to build the libraries. This example shows the commands used on Linux/x86 to perform this task:

```
shell> tar xzf DIS_GPL_2_5_0_SEP_10_2004.tar.gz
shell> cd DIS_GPL_2_5_0_SEP_10_2004/src/
shell> tar xzf ../../SCI_SOCKET_2_3_0_OKT_01_2004.tar.gz
shell> cd ../adm/bin/Linux_pkgs
shell> ./make_PSB_66_release
```

It is possible to build these libraries for some 64-bit processors. To build the libraries for Opteron CPUs using the 64-bit extensions, run make_PSB_66_X86_64_release rather than make_PSB_66_release. If the build is made on an Itanium machine, you should use make_PSB_66_IA64_release. The X86-64 variant should work for Intel EM64T architectures but this has not yet (to our knowledge) been tested.

Once the build process is complete, the compiled libraries will be found in a zipped tar file with a name along the lines of DIS-*<operating-system>-time-date*. It is now time to install the package in the proper place. In this example we will place the installation in /opt/DIS. (**Note**: You will most likely need to run the following as the system root user.)

```
shell> cp DIS_Linux_2.4.20-8_181004.tar.gz /opt/
shell> cd /opt
shell> tar xzf DIS_Linux_2.4.20-8_181004.tar.gz
shell> mv DIS_Linux_2.4.20-8_181004 DIS
```

Network Configuration

Now that all the libraries and binaries are in their proper place, we need to ensure that the SCI cards have proper node IDs within the SCI address space.

It is also necessary to decide on the network structure before proceeding. There are three types of network structures which can be used in this context:

- A simple one-dimensional ring
- One or more SCI switches with one ring per switch port
- A two- or three-dimensional torus

Each of these topologies has its own method for providing node IDs. We discuss each of them in brief.

A simple ring uses node IDs that are non-zero multiples of 4: 4, 8, 12, …

The next possibility uses SCI switches. An SCI switch has 8 ports, each of which can support a ring. It is necessary to make sure that different rings use different node ID spaces. In a typical configuration, the first port uses node IDs below 64 (4 – 60), the next 64 node IDs (68 – 124) are assigned to the next port, and so on, with node IDs 452 – 508 being assigned to the eighth port.

Two- and three-dimensional torus network structures take into account where each node is located in each dimension, incrementing by 4 for each node in the first dimension, by 64 in the second dimension, and (where applicable) by 1024 in the third dimension. See Dolphin's Web site (http://www.dolphinics.com/support/index.html) for more thorough documentation.

In our testing we have used switches, although most large cluster installations use 2- or 3-dimensional torus structures. The advantage provided by switches is that, with dual SCI cards and dual switches, it is possible to build with relative ease a redundant network where the average failover time on the SCI network is on the order of 100 microseconds. This is supported by the SCI transporter in MySQL Cluster and is also under development for the SCI Socket implementation.

Failover for the 2D/3D torus is also possible but requires sending out new routing indexes to all nodes. However, this requires only 100 milliseconds or so to complete and should be acceptable for most high-availability cases.

By placing cluster data nodes properly within the switched architecture, it is possible to use 2 switches to build a structure whereby 16 computers can be interconnected and no single failure can hinder more than one of them. With 32 computers and 2 switches it is possible to configure the cluster in such a manner that no single failure can cause the loss of more than two nodes; in this case, it is also possible to know which pair of nodes is affected. Thus, by placing the two nodes in separate node groups, it is possible to build a "safe" MySQL Cluster installation.

To set the node ID for an SCI card use the following command in the /opt/DIS/sbin directory. In this example, -c 1 refers to the number of the SCI card (this is always 1 if there is only 1 card in the machine); -a 0 refers to adapter 0; and 68 is the node ID:

```
shell> ./sciconfig -c 1 -a 0 -n 68
```

If you have multiple SCI cards in the same machine, you can determine which card has which slot by issuing the following command (again we assume that the current working directory is /opt/DIS/sbin):

```
shell> ./sciconfig -c 1 -gsn
```

This will give you the SCI card's serial number. Then repeat this procedure with -c 2, and so on, for each card in the machine. Once you have matched each card with a slot, you can set node IDs for all cards.

After the necessary libraries and binaries are installed, and the SCI node IDs are set, the next step is to set up the mapping from hostnames (or IP addresses) to SCI node IDs. This is done in the SCI sockets configuration file, which should be saved as /etc/sci/scisock.conf. In this file, each SCI node ID is mapped through the proper SCI card to the hostname or IP address that it is to communicate with. Here is a very simple example of such a configuration file:

```
#host           #nodeId
alpha           8
beta            12
192.168.10.20   16
```

It is also possible to limit the configuration so that it applies only to a subset of the available ports for these hosts. An additional configuration file /etc/sci/scisock_opt.conf can be used to accomplish this, as shown here:

```
#-key                   -type       -values
EnablePortsByDefault                yes
EnablePort              tcp         2200
DisablePort             tcp         2201
EnablePortRange         tcp         2202 2219
DisablePortRange        tcp         2220 2231
```

Driver Installation

With the configuration files in place, the drivers can be installed.

First, the low-level drivers and then the SCI socket driver need to be installed:

```
shell> cd DIS/sbin/
shell> ./drv-install add PSB66
shell> ./scisocket-install add
```

If desired, the installation can be checked by invoking a script that verifies that all nodes in the SCI socket configuration files are accessible:

```
shell> cd /opt/DIS/sbin/
shell> ./status.sh
```

If you discover an error and need to change the SCI socket configuration, it is necessary to use ksocketconfig to accomplish this task:

```
shell> cd /opt/DIS/util
shell> ./ksocketconfig -f
```

Testing the Setup

To ensure that SCI sockets are actually being used, you can employ the latency_bench test program. Using this utility's server component, clients can connect to the server to test the latency of the connection. Determining whether SCI is enabled should be fairly simple from observing the latency. (**Note:** Before using latency_bench, it is necessary to set the LD_PRELOAD environment variable as shown later in this section.)

To set up a server, use the following:

```
shell> cd /opt/DIS/bin/socket
shell> ./latency_bench -server
```

To run a client, use latency_bench again, except this time with the -client option:

```
shell> cd /opt/DIS/bin/socket
shell> ./latency_bench -client server_hostname
```

SCI socket configuration should now be complete and MySQL Cluster ready to use both SCI Sockets and the SCI transporter (see Section 9.4.4.10, "MySQL Cluster SCI Transport Connections").

Starting the Cluster

The next step in the process is to start MySQL Cluster. To enable usage of SCI Sockets it is necessary to set the environment variable LD_PRELOAD before starting ndbd, mysqld, and ndb_mgmd. This variable should point to the kernel library for SCI Sockets.

To start ndbd in a bash shell, do the following:

```
bash-shell> export LD_PRELOAD=/opt/DIS/lib/libkscisock.so
bash-shell> ndbd
```

In a `tcsh` environment the same thing can be accomplished with:

```
tcsh-shell> setenv LD_PRELOAD=/opt/DIS/lib/libkscisock.so
tcsh-shell> ndbd
```

Note: MySQL Cluster can use only the kernel variant of SCI Sockets.

9.8.2 Understanding the Impact of Cluster Interconnects

The `ndbd` process has a number of simple constructs which are used to access the data in a MySQL Cluster. We have created a very simple benchmark to check the performance of each of these and the effects that various interconnects have on their performance.

There are four access methods:

- **Primary key access**

  This is access of a record through its primary key. In the simplest case, only one record is accessed at a time, which means that the full cost of setting up a number of TCP/IP messages and a number of costs for context switching are borne by this single request. In the case where multiple primary key accesses are sent in one batch, those accesses share the cost of setting up the necessary TCP/IP messages and context switches. If the TCP/IP messages are for different destinations, additional TCP/IP messages need to be set up.

- **Unique key access**

  Unique key accesses are similar to primary key accesses, except that a unique key access is executed as a read on an index table followed by a primary key access on the table. However, only one request is sent from the MySQL Server, and the read of the index table is handled by `ndbd`. Such requests also benefit from batching.

- **Full table scan**

  When no indexes exist for a lookup on a table, a full table scan is performed. This is sent as a single request to the `ndbd` process, which then divides the table scan into a set of parallel scans on all cluster `ndbd` processes. In future versions of MySQL Cluster, an SQL node will be able to filter some of these scans.

- **Range scan using ordered index**

  When an ordered index is used, it performs a scan in the same manner as the full table scan, except that it scans only those records that are in the range used by the query transmitted by the MySQL server (SQL node). All partitions are scanned in parallel when all bound index attributes include all attributes in the partitioning key.

To check the base performance of these access methods, we have developed a set of benchmarks. One such benchmark, `testReadPerf`, tests simple and batched primary and unique key accesses. This benchmark also measures the setup cost of range scans by issuing scans returning a single record. There is also a variant of this benchmark that uses a range scan to fetch a batch of records.

In this way, we can determine the cost of both a single key access and a single record scan access, as well as measure the impact of the communication media used, on base access methods.

In our tests, we ran the base benchmarks for both a normal transporter using TCP/IP sockets and a similar setup using SCI sockets. The figures reported in the following table are for small accesses of 20 records per access. The difference between serial and batched access decreases by a factor of 3 to 4 when using 2KB records instead. SCI Sockets were not tested with 2KB records. Tests were performed on a cluster with two data nodes running on two dual-CPU machines equipped with AMD MP1900+ processors.

Access Type	TCP/IP Sockets	SCI Socket
Serial pk access	400 microseconds	160 microseconds
Batched pk access	28 microseconds	22 microseconds
Serial uk access	500 microseconds	250 microseconds
Batched uk access	70 microseconds	36 microseconds
Indexed eq-bound	1250 microseconds	750 microseconds
Index range	24 microseconds	12 microseconds

We also performed another set of tests to check the performance of SCI Sockets vis-à-vis that of the SCI transporter, and both of these as compared with the TCP/IP transporter. All these tests used primary key accesses either serially and multi-threaded, or multi-threaded and batched.

The tests showed that SCI sockets were about 100% faster than TCP/IP. The SCI transporter was faster in most cases compared to SCI sockets. One notable case occurred with many threads in the test program, which showed that the SCI transporter did not perform very well when used for the mysqld process.

Our overall conclusion was that, for most benchmarks, using SCI sockets improves performance by approximately 100% over TCP/IP, except in rare instances when communication performance is not an issue. This can occur when scan filters make up most of processing time or when very large batches of primary key accesses are achieved. In that case, the CPU processing in the ndbd processes becomes a fairly large part of the overhead.

Using the SCI transporter instead of SCI Sockets is only of interest in communicating between ndbd processes. Using the SCI transporter is also only of interest if a CPU can be dedicated to the ndbd process because the SCI transporter ensures that this process will never go to sleep. It is also important to ensure that the ndbd process priority is set in such a way that the process does not lose priority due to running for an extended period of time, as can be done by locking processes to CPUs in Linux 2.6. If such a configuration is possible, the ndbd process will benefit by 10–70% as compared with using SCI sockets. (The larger figures will be seen when performing updates and probably on parallel scan operations as well.)

There are several other optimized socket implementations for computer clusters, including Myrinet, Gigabit Ethernet, Infiniband, and the VIA interface. We have tested MySQL

Cluster so far only with SCI sockets. See Section 9.8.1, "Configuring MySQL Cluster to Use SCI Sockets" for information on how to set up SCI sockets using ordinary TCP/IP for MySQL Cluster.

9.9 Known Limitations of MySQL Cluster

In this section, we provide a list of known limitations in MySQL Cluster releases in the 5.0.x series compared to features available when using the `MyISAM` and `InnoDB` storage engines. Currently, there are no plans to address these in coming releases of MySQL 5.0; however, we will attempt to supply fixes for these issues in subsequent release series. If you check the "Cluster" category in the MySQL bugs database at `http://bugs.mysql.com`, you can find known bugs which (if marked "5.0") we intend to correct in upcoming releases of MySQL 5.0.

The list here is intended to be complete with respect to the conditions just set forth. You can report any discrepancies that you encounter to the MySQL bugs database using the instructions given in Section 1.8, "How to Report Bugs or Problems." If we do not plan to fix the problem in MySQL 5.0, we will add it to the list.

(**Note**: See the end of this section for a list of issues in MySQL 4.1 Cluster that have been resolved in the current version.)

- **Noncompliance in syntax** (resulting in errors when running existing applications):
  - Text indexes are not supported.
  - A `BIT` column cannot be a primary key or part of a composite primary key.
  - Geometry datatypes (`WKT` and `WKB`) are not supported by the NDB storage engine prior to MySQL 5.0.16. (Note that spatial indexes are still not supported in MySQL 5.0.16 and newer.)
- **Non-compliance in limits or behavior** (may result in errors when running existing applications):
  - **Error Reporting**:
    - A duplicate key error returns the error message `ERROR 23000: Can't write; duplicate key in table 'tbl_name'`.
  - **Transaction Handling**:
    - `NDB Cluster` supports only the `READ COMMITTED` transaction isolation level.
    - There is no partial rollback of transactions. A duplicate key or similar error results in a rollback of the entire transaction.
    - **Important**: If a `SELECT` from a Cluster table includes a `BLOB`, `TEXT`, or `VARCHAR` column, the `READ COMMITTED` transaction isolation level is converted to a read with read lock. This is done to guarantee consistency, due to the fact that parts of the values stored in columns of these types are actually read from a separate table.
  - A number of hard limits exist, which are configurable, but available main memory in the cluster sets limits. See the complete list of configuration parameters in

Section 9.4.4, "Configuration File." Most configuration parameters can be upgraded online. These hard limits include:

- Database memory size and index memory size (`DataMemory` and `IndexMemory`, respectively).

- The maximum number of transactions that can be performed is set using the configuration parameter `MaxNoOfConcurrentOperations`. Note that bulk loading, `TRUNCATE TABLE`, and `ALTER TABLE` are handled as special cases by running multiple transactions, and so are not subject to this limitation.

- Different limits related to tables and indexes. For example, the maximum number of ordered indexes per table is determined by `MaxNoOfOrderedIndexes`.

- Database names, table names, and attribute names cannot be as long in NDB tables as with other table handlers. Attribute names are truncated to 31 characters, and if not unique after truncation give rise to errors. Database names and table names can total a maximum of 122 characters. (That is, the maximum length for an NDB Cluster table name is 122 characters fewer the number of characters in the name of the database of which that table is a part.)

- All Cluster table rows are of fixed length. This means (for example) that if a table has one or more VARCHAR fields containing only relatively small values, more memory and disk space is required when using the NDB storage engine than would be the case for the same table and data using the MyISAM engine. (In other words, in the case of a VARCHAR column, the column requires the same amount of storage as a CHAR column of the same size.)

- The maximum number of tables in a Cluster database is limited to 1,792.

- The maximum number of attributes per table is limited to 128.

- The maximum permitted size of any one row is 8KB, *not including data stored in BLOB columns.*

- The maximum number of attributes per key is 32.

- **Unsupported features** (do not cause errors, but are not supported or enforced):

  - The foreign key construct is ignored, just as it is in MyISAM tables.

  - Savepoints and rollbacks to savepoints are ignored as in MyISAM.

- **Performance and limitation-related issues**:

  - There are query performance issues due to sequential access to the NDB storage engine; it is also relatively more expensive to do many range scans than it is with either MyISAM or InnoDB.

  - The Records in range statistic is not supported, resulting in non-optimal query plans in some cases. Employ USE INDEX or FORCE INDEX as a workaround.

  - Unique hash indexes created with USING HASH cannot be used for accessing a table if NULL is given as part of the key.

  - MySQL Cluster does not support durable commits on disk. Commits are replicated, but there is no guarantee that logs are flushed to disk on commit.

- **Missing features**:
    - The only supported isolation level is READ COMMITTED. (InnoDB supports READ COMMITTED, READ COMMITTED, REPEATABLE READ, and SERIALIZABLE.) See Section 9.6.5.5, "Backup Troubleshooting," for information on how this can affect backup and restore of Cluster databases.
    - No durable commits on disk. Commits are replicated, but there is no guarantee that logs are flushed to disk on commit.
- **Problems relating to multiple MySQL servers** (not relating to MyISAM or InnoDB):
    - ALTER TABLE is not fully locking when running multiple MySQL servers (no distributed table lock).
    - MySQL replication will not work correctly if updates are done on multiple MySQL servers. However, if the database partitioning scheme is done at the application level and no transactions take place across these partitions, replication can be made to work.
    - Autodiscovery of databases is not supported for multiple MySQL servers accessing the same MySQL Cluster. However, autodiscovery of tables is supported in such cases. What this means is that after a database named *db_name* is created or imported using one MySQL server, you should issue a CREATE DATABASE *db_name* statement on each additional MySQL server that accesses the same MySQL Cluster. (As of MySQL 5.0.2, you may also use CREATE SCHEMA *db_name*.) Once this has been done for a given MySQL server, that server should be able to detect the database tables without error.
- **Issues exclusive to MySQL Cluster** (not related to MyISAM or InnoDB):
    - All machines used in the cluster must have the same architecture. That is, all machines hosting nodes must be either big-endian or little-endian, and you cannot use a mixture of both. For example, you cannot have a management node running on a PowerPC which directs a data node that is running on an x86 machine. This restriction does not apply to machines simply running mysql or other clients that may be accessing the cluster's SQL nodes.
    - It is not possible to make online schema changes such as those accomplished using ALTER TABLE or CREATE INDEX, because the NDB Cluster does not support autodiscovery of such changes. (However, you can import or create a table that uses a different storage engine, and then convert it to NDB using ALTER TABLE *tbl_name* ENGINE=NDBCLUSTER. In such a case, you must issue a FLUSH TABLES statement to force the cluster to pick up the change.)
    - Online adding or dropping of nodes is not possible (the cluster must be restarted in such cases).
    - When using multiple management servers:
        - You must give nodes explicit IDs in connectstrings because automatic allocation of node IDs does not work across multiple management servers.

- You must take extreme care to have the same configurations for all management servers. No special checks for this are performed by the cluster.

- In order that management nodes be able to see one another, you must restart all data nodes after bringing up the cluster. (See Bug #13070 at http://bugs. mysql.com/13070 for a detailed explanation.)

- Multiple network interfaces for data nodes are not supported. Use of these is liable to cause problems: In the event of a data node failure, an SQL node waits for confirmation that the data node went down but never receives it because another route to that data node remains open. This can effectively make the cluster inoperable.

- The maximum number of data nodes is 48.

- The total maximum number of nodes in a MySQL Cluster is 63. This number includes all MySQL Servers (SQL nodes), data nodes, and management servers.

The following Cluster limitations in MySQL 4.1 have been resolved in MySQL 5.0 as shown below:

- The NDB Cluster storage engine supports all character sets and collations available in MySQL 5.0.

- Prior to MySQL 5.0.6, the maximum number of metadata objects possible was 1600. Beginning with 5.0.6, this limit is increased to 20320.

- Cluster in MySQL 5.0 supports column indexes that make use of prefixes.

- Unlike the case in MySQL 4.1, the Cluster storage engine in MySQL 5.0 supports MySQL's query cache. See Section 4.14, "The MySQL Query Cache."

9.10 MySQL Cluster Development Roadmap

In this section, we discuss changes in the implementation of MySQL Cluster in MySQL 5.0 as compared to MySQL 4.1. We will also discuss our roadmap for further improvements to MySQL Cluster as currently planned for MySQL 5.1.

There are relatively few changes between the NDB Cluster storage engine implementations in MySQL 4.1 and in 5.0, so the upgrade path should be relatively quick and painless.

All significantly new features being developed for MySQL Cluster are going into the MySQL 5.1 tree. We also provide some hints about what Cluster in MySQL 5.1 is likely to include later in this section (see Section 9.10.2, "MySQL 5.1 Development Roadmap for MySQL Cluster").

9.10.1 MySQL Cluster Changes in MySQL 5.0

MySQL Cluster in versions 5.0.3-beta and later contains a number of new features that are likely to be of interest:

- **Push-Down Conditions**: Consider the following query:

```
SELECT * FROM t1 WHERE non_indexed_attribute = 1;
```

This query will use a full table scan and the condition will be evaluated in the cluster's data nodes. Thus, it is not necessary to send the records across the network for evaluation. (That is, function transport is used, rather than data transport.) Please note that this feature is currently disabled by default (pending more thorough testing), but it should work in most cases. This feature can be enabled through the use of the SET engine_condition_pushdown = On statement. Alternatively, you can run mysqld with the this feature enabled by starting the MySQL server with the --engine-condition-pushdown option.

A major benefit of this change is that queries can be executed in parallel. This means that queries against non-indexed columns can run faster than previously by a factor of as much as 5 to 10 times, *times the number of data nodes*, because multiple CPUs can work on the query in parallel.

You can use EXPLAIN to determine when condition pushdown is being used. See Section 6.2.1, "Optimizing Queries with EXPLAIN."

- **Decreased IndexMemory Usage**: In MySQL 5.0, each record consumes approximately 25 bytes of index memory, and every unique index uses 25 bytes per record of index memory (in addition to some data memory because these are stored in a separate table). This is because the primary key is not stored in the index memory anymore.

- **Query Cache Enabled for MySQL Cluster**: See Section 4.14, "The MySQL Query Cache," for information on configuring and using the query cache.

- **New Optimizations**: One optimization that merits particular attention is that a batched read interface is now used in some queries. For example, consider the following query:

```
SELECT * FROM t1 WHERE primary_key IN (1,2,3,4,5,6,7,8,9,10);
```

This query will be executed 2 to 3 times more quickly than in previous MySQL Cluster versions due to the fact that all 10 key lookups are sent in a single batch rather than one at a time.

- **Limit on Number of Metadata Objects**: In MySQL 4.1, each Cluster database may contain a maximum of 1,600 metadataobjects, including database tables, system tables, indexes and BLOBs. Beginning with MySQL 5.0.6, this number is increased to 20320.

9.10.2 MySQL 5.1 Development Roadmap for MySQL Cluster

What is said here is a status report based on recent commits to the MySQL 5.1 source tree. It should be noted all 5.1 development is subject to change.

There are currently 4 major new features being developed for MySQL 5.1:

1. **Integration of MySQL Cluster into MySQL replication**: This will make it possible to update from any MySQL Server in the cluster and still have MySQL Replication handled by one of the MySQL Servers in the cluster, with the state of the slave side remaining consistent with the cluster acting as the master.

2. **Support for disk-based records**: Records on disk will be supported. Indexed fields including the primary key hash index must still be stored in RAM but all other fields can be on disk.

3. **Variable-sized records**: A column defined as VARCHAR(255) currently uses 260 bytes of storage independent of what is stored in any particular record. In MySQL 5.1 Cluster tables, only the portion of the column actually taken up by the record will be stored. This will make possible a reduction in space requirements for such columns by a factor of 5 in many cases.

4. **User-defined partitioning**: Users will be able to define partitions based on columns that are part of the primary key. The MySQL Server will be able to discover whether it is possible to prune away some of the partitions from the WHERE clause. Partitioning based on KEY, HASH, RANGE, and LIST handlers will be possible, as well as subpartitioning. This feature should also be available for many other handlers, and not only NDB Cluster.

In addition, we are working to increase the 8KB size limit for rows containing columns of types other than BLOB or TEXT in Cluster tables. This is due to the fact that rows are currently fixed in size and the page size is 32,768 bytes (minus 128 bytes for the row header). Currently, this means that if we allowed more than 8KB per record, any remaining space (up to approximately 14,000 bytes) would be left empty. In MySQL 5.1, we plan to fix this limitation so that using more than 8KB in a given row does not result in the remainder of the page being wasted.

9.11 MySQL Cluster FAQ

This section answers questions that are often asked about MySQL Cluster.

- *What does "NDB" mean?*

  This stands for "**N**etwork **D**ata**b**ase."

- *What's the difference in using Cluster vs. using replication?*

  In a replication setup, a master MySQL server updates one or more slaves. Transactions are committed sequentially, and a slow transaction can cause the slave to lag behind the master. This means that if the master fails, it is possible that the slave might not have recorded the last few transactions. If a transaction-safe engine such as InnoDB is being used, a transaction will either be complete on the slave or not applied at all, but replication does not guarantee that all data on the master and the slave will be consistent at all times. In MySQL Cluster, all data nodes are kept in synchrony, and a transaction committed by any one data node is committed for all data nodes. In the event of a data node failure, all remaining data nodes remain in a consistent state.

  In short, whereas standard MySQL replication is asynchronous, MySQL Cluster is synchronous.

  We are planning to implement (asynchronous) replication for Cluster in MySQL 5.1. This will include the capability to replicate both between two clusters and between a MySQL cluster and a non-Cluster MySQL server.

- *Do I need to do any special networking to run Cluster? (How do computers in a cluster communicate?)*

  MySQL Cluster is intended to be used in a high-bandwidth environment, with computers connecting via TCP/IP. Its performance depends directly on the connection speed between the cluster's computers. The minimum connectivity requirements for Cluster include a typical 100-megabit Ethernet network or the equivalent. We recommend you use gigabit Ethernet whenever available.

  The faster SCI protocol is also supported, but requires special hardware. See Section 9.8, "Using High-Speed Interconnects with MySQL Cluster," for more information about SCI.

- *How many computers do I need to run a cluster, and why?*

  A minimum of three computers is required to run a viable cluster. However, the minimum **recommended** number of computers in a MySQL Cluster is four: one each to run the management and SQL nodes, and two computers to serve as storage nodes. The purpose of the two data nodes is to provide redundancy; the management node must run on a separate machine to guarantee continued arbitration services in the event that one of the data nodes fails.

- *What do the different computers do in a cluster?*

  A MySQL Cluster has both a physical and logical organization, with computers being the physical elements. The logical or functional elements of a cluster are referred to as "nodes," and a computer housing a cluster node is sometimes referred to as a "cluster host." Ideally, there will be one node per cluster host, although it is possible to run multiple nodes on a single host. There are three types of nodes, each corresponding to a specific role within the cluster. These are:

  - **Management node (MGM node)**: Provides management services for the cluster as a whole, including startup, shutdown, backups, and configuration data for the other nodes. The management node server is implemented as the application ndb_mgmd; the management client used to control MySQL Cluster via the MGM node is ndb_mgm.

  - **Data node**: Stores and replicates data. Data node functionality is handled by an instance of the NDB data node process ndbd.

  - **SQL node**: This is simply an instance of MySQL Server (mysqld) that is built with support for the NDB Cluster storage engine and started with the --ndb-cluster option to enable the engine.

- *With which operating systems can I use Cluster?*

  MySQL Cluster is officially supported on Linux, Mac OS X, and Solaris. We are working to add Cluster support for other platforms, including Windows, and our goal is eventually to offer MySQL Cluster on all platforms for which MySQL itself is supported.

  It may be possible to run Cluster processes on other operating systems. We have had reports from users who say that they have run Cluster successfully on FreeBSD. However, Cluster on any but the three platforms mentioned here should be considered alpha software (at best), cannot be guaranteed reliable in a production setting, and *is not supported by MySQL AB*.

- *What are the hardware requirements for running MySQL Cluster?*

Cluster should run on any platform for which NDB-enabled binaries are available. Naturally, faster CPUs and more memory will improve performance, and 64-bit CPUs will likely be more effective than 32-bit processors. There must be sufficient memory on machines used for data nodes to hold each node's share of the database (see *How much RAM do I need?* for more information). Nodes can communicate via a standard TCP/IP network and hardware. For SCI support, special networking hardware is required.

- *How much RAM do I need? Is it possible to use disk memory at all?*

Currently, Cluster is in-memory only. This means that all table data (including indexes) is stored in RAM. Therefore, if your data takes up 1GB of space and you want to replicate it once in the cluster, you need 2GB of memory to do so. This is in addition to the memory required by the operating system and any applications running on the cluster computers.

You can use the following formula for obtaining a rough estimate of how much RAM is needed for each data node in the cluster:

```
(SizeofDatabase × NumberOfReplicas × 1.1 ) / NumberOfDataNodes
```

To calculate the memory requirements more exactly requires determining, for each table in the cluster database, the storage space required per row, and multiplying this by the number of rows. You must also remember to account for any column indexes as follows:

- Each primary key or hash index created for an `NDBCluster` table requires 21–25 bytes per record. These indexes use `IndexMemory`.

- Each ordered index requires 10 bytes storage per record, using `DataMemory`.

- Creating a primary key or unique index also creates an ordered index, unless this index is created with `USING HASH`. In other words, if created without `USING HASH`, a primary key or unique index on a Cluster table takes up 31–35 bytes per record in MySQL 5.0.

  Note that creating MySQL Cluster tables with `USING HASH` for all primary keys and unique indexes will generally cause table updates to run more quickly. This is due to the fact that less memory is required (because no ordered indexes are created), and that less CPU must be utilized (because fewer indexes must be read and possibly updated).

It is especially important to keep in mind that *every MySQL Cluster table must have a primary key*. The NDB storage engine creates a primary key automatically if none is defined, and this primary key is created without `USING HASH`.

There is no easy way to determine exactly how much memory is being used for storage of Cluster indexes at any given time; however, warnings are written to the Cluster log when 80% of available `DataMemory` or `IndexMemory` is in use, and again when use reaches 85%, 90%, and so on.

We often see questions from users who report that, when they are trying to populate a Cluster database, the loading process terminates prematurely and an error message like this one is observed:

```
ERROR 1114: The table 'my_cluster_table' is full
```

When this occurs, the cause is very likely to be that your setup does not provide sufficient RAM for all table data and all indexes, *including the primary key required by the* NDB *storage engine and automatically created in the event that the table definition does not include the definition of a primary key.*

It is also worth noting that all data nodes should have the same amount of RAM, because no data node in a cluster can use more memory than the least amount available to any individual data node. In other words, if there are three computers hosting Cluster data nodes, with two of these having 3GB of RAM available to store Cluster data, and one having only 1GB RAM, each data node can devote only 1GB to clustering.

- *Because MySQL Cluster uses TCP/IP, does that mean I can run it over the Internet, with one or more nodes in a remote location?*

It is very doubtful in any case that a cluster would perform reliably under such conditions, because MySQL Cluster was designed and implemented with the assumption that it would be run under conditions guaranteeing dedicated high-speed connectivity such as that found in a LAN setting using 100 Mbps or gigabit Ethernet (preferably the latter). We neither test nor warrant its performance using anything slower than this.

Also, it is extremely important to keep in mind that communications between the nodes in a MySQL Cluster are not secure; they are neither encrypted nor safeguarded by any other protective mechanism. The most secure configuration for a cluster is in a private network behind a firewall, with no direct access to any Cluster data or management nodes from outside. (For SQL nodes, you should take the same precautions as you would with any other instance of the MySQL server.)

- *Do I have to learn a new programming or query language to use Cluster?*

No. Although some specialized commands are used to manage and configure the cluster itself, only standard (My)SQL queries and commands are required for the following operations:

  - Creating, altering, and dropping tables
  - Inserting, updating, and deleting table data
  - Creating, changing, and dropping primary and unique indexes
  - Configuring and managing SQL nodes (MySQL servers)

- *How do I find out what an error or warning message means when using Cluster?*

  There are two ways in which this can be done:

  - From within the `mysql` client, use SHOW ERRORS or SHOW WARNINGS immediately upon being notified of the error or warning condition. Errors and warnings also be displayed in MySQL Query Browser.

  - From a system shell prompt, use `perror --ndb error_code`.

- *Is MySQL Cluster transaction-safe? What isolation levels are supported?*

  Yes: For tables created with the NDB storage engine, transactions are supported. In MySQL 5.0, Cluster supports only the READ COMMITTED transaction isolation level.

- *What storage engines are supported by MySQL Cluster?*

  Clustering in MySQL is supported only by the NDB storage engine. That is, in order for a table to be shared between nodes in a cluster, it must be created using ENGINE=NDB (or ENGINE=NDBCLUSTER, which is equivalent).

  It is possible to create tables using other storage engines such as MyISAM or InnoDB on a MySQL server being used for clustering, but these non-NDB tables will **not** participate in the cluster.

- *Which versions of the MySQL software support Cluster? Do I have to compile from source?*

  Cluster is supported in all MySQL-max binaries in the 5.0 release series, except as noted in the following paragraph. You can determine whether your server has NDB support using either the SHOW VARIABLES LIKE 'have_%' or SHOW ENGINES statement. (See Section 4.3, "The `mysqld-max` Extended MySQL Server," for more information.)

  Linux users, please note that NDB is *not* included in the standard MySQL server RPMs. Beginning with MySQL 5.0.4, there are separate RPM packages for the NDB storage engine and accompanying management and other tools; see the NDB RPM Downloads section of the MySQL 5.0 Downloads page for these. (Prior to 5.0.4, you had to use the -max binaries supplied as `.tar.gz` archives. This is still possible, but is not required, so you can use your Linux distribution's RPM manager if you prefer.) You can also obtain NDB support by compiling the -max binaries from source, but it is not necessary to do so simply to use MySQL Cluster. To download the latest binary, RPM, or source distribution in the MySQL 5.0 series, visit `http://dev.mysql.com/downloads/mysql/5.0.html`.

- *In the event of a catastrophic failure—say, for instance, the whole city loses power **and** my UPS fails—would I lose all my data?*

  All committed transactions are logged. Therefore, although it is possible that some data could be lost in the event of a catastrophe, this should be quite limited. Data loss can be further reduced by minimizing the number of operations per transaction. (It is not a good idea to perform large numbers of operations per transaction in any case.)

- *Is it possible to use FULLTEXT indexes with Cluster?*

  FULLTEXT indexing is not currently supported by the NDB storage engine, or by any storage engine other than MyISAM. We are working to add this capability in a future release.

- *Can I run multiple nodes on a single computer?*

  It is possible but not advisable. One of the chief reasons to run a cluster is to provide redundancy. To enjoy the full benefits of this redundancy, each node should reside on a separate machine. If you place multiple nodes on a single machine and that machine fails, you lose all of those nodes. Given that MySQL Cluster can be run on commodity hardware loaded with a low-cost (or even no-cost) operating system, the expense of an extra machine or two is well worth it to safeguard mission-critical data. It also worth noting that the requirements for a cluster host running a management node are minimal. This task can be accomplished with a 200MHz Pentium CPU and sufficient RAM for the operating system plus a small amount of overhead for the ndb_mgmd and ndb_mgm processes.

- *Can I add nodes to a cluster without restarting it?*

  Not at present. A simple restart is all that is required for adding new MGM or SQL nodes to a Cluster. When adding data nodes the process is more complex, and requires the following steps:

  1. Make a complete backup of all Cluster data.
  2. Completely shut down the cluster and all cluster node processes.
  3. Restart the cluster, using the --initial startup option.
  4. Restore all cluster data from the backup.

  In a future MySQL Cluster release series, we hope to implement a "hot" reconfiguration capability for MySQL Cluster to minimize (if not eliminate) the requirement for restarting the cluster when adding new nodes.

- *Are there any limitations that I should be aware of when using Cluster?*

  NDB tables in MySQL are subject to the following limitations:

  - Not all character sets and collations are supported.
  - FULLTEXT indexes and index prefixes are not supported. Only complete columns may be indexed.
  - Spatial data types are not supported.
  - Only complete rollbacks for transactions are supported. Partial rollbacks and rollbacks to savepoints are not supported.
  - The maximum number of attributes allowed per table is 128, and attribute names cannot be any longer than 31 characters. For each table, the maximum combined length of the table and database names is 122 characters.
  - The maximum size for a table row is 8 kilobytes, not counting BLOBs. There is no set limit for the number of rows per table. Table size limits depend on a number of factors, in particular on the amount of RAM available to each data node.
  - The NDB engine does not support foreign key constraints. As with MyISAM tables, these are ignored.
  - Query caching is not supported.

For additional information on Cluster limitations, see Section 9.9, "Known Limitations of MySQL Cluster."

- *How do I import an existing MySQL database into a cluster?*

  You can import databases into MySQL Cluster much as you would with any other version of MySQL. Other than the limitation mentioned in the previous question, the only other special requirement is that any tables to be included in the cluster must use the NDB storage engine. This means that the tables must be created with ENGINE=NDB or ENGINE=NDBCLUSTER. It is also possible to convert existing tables using other storage engines to NDB Cluster using ALTER TABLE, but requires an additional workaround. See Section 9.9, "Known Limitations of MySQL Cluster," for details.

- *How do cluster nodes communicate with one another?*

  Cluster nodes can communicate via any of three different protocols: TCP/IP, SHM (shared memory), and SCI (Scalable Coherent Interface). Where available, SHM is used by default between nodes residing on the same cluster host. SCI is a high-speed (1 gigabit per second and higher), high-availability protocol used in building scalable multi-processor systems; it requires special hardware and drivers. See Section 9.8, "Using High-Speed Interconnects with MySQL Cluster," for more about using SCI as a transport mechanism in MySQL Cluster.

- *What is an "arbitrator"?*

  If one or more nodes in a cluster fail, it is possible that not all cluster nodes will be able to "see" one another. In fact, it is possible that two sets of nodes might become isolated from one another in a network partitioning, also known as a "split brain" scenario. This type of situation is undesirable because each set of nodes tries to behave as though it is the entire cluster.

  When cluster nodes go down, there are two possibilities. If more than 50% of the remaining nodes can communicate with each other, we have what is sometimes called a "majority rules" situation, and this set of nodes is considered to be the cluster. The arbitrator comes into play when there is an even number of nodes: In such cases, the set of nodes to which the arbitrator belongs is considered to be the cluster, and nodes not belonging to this set are shut down.

  The preceding information is somewhat simplified. A more complete explanation taking into account node groups follows:

  When all nodes in at least one node group are alive, network partitioning is not an issue, because no one portion of the cluster can form a functional cluster. The real problem arises when no single node group has all its nodes alive, in which case network partitioning (the "split-brain" scenario) becomes possible. Then an arbitrator is required. All cluster nodes recognize the same node as the arbitrator, which is normally the management server; however, it is possible to configure any of the MySQL Servers in the cluster to act as the arbitrator instead. The arbitrator accepts the first set of cluster nodes to contact it, and tells the remaining set to shut down. Arbitrator selection is controlled by the ArbitrationRank configuration parameter for MySQL Server and management server nodes. (See Section 9.4.4.4, "Defining the MySQL Cluster

Management Server," for details.) It should also be noted that the role of arbitrator does not in and of itself impose any heavy demands on the host so designated, and thus the arbitrator host does not need to be particularly fast or to have extra memory especially for this purpose.

- *What data types are supported by MySQL Cluster?*

  MySQL Cluster supports all of the usual MySQL data types, with the exception of those associated with MySQL's spatial extensions. In addition, there are some differences with regard to indexes when used with NDB tables. **Note**: MySQL Cluster tables (that is, tables created with ENGINE=NDBCLUSTER) have only fixed-width rows. This means that (for example) each record containing a VARCHAR(255) column will require space for 255 characters (as required for the character set and collation being used for the table), regardless of the actual number of characters stored therein. This issue is expected to be fixed in a future MySQL release series.

  See Section 9.9, "Known Limitations of MySQL Cluster," for more information about these issues.

- *How do I start and stop MySQL Cluster?*

  It is necessary to start each node in the cluster separately, in the following order:

  1. Start the management node with the ndb_mgmd command.
  2. Start each data node with the ndbd command.
  3. Start each MySQL server (SQL node) using mysqld_safe --user=mysql &.

  Each of these commands must be run from a system shell on the machine housing the affected node. You can verify the cluster is running by starting the MGM management client ndb_mgm on the machine housing the MGM node.

- *What happens to cluster data when the cluster is shut down?*

  The data held in memory by the cluster's data nodes is written to disk, and is reloaded in memory the next time that the cluster is started.

  To shut down the cluster, enter the following command in a shell on the machine hosting the MGM node:

  ```
  shell> ndb_mgm -e shutdown
  ```

  This causes the ndb_mgm, ndb_mgm, and any ndbd processes to terminate gracefully. MySQL servers running as Cluster SQL nodes can be stopped using mysqladmin shutdown.

  For more information, see Section 9.3.6, "Safe Shutdown and Restart," and Section 9.6.2, "Commands in the Management Client."

- *Is it helpful to have more than one management node for a cluster?*

  It can be helpful as a fail-safe. Only one MGM node controls the cluster at any given time, but it is possible to configure one MGM as primary, and one or more additional management nodes to take over in the event that the primary MGM node fails.

- *Can I mix different kinds of hardware and operating systems in a Cluster?*

  Yes, so long as all machines and operating systems have the same endianness (all big-endian or all little-endian). It is also possible to use different MySQL Cluster releases on different nodes. However, we recommend this be done only as part of a rolling upgrade procedure.

- *Can I run two data nodes on a single host? Two SQL nodes?*

  Yes, it is possible to do this. In the case of multiple data nodes, each node must use a different data directory. If you want to run multiple SQL nodes on one machine, each instance of `mysqld` must use a different TCP/IP port.

- *Can I use hostnames with MySQL Cluster?*

  Yes, it is possible to use DNS and DHCP for cluster hosts. However, if your application requires "five nines" availability, we recommend using fixed IP addresses. Making communication between Cluster hosts dependent on services such as DNS and DHCP introduces additional points of failure, and the fewer of these, the better.

9.12 MySQL Cluster Glossary

The following terms are useful to an understanding of MySQL Cluster or have specialized meanings when used in relation to it.

- **Cluster**:

  In its generic sense, a cluster is a set of computers functioning as a unit and working together to accomplish a single task.

  NDB Cluster:

  This is the storage engine used in MySQL to implement data storage, retrieval, and management distributed among several computers.

  MySQL Cluster:

  This refers to a group of computers working together using the NDB storage engine to support a distributed MySQL database in a *shared-nothing architecture* using *in-memory storage*.

- **Configuration files**:

  Text files containing directives and information regarding the cluster, its hosts, and its nodes. These are read by the cluster's management nodes when the cluster is started. See Section 9.4.4, "Configuration File," for details.

- **Backup**:

  A complete copy of all cluster data, transactions and logs, saved to disk or other long-term storage.

- **Restore**:

  Returning the cluster to a previous state, as stored in a backup.

- **Checkpoint**:

  Generally speaking, when data is saved to disk, it is said that a checkpoint has been reached. More specific to Cluster, it is a point in time where all committed transactions are stored on disk. With regard to the NDB storage engine, there are two types of checkpoints that work together to ensure that a consistent view of the cluster's data is maintained:

  - **Local Checkpoint (LCP)**:

    This is a checkpoint that is specific to a single node; however, LCPs take place for all nodes in the cluster more or less concurrently. An LCP involves saving all of a node's data to disk, and so usually occurs every few minutes. The precise interval varies, and depends on the amount of data stored by the node, the level of cluster activity, and other factors.

  - **Global Checkpoint (GCP)**:

    A GCP occurs every few seconds, when transactions for all nodes are synchronized and the REDO log is flushed to disk.

- **Cluster host**:

  A computer making up part of a MySQL Cluster. A cluster has both a *physical* structure and a *logical* structure. Physically, the cluster consists of a number of computers, known as *cluster hosts* (or more simply as *hosts*). See also **Node** and **Node group** below.

- **Node**:

  This refers to a logical or functional unit of MySQL Cluster, and is sometimes also referred to as a "cluster node." In the context of MySQL Cluster, we use the term "node" to indicate a *process* rather than a physical component of the cluster. There are three node types required to implement a working MySQL Cluster:

  - **Management (MGM) nodes**:

    Manages the other nodes within the MySQL Cluster. It provides configuration data to the other nodes; starts and stops nodes; handles network partitioning; creates backups and restores from them, and so forth.

  - **SQL (MySQL server) nodes**:

    Instances of MySQL Server which serve as front ends to data kept in the cluster's **data nodes**. Clients desiring to store, retrieve, or update data can access an SQL node just as they would any other MySQL Server, employing the usual authentication methods and APIs; the underlying distribution of data between node groups is transparent to users and applications. SQL nodes access the cluster's databases as a whole without regard to the data's distribution across different data nodes or cluster hosts.

  - **Data nodes**:

    These nodes store the actual data. Table data fragments are stored in a set of node groups; each node group stores a different subset of the table data. Each of the nodes making up a node group stores a replica of the fragment for which that node group is responsible. Currently, a single cluster can support up to 48 data nodes total.

It is possible for more than one node to co-exist on a single machine. (In fact, it is even possible to set up a complete cluster on one machine, although you would almost certainly *not* want to do this in a production environment.) It may be helpful to remember that, when working with MySQL Cluster, the term "host" refers to a physical component of the cluster whereas a "node" is a logical or functional component (that is, a process).

Note Regarding Obsolete Terms: In older versions of the MySQL Cluster documentation, data nodes were sometimes referred to as "database nodes," "DB nodes," or occasionally "storage nodes." In addition, SQL nodes were sometimes known as "client nodes" or "API nodes." This older terminology has been deprecated to minimize confusion, and for these reasons should be avoided.

- **Node group**:

  A set of data nodes. All data nodes in a node group contain the same data (fragments), and all nodes in a single group should reside on different hosts. It is possible to control which nodes belong to which node groups.

- **Node failure**:

  MySQL Cluster is not solely dependent on the functioning of any single node making up the cluster; the cluster can continue to run if one or more nodes fail. The precise number of node failures that a given cluster can tolerate depends on the number of nodes and the cluster's configuration.

- **Node restart**:

  The process of restarting a failed cluster node.

- **Initial node restart**:

  The process of starting a cluster node with its filesystem removed. This is sometimes used in the course of software upgrades and in other special circumstances.

- **System crash** (or **system failure**):

  This can occur when so many cluster nodes have failed that the cluster's state can no longer be guaranteed.

- **System restart**:

  The process of restarting the cluster and reinitializing its state from disk logs and checkpoints. This is required after either a planned or an unplanned shutdown of the cluster.

- **Fragment**:

  A portion of a database table; in the NDB storage engine, a table is broken up into and stored as a number of fragments. A fragment is sometimes also called a "partition"; however, "fragment" is the preferred term. Tables are fragmented in MySQL Cluster in order to facilitate load balancing between machines and nodes.

- **Replica**:

  Under the NDB storage engine, each table fragment has number of replicas stored on other data nodes in order to provide redundancy. Currently, there may be up four replicas per fragment.

- **Transporter**:

A protocol providing data transfer between nodes. MySQL Cluster currently supports four different types of transporter connections:

- TCP/IP

This is, of course, the familiar network protocol that underlies HTTP, FTP (and so on) on the Internet. TCP/IP can be used for both local and remote connections.

- SCI

Scalable **C**oherent **I**nterface is a high-speed protocol used in building multiprocessor systems and parallel-processing applications. Use of SCI with MySQL Cluster requires specialized hardware, as discussed in Section 9.8.1, "Configuring MySQL Cluster to Use SCI Sockets." For a basic introduction to SCI, see this essay at dolphinics.com (`http://www.dolphinics.com/corporate/scitech.html`).

- SHM

Unix-style **sh**ared **m**emory segments. Where supported, SHM is used automatically to connect nodes running on the same host. The Unix man page for `shmop(2)` (`http://www.scit.wlv.ac.uk/cgi-bin/mansec?2+shmop`) is a good place to begin obtaining additional information about this topic.

Note: The cluster transporter is internal to the cluster. Applications using MySQL Cluster communicate with SQL nodes just as they do with any other version of MySQL Server (via TCP/IP, or through the use of Unix socket files or Windows named pipes). Queries can be sent and results retrieved using the standard MySQL client APIs.

- **NDB**:

This stands for **N**etwork **D**atabase, and refers to the storage engine used to enable MySQL Cluster. The NDB storage engine supports all the usual MySQL data types and SQL statements, and is ACID-compliant. This engine also provides full support for transactions (commits and rollbacks).

- **Share-nothing architecture**:

The ideal architecture for a MySQL Cluster. In a true share-nothing setup, each node runs on a separate host. The advantage such an arrangement is that there no single host or node can act as single point of failure or as a performance bottleneck for the system as a whole.

- **In-memory storage**:

All data stored in each data node is kept in memory on the node's host computer. For each data node in the cluster, you must have available an amount of RAM equal to the size of the database times the number of replicas, divided by the number of data nodes. Thus, if the database takes up 1GB of memory, and you want to set up the cluster with four replicas and eight data nodes, a minimum of 500MB memory will be required per node. Note that this is in addition to any requirements for the operating system and any other applications that might be running on the host.

- **Table**:

  As is usual in the context of a relational database, the term "table" denotes a set of identically structured records. In MySQL Cluster, a database table is stored in a data node as a set of fragments, each of which is replicated on additional data nodes. The set of data nodes replicating the same fragment or set of fragments is referred to as a *node group*.

- **Cluster programs**:

  These are command-line programs used in running, configuring, and administering MySQL Cluster. They include both server daemons:

  - ndbd:

    The data node daemon (runs a data node process)

  - ndb_mgmd:

    The management server daemon (runs a management server process)

  and client programs:

  - ndb_mgm:

    The management client (provides an interface for executing management commands)

  - ndb_waiter:

    Used to verify status of all nodes in a cluster

  - ndb_restore:

    Restores cluster data from backup

  For more about these programs and their uses, see Section 9.5, "Process Management in MySQL Cluster."

- **Event log**:

  MySQL Cluster logs events by category (startup, shutdown, errors, checkpoints, and so on), priority, and severity. A complete listing of all reportable events may be found in Section 9.6.3, "Event Reports Generated in MySQL Cluster." Event logs are of two types:

  - **Cluster log**:

    Keeps a record of all desired reportable events for the cluster as a whole.

  - **Node log**:

    A separate log that is also kept for each individual node.

  Under normal circumstances, it is necessary and sufficient to keep and examine only the cluster log. The node logs need be consulted only for application development and debugging purposes.

Symbols

A

L

How can we make this index more useful? Email us at indexes@samspublishing.com

How can we make this index more useful? Email us at indexes@samspublishing.com

N

O

How can we make this index more useful? Email us at indexes@samspublishing.com

W